THE PAPERS
OF
JOHN MARSHALL

Sponsored by
The College of William and Mary
and
The Institute of Early American History and Culture
under the auspices of
The National Historical Publications and Records Commission

John Marshall

by an unknown artist (ca. 1797)

Courtesy of Mrs. Benjamin T. Woodruff, Charleston, W. Va.

THE PAPERS
OF
JOHN MARSHALL

Volume III

Correspondence and Papers, January 1796—December 1798

WILLIAM C. STINCHCOMBE, *Diplomatic Editor*

CHARLES T. CULLEN, *Editor*

LESLIE TOBIAS, *Assistant Editor*

The University of North Carolina Press, Chapel Hill
in association with the
Institute of Early American History and Culture
Williamsburg, Virginia

The Institute of Early American History and Culture
is sponsored jointly by The College of William and Mary in Virginia
and The Colonial Williamsburg Foundation

Manufactured in the United States of America
Printed by Heritage Printers, Inc., Charlotte, N.C.
ISBN 0-8078-1337-0
Library of Congress Catalog Card Number 74-9575

The ornament on the title page is based upon John Marshall's personal seal, as it appears on a gold watch fob that also bears the seal of his wife, Mary Willis Marshall. It was drawn by Richard J. Stinely of Williamsburg, Virginia, from the original, now owned by the Association for the Preservation of Virginia Antiquities, Richmond, Virginia, and is published with the owner's permission.

Library of Congress Cataloging in Publication Data

Marshall, John, 1755-1835.
The papers of John Marshall.
Vol. 3- edited by William C. Stinchcombe and Charles T. Cullen.
"Sponsored by the College of William and Mary and the Institute of Early American History and Culture under the auspices of the National Historical Publications Commission."
Includes bibliographical references and index.

CONTENTS: v. 1. Correspondence and papers, November 10, 1775-June 23, 1788. Account book, September 1783-June 1788.—v. 3. Correspondence and papers, January 1796-December 1798.

1. Marshall, John 1755-1835. 2. United States—Politics and government—Revolution, 1775-1783—Sources. 3. United States—Politics and government—1783-1865—Sources. 4. Statesmen—United States—Correspondence. 5. Judges—United States—Correspondence. I. Johnson, Herbert Alan, ed. II. Cullen, Charles T., ed. III. Stinchcombe, William C., ed. IV. Institute of Early American History and Culture, Williamsburg, Va.
E302.M365 347'.73'2634 74-9575
ISBN 0-8078-1233-1 (v. 1)
ISBN 0-8078-1302-8 (v. 2)
ISBN 0-8078-1337-0 (v. 3)

The publication of this volume has been assisted by special grants from the Association for the Preservation of Virginia Antiquities, the William Branch Cabell Foundation, the National Endowment for the Humanities, the John Ben Snow Foundation, and the Windsor Foundation.

CONTENTS

CORRESPONDENCE AND PAPERS
January 1796—December 1798

1796

FOREWORD

The three years covered in this volume represent a turning point in John Marshall's career as an attorney and as a public servant. Between January 1796, when he was just over forty years old, and June 1797, when he left for France, he settled his dispute with the Commonwealth of Virginia over title to the Fairfax lands, continued to take an active role in the annual meetings of the House of Delegates, managed a growing volume of legal business, and strengthened his position as a principal defender of the Federalist administration. By September 1798, when he announced his candidacy for election to Congress, Marshall had completed the transition from state to national politics that established him as one of the leading members of the Federalist party.

When John Adams asked him to accept appointment as an envoy to France in June 1797, Marshall was free from business and professional constraints, such as his legal battle over the Fairfax lands, that had caused him to refrain from accepting previous offers of national office. Marshall accepted the appointment perhaps for financial as well as patriotic reasons. Marshall probably believed that while in Europe he might assist his brother James Markham Marshall negotiate a loan for the purchase of the Fairfax lands. He fully expected to return to his law practice in a few months, but the mission to France lasted twice as long as originally expected.

Marshall's experience as a diplomat and his participation in the so-called XYZ affair catapulted him into the forefront of national politics. George Washington and such other prominent Federalists as John Adams, Timothy Pickering, Theodore Sedgwick, and Rufus King highly regarded his character and ability. Beginning in 1798, Marshall's statements on foreign policy, national defense, the Alien and Sedition Laws, and the Virginia and Kentucky Resolutions received widespread comment, and his addresses appeared in newspapers throughout the country. Marshall's announcement that he would be a candidate for election to Congress and his subsequent election were seen by many as signs of a Federalist resurgence at a time when that party's popularity was declining. By

1799 Marshall had become a leading spokesman for the policies of the Adams administration in its closing years. Politically he never returned to Richmond after the mission to France.

Most of the documents in this volume pertain to Marshall's experience as one of the envoys to France in 1797. Papers dated between June 1797 and June 1798 are almost exclusively diplomatic, and they have received special attention from the editors. In keeping with the announced intention of this project to be as comprehensive and authentic as possible, the editors have republished all of the envoys' dispatches from France, because Marshall had an active part in writing them. Furthermore, previous editions of the dispatches, such as those issued as pamphlets in 1798 and those printed in *American State Papers, Foreign Relations*, do not contain accurate or complete texts. The editors have also deciphered the coded material anew. The most important document in this volume, perhaps, is the journal Marshall kept while in Paris. This document has never appeared in print, although it is a major source of information for the mission.

Professor William C. Stinchcombe, of Syracuse University, prepared the material dealing with the mission to France and wrote the editorial notes and footnotes for these documents. He was part of the editorial staff in Williamsburg from September 1972 to August 1973 and continued his work on the documents upon returning to Syracuse University. He wishes to thank that institution for granting him two leaves of absence and one year in Amsterdam at the Syracuse-in-the-Netherlands Program to facilitate research on the XYZ mission.

For their encouragement since the inception of this volume, the editors wish to thank Stephen G. Kurtz, Thad W. Tate, James Morton Smith, and Bradford Perkins. Brian Morton, William G. Ray, Roger Bruns, and George Billias provided valuable assistance by answering numerous inquiries and sharing documents related to this work. J. Lalloy, director of the Archives des Affaires Etrangères, allowed the editors to microfilm French documents, as did Jean Favier, director of the Archives Nationales. Jill Bourdais de Charbonnière went beyond her role as co-director of the Paris Research Associates in finding new sources on Marshall's stay in Paris. Romuald Szramkiewicz generously shared his knowledge of Jean Hottinguer's career. Special thanks must also go to a French family that furnished Marshall letters previously unknown to scholars. Two former members of the project's staff, Susan H. Elias and

Carolyn D. Hensley, and a former NHPRC fellow in advanced historical editing, W. Allan Wilbur, also made significant contributions, which the editors gratefully acknowledge. The editors also appreciate the work done on the case of *Ware v. Hylton* by the project's research associate, George M. Curtis III, and a former editor, Herbert A. Johnson. Trudi M. Heyer joined the staff as secretary at an important point in our work and contributed her efforts to the task of completing this volume with fidelity and skill. Finally, the editors wish to thank Dorothy H. Cappel for her excellent supervision of the copy editing of the manuscript. Her suggestions resulted in many improvements in the volume, especially in the essays and annotation. The editors appreciate her significant work, but nevertheless accept final responsibility for any errors in the volume.

The editors wish to express special thanks to the project's two sponsoring institutions, the College of William and Mary and the Institute of Early American History and Culture, for their continuing support of this work, and to the National Historical Publications and Records Commission for its constant encouragement.

EDITORIAL APPARATUS

RENDITION OF TEXT

In accordance with modern editorial standards, the editors have attempted to render the text of documents as faithfully as possible. However, the editors have established and consistently applied certain guidelines in transcribing the documents. Each sentence begins with a capital letter and ends with a period, question mark, or an exclamation point. All dashes at the end of sentences and paragraphs have been silently omitted except for those that appear on previously printed documents that are reproduced here. In most cases superscript letters have been lowered to the line. Abbreviated words without apostrophes have been transcribed as written; those with apostrophes have been silently expanded. The ampersand (&) has been retained, but "&c" and "&ca" have been expanded to "etc." The tailed p (ꝑ) has been rendered as either "pro" or "per," depending on the context in which it appears in the original.

The format and typography of each letter and document have been standardized. The dateline, which indicates the place and date of composition, has been set at the top of the document flush with the right margin. Should a letter bear a dispatch number or the designation "private," or both, these have been placed at the left margin above the salutation. The salutation has been set flush with the left margin on the same line as the dateline and has been rendered in capital and lowercase letters, except in the case of previously printed documents, where the original typography has been followed. The complimentary close has been run in with the text of the letter, and the signatures to letters have been set flush with the right margin and have generally been rendered in large and small capital letters. However, where the editors have not examined the original signature or have no reason to believe that the signature on a previously edited document was copied from an original signature, the signature has been rendered as it appears in the text being copied. This usually occurs in the case of printed documents for which the original manuscript copy and all contemporary copies and later transcripts from the original manuscript have been lost. Acknowledgments or jurats to documents have been brought to the left margin, as have the signatures of witnesses or notaries. Postscripts have also been placed flush with the left margin, regardless of their position on the original.

For each document and calendared synopsis the editors have composed a heading that provides a brief key to the nature of the document. These headings, which comprise the table of contents, are designed solely to assist the reader in identifying particular classes of documents. Letters are identified by the name of the individual who wrote to John Marshall or by the name of the person to whom Marshall wrote. Documents other than letters, both printed and calendared, are usually identified by the category of the document, such as "Petition," "Speech," or "Legislative Bill." For printed or calendared legal documents the heading includes not only the category of the document but also the title of the case.

Where interpolation has become necessary, the editors have been sparing and cautious in their exercise of imagination. Omitted letters have been inserted only when necessary to preserve the meaning of a word. If the meaning of a word was clear, although some letters may have been illegible or missing because of mutilation, up to four missing letters have been supplied without the use of brackets; more than four missing letters in a word have been inserted in roman type within square brackets ([ ]) and, if necessary, the editors have explained the insertion in a footnote. Where more than one word was missing, or the text was supplied conjecturally, this material has been inserted in italic type within square brackets. Where material in a manuscript text appears to have been inserted through a slip of the author's pen, the editors have followed the text and explained the error in a footnote. Obvious typographical errors in printed matter that are more likely the compositor's rather than the author's mistakes have been silently corrected.

Matter deleted by the writer has usually been omitted from the text as printed in this edition except when the editors believe that the deletion is sufficiently significant to justify an exception to this policy. In such cases the canceled word or passage has been placed *before* the material that replaced it and enclosed in angle brackets (⟨ ⟩). A deletion within a deletion has been indicated by double angle brackets (⟨⟨ ⟩⟩), and the preceding rule concerning its placement in the text has been followed.

The presentation of seals in a printed edition is a matter of some difficulty. For purposes of clearer rendition, the editors have divided seals into two categories. One group consists of the official and corporate seals, which are rendered [SEAL], provided the document indicates that such a seal was at one time attached to the original. The other seal, be it a wafer seal or simply a signature followed by "L.S.," has been considered a hand seal and rendered "L.S." The editors have treated variations in hand seals as follows:

J. Marshall L.S.	is shown as	J. Marshall L.S.
J. Marshall (LS)	is shown as	J. Marshall (LS)
J. Marshall (Seal)	is shown as	J. Marshall [LS]
J. Marshall (SEAL)	is shown as	J. Marshall [LS]
J. Marshall (L.S)	is shown as	J. Marshall (L.S)

In presenting documents containing seals, the editors have attempted to place the seal on the printed page in the same position as on the original manuscript.

Coded material has been deciphered and rendered in italic type. The editors have silently corrected obvious coding errors and have explained special problems in footnotes. Passages in open brackets (⟦ ⟧) in coded documents indicate segments taken from Marshall's Paris Journal. Words supplied conjecturally within decoded material have been printed in italics within brackets.

ANNOTATION OF DOCUMENTS

While the editors prefer a policy of sparse annotation, they have attempted to give the reader some guidance in interpreting Marshall's papers, including essential explanations and a reasonably complete identification of individuals upon their first mention in the text of the papers. (The volume index facilitates cross-reference to the first mention of a given name or individual.) Biographical references to well-known individuals who are listed in the *Dictionary of American Biography* or *Dictionary of National Biography* are intentionally brief, and the editors similarly have not expansively discussed individuals of slight importance to Marshall's career or those whose identity is not material to an understanding of the text of the document. When the editors have been unsuccessful in identifying a person mentioned in the text, they upon occasion have advanced a supposition based upon knowledge of Marshall's activities and associations, but in most cases they have chosen to leave it to the reader to speculate upon the identity of an unknown person.

In identifying individuals and business firms the editors have frequently relied on several basic reference works and have used information from them without citation. In addition to the *DAB* and the *DNB*, these include Lyon G. Tyler's *Encyclopedia of Virginia Biography* and Earl Gregg Swem's *Virginia Historical Index*. Information derived from the periodicals indexed in the latter has been used without naming the specific source.[1] Definitions of little-used or archaic terms taken from the *Oxford English Dictionary* have not been given a citation, nor have definitions of legal terms obtained from *Black's Law Dictionary*. For all other sources, the editors have provided a full bibliographic citation in the appropriate footnote. Whenever possible, book-length biographies have been cited at the first mention of a given individual in one of Marshall's papers.

The source of each document is identified in full in the line immediately below its heading. In cases where this description is not adequate, the first footnote gives further information and also identifies the writer or recipient if he has not been previously identified. In the case of a particularly delicate problem of documentary analysis, there is, of course, no substitute for seeing the original document, but the editors believe that their annotation policy reduces to a minimum the researcher's need to consult the original documents.

In preparing calendared synopses of documents the editors have tried to summarize concisely the contents of the manuscript or printed source. The synopsis generally includes a notation concerning John Marshall's connection with the document, and an attempt has been made to identify individuals mentioned in the synopsis. Additional details, if available, have been given in footnotes, but these have been kept to a minimum. Synopses dealing with Marshall's law practice include, if possible, sufficient information for the reader to identify the case involved, the nature of the litigation, and the court that heard the case.

The decision to include every identifiable Marshall document in these volumes led to the accumulation of a large number of routine legal documents that have no distinction other than that they were written or signed by John Marshall. Summaries of most of these would demand excessive space and produce little useful information. The editors decided to list them together at the end

1. Lyon G. Tyler, *Encyclopedia of Virginia Biography* (New York, 1915); E[arl] G. Swem, *Virginia Historical Index* (Richmond, 1934).

of each month, with a description of the document and its present location.

When a document or group of documents has required more extended discussion than could be conveniently included in a footnote, an editorial note has been added immediately preceding the document to which it pertains. Although these notes frequently are extensive discussions, they obviously are limited in scope to a consideration of the basic document and the situation that gave rise to the documentary material. The notes also contain editorial commentary about interpretive difficulties that have arisen concerning the paper or papers being edited.

ABBREVIATIONS AND SHORT TITLES

The editors have tried to avoid ambiguous abbreviations and have made short titles in citations sufficiently complete to permit ease in bibliographic reference. The following lists contain, first, explanations of abbreviations that may not be readily understood and that have a special meaning in this series and, second, full citations for short titles that are used frequently throughout this volume. Generally accepted abbreviations, such as months of the year, have not been listed, nor have short titles that occur in a limited section of the volume. The latter can easily be expanded by going to the first reference to a work in each document or editorial note, where a full citation is provided.

ABBREVIATIONS

AD Autograph Document
ADS Autograph Document Signed
AL Autograph Letter
ALS Autograph Letter Signed
DS Document Signed
LS Letter Signed

SHORT TITLES

Amer. State Papers, Foreign Relations — Walter Lowrie and Matthew St. Clair Clarke, eds., *American State Papers. Documents, Legislative and Executive, of the Congress of the United States, . . . Commencing March 3, 1789, and Ending March 3, 1833*, 3 vols. (Washington, D.C., 1833)

Annals of Congress	[*Annals of the Congress of the United States.*] *Debates and Proceedings in the Congress of the United States, 1789–1824 . . .*, 42 vols. (Washington, D.C., 1834–1856)
Beveridge, *Marshall*	Albert J. Beveridge, *The Life of John Marshall*, 4 vols. (Boston, 1916–1919)
JVHD	*Journal of the House of Delegates of the Commonwealth of Virginia. . . .* This short title will be followed by the month and year in which the General Assembly convened.
Miller, ed., *Treaties*, II	Hunter Miller, ed., *Treaties and Other International Acts of the United States of America*, II (Washington, D.C., 1931)
Stinchcombe, "WXYZ Affair," *WMQ*, 3d Ser., XXXIV (1977)	William Stinchcombe, "The Diplomacy of the WXYZ Affair," *William and Mary Quarterly*, 3d Ser., XXXIV (1977), 590–617.
WMQ	*William and Mary Quarterly*

In addition to the foregoing abbreviations and short titles, the editors have followed the policy of using legal form citations when discussing or citing the reports of cases in courts and statutes passed by legislative bodies in England or the United States. These generally conform to *A Uniform System of Citation*, 11th ed. (Cambridge, Mass., 1967), adopted for use by several law reviews. All other legal citations follow the Institute of Early American History and Culture's *Style Sheet for Authors*, with the following exceptions:

Hening	William Waller Hening, ed., *The Statutes at Large; Being a Collection of All the Laws of Virginia . . .* (Richmond, 1809–1823)
Shepherd	Samuel Shepherd, ed., *The Statutes at Large of Virginia, from Oc-*

tober Session 1792, to December Session 1806 . . . (Richmond, 1835–1836)

Stat. *Statutes at Large of the United States of America, 1789–1873* (Boston, 1845–1873)

MARSHALL CHRONOLOGY

1796–1798

February 9–12, 1796	Argued *Ware v. Hylton* before the Supreme Court of the United States.
April 25, 1796	Directed public meeting on Jay Treaty in Richmond.
November 8–December 27, 1796	Served as member of the House of Delegates representing city of Richmond.
April 10, 1797	Elected member of the House of Delegates representing city of Richmond.
June 5, 1797	Appointed United States minister extraordinary to France.
July 18, 1797	Sailed from New Castle, Delaware.
August 29, 1797	Arrived in Holland.
September 27, 1797	Arrived in Paris.
October 8, 1797	Credentials accepted by Talleyrand.
ca. October 18, 1797	Negotiations with WXYZ agents began.
March 6, 1798	Negotiations with Talleyrand began.
April 16, 1798	Departed Paris.
April 23, 1798	Departed Bordeaux.
June 17, 1798	Arrived in New York.
June 19, 1798	Arrived in Philadelphia.
June 28, 1798	Arrived in Winchester.
August 8, 1798	Arrived in Richmond, resumed law practice.
ca. September 5, 1798	Decided to become congressional candidate to House of Representatives.

MARSHALL CHRONOLOGY

CORRESPONDENCE AND PAPERS

January 1796—December 1798

Hunter v. Fairfax

Acknowledgment of Service

ADS, RG 267, National Archives

[*ca. January 15, 1796, Richmond.* JM acknowledges receipt of a citation in the appeal of this case to the U.S. Supreme Court.]

To Thomas Massie

ALS, Massie Family Papers, Virginia Historical Society[1]

Dear Sir [Richmond], January 1796

I have receivd your letter[2] by Mr. Page & will certainly conform to the statement you have now given me in the suit for a title to your land.

I will conclude the business as soon as I can. It depends much on the punctual service of process.[3] I am dear Sir Your obedt. servt.

J Marshall

To Mary W. Marshall

ALS, Marshall Papers, Swem Library, College of William and Mary

My dearest Polly Philadelphia, February 3, 1796

After a journey which woud have been beyond measure tedious but for the agreeable company with which I came I am at length safe at this place. My business woud be spedily determind if Mr. Campbell woud come on. We wait only for him to enter on the cause concerning British debts. My own cause I greatly fear will not be taken up & I shall be under the very disagreeable necessity

1. This is item no. Mss1M3855a605 in the society's collections. JM addressed the letter to "Major Thomas Massie, Frederick."

2. Not found.

3. It is unclear what litigation this pertains to, but JM recorded fees in Massie v. Burwell's Exrs. from 1790 to 1795. See Vol. II, 395, 419, 490. See also Vol. II, 112–116, for JM's opinion on Thomas Adams's will; Massie was one of Adams's executors.

of returning without any decision.[4] It is a cruel thing on me to be kept here extremely against my inclination because Mr. Campbell will not come on.

I have not yet heard from my beloved wife & children. You ought not to keep me in any suspense about you. I was at the play last night & very much admird Mrs. Marshall who is the favorite of the town but with all her good qualities she does not equal our Mrs. Bignal.[5]

No information has yet been receivd of the arrival of the vessel which carried my brother & his wife. We expect every day to receive inteligence from them.[6]

Kiss our children & especially our sweet little Poll for me & tell Tom I expect him to attend to his brother & to write to me. I count on Jaquelines great improvement before my return. I am my dearest Polly your affectionate

J MARSHALL

Ware V. Hylton

EDITORIAL NOTE

John Marshall's argument for the defense in *Ware v. Hylton* was the culmination of his political and legal participation in the British debt controversy that

4. JM was in Philadelphia to argue Ware v. Hylton, in which Alexander Campbell was representing Ware. JM's "own cause" was Hunter v. Fairfax. The latter case was continued because Hunter was not prepared for trial. See Vol. II, 145 n. 8. Robert Morris wrote to James Markham Marshall that JM "could not get your cause brought forward in the Supreme Court of the U.S. at which he was much dissatisfied & I am much concerned thereat, fearing that real disadvantage will result to your Concern thereby." Morris to James M. Marshall, Mar. 4, 1796, Letterbook, Morris Papers, Library of Congress.

By Feb. 6, Campbell had appeared, and the first of six days of argument in Ware v. Hylton began. U.S. Supreme Court Minutes, Feb. 6, 8, 9, 10, 11, and 12, 1796, RG 267, National Archives.

5. Mrs. Marshall, appearing on Feb. 2, 1796, in "The Bank Note; or, Lessons for Ladies" and "Hop in the Well; or the Humours of a Country Wake," has been described as "the *beau ideal* of a comic actress, and . . . *au fait* in every walk of the drama —nay, she was excellent, her romps were a model of perfection." Thomas Clark Pollock, *The Philadelphia Theatre in the Eighteenth Century* . . . (Philadelphia, 1933), 55. See also *Aurora* (Philadelphia), Feb. 2, 1796; Arthur Hornblow, *A History of the Theatre in America from its Beginnings to the Present Time*, I (Philadelphia, 1919), 211–212.

Anne West Bignall, a member of Richmond's Virginia Company, appeared in many plays JM saw in the 1790s. She has been described as the best actress in the country. Suzanne Ketchum Sherman, "Post-Revolutionary Theatre in Virginia, 1784–1810" (M.A. thesis, College of William and Mary, 1950), 87.

6. James M. Marshall and his wife, Hester, had sailed for England late in 1795. See Morris to JM, Dec. 29, 1795, Vol. II, 329 n. 9; Morris to JM, Mar. 8, 1796.

had begun after the Revolution. Since 1774, when Virginia courts ceased hearing debt actions brought by British creditors, all attempts to open the courts to such litigation had failed. As a legislator Marshall had supported reopening the courts to British creditors, but as an attorney he presented a spirited defense of Virginia's strategy to help debtors avoid payment. Among the measures the General Assembly had adopted to assist Virginia debtors was a 1777 law that allowed Virginians to discharge debt liability by paying directly into a state loan office.[7] *Ware v. Hylton* tested the constitutionality of this law against article 4 of the Treaty of Paris of 1783 and the supremacy clause of the United States Constitution.

Marshall had first entered the case for the defense in May 1791, when litigation began as *Jones v. Hylton* in the U.S. Circuit Court for Virginia.[8] From a judgment entered on a 1794 verdict for Daniel L. Hylton, William Jones took a writ of error to the U.S. Supreme Court. While the appeal was pending, Jones died and the action was revived in the name of his administrator, John Tyndal Ware. Marshall was admitted to practice before the Supreme Court on February 2, 1795, in order to participate in the first hearing of the case. A second hearing was held in August 1796, and the third and final arguments occurred in February 1796.[9] This was the only case Marshall ever argued before the Supreme Court.

Marshall's pleadings for his client were elaborate. He invoked, among other things, the Virginia statute of limitations and challenged the binding effect of the 1783 peace treaty upon Virginians, since the British had failed to comply with various provisions of that agreement. The major thrust of his defense of Hylton was that the Virginia statute had the effect of confiscating British book credits. Thus, the voluntary payments to the state under the terms of the 1777 law eradicated his client's liability entirely.[1]

Opposing Marshall and Alexander Campbell in the case were Edward Tilgh-

7. 9 Hening 377–380. See also 11 Hening 75–76, 176–180 (1782), 349 (1783); 12 Hening 528 (1787). In 1784, JM voted against measures to further inhibit compliance with the 1783 peace treaty and the port bill of 1784. See *JVHD*, May 1784, 41, 61, 74–75; Vol. I, 130. In 1787 he voted against amendments that further delayed Virginia's acquiescence to the treaty. *JVHD*, Oct. 1787, 51–52, 79–80. These amendments, introduced and supported by the Patrick Henry faction, not only kept the courts closed to British creditors but also sustained opposition to any final settlement of general wartime disputes. Beginning in 1790, JM joined Patrick Henry as attorney for the defense in Jones v. Walker, a companion case to Ware v. Hylton. See Jones v. Walker, U.S. Circuit Court, Va., Ended Cases (Restored), 1797, Virginia State Library; Robert Douthat Meade, *Patrick Henry: Practical Revolutionary* (Philadelphia, 1969), 403–412. See also Vol. II, 232–235, 293, 294. On court closure in Virginia, see George M. Curtis III, "The Role of the Courts in the Making of the Revolution in Virginia," in James Kirby Martin, ed., *The Human Decisions of Nation Making: Essays on Colonial and Revolutionary America* (Madison, Wis., 1976), 121–146.

8. JM filed an answer on one of his printed forms in May 1791. Although he completed the form, he crossed out his printed name and wrote "James Innes" above it. See Vol. II, 93. The forms JM had printed for federal pleadings in debt cases were applicable for suits where the Sequestration Act of 1777 applied and for suits brought for prewar book debts. The printed form contained three pleas, and JM added or deleted particular pleas depending upon the issues.

9. U.S. Supreme Court Minutes, Feb. 2, Aug. 5, 1795, Feb. 6, 8–12, 23–25, and Mar. 7–8, 1796, RG 267, National Archives.

1. See Jones v. Hylton, U.S. Circuit Court, Va., Ended Cases (Restored), 1794, Va. State Lib.; 3 U.S. (3 Dall.) 199–206.

man and Alexander Willcocks. Tilghman, a prominent Philadelphia lawyer, began his argument with a masterly survey of the international law of war and an attack upon those who construed the 1777 Virginia legislation as a confiscation that would work an alteration in property. Tilghman then appealed to the Supreme Court to consider the operation of article 4 of the 1783 peace treaty. Both nations believed that no confiscations of trade debts had taken place and that the treaty provisions concerning them would be rendered nugatory if debts such as the one in *Ware v. Hylton* were held to be outside their scope. The treaty not only applied to future confiscatory laws but also voided those previously enacted. According to Tilghman, the treaty, "operating as a national compact, is a promise to remove every pre-existing bar to the recovery of British debts. . . ."[2] Marshall disputed his opponents' intrepretation of the international law of war and defended the right of the legislature to confiscate debts. Regardless of the moral connotations of the legislature's act, Marshall argued that it was binding upon the courts. Marshall then proceeded to argue that the 1777 sequestration statute was confiscatory in its nature and thus had destroyed the obligation that existed between the British merchant and the Virginia debtor. The peace treaty of 1783 applied only to subsisting debts, and since the debt in question had been destroyed by payment into the treasury, the treaty did not apply. Alexander Campbell, as Marshall's co-counsel, stressed the failure of the 1783 peace treaty specifically to void state legislative acts that confiscated British property, arguing that "obscure words ought not to be construed as to alter the existing state of things between nations, and involve thousands of individual citizens in ruin." He then referred to the limited federal authority under the Articles of Confederation, and claimed that the treaty itself had not been constitutionally competent to repeal a state statute.[3]

In rebuttal on behalf of the appellant, Alexander Willcocks contended that the treaty was the supreme law of the land, that the words "heretofore contracted" meant precisely those debts that were made before the American Revolution, and that all impediments to the collection of such debts were required to be removed. He was joined in rebuttal by William Lewis, who claimed that the Congress, and not the individual states, possessed the power of wartime confiscation. The war was waged against America as a nation, and the peace had been concluded upon the same principles; consequently all the powers of war and peace were vested in the United States and in the Congress.[4]

Four of the five justices sitting on the Supreme Court decided in favor of the plaintiff. In regard to Virginia's right to confiscate British debts, Justices Samuel Chase, James Iredell, and William Cushing unequivocally upheld the exercise of such power. Justice William Paterson found no intention by the Virginia legislature to confiscate and in fact no occurrence of confiscation of British debts. Justice James Wilson vehemently denounced the confiscation of debts as contrary to international law and practice, basing his opinion on that belief as well as on the failure of Congress to delegate confiscatory authority to the states. Concerning article 4 of the 1783 peace treaty, Justices Chase, Paterson, Wilson, and Cushing believed that it nullified the 1777 Virginia statute and required that collection

2. 3 U.S. (3 Dall.) 207–210.
3. *Ibid.*, 215–217.
4. *Ibid.*, 217–220.

actions be permitted against the original debtors. Justice Iredell, in dissent, repeated the opinion he had rendered in the U.S. Circuit Court for Virginia in favor of Marshall's client, citing British practice to support his conclusion that article 4 was executory only and could not act as a repeal of legislation until the states passed supporting legislation.[5]

The decision in *Ware v. Hylton* thus established the retroactive effect of the Treaty of Paris of 1783 and the supremacy of that treaty over the domestic legislation of the American states. The justices had been circumspect in their statements concerning the right of confiscation and whether that right was vested in the states or in the Congress. Obviously some serious questions about federal-state relations during the Confederation period remained unanswered, but at the same time the preeminence of the central government under the new Constitution was upheld, and the court treated the case as a challenge to the supremacy of treaties entered into by the federal government. Although the justices were not unmindful of the inequity of compelling Virginians to pay their debts a second time, they were willing to sacrifice private property interests to the higher values of international law and peacemaking. While John Marshall lost the decision, he nevertheless succeeded in prolonging the battle on behalf of the Virginia debtors. Viewed in the context of his political positions and his later opinions as chief justice of the United States, Marshall had argued very strongly and effectively a point of view he did not personally embrace. His success on behalf of Jones and Hylton in the lower court and his active defense of his client on appeal offer our only evidence of his ability and capacity for constitutional argument in the federal courts.

Ware v. Hylton

Argument in the Supreme Court of the United States

Printed, Alexander J. Dallas, *Reports of Cases Ruled and Adjudged in the Several Courts of the United States and of Pennsylvania*, III (Philadelphia, 1799), 210–215

Philadelphia, February 9–12, 1796[6]

Marshall, (of *Virginia*) for the Defendant in error. The case resolves itself into two general propositions: 1st, That the act of as-

5. *Ibid.*, 220–285. For a more thorough discussion of the decision, see Julius Goebel, Jr., *The Oliver Wendell Holmes Devise History of the Supreme Court of the United States: Antecedents and Beginnings to 1801*, I (New York, 1971), 748–756.

6. This case was argued from Feb. 6 to 12, and the decision and opinions were handed down on Mar. 7. U.S. Supreme Court Minutes, Feb. 1, 1790–Aug. 4, 1828, RG 267, National Archives. The editors have assumed that JM's argument in reply was heard between Feb. 9 and 12.

Alexander Dallas added the following note to his report of this case: "As I was not present during the argument, I was in hopes to have obtained the briefs of the counsel

sembly of *Virginia*, is a bar to the recovery of the debt, independent of the treaty. 2d, That the treaty does not remove the bar.

1. That the act of Assembly of *Virginia* is a bar to the recovery of the debt, introduces two subjects for consideration: 1st. Whether the Legislature had power to extinguish the debt? 2d. Whether the Legislature had exercised that power?

1st. It has been conceded,[7] that independent nations have, in general, the right of confiscation; and that *Virginia*, at the time of passing her law, was an independent nation. But, it is contended, that from the peculiar circumstances of the war, the citizens of each of the contending nations, having been members of the same government, the general right of confiscation did not apply, and ought not to be exercised.[8] It is not, however, necessary for the Defendant in error to show a parallel case in history; since, it is incumbent on those, who wish to impair the sovereignty of *Virginia*, to establish on principle, or precedent, the justice of their exception. That State being engaged in a war, necessarily possessed the powers of war; and confiscation is one of those powers, weakening the party against whom it is employed, and strengthening the party that employs it. War, indeed, is a state of force; and no tribunal can decide between the belligerent powers. But did not *Virginia* hazard as much by the war, as if she had never been a member of the *British* empire? Did she not hazard more, from the very circumstance of its being a civil war? It will be allowed, that nations have equal powers; and that *America*, in her own tribunals at least, must from the 4th of *July* 1776, be considered as independent a nation as *Great Britain*: then, what would have been the situation of *American* property, had *Great Britain* been triumphant in the conflict? Sequestration, confiscation and proscription would have followed in the train of that event; and why should the confiscation of British property be deemed less just in the event of the

themselves, for a more full display of their learning and ingenuity in this case; but being disappointed in that respect, I have been aided by the notes of Mr. *W*[illiam] *Tilghman*, to whose kindness, it is just on the present occasion to acknowledge. . . ." 3 U.S. (3 Dall.) 207. See also JM to James Iredell, Dec. 15, 1796.

7. Edward Tilghman (1751–1815) had conceded this point, but he had then argued that modern practice in the law of nations was not to confiscate debts of the citizens of a belligerent power. 3 U.S. (3 Dall.) 207.

8. Tilghman had argued that at the time of the Declaration of Independence the creditors in England and the debtors in America were under the same allegiance. Unlike merchants engaged in international trade, British creditors did not anticipate confiscation as a danger in the event of war and hence should not be subjected to its vigors. *Ibid.*, 207–208.

American triumph? The rights of war clearly exist between members of the same Empire, engaged in a civil war. Vatt. B. 3, s. 292, 295.[9] But, suppose a suit had been brought during the war by a *British* subject against an *American* citizen, it could not have been supported; and if there was a power to suspend the recovery, there must have been a power to extinguish the debt: they are, indeed, portions of the same power, emanating from the same source. The legislative authority of any country, can only be restrained by its own municipal constitution: This is a principle that springs from the very nature of society; and the judicial authority can have no right to question the validity of a law, unless such a jurisdiction is expressly given by the constitution. It is not necessary to enquire, how the judicial authority should act, if the Legislature were evidently to violate any of the laws of God; but property is the creature of civil society, and subject, in all respects, to the disposition and controul of civil institutions. There is no weight in the argument founded on what is supposed to be the understanding of the parties at the place and time of contracting debts; for, the right of confiscation does not arise from the understanding of individuals, in private transactions, but from the nature and operation of government. Nor does it follow, that because an individual has not the power of extinguishing his debts, the community, to which he belongs, may not, upon principles of public policy, prevent his creditors from recovering them. It must be repeated, that the law of property, in its origin and operation, is the offspring of the social state; not the incident of a state of nature. But the revolution did not reduce the inhabitants of *America* to a state of nature; and, if it did, the Plaintiff's claim would be at an end. Other objections to the doctrine are started: It is said, that a debt, which arises from a contract, formed between the subjects of two belligerent powers, in a neutral country, cannot be confiscated; but the society has a right to apply to its own use, the property of its enemy, wherever the right of property accrued, and wherever the property itself can be found. Suppose a debt had been con-

9. Emmerich de Vattel defined civil war as "every war between the members of the same political society." He said that once those who rise up against the constituted authorities are strong enough to force the government to make war upon them, a state of civil war must be said to exist. *The Law of Nations or the Principles of Natural Law*, trans. Charles G. Fenwick, III (Washington, D.C., 1916), 338, sec. 292. In sec. 295, Vattel pointed out that once a nation in the course of a civil war becomes divided into two independent parties, the state falls apart, and the conflict is treated as any other public war between nations. At that time all seizures of property belonging to enemy aliens are governed by the international law of war. *Ibid.*, 339–340.

tracted between two *Americans*, and one of them had joined *England*, would not the right of confiscation extend to such a debt? As to the case of the ransom bill, if the right of confiscation does not extend to it, (which is, by no means, admitted) it must be on account of the peculiar nature of the contract, implying a waiver of the rights of war. And the validity of capitulations depends on the same principle. But, let it be supposed, that a government should infringe the provisions of a capitulation, by imprisoning soldiers, who had stipulated for a free return to their home, could an action of trespass be maintained against the gaoler? No: the act of the government, though disgraceful, would be obligatory on the judiciary department.

2d. But it is now to be considered, whether, if the Legislature of *Virginia* had the power of confiscation, they have exercised it?[1] The third section of the act of Assembly discharges the debtor;[2] and, on the plain import of the term, it may be asked, if he is discharged, how can he remain charged? The expression is, he shall be discharged from the debt; and yet, it is contended, he shall remain liable to the debt. Suppose the law had said, that the debtor should be discharged from the commonwealth, but not from his creditor, would not the Legislature have betrayed the extremest folly in such a proposition? and what man in his senses would have paid a farthing into the treasury, under such a law? Yet, in violation of the expressions of the act, this is the construction which is now attempted. It is, likewise, contended, that the act of Assembly does not amount to a confiscation of the debts paid into the treasury; and that the Legislature had no power, as between creditors and debtors, to make a substitution, or commutation, in the mode of payment. But what is a confiscation? The substance, and not the form, is to be regarded. The state had a right either to make the

1. Tilghman had argued that this case was similar to Georgia v. Brailsford, 3 U.S. (3 Dall.) 1 (1794), which held that, with respect to a British creditor, the legislation of the state of Georgia had amounted to a sequestration and not a confiscation. Accepting that argument, the Supreme Court held that, sequestration being a mere suspension of the rights of ownership, the property rights of the indebted British merchant were revived by the end of the war and by the ratification of the 1783 peace treaty. JM's effort here was to distinguish Ware v. Hylton from the binding precedent of Georgia v. Brailsford.

2. Sec. 3 of "An act for Sequestering British Property, enabling those indebted to British subjects to pay off such debts, and directing the proceedings in suits where such subjects are parties" provided that "it shall and may be lawful for any citizen of this commonwealth owing money to a subject of Great Britain to pay the same, or any part thereof, from time to time, as he shall think fit" to the Commonwealth of Virginia; any recourse by British creditors was to be had against the state, and not the debtor. 9 Hening 377–380 (1777).

confiscation absolute, or to modify it as she pleased. If she had ordered the debtor to pay the money into the treasury, to be applied to public uses; would it not have been, in the eye of reason, a perfect confiscation? She has thought proper, however, only to authorize the payment, to exonerate the debtor from his creditor, and to retain the money in the treasury, subject to her own discretion, as to its future appropriation. As far as the arrangement has been made, it is confiscatory in its nature, and must be binding on the parties; though in the exercise of her discretion, the state might chuse to restore the whole, or any part, of the money to the original creditor. Nor is it sufficient to say, that the payment was voluntary, in order to defeat the confiscation. A law is an expression of the public will; which, when expressed, is not the less obligatory, because it imposes no penalty. Banks, Canal Companies, and numerous associations of a similar description, are formed on the principle of voluntary subscription. The nation is desirous that such institutions should exist; individuals are invited to subscribe on the terms of the law; and, when they have subscribed, they are entitled to all the benefits, and are subject to all the inconveniences of the association, although no penalties are imposed. So, when the government of *Virginia* wished to possess itself of the debts previously owing to *British* subjects, the debtors were invited to make the payment into the treasury; and, having done so, there is no reason, or justice, in contending that the law is not obligatory on all the world, in relation to the benefit, which it promised as an inducement to the payment. If, subsequent to the act of 1777, a law had been passed confiscating *British* debts, for the use of the state, with orders that the Attorney General should sue all *British* debtors, could he have sued the defendants in error, as *British* debtors, after this payment of the debt into the treasury? Common sense and common honesty revolt at the idea; and, yet, if the *British* creditor retained any right or interest in the debt, the state would be entitled, on principles of law, to recover the amount.[3]

II. Having thus, then, established, that at the time of entering into the Treaty of 1783, the Defendant owed nothing to the Plain-

3. JM again skirted the question of property rights and stressed the equity of estopping the state from suing a citizen who had already paid into the loan office. Payment into the loan office under the 1777 legislation relieved the Virginia debtor of his obligation, but under the terms of that statute it did not necessarily deprive the British creditor of his property, which was held in safekeeping by the Virginia authorities. *Ibid.* In JM's view the passage of a confiscation act while the debt was held in safekeeping would merely transfer the British creditor's property to the Commonwealth of Virginia.

tiff, it is next to be enquired, whether that treaty revived the debt in favour of the Plaintiff, and removed the bar to a recovery, which the law of *Virginia* had interposed? The words of the fourth article of the Treaty are, "that creditors on either side, shall meet with no lawful impediment to the recovery of the full value, in sterling money, of all *bona fide* debts heretofore contracted "[4] Now, it may be asked, who are creditors? There cannot be a creditor where there is not a debt; and *British* debts were extinguished by the act of confiscation. The articles, therefore, must be construed with reference to those creditors, who had *bona fide* debts, subsisting, in legal force, at the time of making the Treaty; and the word *recovery* can have no effect to create a debt, where none previously existed. Without discussing the power of Congress to take away a vested right by treaty, the fair and rational construction of the instrument itself, is sufficient for the Defendant's cause. The words ought, surely, to be very plain, that shall work so evident a hardship, as to compel a man to pay a debt, which he had before extinguished. The treaty, itself, does not point out any particular description of persons, who were to be deemed debtors; and it must be expounded in relation to the existing state of things. It is not true, that the fourth article can have no meaning, unless it applies to cases like the present. For instance;—there was a law of *Virginia*, which prohibited the recovery of *British* debts, that had not been paid into the treasury: these were *bona fide* subsisting debts; and the prohibition was a legal impediment to the recovery, which the treaty was intended to remove.[5] So, likewise, in several other states, laws had been passed authorizing a discharge of *British* debts in paper money, or by a tender of property at a valuation, and the treaty was calculated to guard against such impediments to the recovery of the sterling value of those debts. It appears, therefore, that at the time of making the treaty, the state of things was such, that *Virginia* had exercised her sovereign right of confiscation, and had actually received the money from the *British* debtors. If debts thus paid were within the scope of the fourth article, those who framed the article knew of the payment; and upon every

4. Miller, ed., *Treaties*, II, 154.

5. See 11 Hening 176 (1782) and 349 (1783). Tilghman had argued that "unless this provision [in the 1783 peace treaty] applied to cases like the present, it will be useless and nugatory. An interpretation, which would render a clause in the treaty of no effect, ought not to be admitted." 3 U.S. (3 Dall.) 209. JM's statement was designed to blunt this argument by demonstrating that some Virginia debtors still owed obligations to British creditors, and that those debts were rendered collectible by the provisions of the 1783 treaty.

principle of equity and law, it ought to be presumed, that the recovery, which they contemplated, was intended against the receiving state, not against the paying debtor. *Virginia* possessing the right of compelling a payment for her own use, the payment to her, upon her requisition, ought to be considered as a payment to the attorney, or agent, of the *British* creditor.[6] Nor is such a substitution a novelty in legal proceedings: a foreign attachment is founded on the same principle. Suppose judgment had been obtained against the Defendants in error, as garnishee in a foreign attachment[7] brought against the Plaintiff in error, and the money had been paid, accordingly, to the Plaintiff in the attachment; but it afterwards appeared that the Plaintiff in the attachment had, in fact, no cause of action, having been paid his debt before he commenced the suit. If the treaty had been made in such a state of things, which would be the debtor contemplated by the fourth article, the Defendants in error, who had complied with a legal judgment against them, or the Plaintiff in the attachment, who had received the money? This act of *Virginia* must have been known to the *American* and *British* commissioners; and, therefore, cannot be repealed without plain and explicit expressions directed to that object. Besides, the public faith ought to be preserved. The public faith was plighted by the act of *Virginia*; and, as a revival of the debt in question, would be a shameful violation of the faith of the state to her own citizens, the treaty should receive any possible interpretion to avoid so dishonorable and so pernicious a consequence. It is evident, that the power of the government, to take away a vested right, was questionable in the minds of the *American* commissioners, since they would not exercise that power in restoring confiscated real estate;[8] and confiscated debts, or other personal estate must come within the same rule. If Congress had the power of divesting a vested right, it must have arisen from the necessity of the case; and if the necessity had existed, the *American* commissioners, explicitly avowing it, would have justified their acquiescence to the nation. But the commissioners could have no

6. This is a restatement of JM's principal argument that recovery should be sought against Virginia and not against the Virginia citizen who had extinguished his debt by payment into the loan office.

7. A foreign attachment is the garnishment of funds or goods in the hands of a third party, which funds or goods are held by him to the credit of a nonresident judgment debtor.

8. This is a reference to art. 5 of the treaty, by which the United States agreed to recommend to the states that restitution be made for confiscated British and loyalist estates. Miller, ed., *Treaties*, II, 154.

motive to form a treaty such as the opposite construction supposes; for, if the stipulation was indispensable to the attainment of peace, the object was national, and so should be the payment of the equivalent: the commissioners, in such case, would have agreed, at once, that the public should pay the *British* debts; since the public must, on every principle of equity, be answerable to the *Virginia* debtor, who is now said to be the victim. The case cited from *Jenkins*, does not apply; as there is no article of the treaty, that declares the law of Virginia void.[9] See *Old Law of Evidence*, 196.[1]

From Samuel Coleman

Letterbook Copy, War 10, Virginia State Library

Sir, Richmond, February 12, 1796

I am directed by the Governor, as Commander in Chief of the Militia, to request, in behalf of the Adjutant General, that you will, with as little delay as possible, cause a Return of your Brigade to be made to his office in Richmond, that a General Return of the militia may be prepared for the Executive, and a duplicate forwarded to the President of the United States, according to law, without delay. I have the honor to be Sir etc.

SAM: COLEMAN.[2]

9. Edward Tilghman, for the plaintiffs in error, had argued that the repeal of a statute did not invalidate mesne acts unless the repealing statute declared the repealed act to be void. 3 U.S. (3 Dall.) 209. He went on to maintain that the 1783 treaty was "a promise to remove every pre-existing bar to the recovery of British debts; and, whatever may have been the previous state of things, this is a paramount engagement. . . ." *Ibid.*, 210. JM contended that an express treaty provision, like an expression of voidness in a repealing statute, was required to invalidate mesne acts, such as Hylton's payment into the Virginia treasury.

The case from Jenkins is Anonymous, Jenk. Cent. 233 (Case 6) 145 Eng. Rep. 162–163 (Exchequer 1567); the case holds that when one statute is repealed by another the acts done in the meantime are valid, but not in any case where the statute is declared void.

1. The reference is probably to [William Nelson], *The Law of Evidence* . . . ,which first appeared in 1717 and was popularly known as the "Old Law of Evidence" to distinguish it from a newer book by Sir Geoffrey Gilbert.

2. This was a circular letter that Gov. Robert Brooke asked to be sent to the brigadier generals of the militia in compliance with the Militia Law of 1792. 1 Stat. 273–274. Coleman (1755–1811) was assistant to the adjutant general, Simon Morgan. See also Coleman to JM, calendared at Aug. 8, 1796.

Bounty Land Grant

DS, Collection of Clarence Dillon, Far Hills, N.J.

[*February 20, 1796, Philadelphia*. JM is given 1,000 acres in the Ohio Territory for his military service during the Revolution.[3]]

To John Nicholson

ALS, Collection of Henry N. Ess III, New York City

Sir[4] Indian Queen,[5] February 24, 1796

I must request your attention to the business concerning which I waited on you yesterday.

Some gentlemen of Richmond in Virginia are possessd of notes drawn by Mr. Allyson[6] & indorsd by you to the amount of about ten thousand dollars of which somewhat less than 2200 dollars being now due were put into my hands for the purpose of obtaining payment. On failure to pay I was directed to put the notes in suit. I informd you that Mr. Allison had been applied to & had faild to pay.

I am very far from being inclind unnecessarily to institute suits. The Gentlemen for whom I act will I am persuaded be content with any arrangements I may make. I therefore suspend any further procedure until I hear from you. Today & tomorrow I remain in Philadelphia. Be pleasd to let me know by what time I may rely on receiving money for the notes I have mentiond. If

3. The land is described in a survey, Nov. 25, 1794, Vol. II, 298. JM sold this tract and an adjacent 1,000 acres to Thomas Underwood, of Richmond, on Apr. 13, 1808. The deed was recorded on Sept. 8, 1808, in the Greene County Deedbook, 509–511, Office of the Greene County Recorder, Xenia, Ohio.

4. John Nicholson (1757–1800) had been comptroller general for Pennsylvania after the Revolution until 1793, when he was impeached by the Pennsylvania legislature for redeeming his own state certificates instead of funding them in federal certificates. He was acquitted in 1794 but resigned from office. After his resignation he became a partner of Robert Morris.

5. The Indian Queen was a tavern on south Fourth Street, above Chestnut Street, in Philadelphia, alleged to have been the site where Thomas Jefferson wrote the first draft of the Declaration of Independence. John E. Watson, *Annals of Philadelphia and Pennsylvania in the Olden Time* . . . , I (Philadelphia, 1844), 466.

6. William Allason (1730–1800) had emigrated from Scotland in 1757 and had established a profitable mercantile business in Falmouth, Va., based on the tobacco industry. See Robert William Spoede, "William Allason: Merchant in an Emerging Nation (1730–1800)" (Ph.D. diss., College of William and Mary, 1973).

the time you name be not unreasonably distant I will wait in the confidence that you will not disappoint me. You will please to observe in naming the day that when the contract was made the sellers counted on punctuality. I am Sir very respectfully, Your obedt. Servt.

J MARSHALL

Fire Insurance Application

DS, Mutual Assurance Society, Richmond

Richmond, *ca.* February 24, 1796

Form of the Declarations for Assurance[7]

I the underwritten Jno. Marshall residing at Richmond in the county of Henrico do hereby declare for Assurance in the Mutual Assurance Society against Fire on Buildings of the State of Virginia, established the 26th December, 1795, agreeable to the several acts of the General Assembly of this state,[8] to wit:

My Five Buildings on Lots No 786 and 792 at the City of Richmond now occupied by Myself situated between the Back Street North and that of A–Street South in the county of Henrico.[9] Their dimensions, situation and contiguity to other buildings or wharves, what the walls are built of, and what the buildings are covered with, are specified in the hereunto annexed description of the said Buildings on the plat, signed by me and the appraisers, and each valued by them as appears by their certificate here under, to wit:

The Dwelling	marked	A. at	5000	Dollars, say	five thousand	Dollars
The Office	do.	B. at	200	do.	Two hundred	do.
The Landra etc.	do.	C. at	400	do.	Four hundred	do.
The Kitchen	do.	D. at	130	do.	One hundred & thirty	do.
The Stable	do.	E. at	170	do.	One hund & seventy	do.
The	do.	F. at		do.		do.
The	do.	G. at		do.		do.
			5900 $			

say Five thousand Nine hundred Dollars in all.

7. This is a printed form, numbered 72, that someone completed for JM. On Feb. 24, JM was in Philadelphia and could not have signed this application; he probably signed it upon his return to Richmond, *ca.* Mar. 10.

8. See 1 Shepherd 307–310 (1794) and 405–406 (1795).

9. This site is now occupied by JM's house and the John Marshall Courts Building. The latter building was dedicated in 1977.

I do hereby declare and affirm that the above mentioned property is not, nor shall be insured elsewhere, without giving notice thereof, agreeably to the policy that may issue in my name, upon the filing of this declaration, and provided the whole sum do not exceed four-fifths of the verified value, and that I will abide by, observe, and adhere to the Constitution, Rules and Regulations as are already established, or may hereafter be established by a majority of the insured, present in person, or by representatives, at a general Meeting to be agreed upon for the said Assurance Society. Witness my hand and seal at Richmond the 24 day of February 1796.

J MARSHALL [LS]

Back Street on the North

Lot No 792

Lot No 787

Lot No 791

Lot No 786

Cross Street on the West

Cross Street on the East

Street Joining on the South

We the underwritten, being each of us House-Owners, declare and affirm that we have examined the above mentioned Property of Jno. Marshall and that we are of opinion that it would cost in cash Five thousand Nine hundred Dollars to build the same, and is now actually worth Five thousand Nine hundred Dollars in ready money, and will command the same as above specified to the best of our knowledge and belief.

City of Richmond Sc.
The foregoing valuation Sworn to in due form before me, a Magistrate for the said City of Richmond. Given under my hand this Eighth day of April in the year 1796.
JNO. BARRET

Residing in Richmond
DABNEY MINOR[1]
WILLIAM GILES
WM. MCKIM[2]

From Robert Morris

Letterbook Copy, Morris Papers, Library of Congress

Dear Sir Philadelphia, March 8, 1796

This moment we have heard of the arrival of the Ship Pennsylvania Captn York at Cowes in which went Mr & Mrs Marshall[3] but no Letter from them as yet. The news comes from London by the December packet in a letter of the 4th of Decemb. I congratulate you upon this Event & Remain, Yrs. etc.

R M

To an Unknown Person

ALS, Dreer Collection, Historical Society of Pennsylvania

Sir[4] Richmond, March 14, 1796

I have seen Mr. Washington[5] & conversd with him on the sub-

1. Minor (*ca.* 1760–1822) was a Richmond joiner and carpenter.
2. McKim was a Richmond carpenter.
3. See Morris to JM, Dec. 29, 1795, Vol. II, 329; JM to Mary W. Marshall, Feb. 3, 1796. Cowes is located on the Isle of Wight off the coast of England.
4. The letter has several endorsements on it but none that indicates clearly to whom JM addressed it. In an unknown hand beneath the dateline is written, "Jno Marshall, And. 8. Apl. (1796)." Robert Gilmor, whose autograph collection was purchased by Ferdinand Dreer in the 1850s, wrote on the verso, "From Wm Sullivan Esqr of Boston July 35 [signed], R. G." Presumably Gilmor obtained the letter from Sullivan in 1835.
5. Bushrod Washington.

ject of your letter. We both think the agreement very carelessly & incautiously drawn but yet suppose your construction to be the right one. If you can adduce in proof those additional circumstances which you mention they will very much aid your exposition of the instrument. It has been said that some declarations you have made will be brought to bear against you. I do not know how this may turn out. I am Sir very respectfully your obedt.

J MARSHALL

From Robert Morris

Letterbook Copy, Morris Papers, Library of Congress

Dear Sir Philadelphia, April 11, 1796

I suppose your Brother has written to you by direct Conveyances to Virginia & informed you of the Birth of his son[6] etc. Accept my thanks for the Communication in your letter of the 15th ulto[7] which is very agreeable to Dr Sir, Yrs

R M

From Charles Lee

ALS, Gray-Glines Collection, Connecticut State Library

Philadelphia, April 17, 1796

How comes it my good friend, that I have received no letter in answer to mine relative to the vacancy of the office of District-Attorney of Virginia?[8]

I wrote to you sometime ago and noted the suits which I wish could wait for me: and the president has put it out of my power to be present term by refusing me leave of absence at this particular

6. Thomas Marshall (1796–1826) was born on Feb. 6, supposedly on a ship in the Thames. He ultimately settled in Winchester, Va., where he practiced law until 1826, when he, his wife, and two children died within hours of one another during an epidemic.

7. Not found.

8. Lee's letter has not been found. Alexander Campbell had resigned as U.S. attorney for Virginia. JM recommended Daniel Call for the position. See Lee to JM, May 5, 1796, for additional information regarding this position.

juncture of our public affairs. If possible obtain a continuance till the next, and for that purpose you may if you please mention the true cause (should you deem this expedient or necessary) to the judges out of court, to whom also present my respects. At the ensuing term I will attend or if absent a longer delay will not be prayed.[9]

Write me how the public mind is impressed respecting the conduct of the President and of the house of representatives concerning the treaty-papers; and whatever you have heard said about this matter at Richmond. Here & to the east and in maryland the President's message refusing the papers is generally approved.[1]

The city gazettes mention every thing that I know of much consequence that relates to public affairs, and the inferences from certain measures, will be made by your own mind more justly perhaps than by mine. 100 members are present and it is said & beleived that 57 members will assuredly vote for Maclay's resolution, or a similar one. It has been supported by Mr. Madison in a lengthy speech;[2] but I own I felt not even a doubt on my mind after hearing him, that his opinion was erroneous and unwise.

The president seems to be well apprized of the possible consequences that may proceed from the measures of the house of representatives, as well to our internal tranquility as to external embarassments and war: but he holds his serenity of mind and if the fair prospects of durable peace and prosperity are blasted by the machinations of the house of representatives, a consolation is afforded that the people whom he loves and whose good he is always promoting, will be able to point to the authors of their calamity. The people have their enemies, and the same persons are his ene-

9. Lee, who had become U.S. attorney general on Dec. 10, 1795, argued at least two cases at the fall 1796 term of the Virginia Court of Appeals. See 2 Va. (2 Wash.) 204, 288.

1. On Mar. 30, Washington refused to submit the papers relating to the negotiation of the Jay Treaty to the House of Representatives. *Annals of Congress*, V, 760–761. For opinion in Richmond, see JM to Rufus King, Apr. 25, 1796, and JM to Alexander Hamilton, Apr. 25, 1796.

2. Samuel Maclay (1741–1811), a Republican congressman from Pennsylvania, introduced a resolution on Apr. 14, 1796, stating that "it is not expedient at this time to concur in passing the laws necessary for carrying the said [Jay] Treaty into effect." Contrary to Lee's interpretation of the speech, James Madison did not favor adopting a resolution but instead advocated voting against a bill that would implement the treaty. *Annals of Congress*, V, 970–971, 975–987; Jerald A. Combs, *The Jay Treaty: Political Battleground of the Founding Fathers* (Berkeley, Calif., 1970), 177, 185–186.

mies: a truth that must be perceived because it is no longer concealed, if the actions of men and not their words are to be regarded. My respects to Mrs. Marshall. Yours most truely

CHARLES LEE

To Andrew Van Bibber

Printed Extract, Kingston Galleries, Inc., Catalog No. 6 (Somerville, Mass., 1963), 25

[*April 18, 1796, Richmond.* "Your[3] suit against Robins has been abated. . . . If you should wish it renewed & will give me notice I will do so. . . . I shall now press it but it will be a considerable time before judgement can be obtained. The suit against Green waits for your answer. . . ."]

To Rufus King

ALS, Hamilton Papers, Library of Congress

Dear Sir Richmond, April 19, 1796

I pray you to excuse my seeming inattention to the subject alluded to in yours[4] by the last mail.

Having never been in habits of correspondence with Mr. H. I coud not by letter ask from him a decision on the proposition I was requested to make him without giving him at the same time a full statement of the whole conversation & of the persons with whom that conversation was held. In doing this I felt some difficulty. I am not positively certain what course that Gentleman might take. The proposition might not only have been rejected but mentiond publickly to others in such manner as to have become an unpleasant circumstance. Genl. Lee[5] corresponds familiarly with

3. Andrew Augustus Van Bibber (*ca.* 1762–1808) was a Baltimore merchant who had settled in Mathews County, Va. See Vol. II, 131, 423.

4. Not found.

5. Henry Lee. Patrick Henry was being asked about his willingness to run for president on the Federalist ticket. See Harold C. Syrett *et al.*, eds., *The Papers of Alexander Hamilton* (New York, 1961–   ), XX, 151–153, 158–159. See also JM to King, May 24, 1796.

Mr. H. & is in the habit of proposing offices to him. I deemd it most adviseable to speak to that gentleman & to request him to sound Mr. H. as from himself or in such manner as might in any event be perfectly safe. He promisd to do so but said confidently that no answer woud be receivd to the letter, nor [*was*] any answer receivd.

Mr. H. will be in Richmond on the 22d. of May. I can then sound him myself & if I find him (I suspect I shall) totally unwilling to engage in the contest, I can stop where prudence may direct. I trust it will not then be too late to bring forward to the public [*view*] Mr. H. or any other gentleman who may be thought of in his stead.

Shoud any thing occur to render it improper to have any communication with Mr. H. on this subject or shoud you wish the communication to take any particular shape you will be so obliging as to drop me a line concerning it. With great & sincere respect & esteem, I am dear Sir your Obedt.

J MARSHALL

To Rufus King

ALS, King Papers, New-York Historical Society

Dear Sir Richmond, April 25, 1796

I take the liberty to avail myself of your aid for forwarding to Mr. Hamilton the inclosd letter.

The ruling party of Virginia are extremely irritated at the vote of today & will spare no exertion to obtain a majority in other counties. Even here they will affect to have the greater number of Freeholders & have set about counter resolutions to which they have the signatures of very many respectable persons but of still a [greater number of] meer boys & altho [some caution has] been usd by us in ex[cluding those who][6] might not be considerd as authorizd to vote they will not fail to charge us with having collected a number of names belonging to foreigners & to persons having no property in the place. The charge is as far untrue as perhaps has

6. The words in brackets were lost when the signature was cut from the verso of the document. The editors have supplied the words from Charles R. King, ed., *The Life and Correspondence of Rufus King . . .*, II (New York, 1895), 45–46.

ever happend on any occasion of the sort. We coud by resorting to that measure have doubled our list of petitioners.[7]

I have endeavord to take means to procure similar applications from various parts of the state. Exitus in dubio est.[8] With very much respect & esteem I am dear Sir Your obedt.

[J MARSHALL]

To Alexander Hamilton

ALS, Hamilton Papers, Library of Congress

Dear Sir[1] Richmond, April 25, 1796

Yours of the 14th[2] only reachd me by the mail of this evening. I had been informd of the temper of the house of representatives & we had promptly taken such measures as appeard to us fitted to the occasion. We coud not venture an expression of the public mind under the violent prejudices with which it had been impressd so long as a hope remaind that the house of representatives might ultimately consult the interest or honor of the nation. But now when all hope of this has vanishd, it was deemd adviseable

7. For the best account of the debate in Virginia over the ratification of the Jay Treaty, see Richard R. Beeman, *The Old Dominion and the New Nation, 1788–1801* (Lexington, Ky., 1972), 140–158, esp. 148–149.

Edmund Randolph observed: "Between 3 & 400 *persons* were present; a large proportion of whom were British merchants, some of whom pay for the British purchases of horses, their clerks, officers, who hold posts under the President at his will, stockholders, expectants of office, and many without the shadow of a freehold. . . . Marshall's argument was inconsistent, and shifting; concluding every third sentence with the horrors of war. . . . Marshall, suspecting, that he would be outnumbered by freeholders, and conscious, that none should instruct, except those, who elect, quitted the idea of instructions, and betook himself to a petition, in which, he said, all the inhabitants of Richmond, though not freeholders, might join." Randolph to James Madison, Apr. 25, 1796, Madison Papers, Library of Congress.

8. "The outcome is uncertain."

1. Hamilton had resigned as secretary of the Treasury on Jan. 31, 1795, and had settled in New York City. Harold C. Syrett *et. al.*, eds., *The Papers of Alexander Hamilton* (New York, 1961–), XVII, 413.

Rufus King apparently showed this letter to John Fenno (1751–1798) before forwarding it to Hamilton, since most of the first paragraph and the first sentence of the second paragraph were printed in Fenno's *Gazette of United States* (Philadelphia), Apr. 30, 1796. See Syrett *et al.*, eds., *Hamilton Papers*, XX, 137, where this letter is also printed.

2. Not found.

to make the experiment however hazardous it might be. A meeting was calld which was more numerous than I have ever seen at this place & after a very ardent & zealous discussion which consumd the day a decided majority declard in favor of a resolution that the welfare & honor of the nation requird us to give full effect to the treaty negotiated with Britain.

This resolution with a petition drawn by an original opponent of the treaty[3] will be forwarded by the next post to Congress. The subject will probably be taken up in every county in the state or at any rate in very many of them. It is probable that a majority of the counties will avow sentiments opposd to ours, but the division of the state will appear to be much more considerable than has been stated. In some of the districts there will certainly be ⟨many⟩ a majority who will concur with us & that perhaps may have some effect. As Man is a gregarious animal we shall certainly derive much aid from declarations in support of the constitution & of appropriations if such can be obtaind from our sister States. The ground we take here is very much that of Mr. Hillhouse.[4] We admit the discretionary constitutional power of the representatives on the subject of appropriations but contend that the treaty is as completely a valid & obligatory contract when negotiated by the President & ratified by him with the assent & advice of the Senate as if sanctiond by the house of representatives also under a constitution requiring such sanction. I think it woud be very difficult perhaps impossible to engage Mr. H.[5] on the right side of this question.

If you have any communications which might promote a concurrence of action we shall be proud to receive them. With much respect & esteem I am dear Sir your obedt.

J MARSHALL

3. For the resolution and a petition drawn by Henry Banks, see *Virginia Gazette, and General Advertiser* (Richmond), Apr. 27, 1796. This account also includes the minutes of the meeting.

4. James Hillhouse (1754–1832), a Federalist congressman from Connecticut, had expressed similar views in a speech before the House of Representatives. *Annals of Congress*, V, 660–676. Hillhouse resigned from the House of Representatives on May 12, 1796, to accept election to the U.S. Senate, where he served until he resigned on June 10, 1810.

5. Patrick Henry.

From Richard Blow

Letterbook Copy, Blow Family Papers, Swem Library, College of William and Mary

Sir Norfolk, May 1, 1796

I shall be glad you will Inform me what Day the suit Wigfall vs. me[6] in The federal Court is set for Tryal, & Inclose me a blank Supena. Yo. Mo. Obt. St.

RICHD. BLOW

From Robert Morris

Letterbook Copy, Morris Papers, Library of Congress

Dear Sir Philadelphia, May 3, 1796

I have received your letter of the 18 ulto & am negotiating for Bank Stock to answer your demand.[7] I have not yet got it, but I hope soon to succeed in obtaining the number of Shares necessary, and the moment I do, you shall be advised thereof. I lately sent a letter by Post from your Brother which no doubt advised you of his having a Son who he says is a remarkable fine lusty Fellow.[8] I am Dr Sir Yrs

R M

From Charles Lee

ALS, Collection of Mr. and Mrs. Morris Login, Bronx, N. Y.

Dear Sir Philadelphia, May 5, 1796

Your two last favors have been duly received: and before this day you must have heard of the resolution of the house to appropriate the sums necessary for keeping our treaty with great Britain.

6. JM received fees in Wigfall v. Blow in 1790 and 1795. See Vol. II, 400, 496. Richard Blow (1746–1833) was a Southampton merchant and partner in the firm Briggs & Blow, which had offices in Williamsburg, Southampton, and Tower Hill. Fredrika J. Teute, "The Commercial Endeavors of a Virginia Merchant during the Confederation Period: The Rise and Fall of Richard Blow, 1781–1791" (M.A. thesis, College of William and Mary, 1976).

7. Not found. See Morris to JM, June 16, 1796.

8. See Morris to JM, Apr. 11, 1796.

A bill has passed the house of representatives on tuesday last to that effect. No debates of consequence attended the passage of the bill and indeed opposition to it ceased when the [*motion*] on the 2d. instant was agreed to.[9]

Congress have agreed that they may finish the business by the 20th. but I rather suppose it will be very near June before they will adjourn.[1] Indeed with such a house of representatives the session cannot be too short; although I am told at this time good temper and harmony reigns among the members.

The wounds given to T.A. Muhlenberg yesterday, proceeded from a wild young man through private motives uninfluenced by political opinions or acts.[2]

Mr Call was named by me to the president, but as Mr. T. Nelson had formerly solicited the office and there was a certainty of his accepting it, and possessed merit as a citizen as well as a lawyer, the choice of the President fell on him.[3] An appointment could not be delayed and there was more uncertainty with respect to Mr. Calls acceptance of the office. I stated my conjecture that he would accept, and I stated his fitness exactly in conformity to your opinion of him as you have since communicated it. Indeed none other but himself & Mr Nelson were much considered by the president. Mr. B.W.[4] you know from Delicacy (blameable in my conception of things) was not contemplated by him.

Fenno has printed, that the "hollow ware company in a late blast have consumed their furnace."[5] This is a mistake as future

9. James Hillhouse reported a bill from the Committee of the Whole and moved that it be engrossed. The bill passed the House of Representatives the next day. *Annals of Congress*, V, 1293, 1295.

The letter has a tear in the last sentence of this paragraph where the editors have inserted a word in italics. The tear extends to the edge of the first word in the next paragraph, "Congress." It is possible that another word is missing and that Lee intended no new paragraph.

1. The first session of the Fourth Congress actually adjourned on June 1, 1796. *Ibid.*, 1516.

2. Frederick A. Muhlenberg (1750–1801) was stabbed, although not fatally, by his brother-in-law, Bernard Schaeffer, on May 4, 1796. A biographer of the Muhlenberg family disagrees with Lee. He says that Schaeffer, prone to emotional instability, broke under popular excitement and attempted to kill the man who, as Speaker of the House of Representatives, had cast the deciding vote in favor of appropriating funds to carry out the provisions of the Jay Treaty. Paul A. W. Wallace, *The Muhlenbergs of Pennsylvania* (Philadelphia, 1950), 285–287.

3. The appointment of Thomas Nelson, Jr., as district attorney for Virginia was announced in Philadelphia on May 5, 1796, in the *Philadelphia Gazette and Universal Daily Advertiser*. See also Lee to JM, Apr. 17, 1796, for evidence of Lee's solicitation of JM's recommendation of Daniel Call.

4. Bushrod Washington.

5. John Fenno, editor of the *Gazette of United States* (Philadelphia), printed the fol-

events well shew. Mrs. Washington in her conversations speaks in all companies of being retired ere long at Mount Vernon once more; The president has signified his disposition to leave the public theatre, upon several occasions when I was present; and it is my conjecture that nothing will induce him to continue in office after the present term shall expire that is to say after the 4th. of next March. I am not authorised to say that this his determination is unalterable; but I fear it. Should this be the case, I have no doubt he will promulgate it soon perhaps after the end of the present Session.[6] Such an event will make it necessary to send men to the house of representatives who are for the independence, and peace of these United States and for measures of the same tenor with his administration. You shall hear from me again upon this point.

To return to the treaty business, the votes on saturday last when the yeas and nays were taken, may appear to some persons unaccountable but they cannot to you. Parker Heath and Claiborne being determined to vote against appropriation in any form, were against Dearborn's amendment,[7] which containing a reprobation of the treaty, made it more possible that a vote of appropriation

---

lowing announcement: "The Hollow Ware Company at the last blast, melted down their furnace—a few articles were saved in the confusion, have been offered for sale, but the ware is all *cracked*, and will fetch no price. The Company is not however dissolved. . . ." *Ibid.*, May 4, 1796.

6. George Washington's Farewell Address, dated Sept. 7, 1796, was not published until Sept. 19, 1796, although he had discussed its preparation with Alexander Hamilton as early as Feb. 1796. *Claypoole's American Daily Advertiser* (Philadelphia), Sept. 19, 1796; Harold C. Syrett *et al.*, eds., *The Papers of Alexander Hamilton* (New York, 1961–), XX, 169–173.

7. By a vote of 50 to 49 on Apr. 30, the House defeated Henry Dearborn's amendment to the resolution supporting appropriations for the Jay Treaty. Dearborn (1751–1829), of the Maine district of Massachusetts, had inserted words criticizing the treaty to make it easier for opponents to vote for the final resolution. Josiah Parker (1751–1810), John Heath (1758–1803), and Thomas Claiborne (1751–1829), all Republicans from Virginia, were obviously opposed to the treaty in any form. *Annals of Congress*, V, 1289.

Parker had served under Lee for a few months in 1776. He resigned his commission in 1778 and returned to his native Isle of Wight County, where he was elected to the House of Delegates in 1778, 1779, 1782, and 1783. He served in Congress from 1789 to 1801.

Heath was one of the organizers of Phi Beta Kappa at the College of William and Mary. After the Revolution he entered the practice of law in Northumberland County and was elected to the House of Delegates in 1782 and 1783. He served in Congress from 1793 to 1797, when he left political office to return to law practice. In 1803 he moved to Richmond to take a seat on the Council of State, an office he held until his death.

Claiborne, a leading citizen of Brunswick County, served in the House of Delegates from 1783 to 1787, was sheriff from 1789 to 1792, and was a member of Congress from 1793 to 1799 and from 1801 to 1805.

would pass in that way rather than in the original one. In this business the end has been better than the most sanguine hoped. Still however the national honor has been deeply tarnished, by those who advocated and voted in favor of a breach of the treaty, & those men ought in my opinion to be for ever excluded from the public councils of america for the part they have taken to disgrace their country.

The british minister Robt. Liston[8] is at new york and will be here soon; he left London about the 23d. of march. I hear nothing remarkable from Europe. My detention here is unspeakably irksome. For being entirely in an unsettled state, without money or the means of getting it conveniently, without servants whom I have in vain most diligently sought, I have passed my time most miserably. Farewell

CHARLES LEE

To Rufus King

ALS, King Papers, New-York Historical Society

Dear Sir[9] Richmond, May 24, 1796

Mr. Henry has at length been sounded on the subject you committed to my charge. Genl. Lee & myself have each conversd with him on it tho without informing him particularly of the persons who authorizd the communication. He is unwilling to embark in the business. His unwillingness I think proceeds from an apprehension of the difficulties to be encounterd by those who shall fill high executive offices. With very much respect & esteem I am dear Sir your obedt.

J MARSHALL

8. Liston (1742–1836) assumed his duties as minister extraordinary and plenipotentiary to the United States on May 16, 1796, after serving in a similar capacity in Madrid, Stockholm, and Constantinople. He replaced British minister George Hammond.

9. The letter is addressed to "The Honble. Rufus King, Philadelphia," and is postmarked at Richmond, May 25. King noted on the address leaf, "Ansd. 1 June, regretting etc. and observing that it wd. be requisite to fix on another person without Delay." See JM to King, Apr. 19, 1796.

From Robert Morris

Letterbook Copy, Morris Papers, Library of Congress

Dear Sir Philadelphia, June 16, 1796

You will receive herein my answer to the Bill filed in your Court of Chancery against me by Alexander John Alexander which I expect will fully refute his pretensions and make the Contriver of that measure shake his head a little more than usual, for I must suppose there can be no other Bill of Exchange than the one of which the Copy is annexed and the Original of which I send to Mr Wm. Wiseham to be kept by him untill Mr Richard returns to Richmond, so that it may be at hand ready to be produced if wanted.[1] I did not succeed in the purchase of the Bank Stock mentioned in my letter of the 3d ulto to you and as Mr Richard tells me in his letter of the 4 Inst that you want the money for the Stock,[2] you may if you please draw upon me for $7000 giving me as much time in the sight as you can & I will most certainly pay your drafts as they become due.

The Brokers shall fix the price of the Stock at the market price at the time I pay the money & I will then state the accot including Dividends & remit you the Balance but if you prefer having the Stock I will buy it on receiving your Answer to this, cost what it may. I am still struggling with want & money so scarce that Sacrifice of Property cannot enable the attainment of it. I hope times will soon mend & remain, Yrs

R M

1. John Alexander, of Loudoun County, Va., representing William Alexander & Co., apparently had filed a bill in chancery against Morris in an attempt to collect money owed the company. Morris's copy of the bill of exchange was marked paid in William Alexander's hand. See Morris to William Wiseham, June 16, 1796, Letterbook, Morris Papers, Library of Congress.

William Wiseham (d. 1805) was a Richmond merchant. John Richard, Jr. (d. 1823), appears to have traveled between New York City and Richmond consulting with various people about pending litigation. See Vol. II, 37. See also Morris to Richard, May 23, 1796, Letterbook, Morris Papers, Lib. Cong.

2. See Morris to JM, May 3, 1796.

Certificate

Copy, Henry Banks Papers, Virginia Historical Society[3]

[Richmond], June 23, 1796

Mr. Henry Banks informs me that he wishes to make a transfer of a part of a demand which he has against the Commonwealth of Virginia and, wishes my opinion thereon.

This is to Certify that at the last District Court there was a Judgment in his favor for a very considerable Sum upon which the Auditor appealed which is now depending. I do expect that the Judgment will be affirmed at the next Court of Appeals, in as much as the said Court have affirmd a Demand which I think precisely in its nature and principals.[4] Certified as my Opinion June 23d. 1796.

JOHN MARSHALL

Deed

ADS, Collection of Robert M. and Leona Skolfield Vaughan, Newtonville, Mass., on deposit at Swem Library, College of William and Mary

[*June 24, 1796, Richmond.* Based on a contract dated Dec. 28, 1794, JM sells John McCreery 1,640 acres of land in Clarke County, Ky., near Strouds Station, which had been patented to JM on Mar. 11, 1784. McCreery pays JM £500 as a down payment, the balance to be remitted as soon as full title is proved. The purchase price is two dollars per acre.]

Law Papers, June 1796

U.S. Circuit Court, Va.

Fontaine v. Henry, declaration in convenant for 6,700 acres, ADS, U.S. Circuit Court, Va., Ended Cases (Unrestored), Virginia State Library.

3. This is item no. Mss1B2264a985 in the society's collections. The copy is endorsed on the verso, "John Marshall, Certificate of Public Debt."

4. On Apr. 11, 1796, the District Court at Richmond ordered a payment of almost £9,682 to Banks. JM was referring to Commonwealth v. Cunningham & Co., a similar case he had argued before the Court of Appeals in 1793. The Court of Appeals decided, however, that the cases were "wholly dissimilar as to the ground of relief" and reversed the district court ruling on May 3, 1799. For a summary of JM's role in the Cunningham case, see Vol. II, 263 n. 3. For Commonwealth v. Banks, see Court of Appeals Order Book, III, 239, 240, 286, 310, Virginia State Library. See also JM to Henry Banks, Dec. 10, 1798.

Fontaine v. Henry, declaration in covenant for 2,000 acres, ADS, U.S. Circuit Court, Va., Ended Cases (Unrestored), Va. State Lib.

To St. George Tucker

ALS, Tucker-Coleman Papers, Swem Library, College of William and Mary

Mr. dear Sir[5] [Richmond], July 7, 1796

In the lifetime of Mr. Donald Campbell[6] I had instituted a suit against him on a bill of exchange which abated by his death. Mr. Wickham defended it. It is now deemd necessary to bring it in chancery & I enclose you the subpoena[7] the service of which you will please to acknowledge. I will have the bill ready by the session of the Genl. court[8] when if you are willing the suit shoud be conducted in that way your answer may be fild. Yours truely

J MARSHALL

From George Washington

ALS, Collection of Dr. Joseph E. Fields, Williamsburg, Va.

(Private)

Dear Sir, Mount Vernon, July 8, 1796

In confidence I inform you, that it has become indispensably necessary to recall our Minister at Paris; and to send one in his place who will explain, faithfully, the views of this government, and ascertain those of France.

Nothing would be more pleasing to me, than that you should be this Organ; if it were only for a temporary absence of a few

5. Tucker endorsed the letter, "John Marshall, enclosing Subpoena, Currie et ux vs Alex. Campbell, July 8, 1796, Answered, July 12, 1796, And same day wrote to Mr. Wickham to defend the suit."

6. Campbell (d. 1795), Tucker's cousin, executed a will in 1784 in which he described himself as "late of the Island of Grenada." His parents, Archibald and Elizabeth Campbell, were described in the same document as "formerly of Norfolk, but now residing in Bermuda." Donald Campbell's will, Feb. 18, 1784, Tucker-Coleman Papers, Swem Library, College of William and Mary. It appears that Campbell was also a nephew of the Richmond attorney, Alexander Campbell.

7. Not found.

8. The General Court was scheduled to meet in Richmond on June 9, 1796. This court, composed of all the district court judges, met at the capital after the spring and fall terms of the district courts. See St. George Tucker, Casebook, June 1796, Tucker-Coleman Papers; 13 Hening 422–423 (1792).

months.[9] But it being feared that even this could not be made to comport with your present pursuits, I have, in order that as little delay as possible may be incurred, put the enclosed letter[1] under cover to be forwarded to its address, if you decline the present offer; or to be returned to me, if you accept it.

Your own correct knowledge of circumstances render details unnecessary, I shall only add therefore that I am, Dear Sir, Your obedt

GO: WASHINGTON

PS. Hearing that you propose to attend the next meeting of the Supreme Court at Philadelphia I should be glad to see you at this place in your way.[2]

To George Washington

ALS, Washington Papers, Library of Congress

Sir Richmond, July 11, 1796

I will not attempt to express those sensations which your letter of the 8th. instant has increasd.

Was it possible for me in the present crisis of my affairs[3] to leave the United States, such is my conviction of the importance of that duty which you woud confide to me, &, pardon me if I add, of the fidelity with which I shoud attempt to perform it, that I woud

9. On July 2 the cabinet had recommended that Washington recall James Monroe from France and replace him with either Patrick Henry, JM, Charles Cotesworth Pinckney (1746–1825), or William L. Smith (1758–1812), the latter two from South Carolina. On July 7, Charles Lee, Washington's attorney general, concurred in the wisdom of recalling Monroe and added, "No person would be fitter than John Marshall to go to France for supplying the place of our minister; but it is scarcely short of absolute certainty, that he would not accept any such office. The same may be said of Mr. Henry." George Gibbs, *Memoirs of the Administrations of Washington and John Adams . . .*, I (New York, 1846), 366–367; Jared Sparks, ed., *The Writings of George Washington . . .*, XI (Boston, 1836), 485–487. See also Harry Ammon, *James Monroe: The Quest for National Identity* (New York, 1971), 150–156.

1. The enclosed letter offered the appointment to Pinckney, who accepted it. See Washington to Pinckney, July 8, 1796, Washington Papers, Ser. 4, Library of Congress (microfilm ed., reel 109); Marvin R. Zahniser, *Charles Cotesworth Pinckney: Founding Father* (Chapel Hill, N.C., 1967).

2. The postscript was not on the letterbook copy but was on the copy printed by John Fitzpatrick. See Washington Papers, Ser. 2, Lib. Cong. (microfilm ed., reel 8), and John C. Fitzpatrick, ed., *The Writings of George Washington from the Original Manuscript Sources, 1745–1799*, XXXV (Washington, D.C., 1940), 128–129.

3. JM was referring to his involvement in the purchase of the Fairfax lands. See Vol. II, 140–149.

certainly forego any consideration not decisive with respect to my future fortunes, & woud surmount that just diffidence I have ever entertaind of myself, to make one effort to convey truely & faithfully to the government of France those sentiments which I have ever beleivd to be entertaind by that of the United States.

I have forwarded your letter to Mr. Pinkney.

The recall of our minister at Paris has been conjecturd while its probable necessity has been regretted by those who love more than all others our own country.

I will certainly do myself the honor of waiting on you at Mount Vernon. With every sentiment of respect & attachment, I am Sir your obedt. Servt.

JOHN MARSHALL

From George Washington

ALS, Washington Papers, Library of Congress

(Private)

Dear Sir, Mount Vernon, July 15, 1796

I have received your letter of the 11th. instant, and regret that present circumstances should deprive our country of the Services which I am confident your going to France, at this time, would have rendered it.

It is difficult to fill some offices with characters which would fit them in *all* respects. Another case ⟨occurs at this time under these circumstances⟩[4] of this sort is now before me, namely that of Surveyor General. A gentleman ⟨in all respects⟩ well qualified to discharge the duties of this office was appointed, ⟨and⟩ but has declined accepting it.[5] Several others have been mentioned, but the recommendations of them have gone more to the general respectability of their characters, than to their scientific knowledge; whilst both are equally essential. For it is a trust, which in the execution requires skill to arrange, instruct ⟨and Inspect⟩ and report correctly

4. The words enclosed in angle brackets were omitted from the letterbook copy.

5. Simeon De Witt, surveyor general of New York, was offered the appointment in June, but declined it. John C. Fitzpatrick, ed., *The Writings of George Washington from the Original Manuscript Sources, 1745–1799*, XXXV (Washington, D.C., 1940), 106, 112. An act "for the sale of lands northwest of the river Ohio" authorized the appointment of a surveyor general on May 18, 1796. Clarence Edwin Carter, comp. and ed., *The Territorial Papers of the United States: The Territory Northwest of the River Ohio, 1787–1803*, II (Washington, D.C., 1934), 552–557.

the conduct of others; & integrity to resist the temptation which opportunities, and an overweening ⟨desire of⟩ fondness for speculating in Lands, may throw in his way.

Among the characters from the State of Virginia who have been presented to my view, on this occasion, are Generals Wood & Posey, & Colonels Tinsley and Anderson;[6] the last of whom is, I believe, an inhabitant of Kentucky; and having been in that line, the presumption ought to be, that his mathematical knowledge (which should extend beyond common surveying) is adequate to the duties which ⟨will⟩ would be required. But how he is in other respects, & what may be the course of his politics, I know *nothing*; and but *little* of those of the other three, particularly of Tinsley's.

The object therefore of writing this letter to you, is, to ask, confidentially, such information as you possess, can acquire, & give me, respecting the qualifications of these Gentlemen; or of any other fit character that may occur to you, for Surveyor General; accordant with the ideas I have expressed above. The office is important and respectable; of course the ⟨person who fills it⟩ incumbent besides, his scientific abilities, should possess a celebrity of character that would justify the appointment.

To learn your sentiments of the characters, and on the points I have mentioned ⟨and on these points⟩ will be in time when I shall have the pleasure of seeing you, on your way to Philadelphia. With very great esteem & regard, I am Dear Sir your Obedt. Servant.

GO: WASHINGTON

6. James Wood, Thomas Posey, Thomas Tinsley (1755–1822), and Richard Clough Anderson. The position was offered to Wood on Sept. 12, 1796, but apparently he also declined. Fitzpatrick, ed., *Writings of Washington*, XXXV, 210–212. In 1794 Posey had moved to Kentucky, where he later served as lieutenant governor before his appointment to the U.S. Senate in 1812. In 1813 he became governor of the Indiana Territory but resigned to become Indian agent in 1816.

After Wood's refusal to accept the office, JM favored William Heth. See Edward Carrington to Washington, Oct. 10, 1796, Washington Papers, Ser. 4, Library of Congress (microfilm ed., reel 109).

Rufus Putnam (1738–1824), appointed superintendent of the Ohio Company in 1788 and judge of the Northwest Territory in 1790, was appointed surveyor general on Nov. 5, 1796. See Roy M. Robbins, *Our Landed Heritage: The Public Domain, 1776–1936* (Gloucester, Mass., 1960), 17.

To Henry Lee

ALS, Sang Collection, Rutgers University Library

Dear Sir Richmond, July 18, 1796

I have receivd yours of the 15th.[7] by the last mail. At the time you purchased the lott on which Mr. Campbell then resided it was made known to you that he had no title to the adjoining ground. The terms of your sale to Mr. Hylton I am unacquainted with. I beleive that there are negroes subject to the balance of Browns debt which will be sufficient to discharge it.

The sale of the property is for a time delayd. Our unfortunate friend is no more. A dose of laudanum taken for the purpose has rid him of the world & of its cares. For him they had so accumulated as to become too heavy to be borne longer. The burthen was laid down on Munday night & yesterday I saw him intered.[8]

While I regret this circumstance as a man I cannot but feel it as it affects us particularly. I fear it will be usd as the instrument of delay for our cause. Mr. Campbell was employd by Mr. Pendleton & relied on by him. It is probable that he will not try the cause without counsel from Virginia & that he will be willing to consider it as now too late to engage another. I have endeavord to carry Mr. Wickham but he will not go unless first applied to.[9] I have written to Mr. Pendleton on the subject & the letter is under cover to Mr. Charles Lee as I suppose it more probable that he will be in Alexandria than yourself. Shoud it be otherwise take out the letter & forward it to Pendleton instantly by express.

I expect to be in Alexandria on Munday evening & propose visiting Mount Vernon on tuesday. By wednesday I hope we may

7. Not found.

8. Apparently JM wrote this and the remaining portions of this letter on July 20, the date it was postmarked in Richmond. Alexander Campbell committed suicide on July 18, the day JM began this letter. See *Virginia Gazette, and General Advertiser* (Richmond), July 20, 1796.

9. In the appeal of Hunter v. Fairfax's Devisee to the U.S. Supreme Court, Campbell had been retained by Philip Pendleton (1752–1802), of Berkeley County, David Hunter's father-in-law. JM asked John Wickham to handle the appeal for Hunter because Wickham had advised the state in Commonwealth v. Fairfax, which was pending before the Court of Appeals. Apparently Wickham refused. At the same time, David Hunter wrote to Alexander Hamilton in an attempt to persuade him to prosecute the appeal of the federal case before the U.S. Supreme Court. When Hamilton refused, Hunter won a motion for continuance by the U.S. Supreme Court on Aug. 6, thus confirming JM's concern about the effects of Campbell's death on the Fairfax litigation. See Vol. II, 140–149, esp. 145 n. 8, for information on the litigation in question.

have an answer from Pendleton. A journey to Philadelphia without arguing the cause is to me a serious calamity. I am dear Sir Your

J MARSHALL

Deed

Record Book Copy, RG 79, National Archives

[*July 22, 1796, Richmond.* JM sells his three shares in the Potomac Company to Charles Higby for £400. JM had bought the shares at £100 each when the company was chartered in 1785.]

From Rawleigh Colston

ALS, Executive Papers, Virginia State Library

Dear Sir, Battletown,[1] August 5, 1796

I wrote you some short time since that my dwelling house had been burnt down on the night of the 18th ulto., by a negro boy we purchased the last winter for a house servant. Mr John Keith of Winchester, who was on a visit to us, by his early discovery of the fire was I believe the means of preserving the lives of the whole family as the stair case soon took fire and would have prevented our escape. There having been no person but this boy in that story of the house during that evening, and Mr Keith having seen him carry the candle into the ajoining room, where he had no kind of business, and where he remained 3 or 4 minutes, and the fire being discovered about 15 or 20 minutes afterward, I had no doubt of his guilt, but did not suppose the wretch had done it by design. The next day he disappeared, and the morning following was apprehended by one of my people, who was directed to set him at liberty. Soon after this I over heard one of my domesticks charge him in the strongest terms with having designedly burn the house, and mentioned a threat she had heard him make about a fortnight before, in consequence of which I had him immediately locked up in a room, untill I could examine into the affair fully. It appeared

1. Battletown, now known as Berryville, is 10 miles east of Winchester, Va. A note on the address leaf indicates this letter was mailed from Winchester on Aug. 12, 1796.

from the testimony of this woman, that about a fortnight before, immediately after having received a slight chastisement for repeated disobedience of orders, she heard him say, looking up to the house, at the corner of which he was standing: "never mind, you shall not enjoy this house long," for which she repremanded him; but not suspecting him of any bad design, she thought no more of it till after the house was set on fire. Another of the house servants declared that she found him setting (on his return from the upper story) on the lower steps of the garret stairs, and on asking him what he did there, he replied, "never mind, I know what I am doing." She then directed him to go down stairs, as she was about to lock the doors. A few minutes afterwards he was seen by another of the servants standing at the corner of the house where the fire first broke out, looking up very attentively at the eaves—being possessed of these and several other suspicious circumstances, I returned to the boy and charged him with the fact on which, without the least threat on my part, he confessed, that after leaving mr Keiths room, he went with the candle into the one adjoining and from there into the most remote part of the cuddy, where he supplied himself with a splinter, which he lighted at the candle and fixed in the shingles. This confession was repeated to mr Keith, & the day after, on his way to prison, he requested the servant who conducted him thither, to call on mr Smith of Battletown, to whom he made the same confession with some other circumstances. He was brought to tryal on the 3rd Inst. before the following judges Viz: Col. Thruston, Col. J. Smith, Mr Woodcock, Mr Mcquire Doct Baldwin, Mr Norton & Mr Dowdall, who appointed Mr Boyed to defend the criminal.[2] After a full investigation of the testimony, and a full discussion of the law arising from the case, he was unanimously found guilty and received sentence of death. A motion was then made by Mr Boyd, to recommend him to mercy, on account of his age (he being between 13 & 14 years of age) but the court unanimously rejected it. To my great surprise I have just heard that a certain set of men, regardless of the many *horrid* acts of the same kind which have lately passed with impunity, for the want of proof—regardless of the future security of individuals,

2. Justices Charles Mynn Thruston, John Smith, Edward McGuire, James Gamul Dowdall, John Shearman Woodcock, Cornelius Baldwin, and George Flowerdew Norton heard the case at the Frederick County Court on Aug. 3. They appointed Elisha Boyd counsel for William. See "Proceedings of the Court on the Trial of Coultson's boy William for burning his Master's house," Aug. 3, 1796, Executive Papers, Virginia State Library.

whose families may be involved in utter ruin, if not involved in the flames, are about to petition the executive for a pardon,[3] under the false pretext of humanity, as if this benign principle had no other objects but those who had been guilty of the most atrocious crimes. I shall here mention a few of the many instances which have lately occurred of this growing evil. About 2 years ago Mr Edward Smiths barn and [*stables*] were malicious consumed by fire, by which he sustained loss in grain and Horses of 6 or 800£. Col. Smiths barn was not long since burnt, and his house set on fire by his own servants, but discovered in time to save it. About three months ago a very spacious and costly new building and a corn house belonging to my neighbour Holker, was maliciously burnt, by which he lost at least £2000. About the same time my neighbour Mr Fauntleroy, lost a nice and valuable dwelling house, but it has not been assertained whether by accident or design. Not long since my neighbour mr Strebling had his dwelling house set on fire designedly by a little negro girl, but saved it by a timely discovery. My own loss, at the present advanced price of work and materials, could not be replacd for less than £2000. For the future safety of others, as well as for my own security, I am compelled to request your good offices in laying a state of this transaction before the executive, from which I expect that justice which is due to a crime of the most distructive and dangerous tendency, and which has lately made the most rapid progress. If any certificates are necessary, be pleased to write me by next post & they shall be furnished. I am yours etc.

RAWLEIGH COLSTON

From Samuel Coleman

Letterbook Copy, War 10, Virginia State Library

[*August 8, 1796, Richmond.* Coleman, for the adjutant general, transmits to JM's brigade of militia a set of forms for reporting militia strength twice a year. The letter cites the 1795 Virginia militia act, secs. 16 and 17. See 1 Shepherd 346–347.]

3. A petition signed by 92 persons was submitted to the executive, but it was rejected by the Council of State on Aug. 31, 1796. See *ibid.*, and "Petition for Pardon of William," *ca.* Aug. 12, 1796, Executive Papers, Va. State Lib. No reference to the action taken by the executive appears in the Journals of the Virginia Council of State.

From George Washington

Letterbook Copy, Washington Papers, Library of Congress

Dear Sir, Mount Vernon, August 10, 1796

If you can recollect by whom, or in what manner the letter for General Pinckney, which went under cover to you,[4] was sent to the Post office in Richmond, I would thank you for information respecting it.

That Letter, with a note enclosed therein, containing three Bank Bills for one hundred Dollars each, for the sufferers by fire in Charleston,[5] had not on the 26th. of July been received by that Gentleman; although duplicates written *after* I had been favored with your answer has been acknowledged by him.

In confidence, I inform you that Genl. Pinckney accepts the appointment to France, and will soon be in Philada. to prepare for the Mission. With very great esteem & regard, I am, Dear Sir, Your Obt Servant

GEO WASHINGTON

To George Washington

ALS, Washington Papers, Library of Congress

Sir Richmond, August 12, 1796

Your letter to General Pinckney was deliverd by myself to the postmaster, the night on which I receivd it, & was, as he says, immediately forwarded by him. Its loss is the more remarkable as it coud not have been opend from a hope that it containd bank notes.

Permit me Sir to express my gratification as a citizen of the United States, that a gentleman of General Pinckneys character will represent our government at the court of France. With every sentiment of respect & attachment I remain Sir, Your obedt. Servt

JOHN MARSHALL

4. See Washington to JM, July 8, 1796.

5. On June 13 a fire destroyed several hundred buildings in Charleston, S.C. See *Gazette of the United States, and Philadelphia Daily Advertiser*, June 24, 1796. The *Virginia Gazette, and General Advertiser* (Richmond) printed the following notice on July 20, 1796: "A subscription has been set on foot in Baltimore for the relief of the Sufferers by the late fire at Charleston. . . . Their loss is enormous, that it must require the general assistance of the large cities throughout the Union to enable them to repair it."

To George Washington

ALS, M. E. Saltykov-Shchedrin State Public Library, Leningrad, U.S.S.R.

Sir Richmond, August 14, 1796

I take the liberty to inform you that the delay experiencd by your letter to Genl. Pinckney is probably producd by its having been inattentively forwarded by the post-master to Pinckney court house instead of Charlestown. This mistake, if it has been committed, will, I trust, produce no other inconvenience than delay. An enquiry into it has been directed. I am Sir with the most respectful attachment Your Obedt. Servt.

JOHN MARSHALL

To Robert Banks

ALS, Collection of Gerald P. Nye, Washington, D.C.

Sir[6] Richmond, August 17, 1796

I have again with all the attention I am master of considerd the papers in your suit with Webb & cannot advise an appeal at present.[7] If it shall be deemd proper after the account the appeal may then be prayed as well as now. It is material to attend to the account. The marriage contract appears to me to be establishd. Its amount however is subject to calculation & opinions may vary much concerning it. I do not conceive that any just objection can be made to allowing Mr. Webb fees where he actually appeard for Mr. Edmondson but at the same time an endeavor shoud be made to charge him with board & with any monies Mr. Edmondson may have paid him.

The great contest is concerning Frank Webbs bond.[8] For that suit ought long since to have been brought & if F. Webb cannot pay it then the deft. Mr. Webb will be accountable for it as the assignor & the one item will balance the other. If he will not agree to take it back this ought immediately to be done. Be careful not

6. The letter is addressed "Robert Banks esquire, Essex." On the verso in an unknown hand is written, "a copy of Edmondsons will."

7. JM recorded a fee for Edmondson v. Webb in Feb. 1792. See Vol. II, 433.

8. Although it was probably not directly related, the case of Francis Webb *et al.* v. Rawleigh Colston in the High Court of Chancery involved some similar issues. See Robert Morris to JM, Dec. 30, 1796, for information regarding that case.

to allow a charge in the account for which there is not a voucher.

Your depositions are: James Throckmorton, Albion Throckmorton, Wm. Gibson, Lewis Carlton, Eliz. Clarke, J F Clarke, Wm. Perkins, John Turner, Sarah Dix, Thomas Dix, Lewis D. Germain, Cary Griggs & Wm. Harwood.[9]

If it was possible to change the present decree it woud only be by obtaining an order for a jury to try the marriage promise & I really think the testimony in its favor coud not be gotten over. I am Sir very respectfully, Your Obedt. Servt.

J MARSHALL

To James McDowell

[*August 22, 1796.* JM sends a legal opinion regarding a claim to land on Martha's Vineyard. Listed in Parke-Bernet Galleries, Inc., Auction Catalog (New York, March 10, 1938), item 126. Not found.]

From Robert Morris

Letterbook Copy, Morris Papers, Library of Congress

Dr. Sir Philadelphia, August 24, 1796

I was much disappointed at not seeing you here and am sorry for the cause, which must be disagreable to you and your Brother and all that are interested with you in the purchase, as delays in such cases are often of mischievous consequences.[1] You will receive herewith enclosed the Certificates for four shares of Bank Stock of the United States placed in your name to enable you to return the four shares to the Gentleman of whom you borrowed them, this I thought better than remitting the money lest some

9. Although few of these individuals can be identified by the editors, an interesting relationship between some of them and the Edmondson and Webb families has been discovered. Albion Throckmorton was married to Mary Webb, the daughter of James and Mary Edmonson Webb. A son was named James Edmonson Throckmorton (1787–1850). Sarah Dix's maiden name was Edmundson. See C. Wickliffe Throckmorton, *A Genealogical and Historical Account of the Throckmorton Family* . . . (Richmond, 1930).

1. JM was in Philadelphia on Aug. 6 to argue Hunter v. Fairfax before the Supreme Court; the case was not argued, however. The court granted David Hunter's motion for a continuance because of the death of his attorney, Alexander Campbell. See Vol. II, 145 n. 8; U.S. Supreme Court Minutes, Aug. 6, 1796, RG 267, National Archives.

difficulty should arise about price of shares. Two other shares in the name of Mr Geo Pickett[2] is also enclosed wherewith and I will go on buying and remitting others untill the number of Ten are completed for him which shall be done before the time limited in your letter of the 12th Inst.[3] The dividends shall also be remitted speedily. Your Brother was in Amsterdam & had hopes of getting Money there the beginning of June. I am Dr. Sir, y. o. h. s

R M

To Zachariah Johnston

ALS, Washington and Lee University Library

Richmond, August 31, 1796

the[4] oldest entry. Yet there are very considera[*ble troubles*] & difficulties in the case. I inclose you a copy of the answer which will show you that some nice points of law arise in it, but independent of them there is great difficulty on the point of the survey conforming to the location. If the survey sent down by Mr. Brown shoud not be correct I can have one made by order of court. If you think such a survey woud be more favorable to you let me know it that I may move for the order. Thinking as I do think that the event is very questionable I showed Mr. Randolph[5] that part of your letter which relates to him. He is disengagd & will take your

2. In the margin Morris wrote, "no. 3656. J Marshall 4, 3657. G Pickett 2, 6 Shares."

3. Not found.

4. The first page of the letter is missing. The verso of this page is the address leaf on which JM wrote, "Zachariah Johnston esquire, Rockbridge county, To go to Lexington." Also on the address leaf in another hand is written, "Marshals Letter & Browns answer." The letter is postmarked Richmond, Aug. 31, 1796.

This case arose from a dispute between Johnston and John Brown over a tract of land. Johnston had bought the parcel from J. Phillips in 1789, surveyed it in 1792, and obtained a patent in 1792. Johnston brought an action in the High Court of Chancery claiming an equitable title superior to Brown's. The date of the decree in favor of Brown is unknown, but a revived decree was issued on May 18, 1799, from which Johnston appealed. The Court of Appeals affirmed the decree on Oct. 19, 1802. See 7 Va. (3 Call) 259, and Court of Appeals Order Book, IV, 207, Virginia State Library.

For a biographical sketch of Johnston, see John G. Paxton, "Zachariah Johnston," *Tyler's Quarterly Historical and Genealogical Magazine*, V (1924), 185–189. See also JM to Johnston, *ca.* 1796.

5. Edmund Randolph, after resigning as U.S. secretary of state, returned to Virginia in Dec. 1795 and resumed the private practice of law. See John J. Reardon, *Edmund Randolph: A Biography* (New York, 1974), 337–347.

business on being applied to by yourself. I wish to hear whether you wish to have an order of court for a survey. I am dear Sir your obedt.

J MARSHALL

Opinion

Minute Book, Mutual Assurance Society, Richmond

Richmond, September 2, 1796

[Declarations for Assurance to the Amount of more than 1,500,000 Dollars upon the Certified Value of Buildings have been lodged with the Principal Agent of the Mutual Assurance Society against fire on Buildings of the State of Virginia, but the premiums upon the Certified Value to the Amount of that Sum have not yet been paid to the Cashier General, or to any other person authorised by the Society.

The Question is; are those persons who have paid or may hereafter pay their respective premiums entitled to the Benefit of Assurance under the Law constituting the Society and the constitution Rules & Regulations[6] thereof before the premiums upon the Certified value of Buildings to the Amount of 1,500,000 Dollars are paid? W: Foushee Pr:. . .]

I feel no Difficulty in answering the above question in the Affirmative on the principals of Justice and convenience Such ought to be the construction of the contract.

Of Justice: Because the person who has paid his premium has done everything which on his part was to be done in order to Secure himself and Carry the Institution into full and complete effect. Tho the other Subscribers have not paid they are all compellable to pay and it is not in the power of the Individual who has paid to control the conduct of others.

Of Convenience: Because if no man was Insured untill others as well as himself had paid, no man would pay untill others had paid

6. Laws relating to the society were adopted in 1794 and 1795. 1 Shepherd 307–310, 405–406. The constitution and rules were approved at a meeting of subscribers on Dec. 24, 1795, after a special committee, which included JM, had examined the draft submitted by William Frederick Ast. The same committee prepared forms to be used for policies. Minute Book, Dec. 17 and 24, 1795, Mutual Assurance Society, Richmond. For JM's earlier involvement with the organization of the society, see Vol. II, 296–297. See also Fire Insurance Application, *ca.* Feb. 24, 1796.

A copy of the constitution and rules with amendments was printed in Richmond in 1802. See *Constitution, Rules and Regulations of the Mutual Assurance Society*, Henry Heth Papers, University of Virginia Library.

and of consequence this construction would entirely destroy the contract. My Opinion is confirmed by the 9th Article which declares that no person shall be entitled to the Benefit of Assurance untill he shall have paid the premium[7] plainly implying that when he has paid the premium he is entitled to the benefit of the Assurance.

It is not shaken by the proviso contained in the first Section of the 15th Article.[8] The right of the Assured does not depend on his possessing the policy, should the President and Directors refuse to give one, or should it be lost after it is given, the title of the assured would be the same. The proviso it must be admitted becomes inoperative, but to give it operation, it must destroy every other part of the contract.

I repeat therefore my decided opinion that in the Case stated, the Assured who has paid his premium is Entitled to the benefit of his Assurance.

Signed J: MARSHALL

From Thomas Marshall

ALS, Marshall Papers, Swem Library, College of William and Mary

Dr. Son. Buckpond, September 9, 1796

I recd. yours by Colo. Fleming[9] as also that by Mr. Dunlap. I am happy to hear that you & your family are well but as all the pleasures of this world are chequerd with evil the same conveyance brings me the news of Mr. Colstons loss & that of the postpone-

7. Art. 9 stated: "Nor shall any person be entitled to the benefit of this assurance until he shall have paid the premiums agreeable to the rates herein before established." *Constitution of the Mutual Assurance Society.*

8. Art. 15 stated in part: "No policy shall be delivered to the assured, until the premiums are paid upon the certified value of the buildings. . . ." *Ibid.*

9. The letter is addressed to "The honble. John Marshall, Richmond, honord by Judge Fleming." William Fleming was a judge on the Court of Appeals and later served as its president, or chief judge. In spite of his profession, he was known familiarly as Col. Fleming, at least by the Marshalls. Fleming traveled to Kentucky each year to inspect his landholdings there. See David J. Mays, "William Fleming, 1736–1824," Virginia State Bar Association, *Proceedings*, XXXIX (1927), 426–435.

This William Fleming is often confused with Dr. William Fleming (1728–1795), of Botetourt County, Va., known also as Col. Fleming. See Edmund P. Goodwin, *Colonel William Fleming of Botetourt, 1728–1795* (Roanoke, Va., 1975). Since he died in 1795 and since Thomas Marshall referred to Fleming as colonel in this letter and as judge on the address leaf, it is clear that he was not referring to the doctor.

ment of yr. intended visit to me.[1] The thoughts of seeing you once more I really believe is a principal means of keeping me alive And I will endeavor to live one year longer in hopes of that event. I am told Mr. J. Ambler talks of coming out with you; Happy shall I be to see him with you, and all my family & friends who may think it worth while to ride out to this country to take leave of me before I close my eyes for ever. The subject of [*your*] letter, though not quite domestic enough, was ve[*ry plea*]sing to me. Next to that of my own family, who you know I am dotingly fond of, The good of my country & our *worthy president* is nearest my heart. And the part you take in the present Storm gives me much pleasure, indeed you never seriously disobliged me in your life. I would ask that your Sons, or as I can say truly from my Heart, my dear Sons Tom & Jaquiline may accompany you out, but am affraid their tender age would prevent their being able to support the fatiegues of such a journey, & the loss of one of them, if occasioned by the attempt, would be more than I could support. If James & Lewis should be returnd from Europe by the time you come out you may concieve but not I desribe how much it would add to my happiness. Charles & Billey never write to me; surly knowing my age and infirmity they cant expect me to write often to them yet I do sometimes. When I write to you I think I write to them all. Tell polley & all my daugters in law, God bless them. When you come out I mean to make a full division of what property God has blessed me with. The Land I have given Susan[2] I have been since offered £3000 for. I think what I shall give Lewis is worth 3 or 4000£ but he will have to wait till mine & his mothers death for it. Mrs. Colston nor my poor daughter Ambler has yet had nothing. The former when you come out shall be rememberd, & the latter or rather her son, god bless him, shall not be forgotten[3] indeed I wish to see you partly on that acctt. as I would willing make all my children as nearly equal as I possibly can.

I have again paid the taxes on your millitary land. But the la[*nd I gave*] my Grandson Tom in Fayette I have [*done*] nothing

1. For Colston's loss, see Rawleigh Colston to JM, Aug. 5, 1796. JM no doubt had to postpone his trip because of developments in the Fairfax case. See Vol. II, 145–147.

2. Susan Tarleton Marshall McClung (1774–1858), Thomas Marshall's fifth daughter, had married William McClung (1758–1811), of Bardstown, Ky., in 1793.

3. The Mrs. Colston referred to was Thomas Marshall's daughter Elizabeth, who had married Rawleigh Colston in 1785. Lucy Marshall Ambler had died in 1795, leaving a son, Thomas Marshall Ambler. Thomas Marshall's will was executed on June 26, 1798, and was probated on Feb. 15, 1803. See Mason County, Ky., Will Book B, 212, Maysville, Ky.

with. You need not be affraid of distressing me by bringing out fr[ ] with you; for of such as I have been accustomed to I have enough.

Colo. Fleming will give you the news [*of*] this Country. I Shall therefore only observe that I think the political Horizon [*about*] to clear up. God Bless you [*all*] once more prays Yr. [*Father*]

T. MARSHALL

P.S. Tell Collo. Carrington that I have sent Mr. Shorts Accts. and other papers to Mr. Walcot.[4] I am unable to write more or would write to him.

T. M

From Thomas Jefferson

[*September 11, 1796.* Listed in Jefferson's "Summary Journal of Letters," Jefferson Papers, Library of Congress. Not found.]

Deed of Emancipation

Deed Book Copy, Office of the Clerk of the Henrico County Circuit Court, Richmond

Richmond, September 22, 1796

I John Marshall do hereby emancipate Peter a black man purchased by me from Mr. Nathaniel Anthony.

Teste. J: MARSHALL (LS)

DAVID LAMBERT[5]
WILLIAM MARSHALL

At a court held for Henrico county at the Courthouse the fifth of December 1796 This Deed of emancipation was proved by the oaths of David Lambert, and William Marshall the witnesses thereto, and ordered to be recorded. Teste

ADAM CRAIG CC.

4. Thomas Marshall, as superintendent of revenue for the Ohio district, was probably transferring papers of Peyton Short (1761–1825) to the secretary of the Treasury, Oliver Wolcott (1760–1833), and notifying Edward Carrington, superintendent of revenue for Virginia, of the transfer. Short had served as collector of the port of Louisville from 1789 to 1790 and had been a business partner of James Wilkinson. Patricia Watlington, *The Partisan Spirit: Kentucky Politics, 1779–1792* (New York, 1972), 203.

5. Lambert (1750–1817), a Richmond merchant and mason, was a recorder for the city of Richmond.

To Thomas Jefferson

[*September 26, 1796.* Listed in Jefferson's "Summary Journal of Letters," Jefferson Papers, Library of Congress. Not found.]

Lottery Notice

Printed, *Virginia Gazette, and General Advertiser* (Richmond), November 9, 1796, 2

[*October 20, 1796, Richmond.* This lottery, offering 1,000 tickets for 342 prizes, seeks $4,000 to aid in the construction of a bridge. The scheme is numbered No. III and is similar to the one JM helped manage on Aug. 2, 1792. See Vol. II, 122.]

To Joseph Jones

ALS, Monroe Papers, New York Public Library

[*October 24, 1796, Richmond.* JM transmits subpoenas to be delivered to witnesses in Jones v. Nathaniel Smith, an ejectment action scheduled to be heard in the General Court on Nov. 7, 1796. A blank subpoena, signed by John Brown on Oct. 22, 1796, and directed to the Loudoun County sheriff, is enclosed.]

Opinion

ADS, Cornell University Library

[Richmond, *ca.* November 13, 1796]

Queries[6]

1st. Will the commencement of an action against an exr. give a priority in any case?

6. This opinion was rendered to William H. Cabell at his request and was enclosed in William H. Cabell to Col. William Cabell, Jr., Nov. 14, 1796, Cabell Family Papers, Swem Library, College of William and Mary. Cabell wrote to his cousin: "Together with this you will receive Mr Marshal's opinion upon the queries proposed to him. I am afraid it is not sufficiently pointed & particular. At the time I gave him the questions, I had but little conversation with him, & when I called at his house this morning, I was informed that he is out of Town. I have however concluded to send the opinion as it is, & obtain more particular information hereafter, I observe his opion upon the first question, differs from what Cousin Landon & myself suggested to you. I suppose it must be founded upon some adjudication of our own Courts, for the law of

2d. Can a creditor who may purchase property belonging to the estate of the deceasd, obtain a preference by injoining the judgement for the purchase money to the amount of his claim against the estate in a case in which he woud not otherwise be intitled to a preference?

3d. If a preference can be thus obtaind can the exr. by prescribing the terms of sale preclude the creditor from such advantage & will it not be adviseable for him so to do if he expects a deficiency of assets?

4th. A suit on a simple contract has been instituted & is now at issue on the plea of non assumpsit. The exr. has reason to fear a deficiency of assets & wishes to know what hazard he is in & what it is most adviseable for him now to do?

A. 1st. The commencement of an action does not give priority to one debt over another which is of equal dignity with itself, so as to prevent the exr. from giving a judgement to the person who may hold such other debt, but a judgement cannot be given on a debt of inferior dignity after the commencement of an action for a debt of superior dignity without subjecting the exr. to the payment of the debt of superior dignity. Among equal debts the person who

---

England is certainly otherwise. I have this morning examined several books upon the subject, & find it to be in England as we had stated. I suppose however according to his own opinion that a preference can be given by Exors. only by a confession of Judgmt. And as he informed me that it is safest for the Exors. to make sale of the property, I shall this day have the advertisement inserted in the papers. I think it most adviseable to sell at 12 months credit, because more money will be made there by, & Mr Mitchel & Buckanan upon their obtaining a preference, would be willing to take a judgemt with a stay of Exon until you could make some collections. If however you think otherwise, give me the information & I will have the advertisemt altered. Let me hear from you by the next post, & suggest any questions you wish proposed to Mr Marshal."

In a subsequent letter, Cabell wrote: "Since writing you last I have had a few minutes conversation with Mr Marshal. He informs me that in a late difficult administration, he had occasion to consult the law arising upon points similar to those which you submitted to him. He says the law is fixed that among debts of equal dignity, the Exor. may give a preference; but that preference can only be given by confessing a judgement, & that he will certainly render himself liable in case of deficiency of assets if he pays a debt without giving a judgemt. when an action has been already brot upon another debt of equal dignity. He informs me that there have been no adjudications in our own Courts to this effect, but that it is a principle of the Common law. I must yield to his superior judgemt. But there certainly are many adjudications to the contrary in England & those of a modern date. The sale he says is highly proper." William H. Cabell to Col. William Cabell, Jr., Nov. 18, 1796, Cabell Family Papers.

The priorities in English ecclesiastical courts are discussed in Thomas Wentworth, *The Office and Duties of Executors . . .* (London, 1728), 32, 116–117, 129–155; and Henry Swinburne, *A briefe Treatise of Testaments and last willes . . .* (London, 1677), 396.

obtains the first judgement, not the person who institutes the first suit is intitled to the preference.

A. 2d. A creditor purchasing at the sale woud not be at liberty to injoin the judgement against him so as to prevent the application of his debt to the payment of debts superior in dignity to his own or of equal dignity but on which judgements had been obtaind; nor do I think (tho this has never been decided) that he coud injoin so as to deprive the exr. of that election which the law gives him to prefer among debts of equal dignity, which he pleases. If the money was only requird for debts of inferior dignity he might certainly injoin.

A. 3d. As such a preference cannot be obtaind a further answer to this question cannot be necessary. I will only add that it may not be improper if the exr. designs a preference for particular debts of a dignity certainly to be paid, to give notice that he will receive them only.

A. 4th. Altho issue be joind in an action on the case yet if the exr. has notice of debts of superior dignity before the rendition of a judgement & has not assets to pay them & also the debt in suit he ought to move for leave to change his plea & show his want of assets unless the plaintiff will take a judgement when assets or if assets. A judgement is questionably in law a confession of assets for its discharge. The person against whom it is renderd must pay it & cannot plead it against debts of superior dignity of which he had notice. What is considerd as notice has been made a question. That the exr. is bound to take notice of all debts of record is certain. With respect to bonds which are not of record it has been determind in England that notice which shall bind the exr. can only be given by action. This has never been decided in this country either way. In England it has also been decided that a court of equity will not interfere to releive the exr. who has permitted a judgement to go against him without having pleaded fully administerd, but if our Judges will adhere to the principle of several decrees they have renderd I think a court of chancery woud interfere here. This however cannot safely be relied on & therefore I advise a change of plea if there is reason to suspect a deficiency of assets & if the creditor shall refuse to receive the judgement before recommended.

J MARSHALL

Commonwealth v. Hamilton

Argument in the General Court

Extract from Casebook, Tucker-Coleman Papers, Swem Library, College of William and Mary

Richmond, November 17, 1796

Commonwealth v. Gawin Hamilton, Clerk of Pendleton County. He was indicted in this Court[7] two or three years ago for misconduct in his office, in cursing the Justices while sitting in Court; and in being drunk, so as to be incapable of performing the Duties of his office. The Jury found him guilty upon both charges, & amerced him in one thousand dollars.

Marshall, for the Deft now moved in arrest of Judgement, and assigned for cause, first that the Court hath not Jurisdiction in this Case, & Secondly, that if they have, they ought not to render Judgement upon this Verdict because of the fine assessed by the Jury: the Court if they have Jurisdiction in the Case, being restrained to pronounce Judgement of Removal from his Office, or not, & no other. And for this he relied on the General Court Law, the District Court law, & the words of the Constitution.[8]

Tucker[9] said. Upon the first of these objections that the Court hath not Jurisdiction of this Cause, the Question was propounded in two ways. First whether the Cognizance of the Case was not by the Acts constituting the General Court, and the District Courts transferred from the former, to the latter; and secondly, if it were not, whether the Cognizance thereof should not be brought before the Court in a different mode, than that which has been observed in this Case.

7. The General Court was composed of the 10 judges of the district courts. They met twice yearly in Richmond after attending their respective districts. 13 Hening 422–423 (1792).

8. Art. 15 of the Virginia Constitution provided that "present and future Clerks shall hold their offices during good behaviour, to be judged of and determined in the General Court." 9 Hening 117 (1776). JM noted that the composition and jurisdiction of that court had changed with various reform acts. The General Court Act of 1792 did not give the court specific jurisdiction over the removal of clerks. *Ibid.*, 424–425. The District Court Act of 1792 gave those courts jurisdiction over everything the General Court had held, "except in . . . such cases as by the constitution of this Commonwealth or some particular statute heretofore made, are . . . reserved to the general court." 13 Hening 431 (1792).

9. St. George Tucker, who took these notes on the argument, was a judge of the General Court.

If I understand the words Cognizance, & Jurisdiction, as applied to Courts of Judicature they are perfectly convertible terms, so far as relates to the right of the Court to *hear*, and to *determine* a Case brought before them. The Court can not take *Cognizance* of any Case which they have not a right to *determine* and *adjudge*, nor can the Court *determine* and *adjudge* any Case of which they have not *Cognizance*. Whenever a Court, therefore, hath a right to *determine* and *adjudge*, that Court must have Jurisdiction, (for *Jus–dicere*, certainly means to adjudge) and whenever it hath *Jurisdiction* it must have *Cognizance*, for without taking knowledge of the fact, it can never decide the Law. These things are so plain, that it seems impossible to have recourse to language simple enough to explain them.

The words of the Constitution are, "The present and future Clerks shall hold their office during good behaviour, to be *judged*, and determined in the General Court." Art: 15.

To my weak Apprehension words can not convey a clearer expression of Jurisdiction: a Jurisdiction which the Legislature neither have power, nor I presume the will to take away. And having Jurisdiction, they have upon the grounds & principles before mentioned undoubted *Cognizance* also of the Case. It remains then to consider whether this Case has been brought before them in such a manner as the law requires: which brings us to the second part of this objection.

It is a principle which I presume will not be contested, that whereever a Court is constituted in this Country, if there be no constitutional, or legislative direction as to the mode of conducting suits therein, the common law mode (in common law Cases) must be pursued. In Cases similar to the present that mode must be by Indictment, or Information. But the Law is not silent as to the mode. The general Court Law (1794, c. 65.) Sect: 14, expressly provides, that the Grand Jury shall be sworn to enquire of and *present* all offences agt. the Commonwealth which are "*cognizable*" in this Court. And if an Indt. be found the like proceedings shall be had here as in district Courts.[1] Can language more plainly describe the mode which has in this Case been pursued?

1. Tucker was referring to the General Court Act of 1792. See 13 Hening 426–427, sec. 14. This act was part of the Revisal of 1792 that Tucker had helped prepare; it was not published until 1794, however, and Tucker consistently referred to the printed version in his notes. See Charles T. Cullen, "Completing the Revisal of the Laws in Post-Revolutionary Virginia," *Virginia Magazine of History and Biography*, LXXXII (1974), 97–98.

The second Objection: That although this Court may have Jurisdiction of the Case, so far as to remove the Defendant from office, they have not power to inflict the Fine, assessed by the Jury, still remains to be considered.

And here it is to be remembered, that whereever a Court hath *Jurisdiction* in any Case, that Court must necessarily pronounce Judgement thereupon according to the nature of that Case: consequently where an offence is *triable*, the measure of *punishment* to be inflicted must also be determinable by the Court. And whereever the Constitution or the laws do not *limit* the punishment for the *Offence*, the Court before whom the *trial* is had must decree the punishment according to the principles of Law. The punishment for *all* Misdemeanours at common law is by Fine, Imprisonment, or corporal punishment, or *all three*, according to the nature and degree of the offence: and the *Measure* of all three, was by the common law left to the Discretion of the Court. To these, where the misdemeanour was by a public officer in the discharge of the duties of his office, the penalty of Forfeiture, or Removal from office, was superadded. The Act of Assembly (1794, c. 74, s. 26.) has transferred the power of fining & amercing upon Indicts. or Informs. for misdemeanours, from the Judges, to the Jury, "by whom the offender shall be convicted," leaving to the Courts the power of superadding the punishment of Imprisonment, Corporal punishment, or Amotion from office, according to the nature of the Case, and their discretion.[2] Here then the Cognizance of the *Offence*, gives to the Jury by whom the offender is convicted the power of fining him: for this Act is a general law of the Land, applying to *all* Courts, and to *all Cases* upon Indictments or Informations in those Courts. The principle that Accessarius sequitur, non ducit suum principale,[3] here applies in full force. The Case of Misbehaviour in Office by the Clerk of a Court is only cognizable in this Court: the *whole* punishment to be inflicted must here be pronounced: no part of the punishment which the common law inflicts in such Cases is taken away, or limited: the Jury are to pronounce

2. See "An act directing the mode of proceeding against free persons charged with certain crimes. . . ." 1 Shepherd 25 (1792).

3. Tucker apparently confused two similar phrases that mean essentially the same thing: "accessorium non ducit, sed sequitur suum principale" and "accessorius sequitur naturam sui principalis," an accessory follows the nature of its principal. In any case, the phrase seems out of place here because it is usually applied to a criminal action wherein an accessory cannot be charged with a higher crime than the principal defendant.

the measure of the fine; the Court, the measure of any further punishment.

Upon a Conference, Nelson & Carrington agreed with me upon all these points. Tyler, Henry & Jones Contra. Winston went off before the Argument.[4] The disagreement was upon the last point, only.

It was finally agreed to set aside the Verdict, as a more adviseable measure than continuing the Case upon the motion for arresting the Judgement, because of the Improbability of a fuller Court, at any future period. This Tucker proposed as the *less of two Evils*, when he found that there was a majority for continuing the Cause upon the motion in Arr: of Judgt.

Verdict set aside, & new trial awarded.

Petition of Thomas Mason

AD, Legislative Petitions, Virginia State Library[5]

[Richmond, *ca.* November 21, 1796]

To the Honble. the speakers & members of the General Assembly the petition of Thomas Mason humbly showeth

That your petitioner is possessd of the negroe slaves herein after namd to wit Alice, Charles, Jenny, Milly, Sam, Bob, Jack & [James], all of whom were born within this commonwealth. Your petitioner is also the owner of lands in Virginia & in Maryland. By the laws of Maryland persons owning lands in both states & residing in either may remove their slaves from Virginia to Maryland for the special purpose of working their own lands but not for the purpose of selling or hiring them to others. About two years past your orator removd the slaves herein before namd to Maryland for the special purpose of working them on his own lands in that state & beleiving at the time that it woud be in his power to bring them back whenever the situation of his affairs shoud make it adviseable for him to do so. Your orator is now sollicitous to cultivate some of his lands in Virginia with the slaves sent from this state to Maryland as above mentiond but is advisd that under the

4. William Nelson, Jr., Paul Carrington, Jr., John Tyler, James Henry, Joseph Jones, Edmund Winston, and Tucker were the only judges attending the court at this term.

5. This petition, in JM's hand, is in Miscellaneous Petitions, Box M. Mason (1770–1806), a son of George Mason, had inherited his father's land in Prince William County.

law of this Commonwealth he woud hazard the loss of them by doing so.[6] Your petitioner therefore humbly prays that an act may pass authorizing him to bring back to Virginia the slaves above enumerated & to hold them in like manner as if they had never been carried into Maryland or in some other manner to suspend the operation of the laws of the commonwealth as to the said slaves. And your petitioner will ever pray, etc.

THOMAS MASON.

To John Wise

Printed, Clarke County Historical Association, *Proceedings*, XIII (Boyce, Va., 1956), 49

Sir,[7] Richmond, November 24, 1796

Being one of the purchasers of the lands of Mr. Fairfax, and authorized to act for them all, I have considered the resolution of the General Assembly on the petition of sundry inhabitants of the counties of Hampshire, Hardy and Shenandoah[8] and have determined to accede to the proposition it contains. So soon as the conveyance shall be transmitted to me from Mr. Fairfax, deeds extinguishing his title to the waste and unappropriated lands in the Northern Neck shall be executed, provided an act passes during this session, confirming, on the execution of such deeds, the title of those claiming under Mr. Fairfax, to lands specifically appropriated and reserved by the late Thomas Lord Fairfax, or his an-

6. In 1778 and 1792 the General Assembly enacted laws that prohibited the importation of slaves into Virginia, providing however that Virginians who owned slaves in other states could return them to Virginia without penalty. Presumably Mason should have been able to return his slaves legally, but perhaps JM saw ambiguity in the law and thus advised Mason to request specific legislation to ensure the return of his slaves. For the General Assembly's action on and JM's role in the resulting legislation, see Legislative Bill, *ca.* Dec. 22, 1796. For the laws regarding slaves, see 9 Hening 471–472 (1778) and 1 Shepherd 122–130 (1792).

7. Wise (1767–1812), a Federalist from Accomack County, was Speaker of the House of Delegates from 1794 until 1799. See Barton H. Wise, *The Life of Henry A. Wise of Virginia, 1806–1876* (New York, 1899); Richard R. Beeman, *The Old Dominion and the New Nation, 1788–1801* (Lexington, Ky., 1972), 211–213. This letter is also printed in 2 Shepherd 23 (1796) and *JVHD*, Nov. 1796, 41. For background information, see Vol. II, 140–149.

8. JM was elected a delegate from Richmond in Apr. 1796. See Election Records, Apr. 1796, Virginia State Library. When the session convened on Nov. 8, JM was appointed to all the important committees, including the Committee for Courts of Justice that considered the petition from the Fairfax leaseholders and recommended the compromise summarized in this letter. *JVHD*, Nov. 1796, 3, 4, 9, 10, 15, 24, 28, 41.

cestors, for his or their use.[9] I remain Sir, with much respect and esteem, your obedient servant.

John Marshall.

Receipt

DS, Foreign Office 5/33, Public Record Office

Duplicate[1]

Richmond, [*ca.* November 30, 1796]

Received from John Hamilton Esquire, His Britannick Majesty's Consul for the State of Virginia through the hands of Messrs. Thomas Hamilton & Co Merchants in Norfolk, the Sum of Two hundred & thirty three & one third Dollars, as a fee for Conducting a Suit, instituted at the instance of the said John Hamilton Esqr. in the Circuit Court of the United States for the District of Virginia by Messrs. Thomas Hamilton & Co. before mentioned, against Cols Thomas Newton and Willis Wilson, the Commanding Officers at Norfolk, for their having detained there certain Horses shipped, and about to be shipped from thence to the Island of Saint Domingo, for the Service of His Britannick Majesty therein.[2]

J Marshall

9. An act to this effect passed on Dec. 10. See 2 Shepherd 23.

1. This document was included in a packet sent to the Foreign Office in London by John Hamilton, British consul at Norfolk, along with a request for reimbursement of expenses incurred in the unsuccessful prosecution of a suit in the U.S. Circuit Court, Va.

2. In Jan. and Feb. 1796, the French consul at Norfolk complained to the governor of Virginia that several British ships were loading horses for military use against the French West Indies, an action prohibited by existing treaties and by the neutrality proclamation. On Jan. 29 the Council instructed the governor to order militia commanders in the area to prevent the shipment of the horses, whereupon Thomas Newton and Willis Wilson led troops onto the ships and seized the horses on Feb. 16, 1796. Apparently the officers did not receive word that the Council had countermanded its orders on Feb. 12.

Hamilton, on behalf of Thomas Hamilton & Co., and on the instructions of the British consul general at Philadelphia, sued Newton and Wilson. From Hamilton's later petition for reimbursement of expenses, it appears he retained JM, Andrew Ronald, and John Wickham to prosecute the suit and paid them each $233.33. Later he added Daniel Call to the battery, paying him $50.00. Call probably entered the case in 1800, when it was argued in court.

A jury found for Newton on May 27, 1800. The suit against Wilson abated by his death in 1798. For documents explaining the case, see John Hamilton to Lord Hawkesbury, Dec. 22, 1801, F.O. 5/33, Public Record Office; Hamilton v. Newton, U.S. Circuit Court, Va., Ended Cases (Restored), 1800, Virginia State Library. See also Journals of the Virginia Council of State, Jan. 29 and Feb. 12, 1796, Va. State Lib.; U.S. Circuit Court, Va., Order Book, III, 67, 151, 294, 301, 366, 368, Va. State Lib.

Law Papers, November 1796

U.S. Circuit Court, Va.

Webster v. Brown's Estate, declaration, ADS, U.S. Circuit Court, Va., Ended Cases (Unrestored), Virginia State Library.

Resolution

Copy, House of Delegates Rough Bills, Virginia State Library

Richmond, December 6, 1796

Resolvd that when this House proceeds by joint ballot with the Senate to elect two members of the privy Council or Council of State to supply the vacancies occasioned by the resignation of two of that Body, it will at the same time proceed by joint ballot with the Senate to the election of a member for the privy Council or Council of State in the room of James Wood Esquire who hath been elected to, and accepted the office of, Governor or Chief Magistrate.[3]

Attest
JOHN STEWART C:H:D

1796 December 6th, Agreed to by the Senate.

H BROOKE C.S

Legislative Report

ADS, Executive Papers, Virginia State Library

Sir Richmond, December 12, 1796

Having been of the committee to whom were refered the proceedings and statement of the commissioners, appointed by the executive to adjust the contested boundary line with the State of Kentucky, we think it may conduce to the publick service to express, and we beg leave thus to declare, our strong approbation of

3. On Dec. 2 the House of Delegates resolved to vote with the Senate to fill two vacancies on the Council of State. Before the election a third vacancy was created when James Wood, president of the Council, was named governor in place of Patrick Henry, who had declined election. After serving on the committee appointed to notify Wood of his election, JM returned to the House and introduced this resolution. The General Assembly immediately elected Meriwether Jones (1766–1806), John Pendleton, Jr., and John Mayo, Jr. (1760–1818), to fill the vacancies. *JVHD*, Nov. 1796, 52–53, 60.

the measures pursued by those commissioners, and our opinions, that it is an object of great importance to procure their aid, in the prosecution of the business. Exclusive of the thorough knowledge of the subject, displayed in their report, they possess a degree of information as to facts, not to be acquired, except in the mode by which they have obtained it; it is therefore extreamly improbable, that any new set of commissioners, by assembling once only at the place, or relying upon the depositions already taken, without viewing the country, can attain a coextensive fitness for the negociation, with the former gentlemen.[4] We are, with great respect, Sir Yr: mo: obt: Serts.

ROBERT ANDREWS
JOHN TAYLOR
J MARSHALL
JAMES BRECKINRIDGE
THOS. MADISON

4. For several years Virginia officials had been trying to settle disputes over the state's boundaries, especially those to the west and south. In 1795 Gov. Isaac Shelby, of Kentucky, wrote to Gov. Robert Brooke complaining that some Virginians had entered land warrants issued by Virginia on land that Kentucky believed to be within its borders. The letter was referred to the General Assembly, which adopted a resolution directing the executive to inform Shelby that the Assembly wished "to ascertain the boundary line between the two states on the most amicable terms," and that commissioners might be appointed for this purpose if Kentucky agreed. At about the same time, the Kentucky legislature adopted a similar resolution providing for the appointment of commissioners to meet with agents from Virginia "relative to the said boundary Line." 1 Shepherd 434 (1795). The Virginia act of 1789 separating Kentucky from Virginia included a clause for appointing commissioners to settle any disputes arising from the separation. 13 Hening 20. H. W. Flournoy, ed., *Calendar of Virginia State Papers . . .*, VIII (Richmond, 1890), 350.

After corresponding with Gov. Shelby, the Council of State in June 1796 appointed commissioners to meet with agents from Kentucky. A report was transmitted to the fall 1796 General Assembly with the governor's annual report. The issue was referred to a special committee of which JM was a member. As a result of the committee's Dec. 12 report, the Assembly adopted a new resolution on Dec. 15, 1796, calling for another meeting of the boundary commissioners and giving them "powers to recommend to their respective governments any amicable adjustment of the difficulty which shall, in their judgments, comport with the real intention of the papers and documents relating to it, or which they may think just and equitable." The Assembly also resolved that "mutual" laws should be passed by both states to settle the disputed titles. The commissioners met, had a line surveyed, and reported to the 1799 General Assembly. A law was passed on Jan. 13, 1800, setting the boundary between the states and assigning title to disputed claims. *JVHD*, Nov. 1796, 7; Journals of the Virginia Council of State, June 30, 1796, and Feb. 8, 1797, Virginia State Library; 2 Shepherd 71 (1796) and 234–235 (1799). See also Flournoy, ed., *Calendar of Virginia State Papers*, VIII, 330, 366–367, 380, 407, 444, 448, 454–455; Clarence Edwin Carter, comp. and ed., *The Territorial Papers of the United States: The Territory South of the River Ohio, 1790–1796*, IV (Washington, D.C., 1936), 155, 200, 208, 241.

To James Wood

Letterbook Copy, War 10, Virginia State Library

[*December 13, 1796, Richmond.* JM, with other members of a board of officers appointed to examine the question of rank for Maj. Edmund Wills of the 49th Regiment, reports that Wills's rank should be 9 instead of 95. With the report are copies of the order appointing the board and Wood's acceptance of the report.]

To James Iredell

ALS, Iredell Manuscripts, Duke University Library

Dear Sir[5] Richmond, December 15, 1796

I had not the pleasure of receiving til yesterday your favor of the 3d. inst.[6] Since then I have seen the votes of North Carolina & you I presume have seen those of Virginia. Mr. Adams woud have receivd one other vote had Mr. Eyre really been elected, but he was left out by accident. There was supposd to be no opposition to him & in consequence of that opinion the people in one county on the eastern shore did not vote at all & in the other a very few assembled. On the day of election the people of Princess Ann whose court day it happend to be assembled in numbers & elected Mr. Nimmo who voted for Mr. Jefferson.[7] For that gentleman you will have heard there were twenty votes, for Mr. Saml. Adams 15, for

5. JM addressed the letter to "The Honble James Iredell, Edenton, North Carolina." Iredell (1751–1799) was born in England but came to North Carolina sometime prior to 1771, at which time he was licensed to practice law in Edenton. After helping revise the state's laws in 1776, he was appointed a superior court judge the following year but resigned after six months. He was elected attorney general in 1779 and a member of the Council of State in 1787. He finished a new revisal of the laws for the state in 1791. Having been appointed to the U.S. Supreme Court in 1790, he traveled the southern circuit that included Richmond. His circuit court opinion in Ware v. Hylton was later filed as a dissent to the Supreme Court's majority opinion. See 3 U.S. (3 Dall.) 199 (1796). See also Don Higginbotham, ed., *The Papers of James Iredell* (Raleigh, N.C., 1976–).

6. Letter not found.

7. The state's electoral districts included one for the Eastern Shore comprised of Accomack, Northampton, and Princess Anne counties. 13 Hening 536 (1792). John Eyre lived in Northampton County, and it was probably there or in Accomack County where no one voted. Princess Anne County, south of the borough of Norfolk, was the home of James Nimmo. That county's court day was the first Monday in each month; electors were to be chosen on the first Monday in November. 13 Hening 70 (1789) and 537 (1792).

Mr. Clinton 3, for Burr 1, Genl. Washington 1, Mr. Pinkney 1, & Mr. John Adams 1.[8] I receivd a letter from Philadelphia stating that five votes south of Potowmack woud be necessary to secure the election of Mr. Adams. It is then certain that he cannot be elected.

Our assembly which you know is in session displays its former hostility to foederalism. They have once more denied *wisdom* to the administration of the President & have gone so far as to say in argument that we ought not by any declarations to commit ourselves so as to be bound to support his measures as they respect France.[9] To what has America fallen! Is it to be hopd that North Carolina will in this particular rather adopt such measures as have been pursued by other states than tread the crooked path of Virginia?

I have receivd a letter from Mr. Dallas & will furnish him with my argument in the case of the British debts.[1]

I expect to be under the necessity of [*getting*] the opinions of the Judges except yours from Mr. Dallas whose report of the case will be publishd before mine. With very much respect & esteem I am dear Sir your obedt

J MARSHALL

8. Virginia had 21 electors, and each was required by the U.S. Constitution to vote for two persons, at least one of whom had to reside outside the elector's state. Virginia thus had a total of 42 electoral votes. According to state law, the electors were to meet in Richmond on the first Wednesday in December, which was Dec. 7 in 1796. 13 Hening 539 (1792). For information on the 1796 election, see Stephen G. Kurtz, *The Presidency of John Adams: The Collapse of Federalism, 1795–1800* (Philadelphia, 1957), 1–191, esp. 161–168; Richard R. Beeman, *The Old Dominion and the New Nation, 1788–1801* (Lexington, Ky., 1972), 159–168.

9. JM and his Federalist colleagues in the House of Delegates tried to insert a phrase in an address to President Washington saying his administration had been "marked by wisdom in the Cabinet, by valor in the field, and by the purest patriotism in both." The attempt failed, and the General Assembly adopted a less complimentary address. See *JVHD*, Nov. 1796, 65, 70, 71; Beeman, *Old Dominion*, 150–151.

1. Alexander James Dallas's letter to JM requesting a copy of his argument in Ware v. Hylton has not been found. Dallas (1759–1817), a native of Jamaica, attended Edinburgh University and was admitted to the bar on his native island. He came to Philadelphia in 1783 and became a U.S. citizen. In 1785 he began practicing in the Pennsylvania courts, and between 1790 and 1807 he edited four volumes of U.S. Supreme Court case reports. After Jefferson became president, Dallas became active in politics, serving as U.S. attorney for the eastern district of Pennsylvania from 1801 to 1814. In the latter year he became secretary of the Treasury. See Raymond Walters, Jr., *Alexander James Dallas: Lawyer, Politician, Financier, 1759–1817* (Philadelphia, 1943).

If JM sent Dallas a copy of his argument, it was not used in the published report. See Ware v. Hylton: Editorial Note, Feb. 9–12, 1796.

Legislative Bill

AD, House of Delegates Rough Bills, Virginia State Library

[Richmond, *ca.* December 22, 1796]

Be it enacted[2] that it shall & may be lawful for any citizen of ⟨this Commonwealth owning land⟩ these United States residing in or owning lands within this State who has carried or may carry any slave or slaves born within this state into any ⟨of these United States⟩ other state & who has ⟨not nor shall hereafter sell⟩ not sold or hird, or shall not hereafter sell or hire out such slave, to bring him her or them back again into Virginia without incurring any penalty therefor, nor shall such slave or slaves be intitled to freedom on that account.

Provided always that if any such slave or slaves be intitled to freedom under the laws of that state to which he she or they may have been or shall hereafter be removd, such right shall remain any thing in this act notwithstanding.

This act shall commence & be in force from & after the passing thereof.

From Robert Morris

Letterbook Copy, Morris Papers, Library of Congress

Dr Sir Philadelphia, December 30, 1796

Your letter of the 10th Instt advises of the compromise you had made with the Commonwealth[3] and altho you were obliged to give up a part of your claim yet it was probably better to do that than to hold a contest with such an opponent. I will give notice to

2. JM wrote on the verso, "A bill concerning certain slaves."

This bill resulted from a petition JM wrote for Thomas Mason. The Committee for Courts of Justice, of which JM was a member, reported that the petition was reasonable, and the House of Delegates ordered a bill drafted. On Dec. 20 the committee introduced a bill designed specifically to aid Mason, and it had received two readings when JM introduced this more general bill as a substitute. JM's bill was adopted immediately by the House and was approved by the Senate on Dec. 23. See Petition of Thomas Mason, *ca.* Nov. 21, 1796; 2 Shepherd 19–20; *JVHD*, Nov. 1796, 45, 67, 88, 90, 92, 95; "A bill Authorizing Thomas Mason to remove certain slaves from Maryland into this commonwealth," Dec. 20, 1796, House of Delegates Rough Bills, Virginia State Library.

3. Morris was referring to the compromise adopted by the General Assembly on Dec. 10. See 2 Shepherd 23, and Vol. II, 147–148. JM's letter has not been found.

Mr Jas Marshall of this compromise and write by the way of New York for we are frozen up here. Your Brother was in Amstm. when my last letters left London. He went thither on the invitation of some Capitalists with whom he was negotiating for a Loan of $400 000 and he had gone determined to submit to the hard terms they had prescribed but I learn that about the time of his arrival, a requisition of 6 per ct. on all property & some other public measures had deterred these Capitalists from fulfilling their agreement. Mr Hottenguer[4] who first put the thing in motion, says it will come on again & he thinks it will be carried into effect, if so your brother will of course be ready for Mr Fairfax and he was trying to raise money from other sources lest that should fail. I am here distressed exceedingly in money matters as indeed every body here are, but I will immediately make such exertions as are in my power to place funds with your brother and I cannot but hope that his and my exertions will produce the needful in proper time to prevent mischief. I expect to send you Certificates for some Bank shares by the next mail. Mr Colston writes that he has empowered you to do the needfull in regard to the judgemt. against Mr Braxton & me,[5] so that I may charge them in the accots now settling by Mr Richard[6] and I hope you will do it within the time necessary. I am Dr Sir, y o. h. S

R M

4. Jean Conrad Hottinguer (1764–1841), a banker, was later X of the XYZ agents. See note at Journal, Oct. 18–19, 1797, for additional biographical information.

5. Rawleigh Colston to Morris, Dec. 9, 1796, Superior Court of Chancery Records, 1784–1820, 180, Frederick County, Virginia State Library. It appears that JM was asked to arrange terms for collecting the judgment that Morris could meet. Colston, as surviving partner of Thomas Webb & Co., had brought suit against Carter Braxton and Morris in the District Court at Richmond to recover money owed the firm for a purchase of arms on which Thomas Webb & Co. had extended credit. JM represented Colston; a judgment for £9,810 was rendered against Braxton and Morris on Apr. 15, 1793.

Colston's difficulty collecting the judgment became an issue in a suit brought against him by Webb's heirs in the High Court of Chancery. Colston had been named administrator of Webb's estate, and Webb's heirs sued him for their inheritance. Colston's defense was based on the complicated partnership he had held with Thomas Webb and on the issue of debts owed the firm. The court did not issue a decree until 1820, by which time the suit had been transferred to the Superior Court of Chancery at Winchester. *Ibid.*, 1–226.

6. John Richard, Jr.

To Zachariah Johnston

ALS, Collection of Matthew W. Paxton, Lexington, Va.

Dear Sir [Richmond, *ca.* 1796]

I receivd your letter directed to Mr. Randolph[7] & myself. I do not think that withdrawing the survey in Philips's entry coud now be done or if done coud be of use to you. If I can perceive any mode of effecting this, I will mention it but really I perceive none at present. Your appeal shall be particularly attended to.[8] Perhaps it may come on this spring. I am extremely sorry for your ill health & am dear Sir very respectfully, Your Obedt

J Marshall

From James Wood

Copy, Executive Letterbooks, Virginia State Library

Sir, Richmond, January 14, 1797

I have the honor to enclose to you an authenticated copy of a Resolution which passed the General Assembly at their late Session, respecting the boundary line between this Commonwealth and the State of Maryland, together with a copy of the Resolution of the Legislature of Maryland on the same subject. I pray you Sir, to have the goodness to acknowledge the receipt of this dispatch as soon as convenient.[9] I have the honor to be with due consideration & respect etc.

James Wood

7. Edmund Randolph. Johnston's letter has not been found.

8. See JM to Johnston, Aug. 31, 1796, for an explanation of this case.

9. The boundary dispute between Virginia and Maryland began in the 17th century and was not resolved until 1910, when the U.S. Supreme Court decided Maryland v. West Virginia. See 217 U.S. 1 (1910). See also Charles Morrison, *The Fairfax Line: A Profile in History and Geography* (Parsons, W.Va., 1970).

In Dec. 1795 the Maryland General Assembly adopted a resolution calling for the appointment of commissioners to settle the boundary between that state and Virginia. The resolution was transmitted to the Virginia General Assembly at its 1796 session, and on Dec. 26 a resolution was adopted appointing Thomas Jefferson, JM, Edmund Randolph, Robert Brooke, Ludwell Lee, Bushrod Washington, and John Taylor of Caroline a committee to obtain information about the Maryland claim from that state's commissioners and to report back to the 1797 session. This copy of Wood's letter is addressed to each appointee. For Maryland's resolution, see H. W. Flournoy, ed., *Calendar of Virginia State Papers . . .*, VIII (Richmond, 1890), 326–327; Virginia's resolution is at 2 Shepherd 69 (1796). See also *JVHD*, Nov. 1796, 7.

From Robert Morris

Letterbook Copy, Morris Papers, Library of Congress

Dr Sir Philadelphia, January 23, 1797

I have delayed any reply to your letter of the 10th Ulto in the hope of being able to send you the Bank Shares which I had agreed for at the date of my last letter, but the Person with whom I had agreed fled from the bargain and disappointed me. I have since been trying to purchase but the demands on me for Money come faster than I can raise it. Money cannot be obtained on any terms, and the distress for want of it is universal. I must pray your patience awhile longer and the shares shall be sent to you. I am anxious to hear from your Brother, you know that he went over to Holland to obtain a loan with a prospect of success, but that some measures of the Dutch Government enterfered and the thing seemed to be over. But by letters from London since, there is again a hope of its being revived. I am however extremely anxious and fearing that it may fall through I am trying to obtain a loan here for the purposes of your Brother in London. This is extremely difficult for those who have money or credit in Europe seem to dread every thing that is American. Whatever I can do shall be done you may rely, for my anxiety on this occasion is beyond what I can express. Mr Alexr Baring[1] a Partner of the House of Hope & Co. could supply the money. I have applied to him but he parries me. He intends soon for the Southward. I will introduce him to you, and write more on this subject about the time he sets out. I am Dr Sir, y. o. h. S.

R M

At the time this committee was appointed, Jefferson had been chosen vice-president of the United States, Randolph had recently resigned as U.S. attorney general, Brooke had just served two terms as governor, Lee was a member of the Virginia senate, Washington was practicing law in Richmond, and JM and Taylor were serving in the House of Delegates. When Jefferson declined to serve, the duties of chairman fell to JM. See Jefferson to JM, Jan. 28, 1797. Because of his mission to France, JM probably did very little work on this committee. There is no record in the journal of the House of Delegates of a report made by the committee members at the 1797 General Assembly and no mention of any results of the committee's work in the governor's annual letter to the General Assembly. See Wood to the Speaker, Dec. 4, 1797, Executive Letterbooks, Virginia State Library.

For JM's reply to this letter, see JM to Wood, Jan. 24, 1797.

1. Alexander Baring (1775–1848), later first Lord Ashburton, was a Philadelphia representative of Hope & Co., bankers in Amsterdam and London.

To James Wood

ALS, Historical Society of Pennsylvania

Sir Richmond, January 24, 1797

I have just receivd your letter of the 14th. inclosing an authentic copy of a resolution which passed the general Assembly at their late session respecting the boundary line between this Commonwealth & the state of Maryland, together with a copy of the resolution of the state of Maryland on the same subject. I have the honor to be with much respect Your obedt. Servt.

J MARSHALL

From Thomas Jefferson

Presscopy, Jefferson Papers, Library of Congress

Dr Sir Monticello, January 28, 1797

[*In a*] letter of the 1[*4*]th. inst. I recieved [*from the governor*] a [*resolu*]tion of the general assembly [*appointing a body of which*] I am named one, to correspond with certain Maryland Commissioners on the dividing boundaries of the two states. The periodical & long absences from the state which I must [*incur,*] with the habitual state of my health obliging me to avoid journies, as much as possible, will I fear render me of little utility in this business.[2] I feel however the less concern as the other names in the resolution leave nothing to desire as to the qualifications proper for it. I pray you therefore to proceed with them, without regarding my inability to attend your meetings. As soon as the points in question, and those on which the Commissioners of Maryland shall rest claims, shall be known, I will undertake to give a thorough examination to such documents as are in my possession, and to give you all the benefit which can be derived from them. Mr Pendleton & mr Wythe[3] are probably acquainted with facts on this subject. The

2. Jefferson had received a letter identical to James Wood to JM, Jan. 14, 1797. By this time Jefferson knew the results of the 1796 election and anticipated his duties as vice-president. See Richard R. Beeman, *The Old Dominion and the New Nation, 1788–1801* (Lexington, Ky., 1972), 168.

3. Edmund Pendleton was president of the Virginia Court of Appeals. George Wythe was serving as the chancellor of the High Court of Chancery.

papers of Colo. Beverley, father of the gentleman [*now living*],[4] those of Ld. Fairfax, of mr Mercer father of mr John Mercer,[5] and especially those of the late Colo. George Mason, will be worthy examination. The last named gentleman had probably committed notes touching on the subject, as he was entirely intimate with it, and in expectation of such a claim.[6] As I can only offer my services as a corresponding member, I pray you to use me freely in that way in all cases where I can be useful. Your name standing first on the list, I avail myself of your address for making this communication to all the gentlemen named, and as far as that circumstance might make it a duty to take measures for putting the business underway, you will be pleased to consider the duty as devolved on you. I am with great respect Dear Sir Your most obedt. servt.

TH: JEFFERSON

To Henry Bedinger

ALS, Knollenberg Collection, Yale University Library

Dear Sir[7] Richmond, January 29, 1797

I have receivd yours of the 9th.[8]

4. Jefferson was probably referring to William Beverley (1696–1756), of "Blandfield," in Essex County, son of the Robert Beverley who wrote a history of Virginia. Beverley had been appointed by Lord Fairfax to act as one of the commissioners to settle the boundary of the Northern Neck. He also had owned large tracts of land in the western part of the state. His brother Harry Beverley (d. 1730) had helped survey the line between North Carolina and Virginia. The Beverley "now living" would have been William's son, Robert (1740–1800), who then resided at "Blandfield."

5. Jefferson probably was referring to John Mercer (1704–1768), of Stafford County, who had come to Virginia from Dublin in 1720. His *An Exact Abridgement of all the Public Acts of Assembly, of Virginia* . . . was published in Williamsburg in 1737. Mercer owned Marlborough Town in what was known as Potomack Neck. He also owned a library of 1,500 volumes, 500 of which were on law. His son, John Francis Mercer (1759–1821), had studied law under Jefferson's tutelage in 1779 and 1780. After serving in the Virginia House of Delegates and the Continental Congress in the 1780s, he moved to Maryland and was one of that state's representatives at the Constitutional Convention. He later served in the U.S. House of Representatives. C. Malcolm Watkins, *The Cultural History of Marlborough, Virginia* . . . , Smithsonian Institution, Bulletin 253 (Washington, D.C., 1968).

6. George Mason had served as a delegate to the Mt. Vernon conference in 1785 and had drafted papers regarding the jurisdiction and navigation of the Potomac and Pokomoke rivers. See Robert A. Rutland, ed., *The Papers of George Mason, 1725–1792*, II (Chapel Hill, N.C., 1970), 812–821.

7. Bedinger (1753–1843) lived in Shepherdstown in Berkeley County (now West Virginia), where JM addressed this letter. He was married to Rachel Strode. The address leaf is endorsed "Alex, 1 Feb.," although it is clear JM dated it Richmond.

There is a bill of review for Mr. Strode to endeavor to obtain a reversal of the former decree against him which I fear will be unsuccessful. In this I am employd & the suit is not yet determind.[9]

I inclose you an execution for Mr. Humphries which I took with me up the country but saw no person to deliver it to & brought it back. That business is finally settled.[1] The old gentleman is dissatisfied at the amount of damages he recovers but it was impossible to obtain more.

I have examind since the receipt of your letter the papers in your suit with Mr. Fairfax.[2] The testimony is not so decisive as to enable me to give it up without further enquiry. I shall write to Mr. Colston concerning it & endeavor to make the most immediate investigation of the subject. If on enquiry the equity & right of the case appears to be against us I can say for myself that I shall not wish to enter into any contest on the subject. Very respectfully I am Sir Your Obedt

J MARSHALL

A typewritten note attached to the letter reads: "Charleston W.Va. Nov. 27, 1929, The within is a copy of a letter, and the indorsements thereon, written by John Marshall, afterwards Chief Justice of the Supreme Court of the United States, to Major Henry Bedinger, my great grand father.

"I received the original letter from my father, the late Henry B. Davenport. He received it from his father, the late Colonel Braxton Davenport, who married a daughter of Major Bedinger. I have this day presented the original letter to Hon. John W. Davis, as a token of my esteem and admiration. [*signed*] Henry Bedinger Davenport."

8. Letter not found.

9. Although this is clearly a chancery suit, it may be related to John Strode v. John Head, Jr., and William Sansum, decided by the District Court at Fredericksburg on Oct. 2, 1794, and affirmed by the Court of Appeals on Oct. 30, 1795. Court of Appeals Order Book, III, 82, Virginia State Library. See also *ibid.*, 202, for a later case.

John Strode was manager of the ironworks located near Falmouth on the Stafford County side of the Rappahannock River.

1. JM had received fees from a Thomas Humphries in 1784 and 1789, but it is not certain they were related to the litigation mentioned here. See Vol. I, 311, and Vol. II, 363.

2. A notice was printed from the High Court of Chancery in Henry Bedinger v. James Strode, Denny Fairfax, late Denny Martin, Robert Stephens, David Hunter, Moses Hunter, and Philip Pendleton under the date June 7, 1797. It was simply publication of notice for Denny Martin Fairfax to appear on the first day of the next term of court to answer a bill filed by Bedinger. No other details of the suit are known, nor have any letters been found between Rawleigh Colston and JM relating to the case. *Virginia Gazette, and General Advertiser* (Richmond), Aug. 2, 1797.

Law Papers, January 1797

U.S. Circuit Court, Va.

Cockran, Donald & Co. v. Pope, declaration, ADS, U.S. Circuit Court, Va., Ended Cases (Unrestored), Virginia State Library.

Donald, Scot & Co. v. Pope, declaration (debt for £196 18s. 2d.), ADS, U.S. Circuit Court, Va., Ended Cases (Unrestored), Va. State Lib.

Donald, Scot & Co. v. Pope, declaration (debt for £171 15s. 10d.), ADS, U.S. Circuit Court, Va., Ended Cases (Unrestored), Va. State Lib.

From James Wood

Copy, Executive Letterbooks, Virginia State Library

Sir Richmond, February 1, 1797

I have been honored with your letter of the 24th. Ultimo. I took the earliest Opportunity of Submitting it to the consideration of the Council of State, who have advised that the interest of the Commonwealth in the Suit of the Indiana Company, should be confided to yourself and General Marshall who is now in Philadelphia,[3] and with whom you will have an Opportunity of con-

3. This letter was actually written to Charles Lee, but a note at the end of the letterbook copy reads, "A Similar letter of the same date was written to John Marshall Esqr. then in Philadelphia, by James Wood." Lee's letter of Jan. 24 has not been found.

Shortly before Wood wrote to Lee and JM, the Council of State had met and discussed Lee's letter and the implications of the suit Hollingsworth v. Virginia. The Council had directed Wood to write to Lee "requesting him to confer with Mr. John Marshall on the Subject of the said suit who the Governor is also requested to retain." The rest of the instructions given by the Council follow almost verbatim the wording of this letter. See Journals of the Virginia Council of State, Feb. 1, 1797, Virginia State Library.

The General Assembly had instructed the governor to take the necessary steps to fight the suit, and the resolution of the legislature had been forwarded to Lee on Jan. 16. The Council of State had then instructed Lee to confer with the senators who represented Virginia in Congress. Apparently Lee's reply of Jan. 24 led the Council to ask him to confer with JM.

The Indiana Company's claim to the land that many believed was within Virginia's borders arose before the Revolution. A 1768 treaty between England and several tribes of Indians at Fort Stanwix awarded to a group of traders almost 2,000,000 acres of land in what is today the northern part of West Virginia and the southwestern part of Pennsylvania. During the war and after, Virginia asserted its claim to the land and denied all petitions for redress from the claimants, who organized as the Indiana Company. In 1792 the company finally sued for damages in the U.S. Supreme Court in an action filed as William Grayson *et al.* v. Virginia. Grayson had died in 1790, a difficulty the company's attorneys rectified in 1793 by amending the bill to name Levi Hollingsworth as plaintiff. Virginia officials refused to respond to the bill until March

ferring on the subject. As the Legislature have already decided on the legality of the claim,[4] and have evidenced an opposition to the principle in the Constitution which is supposed to establish the suability of a State against its consent, the Executive wish you to take such Steps as will bring the suit to trial on these principles, without the Voluntary appearance of the State if such measure can be taken, but if not that you will be pleased to enter an appearance for the Commonwealth, and defend the suit in the manner which you may deem most consistent with its interest. If you should be of opinion that authenticated copies of the petitions presented by the Company to the General Assembly, with the decision of the Legislature thereon is necessary they shall be immediately forwarded to you. I have the honor to be very respectfully etc.

JAMES WOOD.

Bond

DS, Heth Papers, University of Virginia Library

[*March 22, 1797* (*Richmond*). Harry Heth, John Stewart, JM, Hardin Burnley, Samuel Pleasants, and William Randolph bind themselves collectively and severally to John Swann for £2,086 19s., the obligation to be void if Swann is paid half that amount plus 5 percent interest from Dec. 25, 1796, on or before June 25, 1798.][5]

1796, when the Supreme Court began to take steps to allow the company to proceed *ex parte.*

In the meantime the 11th Amendment to the U.S. Constitution was proposed and ratified, and on Feb. 14, 1798, Lee notified the governor that the court had dismissed the suit. See H. W. Flournoy, ed., *Calendar of Virginia State Papers . . .*, VIII (Richmond, 1890), 464. For a detailed explanation of the case and its relationship to Chisholm v. Georgia, the 11th Amendment, and Virginia, see Julius Goebel, Jr., *The Oliver Wendell Holmes Devise History of the Supreme Court of the United States: Antecedents and Beginning to 1801*, I (New York, 1971), 725–726, 734, 737, 738, 741, esp. 756–757. See also 3 U.S. (3 Dall.) 378 (1798).

4. The resolution of the General Assembly, Dec. 27, 1796, is at 2 Shepherd 70.

5. The signatures are partially torn from the document, but enough remains to recognize that all but Pleasants signed the bond. JM's signature was witnessed by John Setchell. Writing on the verso indicates that Swann apparently assigned the bond to William A. Frey on Mar. 3, 1798, but the assignment has been crossed out. An account from 1797 to *ca.* Jan. 17, 1801, also appears on the verso.

Stewart was a clerk of the House of Delegates from 1795 to 1799. Burnley (1762–1809) represented Orange County in the House of Delegates from 1787 to 1790 and then sat on the Council of State until Dec. 7, 1799, when he resigned after a two-year term as lieutenant governor. Pleasants lived in Powhatan County, and Randolph lived in Cumberland County. Swann (d. 1817) also lived in Powhatan County and served for a time as a tax collector there.

Receipt

DS, Morris Papers, University of Virginia Library

[*March 24, 1797* (*Richmond*). The receipt is for £40 5s. ½d. and represents the amount due on judgment, plus interest and costs in Henrico County Court, less costs in the High Court of Chancery and the Court of Appeals. JM apparently represented George Pickett as plaintiff; Col. Richard Morris was the defendant.]

To Thomas Jefferson

[*April 12, 1797*. Listed in Jefferson's "Summary Journal of Letters," Jefferson Papers, Library of Congress. Not found.]

To David Jones

ALS, American Baptist Historical Society, Rochester, N.Y.

Dear Sir[6] Richmond, April 14, 1797

I receivd yours of the 21st. of March & now inclose you a copy of the decree of the court of appeals.[7]

The proceedings in chancery & appeals were on the idea of your being in possession of the property as the suit was brought against you & you had the legal title. Of consequence no process can issue to put you in possession. If it is refusd you must bring an ejectment & must succeed. The decree is only a decision in favor of your equitable title as your legal title was never questiond. I wrote you this some time past & sent the letter to Fort Pitt. I shoud have written to you in Philadelphia after hearing you were there but expected to have seen you there myself in Feby. I coud not however hear of you. I have receivd all the money I desire in the business. I am Sir very respectfully your Obedt.

J Marshall

6. JM addressed the letter to "The reverend David Jones, Philadelphia." "Decree of the Court of Appeals" also appears on the address leaf in a hand other than JM's.

7. Jones's letter has not been found.

This letter concerns the Court of Appeals' decision of Nov. 4, 1793, in Isaac Williams and Joseph Tomlinson v. John Jeremiah Jacob and David Jones, which was appealed from a May 1792 decree of the High Court of Chancery. See George Wythe, *Decisions of Cases in Virginia in the High Court of Chancery* . . . (Richmond, 1795), 145; 1 Va. (1 Wash.) 230; Vol. II, 378, 426.

To Charles Lee

ALS, Adams Papers, Massachusetts Historical Society

My dear Sir Richmond, April 20, 1797

As I think it improbable that you take Pleasants paper I inclose a column or two from it containing an address which I think important both from the matter it contains & its signature.[8] You know well how much the opponents of government in this country act in concert & may consequently judge how far Mr. Pendleton has expressd their general sentiment. I am told, tho not by a person who was present or whose correctness may be depended on, that even the faint & glimmering appearance of American feeling which a microscopic eye with difficulty discerns in one or two passages of this unworthy performance, was produced by a hard election which created a necessity of showing that one of the candidates was not, in case of war & invasion a positive Frenchman. The insiduous attempt which is made to ascribe the aggressions made on us by France to the British treaty & the partiality of our government for Britain, tho it has been provd a thousand times to be the most shameless insult on truth & common sense, still succeeds. That party has laid such fast hold of the public mind in this part

8. Samuel Pleasants, Jr. (1770–1814), changed the title of his newspaper, the *Richmond and Manchester Advertiser,* to the *Virginia Argus* on Nov. 19, 1796.

The address was the product of a meeting in Caroline County of freeholders who had assembled on Apr. 11, 1797, to elect delegates to the General Assembly. Edmund Pendleton had signed the letter, which was addressed to Anthony New, the area's representative in Congress. The citizens of Caroline County were afraid Congress was about to declare war on France, "our magnanimous sister Republic—our first ally—& our faithful preserver." In the letter they expressed their belief that measures taken by the administration, especially the Jay Treaty, had damaged American commerce and, in the process, French trade as well. They also called for the appointment of a minister extraordinary to settle differences with France, just as John Jay had negotiated with England when differences with that country had threatened war. In closing the citizens said: "Let every expedient to avoid war be resorted to. If all fail, they will yet be useful in producing union. May Heaven avert the fatal catastrophe to the God of battles, with that assurance, which the consiousness of a good cause, will never fail to beget. A real, and not a feigned desire of reconciliation, a substantial neutrality, and not a covert design to unite us intimately and injuriously with any particular nation, can alone cement the energies of America. Finally, recollect that the European combinations of kings and princes, was levelled at an elective republic—That the war which mediated its extinction, still rages—That a direct proposition at the commencement of this war, to unite America in the Royal coalition, would have been received with indignation, because its issue might obviously have been an extinction of elective republicanism here, and that by whatever means the same cause is generated, the effect will be the same." *Va. Argus* (Richmond), Apr. 14, 1797.

See Charles Lee to JM, *ca.* May 5, 1797.

of Virginia that an attempt to oppose sinks at once the person who makes it. The elections for the State legislature go entirely go entirely against the foederalists who are madly & foolishly as well as wickedly styled a british party. Tinsly in Hanover is droped & a mad jacobin elected in his place. Mayo in chesterfield has shard the same fate. Baytop of gloster coud not wash out the stain of having voted foederally & in York one or both the old members are to be turnd out I am told for voting against Page.[9] In Fauquier I am apprehensive that Horner & Jennings will supplant Scott & Chilton.[1] I mention these facts to show you the temper of a large portion of our country. The piece which accompanies Mr. Pendletons is the production of a warm & spirited young man[2] & I only send it because it being joind to the other goes without enconvenience.

My brother urges strongly remittances for the purpose of obtaining a title to the land we purchasd by our second contract with Fairfax.[3] I am laboring at it & hope you have made a remittance of your part. If you can I beg you to do so as soon as possible if you have not already. I have been authorizd to offer you to take your interest & besides paying ⟨you⟩ the purchase money to give you four thousand dollars by instalments for your part, but though I

9. Thomas Tinsley was replaced by John Thompson (1777–1799), a Republican attorney from Petersburg. During the Congressional campaign in 1798, Thompson attacked JM in his *Letters of Curtius*. See Congressional Election Campaign: Editorial Note, at Sept. 19, 1798.

George Mayo was defeated by Thomas A. Taylor (1744–1822). James Baytop (d. 1821) was replaced by John Page, of "Rosewell." In York County one of the delegates, William Waller, was replaced by Samuel Shield. Waller had probably voted against Page in the 1796 congressional elections in which Page was defeated.

1. JM was confused about the Fauquier delegates. Augustine Jennings (*ca.* 1746–1815) and Alexander Scott (*ca.* 1762–1819) had represented the county in the 1796 General Assembly. William Chilton (b. *ca.* 1772), a Warrenton attorney whose eldest son was John Marshall Chilton, was elected to Scott's seat in 1797. If Gustavus Brown Horner (1761–1815) ran for election against Jennings in 1797, he lost; Jennings was reelected that year. For information on Chilton, see Ann S. Chilton McDonnell, "The Chilton Family," Fauquier Historical Society, *Bulletin*, III (1923), 321–325.

2. Immediately below Edmund Pendleton's letter in the *Va. Argus*, Apr. 14, 1797, was an essay signed "American" in which the author attacked James Monroe and his address to the French Directory upon his departure from France.

3. The first contract with Denny Martin Fairfax, Feb. 1, 1793, called for the purchase of the Manor of Leeds and South Branch Manor together for a total of £20,000 by Feb. 1, 1794. When that deadline arrived, the Marshalls had failed to raise the money, and JM bought only the South Branch Manor for £6,000. See Vol. II, 143–156. Apparently a second contract was negotiated at that time for the purchase of the Manor of Leeds for £14,000, the amount finally being paid in 1806, but a copy of this contract has not been found.

feel myself bound to mention it I woud rather the original partners shoud retain their shares. I am dear Sir yours etc.

J MARSHALL

From Charles Lee

Printed Extract, *Virginia Argus* (Richmond), May 9, 1797, 2

Philadelphia, *ca.* May 5, 1797

THE[4] letter from the people of Caroline to Mr. New . . . has been noticed here for its abject servility in apologizing for the unjustifiable and insolent proceedings of France. Such sentiments as that paper contains will produce what all the virtuous must and do wish to avoid, the miseries and calamities of war. If there be a respectable minority of the United States, who will avow and act as is contained in that letter we have much to fear. Has Virginia no sense of national honor? Is she so infatuated as not to perceive how rapidly she is meeting the horrors of St. Domingo. That from them, in case of war, nothing can save her but the northern states, and if Virginia prefers France to them, what inducements can they have to make exertions for her? Another war in America will not be conducted with regard to the blacks as the former was, and they who think so, forget the change which has taken place of late years with respect to the rights of man.

Mr. Monroe's valedictory is condemned by all who have expressed any opinion where I have happened to be. Disgraced and injured by France as his country had been, he might have spared it the ignominious wound which this last act inflicted so wantonly and so publicly.

Receipt

ADS, Clark-Hite Papers, The Filson Club

[*June 1, 1797* (*Richmond*). JM gives Gen. George Rogers Clark a receipt for £28 in the case *Hite v. Duff, Green, and McKay*.]

4. This letter is printed as an "Extract of a letter from a gentleman in Philadelphia, to his friend in Virginia," and almost certainly is from Charles Lee to JM. See JM to Lee, Apr. 20, 1797.

Mission to France

EDITORIAL NOTE

John Marshall's acceptance of the position of special envoy to France marked his emergence as a national political leader. Before the appointment Marshall had been content to remain in Richmond tending his burgeoning law practice, securing his future by widespread land speculations, and retaining his seat in the Virginia General Assembly. On his return from France he not only was accorded front rank in the Federalist Party in Virginia but also was admired by Federalists in every section of the country.

The appointment of a mission to France in 1797 came as one of a series of moves made first by George Washington and then by John Adams to preserve American neutrality in the wars of the French Revolution. President Washington issued a proclamation of neutrality when he learned of the renewal of war between France and Great Britain in 1793.[5] The exact terms of the neutrality policy were originally vague, new interpretations being added almost monthly from 1793 until the middle of 1797. Whether the issue was the drawback trade with the French West Indies or the sale of French prizes in American ports, the rationale behind the neutrality policy was to preserve peace with the major European powers while using neutrality to increase American commerce. Washington's cabinet was unanimous on the issue of peace, and neutrality, it was commonly accepted, would ensure peace. The question of how best to preserve neutrality, however, caused a constant struggle among the administration, the Congress, and the public.

France and Great Britain welcomed the American proclamation of neutrality, but each country attempted to impel the United States to interpret neutrality in its favor. Given the insignificant military and naval power of the new federal government, the major task of American diplomacy was to placate one power without alienating the other. Yet Americans could not achieve neutrality in both

5. For background the following works have been especially useful: Alexander DeConde, *Entangling Alliance: Politics and Diplomacy under George Washington* (Durham, N.C., 1958); DeConde, *The Quasi-War: The Politics and Diplomacy of the Undeclared War with France, 1797–1801* (New York, 1966); Bradford Perkins, *The First Rapprochement: England and the United States, 1795–1805* (Philadelphia, 1955); George Athan Billias, *Elbridge Gerry: Founding Father and Republican Statesman* (New York, 1976); Albert Hall Bowman, *The Struggle for Neutrality: Franco-American Diplomacy during the Federalist Era* (Knoxville, Tenn., 1974); Harry Ammon, *James Monroe: The Quest for National Identity* (New York, 1971); R. R. Palmer, *The Age of the Democratic Revolution: A Political History of Europe and America*, 1760–1800, II (Princeton, N.J., 1964); G. Lacour-Gayet, *Talleyrand, 1754–1838*, I (Paris, 1930); E. Wilson Lyon, "The Directory and the United States," *American Historical Review*, XLIII (1938), 514–532; Howard C. Rice, "James Swan: Agent of the French Republic, 1794–1796," *New England Quarterly*, X (1937), 464–486; Georgia Robison, *La Révellière-Lépeaux, Citizen Director, 1753–1824* (New York, 1938); Georges Lefebvre, *The Thermidorians and the Directory: Two Phases of the French Revolution*, trans. Robert Baldick (New York, 1964), James Thomas Flexner, *George Washington: Anguish and Farewell (1793–1799)* (Boston, 1972); Stephen G. Kurtz, *The Presidency of John Adams: The Collapse of Federalism, 1795–1800* (Philadelphia, 1957); Manning Dauer, *The Adams Federalists*, rev. ed. (Baltimore, 1968).

thought and deed. France initially held the advantage, because the Treaty of Alliance of 1778 sanctioned French use of American ports to conduct privateering raids on Spanish and British shipping in the West Indies. Great Britain retaliated by restricting neutral shipping and capturing over three hundred American vessels in 1793 and 1794, thus bringing the two countries to the verge of war.

President Washington sought to lessen the threat of war with England by appointing Chief Justice John Jay as minister extraordinary to Great Britain, superseding the resident minister, Thomas Pinckney. Jay received instructions to sign a commercial treaty with Great Britain and to settle as many of the outstanding differences between the two countries as possible. He succeeded to a limited extent and returned to the United States with the treaty that unofficially bears his name. The terms of the Jay Treaty precipitated a public debate on foreign policy that continued without interruption until Jefferson's election in 1800.

The Jay Treaty was widely condemned for its alleged subservience to Great Britain and faintly praised for being the best that could be achieved. The Federalists, despite many private reservations, generally supported the treaty, while the rising Republicans denounced it. In a South rapidly coming under Republican control, John Marshall first came to national attention through his justification of the Jay Treaty. In the Virginia General Assembly, in public debate, and in pamphlets, Marshall defended the treaty with Great Britain and urged its ratification by Congress.[6]

Despite its shortcomings, the Jay Treaty gave the United States a number of advantages. Yet the advantages of settling the long-standing question of the western posts and of achieving stability in commercial relations with Great Britain were counterbalanced by other features of the treaty that exacerbated problems with France. The United States had agreed to redefine the meaning of neutral rights, reversing the policy of "free ships make free goods" that had been the basis of the commercial treaty with France in 1778. The news that the United States was going to implement the Jay Treaty did not reach France until the last half of 1796. The French, not surprisingly, took exception to the treaty, specifically because it restricted vitally needed neutral shipping, and more generally because it damaged relations with their ally and sister republic.

France's policy toward the United States had already undergone a number of gradual shifts in 1795 and 1796, each change increasing the probability of war. After the Jay Treaty, French policy toward the United States became perceptibly hostile as the former ideological or commercial bonds were replaced by pragmatic considerations. Its navy weakened by desertions and repeated setbacks, the French government relied on privateers to attack British or neutral shipping in European and West Indian waters. Under the Committee of Public Safety, the French had imported vast quantities of grain from the United States to compensate for poor harvests. Following the return of normal harvests in 1795, however, the government, then under the Directory, saw little need or purpose in settling outstanding differences with the United States. American merchants who had contracted with the Committee of Public Safety for foodstuffs and supplies could not collect on their deliveries. The Directory abruptly required authorized manifests of cargo and crews, or a *rôle d'équipage*, for each American ship entering

6. Beveridge, *Marshall*, II, 122–165. See JM to Alexander Hamilton and JM to Rufus King, Apr. 25, 1796.

a French port. Unaware of the new requirement, American captains stood by helplessly as their cargoes and often their ships were confiscated by French tribunals. Despite repeated protests by American officials in France, the Directory refused to alter its policy. In addition, French privateers captured over three hundred American vessels in the West Indies.

The indifference with which the French government treated American complaints was closely linked to French policy toward Great Britain. Buttressed by its vast commerce and indomitable navy, Great Britain pursued a policy of restricting the French fleet and neutral imports into France. The French tried to retaliate by restricting neutral trade with Great Britain wherever possible, but they were handicapped by their lack of sea power and forced to rely on municipal regulations such as the *rôle d'équipage* to constrict British commerce indirectly. The French policy damaged the United States more severely than it harmed Great Britain.

The Directory considered the United States in the context of policy toward Great Britain. Although French policy toward the United States varied, its purpose until mid-1798 was to punish that country for its extensive cooperation with Great Britain. In the eyes of French policymakers, the United States had turned its back on an ally in ratifying the Jay Treaty and had thereby aligned itself with France's ancient and bitter antagonist. It would be useless to make peace with the United States, since this would only serve to strengthen Great Britain.

Another group, though, represented by Talleyrand and a number of his closest advisers in the Foreign Office, viewed the problem differently. This group acknowledged that the United States would naturally be more friendly to Great Britain because of commercial ties, culture, and language. It would be better to have the United States remain neutral and attempt to take advantage of the competing interests of the two English-speaking countries. If France continued its policy of harassment of American shipping, the United States would join the war against France, probably as an ally of Great Britain, creating a hostile bloc in the new world far more powerful than France and Spain. By pursuing a policy of accommodation, France could guard against the entire resources of the United States being added to those of Great Britain.

The advocates of accommodation, including virtually all diplomats or former émigrés who, like Talleyrand, had been in the United States, also wanted to protect French colonies in the Western Hemisphere. Spain had agreed to cede Louisiana to France in the Treaty of Basel in 1795, but the transfer had not yet taken place. In order to be assured of access to Louisiana, the French had to guarantee the continuance of French sovereignty in Santo Domingo, which was in full-scale revolt against the mother country. French interests in the West Indies never received priority from 1793 to 1798, largely due to the exigencies of continental and Mediterranean policies. It was clear, however, that French power in the Western Hemisphere would be more effective if France could avoid war with the United States. Spokesmen for accommodation repeatedly noted American cooperation with Great Britain in aiding the independence movement under Toussaint Louverture in Santo Domingo. They also argued that in the event of war with the United States, one American objective would be to move down the Mississippi and occupy New Orleans, effectively foreclosing the possibility of France regaining control of its former colony.

In July 1797, while Marshall and Elbridge Gerry were on their way to France, Charles Maurice de Talleyrand-Périgord became French foreign minister, succeeding Charles Delacroix de Contant. Whatever Talleyrand's thoughts on accommodation with the United States, the Directory, not Talleyrand, set foreign policy at this time.[7] Talleyrand had returned to France after a four-year absence only the previous year, and this post was his first of ministerial rank. His influence on French foreign policy, vast in later years, was not then sufficient to reverse the Directory's belligerent policy.

Nor did the first commission to France come at a propitious time for a change in French policy. The coup d'etat of 18 Fructidor (September 4, 1797) eliminated the moderates and royalists in the French government. The Treaty of Campo Formio brought an advantageous peace to France by temporarily settling the question of northern Italy. At the same time, the collapse of the peace negotiations with Great Britain at Lille strengthened the position of hard-liners against Talleyrand.[8] Under these circumstances, an accommodation between France and the United States would have been extremely difficult to achieve, no matter who the French foreign minister or the American envoys. Marshall was to find, as had his predecessors Gouverneur Morris, James Monroe, and Charles Cotesworth Pinckney, that negotiating with the French revolutionary government was a sensitive undertaking that could easily harm his political reputation in the United States.

Originally Washington had hoped that a policy of strict neutrality in combination with outspoken appreciation of the French Revolution would enable the United States to maintain friendly relations with France. Until his last year in office, Washington remained more optimistic about the eventual success of the French Revolution than most Federalists, including John Adams.[9] Earlier in the cabinet's struggles over the course of policy toward France, Washington had more often sided with Thomas Jefferson's viewpoint than with Alexander Hamilton's. Washington had received Citizen Edmond Charles Genet over strong objections. He insisted that the French alliance of 1778 remain in effect, although he certainly did not expect that France would ask the United States to guarantee her West Indian possessions. At Jefferson's insistence, Washington recalled Gouverneur Morris as minister to France because of Morris's known contempt for the French Revolution. He appointed James Monroe to succeed Morris primarily because Monroe was favorably inclined toward the French and the French Revolution.[1]

7. R. R. Palmer described the situation in France in late 1797: "The five Directors after Fructidor were Reubell, who exercised the main influence in foreign policy; Barras, whose importance was exaggerated by his ill repute; La Révellière-Lépeaux, of Theophilanthropic fame; Merlin de Douai; and François de Neufchateau. Their foreign minister was Talleyrand, whose actual influence in these years hardly went beyond the writing of magisterial memoranda." Palmer, *Age of Democratic Revolution*, II, 366.

8. Lefebvre, *Thermidorians and the Directory*, 197–201; [James Harris], third earl of Malmesbury, ed., *Diaries and Correspondence of James Harris, First Earl of Malmesbury . . .*, III (London, 1845), 355–575.

9. Compare Flexner, *Washington: Anguish and Farewell*, 19, 257, and Page Smith, *John Adams, 1784–1826*, II (New York, 1962), 785–786, 882.

1. Dumas Malone, *Jefferson and the Ordeal of Liberty* (Boston, 1962), 50–52, 184; Ammon, *Monroe*, 112–117; DeConde, *Entangling Alliance*, 334–341.

The crucial turning point for Washington and for Federalist policy for the remainder of the decade came in the dismissal of Edmund Randolph as secretary of state in 1795. Randolph's indiscreet conversations with Joseph Fauchet, the French minister to the United States who succeeded Genet, forced Washington to demand Randolph's immediate resignation. Concurrent with Randolph's resignation, Washington signed the Jay Treaty and destroyed his image as a man above party. When a number of men declined Washington's offer of the position of secretary of state, the president found himself compelled to select Timothy Pickering, an acidly anti-French High Federalist from Massachusetts.[2] Washington's disillusionment with the prominent Republicans necessitated choosing advisers with decidedly anti-French views. Earlier, however, he had called upon men who saw France as a counterweight to Great Britain. This view of France, commonly associated with Thomas Jefferson and James Madison, but also advanced by Edmund Randolph, Robert R. Livingston, and James Monroe, no longer had an effective advocate in cabinet councils.

Washington now uncritically accepted Pickering's complaints about Monroe as minister to France and agreed to recall him. After Monroe took leave of his post in December 1796, the United States remained without a regularly accredited minister in France until after Jefferson's election in 1801.[3] In seeking a replacement for Monroe, Washington still preferred a man favorably inclined to the French but, more important, a Federalist and a southerner. Knowing, little about Marshall's views toward France, the president narrowed his choice down to John Marshall and Charles Cotesworth Pinckney.[4] Washington stipulated that the minister to France must be one "who will promote not thwart the neutrality policy of the government, and at the same time will not be obnoxious to the People among whom he is sent."[5] Neither Washington, nor Adams later, realized that the two points seemed contradictory to many Frenchmen.[6] After Marshall refused the post, Pinckney accepted it, although he had not supported the Jay Treaty. When Pinckney arrived in Paris, Delacroix refused to accept his credentials and in January 1797 ordered the American to leave Paris immediately. Thus the long-simmering crisis in French-American affairs reached an acute stage just as Washington was completing his term.

Stung by the unfamiliar but growing opposition to his policies, Washington delivered his Farewell Address. In the context of the continuing debate over foreign affairs, the address could only be considered a partisan document defending Federalist foreign policy.[7] By the fall of 1796, Washington had moved into the anti-French ranks of High Federalism. In the Farewell Address he castigated the French and French influence in the United States in indirect but no un-

2. Flexner, *Washington: Anguish and Farewell*, 213–242; W. Allan Wilbur, "Oliver Wolcott, Jr., and Edmund Randolph's Resignation, 1795," Connecticut Historical Society, *Bulletin*, XXXVIII (1973), 12–16.

3. Ammon, *Monroe*, 157–173; DeConde, *Entangling Alliance*, 380–389.

4. George Washington to Timothy Pickering, July 8, 1796, Washington Papers, Ser. 4, Library of Congress (microfilm ed., reel 109).

5. *Ibid.*

6. Max Fajn, "Le 'Journal des hommes libres de tous les pays' et les relations diplomatiques entre la France et les Etats-Unis de 1792 à 1800," *Revue d'Histoire Diplomatique*, LXXXV (1971), 120–126.

7. DeConde, *Entangling Alliance*, 456–500.

certain terms. It is little wonder that the French minister to the United States, Pierre-Auguste Adet, predicted that either Adams or Jefferson as president would be better for France than Washington had been.[8] After Adam's election, French officials waited expectantly for a more accommodating policy.[9] They did not have to wait long for Adams to act.

When Adams became president in March 1797, he faced a number of troublesome decisions concerning French policy. A former diplomat, the new president understood the difficulties with France better than his predecessor or any member of the cabinet. Adams could not put his background to good use, however, because domestic politics circumscribed him. He succeeded a vastly more popular man. Washington had managed, for a time, to convince men of both parties to follow his leadership, something Adams could not equal. Adams's election by a scant three votes over Jefferson dispelled any belief that he had the wide popular support given Washington in his unanimous reelection in 1792. Adams inherited Washington's cabinet intact and decided to make no changes. The Federalists had a solid majority in the Senate to support the president's proposals, but the House was evenly divided. Because the Republican party openly opposed his person and policies, Adams had to hold together the disparate wings of the Federalist party to enact the measures he wanted.[1]

Immediately after taking office, Adams spoke several times with Jefferson about the possibility of cooperation on French policy. The president, strongly backed by Hamilton, wanted to revert to Washington's earlier policy of appointing men favorably inclined toward the French Revolution. The obvious choice for a new mission to France would be either Madison or Jefferson. Unfortunately, Madison urged Jefferson not to cooperate with Adams, advice that Jefferson supinely followed.[2] When the Federalists in the Senate and the cabinet protested the proposed appointment of either Jefferson or Madison, Adams decided not to break with them on this question, although Gerry urged him to do so. At this time, when they still held substantial respect for each other and shared broad agreement in outlook, Adams and Jefferson, perhaps unthinkingly, renounced cooperation in French policy for domestic partisan purposes. Thenceforth, Adams sought to nominate men for foreign policy posts who would receive the approval of the High-Federalists wing of the party, giving this group more influence than its numbers deserved.

Adams also sought to change the tone of foreign policy in a sensitive area, asserting that "we must assume more Decorum than to run after foreign ministers as if We were their Slaves or Subjects."[3] He believed Monroe had been too lavish

8. Pierre-Auguste Adet to Charles Delacroix, Oct. 12, 1796, Frederick J. Turner, ed., *Correspondence of the French Ministers to the United States, 1791–1797*, American Historical Association, *Annual Report, 1903*, II (Washington, D.C., 1904), 954–956.

9. Adet to Delacroix, Dec. 18, 1796, Correspondance Politique, Etats-Unis, XLVI, Archives of the Ministry of Foreign Affairs, Paris. Turner, ed., *Corr. of French Ministers*, 978–980, has the date as Dec. 15, 1796.

1. Kurtz, *Presidency of John Adams*, 261–283.

2. Malone, *Jefferson*, 295–301; Smith, *John Adams*, II, 917–925; Dauer, *Adams Federalists*, 120–128; Franklin B. Sawvel, ed., *The Complete Anas of Thomas Jefferson* (New York, 1903), 184–185.

3. John Adams to Abigail Adams, Jan. 18, 1797, Adams Papers, Massachusetts Historical Society.

in his praise of the French Revolution. Indeed, the new president thought it improper for American diplomats even to comment on the form of government because this indicated a judgment on French internal affairs.[4] In a letter to Gerry, Adams declared, "I would rather fill all foreign places with anti gallicans sooner than with servile fawning base intriguing flatterers of french Jacobins and worthless speculators in french funds and Confiscations."[5] Adams's interpretation of the rules of diplomacy was strict, his underlying hostility to the French Revolution obvious; in the context of 1797, his perspective was narrow. The common interests of France and the United States were very few, and a perfunctory appeal to their mutual republicanism might have helped the envoys in opening negotiations in a less hostile atmosphere.

In the last week of May 1797, Adams asked his cabinet if he should appoint Pinckney as sole envoy extraordinary to France; the answer was no.[6] He then inquired whether it would be preferable to add one or two envoys, and the consensus was to add two in addition to Pinckney. Adams suggested that Gerry be nominated, but the members of the cabinet objected to this man's erratic Federalism and persuaded Adams to mention another name.[7] Adams then suggested Francis Dana, who was selected as the second envoy. If either Gerry or Dana served on the commission, Adams would be assured of a Massachusetts man, a colleague who had served with him during the Revolution and a man whom he could trust.[8]

Adams then sought opinions on the remaining appointment. On the bottom of Adams's questionnaire to the cabinet was a list of suggested names, including James Madison, followed by John Marshall, Ludwell Lee, Thomas Lee, Bushrod Washington, and William Vans Murray.[9] All of these men were from Virginia or Maryland, and the selection of one of them would give the commission the rough geographic balance that Adams desired. Madison had already indicated through Jefferson that he would refuse the appointment; moreover, Madison provoked objections because of his partisanship.[1] After dismissing Madison from consideration, Adams and the cabinet selected John Marshall as the third envoy.

Marshall's alacrity in accepting the appointment was surprising, particularly in view of his previous refusals to accept federal office. Adams had nominated Pinckney, Dana, and Marshall on the last day of May, and the Senate confirmed the appointments within a week. Less than a week after Marshall's confirmation, Secretary of State Pickering knew that Marshall would accept the position, and

4. Draft, undated, *ibid.*

5. Adams to Elbridge Gerry, May 3, 1797, *ibid.*

6. "Questions to be proposed" [May 27–28, 1797], filed under Oct. 1797, *ibid.*

7. Adams to Gerry, June 20, 1797, *ibid.* See James McHenry to Pickering, Feb. 23, 1811, Henry Cabot Lodge, ed., *Life and Letters of George Cabot* (Boston, 1877), 204, for a discussion of Gerry's appointment.

8. Dauer points out Adams's partiality to Revolutionary Whigs in *Adams Federalists*, 89.

9. "Questions to be proposed" [May 27–28, 1797], filed under Oct. 1797, Adams Papers.

1. Dauer, *Adams Federalists*, 125–126; Uriah Tracy to Oliver Wolcott, Sr., May 27, 1797, George Gibbs, *Memoirs of the Administrations of Washington and John Adams . . .*, I (New York, 1846), 537–539. Apparently Adams suggested Madison's name even though he had been informed that Madison would not accept the nomination.

within two weeks of his confirmation, Marshall left Richmond for Philadelphia.[2] The very speed of Marshall's departure suggests that he knew in advance of the appointment and was eager to depart for Europe.

Marshall may have accepted Adams's offer because of the difficulties his brother James had experienced in arranging the financing to purchase the Fairfax lands.[3] James Markham Marshall had been in Europe for almost two years trying to raise credit for the purchase of the Fairfax lands and for other ventures undertaken by his father-in-law, Robert Morris. James M. Marshall had secured a small loan that allowed him to begin the next phase of the Fairfax purchase, but he had not yet been able to raise enough money to buy the Manor of Leeds.[4] Probably because he wanted to assist James in this matter, Marshall informed Pickering that he intended to go to England on business after the completion of the mission.[5] The day after John Marshall arrived in Amsterdam, his brother paid for part of the Fairfax land and arranged terms to purchase the Manor of Leeds, the final transfer of which did not occur until 1806 after eight years of payments. Undoubtedly James informed his brother of the financial arrangements in a letter now lost.[6] Despite Thomas Jefferson's later report that Marshall took the appointment as envoy to arrange his personal finances, it is unlikely that Marshall used his salary from the mission for the Fairfax purchase except, perhaps, for one of the yearly installments.[7]

Marshall's colleagues, Charles Cotesworth Pinckney and Elbridge Gerry, whom Adams had appointed after Dana declined to serve, were men of wider national reputation than Marshall. Both had been prominent in the early stages of the American Revolution and had served together in the Constitutional Convention. Marshall did not know either of them when he departed for Europe in mid-July.

At the start of the mission the three envoys agreed that France had broken both the letter and the spirit of its treaties with the United States. All three also assumed that their country was the aggrieved party in the dispute, and they considered the French government, by contrast, to be capricious, haughty, and arbitrary in its conduct toward the United States and its citizens. The envoys' agreement on the central issues was so complete that they noted no important differences in their attitudes as the mission began. But six months of furtive ne-

2. Pickering to Pinckney, June 12, 1797, Instructions to United States Ministers, IV, RG 59, National Archives; Thomas Jefferson to James Madison, June 1, 1797, Madison Papers, Lib. Cong.; *Columbian Mirror and Alexandria Gazette*, June 20, 1797.

3. See Fairfax Lands: Editorial Note, Vol. II, 140–149.

4. Robert Morris to James Markham Marshall, Apr. 27 and May 30, 1797, and Morris to Henry Lee, June 3, 1797, Letterbook, Morris Papers, Lib. Cong.

5. Pickering to John Quincy Adams, Mar. 17, 1798, Adams Papers.

6. See William Vans Murray to JM, Oct. 5, 1797.

7. For Jefferson's accusation, see Sawvel, ed., *Anas*, 204. JM received $9,000 a year in salary, an additional $9,000 for his outfit, and $1,350 for his secretary. JM collected $19,963.97 for his 13-month mission to France. See Envoy Account, Sept. 30, 1798. While in Paris all three envoys drew between $8,000 and $9,000 for expenses. JM's expenses in Europe were comparable to Gerry's when figured for the same period of time both were in Europe, with each of them drawing about $12,000. After JM returned to the United States, he drew about $6,000 as his final payment, a sum that might have been used to pay off an installment on the Fairfax contract. Envoy Account, Sept. 30, 1798; "United States in Account with Charles C. Pinckney," Nov. 1, 1798, and "United States in Accounts Current with Elbridge Gerry," Nov. 20, 1800, Records of Bureau of Accounts, RG 53, Natl. Arch.

gotiations and their attendant frustrations eventually magnified originally slight divisions until the envoys could no longer work together.

At the time of Marshall's appointment little was known of his views on foreign policy except that he had supported the Jay Treaty. After attending a farewel dinner for him, St. George Tucker, a Francophile Republican, reported, "I had much Conversation with him, & am happy to tell you that of the *t'other Side Men* that I know he appears to me to preserve the best disposition to conciliate & preserve our pacific relations with France."[8] Marshall's desire for peace reflected no sympathy with the French Revolution, however. Even in the revolution's first years he had not shared the enthusiasm for it common among men of all parties in the early 1790s. Marshall did not see any inherent virtue in the French claim of a republican form of government; the form of government mattered less, he thought, than whether France treated the United States fairly.

Marshall's role in defending the Jay Treaty had been noted by both British and French consuls in their reports to their governments.[9] But like many other Federalists who fought in the Revolution, Marshall resented any implication that he belonged to a British party and even denied the existence of such a faction in the United States. His frame of reference was Federalism and Antifederalism, and he saw no validity in the concept of dividing Americans into French or British parties.

Pinckney, who agreed with Marshall on most points while they were in Paris, held beliefs compatible with Marshall's. Pinckney, too, was angered when charged with being a member of the aristocratic or British party in the United States.[1] Perhaps because of his war experience in South Carolina, Pinckney was more appreciative than Marshall of the previous aid that France had given the United States, and as a supporter of the French-American alliance, he had wanted cooperation between the two countries. Unlike Marshall, moreover, Pinckney had remained silent on the ratification of the Jay Treaty.[2] Both Marshall and Pinckney believed that if Americans remained politically united they could convince French officials to act reasonably toward the United States. Implicit in both men's thought was the idea that the Republican party undermined the federal government in its dealings with France. Influenced by the callous treatment given him by Charles Delacroix in 1795 and 1796 when he was refused the right of embassy and ordered to leave the country, Pinckney reacted emotionally to his treatment in France and insisted that he and his country be treated with dignity and respect.

Gerry viewed the situation quite differently from his two colleagues. He saw an identifiable British party in the United States; he alone had many ties with the leading members of the Republican party. Gerry distrusted Secretary of State Pickering and urged President Adams to reappoint Monroe as minister to France.[3] Gerry, moreover, argued vigorously that the outbreak of war with France would

8. Tucker to John Page, June 23, 1797, Collection of Edwin Hutten, Buffalo, N.Y

9. John Hamilton to Lord Grenville, June 16, 1797, F.O. 5/19, Public Record Office; Duhail to Talleyrand, June 8, 1797, Correspondance Politique, Etats-Unis, Supplement, V. Both consuls were stationed in Norfolk.

1. Pinckney to Gerry, June 5, 1797, Gerry Papers, Lib. Cong.; Pinckney to Joseph Pitcairn, June 15, 1797, Pitcairn Papers, Cincinnati Historical Society, Ohio.

2. Marvin R. Zahniser, *Charles Cotesworth Pinckney: Founding Father* (Chapel Hill, N.C., 1967), 124–131.

3. Gerry to Adams, Apr. 25, 1797, Gerry-Knight Papers, Mass. Hist. Soc.

discredit the cause of republicanism and force the United States into closer political and economic relations with Great Britain, which he considered harmful.[4] A man stubborn and persistent in his advocacy of minority viewpoints, Gerry, often referred to as "his oddity" by his detractors, represented the strain of Puritan republicanism arising from the American Revolution.[5]

When Gerry accepted his appointment, he wrote that he would do everything possible to prevent war with France. Believing that he could gain the critical time needed to avert war, he did not object to the prospect of prolonged negotiations. Marshall, however, wanted to finish the mission quickly and hoped it would be over by the end of 1797. Gerry succeeded in prolonging the negotiations, because Marshall and Pinckney wanted unanimity within the commission. Talleyrand's views on the duration of negotiations coincided with Gerry's, and Talleyrand independently planned to prolong the negotiations as long as possible.[6] Thus Gerry persistently debated small points, delayed messages to Talleyrand, refused to sign other documents, and remained more receptive to continued informal negotiations than his colleagues. Pinckney and Marshall began to consider his conduct disgraceful, but it was consistent with Gerry's personality and original strategy.

The envoys' instructions, prepared primarily by Secretary of State Pickering, were neither harsh nor belligerent. The underlying theme of the instructions was the preservation of neutrality. To ensure neutrality, Pickering instructed the envoys to have France accept the legitimacy of the Jay Treaty and of its provisions on contraband. This acceptance, in conjunction with a cessation of maritime abuses, would preserve peace between the two powers. Pickering was willing to allow France to claim territory on the North American continent if France would agree to renegotiate other provisions of the Treaty of Alliance of 1778, particularly the American guarantee of France's West Indian possessions. Pickering advocated this with the full knowledge that France was seeking to obtain Louisiana from Spain. He did not insist that the envoys secure a firm agreement on damages to American merchants caused by French privateers if they could achieve the political goal of French acceptance of the Jay Treaty and a loosening of the ties created by the Treaty of Alliance.[7]

If the instructions that Marshall carried with him to Europe gave him reason to be cautiously hopeful about the mission's outcome, the domestic political situation in the United States quickly undermined any basis for his optimism. The

4. Gerry to Monroe, July 23, 1797, Monroe Papers, Lib. Cong.; Gerry to Adams, July 3 and 14, 1797, Adams Papers; Gerry to Murray, Dec. 28, 1797, Gratz Collection, Historical Society of Pennsylvania; Gerry to Jefferson, Jan. 20, 1801, Russell W. Knight, ed., *Elbridge Gerry's Letterbook: Paris 1797–1798* (Salem, Mass., 1966), 79–85.

5. Gerry and Adams both referred to the Silas Deane affair of 1778–1779 as a symbol of foreign corruption when discussing the mission to France. See Adams to Gerry, May 3, 1797, Adams Papers; and particularly Adams to Gerry, May 30, 1797, Conarroe Papers, Hist. Soc. Pa.; and Gerry to Adams, July 3, 1797, Adams Papers. On Puritan republicanism and the Deane affair, see Edmund S. Morgan, "The Puritan Ethic and the American Revolution," *WMQ*, 3d Ser., XXIV (1967), 25–34.

6. See William Stinchcombe, ed., "A Neglected Memoir by Talleyrand on French-American relations, 1793–1797," American Philosophical Society, *Proceedings*, CXXI (1977), 195–208.

7. See Pickering to American Envoys, July 15, 1797.

closely divided House of Representatives had refused many of Adams's requests for appropriations for military and naval forces even before Marshall left Philadelphia. Clearly, the Republicans did not think the crisis in French affairs as grave as Adams and the Federalists depicted it. The House of Representatives hesitated, modified, and in some cases refused to pass adequate provisions for arming merchant ships, fortifying ports, and raising an army, thus revealing a deep division between the branches of government.

French officials frequently alluded to the lack of majority support in the United States for Federalist policies. Marshall was especially sensitive on this point, perhaps because he knew the charge had a degree of truth. Even if the French were only taunting the envoys, the bitter fact remained that Americans were divided on what was the best policy to pursue toward France. Talleyrand knew it would be difficult to convince the Directory to compromise with the United States, but this did not immediately affect the French negotiating position, because Talleyrand was also confident that the United States would not go to war unless the situation deteriorated further. Talleyrand's assumption that internal divisions in the United States would prevent war was an important consideration in destroying the slim chances for a resolution of the French-American dispute.

The American envoys' dealings with Talleyrand and his agents present a picture of the unremitting French effort to humble the Americans. As Marshall's Journal and the envoys' dispatches make abundantly clear, for every concession that the Americans offered, the French refused to respond in a reciprocal manner. At one time the envoys were willing to discuss the possibility of a loan to France.[8] In return they demanded that the French order a cessation of the privateering raids on American shipping. Acting through his agents, Talleyrand not only refused to do this but also broke off negotiations for six weeks. The douceur requested for Talleyrand by his agents shocked the envoys, who were not given any firm assurances that the bribe would help in achieving peace. Despite Rufus King's recommendation that they at least consider giving the bribe, the envoys refused, not because of their personal aversion to corruption but because they could not see that it would bring any concrete results.[9] Early in their informal diplomacy, the envoys had demonstrated that they wanted serious, formal negotiations. They had shown flexibility and a willingness to disregard their instructions; they had endured indignities and insults. Yet the Directory showed only contempt and continued hostility to the United States.

By January, Marshall saw no hope of ever opening serious negotiations. His last three months in Paris were not pleasant. Marshall believed, and Pinckney agreed to some extent, that France would not act constructively until the United States broke off negotiations. Fully expecting a rupture at any time, Marshall ignored his Journal and worked assiduously on the two papers the envoys presented to Talleyrand.[1] By mid-February, Gerry had agreed to separate and secret negotiations with the French, which at the very least violated the spirit of his instructions. Gerry maintained that any agreements he worked out with Talleyrand must be approved by all three envoys, but he refused to understand that his oath of secrecy to Talleyrand made a mockery of the joint commission. Gerry

8. See Stinchcombe, "WXYZ Affair," *WMQ*, 3d Ser., XXXIV (1977), 599.
9. See Rufus King to American Envoys, Nov. 24, 1797.
1. See American Envoys to Talleyrand, Jan. 17 and Apr. 3, 1798.

thus did not expedite an agreement among the envoys but only embittered his colleagues.[2] Mortified by Gerry's actions, Marshall and Pinckney saw no need for preserving even a facade of unanimity or for remaining in Paris.

The split in the commission was symptomatic of the political divisions in the United States. Gerry assumed that France would go to war if negotiations were broken off; Marshall thought the opposite. Gerry worked to prevent a showdown in French-American relations, while Marshall sought to hasten this result. Although each man later claimed that events vindicated his position, in 1798 neither could forecast the future. France did not seek war with the United States after the proposed invasion of England was canceled. American political unity increased with the publication of the envoys' dispatches. The compromises reached after Marshall's departure could not be attributed to Gerry's continuing efforts. Rather, they reflected Talleyrand's changed assessment of the seriousness of American intentions.

When Marshall left Paris in the spring of 1798, he was distressed by his mission's failure but enamored with the private delights of Paris. Marshall was an avid theater patron, and the Paris opera occupied many of his otherwise empty evenings. The cultivated Madame de Villette enthralled Marshall and Gerry. Acting as hostess, she gave her friends an opportunity to entertain in Parisian style. Marshall was not a cosmopolitan man, nor did he have deep interests in the arts. He viewed the pleasures of Paris with the mixed feelings common to many Americans of his generation. He enjoyed activities unavailable in Richmond, but retained his firm conviction that these urban luxuries should not be too eagerly sought or valued in the United States. Nevertheless, he found the amenities of Paris so alluring that he once mused that if he had to live there he might find it hard to maintain the level of work he considered necessary for success.[3]

Marshall was impressed but not humbled by his reception when he arrived in the United States in June 1798. As the first envoy to return, he served as an emotional symbol of American resistance to corrupt French designs. Although surprised at the intensity of the reception, Marshall did not lose the balanced perception characteristic of him. He refused to be rushed into hasty statements advocating war, saying instead that the United States should await a French declaration of war.[4] Since Marshall believed that France did not want war and would not declare war against the United States, he moderated the more strident war cries heard among many of the High Federalists.

Marshall's relations with Adams after his return have puzzled historians. Despite numerous opportunities, the president did not publicly praise Marshall. Privately Adams had criticized all of the envoys for their handling of the situation.[5] When he finally mentioned the envoys in a public address, the president

2. Gerry to Adams, Apr. 16, 1798, Adams Papers.

3. Mary Pinckney to Margaret Manigault, Oct. 22, 1797, Manigault Family Papers, University of South Carolina; see also C. Vann Woodward, "The Southern Ethic in a Puritan World," *WMQ*, 3d Ser., XXV (1968), 354, 357, 360.

4. All of the information is secondhand, but men of widely divergent viewpoints agreed on the advice JM gave to the Federalists. See Jefferson to Thomas Randolph, June 21, 1798, Jefferson Papers, Mass. Hist. Soc.; George Cabot to King, Oct. 6, 1798, and Feb. 16, 1799, King Papers, XLI, New-York Historical Society.

5. See the document filed under Oct. 22, 1797 (the date of the envoys' first dispatch to Pickering), Adams Papers.

indirectly censured them for remaining in France after they had not been formally received.[6] He did not consider Marshall incompetent, however. Within three months Adams offered him an appointment as an associate justice of the Supreme Court, and within the following two years he offered him the positions of secretary of war and then secretary of state. A critical personal opinion coupled with a public reward was characteristic of Adams's handling of men. Although he privately believed Pinckney should bear primary responsibility for the envoys' mistakes in Paris, Adams approved Pinckney for the post of major general in the Provisional Army even before Pinckney's return. Marshall and Pinckney came from the South, where, Adams noted, it was "very difficult to find gentlemen who are willing to accept of public Trusts and at the same time capable of discharging them."[7] In Marshall's case, Adams probably most appreciated the envoy's intelligent but dispassionate service to the administration. As he had demonstrated in his appointment and support of Gerry, Adams did not demand sycophants in his administration, and Marshall had served his country well in a difficult situation while retaining his personal integrity. To Adams this was ample basis for appointing him to more important positions.

Marshall's experiences in Paris affected his views on the course and direction the United States should take. He grew more suspicious of political leaders who claimed to speak in the name of republicanism and democracy. In France, Marshall had observed many conditions that he feared might some day beset the United States. The performance of a government-controlled press frightened him; the arbitrary power of the Directory and the corruption of the French courts offended his ideals of an impartial judiciary and a limited government. The growing influence of the military in French decision-making was, he believed, a consequence of a system that relied on force over law. Marshall returned to the United States firmly convinced that only the continuation of the Federalists in office could ensure a future free of French influence.

Marshall's nationalism and his foreign policy outlook meshed more closely after his mission. He saw the need for the absolute independence of the United States and warned against entanglements with European powers. Marshall realized that the United States and Europe were interdependent, but by the accident of geographic separation, Americans had the opportunity to develop a different kind of society. Marshall's trip to Europe convinced him that he had to work to protect the distinctive features of American government and society from either European examples or, more important, European dominance.

6. Adams to the Inhabitants of Machias, District of Maine, Oct. 5, 1798, *ibid.*; Cabot to King, Nov. 16, 1798, King Papers, N.-Y. Hist. Soc. Privately Adams expressed a higher opinion of JM's performance. He wrote Pickering that "of the three envoys, the conduct of Marshall alone has been entirely satisfactory and ought to be marked by the most decided approbation of the public." Adams to Pickering, Sept. 26, 1798, Adams Papers.

7. Adams to Abigail Adams, Jan. 7, 1796, Adams Papers.

Commission

Letterbook Copy, RG 59, National Archives

[*June 5, 1797, Philadelphia.* John Adams, with the advice and consent of the Senate, appoints Charles Cotesworth Pinckney, Francis Dana,[8] and JM "Envoys Extraordinary and Ministers Plenipotentiary" to France.]

From Timothy Pickering

Letterbook Copy, RG 59, National Archives

Sir[9]

Philadelphia, June 6, 1797

Yesterday the Senate declared their advice and consent to the appointment of "General Charles Cotesworth Pinckney of South Carolina, Francis Dana, Chief Justice of the State of Massachusetts, and General John Marshall of Virginia, to be jointly and severally Envoys Extraordinary and Ministers Plenipotentiary to the French Republic," and by the President's direction I have the honor to inclose to you their commission.[1]

Your knowledge of the state of the political affairs of the United States, especially in relation to France, renders any explanation of the cause and object of this Extraordinary Commission unnecessary. I need only remark, that the vast importance of the proposed negociation demonstrates the sense entertained by the President and Senate of the talents integrity and patriotism of the gentlemen appointed, and of the high confidence reposed in them by their fellow Citizens; whence they will respectively estimate the extreme disappointment that will be felt and the great disadvantages which will be justly apprehended, if any possible circumstances should prevent their accepting the very honorable and interesting office. I have the honor to be etc.

TIMOTHY PICKERING

8. Dana (1743–1811) had accompanied Adams to Europe in 1779 as secretary of the legation and served in that capacity in France and Holland until Congress named him minister to Russia in 1780. At this time Dana was chief justice of the supreme court of Massachusetts. He declined a special appointment because of ill health.

9. An identical letter was sent to Francis Dana on the same day. See the draft of Pickering to JM and Dana, June 6, 1797, Pickering Papers, Massachusetts Historical Society.

1. See Commission, calendared at June 5, 1797.

Thomas Cheatham's Will

Argument in the General Court

Extract from Casebook, Tucker-Coleman Papers, Swem Library, College of William and Mary

Richmond, June 14, 1797

Being very sick his Brother sent for one Beezley[2] and one or two others—being arrived *William* Cheatham the Brother told if he wished to make a will, Beezley was there present & could do it—desired him to do as he pleased and not regard his presence. T.C. then dictated to Beezley a devise of Slaves[3] to his Brother *Christopher*; Beezley wrote down what he had dictated, but before he had quite done writing T.C. was siezed with a fit of coughing, and expired without speaking again, except saying he was gone; Beezley asked him how he wished to give the rest of his property. T.C. held up his hand & shook his head. The will was never read over to him after it was written, nor did he acknowledge it as his will. In his perfect Senses. *Some* other property.

The notes of the Evidence are among my papers.[4]

Randolph, in favor of the will, cited 3. Co. 31. b, Butler &

2. Thomas Beezley.

3. In the margin of the page St. George Tucker, who took the notes on this case, referred to a case, Freeland v. Freeland's Executor, that he had heard at the Charlottesville District Court in 1795. In that case, on appeal from Amherst County Court, a will devising land had been admitted to record even though it had been proved that the testatrix had not written or signed it. The district court reversed the county court judgment as to the devise of realty but allowed the devise of chattels in the will. See Tucker, Casebook, Sept. 18, 1795, Tucker-Coleman Papers, Swem Library, College of William and Mary. Sometime after this case Tucker also noted the case of Thomas Lipscomb's Will, General Court, Nov. 1798, and Glascock v. Smither & Hunt, 4 Va. (1 Call) 479. Tucker did not record any notes at the Nov. 1798 meeting of the General Court.

While the use of the term "devise" would not necessarily mean that the slaves in question were annexed to realty and therefore to be treated as real property for purposes of inheritance, it appears from the arguments that this was the case. If they were chattels personal, they would be subject to bequest by an oral will, but real property could not be devised without some expression of the testator's intent in writing. The issue presented in the arguments was whether the facts showed that the testator's disposition of the slaves was validly reduced to writing before his death. For further discussion of the status of slaves and their disposition by will, see Vol. I, 186–188, 210, 214–215.

4. Tucker wrote a summary of the evidence in this case in his docket book for the June 1797 General Court. The only information in those notes that he did not include in this record of the case was the fact that Thomas Cheatham spoke these last words to Thomas Beezley in Mar. 1796. He also mentioned the slaves' names as well as those of a few other witnesses. See Docket Book, 1797, Tucker-Coleman Papers.

Baker's Case.[5] If one commands another to write his will and thereby to devise Whiteacre to J.S. and his heirs, and Blackacre to J.N. and his heirs, and he writes the devise to J.S. in the Life of the Devisor, and before the other is written the Devisor dies, yet it is a good will to J.S. But if he commands one to make his will, and to devise White Acre to J.S. & his heirs, upon Condition, and he writes the Devise to J.S. & his heirs, and before he writes the Condition the Devisor dies, this devise is void; for in the one Case the Devises are several and distinct, and in such Case the Devise to J.S. is full and perfect; but in the latter Case the devise is not full but maimed & imperfect, for the whole devise as to J.S. was not fully put in writing, and so Initium in such Case, non fuit plenum. 3. Co. 31. b.

If the Testator when he doth declare his mind doth appoint that the same shall be written, and thereupon the same is written accordingly in the Lifeline of the Testator, this is a good Testament of Lands. Sheppards Touchstone 391.[6] Or if it be written from his mouth by the notary according to his mind, and his mind were to have it written, albeit it not Shewed, or read to him afterwards it is a good Testament. Ibid:—If while the Testator is making his will, and whilst he intended to proceed further at that time, either by adding diminishing or altering, he be suddenly striken with sickness or Insanity of mind whereby he cannot proceed but gives over in the midst and so he die; it seems in this Case the whole will is void. And yet if a man begin his will and make perfect devises to one, and then of *himself* he give over until another time; or if a man make a perfect devise to one, and then die before he can make any devise to any others, it seems these are good Testaments for as much as is done—and then cites the Case put 3. Co. 31. b. ante.

5. Butler and Baker's Case involved the attempted devise of manor lands held directly by the king, subsequent to the enactment of the statutes of wills. In dictum the court cited a precedent which held that to pass title to land under those statutes there must be a writing (termed an "initium"), and that at the time of the testator's death the writing must be effective to dispose of title to the land (that is, it must be "fuit plenum"). In addition the court's opinion set forth the distinction between two separate devises made in Edmund Randolph's argument, one of which might be effective even if the other was void because of lack of a writing, and two dependent devises where the invalidity of a conditional devise would annul the devise predicated upon its effectiveness. 3 Coke Rep. 31b, 76 Eng. Rep. 698, 699 (K.B. 1591).

6. William Sheppard, *The Touch-stone of common Assurances . . .*, 4th ed. ([London], 1780). Significantly neither Randolph nor JM in his reply cited the requirement that in a will of personalty an executor had to be named for the will to be valid. This may have been an oversight, or may be additional evidence that the slaves in question were to be treated as chattels real. *Ibid.*, 390. It is also possible that by this time an executor did not have to be named for the will to be valid.

Shep: Touch: 392. A man may if he please make a Testament of part of his goods and die intestate for the rest, and that Disposition he doth make is good for so much. Ib. 393. If a notary only take certain rude notes or directions from the sick man, which he doth agree unto, and they be afterwards written fair in his Lifetime, and not shewed to him again, or not written fair until after his death these are good Testaments of Lands. Ibid: 391.

M.P. sent for a person to make his will, gave him instructions to do so, when he had wrote it he read it to her, she approved of it, declared it her last will, sent for three witnesses to see her execute it, signed & sealed was written, but she died before any other Execution, yet it was held a good will. Comyn's Rep: 452. cited Vin. abrid: vol: 8, pa. 126.[7]

A will of real and personal Estate was prepared in order to be executed though several blanks in it, and the Testor died before Execution, yet it was held a good will for the personal Estate. Com: Rep. 453, Vin. Ab. Ib.

The Testator on his death bed desired another to write his will who took short notes of it, & went home to write it in form, and soon returnd with it written, but before he came the Testator was dead—adjudged a good will within the Statute, Nelsons Lex. Testamentaria 571.[8]

Keilway 209; 1. And. 34; 1. Brownl. 44; Dyer 72, S.P.[9]

7. This passage and that immediately following are quoted almost verbatim from Charles Viner, *A General Abridgment of Law and Equity* . . . , 2d ed. (London, 1791–1794), VII, 126.

An anonymous case, 1 Comyns 451–456, 92 Eng. Rep. 1155–1157 (C.P. 1734), held that when a testator had made notes in writing on an earlier formal will, it might be held a good will as to his personality, but it would not, in the absence of required formalities, be held to be a revocation of the devise of real property under the older formal will. An earlier case of 1704 was cited in the argument in which it was held that if a will were drawn up and then corrected by the testator in his own handwriting before final engrossing, it would be a valid holographic will even if the testator died before the will was signed or witnessed. 1 Comyns 453.

8. William Nelson, *Lex Testamentaria: or, a compendious system of all the laws of England* . . . , 2d ed. ([London], 1724), 571, is quoted almost verbatim in this paragraph. In addition the related marginal citations in Nelson's work are in the same order and are to the same sources as those cited following this paragraph. Possibly the sole source for Randolph's argument on this point was *Lex Testamentaria*, from which he copied citations to otherwise unavailable authorities.

9. Henry Brown's Will, reported in Keilway 209, 72 Eng. Rep. 389, and 1 Anderson 34, 123 Eng. Rep. 339 (C.P. 1557), involved the classic case of a dying testator dictating the terms of his will to a lawyer and then being unable to sign the document. Such a will, despite the lack of the testator's signature or witnesses attesting his actions was held to be a valid will in writing and thus could pass title under the 1540 statute of wills.

Brown v. Sackville, Dyer 72a–72b, 73 Eng. Rep. 152–154 (K.B. 1552), held that

In this Court, Oct: 16, 1786, the following was established as a will in writing—"Miss Martha Robertson before Doctor Walter Bennet, Jeremiah Keene, Mrs. Keene, Mrs. Ann Eastham and John Roberts. The above Miss Martha Robertson being very sick & weak, Doctor Walter Bennet asked her who she intended to leave her Estate to, her Uncle, Brothers, or Sisters. She answered to my Mama. Sarah Roberts. Test, Walter Bennet, John Roberts, Anne Eastham."

The witnesses swore, that the above instrument of writing was done agreeable to the words of the said M.R. who after it was read to her acknowledged that that was her last will & desire, and that the above persons made oath to the same eight hours after her death. This was upon the record, on an appeal from Halifax Court, where the will was admitted to record.

As to the parol Testimony in the Gen. Court, see my note book no: 1. pa: 15.[1] Judgmente affirmed.

Marshal, Contra insisted, that this will is incomplete. He relied on the Case put Sheppards Touchstone 392. if a person is making his will, and whilst he is intending to proceed, is suddenly taken ill & dies, having given over in the midst etc. the will is void.

June 16, 1796. Per Cur: unanimously.

The will admitted to record, as a will in writing to pass personal Estate.[2]

---

a will prepared from the oral instructions of the testator and written before his death was valid and would be an effective devise of real property even if it was never read to the testator.

The three-witness requirements for valid wills of realty contained in the 1676 English statute of frauds did not apply in colonial Virginia. For a discussion of a similar rule in colonial New York, see Herbert Alan Johnson, "The Prerogative Court of New York, 1686–1776," *American Journal of Legal History*, XVIII (1973), 115–116.

The citation to "1 Brown" does not seem to apply to Brownlow's and Goldsborough's reports or to Brown's chancery cases.

1. JM participated in the argument of this case before the General Court in Oct. 1786. See Vol. I, 184–185.

2. As noted above, the statement of facts and arguments of counsel tend to suggest that the slaves in question were treated as real property. Otherwise they could be bequeathed by an oral will. The General Court's decree in this case, admitting the document as a will in writing to pass personal estate, would also entitle the document to serve as a devise of realty under Virginia law. Although the decree, when taken together with the arguments, is ambiguous as to the status of the slaves, it is clear that the uncertainty did not alter the disposition of the case.

To the District Judges

ALS, Robinson Papers, Swem Library, College of William and Mary

[Richmond, *ca.* June 17, 1797]

Mr. John Robinson was brought up in the office of Mr. Craig & has for some considerable time written in the office of the district court of Henrico.[3]

We beleive him to be well acquainted with the duties of a district clerk & to be very capable of performing properly the duties of that office. We also think very respectfully of his character & principles.

J MARSHALL
JNO: WICKHAM
JOHN WARDEN
ANDW. RONALD

Commission

DS, Pierpont Morgan Library

[*June 22, 1797, Philadelphia.* John Adams, with the advice and consent of the Senate, appoints Charles Cotesworth Pinckney, Elbridge Gerry, and JM "Envoys Extraordinary and Ministers Plenipotentiary" to France.[4]]

3. John Robinson (1773–1850) began serving in 1787 as assistant to Adam Craig, clerk of the Henrico County Court and the Richmond City Hustings Court. Sometime in the early 1790s, he began assisting John Brown, clerk of the District Court at Richmond. When Brown resigned to accompany JM to France, this recommendation was submitted and accepted. Robinson served as a clerk of the district court until 1850, although the court's name was changed to Henrico County Circuit Court in 1809. See F. Johnston, *Memorials of Old Virginia Clerks . . .* (Lynchburg, Va., 1888), 329–332.

According to the 1788 act creating this court, judges had the authority to appoint their clerks. 12 Hening 738. See also 13 Hening 433 (1792).

In his docket book for this term of court, St. George Tucker wrote: "1797. June 17th. John Brown esqr. resigned his office of Clerk of the General Court, and Mr. Wilson Allen, a young man well recommended, was appointed in his stead." Docket Book, June 1797, Tucker-Coleman Papers, Swem Library, College of William and Mary. Since the General Court had been sitting for 10 days when Brown resigned, it is apparent that he was not asked, or did not make his decision, to accompany JM to France until June 17, at which time he probably resigned both court clerkships.

4. This commission is a replacement of JM's commission, June 5, 1797, naming Gerry (1744–1814) in place of Francis Dana.

To Mary W. Marshall

ALS, Marshall Papers, Swem Library, College of William and Mary

My dearest Polly Alexandria, June 24, 1797

I am thus far on my way to Philadelphia & have come without any inconvenience from a starting horse. All your other fears will be as foundationless as this & I shall soon see you again to be the two happiest persons on earth. I came this morning from Mount Vernon where I was pressd to pass the day & which is certainly one of the most delightful places in our country.[5] Had you been with me I shoud have been there as happy as I coud be any where. I shoud have been quite happy as it was coud I have been certain —quite certain that your mind was perfectly at ease. Nothing distresses me but that. Let me hear from you by the time I have been two days at Philadelphia & do tell me & tell me truly that the bitterness of parting is over & your mind at rest—that you think of me only to contemplate the pleasure of our meeting & that you will permit nothing to distress you while I am gone. I cannot help feeling a pang when I reflect that every step I take carrys me further & further from what is to [*me*] most valuable in this world but I will suppress such sensations & will be at quiet if I can only be certain that you are so. Even sending away Dick[6] wounds me because it looks like parting with the last of the family—but I will not yield to these sensations—only let me know that you have conquerd them & all is well. I am now at my unkle Keiths where every body treats me with the utmost affection & friendship.[7] They always have done so. I dine here to day with kind friends who make the time as agreeable as possible—but this is not Richmond.

I shall write to you as soon as I get to Philadelphia & am thinking of you always. Farewell. I never was peremptory but I must now give you one positive order. It is be happy. Once more, Farewell. I am ever your affectionate truely affectionate

J MARSHALL

I brought away by mistake two letters. The [*one to*][8] Genl. Young

5. JM spent the day with George Washington at Mt. Vernon. See Washington to Edward Carrington, June 26, 1797, Cabell Papers, University of Virginia. See also *Columbian Mirror and Alexandria Gazette*, June 27, 1797.

6. JM indicated on the address leaf that the letter was carried by Dick, a slave JM purchased in 1790. See Vol. II, 396.

7. James Keith was an Alexandria merchant.

8. Torn by seal.

send to Mr. Hopkins.[9] That which is unseald send to my brother.[1] Again I am your

J M

Law Papers, June 1797

U.S. Circuit Court, Va.

Backhouse Administrator v. Donald's Executors, declaration, ADS, U.S. Circuit Court, Va., Ended Cases (Unrestored), Virginia State Library.

To Caesar Rodney

ALS, Free Library of Philadelphia

Sir[2] Philadelphia, [July 1, 1797][3]

I had the pleasure of receiving to day your letter to me of the 28th. inst.[4] informing that some papers which had sliped out of my pockett were in possession of Mr. Mc Cullough at New Castle.[5] I have requested that gentleman to forward them to me to this place by the post. Accept sir my thanks for your polite attention in favoring me with information which was so very desirable. I am Sir respectfully Your obedt. Servt.

J MARSHALL

9. The letters are lost. Henry Young and John Hopkins. Hopkins was the U.S. commissioner of loans for Virginia and an active Federalist in Richmond.

1. Thomas Marshall.

2. Caesar Augustus Rodney (1772–1824) was a 1789 graduate of the University of Pennsylvania and a prominent Republican lawyer in Delaware. Rodney later served as a representative in Congress, as attorney general under Jefferson and Madison, as a U.S. senator, and as minister to Argentina under James Monroe. JM addressed this letter to Rodney at Wilmington, Del.

3. JM dated this letter June 31, 1797.

4. Not found.

5. New Castle, Del., south of Philadelphia on the Delaware River, was a frequent embarkation point for ships. JM probably stopped at New Castle to leave off his baggage on his way to Philadelphia.

To Mary W. Marshall

ALS, Marshall Papers, Swem Library, College of William and Mary

My dearest Polly Philadelphia, July [3],[6] 1797

I am here after a passage up the bay from Baltimore which woud have been very unpleasant but for the company of a very agreeable family which greatly alleviated the vexatious calamity of a dead calm under an excessive hot sun. I dind on saturday in private with the President whom I found a sensible plain candid good temperd man & was consequently much pleasd with him.[7] I am not certain when I shall sail nor have I yet taken a vessel but I conjecture it will be early in the next week. Do you however my dearest life continue to write to me as your letters will follow me shoud I be gone before their arrival & as my heart clings with real pleasure & delight only to what comes from you.

I dind yesterday with Mr. Morris. That family receives me with precisely the same friendship & affection as formerly & seems to preserve in a great degree its vivacity but it must be discernible that a heavy gloom hangs around them which only their good sense restrains them from showing.[8] They live what we shoud style most elegantly nor is there in the house any apparent change except in the croud of company which formerly frequented it. I wish most earnestly for their sake they may be able to rtrieve their affairs nor am I without some hope of its being possible.

I was on friday evening at the Vauxhall of Philadelphia. It is

6. JM mistakenly dated this letter July 2, but in it he referred to having dinner with Adams on Saturday, which was July 1, and "yesterday" with Robert Morris, which would have been July 2.

7. This was JM's first meeting with John Adams. JM made a similar impression on each of the Adamses. John Adams described him in a letter to Elbridge Gerry as "a plain Man, very Sensible, cautious, guarded, learned in the Law of Nations. I think you will be pleased with him." See Adams to Gerry, July 17, 1797, Gerry Papers, Henry E. Huntington Library. Abigail Adams wrote to John Q. Adams: "You will find in Genl. Marshal a sensible upright honest man." Abigail Adams to John Q. Adams, July 14, 1797, Adams Papers, Massachusetts Historical Society.

8. Robert Morris had been director of finances during the American Revolution and later served as a U.S. senator from Pennsylvania. His large-scale land speculations had failed, and although he was one of the most eminent merchants in the United States, he was facing bankruptcy at this time. Morris, whose daughter Hester had married James Markham Marshall in 1795, was originally involved in buying the Fairfax lands and had invited JM and his brother to join in the purchase. James M. Marshall was in Europe trying to secure financing for his father-in-law's speculations as well as for the Marshalls' purchase of the Fairfax estate. JM had been Morris's attorney in a number of cases in Virginia. See Morris to JM, Dec. 30, 1796, and Jan. 23, 1797.

indeed a most elegant place. I woud attempt to describe it to you but shoud fail. The amusements were walking, sitting punch ice creams etc. Music & conversation. I rode out yesterday to see Mrs. Heyward[9] but she was not at home. She lives in the neighborhood of Philadelphia on the bank of the schuylkil at one of the most enchanting spots you ever saw.

Thus my dearest Polly do I when not engagd in the very serious business which employs a large portion of my time endeavor by amusements to preserve a mind at ease & [*prevent*] it from brooding too much over my much lovd & absent wife. By all that is dear on earth, I entreat you to do the same. Our separation will not I trust be long & letters do everything to draw its sting. I am my dearest life your affectionate

J MARSHALL

To Mary W. Marshall

ALS, Marshall Papers, Swem Library, College of William and Mary

My dearest Polly Philadelphia, July 5, 1797

I have been extremely chagrind at not having yet receivd a letter from you. I hope you are well as I hear nothing indicating the contrary but you know not how sollicitous how anxiously sollicitous I am to hear it from yourself. Write me that you are well & in good spirits & I shall set out on my voyage with a lightend heart. I beleive I shall sail in the course of the next week for Amsterdam where it is expected that I shall join Genl. Pinckney. I have not taken my passage but I think I shall go in the brig Grace Capt. Wills. However you will hear from me more than once before my departure. I dind yesterday in a very large company of Senators & members of the house of representatives who met to celebrate the 4th. of July.[1] The company was really a most respectable one & I experiencd from them the most flattering attention. I have much reason to be satisfied & pleasd with the manner in which I am receivd here but something is wanting to make me happy. Had I my dearest wife with me I shoud be delighted indeed. Not having

9. This might have been Susan Hayward who was living at "Solitude," outside Philadelphia. Mrs. Hayward was settling her husband's estate at this time. See Richard Claiborne to Henry Banks, May 19, 1797, and Susan Hayward to Banks, July 20, 1797, Henry Banks Papers, Virginia Historical Society.

1. JM attended the celebration at Fouquet's Hotel. See *Gazette of the United States, and Philadelphia Daily Advertiser*, July 5, 1797.

that pleasure why do you not give me what is nearest to it. I am just calld off. Farewell. Your affectionate

J MARSHALL

To George Washington

ALS, Washington Papers, Library of Congress

Sir Philadelphia, July 7, 1797

I have had the pleasure of receiving from Mr. Pickering your letter to me inclosing others for France intrusted to my care, to the delivery of which I shall be particularly attentive.[2]

Receive Sir my warm & grateful acknowledgements for the polite &, allow me to add, friendly wishes which you express concerning myself as well as for the honor of being mentiond in your letters.[3]

I expect to embark in the course of the next week in the Grace for Amsterdam there to join Genl. Pinckney & thence to proceed if we be permitted to proceed to Paris. Mr. Gerry, if he accepts the appointment, which is not yet certain, he having requested some short time for deliberation, will follow. Claypoles papers by the mail of to day exhibit the case of Mr. Blount[4]. Opinions here are as various on this subject as on every other—not with respect to

2. The covering letter to JM is missing. Washington wrote to Guillaume Mathieu, comte Dumas (1753–1837), and Louis-Philippe, comte de Ségur (1724–1801), who had both served in the American Revolution, and to Charles Cotesworth Pinckney. See George Washington to Ségur, June 24, 1797, Washington to Dumas, June 24, 1797, Washington to Pinckney, June 24, 1797, Washington Papers, Ser. 4, Library of Congress (microfilm ed., reel 103).

3. Washington wrote in part: "This letter will be presented you by Genl. Marshall, one of our compatriots in the American War, & now a joint Envoy with Genl. Pinckney & Mr. Gerry (all of whom I beg leave to introduce to your acquaintance as men of honor & worth) appointed for the purpose of adjusting the difference which exist unfortunately, between our two nations; which no man more sincerely regrets than I do—or who more devoutly wishes to have them accommodated upon principles of Equity & justice." Washington to Dumas, June 24, 1797, *ibid.*

4. William Blount (1749–1800) was a U.S. senator from Tennessee until he was expelled on July 8, 1797, for misconduct in office. JM was referring to Blount's letter to James Carey, Apr. 21, 1797, in *Claypoole's American Daily Advertiser* (Philadelphia), July 6, 1797. This letter on Blount's intrigues in the western territories had been submitted to Congress by the president on July 3, 1797. Washington had sent a copy of the letter to Timothy Pickering. See July 3, 1797, *Annals of Congress*, VII, 33–34; Washington to Pickering, July 3, 1797, Washington Papers, Ser. 4, Lib. Cong. (microfilm ed., reel 111). On the Blount affair, see William H. Masterson, *William Blount* (Baton Rouge, La., 1954), 302–323.

Mr. Blount—all concur in giving him up, but with respect to the object of the scheme, the means of execution & the degree of crime or indiscretion attachd to different foreign ministers. It is by some conjecturd that Mr. Blount himself gave to the spanish minister the inteligence on which was founded his application to the government of the United States. I remain Sir with the most respectful attachment, Your obedt. Servt.

J MARSHALL

To Mary W. Marshall

ALS, Marshall Papers, Swem Library, College of William and Mary

My dearest Polly [Philadelphia], July 10, 1797

I have had the pleasure of receiving by the last post your letter of the 30th. of June.[5] I thank Heaven that your health is better. To know that it is so, will take off one half from the unpleasantness of a voyage over the Atlantic. In your next I promise myself the delight of receiving assurances that your mind has become tranquil & as sprightly as usual. Good health will produce good spirits & I woud not on any consideration relinquish the hope that you will possess both. Remember that, if your situation shoud be as suspected, melancholy may inflict punishment on an innocent for whose sake you ought to preserve a serene & composed mind.[6]

Colo. Gamble[7] a day or two before I parted with you expressd the wish of Mrs. Gamble to see you frequently & by her good & cheerful spirits to aid yours but that she felt some difficulty on account of your not encouraging an acquaintance. I mention the fact & leave it to yourself to decide what you will do.

I have been delayd extremely & very much to my mortification. Every day which passes before I set out threatens to make it a day longer before I return & is therefore most irksome to me. If my journey was to be postpond for any considerable time I woud certainly visit Richmond & all that is dearest in the world & which Richmond contains once more before my departure, but I expect to sail in the course of the present week or at any rate in the commencement of the next. This delay is so cruel as to retard my busi-

5. Letter not found.

6. Mrs. Marshall's situation was as expected. John Marshall (1798–1833) was born the following January.

7. Robert Gamble was a Richmond merchant and active Federalist.

ness without the consolation of seeing you. It is as yet out of my power to speak positively concerning my return. Indeed it will not be in my power until I reach Paris. The time depends so much on the course of business there as to make it impossible to know here what its length will be. I still hope however to return as early as we contemplated. Of this I know [*I*] will be certain; All my efforts will be usd [*to*] shorten as much as possible an absence the full misery of which I did not calculate til I felt it. Remember me affectionately to your mother & to all our good friends & relations. Tell the boys I please myself with the hopes of their improvement during my absence & kiss little Mary for your ever affectionate

J MARSHALL

Congress rises to day.[8]

To Timothy Pickering

ALS, Pickering Papers, Massachusetts Historical Society

Sir Philadelphia, July 10, 1797

In conformity with your request I take the liberty now to state to you that I wish to receive in this place about three thousand five hundred dollars. Of this not more than five hundred need be in specie.

Unable to make any calculations of my own on the expence which may be necessarily incured on my arrival in Europe I have only to express a desire that the residue of the money designd for the outfit may be so placed, that I can command it in Amsterdam or in Paris.[9] I remain Sir with very much respect & esteem Your Obedt. Servt.

J MARSHALL

8. The first session of the Fifth Congress adjourned until Nov. 13, 1797. See July 10, 1797, *Annals of Congress*, VII, 46, 466.

9. See Pickering to Oliver Wolcott, July 11, 1797, Domestic Letters, X, RG 59, National Archives; Envoy Account, Sept. 30, 1798.

To Mary W. Marshall

ALS, Marshall Papers, Swem Library, College of William and Mary

My dearest Polly [Philadelphia], July 11, 1797

Altho Mr. Marshall[1] does not go directly to Richmond so that a letter by tomorrows post may perhaps reach you before this yet I cannot avoid writing to you because while doing so I seem to myself to be in some distant degree enjoying your company. I was last night at the play & saw the celebrated Mrs. Merry in the character of Juliet. She performs that part to admiration indeed but I really do not think Mrs. West jr. is far her inferior in it.[2] I saw Mrs. Heyward there. I have paid that Lady one visit to one of the most delightful & romantic spots on the river Schuylkil. She expressd much pleasure to see me & has pressed me very much to repeat my visit. I hope I shall not have time to do so. Tis said she is about to be married to a very wealthy young Englishman named Baring.[3] This I think improbable as he is not more than four & twenty & being rich himself has no temptation to marry meerly for money.

I know nothing more concerning myself than I did yesterday. I am beyond expression impatient to set out on the embassy. The life I lead here does not suit me. I am weary of it. I dine out every day & am now engagd longer I hope than I shall stay. This dissipated life does not long suit my temper. I like it very well for a day or two but I begin to require a frugal repast with good cool water. This is my present situation. I woud give a great deal to dine with you to day on a piece of cold meat with our boys beside us & to see little Mary running backwards & forwards over the

1. This Mr. Marshall might have been Humphrey Marshall, JM's cousin and a U.S. senator from Kentucky, who was probably returning to Kentucky after the Senate adjournment on July 10, 1797. JM wrote "Hond by Mr. Marshall" on the address leaf.

2. *Romeo and Juliet* was performed in the New Theatre on July 10, 1797. On Mrs. Merry (1769–1808), see Gresdna Ann Doty, *The Career of Mrs. Anne Brunton Merry in the American Theatre* (Baton Rouge, La., 1971), 59, 49–63. The other actress, Anne West Bignall, who performed under the names of Mrs. Bignall, Mrs. J. West, and Mrs. West, Jr., regularly appeared in Richmond with the Virginia Company. See JM to Mary W. Marshall, Feb. 3, 1796.

3. Alexander Baring had just announced his engagement to Anne Bingham, daughter of William Bingham (1752–1804), one of the richest Philadelphia merchants and a U.S. senator from Pennsylvania. Henry Baring, who married Bingham's other daughter, Maria, in 1802, is probably the person mentioned. See Robert C. Alberts, *The Golden Voyage: The Life and Times of William Bingham, 1752–1804* (Boston, 1969).

floor playing the sweet little tricks she [*is*] full of. But I can have no s[*uch plea*]sure. I wish to Heaven the time which must intervene before I can repass these delightful scenes was now terminated & that we were looking back on our separation instead of seeing it before us. Farewell my dearest Polly. Make yourself happy & you will bless, your ever affectionate

J MARSHALL

To Mary W. Marshall

ALS, Marshall Papers, Swem Library, College of William and Mary

My dearest Polly. Philadelphia, July 12, 1797

I must beg you immediately to take the trouble to look in one of the outer drawers in the pine desk on the left hand as you go into the office for a parcel of deeds which are bound up together & which are conveyances of land in the upper country from Banks & sundry other persons to Hobe. This parcel of deeds I wish to be lodgd immediately with the clerk of the Genl. court.[4] If there is any difficulty in opening the drawer by putting your hand under to the end & pushing it the difficulty will be over come.

Altho I dine out every day & am treated with much attention I am sick to death of this place. I am impatient to get on board & I find considerable delays still in my way. I hope however to sail this week. The captain of the vessel speaks of going on thursday but those who are best acquainted with the usual course of things suppose we shall not sail til sunday. Every day seems lost & I cannot help regretting that I came so soon from Richmond. Perhaps I have expedited my departure by coming but yet I think I might have remaind one week longer & have been in as much forwardness as I am. That week woud have been worth a year of feasting in Philadelphia. Our Virginians are all gone who filld the home except Mr. Brent[5] & he goes tomorrow. Altho we never agreed in politics my spirits sink at parting with them. I reflect that without being sensible of the happiness they will pass through Richmond [*while*] I who woud prize it so highly [*will be*] going in a different direction.

4. For the law governing conveyances in Virginia, see 12 Hening 154 (1785).

5. Richard Brent (1757–1814), a lawyer from Prince William County, Va., was a Republican member of the U.S. House of Representatives in the Fourth, Fifth, and Seventh Congresses and a U.S. senator from 1809 to 1814.

But only let me hear often that you are well & I shall be happy. I will be so. Farewell my dearest Polly. My heart is incessantly offering prayers for you. I am your ever affectionate,

J MARSHALL

To Mary W. Marshall

ALS, Marshall Papers, Swem Library, College of William and Mary

My dearest Polly Philadelphia, July 14, 1797

Tomorrow the Grace in which I am to embark for Amsterdam will sail from this port. I shall go down to New Castle & go on board there on sunday. All concur that the vessel is a very fine & very safe one & that the season is most favorable for a good voyage. I hope therefore to reach Amsterdam by the latter end of August & from thence I will write to you as soon as possible. My letters however cannot be calculated on till some time in October. You must not therefore after I sail count on hearing from me till october. Unless there shoud be extraordinary & unlookd for delay you will I think receive letters from me in that month. I shall then have it in my power to give you some more certain inteligence concerning my return. At present I can add nothing to what I have always said. My utmost endeavors will be usd to get back by christmass.[6] If that shoud be practicable you will see me; if it shoud be impracticable you must not permit your fears in any situation to subdue you. If you will only give me this assurance I shall be happy. Mr. Brown[7] came in the last stage & says he was too much hurried to give you information of his journey but I am satisfied all was well or he woud have heard it was not so. My son Tom wrote to me on the 6th. of the month & I was pleasd with his letter.[8] I am happy to perceive from it that you retain your better

6. Alexander Maurice Blanc de Lanaute, comte d'Hauterive (1754–1830), former French consul at New York and soon to be Talleyrand's confidential assistant, reported to the French ministry that JM would be anxious to begin negotiations as soon as he arrived in Paris, and he therefore advised the ministry to proceed slowly. See Hauterive to Pierre-Auguste Adet, Aug. 1, 1797, Correspondance Politique, Etats-Unis, XLVIII, Archives of the Ministry of Foreign Affairs, Paris. On Hauterive, see Frances S. Childs, "A Secret Agent's Advice on America, 1797," in Edward Mead Earle, ed., *Nationalism and Internationalism: Essays Inscribed to Carlton J. H. Hayes* (New York, 1950), 18–44.

7. John Brown had resigned as clerk of the Virginia Court of Appeals in Richmond to serve as JM's secretary for his mission to France, although Brown did not understand French. See note at JM to the District Court Judges, *ca.* June 17, 1797.

8. Not found.

health. I flatter myself you do because he does not mention your health. Thus will I continue to please myself concerning you & to beleive that you are well & happy. This beleif smooths the way before me & beguiles the melancholy of many an hour.

I dind yesterday with Mr. Bingham at his celebrated country seat on the Schuylkill. The entertainment was elegant but not by any means so expensive as I had been led to expect. It is the practice here to place in the center of the table a large oval vase almost like the waiter of a tea table but of silver or gold & ornamented with Cupids on which are glasses with flours. The table is then coverd all round with small dishes, none being placed in the center. In consequence of this large dinners here are not so expensive as with us. Mrs. Bingham is a very elegant woman who dresses at the height of the fashion.[9] I do not however like that fashion. The sleeve [*does*] not reach the elbow or the glove come quite to it. There is a vacancy of three or four inches & just [*above*] the naked elbow is a gold clasp. Independent of relationship I like no body so well as the family of Mr. Morris. There is among them throughout a warmth & cordiality which is extremely pleasing. But Virginia & my own dear connections are not only more belovd but appear to me more to deserve love than any body else.

Farewell my much loved wife. Once more before I go on board will you hear from your

J MARSHALL

From Timothy Pickering

Letterbook Copy, RG 59, National Archives

Gentlemen Philadelphia, July 15, 1797

It is known to you that the people of the United States of America entertained a warm and sincere affection for the people of France, ever since their arms were united in the war with Great Britain, which ended in the full and formal acknowledgment of the Independence of these States. It is known to you that this affection was ardent when the French determined to reform their Government and establish it on the basis of liberty; that liberty

9. William Bingham and Anne Willing Bingham were widely renowned for their extravagant tastes and active social life in Philadelphia. See Ethel Elise Rasmusson, "Capital on the Delaware: The Philadelphia Upper Class in Transition, 1789–1801" (Ph.D. diss., Brown University, 1962).

in which the people of the United States were born, and which in the conclusion of the war above mentioned was finally and firmly secured. It is known to you that this affection rose to enthusiasm, when the war was kindled between France and the powers of Europe which were combined against her for the avowed purpose of restoring the monarchy; and every where vows were heard for the success of the French arms. Yet during this period France expressed no wish that the United States should depart from their neutrality. And while no duty required us to enter into the war, and our best interests urged us to remain at peace, the Government determined to take a neutral station: which being taken, the duties of an impartial neutrality became indispensably binding. Hence the Government early proclaimed to our citizens the nature of those duties and the consequences of their violation.

The minister of France, Mr. Genet, who arrived about this time, by his public declaration confirmed the idea that France did not desire us to quit the ground we had taken. His measures, however, were calculated to destroy our neutrality and to draw us into the war.

The principles of the Proclamation of neutrality, founded on the law of nations, which is the law of the land, were afterwards recognized by the national Legislature, and the observance of them enforced by specific penalties, in the act of Congress passed the fifth of June 1794.[1] By these principles and laws the acts of the Executive and the decisions of the Courts of the United States were regulated.

A Government thus fair and upright in its principles and just and impartial in its conduct, might have confidently hoped to be secure against formal official censure: but the United States have not been so fortunate. The acts of their Government, in its various branches, though pure in principle and impartial in operation, and conformable to their indispensable rights of sovereignty, have been assigned as the cause of the offensive and injurious measures of the French Republic. For proofs of the former, all the acts of the Government may be vouched, while the aspersions so freely uttered by the French ministers, the refusal to hear the minister of the United States specially charged to enter on amicable discussions on all the topics of complaint, the Decrees of the Executive Directory and of their agents, the depredations on our commerce

1. For the text of the law, see June 5, 1794, *Annals of Congress*, IV, 1461–1464.

and the violences against the persons of our citizens, are evidences of the latter. These injuries and depredations will constitute an important subject of your discussions with the Government of the French Republic; and for all these wrongs you will seek redress.

In respect to the depredations on our Commerce, the principal objects will be, to agree on an equitable mode of examining and deciding the claims of our Citizens, and the manner and periods of making them compensation. As to the first, the seventh article of the British and the twenty first of the Spanish Treaty present approved precedents to be adopted with France.[2] The proposed mode of adjusting those claims by Commissioners appointed on each side, is so perfectly fair we cannot imagine that it will be refused. But when the claims are adjusted, if payment in specie cannot be obtained, it may be found necessary to agree, in behalf of our Citizens, that they shall accept public securities payable with interest at such periods as the state of the French finances shall render practicable. These periods you will endeavour as far as possible to shorten.

Not only the recent depredations under colour of the decrees, of the Directory of the second of July 1796, and the second of March 1797, or under the decrees of their Agents, or the illegal sentences of their tribunals, but all prior ones not already satisfactorily adjusted, should be put in this equitable train of settlement.[3] To cancel many or all of the last mentioned claims might be the effect of the decree of the Executive Directory of the second of March last, reviving the decree of the ninth of May 1793: but this being an ex post facto regulation, as well as a violation of the treaty between the United States and France cannot be obligatory on the former. Indeed the greater part, probably nearly all the captures and confiscations in question, have been committed in direct violation of that treaty or of the law of nations. But the injuries arising from the capture of enemies property in vessels of the United

2. Both the Jay and Pinckney treaties provided for the establishment of joint citizens' commissions for the purpose of determining the validity of the claims of merchants and the amount of damages due in each case. See Miller, ed., *Treaties*, II, 252–253, 335–337.

3. The Directory decree of July 2, 1796, stated that the French would treat all ships of neutral nations as Great Britain treated them. In the decree of Mar. 2, 1797, the Directory explained the prize court proceedings and specifically stated that U.S. ships were no longer exempt from the May 9, 1793, policy on enemy merchandise. Both decrees were part of the French reaction to the final acceptance of the Jay Treaty by the United States. See July 2, 1796, Correspondance Politique, Etats-Unis, XLVI, Archives of the Ministry of Foreign Affairs, Paris; Mar. 2, 1797, *ibid.*, XLVII.

States may not be very extensive: and if for such captured property the French Government will, agreeably to the law of nations, pay the freight and reasonable demurrage, we shall not on this account, any further contend. But of ship timber and naval stores taken and confiscated by the French, they ought to pay the full value; because our citizens continued their trafic in those articles under the faith of the treaty with France. On these two points we ought to expect that the French Government will not refuse to do us Justice: and the more because it has not, at any period of the war, expressed its desire that the commerical treaty should in these respects be altered.

Besides the claims of our Citizens for depredations on their property, there are many arising from express contracts made with the French Government or its Agents, or founded on the seizure of their property in French ports. Other claims have arisen from the long detention of a multitude of our vessels in the ports of France. The wrong hereby done to our citizens was acknowledged by the French Government, and in some, perhaps in most of the cases, small payments towards indemnifications have been made: the residue still remains to be claimed.

All these just demands of our citizens will merit your attention. The best possible means of compensation must be attempted. These will depend on what you shall discover to be practicable in relation to the French finances. But an exception must be made in respect to debts due to our citizens by the contracts of the French Government and its agents, if they are comprehended in any stipulation, and an option reserved to them, jointly or individually, either to accept the means of payment which you shall stipulate, or to resort to the French Government, directly, for the fulfilment of its contracts.

Although the reparation for losses sustained by the citizens of the United States, in consequence of irregular or illegal captures or condemnations, or forcible seizures or detentions, is of very high importance, and is to be pressed with the greatest earnestness, yet it is not to be insisted on as an indispensable condition of the proposed treaty. You are not however, to renounce these claims of our citizens, nor to stipulate that they be assumed by the United States as a loan to the French Government.

In respect to alterations of the Commercial Treaty with France, in the two cases which have been principal subjects of complaint on her part, viz. enemies property in neutral ships, and the articles contraband of war; although France can have no right to claim the annulling of stipulations at the moment when by both parties they were originally intended to operate; yet if the French Government press for alterations, the President has no difficulty in substituting the principles of the law of nations as stated in the 17th. and 18th. articles of our commercial treaty with Great Britain, to those of the 23d. & 24th. articles of our Commercial Treaty with France: and in respect to provisions and other articles not usually deemed contraband, you are to agree only on a temporary compromise, like that in the 18th. article of the British treaty, and of the same duration.[4] If however, in order to satisfy France *now she is at war*, we change the two important articles before mentioned, then the 14th. article of the French treaty which subjects the property of the neutral nation found on board enemies Ships to capture and condemnation, must of course be abolished.[5]

We have witnessed so many erroneous constructions of the Treaty with France, even in its plainest parts, it will be necessary to examine every article critically, for the purpose of preventing, as far as human wisdom can prevent, all future misinterpretations. The kind of documents necessary for the protection of the neutral vessels should be enumerated and minutely described; the cases in which a sea letter should be required may be specified; the want of a sea letter should not of itself be a cause of confiscation, where

4. The pertinent part of art. 23 stated, "And it is hereby stipulated that free Ships shall also give a freedom to Goods, and that every thing shall be deemed to be free and exempt, which shall be found on board the Ships belonging to the Subjects of either of the Confederates, although the whole lading or any Part thereof should appertain to the Enemies of either, contraband Goods being always excepted." Art. 17 of the British treaty stated, "It is agreed that, in all Cases where Vessels shall be captured or detained on just suspicion of having on board Enemy's property or of carrying to the Enemy, any of the articles which are Contraband of war; The said Vessel shall be brought to the nearest or most convenient Port, and if any property of an Enemy, should be found on board such Vessel, that part only which belongs to the Enemy shall be made prize, and the Vessel shall be at liberty to proceed with the remainder without any Impediment." Miller, ed., *Treaties*, II, 21, 258.

There was also a direct conflict in the definition of contraband. Art. 24 of the French treaty excluded from the definition of contraband cotton, hemp, flax, tar, pitch, ropes, cables, sails, sail cloths, anchors and any parts of anchors, boards, beams, planks, and ships' masts. Art. 18 of the British treaty defined as contraband ship timber, tar, sails, hemp, and cordage. *Ibid.*, 23, 259.

The clause from art. 18 of the British treaty on the changing definition of contraband by the Law of Nations to which Pickering referred provided that the merchants' goods would not be confiscated but would receive full market value plus freight and demurrage charges. *Ibid.*, 259.

5. Art. 14 provided that in case of a declaration of war, enemy goods deemed contraband on board before the declaration of war or by ignorance of the declaration for a period up to two months after the declaration should not be confiscated. *Ibid.*, 14–15.

other reasonable proof of property is produced; and where such proof is furnished, the want of a sea letter should go no farther than to save the captor from damages for detaining and bringing in the neutral vessel. The proportion of the vessel's crew which may be foreigners should be agreed on. Perhaps it will be expedient to introduce divers other regulations conformably to the marine laws of France. Whenever these are to operate on the commerce of the United States, our safety requires that as far as possible they be fixed by Treaty. And it will be desirable to stipulate against any *ex post facto law* or regulation under any pretence whatever.

Great Britain has often claimed a right and practised upon it, to prohibit neutral nations carrying on a commerce with her enemies which had not been allowed in time of peace. On this head it will be desireable to come to an explicit understanding with France; and if possible to obviate the claim by an express stipulation.

Such extensive depredations have been committed on the Commerce of Neutrals, and especially of the United States, by the citizens of France, under pretence that her enemies (particularly Great Britain) have done the same things, it will be desirable to have it explicitly stipulated, that the conduct of an enemy towards the neutral power shall not authorize or excuse the other belligerent power in any departure from the law of Nations or the stipulations of the treaty: especially that the vessels of the neutral nation shall never be captured or detained, or their property confiscated or injured, because bound to or from an enemies port; except the case of a blockaded port, the entering into which may be prevented according to the known rule of the law of nations. And it may be expedient to define a blockaded place or port to be one actually invested by land or naval forces, or both; and that no *declaration* of a blockade shall have any effect without such actual investment. And no commercial right whatever should be abandoned which is secured to neutral powers by the European law of Nations.

The foregoing articles being those which the French Government has made the ostensible grounds of its principal complaints, they have naturally been first brought into view. But the proposed alterations and arrangements suggest the propriety of revising all our Treaties with France. In such revision, the first object that will attract your attention is the reciprocal guaranty in the Eleventh Article of the Treaty of Alliance. This guaranty we are perfectly willing to renounce. The guaranty by France of the Liberty,

Sovereignty and Independence of the United States will add nothing to our security; while, on the contrary, our guaranty of the possessions of France in America will perpetually expose us to the risque and expense of war, or to disputes and questions concerning our National faith.[6]

When Mr. Genet was sent as the minister of the French Republic to the United States, its situation was embarrassed, and the success of its measures problematical. In such circumstances it was natural that France should turn her eye to the mutual guaranty: and accordingly it was required, in Mr. Genet's instructions, to be "an essential clause in the new treaty" which he was to propose; and on the ground "that it nearly concerned the peace and prosperity of the French Nation, that a people whose resources increase beyond all calculation, and whom nature had placed so near their rich Colonies, should become interested, by their own engagements, in the preservation of those Islands." But at this time, France, powerful by her victories and secure in her triumphs, may less regard the reciprocal guaranty with the United States, and be willing to relinquish it. As a substitute for the reciprocal guaranty, may be proposed a mutual renunciation of the same Territories and possessions that were subjects of the guaranty and renunciation in the sixth and eleventh articles of the Treaty of Alliance.[7] Such a renunciation on our part would obviate the reason assigned in the instruction to Mr. Genet before cited, *of future danger from the rapidly growing power of the United States*. But if France insists on the mutual guaranty, it will be necessary to aim at some modification of it.

The existing engagement is of that kind which by writers on the law of Nations is called a general guaranty; of course the *casus foederis* can never occur except in a *defensive* war. The nature of

6. Pickering was paraphrasing art. 11 of the defensive treaty, or the "guarantee" clause, which obligated the United States to recognize and assure French control of her West Indian colonies. *Ibid.*, 39–40.

7. In art. 6, France renounced all claims to Bermuda and any part of the North American continent claimed by the United States. This, of course, left France free to obtain Louisiana from the Spanish without objections from the United States. See *ibid.*, 38, 39–40. For independent French moves to gain Louisiana, see E. Wilson Lyon, *Louisiana in French Diplomacy, 1759–1804* (Norman, Okla., 1934), 79–98; Ronald Dwight Smith, "French Interests in Louisiana: From Choiseul to Napoleon" (Ph.D. diss., University of Southern California, 1964); William Stinchcombe, ed., "A Neglected Memoir by Talleyrand on French-American Relations, 1793–1797," American Philosophical Society, *Proceedings* ,CXXI (1977), 198.

this obligation is understood to be, that when a war *really* and *truly defensive* exists, the engaging nation is bound to furnish an *effectual* and adequate *defence*, in co-operation with the power attacked: whence it follows, that the Nation *may* be required, in some circumstances, to bring forward its whole force. The nature and extent of the succours demandable not being ascertained, engagements of this kind are dangerous on account of their uncertainty: there is always hazard of doing too much or too little and of course of being involved in involuntary rupture.

Specific succours have the advantage of certainty, and are less liable to occasion war. On the other hand, a general guaranty allows a latitude for the exercise of Judgment and discretion.

On the part of the United States, instead of Troops or Ships of war, it will be convenient to stipulate for a moderate sum of money or quantity of provisions, at the option of France: the provisions to be delivered at our own ports, in any future *defensive wars*. The sum of money, or its value in provisions, ought not to exceed two hundred thousand dollars a year, during any such wars. The reciprocal stipulation on the part of France may be to furnish annually the like sum of money or an equivalent in military Stores and cloathing for troops, at the option of the United States, to be delivered in the ports of France.

Particular caution, however, must be used in discussing this subject, not to admit any claims on the ground of the guaranty in relation to the existing war; as we do not allow that the *casus foederis* applies to it. And if the war should continue after your arrival in France, and the question of the guaranty should not be mentioned on her part, you may yourselves be silent on the subject, if you deem it most prudent.

It will be proper here to notice such articles of the treaty of Amity and Commerce between the United States and France as have been differently construed by the two Governments, or which it may be expedient to amend or explain.

Article 2d. The assent of the United States, in their Treaty with Great Britain, to the doctrine of the law of Nations respecting enemies property in neutral Ships, and Ship-timber and naval Stores, and in some cases provisions, as contraband of war, the French Government has chosen to consider as a voluntary *grant of favours*, in respect to commerce and navigation, to Great Britain; and that consequently the same favours have become common to

France.[8] This construction is so foreign from our ideas of the meaning and design of this article, it shows the necessity of reviewing all the articles, and however clear they may appear, of attempting to obviate future misconstructions by declaratory explanations or a change of terms.

Article 5. France has repeatedly contended that the imposition of fifty cents per ton on French vessels arriving in the United States, is contrary to the fifth article of the treaty. The arguments in support of this pretension are unknown; but it is presumed to be unfounded.[9] The reciprocal right of laying "duties or imposts of what nature soever" equal to those imposed on the most favoured nations, and without any other restrictions, seems to be clearly settled by the third and fourth articles. The fifth article appears to have been intended merely to define or qualify the rights of American vessels in France. It is however desirable that the question be understood, and all doubt concerning it removed. But the introduction of a principle of discrimination between the vessels of different foreign nations and in derogation of the powers of Congress to raise revenue by uniform duties on any objects whatever, cannot be hazarded. The naturalization of French vessels will of course be considered as inadmissible.

Article 8. The stipulation of doing us good offices, to secure peace to the United States with the Barbary powers, has never yet procured us any advantage.[1] If therefore the French Government lays any stress on this stipulation, as authorizing a claim for some other engagement from us in favour of France, it may be abandoned; and especially if its abrogation can be applied as a set off against some existing French claim.

8. The disputes over the interpretations of treaties, no matter what the article, generally involved the issue of contraband. Art. 2 is the most-favored-nation clause: "The most Christian King, and the United States engage mutually not to grant any particular Favour to other Nations in respect of Commerce and Navigation, which shall not immediately become common to the other Party, who shall enjoy the same Favour, freely, if the Concession was freely made, or on allowing the same Compensation, if the Concession was Conditional." Miller ed., *Treaties*, II, 5.

9. The long-standing argument over tonnage duties was considered unimportant. The issue had been discussed in more detail than Pickering indicated. See Edmond Genet to Minister of Foreign Affairs, Oct. 5, 1793, Frederick J. Turner, ed., *Correspondence of the French Ministers to the United States, 1791–1797*, American Historical Association, *Annual Report, 1903*, II (Washington, D.C., 1904), 263–264; and esp. Julian P. Boyd *et al.*, eds., *The Papers of Thomas Jefferson*, XVIII (Princeton, N.J., 1971), 516–577.

1. France agreed under art. 8 to "employ his good Offices and Interposition" with the North African Barbary powers. See Miller, ed., *Treaties*, II, 8–9.

Article 14. If the alterations already proposed are made in the 23d. and 24th. articles, then this 14th. article, as before observed, must be abolished.[2]

Article 17. The construction put on this article by the Government of the United States is conceived to be reasonable and just and is therefore to be insisted on. The tribunals of the respective Countries will consequently be justified in taking cognizance of all captures made within their respective Jurisdictions, or by illegal privateers; and those of one Country will be deemed illegal which are fitted out in the Country of the other remaining neutral; seeing to permit such arming would violate the neutral duties of the latter.[3]

It will be expedient to fix explicitly the reception to be given *to public Ships of war* of all nations. The French Ministers have demanded that the public Ships of the enemies of France, which at any time, and in any part of the world, had made prize of a French vessel should be excluded from the ports of the United States, although they brought in no prize with them. In opposition to this demand, we have contended that they were to be excluded only when they came in with French prizes. And the kind of assylum to be afforded in all other circumstances is described in Mr. Jefferson's letter to Mr. Hammond, dated the 9th. of September 1793, in the following words.[4] "Thus then, the *public Ships of war* of both nations (English and French) enjoy a perfect equality in our ports; 1st. in cases of urgent necessity; 2d. in cases of comfort or convenience; and 3d. in the time they choose to continue." And such shelter and accommodation are due to the public Ships of all nations, on the principle of hospitality among friendly nations.

It will also be expedient explicitly to declare that the right of asylum stipulated for the armed vessels of France and their prizes, gives no right to make sale of those prizes.

But when prize Ships are so disabled as to be incapable of putting to sea again, until refitted; and when they are utterly disabled; some provision is necessary relative to their cargoes. Both

2. See n. 4, above.

3. This article dealt with privateers. The argument revolved around whether the French consuls had the right to sell the prizes or whether the sale must be under American jurisdiction. See Miller, ed., *Treaties*, II, 16–17; Genet to Minister of Foreign Affairs, Oct. 5, 1793, Turner, ed., *Corr. of French Ministers*, 253–254; Genet to Thomas Jefferson, May 27, 1793, Jefferson to Genet, June 5, 1793, Genet to Jefferson, June 8, 1793, *Amer. State Papers*, *Foreign Relations*, I, 149–151.

4. Jefferson to George Hammond, Sept. 9, 1793, Jefferson Papers, Library of Congress.

cases occurred last year. The Government permitted, though with hesitation and caution, the cargoes to be unladed, one of the vessels to be repaired, and part of the prize goods sold to pay for the repairs; and the cargo of the vessel that was found unfit ever to go to sea again was allowed to be exported as *prize goods*, even in neutral bottoms. The doubts on these occasions arose from the 24th. article of the British Treaty, forbidding the sale of the prizes of privateers, or the exchanging of the same in any manner whatever. But as French prizes were entitled to an asylum in our ports, it was conceived to be a reasonable construction of it to allow of such proceedings as those above mentioned, to prevent the total loss of vessels and cargoes. The 25th. article of the British treaty demands attention; as it is therein stipulated that no future treaty shall be made that shall be inconsistent with that or the 24th. article. Another doubt arose, whether the British Treaty did not in good faith, require the prohibition of the sale of prizes made by the *national Ships* of France, as well as of those made by her privateers: especially seeing our Treaty with France gave her no right to sell any prizes whatever: but upon the whole, it was conceived that that United States having before allowed the sale of such prizes, and the prohibition in the 24th. article of the Treaty being distinctly pointed against the sale of the prizes of *Privateers*, it was thought proper to permit the former practice to continue, until the Executive should make and publish a prohibition of the sale of all prizes, or that Congress should pass a prohibitory Law.

Article 22d. If in new modelling the treaty with France the total prohibition of the sale of prizes in the ports of the party remaining neutral should not be agreed on, at least the right of each power to make at its pleasure such prohibition whether they are prizes of national Ships or privateers, should be acknowledged, for the reason more than once suggested—to prevent a repetition of claims upon unfounded constructions; such as, under the present article, that a *prohibition* to an *enemy* of either party, is a *grant* to the *other* of the thing forbidden.[5]

Articles 23 & 24. These have been already considered, and the alterations proposed have been mentioned.[6]

There have been so many unjust causes and pretences assigned

5. Art. 22 stipulated that no privateers of any country at war with the United States or France would be allowed to enter the ports of either country except in emergencies. See Miller, ed., *Treaties*, II, 21–22.

6. See n. 3, above.

for capturing and confiscating American vessels, it may perhaps be impossible to guard against a repetition of them in any treaty which can be devised. To state the causes and pretences that have been already advanced by the Government of France, its Agents and Tribunals, as the grounds of the capture and condemnation of American vessels and cargoes, would doubtless give pain to any man of an ingenuous mind who should be employed on the part of France to negociate another treaty, or a modification of the Treaties which exist. It is not desired therefore to go farther into detail on these matters than shall be necessary to guard by explicit stipulations, against future misconstructions and the mischiefs they will naturally produce.

Under pretence that certain ports were surrendered to the English by the treachery of the French and Dutch inhabitants, Victor Hugues and Lebas,[7] the special Agents of the Executive Directory, at Gaudaloupe, have declared that all neutral vessels bound to or from such ports shall be good prize.

Under the pretence that the British were taking all neutral vessels bound to or from French ports, the French Agents at St. Domingo (Santhonax and others)[8] decreed that all *American* vessels bound to or from English ports should be captured; and they have since declared such captured vessels to be good prize. The French Consuls in Spain have on the same ground condemned a number of American vessels—merely because they were destined to or coming from an English port.

Under the pretence that the sea-letters or passports prescribed by the Commercial treaty, for the mutual advantage of the Merchants and navigators of the two nations, to save their vessels from detention and other vexations when met with at Sea, by presenting so clear a proof of the property, are an indispensable document to be found on board, the French confiscate American vessels destitute of them, even when they acknowledge the property to be American.

Because Horses and their military furniture, when destined to any enemy's port, are by the 24th. article of the commercial Treaty declared contraband, and as such by themselves only liable to confiscation, Hugues and Lebas decreed all *neutral vessels* having

7. Hughes (1770–1826) and Lebas were French commissioners to Guadeloupe. See Georges Sainte-Croix de la Roncière, *Victor Hughes, le Conventionnel* (Paris, 1932).

8. Léger Felicité Sonthonax (1763–1813).

horses or any other Contraband goods on board should be good prize; and they accordingly condemned vessels and cargoes.

The ancient ordinances of the French Monarch required a variety of papers to be on board neutral vessels, the want of any one of which is made a cause of condemnation; although the 25th. article of the Commercial Treaty mentions what Certificates shall accompany the merchant vessels and cargoes of each party, and which by every reasonable construction, ought to give them protection.

It will therefore be advisable to guard against abuses by descending to particulars: to describe the Ships papers which shall be required, and to declare that the want of any other shall not be a cause for confiscation: to fix the mode of manning vessels as to the officers, and the proportion of the crews who shall be citizens, endeavouring to provide, in respect to American vessels, that more than one third may be foreigners. This provision will be important to the Southern States, which have but few native seamen.

The marine ordinances of France will show what regulations have been required to be observed by allied as well as neutral powers in general to ascertain and secure the property of neutrals. Some of these regulations may be highly proper to be adopted; while others may be inconvenient and burthensome. Your aim will be to render the documents and formalities as few and as simple as will consist with a fair and regular commerce.

Articles 25 and 27. These two articles should be rendered conformable to each other. The 27th. says, that after the exhibition of the *passport*, the vessel shall be allowed to pass without molestation or search, without giving her chace, or forcing her to quit her intended course. The 25th. requires that besides the *passport*, vessels shall be furnished with certain *certificates*, which of course must also be exhibited. It will be expedient to add, that if in the face of such evidence the armed vessel will carry the other into port, and the papers are found conformable to treaty, the Captors shall be condemned in all the charges, damages, and interest thereof, which they shall have caused. A provision of this nature is made in the Eleventh article of our Treaty with the United Netherlands.

Article 28. The prohibited goods here mentioned have no relation to contraband: but merely to such as *by the laws of the Country are forbidden to be exported*. Yet in the case of exporting Horses from Virginia, which no law prohibited, in the winter of 1796, this article was applied by the French Minister to *Horses* which by the French Treaty are contraband of war. And a letter from the Minister to Victor Hugues and Lebas, informing them that the American Government refused to prevent such export of horses by the British, is made one ground for their decree above mentioned.[9]

Article 30. The vessels of the United States ought to be admitted into the ports of France in the same manner as the vessels of France are admitted into the ports of the United States. But such a stipulation ought not to authorize the admission of vessels of either party into the ports of the other, into which the admission of all foreign vessels shall be forbidden by the laws of France and of the United States respectively. With this restriction, the principles of the 14th. article of the Treaty with Great Britain afford a liberal and unexceptionable precedent. A restriction like that here referred to will be found in the first paragraph of the third article of the British treaty.[1]

The Commerce to the French Colonies in the East and West Indies will doubtless be more or less restricted, according to the usage of other European nations: yet on account of the disarranged condition of the French navigation, probably a larger latitude of trade with their Colonies will be readily permitted for a term of years: and perhaps the mutual advantages thence resulting will be found so great as to induce afterwards a prolongation of that term; to which the course or habit of business may contribute.

While between the United States and France there shall subsist a perfect reciprocity in respect to commerce, we must endeavour to extend our trade to her Colonies to as many articles as possible. Of these the most important are provisions of all kinds, as beef, pork, flour, butter, cheese, fish, grain, pulse, life-stock, and every other article serving for food which is the produce of the Country, horses, mules, timber, planks and wood of all kinds, Cabinet ware and other manufacturers of the United States: and to obtain in return to all the articles of the produce of those Colonies, without exception; at least to the value of the cargoes carried to those Colonies.

9. See "Extrait des registres de l'Agence particulière du Directoire exécutif, aux îles du vent," Dec. 4, 1796, Correspondance Politique, Etats-Unis, XLVI; and "Arrête of Hughes and Lebas," Jan. 1, 1797, *ibid.*, XLVII.

1. Art. 14 of the British treaty was on freedom of commerce and protection of merchants. Art. 3 specifically stated the locations that the ships of the United States and Great Britain could not go in each other's territory in North America. See Miller, ed., *Treaties*, II, 257, 247.

There have been different constructions of the Consular Convention. The French have contended for the execution of their Consular decisions by the Marshal or other Officer of the United States; and their Minister of Justice has formally stated in a report to the Minister of foreign affairs, that the Judicial sentences of the American Consuls in France will be executed by certain officers of Justice in that Country. The legal opinion of the law-officers of the United States which the Government has adopted, opposes such a construction. The French have also contended that deserters from French vessels ought to be apprehended by the Judicial Officers of the United States, upon other evidence than the original shipping paper, or *role d'equipage*: Whereas the District Judges have insisted that the Consular Convention requires the original Roll to be produced. This claim was lately revived by the Consul General of the French Republic. The correspondence on this occasion will be joined to the other documents which accompany these instructions.[2]

The United States cannot consent to the erecting of foreign Tribunals within their jurisdiction. We consider the judicial authority of Consuls as described in the Consular Convention, to be voluntary, not compulsory, in the Country where they reside: and that their decisions, if not obeyed by the parties, respectively, must be inforced by the laws of their proper Country. And such a provision, you will see, has been made in France where a penalty of 1400 Livres is imposed on the Citizen who refuses obedience to a Consular decision in a foreign State.

The Consular Convention will expire in about four years; and if any great difficulties arise in settling the terms of a new one, that which exists must take its course. But if the French Government should be silent on the subject of the Consular Convention, silence may be observed on your part.[3]

The ports of the United States being frequented by the vessels of different belligerent powers, it became necessary to regulate the times of their sailing. The President, therefore, adopted what was understood to be the received rule in Europe; and ordered, that after the sailing of a vessel of one of the belligerent powers,

2. The accompanying documents are not identified. See Pickering to American Envoys, July 15, 1797.

3. This is one of the few places in the instructions where a suggestion from another cabinet member was accepted. In his reply to questions by Adams, Charles Lee, the attorney general, suggested allowing the Consular Convention to lapse. See Lee to John Adams, Apr. 30, 1797, Adams Papers, Massachusetts Historical Society.

twenty four hours should elapse before an armed vessel of the enemy of the former should set sail. This rule has not been duly respected by the armed vessels of France and Great Britain.

As the tranquility of the United States requires that no hostile movements be commenced within their jurisdiction; and the interests of commerce demand an entire freedom to the departure of vessels from their ports, it may be expedient expressly to recognize the above mentioned rule.

It will also be expedient to agree on the extent of Territorial jurisdiction on the sea-coast, and in what situations Bays and Sounds may be said to be land-locked, and within the jurisdiction of the Sovereign of the adjacent Country.

On the supposition that a treaty will be negociated, to alter and amend the Treaties which now exist between France and the United States, the following leading principles, to govern the negociation, are subjoined.

1. Conscious integrity authorizes the Government to insist that no blame or censure be directly or indirectly imputed to the United States. But on the other hand, however exceptionable in the view of our own Government and in the eyes of an impartial world may have been the conduct of France, yet she may be unwilling to acknowledge any aggressions: and we do not wish to wound her feelings or to excite resentment. It will therefore be best to adopt, on this point, the principle of the British Treaty; and "terminate our differences in such manner, as without referring to the merits of our respective complaints and pretensions, may be the best calculated to produce mutual satisfaction and good understanding."

2. That no aid be stipulated in favour of France during the present war.

3. That no engagement be made inconsistent with the obligations of any prior treaty.

4. That no restraint on our lawful Commerce with any other nation be admitted.

5. That no new stipulation be made, under colour of which Tribunals can be established within our jurisdiction, or personal privileges claimed by French citizens, incompatible with the compleat sovereignty and independence of the United States in matters of policy, Commerce and Government.[4]

4. The guidelines for the envoys were developed from papers submitted to the president by his cabinet officers. General agreement within the cabinet makes it difficult to attribute authorship of the instructions to any one person. Oliver Wolcott sug-

It will be expedient to limit the duration of the treaty to a term of from ten to twenty years. Such changes in the circumstances of the two parties are likely to happen within either of those periods, as to give one or both good reason to desire a change in the conditions of the treaty. From this limitation may be excepted such articles as are declaratory of a state of peace, or as are intended to regulate the conduct of the two nations at the commencement of, or during a state of war; or which are founded in morality and justice, and are in their nature of perpetual obligation. Of this kind may be considered the Tenth article of the treaty with Great Britain; which therefore may very properly be introduced into the treaty with France.

Finally, the great object of the Government being to do justice to France and her citizens, if in anything we have injured them—to obtain justice for the multiplied injuries they have committed against us—and to preserve peace—your stile and manner of proceeding will be such as shall most directly tend to secure these objects. There may be such a change of men and measures in France as will authorize, perhaps render politic, the use of strong language, in describing the treatment we have received. On the other hand, the French Government may be determined to frustrate the negociation, and throw the odium on this Country; in which case, anything like warmth and harshness would be made the pretext. If things remain in their present situation, the stile of representation will unite, as much as possible, calm dignity with simplicity, force of sentiment with mildness of language, and be calculated to impress an idea of inflexible perseverance, rather than of distrust or confidence.

---

gested that no fault be acknowledged by the United States, no aid be given to France while the war continued, and all prior treaties be respected. Alexander Hamilton submitted his ideas to James McHenry, who then gave them to the president along with his own memorandum. Charles Lee did not comment directly on instructions for the envoys; nor did Timothy Pickering, who submitted two 20-page reports on the entire issue of French-American relations. Adams apparently condensed Hamilton's many points to four, which included acknowledging no fault on the part of the United States, offering no aid to France during the current war, insisting on consistency with prior treaties, and attempting to modify the guarantee clause in the Treaty of Alliance with France. In another draft Adams, in a note of "minutes to be asked of Secretaries," put great emphasis on consistency with previous treaties. See George Gibbs, *Memoirs of the Administrations of Washington and John Adams . . .*, I (New York, 1846), 502–517; Bernard C. Steiner, *The Life and Correspondence of James McHenry: Secretary of War under Washington and Adams* (Cleveland, Ohio, 1907), 213–223. The responses of other cabinet members are under the dates Apr. 30, May 1 (2 letters), and May 5, 1797, Adams Papers. Adams's condensation of Hamilton's memorandum and his own suggestions are in the drafts of his messages, 1797 to 1801, *ibid.*

With these instructions, you will receive the following documents.

1. The printed State papers containing the correspondence between the Secretary of State and the French Minister Mr. Genet.[5]

2. The letter dated January 16th. 1797, from the Secretary of State to General Pinckney, and the documents therein referred to, in which all the known complaints of the French Government, since the recall of Mr. Genet, are exhibited and discussed.[6]

3. A Report from the Secretary of State to the House of Representatives, dated the 27th. of February 1797, exhibiting the state of American claims which had been presented to the French Government (but few of which had been satisfied) together with some further information relative to the depredations by the officers and people of that nation on the commerce of the United States.[7]

4. A report made by the Secretary of State to the President of the United States, on the 21st. of June 1797, and by him laid before Congress on the 22d.[8]

5. Certain original depositions, protests and other papers relative to the French spoliations on the Commerce, and personal insults and injuries to the Citizens of the United States.[9]

6. The documents laid before the House of Representatives the 17th. of May 1797, relative to General Pinckney's mission to Paris, and comprehending some papers relative to the Capture and condemnation of American vessels by the French.[1]

7. The correspondence with the French Consul General, Létombe relative to the Consular Convention.[2]

TIMOTHY PICKERING
Secretary of State

5. These papers were submitted to Congress on Dec. 5, 1793, and are printed in *Amer. State Papers, Foreign Relations*, I, 141–246.

6. Pickering to Pinckney, Jan. 16, 1797, Diplomatic and Consular Instructions, III, RG 59, National Archives. This paper, which was over 90 pages long, included 149 accompanying documents.

7. See Feb. 27, 1797, *Annals of Congress*, VI, 2769–2777. This printed report does not include the list of vessels. For the list, see *Philadelphia Gazette and Universal Daily Advertiser*, Mar. 2, 1797.

8. See June 22, 1797, *Annals of Congress*, IX, 3115–3127.

9. It is not clear how many documents were transmitted. For an example, see Pickering to American Envoys, July 15, 1797, and the enclosures mentioned in that letter.

1. See May 17, 1797, *Annals of Congress*, IX, 3057–3094.

2. Pickering may have been referring to his letter to Joseph P. Létombe, the French consul general at Philadelphia, which included references to other correspondence and supporting material. See Pickering to Létombe, May 29, 1797, Pickering Papers, Mass. Hist. Soc.; for Létombe's report, see Létombe to Minister of Foreign Affairs, May 16, 1797, Correspondance Politique, Etats-Unis, XLVII.

From Timothy Pickering

DS, Morristown National Historical Park

Gentlemen [Philadelphia], July 15, 1797

Sometime before I received intelligence of Genl. Pinckney's not being received by the Directory, the Messrs. Ketland's of Philadelphia handed me the enclosed papers marked 1 & 2. relating to certain property and credits belonging to them, which were confiscated at Leghorn by the French Consuls, after the French troops entered that city in the latter end of June 1796. The enclosed letters from Mr. Felicchi, dated 7 July and 14th. Septr. 1796, will furnish ample details of the exertions he made to protect this property and of the manner in which his demands were evaded by the French Consuls, as well as of the harsh treatment he received himself from those Gentlemen.[3] The property belonging to citizens of the United States confiscated on this occasion Mr. Felicchi states to be to the amount of 100,000 dollars, a list of which sworn to by Mr. Fantechi the Agent of the English Gentlemen, to whom the proprietors had consigned it, accompanies Mr. Felicchi's letter of the 14 Septr. I have only to add a recommendation of the interest of the concerned to your attention; and that I am, with great respect, Gentlemen, your most obed. servt.

TIMOTHY PICKERING.

To Mary W. Marshall

ALS, Marshall Papers, Swem Library, College of William and Mary

My dearest Polly Bay of Delaware, July 20, 1797

The land is just escaping from my view the pilot is about to leave us & I hasten from the deck into the cabin once more to give myself the sweet indulgence of writing to you. On the 17th. as I mentiond in my last we left Philadelphia in order to join our vessel

3. Thomas and John Ketland were prominent merchants in Philadelphia. There are copies of the letters of Philip Felichy to Pickering, July 7 and Sept. 14, 1796, in Consular Dispatches, Leghorn, I, RG 59, National Archives. The originals that Pickering enclosed appear to be those filed under Miscellaneous-Miscellaneous, F 44, Envelope 1, RG 76, Natl. Arch. These may be the records that JM turned over to Fulwar Skipwith, the U.S. consul general in Paris, as he was leaving France. See JM to Skipwith, Apr. 21, 1798.

at New Castle & on the 18th. we came on board & weighd anchor at about 10 OClock. There has been so little wind that we are not yet entirely out of the bay. It is so wide however that the land has the appearance of a light blue cloud on the surface of the water & we shall very soon lose it entirely. The wind is now fair & tolerably fresh. I have been so long on board that I can form a very tolerable estimate of the accomodations to be expected on the voyage. The cabin is neat & clean, my birth a commodious one in which I have my own bed & sheets of which I have a plenty so that I lodge as conveniently as I coud do in any place whatever & I find that I sleep very soundly altho on water. We have for the voyage the greatest plenty of salt provisions, live stock & poultry & as we lay in our own liquors I have taken care to provide myself with a plenty of excellent porter wine & brandy. The Captain is one of the most obliging men in the world & the vessel is said by every body to be a very fine one.[4] In addition to Mr. Brown Mr. Gamble[5] & myself two dutch Gentlemen are passengers who appear to be intelligent men well disposd to make the voyage agreeable. I have then my dearest Polly every prospect before me of a passage such as I coud wish in every respect but one. At this season of the year there are such frequent calms as to create fear of a lengthy passage. We have met in the bay several vessels. One from Liverpool had been at sea nine weeks, & the others from other places had been out proportionably long. I hope we shall do better but in spite of me fears mingle with my hopes. I shall be extremely impatient to hear from you & our dear children. I have written a letter to Tom which I sent to Winchester in expectation that he might be there.[6] If he is at Fauquier court house let him know it that he may endeavor to have it sent to him. Colo. Carrington or Mr. Hopkins will give your letters a conveyance to me.[7] I think it better for the present that they shoud some go by the way of Lon-

4. JM sailed on the brig *Grace* under Capt. Willis. See *Porcupine's Gazette* (Philadelphia), July 24, 1797.

5. John Brown was JM's secretary; John G. Gamble was the son of Robert Gamble, a close friend of JM's in Richmond, and was 18 years old at the time of this trip. Gamble later attended Princeton University and went into business in Richmond before moving to Florida. See Robert Gamble to Timothy Pickering, Apr. 3, 1800, Pickering Papers, Massachusetts Historical Society.

One of the "Dutch" gentlemen described here was Citizen Gabriel, a former Norfolk businessman and French citizen. See Joseph Létombe to Minister of Foreign Affairs, July 24, 1797, Correspondance Politique, Etats-Unis, XLVIII, Archives of the Ministry of Foreign Affairs, Paris.

6. Not found.

7. Edward Carrington and John Hopkins.

don to the care of [*Rufus*] King esquire our minister there, some by the way of Amsterdam or the Hague to the care of William Vanns Murry[8] esquire our minister at the Hague & perhaps some directed to me as Envoy extraordinary of the United States to the French Republic at Paris. Do not I intreat you omit to write. Some of your letters may miscarry but some will reach me & my heart can feel till my return no pleasure comparable to what will be given it by a line from you telling me that all remains well. Farewell my dearest life. Your happiness will ever be the first prayer of your unceasingly affectionate

J MARSHALL

To Mary W. Marshall

ALS, Marshall Papers, Swem Library, College of William and Mary

My dearest Polly At sea, August 3, 1797

A vessel is just in sight which appears to be sailing for America & with the hope that I may get it on board her I hasten to scribble a few lines to you. We are now 12 or 1300 miles from the capes of Delaware in the direct course for the channel & have had yet a while a favorable voyage except that we have in the general too little wind. We have not made quite a third of our way to Amsterdam. We had for three days a strong breeze but all is calm again & we scarcely creep along. I shoud disregard this if I did not so greatly fear that a long passage may too much delay my return. I have had scarcely any sea sickness & am now perfectly well. My only sollicitudes are for the success of my mission & for the much loved persons I leave behind me in my own country. Sometimes I am melancholy & sink into fears concerning you but I shake them off as fast as possible & please myself with the delightful picture of our meeting on my return. I fancy myself by your side with our children round us & seem to myself to have such a hold on happiness that it cannot slip from me. I have with me more books than I can read during the passage & that circumstance tends very much to diminish the tediousness of such a voyage.[9] The Captain

8. William Vans Murray (1762–1803).

9. While in Philadelphia, JM was advised to purchase Edward Wortley Montagu, *Reflections on the Rise and Fall of the Antient Republicks. Adapted to the present state of Great Britain*, 2d ed. (London, 1760), and Gabriel Daniel, *The History of France, from the*

is remarkably obliging & we have abundant stores of everything which can tend to make our situation comfortable. Indeed if I coud know that you were perfectly well & happy I shoud feel as much content & satisfaction as can be felt with the prospect before me of so long a separation from you. I will indulge the sweet hope of hearing from [*you*] very soon after my arrival in Europe & I will beleive that your letters will all assure me that you are well & happy. Tis that beleif alone which can keep up my spirits.

August 29th. 97

The vessel by which I expected to have sent the above did not give me an opportunity of putting it on board. I have this instant arrived in Holland & seen a vessel whose Captain will sail for america as soon as the wind permits. I sieze the opportunity to let you know that I am safe & perfectly well. I can add nothing further as I have not yet reachd a place where I can collect any inteligence & as I detain the captain while I add with what affection I am your

J MARSHALL

To Edward C. Carrington

ALS, Morristown National Historical Park

My dear Sir Amsterdam, September 2, 1797

I reachd this place in the night of the 29th. of August & shall set out tomorrow for the Hague where I join Genl. Pinckney & from whence I expect to proceed immediately to Paris.

On our passage we did not see a french, spanish or dutch ship of any sort. As we approachd soundings & afterwards while we were on them we were boarded by some english frigates who treated us with much politeness. In the channel the display of the American flag prevented our being even spoken to. The mouth of the Texel is blockd up by a british fleet under Admiral Duncan

time the French monarchy was established in Gaul, to the death of Lewis the Fourteenth . . . (London, 1726), translated from the French original. JM indicated that he wanted to purchase a grammar written by Louis Chambaud, such as *A Grammar of the French Tongue. With a prefatory discourse, containing an essay on the proper method for teaching and learning that language* (London, 1750). *Aurora* (Philadelphia), July 19, 1797. Presumably JM had other books as well as extensive diplomatic correspondence to read during the voyage.

who have for about a fortnight forbid the entrance of any vessel whatever.[1] We were boarded & by some unaccountable accident all the ships papers were lost so that the vessel was lawful prize. It was therefore necessary to exhibit evidence of my being a minister of the United States on which the immediate discharge of the vessel was accompanied with a very polite offer of any service it might be in their power to render us. I mention these circumstances because they manifest a disposition at present in the government of Britain to pursue a system of conduct friendly & conciliatory towards the United States. The conduct of Mr. King has certainly been such as to promote this disposition & I am told that he has obtaind some changes in our treaty relative to the east india commerce which are favorable to the United States.[2]

In the mouth of the Texel lies a dutch fleet at least equal to the british which is said to have receivd orders to sail out, so soon as the wind shall be favorable, & to engage the enemy. I beleive these orders have been really given. Every consideration I can give the subject confirms this opinion. They can never fight with a fairer prospect of success & with less hazard in case of defeat than at present. Their fleet is at least equal to & is much more fully mand than the british. The wind which brings them out of the Texel must be in their favor if they engage immediately. The water about the mouth of that river is shallow & commanded by batteries in which are mounted I know not how many pieces of heavy ordinance, so that in case of defeat a ready shelter is open to the flat bottomed ships of the dutch into a harbor which the british cannot enter. It is of some importance too that the ships of Holland go immediately out of port in excellent order while those of Britain have been four months at sea. These advantages are opposd by considerable disadvantages. The british bottoms being deeper hold water better & consequently as I am told can in a course of maneuvering gain the wind & the dutch fleet has lost its most experiencd officers. Their present Admiral was only a lieutenant in the navy before the revolution. He was a major General in the Army which

1. Adm. Adam Duncan (1731–1804), later Lord Camperdown, of the British navy.

2. It is difficult to determine exactly what changes JM had in mind. He was probably referring to Rufus King's success in getting the British to agree that U.S. ships could stop at non-British ports to pick up and discharge merchandise instead of going directly to India. In addition the British allowed U.S. ships to carry freight from India to China and, if they had local governmental approval, from India to Europe. See King to Timothy Pickering, June 2 and July 4, 1797, Diplomatic Dispatches, Great Britain, V, RG 59, National Archives.

conquered Holland & is considerd as an officer of distinguishd merit in the land service.[3] It is said that he means to board immediately & thereby avail himself of his vast superiority in numbers of men. A considerable body of troops is with the fleet designd for foreign service. You will perceive that the advantages of the Dutch belong to the place where they have it now in their power to fight while their disadvantages follow them every where & are of a permanent nature. Add to these considerations that the influence of Amsterdam of which the trade is at present stopt must be exerted in favor of an action, that the pride of the nation must be wounded by seeing their merchantmen blockd up in port by a fleet not superior to their own & that the bold adventurous temper of the French government the influence of which over the councils of Holland is known to be decisive, will probably be inclind to hazard an action. I am for these reasons decidedly of opinion that only the negotiation at Lisle can prevent an engagement between these fleets if a favorable wind for sailing out of the Texel shoud offer.[4]

Lord Malmsberry[5] is now at Lisle & it seems to be beleivd that peace between France & Britain is rather to be expected than otherwise.

The Dutch have just completed the last payment of the hundred million of Gilders (equal to forty million of dollars) which the French requird of them.[6] It is visible that the merchants of this place are extremely sore under this requisition. They concern themselves less than any people in the world with politics & it is extremely difficult for a stranger to learn the real state of things here. At my lodgings which are in a considerable house I can neither get an english or a french paper, nor are they to be got but at the coffee house. So far from being able to learn on my arrival whether Genl. Pinckney was in town they did not even know who he was

3. JM is confused on this point. The admiral was Jan Willem de Winter (1750–1812). The soldier referred to was Herman Willem Daendels (1762–1818), who was preparing to use the fleet in the projected invasion of Ireland. See Simon Schama, *Patriots and Liberators: Revolution in the Netherlands, 1780–1813* (New York, 1977), 271–310.

4. In the summer and fall of 1797 abortive peace negotiations between France and Great Britain were being held at Lille.

5. James Harris (1746–1820), the first earl of Malmesbury, formerly ambassador to Russia and Holland, headed the British negotiators at Lille. See [James Harris], third earl of Malmesbury, ed., *Diaries and Correspondence of James Harris, First Earl of Malmesbury . . .*, III (London, 1845).

6. By the 1795 Treaty of The Hague, Holland was required to pay France an indemnity of 100,000,000 florins.

& thus an event had taken place which might have involvd their country in a war with a nation with whom they have considerable commercial intercourse, the minister of that nation when expeld from France had taken up his residence among them & the owner of a considerable house knew nothing of the matter. What is still more surprizing I askd the other day a very eminent merchant who politely gave me a ride round the city in his carriage how many french troops there were in Holland. He coud not tell me. I askd who was their general? He coud not tell. I askd some other question to which he answerd that he never meddled with politics. Their constitution, on which they have been two years employed, was rejected when submitted to the primary assemblies by an immense majority of those who voted but by a very small portion of those entitled to vote. Not a tenth of the freeholders assembled.[7]

There has been & is probably still depending in France a very serious conflict between the different departments of the government. I cannot here understand it correctly but the contest has been carried so far as to be laid by the Generals of Italy & of the Rhine before their armies who have taken a decided part with the Directory. The legislature have declard such military consultations to be in future criminal. It is supposd that this contest is subsiding for the present but that the causes of discontent continue. The temper of the Directory is considerd as being inclind to war & that of the council of five hundred to peace.

Taleran Perigord the gentleman supposd to be alluded to in the letters of Genl. Pinckney is minister of foreign affairs.[8] Orders have

7. On the political situation in Holland, see R. R. Palmer, *The Age of the Democratic Revolution: A Political History of Europe and America, 1760–1800*, II (Princeton, N.J., 1964), 177–207. The recorded vote against the new constitution was 108,761 to 27,955. *Ibid.*, 198.

8. Charles Maurice de Talleyrand-Périgord (1754–1838), the former bishop of Autun until his resignation in 1791, was first appointed minister of foreign affairs on July 16, 1797, replacing Charles Delacroix de Contant (1740–1805). Talleyrand had been an early advocate of the French Revolution, but after going to England in 1791 on a diplomatic mission, he was declared an émigré. He was then expelled from Great Britain under the new alien law, and in June 1794 he arrived in the United States, remaining there until June 1796. Never officially received by the U.S. government, Talleyrand concentrated much of his effort in rebuilding his fortune, thus becoming involved with two prominent American land speculators, Henry Knox (1750–1806) and Robert Morris, and with the agent of the Holland Land Company in America, Théophile Cazenove (1760–1811). Stinchcombe, "WXYZ Affair," *WMQ*, 3d Ser., XXXIV (1977), 602–606.

JM was referring to Pinckney's comment in a letter to Pickering that was later printed by Congress. Pinckney wrote, "a late emigrant, now here, has assured them [the Directory] that America is not of greater consequence to them, nor ought to be

been receivd at the different seaports of France to give passports to the American envoys without waiting for an application to Paris.[9] This is civil & ensures the commencement of negotiation. I do not expect to remain any time at the Hague. Present me cordially to my friends & beleive me to be dear Sir very sincerely, Your,

J MARSHALL

From William Vans Murray

Letterbook Copy, Murray Papers, Pierpont Morgan Library

Dear Sir, The Hague, September 2, 1797

Yesterday I congratulated you upon your safe arrival in Holland, & hope you received my letter. General Pinckney (as well as I am) is very anxious to see you. You will find him a clear-sighted and honourable man, & of pleasing friendly manners. He knows you well, though he never saw you, & is prepared to appreciate everything good about you with cordiality & partiality. If the third commissioner is as congenial as I believe you two will be, there is every reason for us all to expect glory from the battle if we do not triumph in success. I mean the battle of words & memorials. Orders have been sent to all the seaports in France to receive the American Commissioners & to furnish them with the necessary passports to Paris—a precaution of extraordinary civility essential to your quiet—for our countrymen in general are repelled from the frontiers by the arrété of April & the passports of the American Ministers expressly made null.

I am sure that the singular appearance of Holland must arrest

---

treated with greater respect than Geneva or Genoa." Pinckney acknowledged that the late emigrant was indeed Talleyrand and gave his own appraisal of him. "From what I can learn of him, he sometimes pretends to be in our favor, and if he does not fully vindicate, he excuses, our conduct, at other times he censures us with asperity. At present he says the measures of the directory with respect to us, have been very impolitic, and pushed a great deal too far. But I am taught to believe, that little reliance is to be placed on him, and that his influence is trifling." See Pinckney to Pickering, Dec. 20, 1796, and June 5, 1797, Diplomatic Dispatches, France, V, RG 59; Pickering to Pinckney, Apr. 4, 1797, Pickering Papers, Massachusetts Historical Society; May 19, 1797, *Annals of Congress*, VII, 67, IX, 3065. On Talleyrand, see G. Lacour-Gayet, *Talleyrand, 1754–1838* (Paris, 1930); Crane Brinton, *The Lives of Talleyrand* (New York, 1936).

9. Talleyrand sent a circular to port officials to admit the American envoys. See July 31, 1797, Correspondance Politique, Etats-Unis, XLVIII, Archives of the Ministry of Foreign Affairs, Paris.

your attention for a little while; but at & about the Hague you will find the same picture reflected which now perhaps arrests you at Amsterdam. I have invited a warm friend of the U. States & a man of much celebrity, talents & worth, to meet you at dinner with me on Wednesday—so that you will see I have a design in preventing your longer stay at Amsterdam. I mean Mr. John Luzac of Leyden, a persecuted worthy, the editor of the very best paper in Europe, in which he has said very handsome things of you, Genl. P. & Mr. *Dana*.[1] If you have any very remarkable point of intelligence & would be good enough to mention it, it would come safe by the post of tomorrow evening. I have engaged two rooms at this house (The Turenne) where I live for you—but entirely conditionally, if you like them.[2] So you can drive up to the Turenne, where I shall rejoice to see you. You do not tell us if you come as a *single* man. Made. T_l_n will like you the more if you have.[3] I am etc.

To Timothy Pickering

ALS, RG 59, National Archives

Dear Sir Amsterdam, September 2, 1797

After a voyage attended with no circumstance deserving your attention we arrived on the morning of the 29th. of August at the mouth of the Texel. A british fleet commanded by Admiral Dun-

1. Jan Luzac (1746–1807), editor of *Nouvelles de Divers Endroits*, popularly known as *Gazette de Leyde*, frequently printed documents given to him by American diplomats. Luzac obviously did not know that Elbridge Gerry had replaced Francis Dana as one of the envoys.

2. While the American minister's house was being refurbished, Murray was living at the Marshall Turenne Tavern. JM waited there for Gerry before setting out for Paris on Sept. 18, 1797. See Murray to Luzac, Sept. 1, 1797, Morristown National Historical Park; Pinckney to Gerry, Sept. 7, 1797, Gerry Papers, Library of Congress; Pinckney to Gerry, Sept. 22, 1797, Gerry Papers, Pierpont Morgan Library.

3. Jeanne Marie Thérésia Cabarrus (1773–1835), a former actress and at that time the wife of Jean Lambert Tallien (1769–1820), was a leader of French fashion and sometimes called "Our Lady of Thermidor." One scholar described her as "tall and lissom, with beautiful shoulders and splendid arms, jet-black hair, tiny feet, and a musical voice. It was she who, in the depths of winter—the hardest winter of the century—started the fashion of wearing Greek robes, with bare arms, transparent tunics, and bare feet shod with sandals." Albert Mathiez, *After Robespierre: The Thermidorian Reaction*, trans. Catherine Alison Phillips (New York, 1965), 88. Apparently JM did not meet Madame Tallien. Mary Pinckney gave a good description of Madame Tallien in her letter to Margaret Manigault, Oct. 22, 1797, Manigault Family Papers, University of South Carolina.

can has, for about four months, maintaind this station, & orders had been given & inforced for about a fortnight, to prevent the entrance of any vessel whatever. In consequence of these orders the Grace was brought to & boarded by a frigate, the Captain of which, on learning that a minister from the United States was on board, immediately dischargd her, & accompanied the discharge with a very polite tender of any service it might be in his power to render us. Within the Texel we saw the dutch fleet consisting of thirty ships of the line & several frigates. Under its protection are a number of transports containing a considerable body of troops designd for foreign service. It is said confidently that the dutch mean to avail themselves of the first favorable wind to sail out & fight the english. So many circumstances concur in support of this opinion that I am much inclined to beleive it well founded. If not prevented by the negotiations now pending at Lisle an engagement, between these two fleets is, I think to be expected.

In the night of the 30th. of August I reachd Amsterdam & was the next day informed that Genl. Pinckney was at the Hague. I am chagrined at being unable to join him til tomorrow evening.

Altho the present moment teems with events extremely interesting to our country & still more nearly so to Europe it is very difficult if not impossible for a stranger to collect suddenly, at this place, materials on which to form opinions at all to be relied on, or to enable himself to deliniate the real situation of things with any tolerable accuracy or precision. I shall not therefore attempt it, nor shoud I at this time even mention any public transaction but for the possibility that the dispatches of Genl. Pinckney & Mr. Murray may from some accident experience greater delays than this letter.

A most serious contest has for some time raged between the executive & legislative departments of the government of France. It has progressed to such a point that the Generals have laid the subject before their armies which have deliberated upon it & have declard warmly & I am told unanimously in favor of the Directory. It is even said that some threatening movements were made towards Paris. The legislature has made it criminal in future for Generals to permit their armies to deliberate & resolve on subjects belonging to the civil power.

I cannot, at present, obtain french papers or such information as woud enable me to state the real points in controversy between the departments, but about this I am the less solicitous, as you have or will receive complete details from General Pinckney. That part of the controversy which most concerns us relates to peace or the continuance & perhaps extension of the war. It is universally understood that the Directory presses as ardently the latter as the council of five hundred does the former system of conduct. One of the best informed men with whom I have conversed here is of opinion that the violence of this contest has subsided for the moment but that it will recommence; that it is not confind to their external concerns but embraces the practice on certain great interior & constitutional principles.

The final peace between the Emperor & France is beleived to have been concluded.

Lord Malmesberry is at Lisle & there was an account last evening, which however is not credited, that the preliminary articles of a peace between France & Britain are agreed on. The negotiations are said to have recommencd at the instance of France, &, though nothing certain has transpird, it is beleived that they rather promise a termination favorable to the repose of the world than otherwise.

Tayleran Perigord is the minister of foreign affairs.

Orders have been dispatchd to the different sea ports of France to give immediate passports for Paris to the envoys from America without subjecting them to the delays which woud be unavoidable if passports were to be applied for after their arrival. I hope that similar orders have been given to the minister of France at the Hague. With very much respect & esteem, I remain Sir your obedt. Servt.

J Marshall

To Mary W. Marshall

ALS, Marshall Papers, Swem Library, College of William and Mary

My dearest Polly The Hague, September 9, 1797

I have just heard that a vessel sails so soon as the wind will permit from Rotterdam for the United States & I sieze the opportunity of writing to you.

I reachd this place on the 3d. instant & immediately saw Genl. Pinckney with whom I am very much pleasd. We had agreed to set out immediately for Paris for which place the minister of France is authorizd to give us passports. Genl. Pinckney however two days after my arrival receivd a letter from Mr. Gerry written at Boston informing of his intention to embark immediately & of his expectation to join us here the latter end of August. He has not yet come but we anxiously wait for him. We shall wait a week or ten days longer & shall then proceed on our journey. You cannot conceive (yes you can conceive) how these delays perplex & mortify me. I fear I cannot return until the spring & that fear excites very much uneasiness & even regret at my having ever consented to cross the Atlantic. I wish extremely to hear from you & to know your situation. My mind clings so much to Richmond that scarcely a night passes in which during the hour of sleep I have not some interesting conversation with you or concerning you.

This place was formerly the residence of the Prince & Princess of orange & being the court was also the residence of all the foreign ministers. It is still the latter. The former palace is bestowd on the Minister from France. There are at the Hague a great many elegant walks which are very unusual in the midst of a city but the pride & boast of the place is a very extensive wood adjoining the city which extends to the sea. This is I beleive the only natural wood in Holland. It is intersected with a variety of walks & is indeed in the summer one of the most delightful situations in the world. The society at the Hague is probably very difficult, to an American it certainly is & I have no inclination to attempt to enter into it. While the differences with France subsist the political characters of this place are probably unwilling to be found frequently in company with our countrymen. It might give umbrage to France. Genl. Pinckney has with him a daughter who appears to be about 12 or 13 years of age. Mrs. Pinckney informs me that only one girl of her age has visited her since the residence of the family at the Hague.[4] In fact we seem to have no communication but with Americans or those who are employd by America or who have property in our country. Near my lodgings is a theatre in which a french company performs three times a week. I have been frequently to the play & tho I do not understand the language I am very much amusd at it. The whole company is considerd as having a great deal of merit but there is a Madame deGazon[5] who

4. Mary Stead Pinckney (1751–1812) was the second wife of Charles Cotesworth Pinckney; Eliza Lucas Pinckney (1783–1851) was her stepdaughter.

5. Louise-Rosalie Lefebvre DuGazon (1755–1821).

is considerd as one of the first performers in Paris who bears the palm in the estimation of every person.

The Directory with the aid of the soldiery have just put in arrest the most able & leading members of the legislature who were considerd as moderate men & friends of peace. Some conjecture that this event will so abridge our negotiations as probably to occasion my return to America this fall. A speedy return is my most ardent wish but to have my return expedited by the means I have spoken of is a circumstance so calamitous that I deprecate it as the Greatest of evils. Remember me affectionately to our friends & kiss for me our dear little Mary. Tell the boys how much I expect from them & how anxious I am to see them as well as their beloved mother. I am my dearest Polly unalterably, Your,

J MARSHALL

To Timothy Pickering

ALS, RG 59, National Archives

Dear Sir The Hague, September 9, 1797[6]

I arrivd at this place on the evening of the 3d. inst. & had immediately the pleasure of seeing Genl. Pinckney. He has been indefatigable in collecting information material to our country & has been liberal in his communications to me. I have very much reason to be pleasd with him & to promise myself from being associated with him, all the satisfaction which an embassy surrounded with so many perplexities & difficulties, with so many circumstances of embarassment & chagrin, can afford. His dispatches & those of Mr Murray which they have been so obliging as to show me, have detaild to the Government all the inteligence which coud be acquired, & have unfolded, so far as we can unfold, the state of parties in France.

We learn today that an event to the last degree interesting has occured in Paris. The majority of the Directory by one bold decisive stroke has probably prostrated the opposition. It is said that Carnot & Barthelemy two members of the Directory, & *Pichegru*,[7]

6. A marginal note indicates the letter was received on Dec. 15.

7. Italics indicate words originally in code. The code used for JM's mission to France was composed of numbers corresponding to approximately 1,600 words, parts of words, letters, symbols, or numerals arranged in columns in alphabetical order.

with about forty leading members of the council of five hundred & *Dumas* with several other members of the council of Antients have been arrested by a detachment of soldiers & that a decree of transportation has been pronounced against them.[8] This inteligence we understand comes by an express from the dutch minister at Paris to the committee of foreign affairs but it is not to be considerd as certainly authentic nor has it receivd confirmation from Mr. Noell[9] but all the diplomatic gentlemen here beleive it. Indeed such materials have been for sometime preparing, that an explosion was to have been expected. After the sense of the armies was fully disclosd &, probably, this measure of the Directory decided on, Genl. Moreau had been orderd to Paris, for the purpose, as was alledgd,

---

By altering the numerical sequence, the code could be changed easily when the need arose.

During the XYZ mission, the envoys apparently used two different sets of codes: one for corresponding with the State Department and the other for corresponding with Rufus King, who as minister to Great Britain handled many administrative problems of other diplomats in Europe. The code between King and the American envoys was apparently used by King to correspond with David Humphreys (1752–1818), William Short, Gouverneur Morris, and James Monroe. Copies of both codes used for JM's mission are in the Gerry Papers, Library of Congress. The editors have been unable to locate the codes in the records of the State Department.

JM used the State Department code when writing to Charles Lee, who either had a copy of the code or, more likely, allowed Pickering to decode JM's letters for him. See JM to Lee, Oct. 12, 1797. When Charles Pinckney sent a letter in code to his brother, Thomas Pinckney (1750–1828), he first sent it to Pickering for deciphering. JM apparently did not establish a code with other American ministers in Europe or correspondents in the United States, with the exception of Lee. See Charles Pinckney to Thomas Pinckney, Feb. 22 and Mar. 13, 1798, Pickering Papers, Massachusetts Historical Society.

8. The Directory with the aid of the army moved against right-wing and royalist-tainted opponents in the coup d'etat of 18 Fructidor by nullifying the results of the 1797 elections and arresting a number of members of the Council of Five Hundred and the Council of Elders. In doing so the Directory eliminated 177 deputies and thus assured themselves continued control of the government. The Directory also moved against the press, closing 42 Paris newspapers, and began a more rigorous enforcement of the laws concerning émigrés. Two directors, Lazare Nicholas Marquerite Carnot (1753–1823) and François, marquis de Barthélemy (1747–1830), were removed and replaced by Philippe Antoine Merlin de Douai (1754–1838) and Nicholas-François de Neufchâteau (1750–1828), former ministers of justice and interior, respectively. See Georges Lefebvre, *The French Revolution from 1795 to 1799*, trans. John Hall Stewart and James Friguglietti, II (New York, 1970), 197–208.

Gen. Jean-Charles Pichegru (1761–1804) fled to Hamburg after his treason was discovered. Guillaume Mathieu, comte Dumas, a member of Gen. Rochambeau's staff in the United States during the American Revolution, also escaped to Hamburg. JM was carrying a letter from George Washington to Dumas. See JM to Washington, July 7, 1797. See also G. Caudrillier, *La Trahison du Pichegru et les intriques royalists dans l'est avant Fructidor* (Paris, 1908).

9. Jean François Noël (1755–1841) was the French minister to Holland at this time. He was replaced by Charles Delacroix de Contant, the former minister of foreign affairs, in Oct. 1797.

of a personal consultation on the means of furnishing his troops with the necessary supplies. His army during his absence from it, as well as that of the interior was we understand, commanded by Genl. Hoche, on whom the Directory implicitly relies.[1] It is probable, tho this forms no part of the circulating report, that Moreau has shard the fate of the chiefs of the party to which he is supposd to be attachd.

If this step has been really taken it is impossible to foresee its results. I am however persuaded that foreign nations will derive no benefit from it. The internal commotions of France produce no external weakness, no diminution of exertion against her enemies. Parties ready to devour each other unite in fighting the battles of their country. In this they display real patriotism. Had the armies been still more du[ ] than they are supposed to be, the vanquishd party woud probably derive no aid from them so long as a foreign war exists. The armies of Italy & of the interior are as you perceive from the papers which have been transmitted to you devoted to the Directory & irritated in a high degree against the Legislature. The army of Moreau following the principles of their General, was supposd to be inclind to support the legislature, but from that Moreau has been withdrawn under the pretext of a consultation. The army of Holland, formerly a part of the army of Pichegru is also supposd to favor the modercis, but the command of it has been given to Reubel the brother of the director of that name. Thus precautions have been taken to prevent any movement of those troops who might be expected to protect the legislature, or support the, at present, defeated party.

This violent procedure seems to produce no shock here. Such are the political tenets of the Republicans of Europe, that a seizure by a military force of two members of the executive & of many leading members of the legislature is spoken of as the masterly execution of a well digested plan by which the royalist party is suppressd & unanimity restord to the counsels of France. That a great majority of the nation was with the fallen party is proved among many other testimonials, by the late elections. But the armies of Italy & those near the scene of action support the three directors & they are too powerful to be resisted. Paris we learn is perfectly tranquil.

1. On the role of Gen. Jean Victor Moreau (1763–1813) and Gen. Louis Lazare Hoche (1768–1797) in the events of 18 Fructidor, see Lefebvre, *French Revolution*, II, 195–196.

Altho the government seems at present to be entirely in the hands of those who have theretofore been considerd as unfriendly to peace, some conjecture that the negotiations will now progress more rapidly than while the conflict between the executive & legislative departments continued. This conjecture must be founded on the expectation that all the demands of France will now be submitted to. However this may be of one melancholy truth I am certain—if there were in France any persons who thought with even the semblance of justice on american affairs, they were only to be sought for among those moderate men who lately composed a majority of the two councils.

On the effect of this extraordinary measure on the constitution of France I cannot hazard a conjecture. The course of this wonderful people sets at defiance all human calculation. Any other nation which coud practice & quietly submit to, such a total subversion of principles, woud be considerd as prepard for & on the eve of experiencing a military despotism. For the sake of human happiness I hope this will not be the lot of France.

I have venturd sir to state this important fact without waiting its complete confirmation or its accurate details, because the vessel which will probably take this to the United States waits only for a favorable wind & may sail before authentic & digested accounts from Paris can reach us.

Genl. Pinckney has receivd a letter from Mr. Gerry informing that he shoud sail from Boston about the 23d. of July & expected to arrive at Rotterdam in August. The receipt of this letter has suspended our departure for Paris. The french minister at this place will deliver us passports when requested, but we are extremely anxious to be joind by Mr. Gerry & deem it proper to wait a week or ten days longer for him. Shoud we be disappointed in seeing him by that time, we shall suppose that some accident has deferd his sailing or changed his rout, & shall consider it as our duty to proceed on our mission. With very much respect & esteem I remain dear Sir Your obedt. Servt

JOHN MARSHALL

P. S. The accounts concerning the recall of Moreau are contradictory.

To Timothy Pickering

ALS, RG 59, National Archives

Dear Sir The Hague, September 15, 1797[2]

In my letter of the 9th inst. I stated to you a revolution reported to have been producd in Paris. That report is now confirmed. I shall not attempt to give you the details because Genl. Pinckney incloses to you those papers which bring us all the inteligence we possess.[3] The constitution of France may survive this wound, but the constitution of no other nation on earth coud survive it. Whether the alledged conspiracy for the reestablishment of royalty did or did not exist, is not for me to say. In my own private mind however I have not even a suspicion of its existence. Shoud I be mistaken the correction of that mistake will by no means remove the cloud which lours over the constitution of France. That constitution will not have been the less vitally & unnecessarily violated by establishing the truth of a conspiracy. In opposition to its mandates the members of the legislature have been seized by an order of the directory, without observing any of the forms it wisely prescribes; Without being brought before that court which alone can try them they have been banishd, unheard, by the remnant of a terrified legislature forbidden in express terms to pronounce such a judgement by the very charter which created it. The same violence in equal opposition to the constitution is practised on a minority of the executive & on several citizens whose only offence was that they had printed free comments on the conduct of the directory & of the armies. These excesses cannot have been necessary. Paris being filled with troops devoted to the victors, & the persons of the accused being securd, the forms of constitutional proceedings might have been observed. A wanton contempt of rules so essential to the very being of a republic coud not have been exhibited by men who wished to preserve it. If there was really a conspiracy to restore royalty which had taken such extensive root

2. JM wrote on the address leaf, "Hond by Capt. Izzard." Someone added on the address leaf, "Genl. Pinckney & Mr. Marshall left Rotterdam the 19th. Septr. for Paris. Mr. Gerry arrived at Rottm. the evening of the same day, & proceeded to France a few days after."

A clerk noted that this letter arrived in Pickering's office on Nov. 22.

3. The information sent on by Pinckney is in Dispatch No. 29, Pinckney to Timothy Pickering, Sept. [14], 1797, Diplomatic Dispatches, France, V, RG 59, National Archives. The dispatch is improperly dated Sept. 24.

that after the conspirators were seized & troops stationed in every quarter of the city, it was yet impossible to bring them before an overawed constitutional tribunal, or even to permit them to be heard in their defence by the trembling ferment of a legislature ready in every thing to obey the conquerors, if it was impossible even to try a few printers, lest a disarmed nation shoud rise in their defence against those armies whose victories have astonishd & almost subdued the world it woud prove that the government is a government of force imposed on the people against their will & only to be preserved by the armies. That the government is to be administerd not according to the public will by representatives chosen to administer it, but according to the will of the Generals & of the armies. Under such a system it requires no political knowledge to perceive that while the name of a republic may be preserved its very essence is destroyd.

However gloomy the present aspect of things may be it is yet possible that French liberty may survive the shock it has sustaind & which seems to have paralyzed it for the moment. The peculiar genius of the people, the immense extent, force & population of the country admit of its extricating itself from difficulties under which republicanism in any other nation of Europe woud sink in dispair & its friends woud abandon it as a phantom they had pursued in vain. While there remains a hope philantropy will cherish it.

I am sensible sir that we have nothing to do with the internal revolutions of a sovereign nation which decides on its own fate. No remark on it will be made by me, nor will any sentiment be utterd which can have the appearance of intermedling, even in thought, with their proper concerns. Our business is to labor the accomodation of differences & to that sole object will all our efforts tend. France may assume what form of government she pleases & may administer it as she pleases—our object & our duty remain the same. It is not however to be conceald that our difficulties appear to increase. All power is now in the undivided possession of those who have directed against us those hostile measures of which we so justly complain.

On Monday next, if Mr. Gerry does not arrive in the meantime, we set out for Paris.

I wrote to you from Amsterdam that peace was beleivd to have been concluded with the Emperor & that report had also signed the preliminary articles with England. Both those pieces of inteligence were announced in the papers but both have been contradicted. The negotiations are still pending & their issue extremely uncertain.

In our permit to go to Paris the rout is prescribed to us. The motive for this most probably is to prevent our passing through Lisle. With every sentiment of respectful esteem I remain Sir your Obedt. Servt.

J Marshall

Merlin[4] is chosen director in the place of Barthelemy, the successor of Carnot is not yet agreed upon. A paper just arrivd says that Francois de Neufchatil[5] is the other director & that peace with the emperor is concluded.

Septr. 17th., 1797

I have opend my letter to inform you that I have just seen Mr. Noell the minister of France at the Hague who disbeleives the account of peace with the Emperor stated in the last paris papers. I just learn too that about 1500 persons have been arrested at Lyons & that resistance is made at Avignon which Genl. Massena is marching to quel.[6]

To George Washington

ALS, Washington Papers, Library of Congress

Dear Sir The Hague, September 15, 1797

The flattering evidences I have receivd of your favorable opinion, which have made on my mind an impression only to wear out with my being, added to a conviction that you must yet feel a deep interest in all that concerns a country to whose service you have devoted so large a portion of your life, induce me to offer you such occasional communications as, while in europe I may be enabled to make, & induce a hope too that the offer will not be deemd an unacceptable or unwelcome intrusion.

Until our arrival in Holland we saw only British & neutral vessels. This added to the blockade of the dutch fleet in the Texel, of the french fleet in Brest & of the spanish fleet in Cadiz manifests

4. Philippe Antoine Merlin de Douai.
5. Nicholas-François de Neufchâteau.
6. Gen. André Masséna (1756–1817).

the entire dominion which one nation at present possesses over the seas. By the ships of war which met us we were three times visited & the conduct of those who came on board was such as woud proceed from general orders to pursue a system calculated to conciliate America. Whether this be occasiond by a sense of justice & the obligations of good faith, or solely by the hope that the perfect contrast which it exhibits to the conduct of France may excite keener sensations at that conduct, its effects on our commerce are the same.

The situation of Holland is truely interesting. Tho the face of the country still exhibits a degree of wealth & population perhaps unequald in any other part of Europe its decline is visible. The great city of Amsterdam is in a state of blockade. More than two thirds of its shipping ly unemployd in port. Other seaports suffer tho not in so great a degree. In the meantime the requisitions made upon them are enormous. They have just completed the payment of the 100,000,000 of florins (equal to 40,000,000 of dollars) stipulated by treaty; they have sunk, on the first entrance of the French, a very considerable sum in assignats; they made large contributions in specifics; & they pay feed & cloath an army estimated, as I am informd, at near three times its real number. It is supposd that France has by various means drawn from Holland about 60,000,000 of dollars. This has been paid, in addition to the national expenditures, by a population of less than 2000,000. Nor, shoud the war continue, can the contributions of Holland stop here.[7] The increasing exigencies of France must inevitably increase her demands on those within her reach. Not even peace can place Holland in her former situation. Antwerp will draw from Amsterdam a large portion of that commerce which is the great source of its wealth, for Antwerp possesses in the existing state of things, advantages which not even weight of capital can entirely surmount. The political divisions of this country & its uncertainty concerning its future destiny must also have their operation. Independent of the grand division between those for & against the stadtholder; between those who favor an indivisible & those who favor a foederal republic, there is much contrariety of opinion concerning the essential principles of that indivisible consolidated republic which

7. JM may have taken his information on Dutch finances from William Vans Murray. Murray had submitted a long report on the costs of the Dutch alliance with France. See Murray to Timothy Pickering, Sept. 10, 1797, Diplomatic Dispatches, Netherlands, III, RG 59, National Archives.

the influence of France imposes on the nation. A constitution which I have not read, but which is stated to me to have containd all the great fundamentals of a representative government, & which has been prepard with infinite labor, & has experienced an uncommon length of discussion was rejected in the primary assemblies by a majority of nearly five to one of those who voted. The objections do not accompany the decision, but they are said to be to the duration of the constitution which was to remain five years unalterd, to the division of the legislature into two chambers, & to its power of definitive legislation. The substitute wished for by its opponents is a legislature with a single branch having power only to initiate laws which are to derive their force from the sanction of the primary assemblies. I do not know how they woud organize their executive, nor is it material how they woud organize it. A constitution with such a legislature woud live too short a time to make it worth the while to examine the structure of its other parts. It is remarkable that the very men who have rejected the form of government proposed to them have reelected a great majority of the persons who prepard it & who will probably make from it no essential departure. Those elected are now assembled in convention at this place, but we know not in what manner they are proceeding. It is also worthy of notice that more than two thirds of those intitled to suffrage including perhaps more than four fifths of the property of the nation & who wishd, as I am told, the adoption of the constitution, withheld their votes on this very interesting question. Many were restraind by an unwillingness to take the oath requird before a vote coud be received; many, disgusted with the present state of things, have come to the unwise determination of revenging themselves on those whom they charge with having occasiond it by taking no part whatever in the politics of their country, & many seem to be indifferent to every consideration not immediately connected with their particular employments.

The political opinions which have producd the rejection of the constitution, & which, as it woud seem, can only be entertaind by intemperate & ill informd minds unaccustomd to a union of the theory & practice of liberty, must be associated with a general system which if brought into action will produce the same excesses here which have been so justly deplored in France. The same materials exist tho not in so great a degree. They have their clubs, they have a numerous poor & they have enormous wealth in the hands of a minority of the nation. On my remarking this to a very rich & inteligent merchant of Amsterdam, & observing that if one class of men withdrew itself from public duties & offices it woud immediately be succeeded by another which woud acquire a degree of power & influence that might be exercisd to the destruction of those who had retired from society, he replied that the remark was just, but that they relied on France for a protection from those evils which she had herself experiencd. That france woud continue to require great supplies from Holland & knew its situation too well to permit it to become the prey of anarchy. That Holland was an artificial country acquird by persevering industry & which coud only be preservd by wealth & order. That confusion & anarchy woud banish a large portion of that wealth, woud dry up its sources & woud entirely disable them from giving France that pecuniary aid she so much needed. That under this impression very many who, tho friends to the revolution, saw with infinite mortification french troops garrison the towns of Holland, woud now see their departure with equal regret. Thus they willingly relinquish national independence for individual safety. What a lesson to those who woud admit foreign influence into the United States!

You have observd the storm which has been long gathering in Paris. The thunder bolt has at length been launched at the heads of the leading members of the legislature & has, it is greatly to be feard, involved in one common ruin with them the constitution & liberties of their country.

The inclosd papers will furnish some idea of a transaction which may be very interesting to America as well as to France. Complete & *impartial* details concerning it will not easily be obtaind as the press is no longer free. The journalists who had venturd to censure the proceedings of a majority of the directory are seizd & against about forty of them a sentence of transportation is pronouncd. The press is placd under the superintendence of a police appointed by & dependent on the executive. It is supposd that all private letters have been seized for inspection.

From some Paris papers it appears that on the first alarm several members of the legislature attempted to assemble in their proper halls, which they found closd & guarded by an armd force. Sixty or seventy assembled at another place & began to remonstrate against the violence offerd to their body but fear soon dispersd them. To destroy the possibility of a rallying point the municipal administrations of Paris & the central administration of the seine were immediately suspended & forbidden by an arrêté of the directoire, to assemble themselves together. Many of the administrators of the departments through France elected by the people, had been previously removd & their places filld by persons chosen by the directory. Moreau who commanded the army of the Sambre & the Meuse by which he was deservedly beloved & who was considered as attached to the fallen party was, as is reported, invited from his army to Paris under the pretext of a personal consultation. We have not heard of his arrival or of his fate. The command of his army during his absence did not, we learn, devolve on the oldest officer but was given to Genl. Hoche who also commands the army of the in[*terior*]. Carnot is at one time said to have been killd in defending himself from some soldiers who pursued & attempted to take him, at another time he is said to have effected his escape. The fragment of the legislature convokd by the directory at L'odeon & L'ecole de santé, hastend to repeal the law for organizing the national guards, & authorized the directory to introduce into Paris as many troops as shoud be judged necessary. The same day the liberty of the press was abolished by a line, property taken away by another & personal security destroyd by a sentence of transportation against men unheard & untried. All this is stild the triumph of liberty & of the constitution.[8]

To give a satisfactory statement of the origin & progress of the contest between the executive & legislative departments woud require more time than coud be devoted to the subject, did I even possess the requisite information, & to you, sir, it woud be unnecessary because I have no doubt of your having received it through other channels. I shall briefly observe that the controversy has embraced a variety of interesting subjects. Since the election of the new third, there were found in both branches of the legislature a majority in favor of moderate measures, &, apparently, wishing sincerely for peace. They have manifested a disposition which threatend a condemnation of the conduct of the directory towards America, a scrutiny into the transactions of Italy, particularly

8. It is not certain to which Paris newspaper JM was referring, but almost all of them carried such news and rumors following the coup of 18 Fructidor. The following Paris papers contain the information: *Journal du Matin*, Sept. 6, 1797; *Le Rédacteur*, Sept. 6 and 7, 1797; *Journal du Soir*, Sept. 6 and 7, 1797. Pinckney sent the *Rédacteur*, Sept. 7, 1797, containing the information in Pinckney to Pickering, Sept. [14], 1797, Diplomatic Dispatches, France, V, RG 59 (the dispatch is improperly dated Sept. 24).

those respecting Venice & Genoa,[9] an enquiry into the disposition of public money & a regular arrangement of the finances as woud prevent in future those dilapidations which are suspected to have grown out of their disorder. They have sought too by their laws to ameliorate the situation of those whom terror had driven out of France, & of those priests who had committed no offence. Carnot & Barthelemy two of the directory were with the legislature.

The cry of a conspiracy to reestablish royalism was immediately raised against them. An envoy was dispatchd to the army of Italy to sound its disposition. It was represented that the legislature was hostile to the armies, that it withheld their pay & subsistence, that by its opposition to the directory it encouraged Austria & Britain to reject the terms of peace which were offered by France & which but for that opposition woud have been accepted, & finally that it had engagd in a conspiracy for the destruction of the constitution & the republic & for the restoration of royalty. At a feast given to the armies of Italy to commemorate their fellow soldiers who had fallen in that country the Generals addressed to them their complaints, plainly spoke of marching to Paris to support the directory against the Councils & receivd from them addresses manifesting the willingness of the soldiers to follow them. The armies also addressd the directory & each other, & addresses were dispatchd to different departments. The directory answerd them by the strongest criminations of the legislature. Similar proceedings were had in the army of the interior commanded by Genl. Hoche. Detachments were moved within the limits prohibited by the constitution, some of which declard they were marching to Paris "to bring the legislature to reason."[1] Alarmd at these movements the council of five hundred called on the directory for an account of them. The movement of the troops within the constitutional circle was attributed to accident & the discontents of the army to the falts committed by the legislature who were plainly criminated as conspirators against the army & the republic. This message was taken up by Tronçon in the council of antients & by

9. The leader in the Council of Five Hundred directing the inquiries toward French policy concerning the United States, Genoa, and Venice was Claude Emmanuel Joseph, marquis de Pastoret (1756–1840), who was removed in the coup of 18 Fructidor. Pinckney discussed Pastoret's actions in Pinckney to Pickering, July 15, 21, and Sept. 21, 1797, Diplomatic Dispatches, France, V, RG 59.

1. As a protection for the Council of Five Hundred and the Council of Elders, the constitution provided that the armies were not to come within 12 leagues, or 36 miles, of Paris without express permission.

Thibideau in the council of five hundred.[2] I hope you have seen their speeches. They are able, & seem to me to have entirely exculpated the legislature. In the mean time the directory employd itself in the removal of the administrators of many of the departments & cantons & replacing those whom the people had elected by others in whom it coud confide, & in the removal generally of such officers both civil & military as coud not be trusted to make room for others in whom it coud rely. The legislature on its part, passed several laws to enforce the constitutional restrictions on the armies & endeavord to organize the national guards. On this latter subject especially Pichegru great & virtuous I beleive in the cabinet as in the field, was indefatigable. We understand that the day before the law for their organization woud have been carried into execution the decisive blow was struck.

To support the general charge of a conspiracy in favor of royalty I know of no particular facts alledgd against the arrested members except Pichegru & two or three others. An abridgement of the paper constituting the whole charge against Pichegru will be found in the inclosd supplement. I have seen the paper at full length. The story at large is still more improbable than its abridgement because Pichegru is made in the first moment of conversation to unbosom himself entirely to a perfect stranger who had only told him that he came from the Prince of Condé[3] & coud not exhibit a single line or testimonial of any sort to prove that he had ever seen that Prince or that he was not a spy employed by some of the enemies of the General.

This story is repeld by Pichegru's character which has never before been defild. Great as were the means he possessed of personal aggrandizement he retird clean handed from the army, without adding a shilling to his private fortune. It is repeled by his resigning the supreme command, by his numerous victories subsequent to the alledgd treason, by its own extreme absurdity & by the fear which his accusers show of bringing him to trial according to the constitution even before a tribunal they can influence & overawe, or of even permitting him to be heard before that prostrate body

2. JM seems to have been referring to Guillaume Alexandre Tronçon de Ducoudray (1750–1798), who made a speech attacking the Directory and the movement of the army under Hoche, and to Antoine-Claire Thibaudeau (1765–1854). Thibaudeau made a number of anti-military and anti-Directory speeches in the two weeks before the coup of 18 Fructidor.

3. Louis Joseph de Bourbon, prince de Condé (1736–1818), was the leader of the émigré army in the Rhineland.

which is still termed the legislature, & which in defiance of the constitution has pronounced judgement on him.

Yet this improbable & unsupported tale seems to be receivd as an establishd truth by those who, the day before [*his*] fall bowed to him as an idol. I am mortified as a man to learn that even his old army which conquerd under him, which adord him, which partook of his fame & had heretofore not joind their brethren in accusing the legislature, now unite in bestowing on him the heaviest execrations & do not hesitate to pronounce him a traitor of the deepest die.

Whether this conspiracy be real or not, the wounds inflicted on the constitution by the three directors seem to me to be mortal. In opposition to the express regulations of the constitution the armies have deliberated, the result of their deliberations addressd to the directory has been favorably received, & the legislature since the revolution has superadded its thanks.

Troops have been marchd within those limits which by the constitution they are forbidden to enter but on the request of the legislature.

The directory is forbidden to arrest a member of the legislature unless in the very commission of a criminal act & then he can only be tried by the high court, on which occasion forms calculated to protect his person from violence or the prejudice of the moment are carefully prescribed. Yet it has seizd by a military force about fifty leading members not taken in a criminal act & has not pursued a single step marked out by the constitution.

The councils can inflict no penalty on their own members other than reprimand, arrest for eight & imprisonment for three days. Yet they have banishd to such place as the directory shall chuse a large portion of their body without the poor formality of hearing a defence.

The legislature shall not exercise any judiciary power or pass any retrospective law. Yet it has pronounced this heavy judgement on others as well as its own members & has taken from individuals property which the law had vested in them.

The members of the directory are personally securd by the same rules with those of the legislature. Yet three directors have deprivd two of their places, the legislature has then banishd them without a hearing & has proceeded to fill up the alledged vacancies. Merlin late minister of justice & François de Neufchatel have been elected.

The constitution forbids the house of any man to be enterd in the night. The orders of the constituted authorities can only be executed in the day. Yet many of the members were seized in their beds.

Indeed sir the constitution has been violated in so many instances that it woud require a pamphlet to detail them. The detail woud be unnecessary for the great principle seems to be introduced that the government is to be administerd according to the will of the armies & not according to the will of the nation.

Necessity the never to be worn out apology for violence, is alledgd—but coud that necessity go further than to secure the persons of the conspirators? Did it extend to the banishment of the printers & to the slavery of the press? If such a necessity did exist it was created by the disposition of the people at large, & it is a truth which requires no demonstration that if a republican form of government cannot be administerd by the general will, it cannot be administerd against that will by an army.

After all the result may not be what is apprehended. France possesses such enormous power, such internal energy, such a vast population that she may possibly spare another million & preserve or reacquire her liberty. Or, the form of the Government being preservd, the independence of the legislature may be gradually recoverd.

With their form of Government or revolutions we have certainly no right to intermeddle, but my regrets at the present state of things are increasd by an apprehension that the rights of our country will not be deemd so sacred under the existing system as they woud have been had the legislature preservd its legitimate authority.

Genl. Pinckney (with whom I cannot but be very much pleasd) have waited impatiently for Mr. Gerry & shall wait until monday the 18th inst. On that day we set out for Paris.

The negotiations with Austria & Britain are still pending & are of very uncertain issue.

This letter has extended itself to an unexpected length. I have fatigued you sir & will only add that I remain, with sincere & respectful attachment, Your obedt. Servt.

J MARSHALL

I just now learn that fifteen hundred persons have been arrested at Lyons. That resistance is made at Avignon & that Massena is marching to quel it.[4]

To Charles Lee

AL, Emmet Collection, New York Public Library

My dear Sir Antwerp, September 22, 1797[5]

We are thus far on our way to Paris to which place we are proceeding slowly in the hope of being overtaken by Mr. Gerry of whose arrival at Helvoet we heard last night.[6]

I have endeavord since my arrival in europe to give the various subjects of inteligence as early as possible & have sometimes found subsequent accounts to contradict those which had been receivd & considerd as certainly true. Thus the attachment of Moreau to the majority of the legislature in opposition to the majority of the directory was generally counted on & has been a general mistake. A letter of his bearing date the 5th of September, the day after the revolution is publishd in which he states himself to have taken with the baggage of an Austrian General captured when he last crossed the Rhine an extensive correspondence proving the verity of a conspiracy for the restoration of royalty. That Pichegru is unquestionably included in this conspiracy. He has been cautious enough not to write a single line himself nor is his name ever mentiond in one of the letters, but there are several letters which must allude to him some by one name & some by another. It is *clearer than the day* says Moreau that Pichegru is engaged in this conspir-

4. Counterrevolutionary activity had again broken out in the south of France but was quickly suppressed by the army under the direction of Gen. André Masséna.

5. A note on the address leaf indicates that the letter arrived on Feb. 3, 1797.

6. Gerry arrived at Hellevoetsluis, south of Rotterdam, on Monday, Sept. 18, 1797. See Gerry to Pinckney, Sept. 20, 1797, Russell W. Knight, ed., *Elbridge Gerry's Letterbook: Paris 1797–1798* (Salem, Mass., 1966), 7–8. Henry Rutledge, Pinckney's secretary and nephew, described the trip to Paris in a letter to his father, Edward Rutledge (1749–1800). "As far as Cambray I accompanied Genl. Pinckny in his carriage, but some accident having happened to Genl. Marshall's wheels, it was thought best to transfer me to his party, as being better able to squabble in French with the blacksmiths, than the gentlemen of his suite. So that I came the remainder of my journey with that gentleman, and assisted at the breaking of three wheels out of the *four.* However after a great deal of imposition and noise, in which there was nothing very remarkable except the good temper of Genl. Marshal, we got through our difficulties, and arrived here a few hours after my Uncle." Henry Rutledge to Edward Rutledge, Oct. 2, 1797, Dreer Collection, Historical Society of Pennsylvania.

acy, but the proofs are not *judicial.* Conspirator or not he has with some others of the legislature, as is stated, set out for the port from which he is to sail for Guiana.[7] These accounts are various. The legislature you know left it with the directory to decide on the place of banishment & the papers have stated at one time Madagascar & at another a part of Portuguese south America as having been fixed on. It is said that some of those who were sentenced to exportation have been *repreivd.* I am uncertain how that fact stands but think it probably true.

Our insulted injurd country has not before it the most flattering prospects. There is no circumstance calculated to flatter us with the hope that our negotiations will terminate as they ought to do. The order made on the motion of Pastoret has been rescinded & the committee dischargd without making a report. Riout on whose motion the order was rescinded without any discussion added to the declaration of its being a diplomatic subject with which the council of five hundred coud not properly mingle, that it had given a discouragement to the privatiers not intended by the legislature.[8]

We understand that all is now quiet in France. The small show of resistance against which Massena marchd is said to have dispersed on hearing of his movement.

To day being the anniversary of the foundation of the republic was celebrated with great pomp by the military at this place. Very few indeed of the inhabitants attended the celebration. Everything in Antwerp wears the appearance of consternation & affright. Since the late revolution a proclamation has been published forbidding any priest to officiate who has not taken the oath prescribd by a late order. No priest at Antwerp has taken it & yesterday commences the suspension of their worship. All the external marks of their religion too with which their streets abound are to be taken down. The distress of the people at this calamity is almost as great as if the town was to be given up to pillage.

The negotiations with the Emperor & with Britain wear for the present rather an unfavorable aspect. The papers now inform us that Buonaparte has lately made some movements which look like preparing for a recommencement of hostilities. It is said that he has

7. Those arrested in the coup of 18 Fructidor were sentenced to exile in Cayenne, French Guiana.

8. A copy of the motion of Sept. 15, 1797, by Joseph François Marie, baron Riou de Kersalaun (1765–1811), is in Correspondance Politique, Etats-Unis, XLVIII, Archives of the Ministry of Foreign Affairs, Paris.

made dispositions to surround the [ ][9] great part of the imperial army. We also learn that Lord Malmsbury has been notified that he must leave the territories of the republic in a week if he is not authorized by his nation to accept the terms offerd by France. What the point of difference is we cannot say with certainty. By the first British officer who boarded us I was told that in addition to the restoration of all the islands & places in both the indies & elsewhere taken from Holland as well as France it is requird that the ships taken at Toulon shoud be restord & those destroyed paid for. A member of the municipality here has added that diminution of the British fleet would be absolutely insisted on. These things are uncertain & therefore I shall not write to the secretary of state til we reach Paris. Present my respects to the President & inform him that I forwarded as early as possible the letters he committed to my charge.[1]

From William Vans Murray

Letterbook Copy, Pierpont Morgan Library

Dear Sir, The Hague, September 24, 1797

Nothing new except the Fête in honour of the fall of the conspirators, as they call Pichegru etc. has occurred here. This fête pervaded all Batavia & probably extended from the mouth of the Rhine to the kingdom of Ulysses, where the flag of the republic now insults his former reign, which though certainly not free was yet wise. These fêtes have a surprising effect. They are among the arcana of french policy. An act of the successful party is thus covered by eclat, by brilliance drums & trumpets, all on the same day, from that scrutiny which an *examination of papers* & evidence would have probably developed into a very different character & shape. They bestow a great but [ ][2] of the magnitude of the event, deride those who doubt by the imposing air of a majority who believe, & divert the public eye from anything except the success that is the cause of them.

9. Torn by seal.

1. These letters, John Adams to John Q. Adams, July 15, 1797, and Abigail Adams to John Q. Adams, July 14, 1797, were carried by JM. See John Q. Adams to John Adams, Sept. 21, 1797, and John Q. Adams to Abigail Adams, Oct. 7, 1797, Adams Papers, Massachusetts Historical Society.

2. At least two words were omitted when the letter was copied.

Mr. Gerry left us this morning. You do not know him personally. You will find him stored with much congressional & general knowledge—not well acquainted with mankind—possessed from his great experience, of resource and alternatives, & with the very best intentions & a tender & friendly heart. He is too, though he appears from a certain hesitation of manners at first, otherwise, a man of cordiality, & will cooperate with you with sincerity & kindness. He seems to believe that which I do not believe, that there is a very powerful british party in America. I have attempted to disabuse him. This I consider as a radical error, productive of great consequences. He mistakes, though Tallyrand did not, our commercial operations for political influence.[3] If there be foreign influence, it is nothing in the estimate of great national affairs if it do not manifest itself & be traceable into acts & facts—if there be this influence at all, it is a french influence—for this there is much food even in the very sources of our best gift, Love of liberty—for the other there is no food. The one is traced in facts; the other has not yet been, & I trust will never be, as I believe it does not exist.

I went with him to Amsterdam, & have been with him & enjoyed the most cordial & confidential conversation with him. I shall be very much gratifyed by a letter from you now & then—short or long as your other affairs may admit.

Lord Malmsbury has left Lille I heard on the 22d Sepr. The Directory ought to have prevented this by some appearance of kindness, for it will certainly strike the nation as one of the first fruits of the late convulsion. I hear nothing of this event except the naked fact. It is questioned whether after such a *revolution* the negotiation could be trusted to. Perhaps the english might so think. I applyed for a passport for your servant & gave him a Certificate of his having been nine years in America—seven of which I knew him personally at Mr. B.s.[4] He will soon be with you I suppose as he obtained one three days since. I am etc.

3. In his "Mémoire sur les relations commerciales des Etats-Unis avec l'Angleterre," read for the Institut national des sciences et arts on Apr. 4, 1797, Talleyrand stressed that common morals, manners, and language, in addition to the nature of the products traded between England and the United States, would naturally make England the primary market for American goods. See Stinchcombe, "WXYZ Affair," *WMQ*, 3d Ser., XXXIV (1977), 196–197.

4. William Bingham.

From John Trumbull

ALS, John Trumbull Papers, Yale University Library

Dear Sir Stuttgard, September 27, 1797

I[5] have the pleasure to inform you that I reachd this place last Evening without delay or interruption; and that I find my Plate of the Battle of Bunker's Hill, finished in a manner perfectly satisfactory. I shall remain here a Week, that is until the 4th: I shall then go to Strasburg, and according to the accounts which I may have by the Newspapers, (which are received here regularly everyday,) I shall either go on to Paris, or go down the Rhine, by the Road which I have come. I hope your Reception will have been such as may justify my taking the former Route, as I have the most earnest Desire to see the National Museum in its present State.

I was very happy to see Mr. Gerry, the Evening after you left Rotterdam; I presume He overtook you before you reached Paris. I earnestly wish success to your Mission, and am Dear Sir, Your much Obliged friend & servant

JNO: TRUMBULL

From Timothy Pickering

Letterbook Copy, RG 59, National Archives

Sir Trenton, September 30, 1797

I think it was Mr. Lee[6] who left the following memorandum from you. "If there have been seizures of American goods in British bottoms let me know it."

No case has come to my knowledge but the one mentioned by Mr. Jefferson in his letter dated the 24th. of July 1793 to Mr. Genet. Holland & Mackie, citizens of the United States, had laden

5. John Trumbull (1756–1843) was an American artist then in London working on American claims arising from the agreements made in the Jay Treaty. Trumbull was combining private business and politics on his trip to Germany and France. See Carl Ludwig Lokke, "The Trumbull Episode: A Prelude to the 'XYZ' Affair," *New England Quarterly*, VII (1934), 100–114; Theodore Sizer, ed., *The Autobiography of Colonel John Trumbull: Patriot-Artist, 1754–1843* (New Haven, Conn., 1953), 216–220.

Trumbull addressed this letter to Pinckney only, in care of the Hotel de Grange Batteliêre in Paris. Pinckney showed it to JM upon receipt.

6. Charles Lee.

a cargo of flour on board a British vessel, which was taken by the French frigate Ambuscade and brought into Philadelphia. Mr. Jefferson claimed a restoration of the flour, on the ground that the shippers were ignorant of the declaration of war, when it was shipped. But Mr. Genet observed, that by the 14th. Article of the treaty of 1778, the plea of ignorance could not be urged after two months from the declaration of war, & Mr. Jefferson finding that this term had elapsed, by a few days, abandoned the claim. You will find this letter from Mr. Jefferson among the State papers published in 1793.[7]

I inclose five letters addressed to you and one to Mr. Gamble[8] which have been transmitted to me for conveyance, but of which the removal to this place has occasioned too long a detention. The removal was in consequence of the yellow fever having again visited Philadelphia. The mortality is not to be compared to that of 1793, owing partly to the early alarm and removal of multitudes of the inhabitants. The burials have been from ten to thirty in a day, for about a month past; but many of course, who were comprehended in those numbers, must have died of other diseases. Some of the inhabitants died in August of this malignant fever. It has also caused many deaths in Baltimore, chiefly at Fellspoint. It has appeared at Norfolk, and at Providence in the State of Rhode Island. The Physicians and others differ, as formally, in their opinions about its origin, and not less in respect to the proper mode of treating it; and on both questions the writings of some partisans appear as malignant as the disease.[9] I have the honor to be etc.

TIMOTHY PICKERING

To Timothy Pickering

LS, RG 59, National Archives

Dear Sir. Paris, October 2, 1797

On the 27th. of September we arrived in this City, and on the next day, in an unofficial manner by verbal message, we notified

7. Thomas Jefferson to Edmond Genet, July 24, 1793, Jefferson Papers, Library of Congress.

8. John Gamble. The letters to JM have not been located.

9. See Martin S. Pernick, "Politics, Parties, and Pestilence: Epidemic Yellow Fever in Philadelphia and the Rise of the First Party System," *WMQ*, 3d Ser., XXIX (1972), 559–586.

it to the Minister of Foreign affairs, and at the same time intimated that, as we expected our Colleague, in a few days, we wished to postpone the official Notification of our arrival until he joined us; the Minister signified his acquiescence, and said he thought it would be proper for us to wait for Mr. Gerry before we officially announced ourselves.[1] We remain with respect & Esteem, Dear Sir, Your most obedient Servants

CHARLES COTESWORTH PINCKNEY
J MARSHALL

Paris Journal

EDITORIAL NOTE

The "hastyly sketchd journal" that Marshall kept on his mission to France is the most important single document for analyzing the American view of the abortive XYZ mission.[2] Although the envoys' eight dispatches to Secretary of State

1. Gerry arrived on Oct. 4, and the envoys announced themselves to Talleyrand on Oct. 6, 1797.

2. JM to Timothy Pickering, Aug. 11, 1798, Pickering Papers, Massachusetts Historical Society. There are other documents that collectively give more information on JM's mission than the Journal. Foremost among the important documents are the dispatches and several of JM's private letters to Pickering and Charles Lee in the Diplomatic Dispatches, France, VI, RG 59, National Archives. An unidentified letterbook of all the dispatches is in the Franklin Collection, Yale University, but it probably is neither Gerry's nor Pinckney's personal copy of the dispatches. It might be JM's, but it is more likely an official letterbook, belonging to the joint commission, that was not sent to the State Department after Gerry left Paris in July 1798. Pinckney had a letterbook, now lost, that contained letters of his first mission to France and his mission with JM and Gerry. It was used by William Henry Trescot, *The Diplomatic History of the Administrations of Washington and Adams, 1789–1801* (Boston, 1857), ix, 87–88n, 172, 177, 180. In addition the Pinckney Family Papers, Library of Congress, contain much information on the mission.

Gerry's papers on the mission are more extensive than JM's or Pinckney's. There are at least three Gerry letterbooks with valuable information, although they often duplicate one another. One is at the Henry E. Huntington Library, and two are in the Gerry Papers, Lib. Cong. One of the Lib. Cong. copies, which was formerly owned by Annette Townsend, was published by Russell W. Knight; see Knight, ed., *Elbridge Gerry's Letterbook: Paris 1797–1798* (Salem, Mass., 1966). Other collections that contain material unavailable elsewhere are: Gerry Papers and Gerry-Knight Collections, Mass. Hist. Soc.; Gerry Papers, Pierpont Morgan Library; and Gerry Papers, Lib. Cong.

After his return from Paris, Gerry defended his conduct in a series of letters that, after the Journal, constitute a good source of information on the joint mission. See Gerry to Pickering, Oct. 1, 1798, Diplomatic Dispatches, France, VI, RG 59; Gerry to John Adams, Oct. 20 and Dec. 29, 1798, Adams Papers, Mass. Hist. Soc. In the middle of 1799, Gerry submitted to Adams two long defenses of his conduct. The first was Gerry to Adams, June 24, 1799, *ibid.* Enclosed in this letter were "Remarks on

Timothy Pickering also included critical information on the negotiations, these dispatches are not as complete or as detailed as the Journal, which is the only document that provides a continuous account of the mission's course. Marshall's Journal also provides a complete record of the conferences with French officials. Indeed, Pinckney and Gerry did not hesitate to insert large portions of the Journal in the public dispatches to the secretary of state. Also, as Marshall's private account of the mission, the Journal best reveals his attitude toward the negotiations.

Marshall was not required to maintain a journal, but because he viewed himself as the junior member of the commission, he might have considered record keeping a suitable task for himself. He may also have feared later controversy, and was therefore determined to keep a systematic record of the negotiations. Although it was not common practice for American diplomats to keep a journal, many did so. In the Paris negotiations in 1782 that ended the American Revolution, John Adams, John Jay, and Benjamin Franklin all kept private journals or diaries, and Jay later continued the practice, keeping a diary in England in 1794. But William Short and Thomas Pinckney, emissaries to Spain in 1794 and 1795, did not keep journals, nor did Charles Cotesworth Pinckney and Elbridge Gerry, who were with Marshall on the XYZ mission. Pinckney and Gerry were aware of Marshall's running account, however, although neither asked to make copies for their own records.[3]

The Journal is Marshall's record of negotiations that failed. Never received officially, the three envoys had only one conference with Talleyrand in which the terms of accommodation between France and the United States were considered. This conference resulted from Gerry's private and informal discussions, not from the efforts of the three envoys acting in unison, as Marshall noted with disdain.[4] The French government's refusal to receive him no doubt strengthened Marshall's belief that the Journal was a private document.

The bulk of the Journal records the approaches of the unofficial French agents, Nicholas Hubbard, Jean Hottinguer, Pierre Bellamy, and of Talleyrand's various secretaries, and their conferences with the American envoys. Other entries are notes of visits made by Americans in Paris who, perhaps at the instigation of Talleyrand, approached the envoys to assist the start of negotiations. The Journal's contents changed slightly when Marshall became involved in preparing the position papers that were delivered to Talleyrand in January and April of 1798.[5] While he was working on these papers, Marshall often allowed as much as a week to go by between entries, and his notations tended to be cryptic and uninformative. By the end of February the Journal again became more detailed as Marshall reported the debates among the envoys while they prepared for their one meeting

---

General Martial's letter of the 12th of Nov. & Mr. Pickering of the 10th of december 1798 to Mr. Gerry: respectfully submitted by the latter to the President of the United States" and "Remarks of Mr. Gerry on Mr. Pickering's report communicated to Congress on the 21st of January 1799 respectfully submitted by the former, to the President of the United States." The second was Gerry to Adams, July 8, 1799, *ibid.* Much of the material cited in this note covers the period after JM and Pinckney left Paris.

3. Adams to Gerry, Dec. 15, 1798, Free Library of Philadelphia; Gerry to Adams, Dec. 29, 1798, and June 24, 1799, Adams Papers.

4. See Journal, Feb. 26 and Mar. 1, 1798.

5. See American Envoys to Talleyrand, Jan. 17 and Apr. 3, 1798.

with Talleyrand on March 6. In the last part of the Journal, Marshall expressed his impatience to see the mission terminated.

In recording his own private negotiations with Caron de Beaumarchais in March and April, Marshall was more circumspect.[6] Although Beaumarchais was acting as an intermediary between Talleyrand and the envoys, Marshall agreed to informal discussions, despite his strong criticism of Gerry for doing the same with Talleyrand's private secretary, Louis Paul d'Autremont.[7] Moreover, Marshall left blanks when discussing Beaumarchais—the only instance in the journal of his trying to shield the identity of any person. Marshall apparently informed Pinckney, but not Gerry, of the conferences with Beaumarchais. Since Marshall was Beaumarchais's attorney for the latter's claim against the state of Virginia, perhaps Marshall did not believe it honorable to refuse to talk with him. More likely, Marshall's own hopes of accommodation with France led him to ignore the admonitions he had given his colleagues about the dangers of personal conferences with French agents.

The Journal does not record the social aspects of Marshall's diplomatic activities in Paris. Marshall did not write about his meetings with other Americans or Pinckney's and Gerry's meetings with various countrymen unless he believed the approach was instigated by Talleyrand.[8] He also did not mention an important dinner party with Talleyrand in Marshall's and Gerry's quarters.[9] In a later dispute with Gerry over a conversation at another dinner party, which included Talleyrand, Hottinguer, Bellamy, and Hauteval, Marshall had to rely on his memory to recall who attended the dinner, who talked to whom, and what was said.[1] Marshall had such respect for his landlady, Madame de Villette, that he accompanied her for a weekend at her chateau, but he gave no indication if he had any reason to believe that she had connections with Talleyrand.[2]

The Journal shows the increasing rigidity of Marshall's thought. In October he was willing to discuss the possibility of a loan to France.[3] After January 1798 he regarded the mission as hopeless and refused to consider proposals for a loan in any form. Marshall's increasing distrust colored his interpretations of all proposals to the extent that he accused Gerry of advising Talleyrand how to ask for a loan from the United States.[4] Certainly Marshall's own moral convictions stood in the way of his giving fair treatment to Gerry's viewpoint on separate negotiations.

When Marshall returned to the United States in June 1798, portions of his Journal that had been included in the envoys' dispatches to the secretary of

6. Fulwar Skipwith wrote that Beaumarchais, "of whose character you I know want no information," was their closest counsellor. Skipwith to [Thomas Jefferson], Mar. 17, 1798, Wolcott Papers, XII, Connecticut Historical Society.

7. See Journal, Feb. 4, 10, 26, Mar. 13, 14, and 26, 1798.

8. Skipwith to [Jefferson], Mar. 17, 1798, Wolcott Papers, XII; William Short to Jefferson, Aug. 6, 1800, Gilpin Papers, Historical Society of Pennsylvania; Joel Barlow to A. Baldwin, Mar. 4, 1798, Barlow Papers, IV, Harvard University.

9. See Journal, Dec. 31, 1797; Gerry to Adams, July 8, 1799, Adams Papers.

1. See JM to Pickering and JM to Gerry, Nov. 12, 1798.

2. See American Envoys to Nathaniel Cutting, Feb. 27, 1798; Mary Pinckney to Margaret Manigault, Mar. 9, 1798, Manigault Family Papers, University of South Carolina.

3. See American Envoys to Pickering, Nov. 8, 1797.

4. See Journal, Mar. 1, 1798.

state had already been published. The Journal entries for December 17 and 18, 1797, had been printed by order of Congress under the title "Extract from General Marshall's Journal."[5] But despite widespread knowledge of the Journal, no demand developed for further publication from it. Marshall received no written inquiries about the Journal from any correspondent except Secretary of State Pickering.

Upon returning to Philadelphia, Marshall agreed to leave the Journal with Pickering, who wanted a copy. As secretary of state, Pickering had copies of all diplomatic papers made for his personal use, and he assigned clerks in the State Department to transcribe the Journal. Pickering's original intentions are not wholly clear, but by the time he returned the Journal to Marshall four months later, at least one of his motives was explicit. "I deemed it important in another point of view," Pickering wrote Marshall. "The President ought to be acquainted with Mr. Gerry's whole conduct."[6] Marshall questioned, but did not veto, Pickering's plans. "I have ever been & still am unwilling that my hasty journal which I have never even read over until I receivd it from you, should be shown to him [John Adams]," Marshall wrote. "This unwillingness proceeds from a repugnance to give him the vexation which I am persuaded it would give him."[7] Such a gentle admonition could hardly deter the vituperative Pickering, who had earlier expressed hopes that Gerry would be guillotined in France.[8] After Adams read the Journal, he showed it to Gerry, but neither of them, surprisingly, made a copy.[1] Gerry argued that the Journal was not official and in any case not very informative, since the envoys had rarely met after January. Gerry added that he would explain to Adams orally "such parts of the curious Journal of General Marshal relating to myself."[2] By the time Gerry completed his voluminious and convoluted defense of his conduct, Adams had appointed a new commission to France composed of William Vans Murray, Oliver Ellsworth, and William R. Davie. The debate over the previous mission faded as Americans waited for the second mission to France to embark.

When Adams dismissed Pickering in May 1800 for continued obstruction of the president's foreign policy, Pickering took his copy of Marshall's Journal with him to his home in Salem. In an era when the boundary line between public and private documents was unclear, Pickering's action was not unusual or even noticed by his successor as secretary of state, John Marshall. Because scholars since that time have relied on Pickering's copy of Marshall's Journal, the fidelity of this copy to the original must be considered. The portions of the Journal included in the envoys' dispatches to the secretary of state can be checked against the passages in Pickering's copy. This material, which constitutes approximately 25 percent of the Journal, includes all of the important conferences but that of October 20, 1797, an omission that Marshall noted.[3] Except for a few minor changes,

5. See *Message of the President of the United States to both Houses of Congress, April 3, 1798* (Philadelphia, 1798), 60–62.

6. See Pickering to JM, Oct. 19, 1798.

7. See JM to Pickering, Nov. 12, 1798.

8. Pickering to Rufus King, June 19, 1798, Pickering Papers.

1. Pickering to Adams, Dec. 11, 1798, Adams Papers; Adams to Gerry, Dec. 15, 1798, Free Lib. Phila.; Gerry to Adams, Dec. 29, 1798, Adams Papers.

2. Gerry to Adams, Dec. 29, 1798, Adams Papers. The quote is from Gerry to Adams, June 24, 1799, *ibid.*

3. See Journal, Oct. 21, 1797.

Pickering's copy appears to be remarkably faithful to what we know of the contents of Marshall's original Journal. Pickering, furthermore, took care to set off in brackets any words he inserted, no matter how minor. In almost all cases the insertions were for clarity. Where Marshall left a blank for Beaumarchais's name in the original Journal, Pickering inserted Beaumarchais's name in brackets. He did this only after Pinckney informed him that JM indeed left blanks where he should have inserted Beaumarchais's name.[4] Another check on Pickering's copy can be made by comparing it with a portion of the Journal that Gerry's secretary inadvertently copied into one of Gerry's letterbooks.[5] In this comparison, Pickering's copy and the Gerry letterbook correspond perfectly.

More than a century later, when Albert Beveridge prepared his biography of Marshall, he asked Worthington C. Ford if Pickering's copy of the Journal could be trusted. Ford, who had long experience with State Department manuscripts, replied that he could think of no reason to suspect Pickering of tampering with the text. Ford surmised that the State Department clerks transcribed the Journal with the expectation of putting it into the files of the State Department.[6] After comparing the Pickering copy with all other contemporary evidence, the editors believe the integrity of the copy appears to be beyond reasonable doubt, with the possible exception of the passage of *ca.* December 2, 1797, which the editors have noted in annotation to the Journal.

The fate of the original Journal is unknown. In the 1830s Marshall told Henry Lee, Jr., who had asked about the Journal, "I believe no copy of the dispatches of the Envoys of whom I was one is now to be found except in the volumes of state papers published by the government." He added, "Our dispatches, which were laid before Congress and published contain all the information it would be in my power to give relative to our communications with the Directory or its agents. I did indeed keep a journal in which was inserted our various conversations with the agents of Mr. Talleyrand."[7]

After the first copies were made, no one appears to have used the original Journal during Marshall's lifetime. In the 1820s, when James Austin was writing a biography of his father-in-law, Elbridge Gerry, he used the Pickering copy of the Journal for his account of the XYZ mission.[8] Almost fifty years after Marshall's death, his great-granddaughter, Sallie E. Marshall Hardy, described some papers in her possession that apparently included the original Journal. "He kept a journal of all that transpired and copies of letters, from which it is easy to see why the mission was fruitless. His handwriting is plain, easy to read, very indicative of the character of the man, as is the simple signature, J. Marshall, to all the papers, placed between Pinckney's and Gerry's."[9]

In the first decade of the twentieth century, historians Waldo Leland and

4. See note at Journal, Mar. 13, 1798.

5. Marginal note for Mar. 3, 1798, Gerry Letterbook, Huntington Lib.

6. Worthington Ford to Albert Beveridge, May 19, 1914, Beveridge Papers, 199, Lib. Cong. On Beveridge's work on JM, see John Braeman, *Albert J. Beveridge: American Nationalist* (Chicago, 1971), 227–231, 244–249, 254–258, 263–269.

7. JM to Henry Lee, Jr., Jan. 29, 1832, Marshall Papers, Lib. Cong.

8. James T. Austin, *The Life of Elbridge Gerry: From the Close of the American Revolution*, II (Boston, 1829), 218.

9. Sallie E. Marshall Hardy, "Chief-Justice John Marshall," *Magazine of American History*, XII (1884), 67.

William Dodd planned to publish Marshall's papers and conducted a systematic search for manuscripts among his descendants. After talking to Mrs. Hardy, Leland wrote Dodd, "Mrs. Hardy has a copy of the Z Y Z [*sic*] papers in Marshall's hand."[1] Leland was unable to get copies of Mrs. Hardy's Marshall documents, however, and when Albert Beveridge, on the advice of William Dodd, asked for copies from Mrs. Hardy, he too was refused on the grounds that the owner was herself intending to write a biography of Marshall. Three years later J. Franklin Jameson asked Beveridge to approach Mrs. Hardy again, in hopes of obtaining her Marshall manuscripts for the Library of Congress, but Beveridge refused to have any further dealings with her.[2] Since that time the original Journal has evidently disappeared. Waldo Leland seems to have been the only scholar to have seen the original manuscript.

Marshall's Journal, as transcribed by State Department clerks, contains not only a vivid, detailed account of the negotiations but also the author's reactions to Europe. Marshall expressed in the Journal his profound dismay at the conduct of the French government. The Directory, which relied on military force to maintain itself in power, had destroyed the French constitution and had exiled many deputies without trial. In the Foreign Office under Talleyrand, bribery had become commonplace. Diplomats in Paris could feel little security. The Portuguese ambassador, Araujo, had been imprisoned and then sent into exile, and Marshall himself repeatedly faced threats of expulsion. The United States and its citizens in Paris were treated with contempt. Ominous warnings from Bellamy and Beaumarchais indicated that the United States would suffer the fate of Venice if it refused to cooperate with France. Given these circumstances, it is little wonder that Marshall became rather self-righteous in the Journal. In the course of the negotiations Marshall redefined his notion of United States independence to mean no compromise with France and, if possible, a lasting isolation of the United States from Europe. His sense of honor had been offended; his personal morality insulted. Marshall returned to the United States a chastened man with an abiding distaste for the French Revolution.

Paris Journal

Copy, Pickering Papers, Massachusetts Historical Society

[*ca.* October 4], 1797

On the 27th. September Genl. Pinckney & my self reached Paris. The next day we notified unofficially our arrival to the Minister of foreign affairs & at the same time signified to him that our collegue Mr. Gerry was on the continent of Europe & was daily expected on which account we were desirous of postponing our entrance on the objects of our mission till we should be joind by him. The Minister expressed his satisfaction at our doing so.[3]

1. Waldo Leland to William Dodd, Apr. 30, 1906, Dodd Papers, V, Lib. Cong.
2. Beveridge to J. Franklin Jameson, Jan. 31, 1916, Beveridge Papers, 206.
3. The first paragraph was probably written at the same time as the dispatch from JM and Pinckney to Pickering, Oct. 2, 1797.

Every day brought to us the complaints of Americans whose vessels had been captured & condemned. By appeals & other dilatory means the money had been kept out of the hands of the captors & they were now waiting on expences in hope that our negotiations might relieve them.

On the night of the 4th. of October Mr. Gerry joined us.

October 5, 1797

We immediately signified the arrival of Mr. Gerry to the Minister of foreign affairs & requested to know when it would be agreeable to receive a letter informing him officially of our arrival, he replied the next day at 12 o'clock. The next day at 12 Major Rutledge waited on him with a letter announcing ourselves to him officially & requesting that he would inform us at what time he would receive us with a copy of our letters of credence. This mode is deemed more respectful than to transmit a copy of the letters of credence & was therefore adopted.[4] We supposed it probable that we should be received immediately but Major Rutledge returned with the information that the minister would see us at his House which is his office on the 8th. at one o'clock.[5]

October 8, 1797

We waited on the Minister precisely at one & were told that he was with the directory & had requested that we would come again at three. At three we again attended after & waiting about ten minutes (during which time the Minister of Portugal[6] was with Mr. Talleyrand) we were admitted into the audience chamber. General Pinckney presented him with a copy of our letters of credence which he read & informed us that the Directory had required a report concerning the existing relations between the two republics on which he was then employed & which woud be finished in two or three days after which its further intentions with respect to us woud be made known.[7] We asked whether cards of

4. For a more detailed description, see JM to Charles Lee, Oct. 12, 1797.

5. Talleyrand lived at 471 rue de Bac, the official residence of the French foreign minister, which was only three blocks from the envoys' apartments.

6. Le Chevalier Antonio de Araujo de Azevedo (1752–1817), later conde da Barca.

7. This report is undoubtedly "Mémoire sur les Relations entre la France et les Etats-Unis de 1792 à 1797," Sept. 1797, Désagés, XXXVI, Archives of the Ministry of Foreign Affairs, Paris. See William Stinchcombe, "Talleyrand and the American Negotiations of 1797–1798," *Journal of American History*, LXII (1975), 575–590; Stinchcombe, ed., "A Neglected Memoir by Talleyrand on French-American Relations, 1793–1797," American Philosophical Society, *Proceedings*, CXXI (1977), 195–208.

hospitality were necessary & were told that they were & that we should be supplied with them. The cards express our characters as ministers plenipotentiary from the United States. The residue of the conversation which continued about fifteen minutes was perfectly unimportant. The Minister in his manners was polite and easy.

October 11, 1797

Nothing further from the minister. Mr. Church an American I believe *by birth*, who had been consul of France, at Lisbon came on a visit to Mr. Gerry who not being at home he with his son called on me.[8] He told me that he had just had a conversation with Mr. Payne[9] who informed him that a plan for some general system concerning neutral powers, which would be extremely advantageous to the United States if adopted, was before the Directory, & advised strongly that we should not urge the objects of our mission at present. He said the present was a most unfavorable moment, & that if we advanced hastily all woud probably be lost. I thanked him for his communications and asked him what the plan was? He said that he had seen but was not just then at liberty to communicate it, but that I might be assured our true policy was, to wait for events. I told him that we brought with us all the sollicitude of our country for a reconciliation with France, & that we could not hurry the Directory, but that the critical situation of our merchants whose vessels were captured, was such that our duty coud not permit us to be inattentive to it. He left me. In the night we received a letter from Mr. Payne inclosing his plan for an unarmd neutrality with his observations on it.[10] This letter made very different impressions on us. I thought it an insult which ought to be received with that coldness which would forbid the repetition of it. Mr. Gerry was of a contrary opinion. He urged that Mr.

8. Edward Church (1740–1816) had been U.S. consul at Lisbon; his son was Edward Church, Jr. Both had resided in Paris for a number of years. Thomas Bulkely succeeded Church as consul in July 1797.

9. Thomas Paine (1737–1809), author of *Common Sense* and *The Age of Reason*, was in Paris after having been released from prison through the aid of James Monroe, former U.S. minister to France. Still active in French-American relations, Paine had advised Talleyrand to receive the American envoys with "a *civil signification of reproach*." See Paine to Talleyrand, Sept. 28, 1797, Correspondance Politique, Etats-Unis, XLVIII, Arch. For. Aff. Paine, in a later letter to Talleyrand, outlined his ideas on what the American government should do to secure an accommodation with France. See Paine to Talleyrand, Sept. 30, 1797, *ibid.* On Paine, see Philip S. Foner, ed., *The Complete Writings of Thomas Paine*, 2 vols. (New York, 1945).

10. See Paine to American Envoys, Oct. 11, 1797.

Payne was in favor with the Directory; that by attention to him we should draw out the views & intentions of the government with respect to America; that by a contrary conduct we might irritate & might be held up as unfriendly to France, whose haughty government might, without hearing us, decide on a war against our country. I, on the contrary, stated my conviction that the proposition was not made without the knowledge of the government & that our answer would be communicated to it: that in the present state of our affairs no policy coud be more mischievous than to create by any means in the government of France an expectation that America woud consent to the adoption of a system which we knew she woud not & could not adopt. That her disappointment would produce more irritation than she woud feel if negotiations were commencd on those calculations only which the public measures of our Government authorized. That the aspersions on our government in a letter addressed to us ought to be receivd in a manner which woud mark our disapprobation of them. That a contrary conduct had contributed very much to produce our present embarassments. Genl. Pinckney thought our answer ought not to be so cold & repulsive as I recommended, or such as Mr. Gerry advisd. The next day he produced the answer which was sent.[11] I proposed to amend it by striking out the words are *thankful for* & inserting will *be properly attentive to*. Mr. Gerry would not agree to it & I gave it up without any further contest. The letter was signed & sent.

October 14, 1797

The minister held a confidential conversation with Mr. Osmont[12] in which he told him that the Directory had decided to demand from us explanations concerning some matters contained in the Presidents speech & not to receive us unless those explanations were satisfactory; that he found the Directory excessively exasper-

11. See American Envoys to Paine, Oct. 12, 1797.

12. Antoine-Eustache, baron d'Osmond (1754–1823), was Talleyrand's personal secretary, though he was paid from ministerial funds, and served in that capacity until 1815. See Stinchcombe, "WXYZ Affair," *WMQ*, 3d Ser., XXXIV (1977), 597.

Talleyrand had a number of secretaries, and none of the American envoys spelled the secretaries' names consistently. The other secretary who had the most extensive contact with the envoys was Louis Paul d'Autremont (1770–*ca.* 1840), who had been in the United States and had traveled back to Europe with Talleyrand. D'Autremont had two brothers who remained in the United States and owned land near Angelica, N.Y. In the Journal and the dispatches, d'Autremont's name was constantly spelled "Dutrimont." For Talleyrand's staff, see *ibid.*, 597–599.

ated against us for which he was extremely sorry & that he had endeavoured in vain to soften them. These observations were communicated to Major Mountflorence, & by him to Genl. Pinckney.[13] Afterwards the Minister mentioned this conversation to the same gentleman & told him that it was purely confidential & therefore ought not to be hinted to any person. Mr. Osmont immediately gave this information likewise to Major Mountflorence with whom we drank tea this evening & he as immediately gave it to Genl. Pinckney. On our return Genl. Pinckney communicated it to us & we had a conference concerning it. It was agreed that the Minister must have intended the conversation for us but that as it came in a form which did not require any apparent attention we woud, not notice it.

October 15, 1797

We read the Presidents speech[14] & were of opinion that explanations coud only be demanded on the conclusion which states his determination to adhere to the system already adopted & to the engagements already made.

We have had several conversations on the extraordinary silence of the Government concerning our reception. The plunder of our commerce sustains no abatements the condemnations of our vessels are pressed with ardor, all the means which have been usd to keep the money out of the hands of the owners of privateers are exhausting & our reception is postpond in a manner most unusual & contemptuous. I urge repeatedly that we ought in a respectful

13. James Cole Mountflorence was an assistant and business partner of Fulwar Skipwith (1765–1839), the U.S. consul general in Paris until 1799. A Frenchman by birth, Mountflorence had fought in the American Revolution, serving as an aide to William R. Davie (1756–1820), a member of the second American commission to France in 1799 and 1800. After the Revolution, Mountflorence was admitted to the North Carolina bar and practiced law until 1791, when he moved to France to be a land agent for William Blount, of North Carolina. See Blount to John Adams, June 3, 1797, Mountflorence to Alexander Martin, Mar. 19, 1797, Martin to Adams, June 30, 1797, and Recommendations and Applications during John Adams's Administration, RG 59, National Archives.

Mountflorence hoped to succeed Fulwar Skipwith as consul general. Skipwith resigned because of his active involvement with James Monroe and his thinly veiled support for Thomas Jefferson in the presidential election of 1796. See Skipwith to James Causten, June 30, and Dec. 28, 1828, Causten-Pickett Papers, V, Library of Congress. While in Paris, JM and Pinckney depended on Mountflorence for contacts in the city, while Gerry relied on Skipwith. See Skipwith to Jefferson, Mar. 17, 1798, Wolcott Papers, XII, Connecticut Historical Society; Pinckney to Pickering, June 13 and 22, 1797, Diplomatic Dispatches, France, V, RG 59; Samuel M. Hopkins's letter in *Pennsylvania Gazette* (Philadelphia), Feb. 11, 1799.

14. Adams's speech of May 16, 1797, *Annals of Congress*, VII, 54–59.

communication to the minister, displaying at the same time the sincerity & ardor of our wishes for a cordial reconciliation with France to pray for a suspension of all further proceedings against American vessels untill the further order of the Directory. In this I woud not be precipitate, but we have already permitted much time to pass away we coud not now be chargd with precipitation & I am willing to wait two or three days longer but not more. France would be content that we shoud remain silent, so long as the season for privateering lasts. The existing state of things is to France the most beneficial & the most desirable, but to America it is ruinous. I therefore urge that in a few days we shall lay this interesting subject before the minister, if in the mean time we receive no further communications from him.

Mr. Gerry is of a contrary opinion. He apprehends that by hurrying we shall irritate the Government. He states further that France experiences a difficulty in taking its ground with respect to us from which difficulty she woud be relieved by any movement on our part & that she might take umbrage at any proposition we might make and break off the negotiations in such manner as to cast blame on us. But in the address I propose I would say nothing which coud give umbrage, & if, as it is to be feard, France is determind to be offended, she may quarrel with our answer to any proposition she may make or even with our silence.

Genl. Pinckney on this subject thinks with me but we are both anxious to proceed with the full assent of Mr. Gerry. We are restraind by a high respect for his opinions & by a wish to preserve unanimity in every thing.

October 17, 1797

Inteligence is this day received of a naval engagement between the British & Dutch fleets in which the latter has been totally defeated & almost destroyed.[15]

In the evening reports are brought to us that the Directory has surmounted some of its strongest objections to peace with the United States & that it was now without question that our differences would be accomodated.

October 18–[19], 1797[16]

We dined with Genl. Pinckney & in the evening a Mr. Hor-

15. JM was referring to the battle of Camperdown, Oct. 11, 1797, in which the British scored a decisive victory over the Dutch.

16. It is clear from the contents that the entry covered two days.

tinguer a native of Switzerland who has been in America called on him.[17] They retird into a private room & after some time Mr. Hortinguer took his leave. Genl. Pinckney stated to Mr. Gerry & my self as the conversation which had passed, that Mr. Hortinguer informd him he came with a message from Mr. Talleyrand. On being requested to proceed, he said that Mr. Talleyrand was extremely sollicitous to accomodate the existing differences between the two countries but that some of the members of the Directoire were highly exasperated at the speech of the President of the United States to Congress & required that it should be disavowed. That he Mr. Hortinguer, had had a confidential conversation with a merchant of Hamburg who was the intimate & confidential friend of Talleyrand & who had directed him to communicate to Genl. Pinckney what the minister had communicated to him, & which if acceded to by us would form the basis of a treaty between the two nations to negotiate which we should be publicly receivd.[18] It was absolutely required that we should give satisfaction to the honor of France wounded by the speech of the president, that we should pay the debts due by contract from France to our citizens that we should also pay for the spoliations committed on our com-

17. Jean Conrad Hottinguer was X of the XYZ agents. Although Hottinguer was born in Switzerland, he did not claim Swiss citizenship when he was suspected by the French government of conspiring to emigrate to Great Britain in 1793. In a statement to the police, Hottinguer said that he had married an American, Martha Elizabeth Redwood (1774–1838), of Newport, R.I. See Sept. 1793, F 7, 4722, Archives Nationales, Paris; Romuald Szramkiewicz, *Les Régents et censeurs de la Banque de France nommés sous le Consulat et l'Empire* (Geneva, 1974), 168–176.

An agent for the Georgia Agricultural Company, Hottinguer had gone to the United States to survey Georgia lands he had purchased from Robert Morris. He had previously met Pinckney in Amsterdam. See American Envoys to Pickering, Oct. 22 and Dec. 24, 1797; Pieter Jan van Winter, *Het aandeel van den Amsterdamschen handel aan den opbouw van het Amerikaansche Gemeenebest*, II (The Hague, 1933), 337–344. Hottinguer was well known to Morris and James Markham Marshall; the latter was in constant contact with Hottinguer concerning business matters. Stinchcombe, "WXYZ Affair," *WMQ*, 3d Ser., XXXIV (1977), 602–603, 607.

18. Pierre Bellamy (1757–1832) conducted informal negotiations for Talleyrand throughout Europe in 1797 and 1798. Wherever Bellamy entered negotiations, reports of bribes flourished. He attempted to extract a bribe from Great Britain, and Araujo, of Portugal, informed William Vans Murray that Bellamy had approached him, demanding money. Araujo indicated that Bellamy was a speculator and adventurer. See John Trumbull to Gerry, [Jan. 1798], Trumbull Papers, Lib. Cong.; Rufus King to American Envoys, Dec. 23, 1797; Dec. 23, 1797, Notebook, King Papers, LXXIII, New-York Historical Society; July 6 and 13, 1798, Commonplace Book, Murray Papers, Lib. Cong.; Journal, Feb. 20, 1798; William Wickham to George Hammond, Feb. 16, 1798, F.O. 27/53, Public Record Office. See Bellamy's defense of his role, June 25, 1798, Correspondance Politique, Etats-Unis, Supplement, II. See also Stinchcombe, "WXYZ Affair," *WMQ*, 3d Ser., XXXIV (1977), 599–605.

merce for which France should be adjudged liable by commissioners to be appointed as in the British treaty & that we should make a considerable loan to an extent not defind in the proposition.[19] Besides this added Mr. Hortinguer there must be something for the pocket. On being asked to explain himself he said that there must be a considerable sum paid for the private use of the Directoire & minister under the form of satisfying claims which did not in fact exist.

This extraordinary communication was fully discussd among ourselves, both this evening and the morning of the 19th. I was decidedly of opinion & so expressed myself that such a proposition could not be made by a nation from whom any treaty short of the absolute surrender of the independence of the United States was to be expected but that if there was a possibility of accomodation to give any countenance whatever to such a proposition would be certainly to destroy that possibility, because it would induce France to demand from us terms to which it was impossible for us to accede. I therefore thought we ought so soon as we could obtain the whole information to treat the terms as inadmissible & without taking any notice of them to make some remonstrance to the minister on our situation & on that of our countrymen. Genl. Pinckney without expressing himself so fully was as decidedly of opinion that such propositions ought not to be considerd as the basis for negotiation as I was. We all agreed that we could not at any rate commit ourselves by saying any thing to such informal propositions which might be denied by the minister & that the business of the douceur was of a very wonderful nature, but we could agree no further. Mr. Gerry contended that we could not understand the propositions & could not decide what was proper to do concerning them, that the success of the whole negotiation depended on what we should now do, that it would entirely be broken off if such an answer was given as I had hinted & there would be a war between the two nations. After considerable discussion it was at length agreed that Genl. Pinckney should see Mr. Hortinguer again & endeavor to obtain fuller details of the plan & should also request him to converse with us all together. This was done. The General returnd & told us that Mr. Hortinguer would put on paper the outlines of his proposition & bring it with him at 6 o'clock this evening.

19. This refers to art. 7 of the Jay Treaty. Samuel Flagg Bemis, *Jay's Treaty: A Study in Commerce and Diplomacy*, 2d ed. rev. (New Haven, Conn., 1962), 463–466.

At six Mr. Hortinguer came & left with us the first set of propositions.[20] The person of note who had the confidence of the Directoire he said was Talleyrand. The amount of the loan he could not ascertain precisely but understood it would be according to our ability to pay. The sum which would be considered as proper *according to diplomatic usage* was about 1200,000 Livres. He could not state to us what parts of the Presidents speech were excepted to but said he would enquire & inform us.

October 20, 1797

We were informd that a Mr. Bellamy a genevoise now residing in Hamburg but in Paris on a visit was the confidential friend of Mr. Talleyrand & instead of communicating with us through Mr. Hortinguer would see us himself. We appointed this evening at 7 to meet him in my room.

We again discussed the conduct we were to observe & I again urgd. the necessity of breaking off this indirect mode of procedure. Genl. Pinckney joined me in thinking that the propisitions were inadmissible & that to countenance them was to cut off every hope of a real & proper accomodation of differences. Mr. Gerry reprobated precipitation, insisted on further explanations as we could not completely understand the scope & object of the propositions & conceived that we ought not abruptly to object to them but might lay them before our government. Genl. Pinckney & my self urged that they were beyond our powers & that if they were not they amounted to a surrender of the independence of our country & to a departure from our neutrality. No impression however was made.

At 7 o'clock Mr. Bellamy & Mr. Hortinguer came in & the first mentioned gentleman being introduced to us as the confidential friend of Mr. Talleyrand immediately stated to us the favorable impression of that Gentleman towards our country, impressions which were produced by the kindness & civilities he had personally received in America. That he was extremely sollicitous of repaying these kindnesses by his good offices with the Directoire to aid us in the present negotiation. That the Directoire not having received us or authorized Mr. Talleyrand to have any communication with us he could not see us himself but had authorized his friend Mr. Bellamy to state to us certain propositions which if acceded to by us as the principles which should form the Basis of the

20. See Statement, Oct. 19, 1797.

proposed treaty, we should signify such assent to him & he would communicate it to Mr. Talleyrand who would then intercede with the Directory to receive us & to open the negotiations. He stated explicitly that he was cloathed with no authority that he was not even a frenchman but that he was the friend of Mr. Talleyrand & trusted by him.

Mr. Bellamy then took out of his pocket a french translation of the Presidents speech the parts of which objected to by the Directory were marked, which he read & stated to us at large the sense of the Directory concerning it & what was positively required from us. He dilated on the resentment of the Directoire. The demand on this point is in substance comprehended in the written paper left with us by him.[21] At half after nine we parted & it was agreed that we should all breakfast with Mr. Gerry at nine the next morning. We again consulted the course of conduct we should pursue. I pressed strongly the necessity of declaring that the propositions were totally inadmissible & that was it even otherwise it was impossible for us to signify our assent to proposals which might afterwards be denied because the persons who made them produced to us no authority which could in any degree bind the government of France: that it was derogatory from the honor & wounded the real interests of our country, to permit ourselves while unacknowledged to carry on this clandestine negotiation with persons who produced no evidence of being authorized by the Directoire or the Minister to treat with us. Mr. Gerry was quite of a contrary opinion & the old beaten ground about precipitation etc. was trodden once again. Genl. Pinckney advocated decidedly the same opinions with myself & we determind that the next morning should positively put and end to these conferences.

October 21, 1797

The conversation is stated at large in our public letter.[22] On our retiring Mr. Gerry began to propose further delays & that we should inform them that we would take their propositions into consideration. I improperly interrupted him & declared that I would not consent to any proposition of the sort, that the subject was already considered & that so far as my voice would go I would not permit it to be supposed longer that we could deliberate on

21. The parts of Adams's speech of May 16, 1797, that offended the French government are included in American Envoys to Pickering, Oct. 22, 1797.

22. *Ibid.*

such propositions as were made to us. Genl. Pinckney declared the same opinion in the same decisive manner. After some little time I said that for the sake of unanimity & out of respect to the opinions of Mr. Gerry I would consent to a consultation of our government for which perpose I would myself immediately return to the U. States but on this express condition only that France should previously & immediately suspend all depredations etc. Mr. Gerry closed with this & I commited it to writing. He thought the expressions too strong & wrote himself the paper which we delivered in.[23]

October [22], 1797[24]

A Mr. Hauteval[25] whose fortune lay in the island of St. Domingo

23. JM was referring to a note by the American envoys composed after their conference with Bellamy and Hottinguer on Oct. 20, 1797. In the note, now lost, Gerry proposed that the negotiations on the propositions could not be discussed until the American envoys were received in their official capacities. Apparently this note was not delivered, and the note composed during the conference on Oct. 21, 1797, was much closer to JM's wishes than Gerry's. For Gerry's note, see Gerry to Pickering, Nov. 21, 1798, Gerry to Adams, June 24, 1799, Adams Papers, Massachusetts Historical Society; Gerry to Jefferson, Jan. 15, 1801, Russell W. Knight, ed., *Elbridge Gerry's Letterbook: Paris 1797–1798* (Salem, Mass., 1966), 74–79; James T. Austin, *The Life of Elbridge Gerry: From the Close of the American Revolution*, II (Boston, 1829), 195–196. For the note that was offered to Bellamy and Hottinguer, see American Envoys to Pickering, Oct. 22, 1797.

24. This entry was incorrectly dated Oct. 24, 1797. This was the only time JM or a clerk in the State Department made such an error. JM identified Lucien Hauteva, in such a way as to indicate that this was the first meeting Gerry had with Hauteval; the date of this meeting was given as Oct. 22, 1797, in American Envoys to Pickeringl Nov. 8, 1797.

JM and Pinckney were probably visiting St. Cloud when Hauteval called on Gerry. Mary Pinckney described a visit to St. Cloud with JM in her letter to Margaret Manigault, Oct. 22, 1797, Manigault Family Papers, University of South Carolina.

25. Lucien Hauteval was Z of the XYZ agents. He had been a resident of Santo Domingo until driven out by the upheavals of 1793. He first moved to Boston, where he became acquainted with John Quincy Adams (1767–1848) and with Gerry. By 1796 he was in Paris and, according to John Q. Adams, hoped to become French minister to the United States succeeding Pierre-Auguste Adet, who was recalled at the end of 1796. Apparently Hauteval knew Talleyrand and frequently submitted memoirs to the Foreign Office on French-American relations and the future policy for Santo Domingo. Hauteval, however, does not appear to have been one of Talleyrand's agents and cannot be connected with the demands for bribes or loans in the same way that Bellamy and Hottinguer can be. See John Q. Adams to Murray, July 17, 1798, Adams Papers; William Lee Diary, Mar. 20, 1796, Lee-Palfrey Papers, Lib. Cong.; Hauteval Mémoire, Feb. 5, 1796, Correspondance Politique, Etats-Unis, XLV; Hauteval to Talleyrand, June 1, 1798, *ibid.*, XLIX; Hauteval Mémoire, July 24, 1798, *ibid.*, L; Hauteval to John Adams, Aug. 26, 1798, Adams Papers; Joseph Pitcairn to King, June 21, 1798, King Papers, XXIX, N.-Y. Hist. Soc.; Talleyrand to the Directory, June 1, 1798, Correspondance Politique, Etats-Unis, XLIX; Stinchcombe, "WXYZ Affair," *WMQ*, 3d Ser., XXXIV (1977), 599.

JM later believed that Hauteval was "a conciliatory character. There are few

& who I believe is sincerely sollicitous of preserving peace between the two republics visited Mr. Gerry & made to him some statements of conversations which had passed between Mr. Talleyrand & himself in which the Minister expressed his wish for a reconciliation between the two countries & his surprize that we did not visit him. He gave too some distant hints of the same sort with those we had already heard.

October 23, 1797

Mr. Hauteval paid a visit to Mr. Gerry while Genl. Pinckney & my self were in company with him & the friendly temper of the Minister was again the subject of conversation. His wish to see us privately was stated & the propriety of visiting him was discussd. Mr. Hauteval declared that it was the wish of the Minister that we shoud call upon him—at private hours & further that the Minister desired this his wish to be communicated to us. We stated our having waited on him & his having told us that we should hear further from him when the Directory had decided on its course respecting us; that we had since heard nothing but had been treated in a manner extremely disrespectful to our country & both Genl. Pinckney & myself declared that in the existing state of things we could not wait on Mr. Talleyrand unless he should expressly signify his wish to see us & would appoint a time & place for the purpose. Mr. Gerry having known Mr. Talleyrand in Boston considered it as a piece of personal respect to wait on him & said that he would do so.[26]

October 23, 1797

Mr. Gerry returnd from his visit with out having seen the Minister, who was with the Directory.

October 26, 1797

In the evening peace with Austria was announced by the dis-

---

frenchmen who are as well disposd to our country—but yet he is devoted to Mr. Talleyrand." See JM to Pickering, Sept. 28, 1798.

26. Talleyrand visited Boston in 1794 and 1795 and must have met Gerry at that time. See Richard M. Brace, "Talleyrand in New England: Reality and Legend," *New England Quarterly*, XVI (1943), 399, 405; see also Edwin R. Baldrige, Jr., "Talleyrand in the United States, 1794–1797" (Ph.D.diss., Lehigh University, 1963); and Hans Huth and Wilma J. Pugh, eds. and trans., *Talleyrand in America as a Financial Promoter, 1794–96: Unpublished Letters and Memoirs*, American Historical Association, *Annual Report, 1941*, II (Washington, D.C., 1942).

charge of canon.[27] About 7 o'clock Mr. Bellamy calld on me. Genl. Pinckney & Mr. Gerry were at the opera. He brought with him the principal articles of the treaty which he read to me & spoke of them as astonishingly advantagious to France. It increased her force he said one fifth. Buonaparte he said had declared in his letter to the Directory that he was now ready to act against England. On this subject we had some conversation & he considered the situation of England as extremely perilous. Concerning America not a syllable was said on either side. He left me about eight. Mr. Gerry informed me on his return that he had received another message from Mr. Talleyrand by Mr. Hauteval expressing his wish to see him. It will not I think be very long before we hear from the Directory. We were informd that orders would be given for the capture of every neutral vessel.[28]

October 27, 1797[29]

About 12 we received another visit from Mr. Hortinguer. He immediately mentiond the great event announcd in the papers & then said that some proposals from us had been expected on the subject on which we had before conversed. That the Directory were becoming impatient & would take a decided course with regard to America if we could not soften them. Genl. Pinckney[30] answered that on that subject we had already spoken explicitly & had nothing further to add. He mentioned the change in the state of things which had been produced by the peace with the Emperor as warranting an expectation of a change in our system: Both Genl. Pinckney & Mr. Gerry answered[31] that this event had been expected by us & would not in any degree affect our conduct. Mr. Hortinguer urged that the Directory had since this peace, taken a higher & more decided tone with respect to us & all other neutral nations than had been before taken. That it had been determined that all nations should aid them or be considerd & treated

27. This refers to the Treaty of Campo Formio. For a brief description of French gains in the treaty, see R. R. Palmer, *The Age of Democratic Revolution: A Political History of Europe and America, 1760–1800*, II (Princeton, N.J., 1964), 302–310.

28. A modified version of the arrête was passed on Jan. 5, 1798. See American Envoys to Pickering, Jan. 8, 1798.

29. This entire entry is included in American Envoys to Pickering, Nov. 8, 1797. JM probably eliminated most of the personal references when he prepared the Journal for copying into the dispatch. All changes mentioned in the notes below were incorporated in the dispatch to Pickering, Nov. 8, 1797.

30. "We" is written above "General Pinckney."

31. "To which we only replied," is written above "Both Genl. Pinckney & Mr. Gerry answered."

as their enemies. Genl. Pinckney replied[32] that such an effect had already been contemplated by us as probable & had not been overlooked when we gave to this proposition our decided answer. Mr. Gerry told him[33] that we had no powers to negotiate for a loan of money. That our government had not contemplated such a circumstance in any degree whatever, that if we should stipulate a loan it would be a perfectly void thing & would only deceive France & expose ourselves. Mr. Hortinguer again expatiated on the power & violence of France: he urged the danger of our situation & pressd the policy of softening them & of thereby obtaining time. The present men he said would very probably not continue long in power & it would be very unfortunate if those who might succeed with better dispositions towards us should find the two nations in actual war. Mr. Gerry told him[34] that if war should be made on us by France it would be so obviously forced on us that on a change of men peace might be made with as much facility as the present differences could be accomodated. Genl. Pinckney told him[35] that all America deprecated a war with France but that our present situation was more ruinous to us than a declared war could be. That at present our commerce was plunderd unprotected but that if war was declared we should seek the means of protection. Mr. Hortinguer said he hoped we should never form a connection with Britain. Genl. Pinckney answered that he hopd so too,[36] that we had all been engagd in our revolution war & felt its injuries, that it had made the deepest impressions on us—but that if France should attack us we must seek the best means of self defense. Mr. H again returnd to the subject of money. Said he Gentlemen you do not speak to the point—it is money—it is expected that you will offer money. Genl. Pinckney[37] said we had spoken to that point very explicitly and had given an answer. No said he, you have not, what is your answer. Genl. Pinckney[38] replied it is No, No, not a sixpence. He again called our attention to the dangers which threatend our country & asked if it would not be prudent tho we might not make a loan to the nation to interest an influential friend in our favor. He said we ought to consider what

32. "We answered" is written above "Genl. Pinckney replied."

33. "And further" is written above "Mr. Gerry told him."

34. "We answered" is written above "Mr. Gerry told him."

35. "We added" is written above "Genl. Pinckney told him."

36. Above "Genl. Pinckney answered he hoped so too" is written "& we answered that we hoped so too."

37. "We" is written above "Genl. Pinckney."

38. "We" is written above "Genl. Pinckney."

men we had to treat with, that they disregarded the justice of our claims & the reasoning with which we might support them, that they disregarded their own colonies & considered themselves as perfectly invulnerable with respect to us. That we could only acquire an interest among them by a judicious application of money & it was for us to consider whether the situation of our country did not require that these means should be resorted to. We observed that the conduct of the French Government was such as to leave us much reason to fear that should we give the money it would effect no good purpose & would not produce a just mode of thinking with respect to us: Proofs of this must first be given us. He said that when we employd a lawyer we gave him a fee without knowing whether the cause could be gaind or not but it was necessary to have one & we paid for his services whether those services were successful or not. So in the present state of things the money must be advanced for the good offices the individuals were to render whatever might be the effect of those good offices. I[39] told him there was no parallel in the cases. That a lawyer not being to render the judgement could not command success, he could only endeavour to obtain it & consequently we could only pay him for his endeavours: but the Directory could decide on the issue of our negotiations. It had only to order that no more American vessels should be seizd & to direct those now in custody to be restored & there could be no opposition to the order. He said that all the members of the Directory were not disposd to receive our money, that Merlin for instance was paid from another quarter & would touch no part of the douceur which was to come from us.[40] Genl. P.[41] replied that we had understood that Merlin was paid by the owners of the Privateers & he nodded an assent to that fact. He proceeded to press this subject with vast perseverance. He told us that we paid money to obtain peace with the Algerines & with the indians & that it was doing no more to pay France for peace. Genl. Pinckney & Mr. Gerry both observed[42] that when our Government commencd a treaty with either Algiers or the indian tribes it was understood that money was to form the basis of the treaty & was its essential article, that the whole nation knew it & was prepared to

39. "We" is written above "I."

40. Merlin de Douai, former minister of justice, was at that time a member of the Directory.

41. "We" is written above "Genl. P."

42. "To this it was answered" is written above "Genl. Pinckney & Mr. Gerry both observed."

expect it as a thing of course, but that in treating with France our Government had supposed that a proposition such as he spoke of would, if made by us give mortal offence. He askd if our government did not know that nothing was to be obtaind here without money? *Genl. P*inckney[43] replied that our government had not even suspected such a state of things. He appeared surprized at it & said there was not an American in Paris who could not have given that information. Genl. P.[44] told him that the letters of our minister[45] had indicated a very contrary temper in the government of France & had represented it as acting entirely upon principle & as feeling a very pure & disinterested affection for America. He looked somewhat surprizd & said briskly to Genl. Pinckney well sir you have been a long time in France & in Holland—what do you think of it? Genl. P. answered that he considerd Mr. H & Mr. B as men of truth & of consequence he could have but one opinion on the subject.

He stated that Hamburg & other states of Europe were obliged to buy a peace & that it would be equally for our interest to do so. Once more he spoke of the danger of a breach with France & of her power which nothing could resist. I[46] told him that it would be in vain for us to deny her power or the sollicitude we felt to avoid a contest with it. That no nation estimated her power more highly than America or wished more to be on amicable terms with her but that our object was still dearer to us than the friendship of France which was our national independence. That America had taken a neutral station. She had a right to take it. No nation had a right to force us out of it. That to lend a sum of money to a belligerent power abounding in every thing requisite for war but money was to relinquish our neutrality & take part in the war, to lend this money under the lash & coercion of France was to relinquish the government of ourselves & to submit to a foreign government imposed upon us by force. That would we make at least one manly struggle before we thus surrenderd our national independence. That our case was different from that of one of the minor nations of Europe. They were unable to maintain their independence & did not expect to do so. America was a great & so far as

43. "We" is written above "*Genl. P*inckney." JM might have originally referred to Pinckney as *Genl. P*, and the clerk in the State Department who copied the Journal for Pickering probably wrote out Pinckney's name.

44. "We" is written above "Genl. P."

45. James Monroe.

46. "We" is written above "I."

concernd her self defence a powerful nation. She was able to maintain her independence & must deserve to lose it if she permited it to be wrested from her. That France & Britain had been at war for near fifty years of the last hundred & might probably be at war for fifty years of the century to come. That America had no motives which could induce her to involve herself in those wars & that if she now preservd her neutrality & her independence it was most probable that she would not in future be afraid as she had been for four years past—but if she now surrendered her rights of self government to France or permitted them to be torn from her she could not expect to recover them or to remain neutral in any future war. He said that France had lent us money during our revolution war & only required that we should now exhibit the same friendship for her. Mr. Gerry[47] answered that the cases were very different. That America sollicited a loan from France & left her at liberty to grant or refuse it—but that France demanded it from America & left us no choice on the subject. Genl. Pinckney & myself[48] told him there was another difference in the cases. That the money was lent by France for great national & french objects. It was lent to maim a rival & an enemy whom she hated. That the money if lent by America would not be for any american object but to enable France to extend still further her conquests. The conversation continued for nearly two hours, & the public & the private advance of money was pressed & repressd in a variety of forms. At length Mr. H said that he did not blame us, that our determination was certainly proper if we could keep it but he showed decidedly his opinion to be that we could not keep it. He said that he would communicate as nearly as he could our conversation to the minister or to Mr. Bellamy to be given by him to the minister I am[49] not certain which. We then separated.

October 28, 1797

Mr. Gerry paid a visit to day with Mr. Hauteval to Mr. Talleyrand. At half past six he sent for us & communicated to us what had passed. After being kept an hour in waiting he was introduced & Mr. Talleyrand told him the Directory had passed an Arrêté demanding from us disavowals explanations & satisfactions concerning the Presidents speech to Congress, which he held in his

47. "We" is written above "Mr. Gerry."
48. "We also" is written above "Genl. Pinckney & myself."
49. "We are" is written above "I am."

hand but did not read.[50] He also said that the Directory would require a loan from the United States. Mr. Gerry expressed the strong sollicitude of our Government for an accomodation with France, said that our powers did not extend to a loan but that the negotiation might proceed & that one of us would return to the United States to obtain instructions on that subject. That with respect to the Presidents speech it was necessary to recollect that the speech of Mr. Barras to our minister had very much insulted our government & that the constitutional duty of the president led to a communication of it to Congress.[51] That it was a subject on which we could say nothing. Mr. Talleyrand said that if we had not powers to make a loan we might assume them. That the Directory was accustomd to dispatch business in a few days & could not wait till we consulted our government. That the loan was an absolute sine qua non & would be insisted on even if we made the required concessions for our President & that he would hold up the Arrêté for a week in order to give us time to find out means which might prevent the directory from insisting on its being transmitted to us. On this being communicated to us in the pres-

50. Talleyrand's demand for an explanation of Adams's speech of May 16, 1797, was a tactic. Stinchcombe, "Talleyrand and the American Negotiations," *JAH*, LXII (1975), 584–586. Although this demand would be renewed from time to time (see Caron de Beaumarchais to JM, Jan. 17, 1798), it was dropped for the time being. There is no record of the arrête in the Archives of the Ministry of Foreign Affairs, Paris.

51. Paul François Nicholas, vicomte de Barras (1755–1829), was a member of the Directory and one of the persons instrumental in bringing Talleyrand into office in 1797. In his speech of May 16, 1797, Adams commented on Barras's speech of Dec. 30, 1796, delivered upon the departure of James Monroe as U.S. minister to France. The offensive passage in Barras's speech was: "The French republic expects, however, that the successors of Columbus, Raleigh, and Penn, always proud of their liberty, will never forget that they owe it to France. They will weigh in their wisdom the magnanimous friendship of the French people, with the crafty caresses of perfidious men, who mediate to bring them again under their former yoke." Dec. 30, 1796, *Amer. State Papers, Foreign Relations*, I, 747. For JM's treatment of the subject, see American Envoys to Talleyrand, Apr. 3, 1798.

Adams said in his speech of May 16, 1797: "The Speech of the President [Barras] discloses sentiments more alarming than the refusal of a Minister; because more dangerous to our independence and union; and at the same time studiously marked with indignities towards the Government of the United States. It evinces a disposition to separate the people of the United States from the Government; to persuade them that they have different affections, principles, and interests, from those of their fellow-citizens, whom they themselves have chosen to manage their common concerns; and thus to provide divisions fatal to our peace." May 16, 1797, *Annals of Congress*, VII, 56. A copy of Adams's speech in which the passage that offended the French is underlined is in Correspondance Politique, Etats-Unis, XLVII, under May 18, 1797. The copy of the speech is from the French paper in Philadelphia, *Courrier Français*, May 18, 1797.

ence of Mr. Hauteval Genl. Pinckney & myself declared that we had no means to arrest the Arrêté unless its injustice & impolicy could stop it & therefore it was perfectly unnecessary to sollicit a weeks suspension. That our situation opinions or powers could not change in a week & it would be to no purpose to practice further delays. We prayd Mr. Hauteval to see the minister to morrow & to inform him that unless there was a hope that the Directory itself might in the course of a week be prevaild on by reason to alter its Arrêté we did not wish to suspend it for an instant. We were as ready to receive it now as we should be eight days hence.

October 29, 1797[52]

Mr. Hortinguer again calld on us. He said Mr. Talleyrand was extremely anxious to be of service to us & had requested that one more effort should be made to induce us to enable him to be so. A great deal of the same conversation which had passd at our former interviews was repeated. The power & the haughtiness of France was again displayd to us. We were told that the destruction of England was inevitable & that the wealth & arts of that nation would naturally pass over to America if that event should find us in peace. To this observation Genl. Pinckney[53] answered that France would probably forbid America to receive them in like manner as she had forbid Switzerland to permit the residence in its country of a British minister. We told him also that we were sensible of the value of peace & therefore sought it unremitingly, but that it was real peace we sought for & real peace only which could be desirable.

The sum of his proposition was that if we would pay by way of *fees* (that was his expression) the sum of money demanded for private use the Directory would not receive us but would permit us to remain in Paris as we now were & we should be received by Mr. Talleyrand untill one of us could go to America to consult our government on the subject of the loan. These were the circumstances he said, under which the minister of Portugal had treated. We asked him if in the meantime the Directory would order the American property not yet passed into the hands of the privateersmen to be restored? He said explicitly that they would not. We askd him whether they would suspend further depredations

52. This entire entry, with the minor changes noted below, was included in American Envoys to Pickering, Nov. 8, 1797.

53. "We" is written above "Genl. Pinckney."

on our commerce? He said they would not but Mr. Talleyrand observd that on this subject we could not sustain much additional injury because the winter season was approaching when few additional captures could be made. We told him that France had taken violently from America more than 15,000,000 of dollars & treated us in every respect as enemies in return for the friendship we had manifested for her, that we had come to endeavour to restore harmony to the two nations & to obtain compensation for the injuries our country men had sustaind & that in lieu of this compensation we were told that if we would pay 1200,000 livres we might be permitted to remain in Paris which could only give us the benefit of seeing the plays & operas of Paris for the winter that we might have time to ask from our country to exhaust her resources for France whose depredations on us would be continued.[54] He again stated that by this procedure we should suspend a war & that perhaps in five or six months power might change hands. We told him that what we wished to see in France was a temper sincerely friendly to the United States & really disposed to do us justice. That if we could perceive this we might not so much regard a little money such as he stated to be usual although we should hazard ourselves by giving it. But that we saw only evidences of the most extreme hostility towards us. War was made upon us so far as France could make it in the present state of things & it was not even proposed that on receiving our money this war should cease. We had no reason to believe that a possible benefit could result from it & we desird him to say that we would not give a shilling unless American property unjustly captured was previously restored & further hostilities suspended & that unless this was done we did not conceive we could even consult our government concerning a loan. That if the Directory would receive us & commence negotiations & any thing occurd which renderd a consultation of the Government necessary one of us would return to America for that purpose. He said that without this money we shoud be obliged to quit Paris & that we ought to consider the consequences. The property of the Americans would be confiscated & their vessels in port embargoed. We told him that unless there was a hope of real reconciliation these evils could not be prevented by us & the little

54. The last phrase in this line might have been changed, because in American Envoys to Pickering, Nov. 8, 1797, it reads, "for France whose depredations would be continued." Without insertions above the line, the phrase in the Journal would have read, "for France depredations would continue."

delay we might obtain would only increase them. That our mission had induced many of our countrymen to trust their vessels into the ports of France & that if we remained in Paris that very circumstance would increase the number & consequently the injury which our countrymen would sustain if France could permit herself so to violate her own engagements & the laws of nations. He expressd a wish that Mr. Bellamy should see us once more. We told him that a visit from Mr. Bellamy as a private gentleman would always be agreeable to us, but if he came only with the expectation that we should stipulate advances of money without previously establish a solid & permanent reconciliation he might save himself the trouble of the application because it was a subject we had considered maturely & on which we were immovable. He parted with us saying if that was the case it would not be worth while for Mr. Bellamy to come. In the evening while Genl. Pinckney & myself were absent Mr. Bellamy & Mr. Hortinguer called & were invited by Mr. Gerry to breakfast with us the next morning.

October 30, 1797[55]

Mr. Gerry requested us to breakfast with him in company with Mr. Bellamy & Mr. Hortinguer. Immediately after breakfast the subject was resumed.

Mr Bellamy spoke without interruption for near an hour. He said that he was desirous of making a last effort to serve us by proposing something which might accomodate the differences between the two nations. That what he was now about to mention had not by any means the approbation of the Directory nor could Mr. Talleyrand undertake further than to make for us the proposition to the Directory & use his influence for its success. That last week Mr. Talleyrand could not have ventured to have offered such propositions but that his situation had been very essentially changed by the peace with the Emperor. By that peace he had acquired in a high degree the confidence of the Directory & now possessed great influence with that body. That he was also closely connected with Buonaparte[56] & the Generals of the army in Italy & was to be considered as firmly fixed in his post at least for 5 or 6 months. That under these circumstances he could undertake to

55. This entire entry, except for the concluding paragraph, is included in American Envoys to Pickering, Nov. 8, 1797.

56. Napoleon Bonaparte (1769–1821).

offer in our behalf propositions which before this increase of influence he could not have hazarded. Mr Bellamy then calld our attention to our own situation & to the force France was capable of bringing to bear upon us. He said that we were the best judges of our capacity to resist so far as depended on our resources & ought not to deceive ourselves on so interesting a subject. The fate of Venice was one which might befall the U. States.[57] But (he proceeded to observe) it was probable we might rely on forming a league with England. If we had such a reliance it would fail us. The situation of England was such as to compel Pitt to make peace on the terms of France. A variety of causes were in operation which made such an effect absolutely certain. To say nothing of the opposition in England to the minister & to the war, an opposition which the fears of the nation would increase, to say nothing of a war against England which was preparing in the north; An army of 150,000 men under the command of Buonaparte spread on the coast of France & aided by all the vast resources of his genius would most probably be enabled to invade England, in which event their government would be overturned, but, should this invasion not be absolutely effected yet the alarm it would spread through the nation the enormous expence it must produce would infallibly ruin them if it was to be continued & would drive them to save themselves by a peace: That independent of this France possessed means which would infallibly destroy their bank & their whole paper system. He said he knew very well it was generally conjectured that Buonaparte would not leave Italy & the army which had conquered under him & which adored him. He assured us nothing could be more unfounded than this conjecture. That Buonaparte had for more than ten days left Italy for Rastadt to preside over the congress which was formd for adjusting the affairs of the empire.[58] He said that Pitt himself was so confident of the absolute necessity of peace that after the naval victory over the Dutch he had signified his readiness to treat on the same terms which he had offered before that action. We could not then rely on the assistance of England. What he asked would be our situation if peace should be made with England before our differences with France would be accomodated? But he continued, if even

57. In the Treaty of Campo Formio, Oct. 18, 1797, France and Austria agreed to divide most of Venice's possessions. See Palmer, *Age of Democratic Revolution*, II, 302–310.

58. The Congress of Rastadt was established after the Treaty of Campo Formio to negotiate the cession of the left bank of the Rhine to the Directory by the Austrian Empire; the congress convened on Nov. 16, 1797.

England should be able to continue the war & America should unite with her, it would not be in our power to injure France. We might indeed wound her ally but if we did it would be so much the worse for us. After having stated the dangers attending us if we should engage in the war he proceeded to the advantages we might derive from a neutral *situation* & insisted at large on the wealth which would naturally flow into our country from the destruction of England.

He next proceeded to detail the propositions which are in substance in the paper annexed marked (A)[59] except that he insisted that we should engage to use our influence with our government for the loan. He stated expressly that the propositions were to be considerd as made by us, that Mr. Talleyrand would not be responsible for the success of any one of them, he would only undertake to use his influence with the Directory in support of them. The proposition he said concerning a suspension of *hostilities* on the part of France was one which proceeded entirely from himself. Mr. Talleyrand had not been consulted upon it & he could not undertake to say that that gentleman would consent even to lay it before the Directory. The proposition for an advance to the government of France of as much money as was due from it to our citizens on contract & as might be determined to be due for vessels improperly captured & condemned was he said indispensable. Unless we made that it was unnecessary to make any other for the others would not be received. He expatiated on the vast advantages we should derive from delay. It was he said absolutely to gain our cause. He returned to the danger of our situation & the policy of making with France any accomodation which France would assent to. Perhaps said he you believe that in returning & exposing to your country men the unreasonableness of the demands of this government you will unite them in their resistance to those demands. You are mistaken. You ought to know that the diplomatic skill of France & the means she possesses in your country are sufficient to enable her with the french party in America to throw the blame which will attend the rupture of the negotiations on the federalists as you term yourselves & on the british party as France terms you: And you may assure yourselves this will be done. He concluded with declarations of being perfectly disinterested & declared that his only motives for speaking thus freely were his

59. JM probably inserted "A" at a later time. The enclosure is not in the Journal, but it is in American Envoys to Pickering, Nov. 8, 1797.

friendship for Mr. Talleyrand & his wish to promote the interests & peace of the U. States.

We told him that the fredom with which he had spoken & which was agreeable to us would induce us to speak freely also & for once to accompany our view of the present state of things with a retrospect of the past. That America was the only nation upon earth which felt & had exhibited a real friendship for the republic of France. That among the empires round her which were compeled to bend beneath her power & to obey her commands there was not one which had voluntarily acknowledged her government or manifested for it spontaneously any marks of regard. America alone had steped forward & given the most unequivocal proofs of a pure & sincere friendship. At a time when almost the whole European world, when Austria, Germany, Prussia Russia Spain Sardinia Holland & Britain were leagued against France, when her situation was in truth hazardous & it was dangerous to hold even friendly intercourse with her, America alone stood forward & openly & boldly avowed her enthusiasm in favor of the republic & her deep & sincere interest in its fate. From that time to the present the government & people of the U States have uniformly manifested a sincere & ardent friendship for France & have as they conceive in no single instance given to this republic just cause of umbrage. If they have done so they wish it to be pointed out to them. After the determination of France to break off all regular intercourse with them they have sent three envoys extraordinary to endeavour to make such explanations as might produce a reconciliation. These envoys are prepared to investigate & wish to investigate any measures which may have given offense[; and are][60] persuaded that they can entirely justify the conduct of their government. To this distant, unoffending friendly republic what is the conduct & the language of France? Wherever our property can be found she seizes & takes it from us: unprovoked she determines to treat us as enemies, & our making no resistance produces no diminution of hostility against us: she abuses & insults our government, endeavours to weaken it in the estimation of the people, recalls her own minister refuses to receive ours & when extraordinary means are taken to make such explanations as may do away misunderstandings & such alterations in the existing relations of the two countries as may be mutually satisfactory &

60. Illegible; the material in brackets was supplied from American Envoys to Pickering, Nov. 8, 1797.

may tend to produce harmony, the envoys who bear these powers are not received they are not permitted to utter the amicable wishes of their country but in the haughty style of a master they are told that unless they will pay a sum to which their resources scarcely extend they may expect the vengeance of France & like Venice be erazed from the list of nations. That France will annihilate the only free republic upon earth & the only nation in the universe which has voluntarily manifested for her a cordial & real friendship. What impression must this make on the mind of America? If with out provocation, France was determined to make war upon us unless we purchased peace we could not easily believe that even our money would save us. Our independence would never cease to give offence & would always furnish a pretext for fresh demands. On the advantages of neutrality it was unnecessary to say any thing: all the efforts of our government were exerted to maintain it & we would never willingly part with it. With respect to a political connection with Britain we told him that America had never contemplated it. Whether the danger he represented that government to be in was or was not real we should not undertake to decide. Britain we believed had much reason to wish for peace & France had much reason to wish for peace also. If peace already existed it would not change the course which America would pursue.

Mr. Bellamy manifested the most excessive impatience. He interrupted us & said this eloquent dessertation might be true. America might have manifested & he believed had manifested great friendship for France & had just complaints against her but he did not come to listen to those complaints. That was not the course which the Directory was accustomed to take. The Minister would on our request make for us certain propositions to the Directory. He had stated them to us & all the answer he wishd was yes or no. Did we or did we not sollicit the Minister to make the propositions for us? We told him that without going further into the discussion we chose to remark one or two things. They were that the existing treaties gave to France certain advantages which were very essential. That especially the American coast afforded a protection near 2000 miles in extent to the prizes made by france on her enemies and refused that protection to the prizes taken from her. That she might be assured that in case of war these advantages would be lost for ever. We also told him we were convinced that France miscalculated on the parties in America. That the extreme injustice offerd to our country would unite every man against her. Mr. Hortinguer informed us that Mr. Talleyrand would not consent even to lay these propositions before the Directory without previously receiving the 50000 £[61] sterling or the greater part of it.

Mr. Bellamy left in writing his propositions & we returnd the answer annexed & marked (B).[62]

Previous to the commencement of these conversations Mr. Hubard & Mr. Willink arrived from Amsterdam. They informed us that they would answer our drafts & Mr. Willink especially said repeatedly touching his palm that there was but one way of doing any thing with this government. The day of their commencement Mr. Hubard informed Genl. Pinckney in my presence that Mr. Hortinguer was a man of truth & reputation & that any communications he should make might be relied on.[63]

November 1, 1797[64]

It was at length agreed for the second time that we would hold no more indirect intercourse with the government.

November 3, 1797[65]

Mr Hortinguer called on us & told Genl. Pinckney & myself (Mr. Gerry not being within) that Mr. Bellamy wished once more to see us. *We* answered that *we* should at any time be glad to see Mr. Bellamy as a private gentleman but that if his object was only to repeat his propositions for money it was perfectly unnecessary to do so because on that subject it was impossible for us to change the answer we had already given. We told him further that we considered it as degrading our country to carry on further such an indirect intercourse as we had for some time submitted

61. Probably because of an encoding error, American Envoys to Pickering, Nov 8, 1797, states that the amount demanded was £15,000. The code number for fifteen is 969, the number for a fifth is 970, and the number for fifty is 971. Furthermore, the sum mentioned earlier in the Journal is £50,000, as it is in American Envoys to Pickering, Oct. 22, 1797. Copies of American Envoys to Pickering, Nov. 8, 1797, Gerry Letterbook, Henry E. Huntington Library, and French Legation Book, Franklin Collection, Yale University, both give the amount as £50,000 rather than £15,000.

62. JM might have inserted this sentence at a later time. The enclosure is not in the Journal, but it is American Envoys to Pickering, Nov. 8, 1797.

63. JM was referring to the conversation between Nicholas Hubbard and Pinckney on Oct. 18, 1797. See American Envoys to Pickering, Oct. 22, 1797. Hubbard, an Englishman, was a junior partner in the Amsterdam banking firm Willink, Van Staphorst & Hubbard, the American government's European bank.

64. This entry was included in American Envoys to Pickering, Nov. 8, 1797, but the words "for the second time" were omitted.

65. This entry was included in American Envoys to Pickering, Nov. 8, 1797.

to & had determined to receive no propositions unless the persons who bore them had an acknowledged authority to treat with us. He said that perhaps Mr. Bellamy might have written powers from the minister & we replied that if he had we should receive his communications with pleasure. He spoke of a probable peace with England & having requested us to be at home in the afternoon left us.

About 3 o'clock he came & after some conversation in which we repeated in substance what is stated above he showed us a paper which was he said a copy of a letter prepared for us by Mr. Talleyrand requiring an explanation of part of the President's speech & which he said would be sent unless we came into the propositions which had been made us. We wished to take a copy of it which he declined permitting, saying he was forbiden to allow it. We spoke of the letter coming to us as a measure we had no expectation of preventing & he said he coud not understand that we wished it delayed to which we answered that the delay of a few days could not be desired unless a hope existed that the Directory might become more friendly to our country. He said that intelligence was received from the United States that if Colo Burr & Mr. Madison had constituted the mission the differences between the two countries would have been accomodated before this time; he added as a fact he was not instructed to communicate that Mr. Talleyrand was preparing a memorial to be sent over to the United States complaining of us as being unfriendly to an accomodation with France.[66]

We replied to his intelligence from the United States that the ministers correspondents in America took a good deal on themselves when they undertook to say how the Directory would have received Colo. Burr & Mr. Madison; & that with respect to the memorial of Mr. Talleyrand it would not be easy for him to convince our countrymen that the statements we should make were untrue. If however we were confident that our conduct would be condemned Mr. Talleyrand might be assured that the fear of censure would not induce us to deserve it but that we should act in a manner which our own judgements & consciences would approve of, & we trusted we should be supported by the great body of candid & honest men.

In this conversation we again stated that America had taken a

66. Stinchcombe, "WXYZ Affair," *WMQ*, 3d Ser., XXXIV (1977), 594.

neutral position, that she had faithfully sought to preserve it, that a loan of money to one of the belligerent powers was directly to take part in the war, & that to take part in the war against her own judgement & will under the coercion of France was to surrender our independence.

November 4, 1797

A conversation was held on the subject of writing to the minister & it was agreed that if we did not hear from him by the 8th. a letter should be prepared & sent to him calling his attention in the most respectful manner to our mission. This is a measure about which I had been for some time extremely sollicitous. It appears to me that for three envoys extraordinary to be kept in Paris thirty days without being received can only be designed to degrade & humiliate their country & to postpone a consideration of its just & reasonable complaints till future events in which it ought not to be implicated shall have determined France on her conduct towards it. Mr. Gerry had been of a contrary opinion & we had yielded to him but this evening he consented that a letter should be prepared.

November 5, 1797

Mr. Gerry appears again to be disinclined to write to the minister untill all our conversations already detailed should be put in cypher & six copies made out & sent by different conveyances to our government & our cypher & other papers either destroyd or in safety.[67] This would on a reasonable calculation require about two or three months.

November 6, 1797

Genl. Pinckney produced to us a letter marked ( ) from Major Mountflorence to which we agreed he should return an answer which is also annexed marked ( ).[68]

November 7, 1797

Major Mountflorence called on the minister & showed him the

67. The envoys did not destroy the cipher or send it out of the country at this time.

68. The parentheses might have been inserted later. Mountflorence's letter to Pinckney, Nov. 1797, has been lost, but for the answer, see American Envoys to Mountflorence, Nov. 6, 1797.

letter received from Genl. Pinckney telling him at the same time that we were much dissatisfied with him (Major Mountflorence) & extremely disgusted with our reception here. That we had said to him that we were the ministers of a republic wishing very earnestly to be on friendly terms with France, that we had come disposed & prepared to do her ample justice if we could be satisfied we had injured her & that we expected a similar disposition on the part of France: that we expected at least to have been heard & felt very sensibly the contempt manifested for our country through us. That we neither came to buy or beg a peace but to treat as an independent nation on the subjects of differences subsisting between us. Mr. Talleyrand expressd his regret that he should have subjected Major Mountflorence to any difficulty with us, said we ought to have called on him & conversed with him, that Lord Malmsbury & the minister from Portugal both did so but that the ministers from the United States were more haughty in their conduct than any other ministers near the republic & he beleived they did not wish to treat. That their business had been very unnecessarily delayed by their declining to come forward properly, that if they had seen him as they ought to have done their treaty might have been finished by this time. Major Mountflorence told him that the ministers of the United States complained that extraordinary delays were imposed on them, that when their letters of credence were delivered they were told they should receive an answer from the Directory, that they did not consider themselves, as at liberty to proceed untill they received that answer or were accredited as ministers. The minister replied that their cards expressd their quality.[69]

I had prepard a letter to Mr. Talleyrand & Genl. Pinckney requested a meeting to day upon it. Mr. Gerry had some particular

69. Talleyrand had become impatient with the American envoys for their refusal to accede to the bribe and loan demands. In November, Talleyrand asked Mountflorence, John Trumbull, and probably Joseph Pitcairn to intercede and plead with the envoys to pay the bribe so that the negotiations could begin. Trumbull, who left Paris in early November, informed Rufus King of a dinner conversation he had had with Talleyrand. "Trumbull dined with Mr. Talleyrand who said that our Envoys were slow, that they must come to some conclusion soon—that frenchmen were impatient, and decided as well as asked with proptitude. . . . Talleyrand said people who were going 3000 miles from home should act on discretion & that they should not be confined by Instructions. The conversation of Talleyrand confirmed the truth of the Proposition made in his name to the american Envoys, and discovered his impatience that they had not acceded to them." Nov. 1797, Notebook, King Papers, LXXIII, N.-Y. Hist. Soc.; see Stinchcombe, "WXYZ Affair," *WMQ*, 3d Ser., XXXIV (1977), 600–602.

engagements which induced him to wish a postponement of it until tomorrow.

November 8, 1797

We again pressed a meeting but could not obtain one untill the evening. In the course of the day a piece evidently from the administration reproaching us with delays & indicating the line of policy with which we had been privately threatened, was published in one of the papers. It is now in the power of the administration to circulate by means of an enslaved press precisely those opinions which are agreeable to itself & no printer dares to publish an examination of them. With this tremendous engine at its will it almost absolutely controls public opinion on every subject which does not immediately affect the interior of the nation. With respect to its designs against America it experiences not so much difficulty as ought to have been expected & as would have been experienced had not our own countrymen labored to persuade them that our government was under a British influence. On this subject a free press would go far in seting the public opinion right provided there were in France Americans who understood perfectly the relative political conduct of the two governments & were inclined to state it truly. In the evening I gave Mr. Gerry the letter I had prepared which is markd ( )[70] and requested his attention to it, so that it might be copied and sent the next day.

November 9, 1797

Mr. Gerry employed the day in a careful consideration and essential change of the letter which had been prepared. We went over his correction and having made some changes in it, directed it to be fairly copied and translated.[71]

November 10, 1797

The letter was copied and a person engaged who made the translation.

70. See American Envoys to Talleyrand, Nov. 11, 1797.

71. All the dispatches from the American envoys to Talleyrand were submitted in French and English. According to Pinckney, JM paid a Mr. Lannoy "for translations made on account of the Mission." See "The United States of America in Account with Charles Cotesworth Pinckney," Oct. 16, 1798, Records of Bureau of Accounts, RG 59. Mr. Lannoy was the tutor of Pinckney's daughter, Eliza. Mary Pinckney stated that five persons in the house were taking French lessons from Mr. Lannoy; so probably JM and his secretary, John Brown, were also taking French. See Mary Pinckney to Margaret Manigault, Nov. 5, 1797, Manigault Family Papers.

November 11, 1797

The letter with the translation were sent to the Minister. The letter is marked.[72]

November 21, 1797

Not having received any answer to our letter transmitted on the 11th Mr. Rutledge was requested to call on Mr. Talleyrand and enquire whether it had been laid before the Directory and whether any answer was given to it. He was informed by Mr. Talleyrand that the letter was laid before the Directory and would be answered so soon as instructions relative to it should be received.

ca. November 22–28, 1797

Mr. Pitcairn, an American, paid me a visit and informed me, that in a conversation with a very influential man whose name he was not at liberty to mention,[73] he had spoken of the Ministers of the United States, and had been requested to know what we would do; that in turn the gentlemen with whom he had conversed had promised to find out the sentiments of the Directory, and by comparing them to endeavour to bring about some accommodation. He asked me what he should say to this gentleman. I told him that the conduct of the United States and our own conduct had manifested the sincerity with which the Government and its Envoys wished the restoration of harmony with France. That it would be impossible for him to declare this wish in terms stronger than the truth would justify, that we were desirous of entering into the discussion of the mutual complaints of the two nations and were entirely disposed to do any thing which was conciliatory and could

72. After this entry the following notation appears in brackets: "No 3, p. 112 Negotiations." This refers to American Envoys to Talleyrand, Nov. 11, 1797, which was included in letter no. 3, American Envoys to Pickering, Nov. 27, 1797, and copied in Duplicate Diplomatic Dispatches, France, V, RG 59.

73. Joseph Pitcairn, of New York, had been appointed vice-consul for Paris but never assumed the post. Adams then appointed Pitcairn as U.S. consul in Hamburg, a post Pitcairn accepted in 1798. Pitcairn had probably been talking to Talleyrand, since he had lived next to Talleyrand in 1796 and knew him well. Because Pitcairn was previously acquainted with Pinckney, Talleyrand asked him to intervene to expedite the negotiations. See Pitcairn to King, Sept. 26, Nov. 3, 1796, and Aug. 3, 1797, King Papers, XXIX, N.-Y. Hist. Soc.; Pinckney to Pitcairn, Apr. 6 and June 15, 1797, Pitcairn Papers, Cincinnati Historical Society, Ohio.

JM apparently was not upset by Pitcairn's approach, since he and the other envoys later asked him to carry personal and highly confidential letters to King when Pitcairn made a trip to England in late December. See JM to King, Dec. 24, 1797.

be shown to be proper; But that we could not and would not make any explicit declarations with respect to particular demands which might be suggested but to a person authorized by the government of France to treat with us. A fews days afterwards Mr. Pitcairn mentioned the same subject to General Pinckney and spoke of a loan. He added that it had occurred to him that a loan might be some how effected in the way of the Dutch inscriptions. Genl. Pinckney told him he was not the first person to whom that had occurred, but that we were not authorized to make a loan in any form. He gave also the same answer concerning indirect negotiations which I had given.

ca. December 2, 1797

Mr. Gerry dined with Mr. Talleyrand. Mr. Bellami and Mr. Hottinguer were both of the party. After dinner Mr. Hottinguer again asked Mr. Gerry in direct terms whether we would now give the douceur which had before been mentioned. Mr. Gerry answered positively in the negative and the conversation dropped.[74]

December 14, 1797

Mr. Gerry and myself called on Genl. Pinckney and found Mr. Hottinguer with him. He said he was glad to see us together, that he had another message from Mr. Bellami, who wished to know

74. This entry describes an event that later became the center of an involved dispute over who attended the dinner and whether it was public or private. In a report to Congress, Pickering asserted that the dinner took place on Dec. 2, 1797. He must have used the Journal for his source, because the date is not mentioned in any of the correspondence. There is no corroborating evidence that the dinner took place on Dec. 2; it probably occurred before that date. See JM to Pickering, Sept. 15, 1798; Jan. 21, 1799, *Annals of Congress*, IX, 3531–3558.

Some pieces of circumstantial evidence about this entry are unsettling. The date is given as "about Dec. 2," which is the only time an indefinite date was assigned to any of the Journal entries. JM may have recalled the dinner only after Hottinguer's visit of Dec. 14, 1797, and Bellamy's of Dec. 17, 1797. See Journal, Dec. 14 and 17, 1797. In addition JM did not mention that Hauteval was at the dinner, although both JM and Gerry later stated that he had attended. Perhaps none of the American Envoys considered Hauteval to be connected with the bribe and loan demands and therefore they failed to mention him. See JM to Pickering, Sept. 15, 1798.

In all the controversy over the dinner, neither JM nor Pickering cited this passage in the Journal, which would have greatly supported JM's contentions. At the time Pickering first published a report of the dinner, JM did not have his Journal, but he had reread it before he answered Gerry's complaints. Pickering had both the original and the copy of the Journal at the beginning of the dispute and, given his vitriolic personal attacks on Gerry in public and private, it is difficult to determine when and, perhaps, by whom this entry was inserted in the Journal. See Pickering to JM, Oct. 19 and Nov. 5, 1798, JM to Pickering, Nov. 12, 1798, and JM to Gerry, Nov. 12, 1798.

whether we were willing again to see him on the same subject. Genl. Pinckney immediately answered that our sentiments respecting it were completely known and had been very explicitly given. Mr. Hottinguer replied that six weeks had elapsed since they were given and they might in that time be changed. We retired for a moment into another room and agreed that Mr. Hottinguer should be informed that if Mr. Bellami could produce a letter from Mr. Talleyrand or any document whatever shewing that he was authorized to treat with us on the part of the French Republic we would immediately enter into negotiations with him, but that unless he was so authorized we could not see him on the subject proposed. Mr. Hottinguer was called in and this determination communicated to him.[75]

December 17, 1797[76]

I stepped into Mr. Gerry's apartment where I saw Mr. Bellami. He expressed his regret at having been disabled to dine with us at Mr. de Beaumarchais by an inveterate toothach. He then asked me whether I had seen Mr. Beaumarchais lately? I told him not since he dined with us and that he had left us much indisposed. He then observed that he had not known until lately that I was advocate for that gentleman in his cause against the State of Virginia, and that Mr. de Beaumarchais in consequence of that circumstance had expressed sentiments of high regard for me. I replied that Mr. de Beaumarchais' cause was of great magnitude and very

75. Pinckney wrote to King explaining the meeting with Hottinguer in more detail. "We are not yet received and I think it is very probable we shall not. It is said Barras and Neufchateau are for receiving us and attempting to obtain money from us by negociation. Merlin and Reubell think it will be in vain and are for sending us away immediately. LaRevelliere is undecided. But the whole of them are undoubtedly hostile to our government and are determined if possible to effectuate a change in our administration and to oblige our present president to resign. With regard to our citizens here it is in contemplation to send away from France every American who cannot produce proof of an implicit approbation of the present measures of France and of a decided aversion to the administration of our government. Attempts are made to divide the envoys and with that view some civilities are shewn to M. G[erry] and none to the two others. I am in hopes such attempts will be without success. The American Jacobins here pay him great court.

"Since writing the above we have received another unofficial message from M. Talleyrand. Agreeable, [*we*] met the same persons as had formerly conversed with us without their being officially authorised. This we have again pointedly and unanimously refused declaring we would have no communication on the subject of our mission with persons not officially authorized to treat with us." Pinckney to King, Dec. 14, 1797, King Papers, Lib. Cong.

76. This entire entry was included in American Envoys to Pickering, Dec. 24, 1797.

uncertain issue and consequently that a portion of the interest he felt in it would very naturally be transferred to his Advocate. He immediately said (low and apart) that Mr. de Beaumarchais had consented, provided his claim could be established to sacrifice 50,000£. sterling of it, as the private gratification, which had been required of us, so that the gratification might be made without any actual loss to the American Government.[77] I answered that a gratification on any terms or in any form was a subject which we approached with much fear and difficulty, as we were not authorized by our Government to make one, nor had it been expected that one would be necessary, that I could not undertake to say (whether my colleagues would consent to it in any state of things but I could undertake to say) that no one of us would consent to it unless it was preceded or accompanied by a full and entire recognition of the claims of our Citizens and a satisfactory arrangement on the objects of our mission. He said it was in the expectation of that event only that he mentioned it. We parted and I stated this conversation to Genl. Pinckney who was disinclined to any stipulation of the sort and considered it as a renewal of the old reprobated system of indirect unauthorized negotiation. Having been originally the Counsel of Mr. de Beaumarchais I had determined and so I informed Genl. Pinckney, that I would not by my voice establish any argument[78] in his favor but that I would positively oppose any admission of the claim of any French Citizen if not accompanied with the admission of the claims of the American Citizens to property captured and condemned for want of a Role d'equipage. My reason for conceiving that this ought to be stipulated expressly was a conviction that if it was referred to Commissioners it would be committing absolutely to chance as complete a right as any individuals ever possessed. Genl. Pinckney was against admitting the claim at any rate. After my return Mr.

77. For JM's relationship with Caron de Beaumarchais, see Vol. II, 124–126. Bellamy later claimed that this offer to JM was part of JM's business dealings with Beaumarchais. See Bellamy's justification, June 25, 1798, Correspondance Politique, Etats-Unis, Supplement, II. A more likely explanation is that given to Pitcairn. "Mr. Bellamy now says that his proposal for Beaumarchais was simply to get the 100,000£ thro his hands—and that he was invited to it from having heard that Marshalls brother had bought one similarly situated for 50 per Cent." Pitcairn to King, July 6, 1798, King Papers, XXIX, N.-Y. Hist. Soc.; Stinchcombe, "WXYZ Affair," *WMQ*, 3d Ser., XXXIV (1977), 607. Bellamy knew from Hottinguer that James M. Marshall was seeking a loan to finance the Fairfax purchase.

78. The word "argument" has been changed to "agreement" in American Envoys to Pickering, Dec. 24, 1797. It seems likely that this is a copying error by one of the secretaries in Paris.

Gerry came into my room and told me that Mr. Bellami had called on him to accompany him on a visit to Mr. Talleyrand. That he proposed seeing Mr. Talleyrand and returning the civility of the dinner and endeavouring to bring about some intercourse between him and us.

December 18, 1797

General Pinckney and Mr. Gerry met in my room and Mr. Gerry detailed to us the conversation mentioned in our public letter.[79] We resolved that we would rigidly adhere to the rule we had adopted to enter into no negotiation with persons not formally authorized to treat with us, and requested Mr. Gerry to give that information to all who should apply and to state that we could not enter into any engagements for money. We came also to the determination to prepare a letter to the Minister of Foreign Relations stating the objects of our mission and discussing the subjects of difference between the two nations in like manner as if we had been actually received and to close the letter with requesting the Government to open the negotiation with us or to grant us our passports.[80] Mr. Gerry wrote a note to Mr. Bellami stating that he would by a given day in the next week give the answer of the Envoys to his last propositions.[81]

December 31, 1797

We had another meeting in my room at which it was again determined that we could give no money and that Mr. Gerry should make this determination known to those who should apply to him.[82]

79. For informal approaches made to all of the envoys separately to determine whether Americans would either pay a bribe or give France a loan, see *ibid.* The envoys believed separate approaches might have been designed to reveal the differences among them. A modified version of this entry is included in the dispatch to Pickering, Dec. 24, 1797.

80. At this time JM wished to terminate the negotiations and to demand passports. See American Envoys to Talleyrand, Jan. 17, 1798. JM changed his mind about demanding the passports and agreed to wait for a response from Talleyrand. See JM and Pinckney to Talleyrand, Feb. 26, 1798, and JM to Lee, Mar. 4, 1798.

81. Bellamy wrote a note to Gerry stating that he would meet him on Dec. 27, 1797. See Bellamy to Gerry, Dec. 26, 1797, Gerry Papers, Pierpont Morgan Library.

82. This conference might have been concerned with Bellamy's meeting with Gerry on Dec. 27, 1797. JM stated that the envoys discussed what Gerry should say, but Bellamy complained that his propositions concerning a loan were still unanswered two weeks later. See Journal, Jan. 15, 1798; Bellamy to Gerry, Dec. 26, 1797, Gerry Papers, Morgan Lib.

It is possible that the conference was provoked by Talleyrand's remarks at a dinner at JM's and Gerry's house the night before. This seems improbable, however, since

January 2, 1798

At my request Genl. Pinckney and Mr. Gerry met in my room and I read to them the first part of a letter to the Minister of Exterior Relations and which consists of a justification of the conduct of the American Government. It was agreed that Mr. Gerry should go over it and suggest such alterations and amendments as he might deem proper, after which it should be submitted to the consideration of Genl. Pinckney.[83]

January 10, 1798

The second part of the letter to the Minister of Exterior Relations, comprehending the claims of the United States upon France, being also prepared, I read it to General Pinckney and Mr. Gerry, this is to go through the same course of consideration with the first.

January 15, 1798

We had a long conversation with Mr. de Beaumarchais who informed us that Mr. Bellamy considered his propositions concerning money as being yet unanswered, and complained that Mr. Gerry practiced delays on the subject.[84]

January 20, 1798

Mr. Gerry informed me that he had had another conversation with Mr. de Beaumarchais which made it proper for him to see Mr. Bellamy and to do away any misunderstanding on the subject of money. He did see Mr. Bellamy, and on his return informed Genl. Pinckney and myself, that he had informed that gentleman positively that we could make no money negotiation whatever. I had so repeatedly pressed Mr. Gerry on the subject of our letter prepared for the Minister of Exterior Relations and manifested such solicitude for its being so completed as to enable us to send it, that I had obviously offended.[85] To-day I have urged that subject and for the last time.

Talleyrand had not yet personally advanced the propositions concerning a loan. At the same dinner Gerry reported that Talleyrand's principal secretary, probably Louis André, baron Pichon (1771–1850), informed him that the Directory would not negotiate with Pinckney. Stinchcombe, "WXYZ Affair," *WMQ*, 3d Ser., XXXIV (1977), 608–609.

83. See American Envoys to Talleyrand, Jan. 17, 1798.

84. Stinchcombe, "WXYZ Affair," *WMQ*, 3d Ser., XXXIV (1977), 608–609.

85. JM was referring to American Envoys to Talleyrand, Jan. 17, 1798. Though dated Jan. 17, the letter was not delivered until Jan. 31, 1798, as can be seen by the following two Journal entries.

January 22, 1798

Mr. Gerry finished the examination of our letter to the Minister of Exterior Relations.

January 31, 1798

Our letter has been translated, and was signed to-day, and committed to Major Rutledge to be delivered by him to the Minister of Exterior Relations.

Mr. Gerry is to see Mr. Talleyrand the day after tomorrow. Three appointments have been made by that gentleman, each of which Mr. Gerry has attended and each of which Mr. Talleyrand has failed to attend, nor has any apology for these disappointments been thought necessary.

February 1, 1798

Dupont de Nemours called on General Pinckney to-day and asked whether we had received any dispatches from our Government. He had just parted with Mr. Talleyrand.[86]

February 2, 1798

Mr. Gerry called on the Minister at the appointed hour, but he was with the Directory.[87]

Mr. de Beaumarchais called on us; after a good deal of conversation he told us that the Government would expect some step on our part. That it still supposed we would perceive our interests so clearly in a connection with France, that we would propose to make the pecuniary advances required from us. I prepared to-day a letter to the Minister remonstrating against the Decree of the Councils subjecting to confiscation all neutral vessels having on

86. Pierre Samuel DuPont de Nemours (1739–1817) was a friend of and a frequent caller on the Pinckneys. DuPont was connected politically and financially with Talleyrand and was one of the informal contacts with the American envoys. Mack Thompson, "Causes and Circumstances of the Du Pont Family's Emigration," *French Historical Studies*, VI (1969), 59–77. For a general treatment of his career, see Ambrose Saricks, *Pierre Samuel DuPont* (Lawrence, Kans., 1965).

87. Earlier in the day Gerry had written Pinckney that he wished to meet with JM and Pinckney before the envoys met with Talleyrand. Pinckney answered Gerry, making his position clear, "but lest any accident should prevent my seeing you, I beg leave to repeat that I adhere to the opinion that a prompt, immediate, & decisive Negative should be given to any proposition that may be made, or insinuation given to obtain money from us in any shape or under any pretense." Gerry to Pinckney, Pinckney to Gerry, Feb. 2, 1798, Pinckney Family Papers, Lib. Cong.

board any article coming out of England or its possessions. The letter closes – – with requesting our passports.[88]

February 3, 1798

One of the Secretaries of Mr. Talleyrand called on Mr. Gerry and made some slight apology for the last disappointment, in saying that Mr. Talleyrand had returned immediately after Mr. Gerry's departure and regreted not meeting with him. He added that they had received a very long letter from us concerning the purport of which he made enquiries (for they could not take the trouble to read it) and he added that such long letters were not to the taste of the French government, who liked a short address coming at once to the point.[89] He again engaged Mr. Gerry to see Mr. Talleyrand tomorrow at 11 o'Clock. A Frenchman has arrived who left the United States early in December and who was dispatched by the French Consul General to this Government.[90]

February 4, 1798

Mr. Gerry returned from his visit to Mr. Talleyrand and informed me that communications and propositions had been made to him by that Gentleman, which he was not at liberty to impart to Genl. Pinckney or myself. That he had also propounded some questions to the minister which had produced some change in the proposition from its original aspect. That he was to give an answer tomorrow or the day after, and that upon it probably depended peace or war.

This communication necessarily gives birth to some very serious reflections. From our first arrival there has been a continuing effort to operate on our fears. We have been threatened with a variety of

88. JM was trying to force the French government to receive the envoys officially or to break off negotiations. He failed to achieve either objective. Gerry refused to sign the letter, thus exposing the irrevocable split among the American envoys, but Pinckney and JM claimed that Gerry had previously agreed to sign the letter. After Gerry refused to sign, Pinckney sent the letter signed by himself and JM to King, who forwarded it to Pickering. See JM and Pinckney to Talleyrand, Feb. 26, 1798, JM to Lee, Mar. 4, 1798, and Pinckney to King, Mar. 14, 1798, King Papers, Lib. Cong.

89. This secretary was probably d'Autremont, who had many conversations with Gerry in the following months. On d'Autremont, see Journal, Oct. 14, 1797.

90. Joseph Philippe Létombe, the French consul general in Philadelphia, identified the messenger as Citizen Grand-Maison. This was probably A. J. Grand-Maison, a Frenchman who was living in New York City in 1795. See Létombe to Talleyrand, Dec. 21, 1797, Correspondance Politique, Etats-Unis, XLVIII; "List of French Citizens Residing in New York," Apr. 6, 1795, *ibid.*, XLV.

ills, and among others with being ordered immediately to quit France. This threat was pronounced three months ago and has not yet been executed. The most haughty and hostile conduct is observed towards us and our country and yet there appears to be an unwillingness to part with us or to profess the war which is in fact made upon us. The state of the contest between France and Britain affords the only probable solution for this enigma. This government is unwilling to act with respect to the United States, [as][91] either to withdraw them from its vengeance in case of a speedy and unsuccessful termination of the war with England, or to force [them][92] to enter immediately into that war when their strength by being allied to that of England could obtain some sort of respect.

The messenger dispatched by the Consul General at Philadelphia and lately arrived in Paris has probably brought with him accurate details of the state of parties in America. To judge from the addresses in answer to the President's Speech to Congress, I should think that if the French Government continues its hostility and does not relax some little in its hauteur its party in the United States will no longer support it. I suspect that some intelligence of this complexion has been received. Whatever may be the views of France with respect to the United States, whether she will be content to leave us our Independence if she can neither cajole or frighten us out of it, or will even endeavour to tear it from us by open war, there can be no doubt of her policy in one respect—she will still keep up and cherish, if it be possible to keep up and cherish, her party in the United States. Whether then she is disposed to treat rather than to part with us, or to part rather than treat with us, she will do the one or the other with a view to this her primary object. She will therefore endeavour to charge Genl. Pinckney and myself who have no foreign attachment, with a disinclination for an accomodation, and will endeavour to throw the blame on us which will attend the rupture of the negotiations, if they are to be broken off, and she will endeavour to give the credit of them to Mr. Gerry if they are to be entered upon. I am led irresistably by this train of thought to the opinion that the communication made to Mr. Gerry in secret is a proposition to furnish passports to General Pinckney and myself and to retain him for

91. Pickering's brackets.
92. Pickering's brackets.

the purpose of negotiating the differences between the two Republics. This in one event will furnish matter of triumph to those who would force our Government into a course it has not yet pursued, and in the other would leave the partizans of France this fruitful seed of discontent that if Genl. Pinckney and myself had been as friendly to the French Republic as Mr. Gerry an accomodation would have taken place and the miseries which may attend a war have been avoided.

There are yet other motives which might induce the Minister to make this proposition. I am firmly persuaded of his unwillingness to dismiss us while the war with England continues in its present uncertain State. He believes that Genl. Pinckney and myself are both determined to remain no longer, unless we can be accredited. I have even understood from Mr. Gerry, that he is of the same opinion, but I am persuaded the Minister does not think so. He would on this account as well as on another which has been the base of all propositions for an accomodation be well pleased to retain only one Minister and to chuse that one.

February 5, 1798

I saw General Pinckney and mentioned to him the suspicions I have detailed. He thought with me and we were both of opinion that we ought to make no sort of objection to the proposition but leave Mr. Gerry to act as his own judgement should dictate.[93] He returned me my draft of a final letter to the Minister with some slight amendment which will be copied and laid before Mr. Gerry. We shall both be happy if by remaining without us, Mr. Gerry can

93. Pinckney shared JM's impression of Gerry's decision to negotiate privately. "Every art is used by Talleyrand and the French Americans here to divide the Envoys, and if possible to detach Mr. Gerry from his colleagues. Confidential communications and proposals are made to him by Mr. Talleyrand, under injunctions to conceal them from us, and he considers himself as pledged to comply with this request. But I understand from a person," perhaps DuPont, "who is well acquainted with Talleyrand, that they would receive Gerry, if he would consent to act without us; but I believe it is clogged with a stipulation, that money in the form of a loan is to make the basis of a treaty. I understand, after having taken time to consider these propositions, he has declined them. Money and the direction of American measures I am convinced is their object. To obtain these ends, they mean to exert themselves to keep up their party in America, and their attention and offers to Mr. Gerry are upon a supposition, that he belongs to that party. I am in hopes he will be firm; but he does not appear to me to be so decided for demanding our passports as he was before. I however still think he will act properly. In every public measure we have yet adopted we have been unanimous, but he is habitually suspicious; and hesitates so much, that it is very unpleasant to do business with him." Charles Pinckney to Thomas Pinckney, Feb. 22, 1798, Pickering Papers, Mass. Hist. Soc.

negotiate a treaty which shall preserve the peace without sacrificing the independence of our country. We will most readily offer up all personal considerations as a sacrifice to appease the haughtiness of this Republic.

February 6, 1798

I delivered to Mr. Gerry to-day the draught I had prepared on the subject of the decree and of our passports and pressed his immediate attention to it. He has had to-day a conference with Mr. Talleyrand the result of which is secret and to-morrow he is to have another.

February 7, 1798

Mr. Gerry has had another private conference with Mr. Talleyrand. We know not what propositions have been made. Mr. Gerry says that upon his decision respecting them probably depends peace or war. That he has rejected one proposition and that he has been considering another which is in some degree modified in consequence of some statements he has made. Of the propositions rejected or modified we know nothing except that Mr. Gerry says they are perfectly new. It must be presumed that he is considering the base of an accomodation between the two Governments. I have stated to him my apprehension that no base will be offered consistent with the Independence of the United States, and that the present extraordinary negotiation is only to prevent our taking decisive measures until the affairs of Europe shall enable France to take them. I have pressed him on the subject of our letter concerning the Decree but he has not yet read it.[94]

February 10, 1798

The private intercourse still continues. Last night after our return from the Theatre Mr. Gerry told me, just as we were separating to retire each to his own apartment, that he had had in the course of the day a very extraordinary conversation with Mr. Dutrimont[95] (a Clerk of M. Talleyrand) which he was not at liberty to communicate; I answered that I did not wish to hear it and was proceeding to my chamber, when he added he was at liberty as from himself to consult Genl. Pinckney and myself again on the

94. JM wrote a letter to Talleyrand protesting the French decree of Jan. 5, 1798, which prohibited any trade with Great Britain by neutrals. Gerry refused to sign the letter. See Pinckney and JM to Talleyrand, Feb. 26, 1798.

95. Louis Paul d'Autremont.

subject of money. I replied that he knew very well it was perfectly unnecessary to consult us on that subject: We had given our ultimate decision upon it more than once. He said he knew it and had so expressed himself both to Mr. Talleyrand and to Mr. Dutrimont, but that Dutrimont in this last conversation had informed him that Talleyrand withheld his (Mr. Gerry's) answer from the Directory but we should be ordered off in four and twenty hours and wished to give us further time for reflection. When this secret business first commenced I thought it my duty to tell Mr. Gerry that I was firmly convinced of the determination of this Government not to leave us our independence but to force us into the situation of her other allies: that all negotiation on their part would have that object in view and that a reconciliation on other terms was unattainable, but that the Government was unwilling to drive us into defensive measures during the present posture of their affairs with England. That its wish was to continue us in an humble state of dependent solicitation whilst it preserved a haughty and an angry distance which would leave it at perfect liberty to exercise its vengeance on us and our Country while we should not have it in our power to reproach France even with duplicity of conduct. I was therefore decidedly of opinion that the object of the present communication was only to amuse us still longer and to prevent our taking those measures which would produce unequivocal explanations on the part of France. Mr. Gerry was not pleased with those sentiments; he said I could not judge of the propositions as they were not known to me and that he had a very different opinion concerning them. I told him it was true I knew nothing of the particular propositions, but I thought I knew something of the general objects of the government and of every man in it respecting our Country, and I did not doubt that every proposition must comport with those objects. Mr. Gerry was a little warm and the conversation was rather unpleasant. A solicitude to preserve harmony restrained me from saying all I thought on the occasion, and from repeating the same ideas continually to him. I could not however avoid saying when he told me of this conversation with Dutrimont, that if we could effect no good I wished very much that the Directory would order us off, but that I was entirely pursuaded their only view was still to play upon and amuse us.

February 14, 1798

To-day Mr. Gerry returned the rough draught of the letter to the Minister with some amendments. It is now under copy and will be given tomorrow to the translator. Mr. Gerry stated in conversation that an advance of money from us was an indispensable [measure][96] on our part, without which no treaty would be made.

February 18, 1798

I signed the letter which is now fully prepared and offered it to Mr. Gerry to sign which he declined. It was not our object to send it under three or four days nor[97] until we should have enquired for an answer to our former letter, but I was desirous of having it entirely completed so as to send it whenever we should chuse. To-day Major Rutledge applied at the Office of foreign affairs for an answer to our letter, but it being Decadi[98] the Minister was not visible.

February 19, 1798

Major Rutledge again waited on Mr. Talleyrand and was informed that there was no answer to our letter (that the Directory had made no arrêté concerning it.) Mr. Talleyrand proceeded to state to him that our powers were too limited, that we ought to have come prepared to advance the money, that our Government had reason to expect that such a demand would be made upon us, and that there was a very strong party in America who were in favor of it. He also mentioned that we ought to take 600 shares in the loan on Britain.[99]

February 20, 1798

Mr. [1] having understood that we were making preparations to leave Paris called on us about 8 o'clock in the evening. Mr. Gerry was not at home. He asked me with much apparent uneasiness concerning our departure. I did not think it proper to tell him that we contemplated the demand of our passports, but I signified that affairs were in such a train as to induce us to suppose that this Government would soon send them to us, in which event

96. Pickering's brackets.

97. The words "and not" are crossed out, and "nor" is inserted above the line.

98. The French revolutionary calendar divided the year into twelve 30-day months, with 5 complementary days from Sept. 17 to Sept. 21. Each month was divided into 10-day segments with *décadi* falling on the 10th, 20th, and 30th of each month. Feb. 18, 1798, was 30 Pluviôse, An VI, in the French calendar.

99. This was the loan to aid the financing of the projected invasion of Great Britain. JM gave more information on the progress of this loan in JM to George Washington, Mar. 8, 1798.

1. Caron de Beaumarchais. See note at Journal, Mar. 13, 1798.

we chose to be prepared to set out on our return so soon as they should be received. He told me that I might be assured that no orders of that sort would be given. That Mr. Bellamy had averred to him that no measures would be taken respecting us or our affairs till his return from Geneva where he is now sent on some private mission, that this Government still counted on our lending money, that our interests led so strongly to an accomodation with France, it was still hoped we would take this only measure to effect it.[2] He then proceeded to say that the only objection which could exist to our making an advance of money was the apprehension of Britain, who with its superior Naval force might be considered by us as more formidable than even France; that Britain without doubt would complain of such a step, but she would not dare to declare war against us: that in the present state of her commerce the consumption of her manufactures in the United States was too important an object for her to lose while it was possible for her to preserve it. On this subject therefore America might be perfectly at ease, for however England might be irritated at the measure she could not make war in consequence of it: that it behoved us on the other side to consider the consequences of our refusal. France most certainly would not forgive it. The descent on England would be attempted and most probably would succeed. What then would be the situation of the United States? England revolutionized would be in the condition of Holland and the Cisalpine Republic, Its fleet would be at the disposition of France, and as well as that of Spain, Holland and Venice might be used against America; That in that event too France would monopolize the commerce of the world as England does at present: It behoved us as *wise* men, trusted by our Country at a distance of more than a thousand leagues to balance these evils well in our minds and to take such measures as would secure the peace of our nation. He also stated the losses we should sustain by the hostilities on our commerce which would certainly continue. I answered that we were perfectly aware of the dangers with which we were environed and were anxious to avoid them, that our Government and ourselves had manifested the most sincere wishes for the preservation of the

2. According to William Wickham, the British secretary of war, Bellamy was in London. Wickham described Bellamy as a "man of abilities clever artful and intriguing." Wickham to George Hammond, Feb. 16, 1798, F.O. 27/53, P.R.O. Bellamy stated he left Paris on Feb. 7, 1798, for two months. See Bellamy's justification of his conduct, June 25, 1798, Correspondance Politique, Etats-Unis, Supplement, II.

friendship of France, that one object only was more dear to us and could not be sacrificed to it, that was our national liberty and independence. If it was a mere question concerning the loss of so much money, if for example the throwing into the Sea the sum demanded by France would of itself prevent all further contest I did not believe there would be any difficulty in doing it; but I could see no end to the demands of this Republic as now made. The only foundation to support those demands were the wants of the nation; those wants would continue and the last shilling of America would not supply them. So soon as one loan was made another might be demanded and we should be still less in a situation to refuse it. I asked him what security we could have that this would not be the case? He said we could have none—but at the same time we could not be certain it would happen and if it did we could refuse to make further advances: I did not think it proper or necessary to go into the argument and therefore assured Mr. [3] that no step would be taken rashly or inconsiderately by us. That however impracticable a loan of money might be we should not take other measures but on the most mature reflection. He expressed with much warmth his attachments to America and his belief that he should endeavour to fix his family and himself in that Country.

February 26, 1798

Mr. Dutrimont, Clerk of Mr. Talleyrand, paid Mr. Gerry a visit yesterday morning and in the evening at six o'clock Genl. Pinckney came by appointment to hold a consultation on the subjects of our mission to this Republic. Mr. Gerry stated to us that Mr. Dutrimont had informed him that perhaps a loan to be stipulated now and paid after a peace should take place between France and Britain might produce an accomodation between the two Governments. He said he did not know that France would accept it but seemed to suppose she would.

General Pinckney declared that a loan in any form was not only beyond but contrary to our powers and that he could not consent to make it. That if we stipulated a loan to be paid in future France would raise money on our stipulation so that it would be to engage actually in the war by furnishing aid to one of the belligerent powers. He said it was the same proposition in essence which had been so often rejected although it had assumed a form somewhat dif-

3. Caron de Beaumarchais. See note at Journal, Mar. 13, 1798.

ferent. I was of the same opinion with Genl. Pinckney and for the same reasons to which I added that we could not even consider this as a proposition from the French Government. That independent of the total want of authority in Mr. Dutrimont which we had so often determined to be a sufficient objection to this sort of negotiation he did not himself pretend to say that he was empowered inofficially to make such a proposition or that it would be acceptable to his Government. I could therefore only enquire whether we ought to offer such a loan in the existing state of things. I had no hesitation in saying that we ought not.

Mr. Gerry supported the proposition very decidedly. He said that he would not pretend to urge any thing in favor of its justice, he admitted that it was perfectly unjust as was the whole conduct of this government towards America: but that we ought to consider the Actual state of things and do that which would conduce most to the interest of the nation. That France had acquired a mass of power never before possessed by any single nation and used that power with a pride and haughtiness never before exhibited by any Government. That if we went to war with her it would cost us at least 200,000,000 and would involve us in miseries and dangers which were incalculable; that we ought to consider whether it would not be true widsom to stand in the *gap* between our Country and France and prevent a war by the stipulation to lend 8 or 10.000.000. when there should be peace between France and England; that by doing so we should save immensly in point of pecuniary calculation, and indeed should lose nothing as the resources of this country were such as to secure its repayment according to the terms which might be stipulated; That by a contrary course of conduct we should lose all the property unlawfully captured and should incur the expenses and dangers of a dreadful war with the most formidable power on earth. That he did not understand our instructions as forbidding us to make the loan, but if they were not sufficient to authorize it one of us ought to return in order to represent the state of things fully to our government and receive orders which should regulate our conduct. He offered to go and to leave Genl. Pinckney and myself in Parris. He added that the loan might be made under an express stipulation not to be used during the war. I told Mr. Gerry that if the real question was a question whether the payment of any sum of money France had required of us, provided such payment involved no other consequences than the mere loss of the money, would certainly prevent a war, I could have no hesitation in deciding that true policy and economy would direct the payment of the money. But that in my judgement a loan under the actual circumstances of our Country would amount to a surrender of our national independence, and further that the proposition he supported would not in my opinion secure us from war. I stated that neither the interest or inclination of America led to a loan of money to either of the beligerent powers. That France had made an unprovoked war upon our commerce as a mean by which to force our Government into measures it disapproved of and deemed highly injurious, that if thus under the leash we adopted the system pressed on us by France, we ceased to mark out our own line of conduct, we no longer acted for ourselves according to our own will but according to the will of France. That in addition to this consideration I was of opinion that the proposition was thrown out for the purpose of amusing us still longer and not with any serious intention of a solid and permanent accommodation. That the conduct of France had manifested an extreme hostility towards the United States accompanied with an indisposition to part with us during the uncertain state of the war with England. That four months past a haughty demand of money had been made upon us accompanied with a thundering threat that in case of refusal we should be ordered out of France; we had refused but the threat had not been executed: It had been repeated three times but had never been executed. This demonstrated the object of the Government to be to keep us here in our present abject state while every species of hostility should be practiced on our country, until France should be in a situation to strike us effectually, and then she could without a charge of duplicity execute whatever her resentments might dictate. That if she found that by varying her informal propositions ever so little she might still keep us here entrapping our countrymen, We need not doubt that she would continue to act as she had acted so long as her situation continued to be the same. That by refusing to lend money to France we did not afford cause of war. That France had not the smallest cause for making war on the United States: if therefore she would without cause make war upon us, and if she would make war without cause under the pretext that we would not lend her money when she had no sort of right to demand it, she would make war upon us whenever we refused to do anything else she might please to insist on. That I did not know whether anything could preserve us from a war with France but such a submission as would destroy our independence, but I was persuaded that if any thing could preserve us from that calamity it was a firm and moderate conduct on our part. That if we should leave France because we could not effect the object of our mission and because we would not lend her money, and a failure of the expedition against England or any furture state of the war should render her desirous of accommodating with the United States we should have the advantage of having impressed her with the conviction that the accommodation could only be made on terms compatible with the liberty of our Country.

General Pinckney again insisted that it was impossible so to fetter the stipulation for a loan as not to leave it in the power of France to avail herself of it immediately by making it a security for borrowing money which was the question we had so often decided, which was directly against our instructions, and which was taking part in the war.

Mr. Gerry insisted that the loan might be so limitted by the form of its grant as to render it impossible for France to avail herself of it during the war, he contended that the liberty and independence of our country had nothing to do with the question and treated that objection as being perfectly irrelative. He considered the whole force of my argument as resting on the suspicion that France would not perform any engagements she might enter into with us—which he said went against any treaty whatever. That our Government by sending us here had manifested a very different opinion and that he conceived as much confidence was to be placed in the engagements of France as of any other Government. He said that it was extremely unwise for a man to deliver himself up entirely to suspicion, and that the person who permitted himself to be governed by it in great national concerns would very often find himself mistaken.

I told him that he had perfectly mistaken and consequently mistated what I had said. That what I had said was that judging from the conduct of France I did not believe she intended to make with us a treaty which would reconcile the two nations on terms compatible with the independence of our country and not that she did not mean to keep such a treaty if made, and that the present proposition appeared to me to be designed, not as a basis for such an accomodation, but merely to amuse us, until the situation of France should enable her to take with advantage those steps which

I was persuaded she contemplated. I admitted that a man who delivered himself up to suspicion would often be mistaken but that none of us possessed a knowledge of the future and to be guided by a confidence that the nation with which we treated would act in conformity to our wishes was as much a suspicion as to suppose that the nation would not so act. The best guide we could take for the future was the past. From what a nation had done in certain situations we might fairly infer the objects of that nation and reason to what it would do in future similar situations. I had done so. I might be mistaken, but I could find no other data to proceed on. Both Genl. Pinckney and myself attempted to take a short view of the conduct of France towards ourselves and towards other nations. Mr. Gerry remained inflexible in his opinion that the loan was proper, that peace or war depended on it, and that on granting the loan we secured all the objects of our mission, the whole of which would infallibly be lost if we refused it. He stated that he believed a loan of money to be paid after the end of the war was no object to the French republic, that as a matter of interest or accommodation it was nothing, but that it was the proudest as well as the most unjust government on the face of the earth, that it was so elevated by its victories as to hold in perfect contempt all the rights of others and that with this disposition it would certainly make war on us if we refused to comply with what its pride would insist on because the measure had been proposed.

I observed that I was perfectly persuaded that such a loan as the United States could make to be paid after a peace and not used during the war, if it was indeed to be repaid, would be no object of desire to the government of France. That this was a strong argument with me for believing that the proposition was not serious. When a government made a proposition perfectly unimportant to itself but distressing to the nation to which it was made and declared that unless that proposition was acceded to, war should be the consequence, there was much reason to doubt the sincerity of the proposition. When I considered the whole conduct of France I could not persuade myself to believe that peace or war depended singly on the stipulation of an unimportant article, that it was designed to lead to extensive consequences or was designed merely to amuse us till France should be inclined to act with respect to us. That the proposition was in my opinion entirely inadmissable, but that I did not think peace or war depended on it and consequently could not view the question in that light.

Mr. Gerry again charged me with being led entirely by my suspicions of this Government. That if it acted on my principles no proposition on either side could be listened to. That France might with as much propriety say that we were not sincere in any propositions made by us and therefore refuse to consider them, as we could say that France was not sincere, and that by such a system all diplomatic intercourse would at once be terminated and their was an end of all negotiation. I told him he had again completely misunderstood and totally mistated what I had said, and that indeed he could not answer the argument but by mistating it. He appeared warm but I repeated with coolness that he had entirely mistated, and that if he would permit me I would point out his mistake. He desired me not to mingle my statements with observations which would entangle them, and I proceeded to say that the sole ground on which I bottomed my opinion of the insincerity of the proposition as he considered it was the total immateriality of that proposition to France, an immateriality which he had himself stated (in former discussions the Agents of France had themselves stated it also) I could not believe that France intended to make war on the United States merely for not doing that, our doing or omitting which was immaterial to France and it was in that view I had considered the question as involving more serious consequences or as not endangering a war by its rejection. That we had not made to France propositions professedly uninteresting to our Country, we had not threatened her with war if she should refuse to comply with a demand acknowledged to be unimportant to us, we had not manifested a disposition at once to intimidate and to beguile this government: on the contrary we had plainly stated our propositions the justice and importance of which to our country were undeniable, and we used no threats of war if those propositions should not be acceded to. The same inferences therefore could not be drawn from our conduct which ought to be drawn from that of France. Mr. Gerry was immoveable and we agreed to meet again the following evening.[4]

4. More than a year later Gerry described his version of this conference in a letter to John Adams: "On the 26th Mr. Talleyrands private secretary called, & said the minister entertained hopes that we should meet on the ground of a loan after the war, & enquired, whether I had conferred with my colleagues on the subject & what was the result? I answered yes, & it did not appear to us, that our powers were adequate. He was struck with the information, changed color, & said 'then I fear the matter is at an end.' In the evening I communicated this to my colleagues, & we agreed to send in a letter to the minister requesting a conference. General Pinckney then desired to know, whether, when we had seen Mr. Talleyrand, I would sign the letter, requiring

Mr. [5] had a long conversation with the Minister of Foreign Affairs last night and we received a note from him this morning inviting us to see him at 10 o'clock. Mr. Gerry did not go and I went alone. He detailed at length the conversation between them, the substance of which was that peace or war depended on a loan. He said that the Hanseatic Towns were obliged now to advance them more money, that Switzerland would be obliged to advance them money, that Spain and Portugal would be compelled to advance them money, that they had no quarrel with their neighbours but because they did not shew sufficient readiness to advance them money, and that the United States must also advance them money or take the consequences. That our powers must be adequate to this object and if they were not we ought to assume them, that our country would approve and honor our conduct when it should be known that by such an exercise of that discretion which must be vested in us we had prevented a war with the most powerful nation on earth. That if we would stipulate a loan the government could immediately raise the money on such stipulation. That our real motive for refusing was that we were English in our hearts, that our Executive was English, that the Washington and Adams administrations were entirely English. That it was in vain for us

---

our passports. I answered, that I could better determine this after the interview, that we were sent to make peace, & I was determined not to quit the object, whilst there were hopes of accomplishing it. That the proposition of a loan after the war was a new one, & this interview would probably inform us of the nature of it. General Martial said, that he & General Pinckney, forming a majority had a right to determine the question. I replyed, that if they were desirous of giving the answer they proposed immediately, I would not object to the measure; provided they would take on themselves the responsibility of their decision: but that it was a matter of such moment, & our powers on this head were so equivocal, that I would not risk a war, which might turn on this answer, without a further view of the subject. Gen. Martial then stated a supposition, that Mr. Talleyrand should not mention a loan after the war, but for the war, I answered, that this point was unalterably decided, we had agreed not to listen to it, & should inform him the measure was impracticable. He then stated another difficulty, if a loan was proposed after the war, how could we ascertain, whether it was intended to be used for raising money before the peace, seeing we could not make this enquiry without compromitting ourselves, to accede to a loan after the war, if not so to be used. I answered I did not wish to compromit him, or myself, either, that we might draw from Mr. Talleyrand, an explanation, if requisite, of his proposition in various ways; one of which might be by saying we understood it, to be a loan not to be used in any way directly or indirectly, before the peace: & I further observed, that there did not appear to be much difficulty in ascertaining his object, without compromitting ourselves in the least. We then drafted the letter to Mr. Talleyrand for a conference & parted." Gerry to Adams, July 8, 1799, Adams Papers. There are slight variations in Gerry to Adams, July 8, 1799, Letterbook, Gerry Papers, Lib. Cong. See also Journal, Feb. 27, 1798.

5. Caron de Beaumarchais. See note at Journal, Mar. 13, 1798.

to hope if we continued to refuse this proof of friendship that our distance would protect us. If they landed 50,000 men in England that Government would be overturned and they would when England should be revolutionized have the command of the British Fleet and of the British funds. He added that France would not permit that cold indifference which we manifested between her and her enemy, she had a right to expect a preference and that America must either be her friend or be considered and treated as her foe. He said that Mr. Talleyrand expressed himself warmly at our not waiting on him and that very heavy complaints against our conduct were preparing and would be transmitted to the United States.[6] That we were very much mistaken if we expected not to be censured by a great body of our countrymen. That it was reported in Town we designed to return by the way of England. He supposed it was for the purpose of taking credit with the English administration for the manner in which we had conducted our mission. This was the substance of a conversation which continued two hours.

February 27, 1798

We met last evening at six o'clock. Genl. Pinckney stated again his objections to the proposed loan. I made objections which were nearly the same with those of Genl. Pinckney. On the subject of our powers particularly I observed that we were not ministers generally but were sent here to effect particular objects, that a loan to France was not within the scope of those objects; that it led to a different state of things from that which we were sent to establish; that therefore if our instructions were silent on the subject we must consider it as beyond our power, since it was not within the line of action which circumscribed us. But I considered our instructions both in their spirit and letter as forbidding the measure. If a loan to France in any form could have been assented to, it would have been in the form of payment to our own Citizens. In that form a loan would not impoverish the nation, it would be incapable of application to the present war and it would be doing justice to our own Citizens and saving from ruin many valuable members of our own community. Yet even in this form we were expressly forbidden to make a loan; *a fortiori* we were forbidden to make it in any other form. Another part of our instructions had directed us to stipulate

6. Stinchcombe, "WXYZ Affair," *WMQ*, 3d Ser., XXXIV (1977), 612–613.

no aid to France during the present war. It was impossible to engage to pay money at a future day in such manner as that money could not be raised immediately on the credit of the stipulation. That France would not receive in mass the money when it should become payable but would authorize some Agent to receive it for her. The person who would lend secretly on the credit of our stipulation might be so authorized or might even be authorized to receive it from the French Minister and if we even had suspicions that money had been raised on it we should not be in a condition to refuse on that account to comply with our engagements. Foreign powers would consider any regulation not to use the loan during the war as a mere veil and would not be its dupe. That I was persuaded our Government would never consent to such a Treaty, and I would not place it in such a situation as it would be placed by rejecting any treaty which might be negotiated with France. That the irritation of France would in such an event be more considerable, there would be more danger of war and the divisions in our own Country would be greater. General Pinckney stated his opinion to be that such a measure would raise the discords of our Country to such a point as actually to endanger civil war. That if such a treaty was ratified a very large portion of our Countrymen would consider it as the surrender of our independence and as making ourselves tributary to France, that if it was rejected the opposition would declare that the Government had plunged us into a war with France.

Mr. Gerry contended that although we were forbidden to pay our own Citizens by way of loan to the French Government for the depredations committed on their property yet we were not forbidden to take this step, which he still supported. The cases were in his opinion essentially different. The depredations on our property amount at least to 20,000,000, the loan would not amount to more than 8 or 10 millions, and might be paid in the produce of our Country by way of supplies to the French Colonies. He still contended that the loan might be made in such manner as might render it impracticable for France to derive any benefit from it during the war, and that consequently such a loan would be within that clause of our instructions which forbid us to stipulate any aid to France during the war. Indeed he drew from that clause an argument in favor of his opinion and urged that a prohibition to stipulate any aid during the present war implied a permission to stipulate aid to be furnished at the end of the war. He did not conceive that our negotiating such a treaty would embarrass our government, nor did he think the Government would disapprove of it. He was far from apprehending that such a measure would endanger a civil war; on the contrary he was of opinion that it would prevent one. He believed the people would be so enraged at understanding we had refused to purchase a peace with France by a loan with the conditions which might be annexed that such refusal would endanger a civil war. The subject was discussed for some time. Genl. Pinckney and myself urged that a Loan to be paid after the war might be negotiated at a future day, after the Government was consulted, and at length we declared positively against the measure and Mr. Gerry in its favor. He still insisted upon it. We asked him in what manner it was to be decided? He said he was unwilling to determine on so important a question hastily. We asked him how the time for its decision could be fixed and when the time was fixed how the question itself could be decided? He hesitated and we observed that there were *three* of us entrusted with the interests of our Country, that in case of division either the majority or minority must govern. That this was a question which had as we conceived been considered more than four months. Two of us were decidedly and unalterably against it. We must either agree that it was decided or that it never was to be decided. Mr. Gerry said that when a difference of opinion arose among us the subject ought to be discussed thoroughly and if we could not agree he supposed the majority must decide: that in matters of small concern he was willing to yield his opinion to the opinion of the majority, but that in the great question of a loan on which depended in his opinion peace or war, if we decided against it and involved our country in war we must take all the responsibility on ourselves and relieve him entirely from it. I told him that I was perfectly willing that each Envoy should state his opinion at length in writing with the reasons on which he formed it, that we should shew our statements to each other and lay them before our Government; That I did not desire this as from myself because I wished to avoid any appearance of division but I was perfectly willing to it if desired by him.

I proposed that we should ask an interview from the Minister of foreign affairs on the objects of our mission. My motive as I stated for making this proposition was that we should know from himself whether nothing but money could form the basis of an accomodation between the two Republics, and that we should in form him definitively that we could not make a loan. It was agreed that we should ask the interview and then Genl. Pinckney requested us to ascertain precisely the language we should use. He and myself both agreed that we ought to inform Mr. Talleyrand that a loan in any form was inadmissible. Mr. Gerry admitted a loan to be paid presently was inadmissible, but would not consent that such a declaration should be made as to a loan payable at the conclusion of the war. This embarrassed us a good deal because we were unwilling to manifest opposite opinions and to make opposite declarations before the Minister. To extricate ourselves from this situation I proposed that if Mr. Talleyrand should mention a loan generally we should answer generally, that we could not make it; that if he should propose a loan to be paid at the close of the war we should agree to take the proposition into consideration and to return an answer by a given day. Mr. Gerry would not assent to this. He said it was to preclude the consideration of the particular question of a loan payable at the close of the war which was an unfair mode of procedure and he insisted on demanding of the Minister an express declaration on this subject. I told Mr. Gerry that if the Minister wished a loan payable at the close of the war he would say so, that his not proposing it would prove he would not be content with it; That for us in a premeditated conversation to suggest it would be considered as conclusive evidence that we were in favor [of it][7] which was directly contrary to the fact and would subject us to the charge of duplicity of conduct. Mr. Gerry showed some resentment and considered me as having charged him with an intention to trick us into a measure we were opposed to. I told him it was not worth while to talk in that manner, that I had said nothing personal and meant nothing personal, that we were discussing a question extremely interesting to our Country and to us all, and that the liberty of speaking freely on it could not be surrendered. I had not said that he designed any thing, but I had said that to suggest to the Minister in a conversation which he could not but consider as premeditated, any particular measure would imply that we had considered that measure and were in favor of it. I was so convinced of this that if he did suggest it I should feel myself bound to say I could not consent to stipulate a loan in any form. Mr. Gerry appeared satisfied as to the personal allusion and I endeavoured to convince him that we ought not

7. Pickering's brackets.

at any rate to propose a loan payable at the close of the war, that if the proposition came from France it would be the measure of this Government and we might pair it down and modify it: if it came from us it would be our measure, it would commit us as to the loan which was the essential thing and would leave France to urge that we ought not to *suffer war* with respect to the modification of the loan as to the time or manner of payment or as to any reasonable difference in the sum. That such of our countrymen as were in favor of a loan would say that having agreed to it we ought not to have quarrelled about any triffling circumstance attending it. That for my own part I could not answer such observations. Mr. Gerry thought there was nothing in them and that it was more proper the offer should be a voluntary offer from us than that it should proceed from France.

At length Mr. Gerry agreed not positively to suggest the loan payable at the close of the war, but if the minister proposed a loan generally to ask whether this was perfectly the same proposition which had before been made to us, and if answered in the affirmative to declare that we could not accede to it: if on the other hand he proposed a loan payable so soon as peace should be made we would take it into consideration. To this for the sake of acting together I consented. Genl. Pinckney said he could not conceive why we might not decide the question before as well as after the conversation with Talleyrand. That it was a subject which could assume no new aspect, and he conceived that a still further postponement of its determination could produce no good and would only serve to embarrass us. Mr. Gerry was decidedly against him. I told him I was perfectly of his opinion but that I was content to yield my opinion for the present for the sake of harmony. Genl. Pinckney desired it might be remembered that he protested against any treaty for a loan in any form, and I told him I protested against it as strongly as he could. The letter to Mr. Talleyrand asking an interview was prepared.[8] To-day we signed it and sent it by Major Rutledge. The Minister returned a verbal answer that he would see us on duodi (the 2nd. of March) at 3 o'clock.

February 28, 1798

I entered Mr. Gerry's appartment where I saw Mr. Dutrimont. After his departure Mr. Gerry informed me that Dutrimont came

8. See American Envoys to Talleyrand, Feb. 27, 1798.

on the part of the Minister to engage him to a particular conversation to-morrow and that he had promised to attend him.

March 1, 1798

Mr. Gerry returned from his visit to Mr. Talleyrand and said that the request which Dutrimont had made was delivered to him by the Minister before the receipt of our letter and that the Minister had not expected to see him alone, or before duodi.[9] That their conversation had not been material. That he had proposed that the Minister should give in a projet and that we should give in a counter projet and that we should search for middle ground on which to meet, that the Minister answered it would not be worth while to trouble the Directory with any thing of the sort unless we first agreed to the essential article. This essential article is a loan.

In the course of the first of the two conversations I have just sketched Mr. Gerry made some allusion to the private communications made to him by the Minister which he was not at liberty to state to us; and General Pinckney observed that he had no wish to pry into those communications but that without any enquiries on his part Mr. Talleyrand had himself given the information, not he believed with any other motive than to excite his jealousy. Mr. Gerry desired to know what the information was and declared that if it was correct he would say so. Genl. Pinckney told him that it had been proposed to send away him and myself and to retain Mr. Gerry alone, to negotiate a treaty. Mr. Gerry said it was true. Genl. Pinckney replied he knew it was true, for that the intelligence came to him through a channel he could not doubt. It was mentioned by Talleyrand himself to a person who Talleyrand knew would communicate it to him Genl. Pinckney.

I am entirely of opinion that the idea of a loan payable at the close of the war is originally the suggestion of Mr. Gerry. It is expected that the war will terminate with this campaign and consequently a loan payable at the close of the war may be negotiated immediately, almost as advantageously as a loan payable as soon as the money could be raised by a tax. It would be a contribution for the purpose of conquering Britain and the world and for the

9. *Duodi* was the second day of the *décade* in the French revolutionary calendar. Since the *décadi*, or tenth day, was often considered a substitute for Sunday, Talleyrand might not have wanted to conduct business that day and perhaps asked Gerry to appear the following day.

purpose of subjugating ourselves. The French speak of England as the only nation on earth which has the hardiness now to oppose them. They consider it as an insolence which ought to be punished. Many speak of a revolution in England as giving them the naval force and the wealth of that nation and the empire of the universe.

March 2, 1798[10]

At 3 o'clock we waited on Mr. Talleyrand and were almost immediately introduced to him. Genl. Pinckney commenced the conversation by saying that our Government and ourselves were extremely anxious to remove the subsisting differences between the two republics, that we had received many propositions through Mr. Bellamy to which we had found it impracticable to accede, and that we had now waited on him for the purpose of enquiring whether other means might not be devised which would effect so desirable an object. The Minister replied that without doubt the Directory wished very sincerely on our arrival to see a solid friendship established between France and the United States, and had manifested this disposition by the readiness with which orders for our passports were given. That the Directory had been extremely wounded by the last Speech of General Washington, made to Congress as he was about to quit the Office of President of the United States, and by the first and last Speech of Mr. Adams.[11] That explanations of these Speeches were expected and required of us. Genl. Pinckney expressed his surprize that the speech of General Washington was complained of and said this was a new complaint. Mr. Talleyrand merely observed that the Directory was wounded at it and proceeded. He said that the original favorable disposition of the Directory had been a good deal altered by the coldness and distance which we had observed. That instead of seeing him often and endeavouring to remove the obstacles to a mutual approach, we had not once waited on him. Genl. Pinckney observed that when we delivered him our letters of Credence he

10. This Journal entry was included in American Envoys to Pickering, Mar. 9, 1798.

11. Talleyrand referred to Washington's Farewell Address of Sept. 17, 1796, in *Claypoole's American Daily Advertiser* (Philadelphia), Sept. 19, 1796. On this speech, see Felix Gilbert, *To the Farewell Address: Ideas of Early American Foreign Policy* (Princeton, N.J., 1961), 115–136, 165–169. Adams's two speeches were given on May 16, 1797, at the opening of the first session of the Fifth Congress, and on Nov. 23, 1797, at the opening of the second session of the Fifth Congress. May 16 and Nov. 23, 1797, *Annals of Congress*, VII, 54–59, 630–634.

informed us that the Directory in a few days would decide concerning us and that when the decision was made he would communicate it to us, that this had for sometime suspended any procedure on our part. He answered that this related only to our public character and not to private visits. Genl. Pinckney said that on[12] application made by his Secretary for a passport for an American under his care he was told that he must apply at the office of police, that America had no minister in France since the recal of Mr. Monroe.[13] The Minister said that was very true and then proceeded to say that the Directory felt itself wounded by the different speeches of Mr. Washington and Mr. Adams, which he had stated and would require some proof on the part of the United States of a friendly disposition previous to a treaty with us. He then said that we ought to search for and propose some means which might furnish this proof, that if we were disposed to furnish it there could be no difficulty in finding it and he alluded very intelligibly to a loan, he said he had several conferences on this subject with Mr. Gerry who had always answered that we had no powers. Mr. Gerry replied that he had stated other objections, that he had particularly urged that it would commit our neutrality and[14] involve us in a war with Great Britain. He made no reply and Genl. Pinckney observed that a loan had been repeatedly suggested to us, but that we had uniformly answered that it exceeded our powers. Mr. Talleyrand replied that persons at such a distance as we were from our Government and possessed as we were of the public confidence must often use their discretion and exceed their powers for the public good. That there was a material difference between acting where instructions were silent and doing what was particularly forbidden. That if indeed a loan was positively forbidden we might consider ourselves as incapable of making one; but, if as he supposed was the case (and he looked the question) our instructions were only silent that it must be referred to us to act in a case not provided for according to the best of our judgement for the public good. That in almost all the treaties made during the revolution the negotiators had exceeded their powers although the Government appointing them was at no considerable distance. He particularized

12. In American Envoys to Pickering, Mar. 9, 1798, "an" is inserted at this point.

13. Henry Rutledge was Pinckney's secretary on his first mission to France. Monroe took his formal leave on Dec. 30, 1796. See Harry Ammon, *James Monroe: The Quest for National Identity* (New York, 1971), 157.

14. The words "commit our neutrality and" are omitted in American Envoys to Pickering, Mar. 9, 1798.

the treaty with Prussia and several others. Genl. Pinckney told him that our powers did not extend to a loan and perhaps might forbid it. The minister still urged the difference between an express prohibition and mere silence. He then proceeded to state that the principal objection on the part of our Government to a loan must be that it would draw us out of that neutral situation in which we wished to continue, that there were various means of avoiding this, first the secrecy of France which might be relied on; and secondly means of disguising the loan might be devised which would effectually prevent its being considered as an aid during the present war. That if we were truly and sincerely desirous of effecting the thing we should experience no difficulty in finding the means. He again stated a proposition of this sort on our part as being absolutely necessary to prove that the Government was not about entering into a treaty with persons of a temper hostile to it. Mr. Gerry not well hearing Mr. Talleyrand who spoke low asked him to explain himself with respect to the proposition which he had alluded to, supposing it to be a new one; and he answered that one of them was secrecy, but that there were besides various ways which might easily be suggested to cover the loan as an immediate one, by limiting the time of advancing it to distant instalments.

Mr. Gerry observed that Dutrimont had suggested that a loan was proposed to be made payable after the war and in supplies to St. Domingo: Mr. Talleyrand signified that that might be one of the means used and said that if we were only sincere in our wish it would be easy to bring about the end. I[15] told Mr. Talleyrand that if the Ministers of the United States had manifested any unwillingness to take all proper means to reconcile the two republics or any coldness or indifference on the subject they had very badly represented the feelings and wishes of their Government. That the Government of the United States was most sincerely desirous of preserving the friendship of France and had in my opinion unequivocally manifested that desire by having deputed us under the extraordinary circumstances attending our mission and by having so long patiently borne the immense loss of property which had been sustained, that we had endeavoured according to the best of our judgement to represent truly this disposition of our Government but that we understood that France would consider nothing as an evidence of friendship but an act which would transcend and violate our powers and at the same time operate the most serious in-

15. "Genl. Marshall" is inserted in place of "I," *ibid.*

jury to our Country. That neutrality in the present war was of the last importance to the United States and they had resolved faithfully to maintain it. That they had committed no act voluntarily which was a breach of it and could do nothing in secret which if known would justly arrange them among the belligerent powers. That in the present state of things if America was actually leagued with France in the war she would only be required to furnish money. That we had neither ships of war or men to be employed in it and could consequently as a belligerent power only be asked for money. That therefore to furnish money was in fact to make war which we could by no means consent to do and which would absolutely transcend our powers, being an Act altogether without the view and contemplation of our Government when our mission was decided on. That with respect to supplies to St. Domingo no doubt could be entertained that our merchants would furnish them very abundantly if France would permit the commerce, and a loan really payable after the close of the war might then be negotiated. Mr. Talleyrand again marked the distinction between silence of instructions and an express prohibition and again insisted on the necessity of our proving by some means which we must offer our friendship for the republic. He said he must exact from us on the part of his government some proposition of this sort, that to prove our friendship there must be some immediate aid or something which might avail them. That the principles of reciprocity would require it. I[16] understood him by this expression to allude to the loan formerly made by France to the United States. Mr. Gerry at the time thought he alluded to the treaty to be made, and said all treaties should be founded in reciprocity, and then asked him whether a loan was the ultimatum of this Government. Mr. Talleyrand did not give a direct answer to the question, he said, as he was understood, that the government insisted on some act which would demonstrate our friendly disposition towards and our good wishes for the republic. This once done he said the adjustment of complaints would be easy. They would be matter of enquiry, and if France had done us wrong it would be repaired; but that if this was refused it would increase the distance and coldness between the two republics. The conversation continued in this stile until 4 o'clock when we took our leave and agreed to meet in the evening. In the course of it and in reply to some observations of Mr. Talley-

16. "Genl. Marshall and Genl. Pinckney" are inserted in place of "I," *ibid.*

rand respecting the proofs of friendship required by France, Genl. Pinckney observed that our being here was a mark of the friendly disposition of our Government, and that while we were here the government had passed a decree for seizing neutral vessels having on board any article coming out of England which in its operation would subject to capture all our property on the ocean. Mr. Talleyrand replied that this was not particular to us but was common to all the neutral powers. At another time in answer to his demands of some marks of our friendship I[17] observed that we considered the mutual interests of the two nations as requiring peace and friendship and we relied on finding sufficient motives in the interest of France to perserve that friendship without forcing us to an Act which transcended our powers and would be so injurious to our country. As we were taking our leave Mr. Talleyrand again noticed our not visiting him and said that he conceived our not having had an audience from the Directory ought not to have prevented it. I[18] told him that our seeing the Directory or not was an object of no sort of concern to us. That we were perfectly indifferent with regard to it, but that we conceived that until our public character was in some degree recognized and we were treated as the Ministers and representatives of our Government we could not take upon ourselves to act as Ministers, because by doing so we might subject ourselves to some injurious circumstances to which we could not submit. He said that was very true but that we might see him as private individuals and discuss the objects of difference between us.

March 3, 1798

We met last evening in conformity with our appointment. The subject was discussed pretty nearly in the same manner as on former occasions. Genl. Pinckney and myself were decidedly of opinion that our instructions forbid us to negotiate a loan payable after the war, and that the ideas suggested by Talleyrand did not in fact vary the case at all. We contended that a loan payable at a future day would serve as a pledge on which to raise money immediately, that it was in fact to aid the descent on England, to subjugate our own country and to forge chains with which to manacle ourselves. Mr. Gerry on the contrary that our instruc-

17. "Genl. Marshall" is inserted in place of "I," *ibid.*
18. "Genl. Marshall" is inserted in place of "I," *ibid.*

tions implied the power to stipulate the loan payable at a future day, that it would prevent a war and that the people of the United States would certainly approve the measure. We parted, neither having made any sort of impression on the other.[19]

Mr. Gerry came into my room this morning, and we had another conversation on the subject of our instructions. He still showed an expectation, that his opinion might be acceded to. I told him, that my judgment was not more perfectly convinced that the floor was wood, or that I stood on my feet and not my head, than that our instructions would not permit us to make the loan required: that being both my opinion and the opinion of Genl. Pinckney, formed upon the most mature and attentive consideration we were able to give the subject, it was certain we should not change; and he might rely upon it, that we would neither of us consent to stipulate a loan. This being the case, the only alternatives were, since he would not accede to our proposition, which was to say positively we would not make the loan required, in any form whatever, to negociate the loan singly, or to consult our government on the subject. He said I need not expect he would negociate the loan himself: I told him I did not advise him to do so; that on the contrary I should think he acted very improperly in doing so. I only named it as an alternative. He might negociate the loan separately, or he and myself would return to the United States and make a fair statement of the situation of our affairs here, leaving General Pinckney to keep up the relations between the two governments, to avail himself of any favourable circumstances, and to receive the orders which might be given by the United States. Mr. Gerry assented to this, and said he would go alone or with either of us, or he would stay with either of us. I told him it was most proper he should go, because he had communications from this government, which we did not possess; and because, being of a different opinion from his colleagues, it would be doing justice to those opinions, to state them himself fully to his government: that it was most proper Genl. Pinckney should remain, because he was the permanent Minister and would continue in the event of a favourable issue of the negociation. We meet again to morrow, when I shall propose this measure.

19. This paragraph is identical to the one in Gerry's letterbook, which has a marginal note by Gerry: "this by mistake of Mr. Foster [Gerry's secretary] is entered as part of the dispatch, being a part of Mr. Marshals minutes respecting it." See American Envoys to Pickering, Mar. 9, 1798, Gerry Letterbook, Huntington Lib.

March 4, 1798

We met to day, but employed the time in the correction of the notes I had taken of our conversation with the Minister: Mr. Gerry had some engagements and was besides desirous of reading that part of the correspondence of Colo. Monroe, which related to a loan.[20] We agreed to meet again to morrow, and in the mean time to request another interview with Mr. Talleyrand, the day after to morrow. The letter was immediately written and sent.

March 5, 1798

We met according to the appointment of yesterday. Mr. Gerry read to us our instructions and our powers, and then argued our right to make a loan payable at the close of the war. Genl. Pinckney and myself opposed him on nearly the same ground as heretofore. Mr. Gerry said, that if we chose to take the responsibility of a war upon ourselves, we might deliver the opinion of the commission, and he would not inform the French Government of the difference of opinion between us; but it was to be remembered in America, that no share of the blame was attributable to him. I then stated the importance of unanimity; that a division among us would tend greatly still more to divide our country; that to preserve it, I would still sacrifice the opinion I entertained, and accede to a proposition Mr. Gerry had formerly made of going to America to consult our government: Mr. Gerry had offered to go alone: I would accompany him and leave General Pinckney here to keep up the relations between the two governments, and to receive and conform to any instructions, which might be transmitted from the United States. After some little conversation, this was acceded to. We then sat down to put in writing what would be said to Talleyrand to morrow; and Mr. Gerry stated, that considering no other proposition as having been made than a loan payable immediately, we could not make such a loan.[21] That was agreed to. I then asked what we should say, if Mr. Talleyrand should propose a loan payable at the end of the war. I could not obtain any decisive answer; and to procure one, wrote on the paper on which Mr. Gerry had before written, that to such a proposition the answer should be, that we had maturely considered the subject, and could not make a loan in any form; but if this was positively insisted on by France, that we were so solicitous to

20. On the French request for a loan in 1794, see Ammon, *Monroe*, 128–130.
21. See Memorandum, Mar. 5, 1798.

restore harmony between the two Republics, that Mr. Gerry and myself would proceed immediately to America, to receive the instructions of our government. Some conversation was had about the person, who was to remain; but we all agreed, that General Pinckney must continue here, as he was the permanent Minister, who was trusted by the Government to continue to guard its interests in France. I then declared positively, that I would not return without Mr. Gerry; because if the Government should decline making the loan, as it was notorious that I differed from Mr. Gerry not only with respect to the measure itself, but with respect to the consequences, and as we had different views of the intentions and objects of this government, I should be charged with stating unfairly the proposition itself and the circumstances attending it. To this I would not subject myself, and therefore as Mr. Gerry had himself proposed to go, I deemed it proper, that we should go together. The Government might then be fully possessed of the ideas of the whole commission.

Mr. Gerry then objected to the declaration, that we had maturely considered the subject, and could not make a loan in any form: he would not consent to say this. I insisted upon it as inevitable; because if we did not declare against a loan to be made by ourselves, the proposition to consult our government would be answered by insisting on our making the loan ourselves, which we must do or refuse to do. Mr. Gerry was for negociating about it. He at length agreed, that it would be improper to make the loan without explanatory instructions, but insisted on our waiting for those instructions. I still insisted on retaining the words; and he declared, that if we did retain them, we must retain them on our own responsibility, that he was decidedly against them, and was to be acquitted of the war they would produce. Genl. Pinckney was disposed to let them be struck out, supposing the sense to be implied. I reluctantly consented to it. Mr. Gerry then proposed, that we should add, that we expected to receive instructions soon from our government, and that we would wait for those instructions. Genl. Pinckney and myself told him that we could not say so, because we did not expect soon to receive instructions. We knew certainly, that our letters had not reached our government in the beginning of January, and all probabilities considered, it was an even chance, that we should not receive letters acknowledging them till May or late in April. Mr. Gerry was of a contrary opinion. However we separated without going further than to modify our proposition to consult our government, so as to make it dependent on the wish of France. It is not difficult to foresee considerable impediments in the way of our departure. To morrow, at half past eleven, we see the Minister.

March 6, 1798

Just before we sat out on the visit to Mr. Talleyrand, Mr. Gerry came into my room and said that dissatisfaction had been repeatedly expressed by the French government at the speeches of our Presidents, and that if General Pinckney and myself were willing, he would propose to insert in the treaty we might enter into, a clause declaring that the complaints of the two governments had been founded in mistake. I told him, that I did not wish to say any thing which might wound France, but on the contrary would chuse to avoid it: but I could not say the complaints of our government were founded in mistake: It would be impossible for me to say so: with my view of things, I should tell an absolute lye, if I should say that our complaints were founded in mistake.[22] He replied hastily and with warmth, that he wished to God, I would propose something which was accommodating: that I would propose nothing myself and objected to every thing which he proposed. I observed that it was not worth while to talk in that manner; that it was calculated to wound but not to do good; that I had proposed every thing which in my opinion was calculated to accommodate differences on just and reasonable ground. He said that he had heard nothing from me yet, which was accommodating; and if there was, he should be glad I would point it out; that to talk about justice was saying nothing; that I should involve our

22. This argument reflected the personal differences between JM and Gerry. Without any tangible action by the French to lessen tension, Gerry still believed that by negotiating on each individual item, success might perhaps be obtained. JM by this time viewed the mission as hopeless and any further negotiation as fruitless. Both JM and Gerry could point to their instructions to bolster their particular position, since Pickering had written, "Conscious integrity authorizes the Government to insist that no blame or censure be directly or indirectly imputed to the United States. But on the other hand, however exceptionable in the view of our own Government and in the eyes of an impartial world may have been the conduct of France, yet she may be unwilling to acknowledge any agressions: and we do not wish to wound her feelings or to excite resentment. It will therefore be best to adopt, on this point, the principle of the British Treaty; and 'terminate our differences in such manner, as without referring to the merits of our respective complaints and pretensions, may be the best calculated to produce mutual satisfaction and good understanding.' " Pickering to American Envoys, July 15, 1797. Gerry was certainly not violating his instructions by negotiating informally, but JM was not willing to explore the possibility of informal but substantive negotiation with French officials.

country in a war, and should bring it about in such a manner, as to divide the people among themselves. I felt a momentary irritation, which I afterwards regretted, and told Mr. Gerry, that I was not accustomed to such language, and did not permit myself to use it, with respect to him or his opinions: that I did not believe any part of his conduct or any propositions he made were calculated to accommodate or to unite the people of America, but the contrary: that what he now proposed had in my opinion no such tendency, and was inadmissible because untrue: that our complaints of depredation on our commerce were not founded on mistake. He said I might think of him as I pleased. I told him, that whatever I might think of his opinions, I had not thought myself authorized to apply to him such language as he had bestowed upon me. He then said, that he had not intended his proposition to extend to the depredations on our commerce, but merely to the expressions which the Presidents, on each side, had used, and which were mutually complained of. The conversation thus ended.

Immediately[23] after our arrival at his office, we were introduced to the Minister; and General Pinckney stated, that we had considered with the most serious attention the conversation we had had the honor of holding with him a few days past: that the propositions he had suggested, appeared to us to be substantially the same with those which had been made by Mr. by Mr. [24] and also to Mr. Gerry, with an intention that they should be communicated to his colleagues; that we considered it as a proposition, that the United States should furnish aid to France, to be used during the present war: that though it was unusual to disclose instructions, yet we would declare to him, that in addition to its being a measure amounting to a declaration of war against Great-Britain, we were expressly forbidden by our instructions to take such a step.[25]

23. The remaining portion of the Journal entry was included in American Envoys to Pickering, Mar. 9, 1798. Pickering submitted a slightly modified version of the dispatch to Congress on June 5, 1798. *Annals of Congress*, IX, 3418–3425.

24. "Hottinguer" and "Bellamy" were inserted later without any indication when or by whom. Since all the contemporary copies of this entry contain the insertions, JM probably wrote both names in the original. See American Envoys to Pickering, Mar. 9, 1798, Gerry Letterbook, Huntington Lib.; American Envoys to Pickering, Mar. 9, 1798, French Legation Book, Franklin Collection.

25. In his letterbook Gerry commented on this paragraph: "All between the indexes was proposed & committed to writing by Mr. Gerry in the morning before we met Mr. Talleyrand & repeated carefully by G. Pinckney, who after the meeting said 'he thot he had got his lesson very well by heart.'" American Envoys to Pickering,

The Minister said, in the tone of a question, he supposed our instructions were, to do nothing which would amount to a departure from our neutrality.

General Pinckney said that we were so instructed, and that they were still more particular. Mr. Talleyrand then proceeded to argue, that it would be no departure from neutrality, to stipulate a loan payable after the war; and spoke of it clearly as admitting of application to immediate use. He said a good deal of the secrecy with which the transaction might be cloathed, and observed further, that a loan payable after the war would be a proof of our faithful observance of the duties of neutrality, since it would be considered as proving that we had rejected propositions for an immediate loan. General Marshall replied, that we thought differently; that in our opinion, any act, on the part of the American Government, on which one of the belligerent powers could raise money for immediate use, would be furnishing aid to that power, and would be taking a part in the war. It would be, in fact, to take the only part, which, in the existing state of things, America could take. This was our deliberate opinion: and in addition to it, we considered our instructions as conclusive on this point.

He observed, that we had claims on the French Government, for property taken from American citizens. Some of those claims were probably just. He asked if they were acknowledged by France, whether we could not give a credit as to the payment—say for two years? We answered that we could. He then insisted that it was precisely the same thing; that by such an act, we should consent to leave in the hands of France, funds to which our citizens were entitled, and which might be used in the prosecution of the war. General Pinckney said there was a difference between the cases; that such prizes were now actually in the power of the French, without our consent, we could not prevent it or get them out, but the granting or not granting a loan was in our own power. He repeated his observation; and General Marshall said that the property for which money was due to American Citizens from the French Government, was taken into the possession of that government, without any co-operation on the part of the United States. No act of any sort was performed by our government, which in any degree contributed to place those funds in the hands

---

Mar. 9, 1798, Gerry Letterbook, Huntington Lib. Gerry claimed that he had written this passage when he prepared a defense of his actions. See Gerry to John Adams, July 8, 1799, Adams Papers. For Pinckney's copy, see Memorandum, Mar. 5, 1798.

of France, nor was there any consent towards it; but in the case proposed, the act would be the act of the government; the government would itself place the funds in the hands of France, and thereby furnish means which might be employed in the prosecution of the war. This was the distinction between the cases, and in a question of neutrality, it appeared to us to be all important. The Minister then proceeded to state the case of our assuming the debt to our citizens, and of paying money in that manner; but General Pinckney and Mr. Gerry told him we were positively forbidden to assume the debt to our own citizens, even if we were to pay the money directly to them. He seemed surprized at this. General Pinckney observed, that contrary to usage we had deemed it proper, in the existing state of things, to state candidly our powers to him, that he might know certainly that we could not secretly, or under any disguise whatever, make a loan which might be used during the war. Mr. Talleyrand said, he must resume his position, that there was a difference, which he must insist upon, between a loan payable immediately, and a loan payable in future; and he still insisted there was no difference between a loan payable in future, and a credit for the money which might be due to our citizens. Mr. Gerry observed, that his colleagues had justly stated the distinction between the debt which will be due to the citizens of the United States from France, in case of her recognizing the claim which we shall make in their behalf, and a debt which might arise from a loan by the government of the United States to that of France, during the war. The one is the result of an arrest of their property without their consent, the other would be a voluntary act of the government of the United States, and a breach of their neutrality. There is an additional objection to the latter: if the United States should make such a loan, it would give too much reason to suppose that their government had consented in a collusive manner, to the capture of the vessels of their citizens, and had thus been furnishing France with supplies to carry on the war. Our instructions are express not to stipulate for any aids to France, either directly or indirectly during the war. With respect to a secret stipulation, a loan cannot be made without an act of the Legislature: but if the executive were adequate to it, we have had an instance of an injunction of secrecy on members of the senate, on an important subject, which one of the members thought himself warranted in publishing in the news-papers; and of frequent instances of secrets, which have otherwise escaped: secrecy, in this instance might therefore be considered, if the measure was in itself admissable, as being impracticable. General Marshall observed, that we had considered the subject with great solicitude, and were decidedly of opinion, that we could not, under any form make a loan which could be used during the war; that we could not tell what our government would do if on the spot, but we were perfectly clear, that without additional orders, we could not do what France requested. Mr. Gerry observed that the government, and nation of the United States, as well as ourselves, were earnestly solicitous to restore friendship between the two republics; that as General Marshall had stated, we could not say what our government would do if on the spot; but that if this proposition met the wishes of the government of France, General Marshall and himself had agreed immediately to embark for the United States, and lay before our Government the existing state of things here, as it respected our nation, to enable them to determine whether any, and what other measures on their part were necessary. Mr. Talleyrand made no observation on this proposition: but enquired whether we expected soon to receive orders. Mr. Gerry mentioned an answer he had received to a letter sent by him in November; and General Pinckney stated that our first dispatches were put on board two vessels at Amsterdam, on the 20th. of November; from which Mr. Talleyrand could form as just an idea as we could, when an answer might be expected; but he did not think it probable one would arrive for a month to come. General Marshall told him, that we knew our government had not received our dispatches on the 8th. of January: and we could not tell when they might be received. He asked if our intelligence came through England? General Marshall answered that it did not; and General Pinckney said that American papers as late as the 8th. of January had mentioned the fact.

There was some conversation about the time when these instructions might be expected; and General Marshall suggested a doubt whether our government might give any instructions? He asked with some surprize if we had not written for instructions? and we answered that we had not; that those who had communicated with us had told us, that we should be ordered out of France immediately and we had supposed, that we should be ordered out before our letters could reach our government.

Mr. Gerry then observed, that the government of France must judge for itself, but that it appeared to him a treaty on liberal principles, such as those on which the treaty of commerce between the two nations was first established, would be infinitely more advantageous to France than the trifling advantages she could derive from a loan: such a treaty would produce a friendship and attachment on the part of the United States to France, which would be solid and permanent, and produce benefits far superior to those of a loan, if we had powers to make it. To this observation Mr. Talleyrand made no reply. We parted without any sentiment delivered by the Minister on the subject of our going home to consult our government.

As we were about leaving Mr. Talleyrand, we told him, that two of us would return immediately to receive the instructions of our government, if that would be agreeable to the Directory: if it was not, we would wait some time in the expectation of receiving instructions.

March 13, 1798

About 9 O Clock last evening, Mr. [26] called on me and told me, that he had just understood the effects of the Americans in France were to be sequestered. He expressed much sorrow at this fact, and turned the conversation on the payment of money, which was required by the government as the only means of preventing this unpleasant measure, and the still more unpleasant consequences which would attend it. After some further conversation of the same complexion with what had been so often held, he informed me, that he should see the Minister of exterior relations to day, and would call on me this evening and state the result of the conversation. He then took his leave.

March 14, 1798

Mr. [27] called on me late last evening. He had just parted from the Minister. He informed me, that he had been told confi-

26. Caron de Beaumarchais. Above the Journal entry of Mar. 13, 1798, Pickering wrote, "I have inserted the name Beaumarchais in the blanks left in this and the following pages by Genl. Marshall. I have done it on the information of Genl. Pinckney." When Pinckney was in Trenton, N.J., in the first part of Nov. 1798, he probably told Pickering that JM left blanks in the Journal rather than using Beaumarchais's name.

Because of his previous business connections with Beaumarchais, JM perhaps used more discretion in discussing him than he did in discussing Bellamy or Hottinguer. Beaumarchais, who was in communication with Bellamy and Talleyrand, approached JM in one of the last attempts to secure a loan from the United States, but this was not reported in JM's letters or the official dispatches.

27. Caron de Beaumarchais.

dentially, and could only communicate it to me under an injunction of secresy, except as to my colleagues, that the Directory was determined to give passports to General Pinckney and myself, but to retain Mr. Gerry: that this order would be kept up a few days to give us time to make propositions conforming to the views of the government: that if they were not made, Mr. Talleyrand would be compelled to execute the order. I told him, that if the proposition, in expectation of which the order was kept up, was a loan, it was perfectly unnecessary to keep it up a single day: that the subject had been considered for five months, and our opinions with respect to the injunctions of positive duty concerning it were incapable of being shaken: that for myself if it was impossible to effect the objects of our mission, I did not wish to stay another day in France, and would as cheerfully depart the next day as at any future time. He reasoned, as often before, on the propriety of our assuming the powers which were required, as being indispensably necessary for the welfare of our country. On my repeating remarks which had been often made, he said that he did not pretend to say the demands of France were just, nor did the Minister pretend to place the demand on that ground, or to expect our compliance with it on that account; but because a compliance would be useful to our country: that France thought herself sufficiently powerful to give the law to the world, and exacted from all around her money to enable her to finish successfully her war against England. All the nations around her (and he enumerated them) had been compelled to contribute to this object: there was no instance in which France had desisted from a demand once made, and it might be relied on, that she would not recede from the demand made on us. After some further conversation, in which I persisted to declare, that no money stipulation would or could be made, he returned to the subject of dividing us and retaining Mr. Gerry: he said that it was expected America would consider this as manifesting an unwillingness on the part of France to break entirely with us, and that the government would annex to Mr. Gerry two other persons who might have more courage to do what was necessary for our country, or a stronger disposition to reconcile the two Republics. He hinted a desire that some proposition of the sort should come from us. I told him, that if two of us should return, our government would act, as its own judgment should dictate, that if France was desirous that two of us should return to represent fully to our government the state of politics in this country, and meant to leave to our decision who should stay or go, we should arrange that matter, as might comport with our own opinion of propriety and the interests of our country: that if on the contrary France chose to decide for us, and to select for the United States the Minister who should represent them, the act must be entirely the Act of France, and I should not have the smallest concern with it. He knew very well that if any of us returned to the United States, I was resolved to return, but that I would contribute to no arrangement of the sort proposed, because I conceived that a minister ought to represent the country and the interests of that country which deputed him, and not that to which he was deputed and consequently, that he ought to be chosen by those who deputed him and not by those to whom he was deputed. Mr. [28] replied that my observation was very just in itself and would apply if France rejected us all and required a fourth man from America; but that we were all three equally trusted and chosen by the government of the United States, and France only selected from among us one whose dispositions were believed to be friendly to this government and who might safely be permitted to stay among them: that General Pinckney and myself, and especially me, were considered ⟨as being sold to the⟩ entirely English. He would not conceal from me, that our positive refusal to comply with the demands of France was attributed principally to me, who was considered as entirely English: that he had assured the Minister that he was mistaken, that I was restrained from agreeing to the loan by want of power, and not by want of will, but the opinion was persisted in. I felt some little resentment and answered, that the French government thought no such thing: that neither the government nor any man in France thought me English, but they knew I was not French: they knew I would not sacrifice my duty and the interests of my own country to any nation on earth, and therefore I was not a proper man to stay, and was branded with the epithet of being English; that the government knew very well I loved my own country exclusively, and it was impossible to suppose any man, who loved America, fool enough to wish to engage her in a war with France, if that war was avoidable. After some further conversation, he spoke of taking a passage with me to the United States. I told him I should be much pleased with his company. He said he should have no public mission, nor should he

28. Caron de Beaumarchais.

concern with the affairs of the government (he had in a former conversation hinted at endeavouring to obtain the confidence of this government, and of endeavouring while in America to reconcile the two Republics) further than to testify if necessary to the moderation of my conduct, and to the solicitude I had uniformly expressed to prevent a rupture with France. He hinted very plainly at what he had before observed that means would be employed to irritate the people of the United States against me, and that those means would be successful. I told him that I was much obliged to him, but that I relied entirely on my conduct itself for its justification, and that I felt no sort of apprehension for consequences, as they regarded me personally: that in public life considerations of that sort never had and never would in any degree influence me. We parted with a request on his part, that whatever might arrive, we would preserve the most perfect temper, and with my assuring him of my persuasion, that our conduct would always manifest the firmness of men who were determined, and never the violence of passionate men.

I have been particular in stating this conversation, because I have no doubt of its having been held at the instance of the Minister, and that it will be faithfully reported to him.

I mentioned to day to Mr. Gerry, that the government wished to detain him and to send away General Pinckney and myself. He said he would not stay; but I find I shall not succeed in my efforts to procure a serious demand of passports for Mr. Gerry and myself.

March [19]–20, 1798

Mr. Gerry brought in, just before dinner, a letter from the Minister of exterior relations purporting to be an answer to our long memorial criminating in strong terms our government and ourselves, and proposing that two of us should go home, leaving for the negociation the person most acceptable to France. The person is not named but no question is entertained that Mr. Gerry is alluded to.[29] I read the letter and gave it again to Mr. Gerry.

I waited on General Pinckney with the letter of the Minister,

29. See Talleyrand to American Envoys, Mar. 18, 1798. The key passage in the Talleyrand letter to which JM alluded reads as follows in the translated version submitted to Congress: "The Executive Directory is disposed to treat with that one of the three, whose opinions, presumed to be more impartial, promise, in the course of the explanations, more of that reciprocal confidence which is indispensable." June 18, 1798, *Annals of Congress*, IX, 3432.

and we read it together. Mr. Gerry having some engagements, it was proposed that we should meet to morrow in order to consider what should now be done.

March 21, 1798

We met and the letter was read entirely through. Mr. Gerry declared explicitly that he would not on any consideration stay and negociate alone on subjects entrusted by our country to all three of us: that in his secret communications with Mr. Talleyrand he had explicitly and unequivocally declined this decision, and he expressed much surprize, that such a proposition should be made when there was a perfect previous knowledge, that it would not be acceded to. That is probably the very reason why it was made.

March 22, 1798

We met again and Mr. Gerry told us, that in a conversation with Dutrimond this morning, he had expressed the impropriety of permitting a foreign government to chuse the person who should negociate etc. as an objection to his staying; and Dutrimond had informed him, that it would not be expected that he should treat, and that he would only be required to remain in Paris to keep up a communication between the governments until instructions could be given on the requisitions of France. Mr. Gerry said he would sooner be thrown into the Seine than consent to stay under the actual circumstances. We agreed that the letter should be immediately copied for the purpose of being forwarded to our government, and that so soon as it was copied I should take it and prepare an answer to it, in which I should state, that no one of the Ministers could consent to remain on a business committed to all three, and that none of us felt ourselves at liberty to withdraw, but by the direction of our own government, from a service which had been entrusted to us, and that at a time when there existed a prospect of performing it.[30] Genl. Pinckney gave his opinion very freely to Mr. Gerry, that he ought not to stay, with which opinion Mr. Gerry entirely accorded. I was perfectly silent.

March 23, 1798

Mr. Dutrimond came to visit Mr. Gerry and breakfast with him, but he being at Patough, Mr. Dutrimond for the first time called

30. The reply to Talleyrand is in American Envoys to Talleyrand, Apr. 3, 1798.

on me. We had a good deal of conversation on the affairs of the two nations in which he manifested clearly, that the object of his visit was to prevail on me to agree to an application to the French government to permit Genl. Pinckney and myself to return to enlighten the minds of our government and fellow citizens on the politics of Europe, while Mr. Gerry should remain until such powers should be received, as would enable him to take those measures, which would preserve peace with France. He said that the Directory were very much irritated against us and hinted that the course of the elections which run too much in favor of Jacobins had encreased the irritation against us.[31] He said that the Directory supposed we must be doing harm, since they could not conceive for what object we remained in France, as we were not progressing in our negociation, and that Mr. Talleyrand would be compelled, though very reluctantly, to order us in three days at furtherest to leave the Republic. He said that it gave Mr. Talleyrand a great deal of pain, and gave him a great deal of pain also. I told him that personally nothing could be more desireable to me than to return immediately to the United States: that I regretted the order, but only regretted it as it manifested an encreasing hostility on the part of France towards the United States. He said that this measure might be softened by giving it the appearance of having been taken on our application, and he strongly recommended the procedure I have mentioned. We had a lengthy conversation on this subject, in the course of which he spoke of General Pinckney, as being particularly objectionable to the Directory. I entered into a representation of Genl. Pinckney's character and opinions, and shewed him that one motive for the appointment of Genl. Pinckney was that while he was a man of honor in whom his own government could confide, his politics had been of a complexion which ought to render him acceptable to France.

Mr. Gerry returned about 2 O Clock, and I informed him, that Mr. Dutrimond had said that unless we sent in an application in two or three days, we should be all three ordered off. He said the letter ought to be written and sent immediately. I told him it was impossible: he then said that to prevent a war he would stay. I made no observation on this declaration of Mr. Gerry.

31. On the Jacobin resurgence, see Isser Woloch, *Jacobin Legacy: The Democratic Movement under the Directory* (Princeton, N.J., 1970).

March 26, 1798

I had another conversation with Mr. Beaumarchais,[32] in which he repeated his representations of the power of France and of the policy of acceding to her propositions. He spoke to me of my return to the United States. I told him, that if I could obtain letters of safe-conduct and a vessel which could afford me a commodious passage from France immediately to the United States, I should, though I had private business of very considerable consequence in England, embrace the direct passage to America.[33] If this was unattainable I should embark immediately for England. He advised me strongly against passing through England, said it would give great offence to this government, and would injure me in the opinion of my own countrymen. I observed to this, that I did not mean to take England in my way, if I could obtain a safe passage from France, but that I would not risk being taken to the West Indies and exposed to the dangers of that climate: that I was by no means certain a letter of safe-conduct would protect me, though I was disposed to trust to it; but I was certain that my character as minister would not protect me, since I knew that the Captains of privateers had received orders to cruize for us on our passage outwards, and take us to the West Indies. He said the Government could not have countenanced such an Act of violence. I replied that I did not believe the government had countenanced it but I was well assured of the fact.[34] He said he should see Mr. Talleyrand to morrow evening and would state to him what conversation had passed between us and know whether letters of safe-conduct would be granted. I also mentioned to him the situation of Miss Pinckney, and observed that her physicians had prescribed a residence of some time in the South of France as being indispensable to her recovery. Mr. De Beaumarchais said there could be no doubt but that the government would permit Genl. Pinckney to conduct his daughter to the place advised by her physicians; but that he would mention this circumstance also to the Minister.

32. Beaumarchais's name is used twice in this entry, and Pickering did not put brackets around Beaumarchais's name to indicate that JM had left a blank space. Perhaps Beaumarchais was not attempting to secure a loan or a bribe, so JM saw no harm in leaving his name in the Journal.

33. JM was referring to his need to secure credit for the Fairfax purchase that James Marshall had been seeking in Amsterdam and London in 1797.

34. JM reported this rumor in JM to Lee, Oct. 12, 1797. Gerry heard the same rumor and reported it to his wife. See Gerry to Ann Gerry, Oct. 9, 1797, Knight, ed., *Gerry's Letterbook*, 13.

March 29, 1798

I received this morning a billet from Mr. De Beaumarchais, requesting to see me. He informed me, that he had seen the Minister, who expressed himself very doubtfully on the subject of permitting General Pinckney to conduct his daughter to the South of France, and also on that of granting to us letters of safe-conduct. He expressed himself however in very strong terms against my taking England in my way to the United States. He said it would greatly irritate this government, and increase the difficulties of an accommodation; that it would also affect my reputation, as it would immediately be published by this government, that I was gone to England to receive the wages I had earned by breaking off the treaty with France. I told him in reply that my searching for that safety to which I was entitled, but which the Directory refused to afford me against its own cruizers, was no just cause of irritation, and ought not to encrease the difficulties of accommodation; that the calumny threatened against myself was too contemptible to be credited for a moment by those who would utter it, and was too much despised by me to be permitted to influence the smallest of my actions, that I could tell him plainly, and he might so inform the Minister, that if letters of safe-conduct were not furnished me, I should certainly endeavour to obtain personal safety by going to England.

March 30, 1798

Mr. Dutrimond called to see Mr. Gerry, and entered my apartment, Mr. Gerry being in the town. He showed an expectation, that we would demand our passports. I told him that we were ready to receive our passports, but that we could not demand them, because the letter of Mr. Talleyrand had held out the idea of treating, as being yet possible, and so long as such a possibility existed we could not demand permission to go away. He said that if we wished rather to be ordered away than to demand permission to leave the country, the order would soon be received. I told him, that if it was impossible to effect the objects of our mission, the order could not come too soon: that our letter to Mr. Talleyrand was finished, and only required to be corrected and copied, and that so soon as it was sent in I should be ready for myself to quit France, but that the situation of his daughter was extremely embarrassing to Genl. Pinckney, as it would prevent him from acting as promptly, as it was in my power to act.[35] He said that the Directory had given to Mr. Talleyrand a direction to send two physicians to inspect Miss Pinckney's health, and to report on the practicability of her going out of France; that for myself I might depend on receiving my passports. I mentioned to him the necessity of letters of safe-conduct, without which I would certainly go by England, and also stated my apprehension that the privateers, having rights under an Act of the legislature would disregard a mere letter of safe-conduct. He left me without answering these observations.

April 3, 1798

Mr. Gerry having finished his examination and corrections of the concluding part of our letter to the Minister, we met last night for the purpose of considering them. He prefaced his observations on the letter itself with a dissertation on himself and his own motives of conduct. This had been very frequently made and had been usually understood as implying a censure, not expressed, on his colleagues. It was again so understood and produced a warm conversation between him and General Pinckney. The Genl. told him, that he thought his conduct calculated to embarrass our government, and to encrease instead of diminishing the danger of war between the two nations: that if his conduct and his separation from us should be disapproved of in America (and he believed it would) that would furnish a better pretext for quarrel than could have been given by our acting and going together. Mr. Gerry charged Genl. Pinckney and myself with being embittered against him, and with having views and objects which were not candidly communicated to him. General Pinckney replied, "it is false sir:" he added that every thing known respecting the negociation had been communicated to him, but that Mr. Gerry himself had not used the same candour. Mr. Gerry called on him to state a fact in support of this opinion, and the General stated his holding long and repeated conversations with Mr. Talleyrand and his agents on the subjects of our country, which were jointly entrusted to us, and which he concealed from us. Mr. Gerry said that he had given his word not to reveal the purport of those conversations: that he had pressed the Minister to relieve him from the promise, but had not succeeded in obtaining permission to make the communication.

35. See American Envoys to Talleyrand, Apr. 3, 1798.

Genl. Pinckney replied that he ought never to have given such a promise; that similar applications had been made to him, and he instanced the case of Mr. Hottinguer, but he had refused to hear any thing which was not imparted also to his colleagues: that after having made the promise and obtained a knowledge of the matter to be disclosed, he ought to have refused to hold any further intercourse with Talleyrand respecting that or any other subject relating to the objects of our joint mission unless he was allowed to communicate it to us.

General Pinckney also told him, that he had deceived us with respect to the letter demanding our passports: that he had pretended to agree with us in writing that letter and in sending it, that he had corrected it to his own taste, had it translated and then refused to sign it.[36] Mr. Gerry said he had been told by Talleyrand, that if he sent the letter there would be a war:—he was proceeding, but General Pinckney interrupted him by observing, that this proved he had kept up to us the appearance of signing a letter, which his private communications with the Minister had decided him not to sign. Mr. Gerry corrected himself: he did not mean to say, that the Minister had told him, if he sent that letter, there would be a war; but that if we all left France there would be war. General Pinckney insisted that this was the same thing; because if that declaration of the Minister governed him, the declaration had been made while he held out the appearance of signing the letter. Mr. Gerry said, that he had always entertained a hope of bringing the Minister to treat with us together, and had intended to sign the letter; but that his intention was changed by a change of circumstances. General Pinckney insisted there was no change of circumstances. The conversation embraced several parts of the conduct of all the Ministers, and throughout General Pinckney challenged Mr. Gerry to produce a single act on his part, which was not perfectly open and candid, and insisted in plain terms on the duplicity; which had been practised upon us both. Mr. Gerry said we were wounded, and he was not surprized at it, by the manner in which we had been treated by the government of France, and the difference which had been used with respect to him: that it was, he believed, to be entirely attributed to his having paid to Mr. Talleyrand a private visit, which we had refused to pay: that he

36. See Journal, Feb. 2, 1798; see also JM and Pinckney to Talleyrand, Feb. 26, 1798, JM to Lee, Mar. 4, 1798; and Pinckney to King, Mar. 14, 1798, King Papers, Lib. Cong.

had acted in this by our advice. General Pinckney told him, that he had not acted by our advice; that we had not advised him to go (the fact is that I gave as strong an opinion against it as a man could give on a subject of that sort) that he knew very well that at that time and long afterwards he found his visit and himself so slighted that he was extremely sore under it, and had declared he would not go again. There was some consideration on this subject; and at length this unpleasant conversation terminated with some declarations on the part of Mr. Gerry of the strong attachment he had always felt for Genl. Pinckney, which he said could alone have prevailed on him to have accepted the mission. We at length entered on the letter and agreed on some corrections. To day between 12 & 1 the letter was sent in.

April 10, 1798

Having received letters from Bourdeaux[37] and from Nantz informing me, that the vessels at both those places would all sail in a few days, and being very much dissatisfied with the situation in which I found myself respecting my return to the United States or longer continuance in France I called on Mr. [38] to enquire whether he knew any thing of the resolution of the government respecting passports: he knew nothing, but said that he was about to visit the Minister to night, and that he would make a point of enquiring into the fact, and as he supposed it could not be a secret of informing me what ⟨was⟩ should be the result of the enquiry. I had represented to him that the private intimations I had received on the subject were of such a sort that I had packed up entirely, that I might be in readiness to depart so soon as the will of the government should be signified to me; that I could not even lay in a moderate stock of wine or send my foul linen to be washed; that I asked nothing of the government but a frank declaration whether I was to go or stay, that my private arrangements might conform with my situation; this I had a right to expect, because it would answer no national purpose to render my particular situation unnecessarily unpleasant. I also informed him that in a very few days no vessel destined for the United States would be in the ports of France.

37. See JM to James Hooe, Apr. 9, 1798.
38. Caron de Beaumarchais.

April 11, 1798

Mr. [39] called on me this morning after having seen the Minister. He told me that our departure was expected; that on his saying I complained of not receiving my passports, while it was privately intimated to me, that I must leave the country, and that this was not the manner in which a foreign minister ought to be treated, Mr. Talleyrand replied that I was no foreign minister, that I was to be considered as a private American citizen, to obtain my passport in the manner pursued by all others through the Consul. Mr. [40] replied that I was a foreign minister, and that this government could not deprive me of that character; that it was conferred upon me not by Mr. Talleyrand, but by the government of the United States; and though the Directory might refuse to receive or to treat with me, still my country had clothed me with the requisite powers, and I held them independent of France; that if I was unacceptable to this government, and in consequence thereof it was determined to send me away still I ought to be sent away like a minister; I ought to have my passports with letters of safe conduct, which would protect me from the cruizers of France: he added that I was informed that all the American vessels would soon quit the ports of France, and that I should be compelled to search elsewhere for a passage, which I could not obtain here. Mr. Talleyrand replied, that if I wished a passport, I must give my name, stature, age, complexion etc. to our Consul, who would obtain a passport for me; that with respect to a letter of safe-conduct, it would be unnecessary as no risk from the cruizers would be incurred; that it was well known I was determined to return through England, and had published that intention to every body with whom I had spoken. Mr. [41] replied that he knew perfectly I did not intend to return through England, unless forced to do so; that though I had private business there of very much importance, which would certainly be sufficient to induce me to take England in my way home, if I was a private individual, yet circumstanced as I was, I had determined to sacrifice my private interests to a public object; that the measures pursued would force me to go to England, and then I should hear it said by this government, that I had gone to England, in order to receive the reward

39. Caron de Beaumarchais.
40. Caron de Beaumarchais.
41. Caron de Beaumarchais.

of my perfidy; that it was an unworthy manner of treating a foreign minister, to whom this government was pleased to attribute sentiments which he denied holding. There was much other conversation of the same sort, which ended in a plain demonstration of the intention of the Minister, that in consequence of his letter I should demand my passport like any other citizen through our Consul, and embark for the United States.[42]

I told Mr. [43] that the Minister had written in such a style as to render this impossible; that he had not signified the wish of his government, that we should depart or selected the person that was to stay. At this he seemed surprized, and I shewed him that part of Mr. Talleyrand's letter.[44] He read it over two or three times, and I then observed to him, that if on that letter Genl. Pinckney and myself should return, our government would very properly say to us, that we had ourselves taken the character which the Minister had drawn generally, and had appropriated it to ourselves. I stated to him the purport of the answer we had given to this part of the letter, and he agreed that nothing could be more proper or reasonable. After some conversation on this subject he determined to revisit Mr. Talleyrand, and on his return to state to me the result of his visit.

In about three quarters of an hour he returned and informed that he had spoken with Mr. Talleyrand alone and had made to him the representations, which he stated with great force and which the subject naturally suggested. Mr. Talleyrand was warm in reply and charged him with being more attached to the Americans than to France. Mr. [45] said he was not more attached to the Americans than to France; that he thought himself serving his own country, when he was endeavouring to diminish the disgusts unnecessarily given to a man, who had rendered him great services, for whom he had a friendship, who had come to France for the purpose of endeavouring to reconcile the two Republics to each other, and who notwithstanding the sentiments ascribed to him was as much impressed with the importance of preventing a rupture as any man with whom he had conversed; that all I wanted was to know whether I was to go or to stay; that instead of acting

42. In a report to Congress on Jan. 21, 1799, Pickering used the information given in this entry and cited the Journal as his source. See Jan. 21, 1799, *Annals of Congress*, IX, 3537–3538.

43. Caron de Beaumarchais.

44. See Talleyrand to American Envoys, Mar. 18, 1798.

45. Caron de Beaumarchais.

plainly with me, they kept me in the situation of the statue in bronze—a foot in the air, without moving a step. Mr. Talleyrand said that he was mistaken in me; that I prevented all negociation, and that so soon as I was gone the negociation would be carried on; that in America I belonged to the English faction, which universally hated and opposed the French faction; that all I sought for was to produce a rupture in such a manner as to throw the whole blame on France; that this would be brought about, if the French government should order us out of the country. Mr. [46] replied that it was unjust to attribute to men intentions which they absolutely disavowed; that I had no desire of throwing blame upon France; but was unwilling to take blame to myself which was unmerited; that I had been sent to Paris by my nation for public purposes; that I was desirous of accomplishing the objects of my mission; and consequently at Paris was in my place and in my duty; but that the government of France alleged personal objections to me and refused to treat with me: the government wished me to leave the country; it was fair that they should tell me so: it was reasonable that my departure should appear to be produced by the will of the government, by which it was in reality produced; and not by my own will, which did not produce it; that it was true this had been verbally communicated to me repeatedly, but that diplomatic transactions required writing; that unless I received a communication in writing, signifying the positive objection of the government to me, I should remain while there was a hope of treating. Mr. Talleyrand persisted warmly in asserting that I only wished to receive the order for my departure for the purpose of throwing the blame on France: he said that he could easily devise means which would force me off; that he would send for Mr. Gerry and open negociations with him.[47]

I told Mr. [48] that whatever the powers of Mr. Gerry might be, when Genl. Pinckney and myself should be absent, he certainly had none to act separately while we were present; and that I was entirely confident he would not venture to act in any manner not approved of by us.

I told him that I believed the Minister endeavoured to make our

46. Caron de Beaumarchais.

47. Neither Talleyrand nor JM achieved their wishes to have the other bear the onus of breaking off the mission. Since Gerry remained in Paris until late July, the debate was without substance. Talleyrand did send passports to JM and Pinckney two days later. See Talleyrand to JM and Pinckney, Apr. 13, 1798.

48. Caron de Beaumarchais.

situation more unpleasant than his orders required in order to gratify his personal feelings; that I should, if orders for our departure were not given, take it for granted that the government had not authorized it, and should make my arrangements accordingly.

From William Vans Murray

Letterbook Copy, Murray Papers, Pierpont Morgan Library

Dear Sir, The Hague, October 5, 1797

The enclosed letter from your brother came to me yesterday & I think it safest to enclose it to you with a more appropriate address.[1] He tells me he goes to the U.S. and Mr. Foster[2] just from London, says they sailed about the middle of September. I admire secrecy—it is the soul of Love & War—and e'er this doubtless love letters extremely sincere, have past between the Directoire & you & your colleagues; but at least you might tell me to what lengths the Fishwomen proceeded *publicly* with you.[3] I am etc.

To Talleyrand

LS, Archives of the Ministry of Foreign Affairs, Paris

Citizen Minister Paris, October 6, 1797

The United States of America being desirous of terminating all differences between them and the French Republic and of restor-

1. The letter from James Markham Marshall, who was in London, has not been found.

2. Bossenger Foster, Jr. (1768–1816), the son of a Boston merchant, was Gerry's first secretary.

3. The women of Paris customarily performed a greeting ceremony for new ministers. Henry Rutledge, who participated in this boisterous affair in place of JM, described the event in a letter to his father. "The morning after our arrival, I had the satisfaction of going once more, through the ceremony of the Poissardes, for the benefit of Genl. Marshall—An honor which was conferred upon me, in consideration I suppose of my being more 'au fait' than his own Secretary, whom I contrived however to let in for a share of the 'embrassades'—being naturally of too generous a temper to aspire at a monopoly of any description. It would have afforded you no doubt a great deal of diversion to have beheld me in the midst of 40 or 50 strapping lasses deputed from all the Markets of Paris, endeavoring to return the handsome compliments I received, and buffetted about every now & then from one to the other—first one cheek & then the other, & sometimes both at once." Henry Rutledge to Edward Rutledge, Oct. 2, 1797, Dreer Collection, Historical Society of Pennsylvania.

ing that harmony and good understanding and that commercial and friendly intercourse which from the commencement of their political connection until lately have so happily subsisted, the President has nominated, and by and with the advice and consent of the Senate, has appointed us, the undersigned, jointly, and severally, Envoys extraordinary & Ministers Plenipotentiary, to the French Republic, for the purpose of accomplishing these great objects. In pursuance of such nomination and appointment and with such view having come to Paris, we wish, Citizen Minister, to wait on you at any hour you will be pleased to appoint, to present the copy of our Letters of Credence and whilst we evince our sincere and ardent desire for the speedy restoration of friendship and harmony between the two Republics we flatter ourselves with your concurrence in the accomplishment of this desirable event. We request you will accept the assurance of our perfect esteem and consideration.

CHARLES COTESWORTH PINCKNEY
JOHN MARSHALL
ELBRIDGE GERRY

From Thomas Paine

ALS, Pinckney Family Papers, Library of Congress

Gentlemen Paris, October 11, 1797

I drew up the enclosed plan about four months ago intending to shew it to Mr Madison as there was then a report that he was coming.[4] I have sent a french translation of it to the Swedish and Danish Ministers and I have sent an English Copy to the Minister for foreign Affairs.[5] I shall in a few days know their opinions, and also that of the prussian Minister. I have not yet spoken of it to the Directory but as soon as I can collect together some opinions respecting it I shall take the opportunity of doing so.

I know not what your instructions are nor do I wish to know them; but it may be convenient to you to be informed of the en-

4. For the background of this letter, see Journal, Oct. 11, 1797. See Paine to Fulwar Skipwith, Apr. 24, 1797, and Paine to James Madison, Apr. 27, 1797, Historical Society of Pennsylvania.

5. Paine to Talleyrand, Sept. 30, 1797, Correspondance Politique, Etats-Unis, XLVIII, Archives of the Ministry of Foreign Affairs, Paris. See JM to Charles Lee, Oct. 12, 1797.

closed plan. If it should take place, America can draw herself out of the Scrape she is in by the English Treaty, because it will supercede that treaty, and I see no other way by which she can be extricated. An expression in the Answer of the house of Representatives to the Message of Mr. Adams speaks something of making the Treaties equal if there being any inequalities, meaning thereby to cede to France the same things as are ceded in Jay's treaty to England. Mr. Nichols might mean honestly when he said this, but they are already ceded.[6] France takes them as her right in consequence of the 2 article in the treaty of Commerce of 1778. Besides, there is no good policy in mending one mischief by another; neither is this sacrifice of Neutral Rights consistent with the good of Neutral Nations considered collectively and as forming a common interest. Sweden and Denmark have already some reproaches to make to America for having deserted and betrayed the common cause of Neutrals in Jay's treaty, and that at the time when these two Nations had made proposals to the American administration to concert some method for common protection.

I know that france very sincerely hated the appearance of a rupture between the two republics, and this [ ] sensation on her part held her back in her resentment for a considerable time; but it was easy to see that when this delicacy was got over, America had nothing to expect from her but a high toned indignation.

As to compensation for the Vessels and Cargoes, it will not be good policy to press that subject too much at first; for as America has made a *merit* of disowning all gratitude to france for the aid received in the American Revolution it is problematical that she

6. During the congressional debate concerning an answer to John Adams's speech of May 16, 1797, John Nicholas (*ca.* 1763–1819), of Virginia, offered an amendment. "We therefore receive with the utmost satisfaction, your information, that a fresh attempt at negotiation will be instituted; and we expect with confidence that a mutual spirit of conciliation, and a disposition on the part of the United States to place France on the footing of other countries, by removing the inequalities which may have arisen in the operation of our respective treaties with them will produce an accommodation compatible with the engagements, rights, duties, and honor of the United States." The amendment was defeated, and the final version read: "We, therefore, receive with the utmost satisfaction your information that a fresh attempt at negotiation will be instituted; and we cherish the hope that a mutual spirit of conciliation, and a disposition on the part of France to compensate for any injuries which may have been committed upon our neutral rights; and, on the part of the United States, to place France on grounds similar to those of other countries in their relation and connection with us, if any inequalities shall be found to exist, will produce an accommodation compatible with the engagements, rights, duties, and honor of the United States." See May 22, 29, and June 3, 1797, *Annals of Congress*, VII, 69–70, 193, 236–237.

(france) may propose a settlement of those expences. There are many thousands in france who subscribed to the loans which enabled the french Government to carry on that war that have not now bread to eat. I have often heard this matter spoken of in conversation, and I observe that conversation grow into politics.

I know however that the french Government would be glad that the breach could be healed, but the english treaty lies so much in the way that I see not how it is to be got over, otherwise than by a general measure such as is proposed in the plan. I have said thus much to Talleyrand; and offered any aid I could give, taking that as a ground. In his answer to me he said—Je n'ai pas besoin de vous assurer de la reconnaissance avec laquelle Je recevrai les renseignmens ulterieurs que vous m'y annoncez sur les moyens de terminer d'une maniere durable des differens qui doivent exciter votre interet comme patriote et comme republicain. Animées d'un pareil principe vos Idees ne peuvent que jetter un jour précieux sur la discussion qui va s'ouvrir *et qui doit avoir pour but de reunir deux Republiques dont la division serai le triomphe des Ennemis de la Liberté.*

I enclose you some proof pages of a letter to the people of france. It will give you some insight into the cause of the event of the 18 Fructidor.[7] It will be translated into french by Mr Adet (American Minister).[8] The remainer of the letter will be five or six pages more. I leave the last half sheet open in order to close with whatever Circumstance the Negociation at Lille may be in, and of which I expect some account in two or three days.

Please to return me the plan and the observations. You are welcome to take a Copy if you please, but I cannot spare mine as I am obliged to do all my writing myself. Salut et fraternité

THOMAS PAINE

To Thomas Paine

Copy, Pinckney Family Papers, Library of Congress

Sr: Paris, October 12, 1797

We yesterday received your letter with the enclosures & are

7. Paine's essay, "The Eighteenth Fructidor," is printed in Philip S. Foner, ed., *The Complete Writings of Thomas Paine*, II (New York, 1945), 594–613.

8. Pierre-Auguste Adet (1763–1834).

thankful for every information relative to the affairs of our Country. We have availed ourselves of your permission in taking the copies mentioned, & agreeably to your desire return the originals. We have the honour to be, Your most obedt: hble Sert:

Signd C: C: PINCKNEY
J: MARSHALL
E: GERRY

To Charles Lee

AL, RG 59, National Archives

Dear Sir Paris, October 12, 1797

General Pinkney and myself reached Paris on the 27th. of September and our arrival was the next day unofficially notified to the Minister of foreign affairs, who was at the same time informed that Mr Gerry was on the continent of Europe and would join us in a very few days, when we should announce ourselves formally to him. We have been induced, though delay is calamity perhaps to us, to wait sometime at the Hague and afterwards at this place for our colleague; from a sollicitude to give our Country the aid of all its agents and because we conceived it too to be a mark of personal respect to which that Gentleman was intitled and which would contribute to perserve in the commission that harmony which is so very essential, which at present exists, and which I am persuaded will continue to exist.

In the night of the 4th. inst. we had the pleasure of seeing Mr. Gerry and the next day ⟨Major Rutledge and Major Mountflorence waited on the Minister of foreign affairs to inform him of⟩ our arrival was signified to the minister, who was asked to name a time when it woud be agreeable to him to receive a letter notifying him officially of our arrival & asking an audience for the purpose of delivering a copy of our letters of credence. He appointed the next day at 12 at which hour Major Rutlege waited on him with a letter announcing our arrival and soliciting permission to wait on him with a copy of our letters of credence. He appointed the 8th: at 1 OClock our reception. We attended and were a little surprized at being informed that the Minister was with the Directory but would see us at three OClock. At three we again attended and were in a short time admitted. General Pinkney delivered him a copy of our full powers and he informed us that the Directory had ordered a report on the existing relations between France & the United States on which he was then employed, and which would be completed in a few days; that after the receipt of that report the Directory would decide concerning us, which decision should immediately be communicated to us. We were without any hesitation furnished with cards of hospitality which Cards express the public character we bear. The residue of the conversation was perfectly unimportant. The personal demeanor of the Minister was polite and easy. We have not since heard from him in any manner whatever. It will appear strange to you as it does to us that this delay should be experienced. The relations between the two countries are notorious, the proceedings of our Government complained of by France have been long since acted upon and therefore one would suppose had been considered; Those of the french Government towards us have emanated from the Directory itself and therefore ought also to have been considered and understood. Our appointment was known in the beginning of August and my arrival in Holland with the commission was communicated very early in September. Yet our reception and the commencement of our negociations are delayed in order to receive a report. In the meantime our vessels are every day condemned and the money will soon be every day passing into the hands of the Captors. Some of the owners of privateers have been in Paris since our arrival and I think it not improbable that their object *has*[9] *been to exert their influence* which unfortunately is *very considerable to prevent any accommodation* which may *rescue from them the specie they have not yet received. I greatly fear they will be successful.* It is said that *Merlin when Minister of Justice received four thousand Louis from the owners of privateers for the direction concerning the role d'equipage* and it is said publickly by them that *money influences the Tribunals.* However this may be I am entirely persuaded that the *courts even in the last resort are political and will carry into effect the will of the Directory without any respect to its legality. This is ensured by the nice appointments made since the last revolution.* The members of the tribunals who judge in the first instance are, generally speaking, themselves the captors. The Ministers of France at Lisle had declared that they should wait till the 16th. of October for the return of Lord Malmsbury. A letter has been received informing them that he should not return. This you will see in the papers. There was a possibility that the directory

9. Italics indicate words originally in code.

might in some degree regulate its conduct toward us by the probability of a Peace with England and might therefore have designed this postponement of our reception for the purpose of fashioning it according to existing circumstances after the 16th. of October. However this may be the situation of our affairs seems to me to render some movement on our part indispensably necessary and I believe if we do not hear from the Minister in a few days we shall address to him unofficially a note requesting that all proceedings against our Captured Vessels may be suspended untill the result of our negociations is known.

I inclose you a letter we received from Mr Paine on the 11th. inst.[1] The plan he proposes is a combination of the United States with any of the nations of Europe for the support of the principles that neutral bottoms make neutral Goods etc. The practice is to be enforced absolutely cutting off all commercial intercourse of every sort with any nation which shall violate the principle, untill such nation shall pay three times the value of the goods it may have seized. A copy of the plan will be transmitted to you with our public letter. Our answer merely acknowledged the receipt of his letter with its enclosures and declared that we were *thankful* (a word I do not like) for any communications which might concern our country. We have not since heard further from him. *I think material to forward this paper to you because from the countenance this man receives one has reason to suppose it was not written without the knowledge and approbation of the government. However it may tend to develope the views of this nation with respect to us, I own it has not tended to remove the fear I before entertained concerning the issue of our negotiation.*

I am apprehensive that our countrymen have in some degree been lulled into a fatal security by the unfortunate decision of one of the tribunals in favor of our Commerce. I term it unfortunate because it was reversed and because from the universality of its publication I apprehend it has done mischief by putting our merchants off their guard. It ought to be remembered that there are very many merchants, and, to their eternal infamy be it said, many Americans, who are concerned in this Wicked and disgraceful business of plunder. These men will write letters encouraging our vessels from a hope that their intelligence will bring a number of them within their reach, and if even this was not the case the Merchants of a Sea Port catch at any favorable circumstance which

1. See Paine to American Envoys, Oct. 11, 1797.

may induce our Merchants to push our commerce to the Ports of France since it is for their profit and at our risk. These letters are not to be credited. There does not at present exist a single circumstance so far as facts are known to us, from which an inference is to be drawn in any degree flattering. It is notorious that a greater number of privateers are now fitting out than have been employed in any former period of the war and the government is consigned to the Merchants the National Ships of war for the purpose of cruising. It is also said that the rancor of these men against the Americans is still more violent than against the English. This I can believe—for Nations or individuals seldom forgive those they have greatly injured.

The campaign in Italy and on the Rhine it is expected is about opening. Great preparations are making and have been made on both sides. The French Armies are very strong, well disciplined, Accustomed to Victory, commanded by the most celebrated General in the world and can be recruited to any number. The government draws out at pleasure any portion of its enormous population to supply the places of those who may fall in Action or be taken off by disease. You cannot figure to yourself a government which more perfectly commands all the resources of the nation than that of France. Its resources of men and provisions are abundant. Money it will be found very difficult to raise. *The government has no credit. I am told that it occasionally borrows for emergencies at an enormous* premium *and makes deposits to secure repayment. On one great occasion* [*in*] *the last revolution the three Directors forcibly took from a company of bankers eight hundred thousand livres. The complete and perfect discredit of the government is effected by the late operation on the public debt two thirds of which they have in fact struck off under the pretext of mobilising it. This is supposed to have been unnecessary because it is believed that the national debt of France was not greater that than of the United States in proportion to the respective ability of the two nations. It is also in part effected by some suspicions concerning the continuance of the power of those who at present hold it. I sometimes hear that on this subject great doubts are entertained, tho was I to judge from what publicly appears I should suppose there could be none. The press is so entirely enslaved that it announces nothing which the Directory does not authorise and of consequence it exhibits only the universal joy of France at their having saved liberty by their late bold and decided measures. Strong violent and sanguinary means are used for their establishment and these means are applauded by the papers. I see nothing which would not appear to be dictated by the government itself and yet very frequently presses types and papers make a bonfire in the streets which lights the unfortunate printer, who knows not how he has offended, to the confinement to which he is doomed.*

We have some reason to believe that the effort of the government here be to break off or indeed prevent the commencement of negotiation here in such a manner as to leave it in the power of those whom it thinks its, I hope untruely its partisans in America to cast blame and thus the system of dividing us is to be kept up. Is it possible that it can be yet successful?

It is communicated to us indirectly that the Directory is excessively exasperated against the United States and will before our reception demand explanation of the speech made by the president to the last Congress.

October 19th *Inteligence has been received of the naval engagement with the Dutch. It has been stated to us that the Directory is now better disposed toward us. After this inteligence their change of disposition had been communicated indirectly. A gentleman*[2] *waited on General Pin*[ckney] *the evening of the eighteenth and told him that he brought a message from Talayran. that France would now consent to treat with America without demanding for her wounded honor on certain terms. They were that America should pay the debt due France by contract and otherwise to American citizens to be repaid in fifteen years. But said the gentleman this is not all there must be something for the pocket too. On to explain himself he said that the persons now in power must receive something for themselves: that claims beyond those really due could be made out, the money for which might pass into the private purse of the Directory and Minister. This proposition is not direct. The bearer of it received it from a Hamburg merchant*[3] *who received it from Talayran.*

October 25th

Our public letter states at length the *transaction hinted above. We hope the names of the parties will be kept secret. The proposition varying somewhat in* form *has been renewed by distant hints. I think the object to while away the time till some events in Europe shall decide France on the* [*measures*] *to be pursued with us. With her present government she* requires *only to be able to reach us to rule us with a rod of iron. Does it comport with the dignity of the American government that its ministers should remain thus suspended receiving indirectly propositions so disgraceful to the United States as well as to those who make them? Be assured this is* not the first *time the question has been asked but we have a delicate part to play* &

2. Jean Conrad Hottinguer. See Journal, Oct. 18–19, 1797.
3. Pierre Bellamy. See *ibid.*

well considered opinions must *sometimes be relinquished* for a substantial object. *The men now in power are personally hostile to our country. They do not possess the confidence of their own but they may* notwithstanding *retain their power for a considerable time unless* (*which is* extremely probable) *they quarrel among themselves. The party which reigns is supported by the private interests of a* bold & active *class of individuals. Half the surface of France yielded in doing this* an immensity of injustice has been practisd. *The return of moderate republicanism would soften the fate of those who have been punished without cause. The purchasers of national property consider this as endangering their* acquisitions *and will of course support the most violent. Such are the men now in power. Dreading the next elections if free they prepare for them by disfranchising* a large portion of the *citizens whose rights were* sanctioned by the *constitution and France is prepared to submit to this or any other violation of the most* sacred principles. *That she is not and never will be a republick is a truth which I* scarcely *dare* whisper *even to myself. It is in America and America only that human liberty has* found an *asylum. Let our foreign factions banish her from the United States and this earth affords her no longer a place of refuge. It is my decided opinion that the peace with the Emporor settles our negotiation and that our next letters will be dated from some other place than Paris.*

October 27

A bold and persevering effort has been repeated for money for private and public purposes. It has been repelled and I expect the result will be that we shall receive marching orders in a week. It is hardly worth mentioning except as it shows what the owners of privatiers can venture to do, that one of them who is in high favor has declard seriously that he had orderd his vessels to cruise for the envoys from the United States & to carry them to the West indies.

From William Vans Murray

Letterbook Copy, Murray Papers, Pierpont Morgan Library

Dr. Sir, The Hague, October 17, 1797

Considering the immense importance of your mission you may suppose I remained in great anxiety for a line of intelligence from you, & yours of the 10th.[4] was the first & only one I have received

4. Not found.

since you arrived at Paris. You attribute certain delays in prize causes to their true cause I dare say. The delay in your reception may be imputed to the same policy.

Mr. Gilpin of Philada. has obtained a passport & goes on to Paris, & I write by him.[5] The Dutch fleet has been dreadfully shattered.[6] Nine of their line are taken & one more missing. This affects parties differently. The Orangists among the vulgar enjoy it with a stupid triumph. There are on the stocks five of the line which will be ready next spring. I should hope that this disaster would be convertible to our good. The Dutch fleet kept to this coast a very large & expensive squadron from 16 to 20 sail of the line of british ships. At present five may do. The french will perceive that the british naval force to such an extent when liberated from Europe, may & probably will go to the W. Indies. All this renders our countenance & neutrality the more important. I am Dear Sir etc.

Statement

AD, Pinckney Family Papers, Library of Congress

Paris, October 19, 1797[7]

Une personne de marque qui a la confiance du directoire sur ce qui concerne les affaires de l'Amerique, convaincue de l'avantage mutuel qui resulteroit du rétablissement de la bonne intelligence

5. Joshua Gilpin (1765–1840) was a Philadelphia businessman who arrived in Paris on Nov. 12, 1797. See Joshua Gilpin Journal, XXXV, Joshua and Thomas Gilpin Papers, Pennsylvania Historical and Museum Commission, Harrisburg.

6. Murray was referring to the battle of Camperdown, in which the Dutch admiral, Jan de Winter, was taken prisoner by Adm. Adam Duncan, of the British navy.

7. These propositions were delivered by Jean Conrad Hottinguer to the American Envoys. For the background and English summaries of these propositions, see American Envoys to Timothy Pickering, Oct. 22, 1797.

Gerry later claimed that he wrote a response to these propositions and that Pinckney added a marginal note, "intended to be given saturday, the 21st of october." Gerry wrote: "To the question, whether the propositions, informally & confidentially communicated to us as private citizens, at the request, as is stated, of Mr. Talleyrand in his private capacity, will be adopted as the basis of a treaty? This answer is given—That it is highly probable, some of the propositions communicated on the evenings of the 19th & 20th of october (being the 28 & 29 Vendemiaire) will be considered as the basis of the projet of a treaty & others as inadmissible, but that it is impossible to discuss them, or come to a decision on them untill they are presented to us, in our *official characters*." Gerry to John Adams, June 24, 1799, Adams Papers, Massachusetts Historical Society. Gerry claimed he had authored the note in Gerry to Pickering, Nov. 21, 1798, *ibid*. See also Journal, Oct. 21, 1797.

entre les deux Nations se propose d'employer toute son influence pour parvenir à ce but.[8]

Elle assistera les Commissaires des Etats Unis dans toutes les demandes qu'ils pourront avoir à faire auprès du gouvernement de France en tant qu'elles ne contrarieront pas celles que le dernier se propose de former lui même, & dont on va comuniquer confidentiellement les principales.

On désire que dans les communications officielles on donne une tournure adoucissante à une partie du discours du président au Congrès qui a fortement irrité. L'on craint qu'en ne satisfaisant pas certains Individus à cet égard qu'ils se livreroient à tous leurs réssentimens.

On consentira à la nomination de Commissaires sur le même pied qu'il en a été nommé dans le traité avec l'Angleterre pour décider des réclamations qui peuvent faire des Individus americains sur le gouvernement de France, ou sur des Individus francais.

Les payemens qui d'après les décisions de ces commissaires tomberont à la charge du gouvernement de France, devront être avancés par le gouvernement americain même.

L'on desire que les fonds qui rentreront de cette manière au Commerce americain soyent employés à des nouvelles fournitures aux Colonies françaises. Des engagemens de cette nature de la part des Individus réclamans hateront probablement toujours les décisions des Commissaires français—& peut être desire-t-on que cette clause fasse partie des Instructions que le gouvernement des Etats Unis donnera aux Commissaires de son choix.

Le gouvernement français désire en outre de pouvoir obtenir un Emprunt de la part de celui des Etats Unis. Mais afin que cela ne puisse point donner de jalousie au gouvernement anglais & nuire à la neutralité des Etats Unis, on masquera cet Emprunt, en stipulant.

"Que le gouvernement des Etats Unis consent à faire les avances pour le payement des dettes contractées par les agens du gouvernement français vis à vis des Citoyens des Etats Unis, & qui sont dejà réconnues & le payement ordonné par le directoire, mais n'a point encore pu être effectué. Il dévra être rémis une note arretée du montant de ces créances.

Probablement que cette note pourra être accompagnée de pieces

8. Hottinguer informed the envoys that it was Talleyrand who had the confidence of the Directory. See American Envoys to Pickering, Oct. 22, 1797, and Journal, Oct. 18–19, 1797.

ostensibles, qui garantiront les agens de la comptabilité des Etats Unis, en cas de quelques ombrages qui donneroient lieu à des réchèrches.

Il sera aussi prélévé sur cet Emprunt certaines sommes pour faire les distributions d'usage en affaires diplomatiques.

To William Vans Murray

Copy, RG 59, National Archives[9]

My dear Sir, [Paris], October 21, 1797

We are not & I believe shall not be received. I cannot be explicit with you; but I am persuaded that, however unsuccessful our mission may be, our conduct can never be disapproved by our Country. I am preparing for orders, which I daily expect, to leave France.[1] Direct the person who distributes the Leyden Gazette at the Hague to send no more to me. With my very respectful compliments to Mrs. Murray, I remain, My Dr. Sir, Yr. sincere & affectte.

(Signed) J MARSHALL

9. Murray later enclosed this letter in Murray to Timothy Pickering, Oct. 28, 1797, Diplomatic Dispatches, Netherlands, III, RG 59, National Archives.

1. All of the envoys were depressed and expected a rapid termination of the negotiations. Mary Pinckney and Henry Rutledge expected to make a quick departure from Paris. See Mary Pinckney to Margaret Manigault, Oct. 22, 1797, Manigault Family Papers, University of South Carolina; Henry Rutledge to Edward Rutledge, Nov. 3, 1797, F 7, 4269, Archives Nationales, Paris. Pinckney believed the negotiations had reached a critical stage. In a letter to Murray, Pinckney's pessimism was equal to JM's. "When I dropt you a line the other day, I did not expect to have been thus long in Paris—nor do I now expect to remain here a week longer, & yet it may happen that I shall not leave it for the winter. . . . We experience a haughtiness which is unexampled in the history & practice of nations, and feel ourselves under the necessity of submitting to circumstances which make an impression to be worn out, you may be assured, only with life. I would give a handsome fee for one half hour with you. 'I could a tale unfold etc.' but no more of this." See Pinckney to Murray, Oct. 30, 1797, copy enclosed in Murray to Pickering, Nov. 10, 1797, Diplomatic Dispatches, Netherlands, III, RG 59.

Gerry's assessment of the situation at this time was remarkably similar to JM's and Pinckney's. "The ministers of the U. States here are in a very unpleasant situation. They are not to be received by the Directoire, & having no powers to negociate upon certain propositions *informally* made, which the most extravagant imagination of any citizen of the United States could never have suggested, they expect every moment a *formal* hint to depart, & if made, will promptly obey it. . . . The fact is, as I conceive it, that a small cargo of mexican dollars would be more efficient in a negociation at present than two Cargoes of Ambassadors." Gerry to Murray, Oct. 30, 1797, enclosed in Murray to Pickering, Nov. 10, 1797, *ibid.*

To Timothy Pickering

LS, RG 59, National Archives

No. 1

Dear Sir Paris, October 22, 1797[2]

All of us having arrived at Paris on the evening of the fourth instant, on the next day we verbally and unofficially informed the Minister of Foreign Affairs therewith, & desired to know when he would be at leisure to receive one of our Secretaries with the official notification; he appointed the next day at two o'Clock, when Major Rutledge[3] waited on him with the following Letter.

Citizen Minister,

The United States of America being desirous of terminating all differences between them and the French Republic, and of restoring that harmony and good understanding, and that commercial and friendly intercourse which from the commencement of their political connection until lately have so happily subsisted, the President has nominated and by and with the advice and consent of the Senate has appointed us, the undersigned, jointly and severally Envoys extraordinary and Ministers Plenipotentiary to the French Republic, for the purpose of accomplishing these great objects. In persuance of such nomination and appointment and with such view having come to Paris, we wish, Citizen Minister, to wait on you at any hour you will be pleased to appoint, to present the Copy of our Letters of Credence; and whilst we evince our sincere and ardent desire for the speedy restoration of friendship and harmony between the two Republics, we flatter ourselves with your concurrence in the accomplishment of this desirable event. We request you will accept the assurances of our perfect esteem and consideration.

Paris October 6th. in the 22d. year of American Independence

Signed, CHARLES COTESWORTH PINCKNEY
JOHN MARSHALL
ELBRIDGE GERRY

To this letter the Minister gave a verbal answer that he would see us the day after the morrow (the 8th.) at one o'Clock. Accordingly at that hour and day we waited on the Minister at his home where his office is held, when being informed he was not at home, the Secretary General[4] of the Department told Major Rutledge that the Minister was obliged to wait on the Directory &

2. A note on the verso indicates this letter arrived in Pickering's office on Mar. 4, 1798, "at 10. P.M."

3. Henry Rutledge.

4. Pierre Paganel (1745–1826) was chief secretary at this time.

requested we would suspend our visit till three o'Clock. At which hour we called; the Minister we found was then engaged with the Portuguese Minister,[5] who retired in about ten minutes, when we were introduced and produced the copy of our Letters of credence, which the Minister persued and kept. He informed us "that the Directory had required him to make a report relative to the situation of the United States with regard to France which he was then about, and which would be finished in a few days, when he would let us know what steps were to follow." We asked if cards of hospitality were in the mean time necessary, he said they were and that they should be delivered to us: and he immediately rung for his Secretary and directed him to make them out. The Conversation was carried on by him in French, and by us in our own language.

The next day Cards of Hospitality were sent to us and our Secretaries, in a Style suitable to our official Character.

On Saturday the 14th Major Mountflorence informed General Pinckney that he had a conversation with mr. Osmond,[6] the private and confidential Secretary of the Minister of Foreign Affairs, who told him that the Directory were greatly exasperated at some parts of the President's Speech at the opening of the last Session of Congress, and would require an explanation of them from us. The particular parts were not mentioned. In another Conversation on the same day the Secretary informed the Major that the Minister had told him it was probable we should not have a public Audience of the Directory till such time as our negociation was finished; that probably persons might be appointed to treat with us, but they would report to him, and he would have the direction of the negociation. The Major did not conceal from mr. Osmond his intention to communicate these conversations to us.

In[7] *the morning of October the eighteenth M. Hubbard*[8] *of the House of Van Stophorsts and Hubbard of Amsterdam called on General Pinckney and informed him that a Mr. Horttinguer who was in Paris and whom the General had seen at Amsterdam was a gentleman of considerable credit* and *reputation; that he had formerly been a banker at Paris* and *had settled his affairs with honor; that he had then formed connections in America; had married a native of that country; intended to settle there; was supported by some capital houses in Holland; and that we might place great*

5. Le Chevalier Antonio de Araujo de Azevedo.
6. See Journal, Oct. 14, 1797.
7. Italics indicate words originally in code.
8. Nicholas Hubbard, later identified as W of the WXYZ agents.

reliance on him.[9] *In the evening of the same day M. Horttinguer called on General Pinckney and after having sat some time in* a *room full of company whispered* [*to*] *him that he had a message from M. Talleyrand* to *communicate when he was at leisure. General Pinckney immediately withdrew with him into another room; and when they were alone, M. Horttinguer said that he was charged with a business in which he was a novice; that he had been acquainted with M. Talleyrand in America; and that he was sure he had a great regard for that country* and *its citizens*; and *was very desirous that a reconciliation should be brought about with France: that to effectuate that end, he was ready*, if it *was thought proper, to suggest a plan, confidentially, that M. Talleyrand expected would answer the purpose. General Pinckney said he should be glad to hear it. M. Horttinguer replied, that the Directory*, and *particularly two of the members of it, were exceedingly irritated at some passages of the President's speech*, and *desired that they should be softened;* and *that this step would be necessary previous*

9. When a copy of this dispatch was submitted to Congress on Apr. 3, 1798, Pickering substituted W for Hubbard and X for Hottinguer. In addition all descriptive information about Hottinguer was omitted. See Apr. 3, 1798, *Annals of Congress*, IX, 3338.

The meeting with Hottinguer may have been the one that Francis Childs (1763–1830), formerly a New York printer who was in Europe to secure the release of Lafayette, described in a letter to William Vans Murray. Childs's letter convinced Pinckney and JM that they should leave for Paris without waiting for Gerry. Childs wrote: "A friend (This was a Hamburg banker who had lived some years in Paris—a man friendly to the US) of mine, who had the honor of dining with you at the H (Hague) in company with myself & Genl. P[inckne]y, yesterday dined at a party wholly of Government Bankers, ministers etc. where, as he was connected with them, the conversation turned generally on the general affairs of the nation. Among other topics the situation of our poor Country occupied them a few moments. They were quite unreserved & spoke freely. They had no objection to *make peace* with A[merica] but then the A[mericans] must wholly abandon their claims; they must just make such acknowledgements and sign just such papers as should be offered to them. We were not even spoken of as having the right *to ask* for anything. They look on our political situation as desperate at home, assuring themselves of a strong party amongst us, at least equal to counteract the operations of our Government, if not sufficient wholly to overturn it and destroy the Union. This was not the opinion of one but of all of them—& they had in company the late secretary of the mission to our country [Brunet], who thought that if we went to war with F[rance] our union would not last us six months, and that leaving us unattacked would be a great favor." See [Francis Childs] to Murray, Sept. 11, 1797, enclosed in Murray to George Washington, Sept. 17, 1797, Washington Papers, Ser. 4, Library of Congress (microfilm ed., reel 109); several illegible words have been supplied from another copy of Childs's letter enclosed Murray to Pickering, Sept. 23, 1797, Diplomatic Dispatches, Netherlands, III, RG 59, National Archives. For the identification of Childs as the author of the letter, see Murray to Childs, Sept. 24, 1797, Murray Papers, Pierpont Morgan Library. For Childs's activities in Europe, see Rufus King to Samuel Williams, Sept. 1, 1797, enclosed in King to Pickering, Sept. 3, 1797, Diplomatic Dispatches, Great Britain, V, RG 59. A biographical sketch of Childs is in E. James Ferguson *et al.*, eds., *The Papers of Robert Morris, 1781-1784*, I (Pittsburgh, 1973), 114 n. 6.

to our reception; that besides this, a *sum of money was required for the pocket of the Directory* and *ministers, which would be* at *the disposal of M. Talleyrand;* and *that a loan would also be insisted on. M. Horttinguer said if we acceded to these measures, M. Talleyrand had no doubt that all our differences with France might be accommodated. On enquiry, M. Horttinguer could not point out the particular passages of the speech that had given offence, nor the quantum of the loan; but mentioned that the douceur for the pocket was twelve hundred thousand livres, about fifty thousand pounds sterling. General Pinckney told him his colleagues* and *himself from the time of their arrival here had been treated with great slight and disrespect; that they earnestly wished for peace and reconciliation with France;* and *had been entrusted by their country with very great powers to obtain these ends on honourable terms; that with regard to the propositions made, he could not even consider of them before he had communicated them to his colleagues; that after he had done so, he should hear from him. After a communication and consultation had, it was agreed that General Pinckney should call on M. Horttinguer and request him to make his propositions to us all; and for fear of mistakes or misapprehension, that he should be requested to reduce the heads into writing. Accordingly, on the morning of October the nineteenth, General Pinckney called on M. Horttinguer, who consented to see his colleagues in the evening, and to reduce his propositions to writing. He said his communication was not immediately with M. Talleyrand, but through another gentleman, in whom M. Talleyrand had great confidence: this proved afterwards to be M. Bellamy, a native of Geneva, of the house of Bellamy Riccia and Company of Hamburg.*[1]

At six in the evening, M. Horttinguer came and left *with us the first set of propositions which, translated* from the *French, are as follows.* "A *person who possesses the confidence* of the *Directory,* on what *relates to the affairs of America, convinced of the mutual* advantages which *would result from the reestablishment of* the *good understanding between two nations, proposes to employ* all of *his influence to obtain this object.* He will *assist the commissioners of the United States* in all the *demands which they may have* to *make from the government of France, in as* much as they *may not be contradictory* to *those which he proposes* himself *to make,* and *of which the principal will be communicated confidentially.* It is desired *that in the official communications* there should *be given a softening turn* to a *part of the President's speech to Congress, which has caused much irritation.* It is *feared* that in *not satisfying certain individuals* in *this re-*

1. In the printed dispatch, Y was substituted for Bellamy, and the name of his banking house in Hamburg was omitted. See Journal, Oct. 18–19, 1797.

spect, they may *give way to all their resentment.* The *nomination of commissioners* will *be consented to on the same footing* as they have *been named in the treaty with England, to decide on the reclamations which individuals of America may make on the government of France*, or on *French individuals.* The *payment which* agreably *to the decisions of the commissioners, shall fall to the share of the French Government, are to be advanced by the American government* itself. It is *desired that the funds which* by this *means shall enter again into* the *American trade, should be employed in new supplies* for the *French colonies.* Engagements *of* this *nature* on *the part of individuals reclaming will* always *hasten in all* probability *the decisions of the French commissioners;* and perhaps *it may be desired that this clause should make* a *part of* the *instructions which the government* of the *United States should give to the commissioners they may chuse.* The *French government desires besides to obtain a loan from the United States;* but so that *that should not give any jealousy* to the *English government, nor hurt the neutrality of the United States this loan shall be masked*, by *stipulating* That the *government of the United States consents to make* The *advances* for the *payment of the debts contracted by the agents of* the *French government with the citizens of* the *United States; and which are* already *acknowledged*, and *the payment ordered by the Directory, but without having been yet effectuated.* There *should be delivered* a *note* to the *amount of these debts.* Probably *this note may be accompanied* by *ostensible peices which will guarantee to the agents* the *responsability of the United States in case any umbrage should cause an enquiry.* There shall *also be first taken* from *this loan certain sums for the purpose* of making *the customary distributions in diplomatic affairs.*"[2] The *person of note mentioned in* the *minutes who had* the *confidence* of *the Directory*, he *said before us all, was M. Talleyrand.* The *amount of the loan he* could not *ascertain precisely* but understood it *would be according* to *our ability to pay.* The *sum which would be considered* as *proper according to diplomatic usage* was *about twelve hundred thousand livres. He* could not *state to us what parts* of the *President's speech* were *excepted to*, but *said he would enquire* and *inform us. He agreed to* break*fast* with *M. Gerry the morning of the twenty first* in *order to make such explanations* as *we had then* requested or *should* think *proper to request: but* on *the morning of the twentieth M. Horttinguer called and said* that *M. Bellami*, the *confidential friend* of *M. Talleyrand*, instead of *communicating with us through M. Horttinguer, would see us himself* and *make* the *necessary explanations. We*

2. See Statement, Oct. 19, 1797, for a copy of the original.

appointed to *meet him the evening* of the *twentieth, at seven o'clock, in General Marshalls room.* ⟦At[3] *seven M. Bellami* and *M. Horttinguer entered:* and the *first mentioned gentleman* being in*troduced to us* as the *confidential friend of M. Talleyrand, immediately stated to us* the *favorable impressions of* that *gentleman toward our country, impressions which* were made *by the kindness* and *civilities he had personally received in America.* That *impressed* by *his solicitude* to *repay these kindness, he was willing to aid us* in the *present negociation by his good offices* with the *Directory, who* were, *he said, extremely irritated against the government of* the *United States, on account of some parts of the Presidents speech,* & *who* had *neither acknowledged nor received us,* and consequently have not *authorised M. Talleyrand to have any communications* with *us.* The *Minister therefore could not see us himself* but had *authorized his friend M. Bellami to communicate to us certain propositions* and *to receive our answers to them,* and to *promise on his part that if we would engage* to *consider them as the basis of the proposed negociation, he would intercede* with the *Directory to acknowledge us* and *to give us a public audience. M. Bellami stated to us* explicitly and repeatedly *that he was cloathed with no authority; that he was not a diplomatic character;* that *he was not even a Frenchman; he was only the friend of M. Talleyrand,* and *trusted by him.*⟧ That with regard to *himself, he had landed property in America* on *which he hoped his children would reside:* and that *he earnestly wished well to the United States.*[4] He then *took out of his pocket* a *French translation of the President's speech,* the *parts of which objected to* by *the Directory* were *marked* agreeably to *our request to M. Horttinguer* and are *contained in the exhibit* A. *Then he made us* the *second set of propositions,* which were *dictated by* him & *written by M. Horttinguer* in *our presence,* and *delivered* to *us,* and which, *translated from the French, are as follows:*[5] "*There is demanded a formal disavowal in writing, declaring* that the *speech of the citizen President Barras did not contain any thing offensive* to the *government of the United States,* nor *any thing which deserved* the *epithets contained in the whole paragraph.* Secondly, *reparation is demanded* for the *article by which* it *shall be declared* that the *decree of the Directory* there *mentioned did not contain* any *thing contrary to the treaty of 1778,* and had none *of those fatal consequences* that *the paragraph reproaches to it.* Thirdly, it is *demanded* that *there should be*

3. Material in open brackets (⟦ ⟧) is a slightly modified passage taken from the Journal, Oct. 20, 1797.

4. The statement that Bellamy owned property in the United States was omitted in the copy of the dispatch turned over to Congress on Apr. 3, 1798.

5. For a discussion of the suggested answer to Hottinguer's proposals, see Journal, Oct. 21, 1797, and Statement, Oct. 19, 1797.

an acknowledgement in writing of the *depredations* exercised *on our trade by the English* and *French privateers*. Fourthly, the *government of France, faithful to the profession of public faith which it* has *made not to intermeddle in* the *internal affairs of foreign governments* with which it *is at peace, would look upon* this *paragraph as an attack upon its loyalty*, if this *was intended by the President*. It *demands, in consequence, a formal declaration* that it is *not the government of France, nor its agents* that *this paragraph meant to designate. In* consideration *of these reparations, the French Republic disposed to renew* with the *United States of America*, a *treaty which shall place them reciprocally in the same state* that they were *in 1778*. By *this new treaty, France shall be placed, with respect to the United States, exactly on* the *same footing* as they *stand with England, in virtue of* the *last treaty which has been concluded between them*. A *secret article of this new treaty would be* a *loan*, to *be made by* the *United States to the French Republic:* and *once agreed upon the amount of* the *loan*, it would be *endeavoured to consult the convenience* of the *United States with respect to the best method of preventing its publicity*." On reading *the speech, M. Bellami dilated very much* upon the *keenness of the resentment it had produced, and expatiated largely* on the *satisfaction he said was* indispensably *necessary as a preliminary to negociation*. But said *he, gentlemen, I will not disguise* from you, that *this satisfaction, being made*, the *essential part of the treaty remains* to be *adjusted: "il faut de l'argent —il faut beaucoup d'argent." You must pay money—you must pay a great deal of money*. He *spoke much of the force*, the *honor* and the jealous *republican pride of France;* and *represented to us strongly the advantages which we should derive from the neutrality* thus to *be purchased. He said that the receipt of the money might be so disguised* as to *prevent its being considered* as a *breach of neutrality by England;* and thus *save us from being embroiled* with that *power*. Concerning *the twelve hundred thousand livres, little was said;* that being *completely understood, on all sides, to be required for* the *officers of government;* and *therefore needing no* further *explanation*. These *propositions, he said, being considered* as *the admitted basis of the proposed treaty, M. Talleyrand trusted* that, *by his influence with the Directory, he could prevail on the government to receive us. We asked whether we were to consider it* as certain *that without previous stipulation to the effect required we were not to be received. He answered, that M. Talleyrand himself was not authorised to speak to us the will of the Directory* and consequently *could not authorise him*. The *conversation continued until after nine, when they left us;* having *engaged to breakfast with M. Gerry the next morning. October the twenty first, M. Hortinguer came before nine o'clock. M. Bellami did not come until ten: he had passed the morning with M. Talleyrand.* After *breakfast the subject was immediately resumed. He represented to us, that we were not yet acknowledged or received; that the Directory were so exasperated against the United States,* as to have *come to a determination to demand from us, previous to our reception, those disavowals, reparations* and *explanations, which were stated at large last evening. He said that M. Talleyrand* and *himself were extremely sensible of the pain we* must *feel in complying with this demand*: but that the *Directory would not dispense with it: that therefore we must consider it as the indispensable preliminary, to obtain our reception: unless*[6] *we could find the means to change their determination in this particular.* That *if we satisfied the Directory in these particulars, a letter would be written to us to demand* the *extent of our powers,* and to *know whether we were authorized to place them precisely on the same footing with England: whether, he said, our full powers were really* and *substantially full powers; or, like those of Lord Malmesbury, only illusory powers.* That *if, to this demand, our answer should be affirmative,* then *France would consent that commissioners should be appointed to ascertain the claims of the United States, in like manner as under our treaty with England:* but from their *jurisdiction must be withdrawn those which were condemned for want of a rôle d'equipage*; that being a *point on which Merlin, while minister of justice, had written* a *treatise* and on *which the Directory were decided.* There *would however be no objection* to *our complaining of these captures* in the *course of the negociation;* and *if we could convince Merlin by our reasoning,* the *Minister would himself be* satisfied *with our so doing.* We *required an explanation of that part* of the *conversation in which M. Bellami had hinted at our finding means to avert the demand concerning the President's speech.* He *answered that he was not authorised to state those means; but that we* must *search for them* and *propose them ourselves.* If however *we asked his opinion* as *a private individual,* and *would receive it as coming from him, he would suggest to us the means which in his opinion would succeed.* On *being asked to suggest the means, he answered—money.* That the *Directory were jealous of its own honor* and of the *honor of the nation;* that *it insisted on* receiving *from us the same respect with which we had treated the king;* that *this honor must be maintained in the manner before required; unless we substituted* in the *place* of those *reparations something perhaps more valuable that was money.* He *said further, that if we desired him to point out the sum which he believed would be satisfactory, he would do so.* We *requested him to proceed:* and *he said that there were thirty two millions of florins of Dutch inscriptions, worth ten shillings in*

6. This word and the remainder of the sentence are underlined in the manuscript.

the pound, which might be assigned to us at *twenty shillings in* the *pound:* and he *preceeded to state to us the certainty*, that *after a peace* the *Dutch government would repay us the money; so that we should ultimately lose nothing:* and *the only operation of the measure would be, an advance from us to France of thirty two millions, on the credit of the government of Holland. We asked him whether the fifty thousand pounds sterling, as a douceur to the Directory*, must *be in addition to this sum. He answered in the affirmative. We told him, that on the subject of the treaty, we had no hesitation in saying that our powers were ample: that on the other points proposed to us, we would retire into* another *room, and return in a few minutes with our answer.*

We committed immediately *to writing the answer we proposed, in the following words: "Our powers respecting a treaty are ample: but the proposition of a loan, in the form of Dutch inscriptions, or in any other form, is not within the limits of our instructions: upon this point therefore the government* must *be consulted: one of the American Ministers will for the purpose forthwith embark for America: provided the Directoire will suspend all further captures on American vessels*, and *will suspend proceedings on those already captured, as well where they have been already condemned, as where the decisions have not yet been rendered:* and *that where sales have been made, but the money not yet received by the captors, it shall not be paid until the preliminary questions proposed to the ministers of the United States be discussed* [*and*] *decided:" which was read as a verbal answer;* and *we told them they might copy it if they pleased. M. Bellamy refused to do so; his disappointment was apparent: he said we treated the money part of the proposition as if it had proceeded from the Directory; whereas in fact* it *did not proceed even from the Minister but was only a suggestion from himself, as* a *substitute to be proposed by us, in order to avoid the painful acknowledgement that the Directory had determined to demand of us.* It *was told him, that we understood that matter perfectly; that we knew the proposition was in form to be ours; but that it came substantially from the minister. We asked what had led to our present conversation? And General Pinckney* then *repeated the first communication from M. Horttinguer* (*to the whole of which that gentleman assented*) and *we observed that those gentlemen had brought no testimonials of their speaking any thing from authority; but that relying on the fair characters they bore, we had believed them when they said they were from the minister;* and *had conversed with them in like manner as if we were conversing with M. Talleyrand himself; and that we could not consider any suggestion M. Bellamy had made, as not having been previously approved of: but yet, if he did not choose to take a memorandum in writing of our answer, we had no wish that he should do so:* and *further*, if *he chose to give the answer to his proposition the form of a proposition* from *ourselves, we* could only *tell him that we had no other proposition to make*, relative *to any advance of money on our part*. That *America had sustained deep* and *heavy losses by French depredations on our commerce*, and that *France had alledged* [*some*][7] *complaints against* the *United States*, that on those *subjects we came fully prepared;* and were *not a little surprized to find France unwilling to hear us;* and making *demands upon us which* could *never have been suspected by* our *government;* and *which had the appearance of our being the aggressing party. M. Bellami expressed himself vehemently* on the *resentment of France;* and *complained that instead of our proposing some substitute* for the *reparations demanded of us, we were stipulating certain conditions to be performed by* the *Directory itself*. That *he could not take charge of such propositions* and that the *Directory would persist in its demand* [*of*] *those reparations which he at first stated. We answered, that we could not help it; it was for the Directory to determine what course its own honor and the interests of France required it to pursue: it was for us to guard the interests and honor of our country. M. Bellamy observed, that we had taken no notice of the first proposition, which was, to know whether we were ready to make the disavowal reparations and explanations concerning the President's Speech. We told him that we supposed it to be impossible that either he or the minister could imagine that such a proposition could require an answer: that we did not understand it as being seriously expected; but merely as introductory to the subjects of real consideration.*

He spoke of the respect which the Directory required, and repeated, that it would exact as much as was paid to the antient kings. We answered, that America had demonstrated to the world, and especially to France, a much greater respect for her present government than for her former monarchy; and that there was no evidence of this disposition which ought to be required, that we were not ready to give. He said that we should certainly not be received; and seemed to shudder at the consequences. We told him that America had made every possible effort to remain on friendly terms with France; that she was still making them: that if France would not hear us; but would make war on the United States; nothing remained for us, but to regret the unavoidable necessity of defending ourselves.

7. The code reads "so," but both letterbook copies of the dispatch read "some complaints." This was probably a simple decoding error, since 1187 was the number for "so" and 1188 for "some." Pickering misinterpreted the code, making it read "so [many] complaints," rather than "some complaints." See Apr. 3, 1798, *Annals of Congress*, IX, 3334; American Envoys to Pickering, Oct. 22, 1797, Franklin Collection, Yale University; Gerry Letterbook, Gerry Papers, Henry E. Huntington Library.

The subject of our powers was again mentioned; and we told him, that America was solicitous to have no more misunderstandings with any republic, but especially with France; that she wished a permanent treaty; and was sensible that no treaty could be permanent which did not comport with the interests of the parties; and therefore that he might be assured, that our powers were such as authorized us to place France on an equal ground with England, in any respects in which an inequality might be supposed to exist at present between them, to the disadvantage of France. The *subject of the rôle d'equipage was also mentioned; and we asked what assurance we could have, if France insisted on the right of adding to the stipulations of our our treaty, or of altering them by municipal regulations, that any future treaty we could make should be observed. M. Bellamy said, that he did not assert the principle of changing treaties by municipal regulations; but that the Directory considered its regulation concerning the rôle d'equipage as comporting with the treaty. We observed to him, that none of our vessels had what the French termed a rôle d'equipage; & that if we were to surrender all the property which had been taken from our citizens in cases where their vessels were not furnished with such a rôle, the government would be* responsible *to its citizens for the property so surrendered; since it would be impossible to undertake to assert that there was any plausibility in the allegation, that our treaty required a rôle d'equipage.*

The *subject of disavowals* etc. *concerning the Presidents speech was again mentioned; and it was observed, that the constitution of the United States authorised and required our President to communicate his ideas on the affairs of the nation; that in obedience to the constitution he had done so; that we had not power to confirm or invalidate any part of the President's speech; that such an attempt could produce no other effect than to make us* ridiculous *to the government and to the citizens at large of the United States; and to produce, on the part of the President, an immediate disavowal* and *recall of us as his agents: that independent of this, all America was acquainted with the facts stated by the President; and our disavowing them would not change the public sentiment concerning them.*

We *parted with mutual professions of personal respect, and with full indications, on the part of M. Bellamy, of his expectation that we should immediately receive the threatened letter.*[8]

The *nature of the above communication will evince the necessity of secrecy;* and we *have promised Messrs. Horttinguer* and *Bellami that their names shall in no event be made public.*

8. This report on the conversation is much more extensive than that in the Journal, in which JM noted, "The conversation is stated at large in our public letter." See Journal, Oct. 21, 1797.

We have the honor to be, with great respect & esteem, your most obedient humble Servants

CHARLES COTESWORTH PINCKNEY
J MARSHALL
E GERRY

P. S. October 27th. 1797. The Definitive Articles of Peace are signed between the French Republic and the Emperor, the particulars you will find in the public prints. The Portuguese Minister[9] is ordered to quit France as the Treaty with Portugal has not been yet ratified by the Queen. The Treaty itself is declared by the Directory to be void. Since our arrival at Paris the Tribunal of Cassation has rejected Capt: Scott's petition complaining of the condemnation of his vessel by the Civil tribunal for the want of a Role d'Equipage. Mr. Duclos,[1] the Advocate employed in behalf of the owners of the American Vessels who have appealed in the last report to the Tribunal of Cassation, informs that notwithstanding all the arguments he made use of to the Reporter and Commissary of the Executive Directory to put off the hearing of the Rosanna as a diplomatic case, till the issue of our negociations is known, that case is set down for hearing and will come on the 29th. or 30th. instant. The same Advocate also says that it is obvious that the Tribunal have received instructions from the Officers of the Government to hasten their decisions, and that it was hardly worth while to plead, for all our petitions in Cassation would be rejected. Our Advocates however decline giving their Sentiments on this subject in writing under an apprehension of committing themselves.

Exhibit A[2]

No. 1. With this conduct of the French Government, it will be proper to take into view, the public audience given to the late minister of the United States, on his taking leave of the Executive Directory. The speech of the President discloses sentiments more alarming than the refusal of a Minister, because more dangerous to our independence and union, and at the same time studiously

9. The Treaty of Campo Formio. The Portuguese minister, Araujo, moved to Holland to await word from his government.

1. In the copy of the dispatch sent to Congress on Apr. 3, 1798, Pickering omitted Duclos's name and all references to his being an advocate. See Apr. 3, 1798, *Annals of Congress*, IX, 3345–3346.

2. The enclosure is dated Oct. 20, 1797, and is entitled, "Paragraphs of the President's Speech, referd to in letter no. 1 under title of Exhibit A."

marked with indignities towards the Government of the United States. It evinces a disposition to separate the people of the United States from the Government; to persuade them that they have different affections, principles and interests from those of their fellow citizens, whom they themselves have chosen to manage their common concerns; and thus to produce divisions fatal to our peace. Such attempts ought to be repelled, with a decision which shall convince France & the world, that we are not a degraded people, humiliated under a colonial spirit of fear and sense of inferiority, fitted to be the miserable instruments of foreign influence and regardless of national honor, character & interest.

No. 2. The diplomatic intercourse between the United States & France being at present suspended, the Government has no means of obtaining official information from that Country: nevertheless there is reason to believe that the Executive Directory passed a decree on the second of March last, contravening in part the treaty of Amity and Commerce of 1778, injurious to our lawful commerce and endangering the lives of our Citizens. A Copy of this Decree will be laid before you.

No. 3. While we are endeavoring to adjust all our differences with France; by amicable negociation, the progress of the war in Europe, the Depredations on our Commerce, the personal injuries to our Citizens and the general complexion of affairs, render it my indispensable duty to recommend to your consideration effectual measures of defence.

No. 4. It is impossible to conceal from ourselves or the world, what has been before observed, that endeavors have been employed to foster & establish a division between the Government and the people of the United States. To investigate the causes which have encouraged this attempt is not necessary. But to repel by decided and united Councils, in situations so derogatory to the honor, and agressions so dangerous to the Constitution, Union, and even Independence of the nation, is an indispensable duty.

To George Washington

AL, Washington Papers, Library of Congress

Dear Sir Paris, October 24, 1797

I did myself the honor of addressing to you from the Hague by

Capt Izzard, a very long letter which I hope you have received.[3] The offer therein made of occasionally communicating to you my observations on the great & interesting events of europe was not even intitled to the small value which in my own mind I had bestowd upon it. Causes, which I am persuaded you have anticipated, forbid me to allow myself that free range of thought & expression which coud alone apologize for the intrusive character my letters bear. Having however offerd what I cannot furnish, I go on to substitute something else perhaps not worth receiving.

You have heard it said in the United States that the agriculture of France has in the course of the present war been considerably improved. On this subject I am persuaded there has been no exaggeration. In that part of the country through which I have passd the evidences of plenty abound. The whole earth appears to be in cultivation & the harvests of the present year appear to be as productive as the fields which yield them are extensive. I am informd that every part of the country exhibits the same aspect. If this be the fact, there will probably remain, notwithstanding the demands of the armies, a surplus of provisions. Manufactures have declind in the same ratio that the cultivation of the soil has increased. War has been made upon the great manufacturing towns & they are in a considerable degree destroyed. With manufactures France does not supply herself fully from her internal resources. Those of Britain flow in upon her notwithstanding the most severe prohibitory laws. The port of Rotterdam is purposely left open by the English & their goods are imported by the Dutch under Prussian & other neutral colors. They are smuggled in great quantities into France. Peace then will find this nation entirely competent to the full supply of her colonies with provisions & needing manufactures to be imported for her own consumption. This state of things will probably change; but it is unquestionably the state of things which will exist at, & for some time after the termination of the present war. France can take from America tobacco & raw cotton, she can supply us with wines, brandies & silks.

The papers which I transmitted to you contained the evidence on which were founded the transactions of the 18th. fructidor or 4th of September.[4] Since then a letter has been publishd bearing

3. See JM to Washington, Sept. 15, 1797. Capt. Henry Izard (1771–1826), of Charleston, S.C., was the son of Ralph Izard (1742–1804), a former member of the Continental Congress and a U.S. senator from 1789 to 1795. Henry Izard pursued a career in the U.S. Navy.

4. *Ibid.*

the signature of Genl. Moreau[5] & produced as an unequivocal testimonial of the treason alledged to have existed. You will have seen the letter & have made upon it your own comments, but you will be astonishd to hear that perhaps a majority of the people do not beleive that Moreau ever wrote it.

The existing political state of France is connected with certain internal & powerfully operating causes by which it has been & will continue to be greatly influenced. Not the least of these is the tenure by which property is held.

In the course of the revolution it is beleivd that more than half the land of France has become national. Of this a very considerable proportion has been sold at a low rate. It is true that much of this property formerly belonged to the church but it is also true that much of it belongd to those who have fallen under the guillotine or have been termd emigrants. Among the emigrants are many whose attachments to their country has never been shaken; & what is remarkable, among them are many who were never out of France. The law upon this subject is worthy of attention. Any two persons, no matter what their reputation, may, to some authority, I beleive the municipality of the district, write & subscribe against any person whatever a charge, that such person is an emigrant, on receipt of which the person so chargd is without further investigation inscribd on the list of emigrants. If the person so inscribed be afterwards apprehended while his name remains on the list, the trial, as I understand, is not of the fact of emigration, but of the identity of the person, & if this identity be establishd, he is instantly fusillerd. This law is either rigidly executed or permited to be relaxed, as the occasion or the temper of the times may direct.

During intervals of humanity some disposition has been manifested to permit the return of those who have never offended, who have been banishd by a turn which the government itself has reprobated, & to permit in cases of arrestation, an investigation of the fact of emigration as well as of the identity of the person accused.

There is too a great deal of property which has been sold as national but which in truth was never so, & which may be reclaimd by the original proprietors.

In this state of things the acquirers of national property are of course extremely suspicious. They form a vast proportion of the population of France. They are not only important in consequence of their numbers, but in consequence of their vigor, their activity

5. Jean Victor Moreau.

& that unity of interest which produces a unity of effort among them. The armies too have been promisd a milliard.[6] This promise rests upon the national property for its performance. The effect of these circumstances cannot escape your observation. Classes of citizens are to be disfranchisd against the next elections.

Our ministers have not yet, nor do they seem to think it certain that they will be, receivd. Indeed they make arrangements which denote an expectation of returning to America immediately. The captures of our vessels seem to be only limited by the ability to capture. That ability is increasing, as the government has let out to hardy adventurers the national frigates. Among those who plunder us, who are most active in this infamous business, & most loud in vociferating criminations equally absurd & untrue, are some unprincipled apostates who were born in America. These sea rovers by a variety of means seem to have acquird great influence in the government. This influence will be exerted to prevent an accommodation between the United States & France & to prevent any regulations which may intercept the passage of the spoils they have made on our commerce, to their pockets. The government I beleive is but too well disposd to promote their views. At present it seems to me to be radically hostile to our country. I coud wish to form a contrary opinion, but to do so I must shut my eyes on every object which presents itself to them, & fabricate in my own mind nonexisting things, to be substituted for realities, & to form the basis of my creed. Might I be permited to hazard an opinion it woud be that the Atlantic only can save us, & that no consideration will be sufficiently powerful to check the extremities to which the temper of this government will carry it, but an apprehension that we may be thrown into the arms of Britain.

The negotiations with the Emperor[7] are said not to have been absolutely broken off. Yesterday it was said that peace with him was certain. Several couriers have arrivd lately from Buonaparte & the national debt rose yesterday from seven to ten livres in the hundred. Whether this is founded on a real expectation of peace with Austria or is the meer work of stock jobbers is not for me to decide. We are told that Mantua is no longer the obstacle to peace,

6. JM was referring to grants of money the Directory promised to disabled soldiers and to dependents of soldiers killed on active duty. The money was to be raised by selling the property of parents of émigrés.

7. Francis II, emperor of the Austro-Hungarian empire.

that it is surrenderd by the Emperor & that the contest now is for Istria & Dalmatia.

October 27th.
The definitive peace is made with the Emperor.[8] You will have seen the conditions. Venice has experiencd the fate of Poland. England is threatend with an invasion.

From H. M. Bears

ALS, RG 84, National Archives

Gentlemen! Brussels, October 27, 1797

Being informed through the Channell of the public papers, of your Arrival in Paris; And the great hopes I entertain of your Success, in your present undertaking, I take the Liberty to Communicate to you, certain Circumstances relating to Several Ships & Vessells, belonging to Citizens of the United States, now in India.

Since the commencement of the present War, upwards of Twenty Sail of American Vessells, has been constantly employed, from the Different States, [*to*] supply the Isle of France, & Bourbon, with Provisions, during these *last* two Years, *Cash* became so rare, & the Paper money depreciating so fast, that many of our fellow Citizens were forced to receive Prize Vessells, at a certain Valuation for their respective Cargoes; As most of those Vessells have since been Employd in Victualling those Colonies, from the Different Ports in India, & are now, some of them, on their return to America, & Europe; it was utterly impossible for them to have knowledge, of the Law respecting the *Role d'Equipage*, as proscribed by the french government. I have therefore taken the Liberty of mentioning particulary, the above circumstances, (being unfortunately a Part owner in some of them) And most sincerely wish it may be in your power to obtain a Clause, in favour of Ships, which has not had an opportunity of receiving information concerning those regulations adopted since their departure from America.

In doing which you will greatly serve the Interest of several

8. The Treaty of Campo Formio, signed on Oct. 18, 1797, between the French and Austrians, made provisions for dividing northern Italy.

Mercantile Houses in America, as Well as Gentlemen, with the greatest respect, Your mt. Oe. & hble. Servt.

H: M BEARS
A Citizen of the U: S:

From William Vans Murray

Letterbook Copy, Murray Papers, Pierpont Morgan Library

My dr. Sir, The Hague, November 2, 1797

On the 28 Oct. I received you favour of 21.[9] I did expect that you would be received & never any further. Their late conduct to Venice confirms with the weight of a mountain, all that I have thought of their character, policy & ambition. Burke could not illustrate this, nor could Ames make it more pathetic or terrible.[1] The treaty is the most poignant satire ever written against those *republicans*—those holy of holies in the temple of Liberty.

I have taken every opportunity to urge these points where they might work well, & under the idea that the negotiation might possibly fail, to the Spanish Minister & the Dutch.

1. that as allies of France they are bound by principle & policy to demand a participation in the Councils of France upon points leading to a war with any new enemy—because they cannot be bound to enter into an unjust war, & ought to prevent her from so doing.

2. that if there is war between F. & the US, they can have no object;

1. If to injure G:B. by diverting the Amer. trade, if they succeeded *they* would not be benefitted, as a coerced commerce would be confined to France.

2. If to conquer America, france alone would be benefited.

3. To divide the Union & erect a Southern Republic—If succeeding, Spain would be ruined by such a neighbour under the french direction. If they succeeded france alone would be aggrandised—

9. See JM to Murray, Oct. 21, 1797.

1. Edmund Burke (1729–1797) was one of the leading British critics of the French Revolution and the author of the widely read *Reflections on the Revolution in France . . .* (London, 1790), which went through many printings in the United States. Fisher Ames (1758–1808) was a former congressman from Massachusetts who had been one of the leading anti-French orators in Congress. See Winfred E. Bernhard, *Fisher Ames: Federalist and Statesman, 1758–1808* (Chapel Hill, N.C., 1965).

& if they *did not*, as they would not, they would be ruined, though france would not, as at a peace she by her land influence would get some of her possessions restored. That their colonies wd. fall—that they would be to the aggrandizement of G:B. not of the U.S.

These heads comprehend a very extensive compass of reflexion, & seem to make an impression, of course I keep up the idea of success to your negotiation & attribute the delay to the great events which distract & engage the whole attention of the Directory at present, but make them as things to be thought of and as including motives that should lead both to aid the amicable side of the negotiation & ensure success to it as far as relates to Peace. I am etc.

To Charles Lee

AL, Marshall Papers, Library of Congress

My dear Sir Paris, November 3, 1797

When I closd my last letter I did not expect again to address you from this place. I calculated on being by this time on my return to the United States. The decision concerning us has not however been so rapid as I had supposd & my own opinion is that France *wished*[2] *to retain america in her present situation until her negotiation with Britain which it is beleived is about to recommence shall have been terminated & a present absolute rupture with america might encourage England to continue the war and peace with England & pending her differences with us will put us more* absolutely *in her power. A continuance of this state of things ought not to be permitted, but our situation is more intricate and difficult than you can believe. Since my last the demand for money has been yet again repeated. The last address to us which was extremely interesting concluded with uttering this remarkable sentiment, that if we beleivd that America would be united, by any representation we could make of the hostile temper of france, we should be mistaken. That we ought to know the diplomatic skill of france and her means in our country, sufficiently to be convinced that the French party in America would throw all the blame of rupture on the federalists as we stiled ourselves on the british party as they style us. We were warned too of the fate of Venice.*[3] *All these conversations are preparing for a public letter but the delay and the necessity*

2. Italics indicate words originally in code.

3. See Journal, Oct. 30, 1797. Pierre Bellamy was the emissary who threatened the United States.

of writing only in cypher prevents our sending it by this occasion. A triplicate of our first public letter goes by this conveyance and will give the government some idea of the state of things here. I fear that the permitting of these indirect communications and the sort of countenance given to the idea of a bribe and the admission that the demand of a loan was even a subject on which our government should be consulted will be disapproved of.[4] *We have at length come to the determination positively to refuse to hold any further indirect intercourse, unsanctioned by written authority. I wish we could likewise determine to address the minister concerning our reception. We despair of doing anything. If at any future time during the present goverment in france, negotiations should recommence it will be necessary for America to determine what money, is to be bestowed, for no person here seems to think that peace ought to be demanded, but by ministers with full hand. Mr. Putnam an American citizen has been arrested and sent to gaol under the pretext of his cheating frenchmen.*[5] *By those Americans who have mentioned the subject to me this is understood to be a mere pretext. It is considered as ominous towards Americans generally. He like most of them is a creditor of the government.*

4. See American Envoys to Timothy Pickering, Oct. 22, 1797. John Adams did disapprove of the manner in which the envoys handled the situation, although he apparently did not make his views known to his cabinet. Adams strongly criticized the letter of the American Envoys to Talleyrand, Oct. 6, 1797. "This is a pedantical, timorous Thing. They ought to have Sent a Card to inform the Minister, that they had arrived in Paris, as Envoys Extra to the Executive Directory, and have asked for an hour, when to wait upon him and no more. The long canting Preamble is not only weak, but ridiculous and mischievous.

"The Conversation of Mountflorence and Osmond was beneath the Envoys to take notice of in their dispatches. They should have been put upon their guard by it, however, against the subsequent Errors into which they fell.

"Hubbard (W) and X, with all their Tittle Tattle ought to have been not attended to nor any word said to them, till the Envoys were received by the Directory and some one [*elected*] with full Powers to treat. Pinckneys answer to X should have |been We will not say one word in answer to any Proposition till We are recd and meet a Minister on equal ground." See "Remarks," Oct. 22, 1797, Adams Papers, Massachusetts Historical Society.

Abigail Adams (1744–1818) was less political but more pungent in her remarks. "I hope it will be the *last dispatch* from our Lamb like Envoys. I fear they will find wolves to devour them. How could they Stay? How could they bear to hold converse with that depraved and venal wretch Talleyrand?" Abigail Adams to Cotton Tufts, June 8, 1798, *ibid.*

5. Jesse Putnam was a merchant from Boston. He acted as an agent for William Lee (1772–1840), also a Boston merchant, to collect claims against the French government. See Fulwar Skipwith to Talleyrand, Nov. 4, 1797, and William Lee to Talleyrand, Nov. 6, 1797, Correspondance Politique, Etats-Unis, XLVIII, Archives of the Ministry of Foreign Affairs, Paris. Talleyrand requested Putnam's immediate release but was unsuccessful. See Talleyrand to Minister of Police, Nov. 7, 1797, *ibid.* On William Lee, see Mary Lee Mann, ed., *A Yankee Jeffersonian: Selections from the Diary and Letters of William Lee of Massachusetts, Written from 1796–1840* (Cambridge, Mass., 1958).

To James C. Mountflorence

Draft, Gerry-Knight Papers, Massachusetts Historical Society

Sir,[6] Paris, November 6, 1797

Your letter of the 5th I have received & communicated to my collegues General Marshal & Mr Gerry: ⟨their⟩ our answer ⟨which is perfectly correspondent with my own opinion⟩, is, that the same propositions having been repeatedly made to us & as often answered by us, we have nothing to add except, that we cannot consistently with the dignity of our Government or with own honor receive any more communications relative to our mission unless they are officially made. We are Sir with great respect & sincere esteem, Your most hum. Serts.

signed CHARLES COTES. PINCKNEY[7]

From Caron de Beaumarchais

Draft, Private Collection

[Paris, November 7, 1797][8]

Mes lettres d'amerique, Monsieur, m'apprennent qu'un des trois plenipotentiares envoyés par Votre République à la Notre, Est l'avocat célébre qui a [*bien*] plaidé ma cause à qui je dois de la reconnaissance, est le général *John Marshall*. Entre nous, Monsieur, et pardon, si je ne l'ai pas [*cité*] plustot, dupuis que j'ai reçu cette interessante instruction, je me suis occupé de connaître votre [*mission*], et je vous prie demander, si la visite d'un citoyen français qui l'honore depuis j'ai pu avoir servi l'un des 1ers la liberté de l'amerique, Et qui vous a, Monsieur, des obligations particulières, ne vous importunera pas, [ ] vous faire ses remerciemens personels.

6. This draft is in Gerry's hand; on the verso of the document is the notation, "Letter to Major Mountflorence 6 Nov: 1797—& his Letter mentioning his conversation with Mr. Taleyrand of the 5th Novr."

7. The American envoys held joint powers on all matters relating to the negotiations. Although Gerry's draft shows only Pinckney's signature, it is clear that JM approved of the note and probably signed the original.

8. Beaumarchais dated his draft "16 Brumaire," which was Nov. 6. The letter sent appears to have been dated Nov. 7. See JM to Beaumarchais, Nov. 7, 1797.

For Beaumarchais's entrance into the negotiations at the behest of Talleyrand and Bellamy, see Stinchcombe, "WXYZ Affair," *WMQ*, 3d Ser., XXXIV (1977), 601.

Je felicite votre pays d'un aussi bon choix que le votre. Beaucoup [*d'experience*] m'ont trop appris, monsieur, que tous les governements d'Europe n'ont pas été aussi éclairé dans le choix de leurs graves representans, que l'amerique a pu s'enflatter quand elle a nommé John Marshall. Salut, honneur, et gratitude

To Caron de Beaumarchais

ALS, Private Collection

Sir: Paris, November 7, 1797

Your very polite & flattering letter of to day is just receivd. I felicitate myself on the prospects of knowing personally a gentleman whose merit has given him so high a rank in Europe & America as is assigned in both to M. de Beaumarchais. I shall expect you sir tomorrow with real pleasure & beg leave to assure you that I am with very much respect, Your Obedt Servt

J MARSHALL

To Timothy Pickering

LS, RG 59, National Archives

No. 2

Dear Sir Paris, November 8, 1797

We now enclose you in thirty six quarto pages of Cypher, and in eight pages of cyphered exhibits the sequel to the details commenced in No 1 dated the 22d of last month, and have the honor to be Your most obedt hble Servts

CHARLES COTESWORTH PINCKNEY
J MARSHALL
E GERRY

Account of Negotiation Proceedings

[Paris, October 27–November 3, 1797]

October 27, 1797[9] ⟦*About twelve we received another visit from M.*

9. See Journal, Oct. 27, 1797. Over 80% of this dispatch was taken directly from the Journal; only Gerry's conference with Talleyrand is not recorded there. Passages from the Journal are printed here in open brackets (⟦ ⟧). See Journal, Oct. 27, 29, 30, Nov. 1, and 3, 1797. Italics indicate words originally in code.

Horttingguer. He immediately mentioned the great event announced in the papers and then said that some proposals from us had been expected on the subject on which we had before conversed; that the Directory were becoming impatient and would take a decided course with regard to America, if we could not soften them. We answer[ed], that on that subject we had already spoken explicitly, and had nothing further to add. He mentioned the change in the state of things which had been produced by the peace with the Emperor, as warranting an expectation of a change in our system: to which we only replied, that this event had been expected by us, and would not in any degree affect our conduct. M. Horttinguer urged that the Directory, had since this peace, taken a higher and more decided tone with respect to us and all other neutral nations, than had been before taken; that it had been determined that all nations should aid them, or be considered and treated as their enemies. We answered, that such an effect had already been contemplated by us as probable; and had not been overlooked when we gave to this proposition our decided answer: and further that we had no powers to negociate for a loan of money; that our government had not contemplated such a circumstance in any degree whatever; that if we should stipulate a loan, it would be a perfectly void thing, and would only deceive France and expose ourselves. M. Horttinguer again expatiated on the power and violence of France; he urged the danger of our situation; and pressed the policy of softening them, and of thereby obtaining time. The present men he said would very probably not continue long in power and it would be very unfortunate if those who might succeed, with better dispositions towards us, should find the two nations in actual war. We answered, that if war should be made on us by France, it would be so obviously forced on us, that on a change of men, peace might be made with as much facility as the present differences could be accomodated: we added, that all America deprecated a war with France; but that our present situation was more ruinous to us than a declared war could be; that at present our commerce was plundered unprotected; but that if war was declared, we should seek the means of protection. M. Horttinguer said he hoped we should not form a connection with Britain; and we answered that we hoped so too; that we had all been engaged in our revolution war, and felt its injuries; that it had made the deepest impression on us; but that if France should attack us we must seek the best means of self-defence. M. Horttinguer again returned to the subject of money: said he, gentlemen you do not speak to the point; it is money; it is expected that you will offer money: we said we had spoken to that point very explicitly: we had given an answer. No, said he, you have not: what is your answer? We replied, it is no, no, not a six pence. He again called our attention to the dangers which threatened our country; and asked if it would *not be prudent, though we might not make a loan to the nation, to interest an influential friend in our favor. He said we ought to consider what men we had to treat with; that they disregarded the justice of our claims and the reasoning with which we might support them; that they disregarded their own colonies; and considered themselves as perfectly invulnerable with respect to us; that we could only acquire an interest among them by a* judicious *application of money; and it was for us to consider whether the situation of our country did not require that these means should be resorted to. We observed, that the conduct of the French government was such as to leave us much reason to fear, that should we give the money, it would effect no good purpose; and would not produce a just mode of thinking with respect to us. Proof of this must first be given us. He said, that when we employed a lawyer, we gave him a fee, without knowing, whether the cause could be gained or not; but it was necessary to have one; and we paid for his services, whether those services were successful or not: so in the present state of things, the money must be advanced for the good offices the individuals were to render, whatever might be the effect of those good offices. We told him there was no parallel in the cases; that a lawyer not being to render the judgement, could not command success: he could only endeavor to obtain it; and consequently we could only pay him for his endeavours: but the Directory could decide on the issue of our negociation. It had only to order that no more American vessels should be seized, and to direct those now in custody to be restored; and there could be no opposition to the order. He said that all the members of the Directory were not disposed to receive our money; that Merlin, for instance, was paid from another quarter, and would touch no part of the douceur which was to come from us. We replied that we had understood, that Merlin was paid by the owners, of the privateers; and he nodded an assent to the fact. He proceeded to press this subject with vast perseverance. He told us that we paid money to obtain peace with the Algerines and with the Indians; and that it was doing no more to pay France for peace. To this it was answered, that when our government commenced a treaty with* either *Algiers or the Indian tribes, it was understood that money was to form the basis of the treaty and was it's essential article; that the whole nation knew it, and was prepared to expect it, as a thing of course; but that in treating with France, our government had supposed that a proposition, such as he spoke of, would, if made by us, give mortal offence. He asked if our government did not know that nothing was to be obtained here without money? We replied, that our government had not even suspected such a state of things. He appeared surprized at it, and said, there was not an American in Paris who could not have given that information. We told him that the letters of our Minister had indicated a very contrary temper in the government of France;*

and had represented it as acting entirely upon principle, and as feeling a very pure and disinterested affection for America. He looked somewhat surprized; and said briskly, to General Pinckney—Well; Sir; you have been a long time in France and in Holland, what do you think of it? General Pinckney answered, that he considered M. Horttinguer and M. Bellamy as men of truth, and of consequence he could have but one opinion on the subject. He stated, that Hamburg and other States of Europe were obliged to buy a peace; and that it would be equally for our interest to do so. Once more he spoke of the danger of a breach with France, and of her power which nothing could resist. We told him, that it would be in vain for us to deny her power, or the solicitude we felt to avoid a contest with it; that no nation estimated her power more highly than America, or wished more to be on amicable terms with her; but that one object was still dearer to us than the friendship of France, which was our national independence: that America had taken a neutral station: she had a right to take it: no nation had a right to force us out of it: that to lend a sum of money to a belligerent power abounding in everything requisite for war but money, was to relinquish our neutrality, and take part in the war: to lend this money under the lash and coercion of France, was to relinquish the government of ourselves, and to submit to a foreign government imposed upon us by force: that we would make at least one manly struggle before we thus surrendered our national independence: that our case was different from that of one of the minor nations of Europe; they were unable to maintain their independence, and did not expect to do so: America was a great, and so far as concerned her self defence, a powerful nation: She was able to maintain her independence; and must deserve to lose it, if she permitted it to be wrested from her; that France and Britain had been at war for near fifty years of the last hundred; and might probably be at war for fifty years of the century to come: that America had no motives which could induce her to involve herself in those wars; and that if she now preserved her neutrality and her independence, it was most probable that she would not in future be afraid, as she had been for four years past: but if she now surrendered her rights of self government to France, or permitted them to be torn from her, she could not expect to recover them, or to remain neutral in any future war. He said that France had lent us money during our revolution war, and only required that we should now exhibit the same friendship for her. We answered that the cases were *very different; that America solicited a loan from France, and left her at liberty to* grant *or refuse it; but that France demanded it from America, and left us no choice on the subject. We also told him there was another difference in the cases; that the money was lent by France for great national and French objects. It was lent to maim a rival, and an enemy whom she hated; that the money, if lent by America, would not be for any American objects, but to enable France to extend* still *further her conquests. The conversation* continued *for nearly two hours and the public & private advance of money was pressed and repressed in a variety of forms.* At length *M. Horttinguer said that he did not blame us; that our determination was certainly proper, if we could* keep *it: but he showed decidedly his opinion to be, that we could not keep it. He said that he would communicate, as nearly as he could, our* conversation *to the Minister; or to M. Bellamy, to be given by him to the Minister;* we are *not certain which. We then separated.*] On *the 22nd of October, M. Hautval a French Gentleman of respectable character,* informed *Mr. Gerry, that M. Talleyrand, Minister of foreign relations, who professed to be well disposed towards the United States had* expected *to have seen the American Ministers frequently, in their private capacities, and to have confered with them* individually *on the objects of their mission; and had* authorized *M. Hautval to make this communication to M. Gerry. The* latter *sent for his colleagues; and a conference was held with M. Hautval on the subject; in which General Pinckney and General Marshall expressed their opinions, that not* being *acquainted with M. Talleyrand, they could not with propriety call on him; but that* according to the *custom of France, he might expect this of M. Gerry, from a previous acquaintance in America. This M. Gerry reluctantly complied with on the 23rd; and with M. Hautval called on M. Talleyrand; who not* being *then at his office, appointed the 28th for the interview. After the first introduction, M. Talleyrand began the conference. He said, that the Directory had passed an arrête, which he offered for perusal, in which they had demanded of the envoys an explanation of some parts, and a reparation for others, of the President's speech to Congress, of the 16th. of May last: he was sensible, he said, that difficulties would* exist *on the part of the envoys relative to this demand; but that by their offering money, he thought he could prevent the effect of the arrête. M. Hautval, at the request of M. Gerry, having stated that the envoys have no such powers; M. Talleyrand replied; they can in such* case *take a power on themselves: and proposed that they should make a loan. M. Gerry then addressed M Talleyrand* distinctly *in English, which he said he understood and stated, that the uneasiness of the Directory resulting from the Presidents speech, was a subject unconnected with the objects of the mission; that M. Barras in his speech to M. Munroe, on his recall, had expressed himself in a manner displeasing to the government and citizens of the United States;* that *the President, as the envoys conceived, had made such observations on M. Barras's speech as were necessary* to *vindicate* the *honor of the United States;* that *this was not considered by our government as* a *subject of dispute between the two nations;* that having *no instructions respecting it, we could not make any explanations* or *reparations relating to it;* and that *M. Talleyrand himself was* sufficiently *acquainted with the constitution of the United States to be convinced of the truth of these observations. M. Gerry further stated,* that the *powers of the Envoys, as they conceived, were adequate to the discussion* and *adjustment of all points of real difference between the two nations;* that *they could alter* and *amend the treaty;* or if *necessary, form a new one: that the United States were* anxiously *desirous of removing all causes of complaint between* themselves and *France,* and *of renewing their former friendship* and *intercourse,* on *terms which should be mutually honorable* and *beneficial to the two nations;* but *not on any other terms: that as to a loan, we* had *no powers whatever to make one;* that *if we were to attempt it, we should deceive himself* and *the Directory likewise, which as men of honor we could not do;* but that *we could send one of our number for instructions on this proposition, if deemed expedient; provided that the other objects of the negociation could be discussed* and *adjusted:* that *as he had expressed a desire to confer with the envoys individually, it was the wish of M. Gerry that such* a *conference should take place,* and *their opinions thus be ascertained, which he conceived corresponded with his own in the particulars mentioned. M. Talleyrand, in answer, said he* should be *glad to confer with the other envoys individually, but that this matter about the money* must *be settled directly, without sending to America;* that *he would not communicate the arrête for a week;* and that *if we could adjust the difficulty respecting the speech,* an application *would nevertheless go to the U. States for a loan.* A *courier arriving at this moment from Italy* and *M. Talleyrand appearing impatient to read the letters, M. Gerry took leave of him* immediately. *He followed to the door,* and *desired M. Hautval to repeat to M. Gerry* what *he, M. Talleyrand, had said to him. M. Gerry then rereturned to his quarters, with M. Hautval, took down the particulars* of this *interview, as before stated, sent for Generals Pinckney* and *Marshall,* and *read it to them in the presence* of *M. Hautval, who confirmed it. Generals Pinckney* and *Marshall then desired M. Hautval to inform M. Talleyrand, that they had nothing to add to this conference;* and did not *wish that the arrête might be delayed* on *their account.*[1]

¶*October the twenty ninth,*[2] *M. Horttinguer again called on us.* He *said M. Talleyrand was extremely* anxious *to be of service to us,* and *had re-*

1. For a description of Talleyrand's meeting with Gerry and Hauteval, see *ibid.*, Oct. 28, 1797. Gerry's more extended recapitulation of the meeting in this dispatch unquestionably established that Bellamy, Hottinguer, and Hauteval were negotiating, though unofficially, with Talleyrand's knowledge and approval.

2. See *ibid.*, Oct. 29, 1797.

quested that one more effort should be made to induce us to enable him to be so. A great deal *of the same conversation which had passed at our former interviews was repeated.* The *power* and *the haughtiness of France was again displayed to us. We were told* that the *destruction of England was inevitable;* and that the *wealth* and *arts of that nation would naturally pass over to America, if that event should find us in peace.* To *this observation we replied;* that *France would* probably *forbid America to receive them, in like manner as she had forbid Switzerland to permit the residence in its country of a British Minister. We told him also, that we were sensible of the value of peace*, and *therefore sought it* unremittingly, *but that it was real peace we sought for;* and *real peace only which could be desirable.*

The *sum of his proposition was*, that *if we would pay, by way of fees*, that was *his expression, the sum of money demanded for private use, the Directory would not receive us; but would permit us to remain in Paris as we now were;* and *we should be received by M. Talleyrand, until one of us could go to America* and *consult our government on the subject of the loan.* These were *the circumstances he said under which the minister of Portugal had treated.* We *asked him if in the mean time the Directory would order the American property not yet passed into the hands of the privateersmen, to be restored? He said* explicitly, that *they would not. We asked him whether they would suspend further depredations on our commerce? He said they would not:* but *M. Talleyrand observed, that on this subject we could not sustain* much *additional injury, because* the *winter season was approaching, when few additional captures could be made.* We *told him that France had taken violently from America more than fifteen millions of dollars*, and *treated us in every respect as enemies*, in *return for* the *friendship we had manifested for her;* that *we had come to endeavour to restore harmony to the two nations*, and to *obtain compensation for the injuries our countrymen had sustained;* and that in *lieu of this compensation, we were told* that *if we would pay twelve hundred thousand livres, we might be permitted to remain in Paris (which would only give us the benefit of seeing the plays* and *operas of Paris, for the winter*), that *we might have time to ask from our country to exhaust her resources for France*, whose *depredations would be continued.* He *again stated, that by this procedure we should suspend a war;* and that *perhaps in five or six months, power might change hands.*

We told him, that what we wished to see in France, was a temper sincerely *friendly to the United States*, and *really disposed to do us justice.* That *if we could perceive this, we might not so* much *regard a little money, such as he stated to be usual; although we should hazard ourselves by giving it.* But that *we saw only evidences of the most extreme hostility toward us. War was made upon us so far as France could make it in the present state of things;* and it was not *even proposed that on receiving our money this war should cease.* We *had no reason to* beleive *that a possible benefit could result from it;* and *we desired him to say* that *we would not give a shilling, unless American property unjustly captured was previously restored,* and further *hostilities suspended;* and that *unless this was done, we did not conceive that we could even consult our government concerning a loan.* That *if the Directory would receive us* and *commence negociations,* and *any thing occurred which rendered* a *consultation of the government necessary, one of us would return to America for that purpose. He said, that without this money we should be obliged to quit Paris;* and *that we ought to consider the consequences.*

The property of the Americans would be confiscated, and *their vessels in port embargoed.* We *told him that unless there was* a *hope of real reconciliation, these evils could not be prevented by us;* and the *little delay we might obtain would only increase them.* That *our mission had induced many of our countrymen to trust their vessels into the ports of France;* and that *if we remained in Paris, that very circumstance would increase the number;* and consequently the *injury which our countrymen would sustain, if France could permit herself so to violate her own engagements* and the *laws of nations. He expressed a wish that M. Bellamy should see us once more. We told him* that a *visit from M. Bellamy, as a private gentleman would* always *be agreeable to us;* but *if he came only with the expectation that we should stipulate advances of money, without previously establishing a solid* and *permanent reconciliation, he might save himself the trouble of the application; because it was a subject we had considered* maturely, and *on which we were immovable. He parted with us, saying if that was the case, it would not be worthwhile for M. Bellamy to come.* In the *evening, while Genl. Pinckney* and *Genl. Marshall were absent, M. Bellamy* and *M. Horttinguer called,* and *were invited by M. Gerry to* break*fast with us the next morning.*⟧

⟦*October the thirtieth.*[3] Immediately *after breakfast, the subject was resumed. M. Bellamy spoke without interuption for near* an *hour. He said that he was* desirous *of making a last effort to serve us, by proposing something which might accomodate the differences between the two nations.* That what *he was now about to mention had not by any means the approbation of the Directory;* nor could *M. Talleyrand undertake further than to make from us the proposition to the Directory,* and *use his influence for its success.*

3. See *ibid.*, Oct. 30, 1797.

That *last week, M. Talleyrand could not have ventured to have offered such propositions;* but that *his situation had been very materially changed by the peace with the emperor.* By *that peace he had acquired,* in an *high degree, the confidence of the Directory,* and *now possessed great influence with that body;* that *he was also closely connected with Bonaparte* and the *generals of the army in Italy;* and *was to be considered as firmly fixed in his post, at least for five or six months.* That *under these circumstances, he could undertake to offer in our behalf, propositions* which before *this increase of influence he could not have hazarded. M. Bellamy then called our* attention to *our own situation,* and *to the force France was capable of bringing to bear upon us. He said* that *we were the best judges of our capacity to resist,* so far as depended on *our own resources;* and *ought not to deceive ourselves on so interesting* a *subject.*

The *fate of Venice was one which might befall the United States.* But, *he proceeded to observe, it was probable we might rely on forming* a *league with England: If we had such a reliance, it would fail us.* The situation *of England was such as to compel Pitt to make peace on the terms of France.* A variety of causes were *in operation which made such an effect* absolutely *certain.* To *say nothing of the opposition in England to the minister* and *to the war, an opposition which the fears of the nation would encrease;* to *say nothing of* a *war against England which was preparing in the north;* an *army of one hundred* and *fifty thousand men, under the command of Bonaparte, spread* upon the *coast of France;* and *aided by all the vast resources of his genius, would* most probably *be enabled to invade England; in which event their government would be overturned:* but *should this invasion not be* absolutely *effected, yet the alarm it would spread through the nation,* the en*ormous expence it* must *produce, would infallibly ruin them, if it was to be* continued, and *would drive them to save themselves by a peace:* that *independant of this, France possessed means which would infallibly destroy their bank* and *their whole paper system. He said he knew very well* it was generally *conjectured that Bonaparte would not* leave *Italy,* and *the army which had conquered under him,* and *which adored him; he assured* [us that][4] *nothing could be more* unfounded *than the conjecture; that Bonaparte had for more than ten days left Italy for Rastadt, to preside over the Congress which was formed for adjusting the affairs of the empire. He said that Pitt himself was so confident of the absolute necessity* of *peace, that after the naval* victory *over the Dutch, he had* signified *his readiness to treat* on *the same terms which he had offered*

4. These two words were inserted by Pickering for clarity before he released this dispatch to Congress on Apr. 3, 1797.

before that action: we could not then rely on the assistance of England. What, he asked, would be our situation if peace should be made with England before our differences with France would be accommodated? But he continued: if *even England should be able to continue the war, and America should unite with her, it would not be in our power to injure France. We might indeed wound* her *ally; but* if *we did, it would be so much the worse for us. After having stated the dangers attending us, if we should engage in the war, he proceeded to the advantages we might derive from a neutral situation: and insisted* at *large on the wealth which would naturally flow into our country from the destruction of England. He* next *proceeded to detail the propositions which are in substance in the paper annexed marked* (A;)[5] *except that he insisted that we should engage to use our* influence *with our government for the loan. He stated expressly that the propositions were to be considered as made by us; that* Mr *Talleyrand would not be* responsible *for the success of any one of them: He would only undertake to use his* influence *with the Directory in support of them. The proposition, he said, concerning* a *suspension of hostilities on the part of France, was one which proceeded* entirely *from himself:* Mr *Talleyrand had not been consulted upon it; and he could not undertake to say that that* Gentleman *would consent even to lay it before the Directory. The proposition for an advance to the government of France of as much money as was due from it to our citizens on contract, and as might be* determined *to be due for* Vessels *improperly captured and condemned, was, he* said *indispensible: unless we made that, it was unnecessary to make any other; for the others would not* be *received. He* expatiated *on the vast advantages we should derive from delay: it was, he said, absolutely* to *gain our cause. He* returned *to the danger of our* situation, *and the policy of making with France any accommodation which France would assent to. Perhaps, said he, you* believe *that in returning and exposing to your countrymen the unreasonableness of the demands of this government, you will unite them in their resistance to those demands: you are mistaken: you ought to know that the* Diplomatic *skill of France*, and the *means she possesses in your country, are* sufficient *to enable her, with the French party in America*, to *throw* the *blame which will attend* the *rupture* of *the negociations on the Federalists, as you term yourselves, but on the British party*, as *France* terms *you: and you may assure yourselves this will be done. He concluded with* Declarations *of being perfectly disinterested; and declared that his only motive for* speaking *thus freely were his friendship for* Mr *Talleyrand* and *his wish*

5. See Exhibit A in this document. Gerry copied Bellamy's proposal in French into his letterbook. See American Envoys to Pickering, Nov. 8, 1797, Letterbook, Gerry Papers, Henry E. Huntington Library.

to *promote the* Interests *and peace of the United States. We told him that the freedom with which he had spoken,* and *which was agreeable* to *us, would* induce *us to speak freely also; and for once to* accompany *our view* of *the present state* of *things with a retrospect* of *the past: that America was the only nation upon earth which felt* and *had* exhibited *a real friendship for the Republic of France:* That *among the empires round her which were* compelled *to bend beneath her power and to obey her commands, there was not one which had* voluntarily *acknowledged her government; or manifested for it,* spontaneously, *any mark of regard: America alone had* stepted *forward and given the most* unequivocal *proofs of* a *pure* and *sincere friendship,* at a *time when almost the whole European world, when Austria, Germany, Prussia, Russia, Spain, Sardinia, Holland* and *Britain were leagued against France; when her situation was in truth* hazardous, *and it was dangerous to hold even friendly intercourse with her, America alone stood forward* and *openly and* boldly avowed *her enthusiasm in favour of the Republic,* and *her deep* and *sincere interest in* its *fate. From that time to the present, the government* and *people* of *the United States have* uniformly *manifested a sincere* and *ardent friendship for France,* and *have, as they conceive,* in *no single* instance *given to this Republic just cause of* umbrage: if *they have done so, they* wish *it to be pointed out to them. After the* Determination *of France to break off all* regular *intercourse with them, they have sent three Envoys* Extraordinary *to endeavour to make such explanations* as *might produce reconciliation: these Envoys are prepared to* investigate, *and wish to* investigate *any measures which may have given offence; and are* persuaded *that they can entirely justify the conduct of their government. To this distant, unoffending, friendly Republic what is the conduct and the* Language *of France? Wherever our property can be* found *she seizes and takes it from us;* unprovoked, *she determines to treat us as enemies; and our making no resistance produces no* Diminution *of hostility against us; she abuses and insults our government,* Endeavours *to weaken it in the estimation of the people, recalls her own minister,* refuses *to receive ours, and when* Extraordinary *means are taken to make such explanations as may do* away *misunderstandings, and such* alterations *in the existing relations of the two* countries as *may be mutually satisfactory,* & *may tend to produce harmony,* the *Envoys who bear these powers are not received; they are not permitted to utter the amicable* wishes *of their country, but in the haughty* style *of a master, they are told that unless they will pay a sum to which their* resources *scarcely extend, that they may expect the vengeance of France, and like Venice be* erazed *from the list of nations; that France will* annihilate *the only free Republic upon earth, and the only nation in the* universe *which has* voluntarily *manifested for her a cordial and real friendship! What impression* must *this make on the mind* of *America, if without provocation France was determined* to *make war upon us, unless we* purchased *peace? We could not* easily *believe that even our money would save us: our independence would never* cease *to give offence;* and *would* always *furnish a pretext for fresh demands. On the* advantages *of neutrality it was unnecessary to say any thing: all the efforts* of *our government were* Exerted *to maintain it; and we would* never *willingly part with it. With respect to* a *political connection with Britain, we told him that America had never* Contemplated *it. Whether the danger he represented that government to be in was or was not real we should not undertake to decide: Britain we* believed *had much reason to wish for peace;* and *France had much reason to wish for peace also:* if *peace already* existed *it would not change the course America would* pursue. Mr *Bellamy manifested the most excessive impatience: he interrupted us and said, This* eloquent *dissertation might be true: America might have manifested*, and *he* believed *had manifested great friendship for France, and had just complaints against her; but he did not come to* listen *to those complaints.* The *Minister would on our request make for us certain propositions to the Directory: he had stated them to us*; and all *the answer he* wished *was yes or no: did we or did we not* sollicit *the Minister to make the propositions for us? We told him that without going farther into the discussion we* chose *to remark one or two things: they were, that the* existing *treaties gave to France certain advantages which were very* essential; *that* especially *the American coast afforded a protection near two thousand miles in extent to the prizes made by France on her* Enemies, *and refused that protection to the prizes taken from her; that she might* be assured *that in case of war these advantages would be lost for ever. We also told him we were convinced that France* miscalculated *on the parties in America: that the extreme injustice offered to our country would unite every man against her.* Mr. *Hortinguer informed us, that* Mr *Talleyrand would not consent even to lay this* proposition *before the Directory without* previously *receiving the fifteen thousand pounds,*[6] *or the greater part of it.* Mr *Bellamy left in writing his* propositions; *and we returned the answer annexed and marked*]] (B).[7]

6. This is a coding error for £50,000, an amount that had been previously mentioned in this dispatch and in American Envoys to Pickering, Oct. 22, 1797. The other contemporary copies of the dispatch all contain the figure £50,000. See American Envoys to Pickering, Nov. 8, 1797, Letterbook, Gerry Papers, Huntington Lib.; Journal, Oct. 30, 1797; American envoys to Pickering, Nov. 8, 1797, Legation Book, Franklin Collection, Yale University.

7. See Exhibit B in this document. It is not certain that the envoys gave their reply to Bellamy on Oct. 30, 1797. The counterproposal was the closest the envoys came to

significant negotiations. The tone in Exhibit B was milder than JM had wanted. Although the envoys refused to consider paying a bribe or assuming French debts to American citizens, they agreed to discuss the possibility of a loan.

Before their next conference with Bellamy, the envoys had again decided not to enter into informal negotiations, but all three immediately violated this agreement. It is unclear whether the cause of the breakdown in negotiations was the Americans' decision to demand formal negotiations or their decision to await an answer to their counterproposal, which they never received. On Nov. 3, however, Bellamy renewed the French demand for an explanation of Adams's speech to Congress on May 16, 1797. Gerry had previously refused to discuss any apology for the speech in his conference with Talleyrand on Oct. 28, 1797.

The French demand for an explanation of Adams's speech was a tactic designed to gauge how sincere the envoys were in desiring a settlement. Talleyrand, unlike the Directory, did not seriously expect an apology, and he therefore took a quite different view of Adams's speech. "While overlooking those expressions which a wounded pride had dictated to him following the refusal with which Mr. Pinckney had met," Talleyrand wrote in a report to the Directory, "it is difficult to imagine him taking up his predecessor's errors by denouncing us to America as wanting to take over a leading role in its internal affairs and cause dissention there between the government and the people. Nevertheless, beneath these accusations and the arrogance of the rest of the speech, a strong desire for reconciliation can be detected as well as firm intentions to seek out all possible means." William Stinchcombe, ed., "A Neglected Memoir by Talleyrand on French-American Relations, 1793–1797," American Philosophical Society, *Proceedings*, CXXI (1977), 204.

The Directory often ignored Talleyrand's advice, and they ignored his memorandum. See *ibid.*, 195–208. Joseph Pitcairn, an acquaintance of Talleyrand who later tried to reopen the stalled negotiations, did not believe Talleyrand was directing French foreign policy at this time. Pitcairn must have given his opinion of Talleyrand to the envoys, but the envoys were hesitant to give an apology that would have put the United States in a position of being a supplicant instead of an independent power with legitimate grievances with France. See Journal, Nov. 22–28, 1797; John Q. Adams to Pitcairn, Aug. 14, 1797, Pitcairn Papers, Cincinnati Historical Society, Ohio; and Pitcairn to John Q. Adams, Oct. 13, 1797, Adams Papers, Massachusetts Historical Society.

Talleyrand had to negotiate with the Americans while still complying with the Directory's demand for an apology for Adams's speech. In early November, Talleyrand wrote another memorandum to the American envoys that evidently was not sent. It is undated and inserted after Nov. 11, 1797, Correspondance Politique, Etats-Unis, XLVIII, Archives of the Ministry of Foreign Affairs, Paris. In this memorandum Talleyrand considerably moderated his previous demands for an apology, and he asked only for an explanation of the following passage from Adams's speech of May 16, 1797. "While we are endeavoring to adjust all our differences with France by amicable negotiations, the progress of the war in Europe, *the depredations on our commerce*, the personal injuries to our citizens, and general complexion of affairs, render it my indispensable duty to recommend to your consideration effectual measures of defence." *Annals of Congress*, VII, 56. Emphasis appears in the French version, following Nov. 11, 1797, Correspondance Politique, Etats-Unis, XLVIII. Talleyrand, perhaps seeking a way out of an impasse he did not consider necessary, further asked if Adams meant to accuse individuals or the state for the depredations on commerce and if the defense measures were directed against France. The evidence is indecisive, but this memorandum might have been the document that Bellamy refused to give to the American envoys on Nov. 3, 1797. Nonetheless, Talleyrand's demand was noticeably less strident than his previous requests for an explanation of Adams's speech. For a comparison of the difference in tone, see American Envoys to Pickering, Oct. 22, 1797, Exhibit A. The best chance for constructive negotiations faded as the American counterproposal went unanswered and Talleyrand's memorandum remained undelivered.

[*Novr. 1st.*[8] *It was at* length *agreed that we would hold no more indirect intercourse with the government.*]

[*Novr. 3d.*[9] Mr. *Hortinguer called on us* and *told General Pinckney and General Marshall* (Mr *Gerry not being within*) *that* Mr *Bellamy* wished *once more to see us. We* answered, *that we should at any time be glad to see* Mr *Bellamy as* a *private* Gentleman: *but that* if *his object was only to repeat his* propositions *for money, it was perfectly unnecessary to do so; because on that subject it was impossible for us to change the* answer *we had already given. We told him further, that we considered it* as *degrading our country to carry on farther such an indirect intercourse as we had for sometime submitted to, and had* determined *to receive no* propositions, *unless the persons who bore them had* acknowledged *authority to treat with us.* He said *that perhaps* Mr *Bellamy might have written powers from the Minister;* and *we replied, that if he had, we should receive his communications with pleasure. He* spoke *of a probable peace with England; and having* requested *us to be at home in the afternoon, left us.*

About *three* o Clock *he came; and after some conversation, in which we* repeated *in substance what is stated above, He* shewed *us a paper which he* said *was a copy of a letter prepared for us* by Mr. *Talleyrand, requesting an explanation of part of the President's* speech, *and which he* said *would be sent, unless we came into the propositions which had been made us. We* wished *to take a copy of it; which he* declined *permitting, saying he was forbidden to* allow *it.*[1] *We* spoke *of the letter coming to us* as *a measure we had no expectation of preventing: and he* said *he could not understand, that we* wished *it delayed. To which we answered, that the delay of* a *few* days *could not be desired; unless a hope* existed *that the Directory might become more friendly to our country. He said that* intelligence *had been received from the United States that if Colonel Burr and* Mr *Madison had constituted the mission, the differences* between *the two nations would have been accommodated before this time.*[2] *He added, as* a *fact he was not instructed to communicate, that* Mr *Talleyrand was preparing a memorial to be sent out to the United States complaining of us as being unfriendly to an accommodation with France. We replied to his* intelligence *from the United States that the Ministers correspondents in America took* a *good deal*

8. See Journal, Nov. 1, 1797. The entry at this date is slightly different: "It was at length for the second time agreed that we would hold no more indirect intercourse with the government."

9. See *ibid.*, Nov. 3, 1797.

1. This might be a reference to Talleyrand's memorandum discussed in n. 7 immediately above, inserted undated after Nov. 11, 1797, Correspondance Politique, Etats-Unis, XLVIII.

2. Stinchcombe, "WXYZ Affair," *WMQ*, 3d Ser., XXXIV (1977), 592.

on themselves when they undertook to say *how the Directory would have received Colonel Burr and* Mr *Madison and that with respect* to *the memorial of* Mr *Talleyrand, it would not be* easy *for him to convince our countrymen, that the statements we should make were untrue: if however we were confident that our conduct would* be *condemned,* Mr *Talleyrand might be assured that the fear of* Censure *would not induce us to deserve it: but that we should act in* a *manner which our own* Judgments *and consciences would approve of; and we trusted we should be supported by the great body of candid and honest men. In this conversation we again stated that America had taken* a *neutral position; that she had faithfully* sought *to preserve it; that a loan of money to one of the belligerent powers was directly to take part in the war;* and *that to take part in the war against her own* Judgment *and will, under the coercion of France, was to surrender our independence.*⟧

Exhibit A

[Paris, October 30, 1797]

1. The *American envoys shall remain here for six months in the same manner* and *upon the same footing* with regard *to etiquette as did M. D'Aranjo the envoy of Portugal.*

2. *There shall be named a commission of five members,* agreably *to a form to be established, for the purpose of deciding upon the reclamations of the Americans relative to the prizes made on them by the French privateers.*

3. The *American envoys* will *engage that their government shall pay the indemnifications,* or *the amount of the sums already decreed to the American creditors of the French republic,* and those which *shall be adjudged to the claimants by the commissioners.* This *payment shall be made under the name of* an *advance to the French Republic, who will repay it in* a *time* and *manner* to be *agreed upon.*

4. *One of the American envoys shall return to America to demand* of *his government the necessary powers to purchase for cash the thirty two millions of dutch rescriptions belonging to the French Republic,* in case the *envoys should conclude a treaty which shall be approved by the two nations.*

5. In the *interval, the definitive treaty shall proceed* for the *termination of all differences existing between the French republic* and *the United States;* so as *that the treaty may be concluded* immediately *on the return of the deputy.*

6. *The question of the rôle d'equipage shall remain suspended,* untill the *return of the deputy* and the *commission shall not pronounce upon any reclamation* where *this point shall be in question.*

7th. *During the six months granted for the going* and *returning of the deputy, hostilities against the Americans shall be suspended,* as well as the *process for condemnation before the tribunals;* and the *money of the prizes already condemned, in the hands of the civil officers of the nation, shall* remain there *without being* deliverd *to the privateers-men until the return of the deputy.*

Exhibit B

[Paris, October 30–31, 1797]

The envoys extraordinary and ministers Plenipotentiary of the United States cannot avoid observing the very unusual *situation in which they are placed by the manner in which they are alone permitted to make communications on the objects of their mission. They are called upon to* pledge *their country to a very great amount, to answer demands which appear to them as extraordinary as they were unexpected, without being permitted to discuss the reason, the* justice, *or the policy on which those demands are founded, and not only without assurances that the rights of the United States will in future be respected, but without a document to prove that those to whom they are required to open* themselves *without reserve, and at whose instance they are called on to* sacrifice *so much, are empowered even by the Minister to hold any communication with them: yet such is the* anxious *and real solicitude of the envoys to seize any occasion which may afford a hope, however distant, of coming to those explanations which they so much wish to make with this Republic, that they pass over the* uncommon *and informal modes which have been adopted, and will only consider the propositions* themselves.

1. *The Ministers of the United States will permit no personal considerations to influence their negociations with the French Republic. Although they expected that the extraordinary means adopted by their government to reconcile itself to that of France would have been received with* some *degree of attention, yet they are too solicitous to enter upon the important and* [*inter*]*esting duty of their mission to permit* themselves *to be restrained by forms or etiquette.*

2. *On this article it is* believed *there can be no disagreement.*

3. *This Article, as* explained, *would oblige the United States to advance, not to their own citizens, but to the government of France, sums equivalent to the depredations made by the corsaires of the Republic on the American commerce and to the contracts made with their citizens by France, and this advance, instead of benefiting the citizens of the United States would leave them* precisely *what they now are, the creditors of the French Republic: the more extensive the depredations* and *the more considerable the contracts* uncomplied with, *the more would the government of France re-*

ceive from the United States. Independant of these objections, the Ministers of the United States cannot engage *to assume in* any form *the debts due from France to their* fellow *citizens: they have no such power.*

4th. If the *negociations be opened, and the propositions for a loan, or any other propositions exceeding the powers* of *the Ministers* be *made, the government of the United States will be consulted thereon with* expedition.

5th. *This or any proposition having for its object the claims* of *the two nations on each other*, or *an* accommodation *of differences, will be embraced with ardor* by *the Ministers of the United States.*

6th. It cannot *escape notice that the question of the role d'equipage may* involve *in it every vessel taken from the United States: the Ministers however consider* it, & wish *to take it up as* a *subject of negociation.*

7th. On this *Article it is only to be observed, that the season of the year* is *such* as *probably to render* a *return, within six months,* of *the envoy who might* sail *to the United States* impracticable; *provision should be made* for *such an event.*

If the *difficulties* attending *the propositions for* a *loan and a compensation* for *past* Injuries *be such as to require time for their removal, the Ministers* of *the United States propose that the* discussions *on the relative* situation *of the two countries may commence in the* usual *forms; that the relation to each other may be so* regulated *as to obviate future misunderstandings; and that the* adjustment *of the claims of the citizens of the United States whose* vessels *have been captured, may be made, after* a *decision on the point first mentioned.*

No diplomatic *gratification can precede the ratification of the treaty.*

From William Vans Murray

Letterbook Copy, Murray Papers, Pierpont Morgan Library

Dear Sir, The Hague, November 9, 1797

A report is here that Ld. St. Vincent has sunk & taken 11 ships, spanish, of the line.[3] I send this by a countryman of mine.

Today I learn that our *fellow citizen* who stands so high in the Republic & who was out when you all first called on him, wrote a letter to the Lady mentioned in my last & whom Mrs. P. saw once at our lodgings, in the most friendly manner, pressing her to come

3. John Jervis, Lord St. Vincent (1735–1823), was a British admiral conducting a blockade of Cadiz. The report on Lord St. Vincent's victory was exaggerated.

on to Paris.[4] In my last I mentioned to you the importance of knowing & being well with a particular gentleman—at all events *for information.*[5]

The Directoire I see by my Paris papers have included America the suite of England, in that burlesque sublime which they lately gave upon the separation of the british government from their nation. This infamous slander is worthy of them & will have a good effect in America.

The letter I alluded to came yesterday, but she had been gone some days. A friend who was empowered to open her letters told me. Through another channel I hear you were not received on the 1st. The british governt. did not know of the peace on the 31. Octr. and published its manifesto on the failure of negotiation—which is an address to the nation in fact—pity it had not had the 1st act of the Plot unfolded, or Venice, a *democracy*, sold to a *crowned* head, by the *republic* of france.[6] I am etc.

To Talleyrand

LS, Archives of the Ministry of Foreign Affairs, Paris

Citizen Minister, Paris, November 11, 1797

The undersigned Envoys extraordinary and Ministers Plenipotentiary of the United States of America to the French Republic had the honor of announcing to you officially, on the sixth of October, their arrival at Paris, and of presenting to you on the eighth a copy of their Letters of Credence. Your declaration at that time that a report on American Affairs was then preparing and would in a few days be laid before the Directory, whose decision thereon should without delay be made known, has hitherto imposed silence

4. It is difficult to determine the identity of the "Lady." The French minister to Holland, Jean François Noël, warned Talleyrand that Madame de Nadaillac, a former acquaintance of Talleyrand and Gouverneur Morris, was headed for Paris. See Noël to Talleyrand, Oct. 29, 1797, Correspondance Politique, Netherlands, 596, Archives of the Ministry of Foreign Affairs, Paris. Because of her association with Talleyrand, Madame de Nadaillac is probably the person referred to by Murray.

5. Murray was referring to his letter to JM of Nov. 2, 1797. Unfortunately, Murray's letterbook and autograph letters are quite different, since Murray had the habit of adding a long postscript or another page without inserting the additions in his letterbook. No persons are discussed in the letterbook copy of Murray to JM, Nov. 2, 1797.

6. The Treaty of Campo Formio between Austria and France, signed on Oct. 18, 1797, provided for the cession of the Venetian hinterlands in northern Italy to Austria.

on them. For this communication they have waited with that anxious solicitude which so interesting an event could not fail to excite and with that respect which is due to the Government of France. They have not yet received it, and so much time has been permitted to elapse, so critical is the situation of many of their Countrymen, and so embarrassing is that of the undersigned, both as it respects themselves and the Government they represent, that they can no longer dispense with the duty of soliciting your attention to their mission.

The United States, Citizen Minister, at an epoch which evinced their sincerity, have given incontestable proofs of their ardent friendship, of their affection for the French Republic. These were the result not of her unparallelled prowess and power, but of their confidence in her justice and magnanimity; and in such high estimation was the reciprocity of her friendship held by them, as to have been a primary object of national concern. The preservation of it was dear to them, the loss of it a subject of unfeigned regret, and the recovery of it, by every measure, which shall consist with the rights of an independent nation, engages their constant attention. The Government of the United States, we are authorized to declare, has examined, with the most scrupulous justice, its conduct towards its former friend. It has been led to this by a sincere desire to remove of itself every just cause of complaint; conceiving that with the most upright intentions, such cause may possibly exist; and although the strictest search has produced no self reproach, although the Government is conscious that it has uniformly sought to preserve with fidelity its engagements to France; yet far from wishing to exercise the privilege of judging for itself on its own course of reasoning and the lights in its own possession, it invites fair and candid discussion, it solicits a reconsideration of the past; it is persuaded its intentions, its views and its actions must have been misrepresented and misunderstood; it is convinced that the essential interests of both nations will be promoted by reconciliation and peace, and it cherishes the hope of meeting with similar dispositions on the part of the Directory.

Guided by these Sentiments, the President of the United States has given it in charge to the undersigned to state to the Executive Directory the deep regret, which he feels at the loss or suspension of the harmony and friendly intercourse which subsisted between the two Republics, and his sincere wish to restore them; to discuss candidly the complaints of France, and to offer frankly those of the

United States: & he has authorized a review of existing treaties and such alterations thereof as shall consist with the mutual interest and satisfaction of the contracting parties.

This task the undersigned are anxious to commence; & truly happy will they be if their exertions can in any degree contribute to restore that friendship, that mutual interchange of good offices, which it is alike their wish and their duty to effect between the Citizens of the two Republics.

The undersigned pray you, Citizen Minister, to present this communication to the Executive Directory; and to receive the assurances of their most perfect consideration.

CHARLES COTESWORTH PINCKNEY
J MARSHALL
ELBRIDGE GERRY

From Rufus King

LS, Gerry Papers, Pierpont Morgan Library

Gentlemen,[7] London, November 15, 1797

Mr.[8] *Trumbull returned on the eleventh. I employed the two next days in copying your dispatch for the Secretary of State though I was unable to decypher it.*[9] *Yesterday I deliverd it to a confidential person who immediately set off for Falmouth where he will embark in the packet which will sail for New York as soon as he arrives there. I have sent two copies of your dispatch to Liverpool from which two vessels will sail for the United States in the course of a week.*

Though my expectation of a satisfactory issue of your mission was materially weakened by the revolution fourth of September yet I must confess that I was not prepared for the accounts which Col. Trumbull has given me. I will not, however, allow myself yet to despair of your success though my apprehensions are greater than my hopes. I annex the copy of my number fifty two to the Secretary of State.[1] *It is in the cypher established between*

7. Italics indicate words originally in code.

8. The symbol for "lose" instead of "Mr." was used at this point in the coded letter. King's secretary made the same mistake before Talleyrand's name later in this letter.

9. See American Envoys to Timothy Pickering, Nov. 8, 1797.

1. See King to Pickering, Nov. 9, 1797, Diplomatic Dispatches, Great Britain, V, National Archives, printed in Charles R. King, ed., *The Life and Correspondence of Rufus King . . .*, II (New York, 1895), 237–238. Acting on information from William Wyndham, Lord Grenville (1759–1834), King informed Pickering that Spain would no longer be able to resist the French demands for Louisiana.

General Pinckney and me and may be considered as a communication of considerable importance in enabling you to judge of the views of the French government. The Envoy of Portugal[2] *confirmed to me today this information so far as regards the demand which he said had been made in the shape of a note and not as heretofore verbally. He knows nothing of the answer that was given by the Minister of Spain. I likewise send you the copy of a letter that some months past I wrote to Mr. Talleyrand to which I received no answer.*[3] *I have before mentioned this letter to General Pinckney. Slight circumstances sometimes assist us in the discovery of important decisions.*

I have lately received a letter from LaFayette who passes the winter in Holstein which expresses much anxiety concerning our affairs and an earnest desire of such information as will enable him to employ himself in our service. I have returned *a prudent answer.*[4] *As I knew* nothing *I could communicate* nothing *of what was doing at Paris. I mention this circumstance in order that you may make use of the services of LaFayette if there is any way which I do not perceive to be the case in which they can be* advantageously *employed. The failure of the negociation at Lisle has* undoubtedly *added strength to this government. The two houses of Parliament this day made a joint and unanimous*[5] *address to the King in reply to his speech pledging the wealth and strength of the nation in language of uncommon solemnity and force to support the Crown in the prosecution of the* [war against an enemy whose enmity says the][6] *address is directed against their laws religion and liberty. What another revolution in France may effect, nay, to what the corruption of those who are now in power may lead them to agree it is not easy to pronounce* [but here, there is every appearance][7] *of a firm and steady perseverance in the war. I send by Cap.* Clough *who is the bearer of this letter a copy of Lord Malmesbury's correspondence.* With perfect respect & Esteem, I have the honor to be, Gentlemen, Your ob: & faithful Servant,

RUFUS KING

2. The Portuguese envoy to Great Britain was Don Juan de Almeida, conde das Galveas (1757–1814).

3. See King to Talleyrand, Aug. 3, 1797, King Papers, LXIII, New-York Historical Society.

4. See King to Lafayette, Nov. 7, 1797, King, ed., *Corr. of King*, II, 238–239.

5. This word is underlined in the manuscript.

6. The words in brackets were omitted in the coded copy sent to the envoys and have been supplied from the letterbook copy, King Papers, LXIII, N.-Y. Hist. Soc.

7. The words in brackets were omitted in the coded copy sent to the envoys, and have been supplied from the letterbook copy. *Ibid.*

From Rufus King

Copy, King Papers, New-York Historical Society

Gentlemen London, November 24, 1797

No one detests more than I do the conduct of France towards our Country still I earnestly desire that we may remain in peace. War would retard our progress—which with all the disadvantages to which we are exposed brings daily additions of riches and strength, and to the oeconomical and moral motives which should influence Nations to cultivate peace we may add the danger to be apprehended from the division of our people. I make these observations in order that you may the more justly estimate such information as with a view to the negociation in your hands, I may send you, for with all our impartiality our prejudices will sometimes colour not only what passes through our minds, but even the objects which pass beneath our senses. Portugal gave money as a preliminary to the negociation of the late Treaty with France by a secret Article in which she stipulated a loan a part of which was paid at the Signature of the Treaty.[8] This money enabled the Directory to march the Army which effected the revolution of the 18th. of Fructidor. Spain is alarmed and Portugal trembles. England cannot furnish troops, without which Portugal must fall. The Court of Vienna have at this moment little confidence in the solidity of their peace. The complicated interests of Germany remain to be settled. This is no easy task, and the war may again burst out. The Directory are not at ease on this point. England sees all this and notwithstanding the disaffected state of Ireland is resolved with firmness to continue the war. I cannot give you my sources of information but I am not deceived. I am with perfect respect & esteem, Gentlemen, Your obt. & faithful Servant

From William Vans Murray

Letterbook Copy, Murray Papers, Pierpont Morgan Library

Dr. Sir, The Hague, November 26, 1797

This moment I received the enclosed & must run the risk of the

8. King indicated in his notebook that he had received this information on Portugal from Lord Grenville. See Nov. 1797, Notebook, King Papers, LXXIII, New-York Historical Society.

post—it goes under cover to Genl. Pinckney's banker etc.[9]

Your letters enclosed to the Willincks would come safe to me—but it is perfectly in vain to expect anything from the university of Dublin[1] to me so I can only pray God that you may succeed—my prayer will succeed I believe, though your's of the 11th. did not.[2] Your Jupiter wants incense & sacrifices, the offerings of a "broken heart & a contrite spirit." I would give my best silk breeches to look only at Genl. P. & Mr. G. while the *republicans* had in the face of America the grace of *parcere subjectos*.[3] The benevolent mind of the last seemed to think that they were *republicans*. Oh God, how bitter is experience when the reluctant mind is forced from suffering to give up its visions of philanthropy & its systems of universal Liberty.

But I beg your pardon. I had enjoined upon myself the maxims of that severe monastery; which I believe is abolished, but which has some hopes in our commissioners. I mean that of la Trappe.[4] I am etc.

9. The enclosure is unidentified and is apparently lost.

The American envoys used the bankers Willink, Van Staphorst & Hubbard, of Amsterdam, whose Paris agency was the firm of Vanderyrer, Villemont & Schwartz.

1. The allusion is unclear; this might be a reference to Talleyrand.

2. Murray was alluding to the opening of negotiations that the American envoys had requested in their letter to Talleyrand. See American Envoys to Talleyrand, Nov. 11, 1797. Pinckney described the situation to Murray in detail in his letter of Nov. 15, 1797. "On the 11 instant we again requested the Minister of foreign affairs to attend to the business of our mission. The letter was written in the mildest terms & showed an anxious disposition on our part for peace & reconciliation, but at the same time it contained nothing abject, mean or dishonourable. To this letter we have not recd hitherto any reply. The condemnation of our vessels is unremittingly continued—our lawyers have given up all hopes & say it is useless to make any defence. The newspapers are filled with invectives against America, as if it was intended to prepare the public mind for a declaration of war. Some of our Citizens [Jesse Putnam] are arrested by the police under pretence of having defrauded french citizens in Stockjobbing, when if guilty they ought to be tried by regular judicial proceedings. In short every thing here bears the appearance of hostility to America, & I have no hopes of success in our negotiation." See Pinckney to Murray, Nov. 15, 1797, enclosed in Murray to Timothy Pickering, Nov. 29, 1797, Diplomatic Dispatches, Netherlands, III, RG 59, National Archives.

3. Murray was quoting Vergil *Aeneid* 6. 847, "parcere subjectis, et debellare superbos" (to spare the vanquished and subdue the proud).

4. Murray was apparently referring to the vows of silence and seclusion from the world required of Trappist monks.

To Mary W. Marshall

AL, Marshall Papers, Swem Library, College of William and Mary

My dearest Polly Paris, November 27, 1797

I have not since my departure from the United States receivd a single letter from you or from any one of my friends in America. Judge what anxiety I must feel concerning you. I do not permit myself for a moment to suspect that you are in any degree to blame for this. I am sure you have written often to me but unhappily for me your letters have not found me. I fear they will not. They have been thrown over board or intercepted. Such is the fate of the greater number of the letters addressed by Americans to their friends in France, such I fear will be the fate of all that may be addressed to me.

In my last letter I informd you that I counted on being at home in march. I then expected to have been able to leave this country by christmass at furthest & such is my impatience to see you & my dear children that I had determined to risk a winters passage: I now apprehend that it will not be in my power to reach America til April or May—but on this subject all is yet uncertain. I wish you woud present my compliments to Mr. Wickham & express to him my wish that the case of Randolphs exrs. & Colo. Meade may ly til my return.[5] I think nothing will prevent my being at the chancery term in May. Oh God how much time & how much happiness have I thrown away!

Paris presents one incessant round of amusement & dissipation but very little I beleive even for its inhabitants of that society which interests the heart. Every day you may see something new magnificent & beautiful, every night you may see a spectacle which astonishes & inchants the imagination. The most lively fancy aided by the strongest description cannot equal the reality of the opera. All that you can conceive & a great deal more than you can conceive in the line of amusement is to be found in this gay metropolis but I suspect it woud not be easy to find a friend. I woud not live in Paris to be among the wealthiest of its citizens.

5. John Wickham, a Richmond attorney, was involved in the case of Randolph's Executors v. Randolph's Executors before the High Court of Chancery, and this may be the case JM intended to mention. A bill had been filed in 1796, and in Jan. 1797 the cause was set for hearing. Inasmuch as the decree was not issued until Mar. 1799, the case may have been continued until JM's return. See 6 Va. (2 Call) 537–546 (1801).

I have changed my lodgings much for the better. I lived till within a few days in a house where I kept my own apartments perfectly in the style of a miserable old batchelor without any mixture of female society.[6] I now have rooms in the house of a very accomplishd a very sensible & I beleive a very amiable lady whose temper, very contrary to the general character of her country women, is domestic & who generally sets with us two or three hours in the afternoon.[7] This renders my sitation less unpleasant

6. Gerry described his lodging to his wife in a more explicit fashion. "Six weeks, I lived in the same house with my collegues, with only a bed room & parlour, for myself, & antechamber for my servants. General Marshal had just such a suite of apartments, & both his & mine were badly furnished, not even having a carpet, & being on the lower floor. My chimnies smoaked, & to compleat my happiness, there was a stable under ground, in which there was a constant noise, as of persons breaking thro the wall: which at the same time that it disturbed my rest, rendered it necessary to have a pair of pistols under my pillow." Gerry to Ann Gerry, Nov. 25, 1797, Gerry Papers, Library of Congress. Gerry's and JM's first residence was described in more delicate terms by Mary Pinckney. "At the front door on the ground floor you enter a vestibule—on the right & left are a small antichamber, drawing room, & bed chamber, furnished with sattin furniture & glasses, neat, but the furniture not very fresh—these are the apartments of Genl. Marshal & Mr. Gerry each exactly the same." Mary Pinckney to Margaret Manigault, Oct. 5, 1797, Manigault Family Papers, University of South Carolina. Gerry and JM moved from 1131 Rue Fontaine Grenelle to 70, currently 54, Rue Vaugirard.

7. JM is speaking of Reine-Philiberte Rouph de Variacourt, Madame de Villette (1757–1822), the famous landlady of JM and Gerry for the remainder of their stay in Paris. Gerry was more effusive in his description. "Madam Villette is a Widow lady of about 35 years old. Her husband died about 4 years ago at the age of 55 & left her a daughter who is now about 12 & a son about 9 years old. She is to continue in the house during the winter, it being an immense chateau, large enough to hold General Pinckneys family in addition to those which now inhabit it. Madam Villette is I think one of the finest Women in Paris: on account of the goodness of her heart her excellent morals, & the richness of her mind. She was the daughter of Voltaire's particular friend, & lived with the former. He was charmed with her disposition & amiable qualities, & in his writings frequently speaks of her as the *belle* & *bonne*; by which name she is distinguished here." Gerry to Ann Gerry, Nov. 25, 1797, Gerry Papers, Lib. Cong. Mary Pinckney viewed the situation somewhat differently. "Did I ever tell you that she was the landlady of two of the American ministers? She was the niece & adopted daughter of Voltaire, & lived with him at Terney. She is an agreeable pleasing woman, about 32 years of age. She always dines with the two *batchelors*, & renders their situation very agreeable. She called on me a few evenings ago & invited me to a little musical party for to-morrow, when some of the first artists of Paris are to perform, & a heavenly voice is to sing." Mary Pinckney to Margaret Manigault, Mar. 9, 1798, Manigault Family Papers. For a biography of Madame de Villette, see Jean Stern, *Belle et Bonne, une fervente amie de Voltaire (1757–1822)* ([Paris, 1938]).

Fulwar Skipwith, who had known Madame de Villette for at least two years, probably found the new apartments for JM and Gerry. Madame de Villette maintained close connections with the American community in Paris. Among others, Thomas H. Perkins (1764–1854), a Boston merchant, mentioned meeting her at a party at James Monroe's. At a later party, Perkins, as captivated by Madame de Villette as JM and Gerry were to be, called her "as fine a woman as I ever knew." Apr. 3, 1795, Thomas H. Perkins Diary, Perkins Papers, Massachusetts Historical Society. Joel Barlow (1754–1812) reported that Madame de Villette had attended a party at his house celebrating

than it has been but nothing can make it eligible. Let me see you once more & [*then I*][8] can venture to assert that no consideration will induce me ever again to consent to place the Atlantic between us. Adieu my dearest Polly. Preserve your health & be as happy as possible till the return of him who is ever yours.

I inclose this letter under cover to Colo. Carrington.[9] Whenever that happens you will advert to paying the postage.

To Timothy Pickering

AL, RG 59, National Archives

Dear Sir Paris, November 27, 1797[1]

I send you by this conveyance the conservative, an official paper,[2] which however is not otherwise interesting than as it exhibits a specimen of the real situation of the press. You will perceive in it the manifesto of the Directory in answer to that of the King of England & will perceive also that such an opportunity to insult America was not passd over. It is not often that we are noticed in the Paris papers & when we are it is only to be insulted & abused. The Americans have been threatend personally & some of them apprehended. A Mr. Putnam[3] from one of the New England states with whom I am not acquainted but who is spoken of in a favorable manner by those of our countrymen who are most attachd to France has been siezed on the complaint of a broker who pretends to be his creditor, but who, as I am informd, is in fact his debtor on some stock jobbing account, & has been committed to jail by the officer of the police without any examination of the case or regard to forms usual between creditor & debtor. The proceeding as stated is not in nature of a civil suit but of a governmental transaction. The committment was accompanied with expressions of rage & with threats which produced an extensive alarm. It is now pretended to examine him as a state prisoner & I am not without the expectation that this change of plan forebodes

the defeat of royalism. See Barlow to Skipwith, Aug. 9 [1798 or 1799], Beinecke Library, Yale University.

8. Torn by seal.

9. Edward Carrington. The covering letter has not been found.

1. A note on the verso indicates this letter arrived in Philadelphia on Mar. 6, 1798.

2. It is unclear what issue of *Conservateur* (Paris) JM sent to Pickering. None of the enclosures JM mentioned has been found.

3. On Jesse Putnam's case, see JM to Charles Lee, Nov. 3, 1797.

his liberation & is designd to cover the illegality & violence of the first step. A Mr. Murray[4] from New York who has been some time in England & who came to Paris under the protection of a passport has, without the assignment of any cause, been apprehended & thrown into the common jail of felons from which he was taken after a few days confinement covered with filth & lice & sent under guard out of France. It is said that the motive for this procedure was that the government had receivd inteligence from some of its spies in England that Mr. Murray entertaind sentiments unfriendly to this republic. The brother of the last mentiond gentleman who has resided in Paris for a considerable time & against whom no complaint so far as I can learn, is even whispered is likewise apprehended & comittd to jail. I am informd by the consul that upon an inquiry into his case, it turns out that he may be discharged on the payment of about 50 or 100 louis. This therefore may be the commencement of a system of *forced gifts* bearing some affinity to the *forced loans* which have by some governments been levied on its citizens. On this account Mr. Murray has been advised not to give the money. The situation of many Americans is by no means pleasant. They are creditors of the government to a very great amount for supplies furnished, they have acquird real property in the country to a considerable amount which they cannot easily sell & they have purchasd largely into the public funds which have lost about ¾ of the value they held when most of those purchases were made. Having sustaind this loss from their confidence in the government they are now very freely abused as being the depreciators of the funds into which they have purchasd & by the depreciation of which many of them are ruined. Whatever they may deserve from their own country they do not merit injury from France.

Among the many mischiefs resulting from the unparaleld depredations commited on our unoffending & defenseless commerce is

4. James V. Murray, of New York, was in France trying to collect payments on supplies shipped to the French government. His brother George W. Murray had been in Paris for several years. Earlier the French government had been angry with James V. Murray for signing a petition in support of the Jay Treaty, and this might have been one of the reasons why he was in disfavor with the Directory. See "Convention of 1803," F 39, Envelope 2, RG 76, National Archives, for an affidavit by James V. Murray stating that George W. Murray was indeed his brother and that the latter had resided in Paris for a number of years. See also George W. Murray to James Monroe, June 20, 1795, Correspondence, American Embassy, Paris, RG 84, Natl. Arch. On the French displeasure with James V. Murray, see James Swan to Pierre-Auguste Adet, Sept. 11, 1795, Correspondance Politique, Etats-Unis, Supplement, XXII, Archives of the Ministry of Foreign Affairs, Paris.

one which well deserves the attention of government. The sailors belonging to the captured vessels who are thrown on shore without adequate support & without the means of returning to their country are very frequently seduced by the owners of privatiers to engage in their nefarious employment. The pressure of present want added to the hope of considerable tho illicit & wicked gain has the operation of an impressment & carries into the service of these sea rovers a very considerable number of our sailors who woud certainly return home if the means of returning coud be provided for them. Poisoned by habits of turpitude to be acquird in this immoral & flagitious employment, they will be lost perhaps forever, but certainly during the present war, to their country. France resounds with the proposd invasion of England. This has been very long & still is a favorite national object. It may perhaps be seriously the intention of the government to effect its execution. To me however it appears not probable that such is its intention. I do not perceive means adequate to such an object. An Army passing the channel unprotected by a sufficient fleet woud risk a great deal in its passage & shoud it even effect a landing it must succeed or perish. I cannot beleive its success woud be certain. It appears to me that a proud & brave nation as powerful as Britain cannot be conquerd if its national spirit be preserved. It seems more probable therefore that this show of invasion is designd to alarm & to force Britain into a peace on the terms prescribed by France or in case of failure, to increase her expenses in such a manner as to produce a national bankruptcy. It may cover another plan which is mentiond & seems more probable. It is to annex Holland & Hamburg to France with that portion of the dominions of Prussia lying on this side the Rhine & to assign Hanover to Prussia. No consideration of justice or of the rights of nations will have an influence on the execution of these designs. Justice is an item which the great nations of this continent seem to think unfit to be inserted in their calculations. It is even conjecturd that neither the courage the hardihood or the poverty of Switzerland will protect it from partition. Portugal too is threatend seriously with annihilation. If the war continues a French army will probably invade that country through Spain. On this subject however we can only conjecture. I cannot easily beleive myself that Spain woud be pleasd with having a French army pass through her dominions or in possession of Portugal. I know not how to beleive that a jealous haughty impotent monarchy can consent to see itself penetrated & almost surrounded by the troops of a nation whose sword & whose principles must be equally dreaded. I shoud think Spain woud rather make one national effort to close her present calamitous war in the prosecution of which she performs so subservient a part, & for the commencement of which she had not motive, by a separate peace.

It is beleivd that the arrangements relative to the elections in the spring constitute to this government an object of serious concern. The people of France must be wearied with war. Their taxes are of necessity so very heavy that they must wish, notwithstanding the military genius of the nation & its excessive hate of England, for peace. This temper woud probably give to the next elections, if free, the same complexion, with the last. This is to be guarded against, but in what manner it is not easy to say. Whether the elections will be overawd by armd troops or influencd by disfranchising certain classes of citizens, or whether they may be intirely dispensed with are matters for speculation but on which no solid ground of opinion is afforded. The subject is one of the most interesting to this nation that can occur, nor is it altogether unimportant to the rest of the world.

I send you also the Leyden gazette. In that of the 7th. of November you will perceive some effort has been made by D'Antraigues[5] to publish in Vienna but the effort has been unsuccessful. In a subsequent paper about the 14th. of November is to be found a letter of Fauche[6] in which he most explicitly contradicts the story of his having been concerned in corrupting Pichegru. This paper is mislaid but I the less regret that circumstance as I suppose you will receive it from others. I send you also the reports of Thibidau & Tronçon de coudray as containing a statement of the conduct of the two councils prior to the revolution of the 4th. of September which was not then & has not since been controverted.[7] I am inducd to think a proper understanding of that event very material

5. Emmanuel Louis Henri Alexandre de Launay, comte d'Antraigues (1753–1812), was one of the royalist exile leaders living in Vienna, and was connected with the treason of Gen. Jean-Charles Pichegru. See JM to Pickering, Sept. 9, 1797. On d'Antraigues, see Jacques Godechot, *The Counter-Revolution: Doctrine and Action, 1789–1804,* trans. Salvator Attanasio (New York, 1971), 177–200.

6. This was Joseph Fouché (1759–1820), later the minister of police. At this time Fouché was in Barras's favor and was obviously trying to allay any suspicions that he had connections with the royalists.

7. On Thibaudeau and Tronçon Ducoudray, see JM to George Washington, Sept. 15, 1797.

to our country & therefore forward you these two speeches altho I suppose you to be already possessd of them.

As I suppose our ministers write very fully to you I will only say with respect to them & their affairs that if one may be permited to judge from appearances their prospects are by no means flattering. My own private opinion is that this haughty ambitious government is not willing to come to an absolute rupture with America during the present state of the war with England but will not condescend to act with justice or to treat us as a free and independent nation.

To Timothy Pickering

LS, RG 59, National Archives

No: 3.

Dear Sir, Paris, November 27, 1797[8]

On the 11th. instant we transmitted the following official letter to the minister of Foreign Affairs,

Citizen Minister

The undersigned Envoys extraordinary and Ministers Plenipotentiary of the United States of America to the French Republic had the honor of announcing to you officially, on the sixth of October, their arrival at Paris, and of presenting to you on the eighth a copy of their letters of credence. Your declaration at that time that a report on American affairs was then preparing and would in a few days be laid before the Directory, whose decision thereon should without delay been made known, has hitherto imposed silence on them. For this communication they have waited with that anxious solicitude which so interesting an event could not fail to excite, and with that respect which is due to the Government of France. They have not yet received it, and so much time has been permitted to elapse, so critical is the situation of many of their Countrymen, and so embarrassing is that of the undersigned, both as it respects themselves & the Government they represent, that they can no longer dispense with the duty of soliciting your attention to their mission.

The United States, Citizen Minister, at an epoch which evinced their sincerity, have given incontestable proofs of their ardent friendship, of their affection for the French Republic: These were the result not of her unparallelled prowess and power, but of their confidence in her justice

8. A note on the address leaf indicates this letter arrived on Mar. 6, 1798.

and magnanimity; and in such high estimation was the *reciprocity* of her friendship held by them, as to have been a primary object of national concern. The preservation of it was dear to them, the loss of it a subject of unfeigned regret, and the recovery of it by every measure, which shall consist with the rights of an independent nation engages their constant attention. The Government of the United States, we are authorized to declare, has examined with the most scrupulous justice its conduct towards its former friend. It has been led to this by a sincere desire to remove of itself every just cause of complaint; conceiving that with the most upright intentions such cause may possibly exist; and although the strictest search has produced no self reproach, although the Government is conscious that it has uniformly sought to preserve with fidelity its engagements to France, yet far from wishing to exercise the priviledge of judging for itself on its own course of reasoning and the lights in its own possession, it invites fair and candid discussion, it solicits a reconsideration of the past; it is persuaded its intentions, its views and its actions must have been misrepresented and misunderstood; it is convinced that the essential interests of both nations will be promoted by reconciliation and peace, and it cherishes the hope of meeting with similar dispositions on the part of the Directory.

Guided by these sentiments, the President of the United States has given it in charge to the undersigned to state to the Executive Directory the deep regret, which he feels at the loss or suspension of the harmony and friendly intercourse which subsisted between the two Republics, and his sincere wish to restore them; to discuss candidly the complaints of France, and to offer frankly those of the United States: and he has authorized a review of existing treaties & such alterations thereof as shall consist with the mutual interest and satisfaction of the contracting parties.

This task the undersigned are anxious to commence: and truly happy will they be if their exertions can in any degree contribute to restore that friendship, that mutual interchange of good offices which it is alike their wish and their duty to effect between the Citizens of the two republics.

The undersigned pray you, Citizen Minister, to present the communication to the Executive Directory, and to receive the assurance of their most perfect consideration.

Paris Novr: 11th. in the 22d. year, of American Independence.

signed, CHARLES COTESWORTH PINCKNEY
J MARSHALL
ELBRIDGE GERRY

To the minister of Foreign Affairs of the French Republic

No answer having been given to it on the 21st. instant, we requested Major Rutledge to wait on the Minister and enquire of him whether he had communicated the letter to the Directory, and whether we might expect an answer; he replied that he had submitted our letter to them, and that they would direct him what steps to pursue, of which we should be informed. We have not however hitherto received any official intimation relative to this business; we are not yet received, and the condemnation of our Vessels for want of a role d'Equipage is unremittingly continued. *Frequent*[9] *and urgent attempts have been made to inveigle us again into negociation with persons not officially* authorized, *of which the obtaining money is the basis: but we have persisted in declining to have any further communication relative* to diplomatic *business with persons of that description:* and *we mean* to *adhere* to *this* determination. *We are sorry* to *inform you, that the present disposition* of *the government of this country appears* to be *as unfriendly toward ours as ever;* & *that we have very little prospect of succeeding in our mission.* We have the honor to be, Your most obedt. hume. Servts.

CHARLES COTESWORTH PINCKNEY
J MARSHALL
E GERRY

From George Washington

Letterbook Copy, Washington Papers, Library of Congress

Dear Sir, Mount Vernon, December 4, 1797

Your very interesting and obliging favour of the 15th. of Septr. from the Hague came duly to hand,[1] and I thank you sincerely for the important details with which it is fraught, and pray for the continuation of them.

I congratulate you too on your safe arrival from Ship-board, and as the News Papers tell us at Paris; and I wish in a little while hence I may have it in my power to do the same on the favorable conclusion of your Embassy, and happy return to your family and friends in this Country. To predict the contrary might be as unjust as it would be impolitic and therefore—mum—on that Topic. Be the issue however what it may, three things I shall be perfectly satisfied of & these are that nothing which Justice sound reasoning and fair representation would require, will be wanting to render it Just and honorable; and if it not so, that the eyes of all in this Country, who are not wilfully blind, and resolved to remain so

9. Italics indicate words originally in code.
1. See JM to Washington, Sept. 15, 1797.

(some from one motive, and some from another) will be fully opened, and lastly, that if the French Directory proceed on the supposition, that the parties in these United States are nearly equal, and that one of them would advocate their measures in the dernier resort, they will greatly deceive themselves; for the *mass* of our Citizens require no more than to understand a question, to decide it properly, and an adverse conclusion of the negociation will effect this. Indeed I believe it may be said with Truth, that a very great change in the public mind has taken place already. The leaders it is true attempt to keep up the Ball, which is evidently declining; but as both houses of Congress have formed quorams, and received the Presidents speech, the Response of the Representative branch; will be some criterian by which this opinion of mine may be tried, though not a conclusive one.

The situation of things in Holland is a good lesson for us if we are disposed to profit by it; but unfortunately the nature of man is such, that the experience of others is not attended to as it ought to be: we must *feel ourselves* before we can think, or perceive the danger which threattens, but as this letter (after it quits the office of the Secretary of State to whose care I shall send it) may pass through many hands, I shall dwell very little on European Politics. It is laughable enough however, to behold those men *amongst us* who were reprobating in the severest terms, and sounding the Tocsin upon every occasion that a wild imagination could *torture* into a stretch of power, or unconstitutionality, in the Executive of the United States, all of a sudden become the warm advocates of those high handed measures of the French Directory, which *succeeded* the arrestation on the 4th. of Septr.: and this too without *denying* that the barries of the Constitution, under which they acted have been *overleaped* but do it on the ground of *tender mercy* & an unwillingness to shed blood. But so it always has been and I presume ever will be with men who are governed more by passion, and party Views than by the dictates of Justice temperance & sound policy. If there were good grounds to suspect that the proscribed & banished Characters, were engaged in a conspiracy against the Constitution of the peoples choice, to seize them even in an irregular manner, might be justified upon the ground of expediency of self preservation. But after they were secured and amenable to the laws, to *condemn them without a hearing, and consign them to punishment more rigorous perhaps than death* is the summet of Depotism.

A very severe winter has commenced, since the first of November, we have hardly experienced a moderate day; heavy rains following severe frosts have done more damage to the winter grain now growing, than I recollect ever to have seen. At this moment and for several days past all the Creeks and small waters, are hard bound with ice and if the Navigation of the River is not entirely stoped, is yet very much impeded by it. The Crops of Indian Corn in the lower parts of the State, have been uncommonly great: midway of it tolerably good; but under the mountains and above them, extremely bad—with partial exceptions. The Wheat in Crop & in quantity turned out better than was expected; in quality remarkable fine: the white and early wheat weighing from 60 to 64 lb. per bushel.

The Virginia Assembly is or ought to be in Session, but what the temper of it is I know not. Its composition you must be better acquainted with than I am.

Young Layfayette[2] too fondly led by his eagerness to embrace his Parents & Sisters in the first moments of their releasement from Prison; and unintentially deceived by premature accouts from his friends at Hamburgh, that this event had actually taken place, embarked for this purpose on the 26th. of October at New York for Harve De Grace. Since which official acct. having been received of the terms on which his liberation was granted by the Emperor, the meeting in Europe is become problematical; a circumstance should it happen, which will be sorely regretted on both sides. I said all I could to induce him to wait here, until he should receive *direct* advice from his father, but his impatience on one hand, his confidence in the information he had received, that his Parents were on their way to Paris on the other, his apprehensions from a winters passage, and belief that he would not be illy recd: in France, even if they were not there turned the scale against my opinion & advice, that he should postpone his departure until he heard from him or one of the family. With very great Esteem & Regard I remain, Dear Sir, Your most Obedt. and Obliged Hble. Servt.

GO: WASHINGTON

2. George Washington Lafayette (1779–1849), the eldest son of the marquis de Lafayette, had been sent to the United States after his father's imprisonment in Austria. After Washington retired from the presidency, young Lafayette and his tutor stayed with Washington at Mt. Vernon until Lafayette learned of his father's release.

From Rufus King

LS, Archives Nationales, Paris

Confidential

London, December 7, [1797]

Lord[3] *Grenville last* [*night*] *sent Hammond*[4] *the following information that had been just received* [*by*] *this government.*

Coast of France, November 26: the Minister of Marine Pleville LePeley has recommended to the marine officers at Granville [*and*] *St. Maloes to throw every secret* [*im*]*pediment without open force to delay the departure of American ships and the exportation of American property which they daily expected orders to sequester.*

Hammond said that he was ordered to declare that this [*in*]*formation was authentic, and such as they should act upon in a case that concerned them.*[5] *You will judge whether you can give notice to our people to withdraw their property. With great truth.* Yours etc.

R KING

From David Humphreys

LS, William L. Clements Library, University of Michigan

Gentlemen, Madrid, December 8, 1797

I[6] took the liberty of addressing a letter to you on the 28th of October, of inclosing certain documents which had been sent to me from Cadiz, and of expressing a desire of being acquainted with the success of your negociations, as I apprehended such an event might have a favorable influence on the conduct of this government in their treatment of the flag of the United States.[7] I

3. Italics indicate words originally in code. Printed under Dec. 9, 1797, in Charles R. King, ed., *The Life and Correspondence of Rufus King . . .*, II (New York, 1895), 247-248.

4. George Hammond (1763–1853), former British minister to the United States and at this time undersecretary for foreign affairs, was a close friend of King.

5. King recorded in his notebook that Lord Grenville had sent Hammond to King's house to give him the information. See Dec. 9, 1797, Notebook, King Papers, LXXIII, New-York Historical Society.

6. David Humphreys was U.S. minister to Spain. See Frank Landon Humphreys, *Life and Times of David Humphreys: Soldier, Statesman, Poet*, 2 vols. (New York, 1917).

7. The letter Humphreys referred to has not been found. Humphreys included a copy of his letter to Joel Barlow, Oct. 28, 1797, in Humphreys to Timothy Pickering, Nov. 7, 1797, Diplomatic Dispatches, Spain, IV, RG 59, National Archives. In his letter to Barlow, Humphreys discussed several of the issues mentioned in his letter to the American envoys.

have not yet had the pleasure of being informed that my letter has reached you: and therefore I beg leave to repeat my anxiety to be informed of the result of the business, as soon as it may be communicated without indiscretion.

In the mean time, in consequence of a sollicitation from our consul at Cadiz,[8] I take the occasion of recommending to your protection the case of the brig Amiable Matilda, captain Willm. Brown bound from Philadelphia to Bilboa with a valuable cargo of cacao, lately taken by a French privateer in that harbour, and carried for adjudication to Bayonne . . . in which port I know not whether we have any consul or agent.

I have, within a few days past, received two notes from the Prince of the Peace[9] on the subject of the complaints which I had made respecting the capture of vessels belonging to citizens of the United States, taken by Spanish privateers and condemned as prizes in the inferior maritime tribunals. From these notes nothing very definitive is to be deduced. The tryals on appeals are proceeding slowly in the supreme tribunals of this capital.

I request you will have the goodness to cause the inclosed letters to be delivered, and to believe me, With sentiments of perfect consideration and esteem, Gentlemen, Your most obedt. & most humble servt.

D. Humphreys.

To Charles Cotesworth Pinckney

ALS, Middleton Collection of Pinckney Papers, South Carolina Historical Society

Dear Sir [Paris, December 17, 1797]

I was for the first time extremely chagrind to find your card on my return from the play this evening. I had hopd you woud not come. I was placed in a situation which obliged me to go out. Mr. Gerry was not here & Madam Villet had taken a box at the Odeon where Voltaires Mahomet was performd of which she gave me notice at night & invited me to accompany her.[1] What coud I do? You will excuse my going but will think I ought to have sent to

8. Josef Yznardy, of Baltimore, was U.S. consul at Cadiz.

9. Manuel de Godoy Alvarez de Faria (1767–1851).

1. The only time the play was performed at the Odeon was the evening of Dec. 17. *Moniteur Universel* (Paris), Dec. 17, 1797.

stop you. I am sure I ought, but it did not occur to me. I pray you to excuse me & to beleive that I am, very sincerely your

J MARSHALL

To Fulwar Skipwith

LS, Norcross Papers, Massachusetts Historical Society

Sir, Paris, December 20, 1797

We have received your letters, requesting our opinion on several subjects interesting to the Consuls of the United States, in the several ports of France.[2]

We are very strongly impressed with the justice of refunding immediately to mr. Daubry,[3] and to such other Consuls as may be in the same situation, any monies they may have advanced for the use of the United States. We are sensible of the utility of those advances and of the patriotism of the motives, which dictated them; and we regret very sincerely that we have not the power of having their accounts settled, and of paying immediately those sums, to which they are so well entitled. Full representations on this subjet have been made to the Government of the United States, and we expect soon to receive instructions concerning it. We doubt not that they will be such as justice dictates, and we shall feel much pleasure in hastening to obey them.

The situation of our Sailors demands the immediate attention of our Government. We consider it as indispensably necessary to provide the means of their return to their Country. You will therefore please to inform the different Consuls that wherever opportunities of sending our Sailors home shall occur such opportunities shall be seized, & the necessary advances, not exceeding [4] per man, be made, for which the drafts of the Consul on the Ministers of the United States will be paid. Such drafts, however, must be accompanied with the vouchers necessary to justify the ministers in making such payment; and in the application of this money other vouchers must be taken by the Consuls and Vice-Consuls, to be

2. The letters from Skipwith to the American envoys have not been found.

3. Pierre Frédéric Dobrée was U.S. consul at Nantes and was active in French-American trade. Dobrée's name is spelled correctly in the copy in Diplomatic Dispatches, France, VI, RG 59, National Archives. See Ulane Z. Bonnel, "The Dobrée Papers at Nantes," *Quarterly Journal of the Library of Congress*, XXVIII (1971), 253–259.

4. The amount of aid per seaman was left blank in all copies.

exhibited to the treasury department of the United States, when they adjust their respective accounts; & duplicates of the vouchers last mentioned must be transmitted to and filed in your office. The forms of the vouchers you will please to prescribe.

The Congress at their last Session has passed an act relative to American vessels condemned in the Courts of France & purchased by American citizens other than the original owners. You will please to have the necessary number of these laws printed, & each Consul furnished with a copy, which you will accompany with instructions desiring him to consider the act as his sole guide on the subject to which it relates.

Although we have very little hope that a certificate of the seamen and passengers on board can be of any service to our oppressed and injured commerce, yet we think it adviseable to give such certificates, if requested. We conceive that no injury can result from it, and we are the more inclined to advise it, as such a practice has, we understand, prevailed in some of the ports of the United States. Although we give this opinion, we deem it unquestionable that our Treaty with France dispenses with the necessity of any such paper, and therefore care must be taken to avoid any expression, which might be construed to imply such necessity. We are your obedt.

Charles Cotesworth Pinckney
J Marshall
E Gerry

From Rufus King

LS, Archives Nationales, Paris

Gentlemen, London, December 23, 1797

I[5] *hope that my letters of November fifteenth and twenty-fourth and of the seventh instant have come to hand in that of November twenty-fourth. I took notice of those considerations which render the preservation of peace so important. More might be added on the same subject, but France perseveres in the capture and condemnation of our ships. She continues to decline to treat with us and even to receive our envoys, while she employs all the influence left her to discredit our government and to divide our people.*

If we are denied the right of embassy, if we cannot navigate the ocean in security, and if, moreover, we are not free to choose our own governors un-

5. Italics indicate words originally in code.

less they are agreeable to France and at the same time to remain in peace, our rep[ut]ation in the eyes of others, our duty to ourselves and above all self-respect and national independence command us to endeavour to protect and preserve these high privileges even at the expen[se] of peace.

As we desire the preservation *of peace, the time is near at hand when we must look and act with firmness. Upon the* alternative *France may be inclined to practice a dilatory and insidious policy. It is in your power to* disappoint *the former, and I have the* consolation *to believe that the latter will be [attempted] in vain. Confidence on this point is derived as well from the respect due to your judgment as from the persuasion that you will think and act in concert, the want of which in [some] of our former commissions has been injurious as well as disreputable to our country.*[6] *The events of every day confirm the propriety of your resolution not to treat with any unauthorized persons, and on the [sub]ject of bribes and loans I do not perceive that under any circumstances you consent to them. To ransome our country from injustice and power would be to invite dishonor and injury because there can be no guaranty against them. This cabinet last night after several days' consideration gave a decided negative to a proposal of peace from the Directory thro. Talleyrand. The [pro]ject was detailed and the terms more favorable than those demanded by Lord Malmsbury at Lisle. The price was a bribe of a million sterling to be divided among directors, ministers & others, Talleyrand's department to have shared one hundred thousand pounds. I could name the agents, the stages, and every circumstance of the overture.*[7] *You may place entire confidence in the fact. This re-*

6. John Trumbull had informed King of the divisions in the American delegation. In a private letter written to Pinckney on Dec. 24, 1797, King was much more explicit. "If I do not mistake its import, we are in danger from a quarter [Gerry] in which I confess I have not felt wholly secure, but where I thought integrity and honest though sometimes mistaken patriotism would overcome my miserable vanity and a few little defects of character that I have [*known*] for a long time to exist, and which I now fear have been discovered by those who will be assiduous to turn it to mischief. You must not appear to suspect what you may really know. You must appear to act as you would do, did the most perfect harmony exist. You must in short save him and in doing so prevent the division that would grow out of schism in your commission." Later in the letter King urged Pinckney to "take care that means are not employed to protract the negotiation till commerce ruined by depredation shall not be worth protecting." On the same day King wrote a personal letter to Gerry in which he made only one political point: "The continued depredation upon our commerce has the effect that might naturally have been looked for, and temperate men have become anxious least a long and patient negotiation should be followed by an open rupture." See King to Pinckney, King to Gerry, Dec. 24, 1797, F 7, 4269, Archives Nationales, Paris.

7. King recorded in his notebook that his information had come from Trumbull, and that Hottinguer and Bellamy had been the intermediaries in this bribe attempt. Mr. Williams, a British banker in Paris, had made a down payment of £10,000 while the British were debating the possibility of reopening negotiations with the French. Dec. 23, 1797, Notebook, King Papers, LXXIII, New-York Historical Society.

fusal has been made at a time when the part that shall be taken by the new King of Prussia[8] *is unknown, when England would be glad to obtain a solid peace, & if economy alone influenced her, would have paid the bribe to procure it in case she could have put confidence in the* [*cor*]*rupt agents with whom she might have made the bargain.* With great Respect & Esteem, I am Your ob: & faithful servant

RUFUS KING

To Rufus King

LS, King Papers, Library of Congress

Dear Sir Paris, December 24, 1797

We[9] *have remained thus long in Paris without being accredited as ministers because we would really submit to any situation however irksome, while a hope remained that such submission could produce good and because too, we deem it necessary to satisfy our country and our government as well as ourselves that we have made every effort for accommodation which is compatible with the independence of our nation. But submission has its limits and if we have not actually passed, we are certainly approaching them. Repeated efforts for a bribe and for a loan continue to be made. We are assured that if we remain here six months longer we shall not be received but on condition of complying with these demands. We are convinced that this information is well-founded. We are also convinced that it is the intention of this government to detain us in Paris thus unacknowledged until the descent on England, which almost entirely occupies it, shall have been attempted. On the success of that attempt would depend their future treatment of us and of our country. They think we dare not leave them without being ordered away because as they say themselves such a step would produce a rupture and we know* [*that*] *they can count on a very strong party in America to support them in such an event. I think them mistaken, but they are of a different opinion. Under these circumstances what ought we to do? We regret the impossibility of consulting our government or of those in whom we can confide. We must act upon our own judgments and our opinion is that we ought not to remain much longer. We have determined to make a full representation to the government of the objects of our mission, and if it will not enter upon the discussion of them, to demand our passports. We shall do this in a manner as well calculated as possible to assuage the pride and*

8. Frederick William III succeeded Frederick William II as king of Prussia.
9. Italics indicate words originally in code.

anger of this government, but in a manner not totally unmindful of what is [due] to our own. If they grant us our passports and will permit it, we shall set out for England in January in order to take a passage for the United States. The resolution mentioned of demanding a passport in January is not so positively taken as I had supposed it to be.[1] *There is now some hesita-*

1. With virtually the same outlook, Pinckney wrote King on Dec. 27, 1797. "I have not now the least hope that we shall make any treaty with this government, for in order to do so, tribute, under the disguise of a loan, or some other disguise, and a private douceur of fifty thousand pounds sterling must be stipulated: and these degrading terms must be humbly offered by us even before we can be received, and I have been given to understand by a person who wishes us well, and is intimate with Mr. Talleyrand, that if we were to remain here for six months longer, we should not advance a step further towards our negociation, till these matters are agreed on. In the mean time, depredations on our commerce are threatend to be continued, and that frigates and armed vessels from St. Domingo shall ravage our coasts. In a conversation which Mr. Gerry had with Mr. Talleyrand, he told him the offer of a loan must come from us. We still intend to prepare, and transmit by the tenth of next month, to the minister of foreign affairs, a statement of the claims of our country, and declare our desire to enter into a discussion of their complaints. And to do justice on all the points wherein we shall be convinced that justice is due; and if they shall still continue not to receive us and enter into an investigation of the objects of our mission; and matters remain as they are; it is my opinion, and my colleagues tell me, that it is theirs also, that we ought to request our passports; and no longer exhibit to the world the unprecedented spectacle of three envoys extraordinary from a free and independant nation, in vain soliciting to be heard. It is our present intention to require passports for Calais, and remain on your side of the channel till March, and then embark for America: but passports to go by Calais may be refused us: and we are not decided to what port we shall then go to embark." See Pinckney to King, Dec. 27, 1797, Pickering Papers, Massachusetts Historical Society.

Joseph Pitcairn had permission to go to England, thus giving the envoys an opportunity to safely correspond with King. In his letter to King, however, Gerry did not discuss the political situation in France but dwelt on personal matters. Gerry was not necessarily hiding information from King, but since their differences during the debates over the Constitution in the mid-1780s, Gerry and King had not been politically close. See Gerry to King, Dec. 28, 1797, King Papers, Henry E. Huntington Library.

Gerry was more explicit in a letter to William Vans Murray. Gerry's description of the situation was slightly more accommodating and less indignant than JM's or Pinckney's. "The aspect of our affairs is unpleasant, & the crisis approaches. If the event should be favorable, of which I see no prospect at present, I shall be amply repaid for all the embarassments & vexations wch we have experienced, since our arrival in Paris: if unfavorable, I shall reflect with pleasure on the personal mortifications which I have voluntarily submitted to, for the restoration of friendship between the two republicks & their governments. I deprecate a war with France, but if she should adopt such an impolitic measure, which would inevitably produce on her part as well as ours, an immense Expence of men & money, without an object to be attained by either party, we must fight her into good humour, & thus convince her of her unparallelled policy. She may ravage in some degree, our coasts, & distress our commerce; but it is not, in my opinion, in the power of France & her allies, to transport to the U States men enough to conquer them. We will take care to dispatch one army, before she can send another. The conflict indeed would disgrace republicanism, & make it the scoff of despots: it would likewise, unite us with G Britain, & thus produce an alliance which might bid defiance to Europe: for with the support which the british navy would have, by our commerce & seamen, it would be forever triumphant. God

tion concerning it. With very much respect & esteem, I am dear Sir your obedt.

J MARSHALL

To Timothy Pickering

LS, RG 59, National Archives

No. 4

Dear Sir, Paris, December 24, 1797

We have not yet received *any*[2] *answer to our official letter to the Minister of foreign affairs, dated 11th. of last month,* and *mentioned in number three*; but reiterated *attempts have been made to engage us in negociation with persons not officially authorized*; and you will *find by the* Exhibits marked A B & C herewith sent, *some important information relative to the views and intentions of the french government with respect to ours.*[3] We are *all of opinion, that if we were to remain here for six months longer, without we were to stipulate the payment of money,* and a great deal *of it, in some shape or other, we should not be able to effectuate the objects of our mission, should we be even officially received,* unless the *projected attempt on England was to fail,* or a *total change takes place in the persons who at present direct the affairs of this government.* In[4] this situation of matters, *we are determined by the tenth of next month, should they, remain as they are, to transmit another letter to the minister, representing,* as far as may be expedient, *the views of our government.* We have the honor to be with great respect and regard, Your most Obedient, humble Servants

CHARLES COTESWORTH PINCKNEY
J MARSHALL
E GERRY

---

grant that none of these events may take place." Gerry to Murray, Dec. 28, 1797, Gratz Collection, Historical Society of Pennsylvania.

2. Italics indicate words originally in code.

3. See American Envoys to Talleyrand, Nov. 11, 1797, and American Envoys to Pickering, Nov. 27, 1797.

4. Another copy of this dispatch, received 10 days later on Mar. 30, 1797, ended somewhat differently. "In this situation of matters we are determined by the tenth of next month, should they, remain as they are, to transmit another letter to the minister representing as far as may be expedient, the view of our government in the mission they have entrusted to us. A copy whereof [will] be transmitted to you." American Envoys to Pickering, Dec. 24, 1797 (triplicate copy), Duplicate Diplomatic Dispatches, France, V, RG 59, National Archives.

Exhibit A: General Pinckney's Memorandum

[Paris], December 21, 1797

On the fourteenth of December, M. Horttinguer called on me, in order, as he said, to gain some information relative to some *lands in Georgia purchased by* a *Dutch company, for whom he was Agent.*[5] Soon afterwards *General Marshall came in* and *then M Gerrys carriage drove into the yard.* Here *is M. Gerry said General Marshall.* I *am glad of it, said M. Horttinguer, for* I *wished to meet all of you gentlemen, to inform you that M. Bellamy had another message to you from M. Talleyrand.* I immediately *expressed my surprize at it as M. Talleyrand, M. Bellamy and he all knew our determination to have no further communication on the subject of our mission with persons not officially authorised.* He *replied, that determination was made six weeks ago* and it was *presumed that we had changed our opinion.* I *said that* I *had not; and* I *did not* believe *my colleagues had. At that moment M. Gerry entered the room,* and I *privately acquainted him with the object of M. Horttinguer's visit. General Marshall, M. Gerry* and *myself then withdrew into another room;* and immediately *agreed to adhere* to *our former resolution. M. Horttinguer was then called in; when* I *acquainted him, in a few words, with our determination;* and *M. Gerry expatiated more at large on the propriety of our acting in this manner,* and on the very *unprecedented way in which we had been treated since our arrival.*[6]

On the twentieth of December, a lady,[7] *who is well acquainted with M. Talleyrand, expressed to me her concern, that we were still* [in][8] *so un-*

5. Pickering omitted the information on Hottinguer's business activities in the United States when he submitted a copy of this dispatch to Congress. Hottinguer was apparently referring to the Georgia Agricultural Company. See Pieter Jan van Winter, *Het aandeel van den Amsterdamschen handel aan den opbouw van het Amerikaansche Gemeenebest*, II (The Hague, 1933), 337–345.

6. See Exhibit C in this document for Gerry's account of the meeting.

7. The "lady" who made this remark to Pinckney has long been identified as Madame de Villette. See Beveridge, *Marshall*, II, 291; Marvin R. Zahniser, *Charles Cotesworth Pinckney: Founding Father* (Chapel Hill, N.C., 1967), 175; Alexander DeConde, *The Quasi-War: The Politics and Diplomacy of the Undeclared War with France, 1797–1801* (New York, 1966), 52. There is no evidence, however, to prove that Madame de Villette was the "lady" referred to here. Mrs. Pinckney acknowledged that she met Madame de Villette often, but she gave no hint of a close connection between the "lady" and her husband, as Talleyrand later charged. See Mary Pinckney to Margaret Manigault, Mar. 9, 1798, Manigault Family Papers, University of South Carolina; for Talleyrand's comment, see *Amer. State Papers, Foreign Relations*, II, 225–226. If the "lady" were Madame de Villette, it is unlikely that Gerry and JM would have retained such high respect for her after Pinckney reported the conversation. See JM to Fulwar Skipwith, Apr. 21, 1798; JM to Beaumarchais, Nov. 20, 1798; Gerry to Skipwith, June 22, 1807, Causten-Pickett Papers, VII, Library of Congress; Stinchcombe, "WXYZ Affair," *WMQ*, 3d Ser., XXXIV (1977), 609–610.

8. This word was omitted in the original coded letter; it was inserted later, probably by Jacob Wagner, the chief clerk in the State Department.

settled a *situation, but adds she, why will not you lend us money? if you would but make us a loan, all matters would be adjusted:* and *she added* when you were *contending for your revolution we lent you money.* I *mentioned the very great difference there was between the situation of the two countries at that period* and the *present,* and *the very different circumstances under which the loan was made us and the loan was now demanded from us. She replied, we do not make a demand; we* think it more *delicate that the offer should come from you: but M. Talleyrand has mentioned to me (who am surely not in his confidence) the necessity of your* making *us a loan; and I know that he has Mentioned it to two* or *three others;* and *that you have been informed of it;* and *I will assure you, that if you remain here six months longer, you would not advance a single step further in your negociations without a loan. If that is the case* I *replied, we may as well go away now.* Why that possibly, *said she, might lead to a rupture, which you had better avoid; for we know we have a* very considerable *party in America who are strongly in our interest.*

There is no *occasion to enter into a further detail of the conversation; I have only noted this part of it,* as expressive *of what I* believe (*as far as relates to the loan and a party in America in their favor) to be the sentiments of the french government with regard to us.*

CHARLES COTESWORTH PINCKNEY

Exhibit B: Extract From Genl. Marshall's Journal

[Paris, December 17, 18, 1797]

December seventeenth one thousand seven hundred ninety seven. I stept into M. Gerry's apartment, where I saw M. Bellamy. He expressd his regret at having been disabled to dine with us at M. de Beaumarchais by an inveterate tooth-ache. He then asked me whether I had seen M: de Beaumarchais lately? I told him not since he dined with us and that he had left us much indisposed. He then observed that he had not known until lately, that I was the advocate for that gentleman in his cause against the State of Virginia; and that M. de Beaumarchais, in consequence of that circumstance, had expressed sentiments of high regard for me.[9] *I replied, that M. de Beaumarchais' cause was of great magnitude and very uncertain issue, and consequently, that a portion of the interest he felt in it would very naturally be transfered to his advocate. He* immediately *said (low and apart) that M. de Beaumarchais had consented, provided his claim could be established to sacreifice 50,000 pounds sterling of it, as the private gratification which had been required of us; so that the gratification might be made with-*

9. JM had been Beaumarchais's attorney in Virginia. See Vol. II, 124–126.

out any actual loss to the American government.[1] *I answered, that a gratification on any terms, or in any form, was a subject which we approached with much fear and difficulty, as we were not authorised by our government to make one; nor had it been expected that one would be necessary: that I could not undertake to say whether my colleagues would consent to it, in any state of things; but I could undertake to say, no one of us would consent to it, unless it was preceeded, or accompanied, by a full and entire recognition of the claims of our citizens, and a satisfactory arrangement on the objects of our mission. He said it was in the expectation of that event only that he mentioned it. We parted; and I stated the conversation to General Pinckney, who was disinclined to any stipulation of the sort, and consider it as a renewal of the old reprobated system of indirect, unauthorized negociation. Having been originally the counsel of M. de Beaumarchais, I had determined, and so I informed General Pinckney, that I would not, by my voice, establish any agreement in his favor; but that I would* possitively *oppose any admission of the claim of any french citizen, if not accompanied with the admission of the claims of the American citizens of property captured and condemned for want of a role d'equipage. My reason for conceiving, that this ought to be stipulated expressly, was a conviction, that if it was refered to commissioners, it would be committing* absolutely *to chance as complete a right as any individual ever possessed. General Pinckney was against admitting the claim at any rate. After my return, M. Gerry came into my room, and told me that M. Bellamy had called on him, to accompany him on a visit to M. Taleyrand; that he proposed seeing M. Taleyrand; and returning the civility of the dinner; and endeavoring to bring about some intercourse between him and us.*

December eighteenth. General Pinckney and M. Gerry met in my room; and M. Gerry detailed to us the conversations mentioned in our public letter. The proposition relative to the claim of M. de Beaumarchais is entirely *different from my understanding of it, in the very brief statement made to me by M. Bellamy.*[2] *We resolved that we would rigidly adhere to the rule we had adopted, to enter into no negociation with persons not formally authorised to treat with us. We came also to the determination to prepare a letter to the Minister of foreign relations, stating the object of our mission, and discussing the subjects of difference between the two nations, in like manner as we had been actually received; and to close the letter with requesting the government to open the negociation with us, or to grant us our passports.*

1. See Journal, Dec. 17, 1797.
2. This sentence is not included in the Journal, Dec. 18, 1797.

Exhibit C: Gerry's Memorandum

[Paris, Dec. 14, 17, 1797]

December [*14*]*th.*[3] Accidentally *calling on General Pinckney Mr. Gerry there found* Mr *Horttinguer* and *was soon informed that his object was to obtain another interview between the Ministers* and Mr. *Bellamy on the affairs of their mission. General Marshall happening also to be there we retired into another room and* immediately *agreed to adhere to our former* determination *not to have any more informal communications. Mr Horttinguer having been called in, General Pinckney* briefly *communicated our* Determination *and* Mr. *Gerry observed that he was much hurt by this proposition: that the ministers had already proceeded further in this mode of communication than perhaps they could* justify; *that they had refused six weeks ago to renew it;* and *that some regard ought to be paid to their* feelings, *which had been* sufficiently *mortified; that the proposition was disrespectful to the Envoys as it* betrayed *a belief that they had lost the Sense of their dignity* and *were indeed* incompetent *to their office; that had there been but one Envoy* extraordinary *he ought to have had an audience in* a *few days;* and *that for three to* remain *between two* & *three months in this* Situation *was too humiliating, too debasing for any nation to* submit to *it; that for his own part had he been sent to any other nation in Europe with two other Envoys he would not have consented to have* remained *in such a state ten days, but knowing the great desire of the Government and nation of the United States to be at peace with France he had with his* Collegues *submitted to this indignity* at *the* risque *of the severe censure of both the former.* Having *also enquired of* Mr *Horttinguer* at *what time* Mr *Talleyrand could be seen, the former said he would inquire of* Mr. *Bellamy, who on the sixteenth in the evening sent,* in Mr *Gerry's absence from his* lodgings, *a billet as follows* "Mr B. *has the honor to present his respects to Mr Gerry and to inform him that he will have the honor to wait on him tomorrow morning at ten* O Clock *to go together to the minister of Foreign Relations. He is with respect,* etc." *On the morning of the seventeenth* Mr B *came in whilst* Mr *Gerry was* at breakfast, *not having received an* answer *to his note;* & *Mr Marshall coming in* Mr *Bellamy took him aside* & *conferred with him* a *considerable time—after which the former and the rest of the* family *left the room,* and Mr *Bellamy and Mr Gerry being together,* Mr *Gerry told him, that his object in seeing* Mr *Talleyrand was to return* a civility *by requesting him to fix* a *day for dining with* Mr G. *who intended to* in-

3. Gerry incorrectly gave the date as Dec. 13, 1797. Both Pinckney in Exhibit A of this dispatch and JM in his Journal, Dec. 14, 1797, recorded that the conversation took place on Dec. 14, 1797.

vite *his colleagues,* and *by this interview to promote, if possible,* a *better* understanding *between the minister* and *the American Envoys;* and Mr *Gerry also proposed to confer with the minister on the disagreeable* situation *the Envoys were in* and *so state to him some reports which appeared to be* founded *respecting* a *proposition before the Directory for sending off all Americans in* a short period; *but,* Mr *Gerry added, he could not hear* a *word on the subject of the mission or the* preliminaries *to a negociation, as the Envoys had determined* unanimously *against any informal cummunication* on *the subject.* Mr *Bellamy in* answer *said that* Mr *Marshall had* Just *heard him on* a *subject of this* kind and *that we might consider it as he did* merely *a* conversation *between ourselves. He then stated that two measures, which* Mr *Talleyrand proposed, being* adopted, *a restoration of friendship between the republics would follow* immediately, *the one was* a *gratuity of £50000 Sterling, the other* a *purchase of sixteen instead of thirty two millions of the Dutch rescriptions; that as to the first Mr de Beaumarchais had* recovered *in a cause depending in Virginia between that State and himself £145,000 Sterling,* that there was an appeal from the Judgement; that he would sign an act to relinquish £*45,000 if the whole should be finally recovered, leaving only* £*100,000 for himself: that the* £*45,000. might* accrue *to the United States who would in this case lose but a small part of the* £*50,000; that the* purchase *of sixteen millions of rescriptions would amount to but* £*1,333,333.6.8 Sterling which, with an interest of five per cent, would be certainly paid by the Government of Holland to the United States & leave them without any loss; that more than half the sum may now be* hired *in Holland on the credit of the Rescriptions and an easy arrangement be made for paying, by short instalments, the other half, which might be obtained also by a loan; that it was worthy the attention of the Envoys to consider whether by so small a sacrifice they would establish a peace with France, or whether they would* risk *the consequences; that if nothing could be done by the envoys,* arrangements *would be made forthwith to ravage the coasts of the United States by frigates from St. Domingo; that small States which had offended France were suffering by it; that Hamburg and other Cities in that quarter would within a month or two have their Government changed; that Switzerland would undergo the same operation, and that Portugual would probably be in a worse predicament; that the expedition against England would be* certainly *pursued; and that the present period was the most favorable, if we wished to adopt any measures for a pacification. Mr. Gerry in answer said that if the French were disposed to pursue with vengence the United States they might perhaps ravage their Coasts and* injure *them in this way, but they could never subdue them; the measure he thought utterly* impracticable *even if attempted by*

France and her allies; to which Mr Bellamy assented. Mr. Gerry observed further that the revages alluded to would undoubtedly *closely connect the United States and Great Britain, and prevent the former from returning to the friendship which they have ever had for France; that as to the propositions he should express no opinion on them; that his situation and that of his Colleagues was extremely difficult; that the Directory were* Excessively *prejudiced against the Government of the United States and considered them as the friends of Great Britain that if the Envoys could have an opportunity of being heard they could remove such impressions and show that the Government were the friends of France as much as of Great Britain; but that the Envoys were now in the most painful* Situation. That they were *treated by the Directory in the eyes of all* Europe *and of the American Government and nation with the utmost contempt, and were submitting to indignities which they could not reconcile to their own feelings* or *justify to their Constituents. Mr. Bellamy said that the observations were just;* But that the *American Envoys had not* experienced *worse treatment than other ministers, nor indeed as bad; that the minister of Portugual was again ordered to depart* and that but *little Ceremony was observed to the ministers in general. Mr. Bellamy and Mr Gerry took then a ride to Mr Talleyrand's bureau who received them politely; and after being seated Mr Gerry observed to Mr Talleyrand in English* slowly that *Mr Bellamy had stated to him that morning some propositions as coming from Mr Talleyrand respecting which Mr Gerry could give no opinion;* That *his object at this interview was to request of him information whether he would fix a time for* taking a *dinner with Mr Gerry at which he proposed to invite his Colleagues; that he* wished *for more frequent interviews of some kind or other between himself and the Envoys,* conceiving that *many imaginary difficulties, which obstructed the negociation, would* vanish by *these means and that those which were real would be surmounted;* that conceiving *the delicate part which the ministers of France had to act at this time he did not wish Mr. Talleyrand to accept the invitation if it would subject him to inconveniences.* That *he wished to speak on another subject* and it *was painful to him to acknowledge that the precarious situation of the Envoys was such as to render it impossible for them to take measures for decent arrangements;* That *a short time since he had supposed measures were* taking a *favorable turn, but that lately he had received from* various *quarters information of a report made by the minister of the interior and under the consideration of the Directory for sending all Americans from Paris in twenty-four hours; that he could not be* responsible *for the truth of the information, but it appeared to him as well from the various quarters from which it came as from the* intelligence *of the persons who gave it to be highly probable;* That *if this was the case it was unnecessary for the Directory as he conceived to pass any arrêté as it respected the envoys* for that *they would depart from Paris whenever it was hinted as the wish of the Directory;* that for *his own part he should feel more at ease, until we were received, to reside in a City of some other nation, than that of France* and to *return to Paris* on *notice that the Directory were disposed to open the negotiation. Mr. Talleyrand appeared to be very uneasy at this declaration but* avoided *saying a word* on it; *he said that the information which Mr. Bellamy had given me was just* and *might always be relied on, but that he would reduce to writing his propositions which he accordingly did* and after *he had shewn them to Mr Gerry he burnt the paper.* The *substance was as follows* marked No. 1.

He *then said that he* accepted *of the invitation; that he would dine* with *him the decade*[4] *after the present* in which *he was engaged.*

Mr. Gerry did not repeat all that he had said to Mr. Bellamy having no doubt *that he would communicate the whole to Mr. Talleyrand;* and after *expressing* a friendship *for the french Republic* and a *warm desire to renew the former* attachments *of the two Republics, which Mr. Talleyrand warmly* reciprocated, *Mr Gerry bid Mr. Talleyrand* adieu *leaving with him Mr. Bellamy.*

No. 1 Referred to in Exhibit C

[Paris, December 17, 1797]

That the envoys should come forward generally *and say:*

"*France has been* serviceable *to the United States;* and *now they wish to be* serviceable *to France: understanding that the French republic has sixteen million of dutch rescriptions to sell, the United States will* purchase *them at par,* and *will give her further* assistance *when in their power.*

The first arrangement *being made, the French government will take measures for* reimbursing *the equitable demands of America; arising from prizes,* and *to give free navigation to their ships in future.*"[5]

From Rufus King

ALS, Archives Nationales, Paris

London, December 30, 1797

I find it difficult to send my Letters to you—the vessels are searched and the Letters taken out. I yesterday had returned to me

4. The next *décade* would be Dec. 30, 1797.

5. Gerry started a sentence here that he crossed out. "Mr. Gerry did not repeat all that he . . . ."

tho the Post Office the Orig. and trip of my Letter to you of Dec. 7. I hope the Dup. of that, as well as some one of the Copies of a Letter that I wrote to you early in Novr. may have reached you. I have nothing new to add. The repeated Declarations concerning the invasion of this country have an opposite Effect from what is wished—they say here those who talk much, do little. We understand that the army of Italy is to take Paris on its way to the Coast of the Ocean. What does this mean? Are you to see another 18th. fructidor?

I sent you in my last the only copy I had of the Pr. Speech. Yours etc.

R K.

From Rufus King

ALS, Wendell Collection, Harvard University

No. 4.

Gentlemen London, January 3, 1798

I have great pleasure in sending you copies of the Answers of the Senate and H. of R. to the presidents Speech, they display an excellencent Spirit, and are very satisfactory Evidence of the good State of the pub. Mind of our Country.[6]

I have only a moment to add the assurance of my sincere Regard, and am Genn. yr. ob. & faithful ser.

RUFUS KING

To Timothy Pickering

LS, RG 59, National Archives

(Triplicate)

No. 5

Dear Sir, Paris, January 8, 1798[7]

We embrace an unexpected opportunity to send you the "Redacteur" of the fifth instant, containing the message of the Direc-

6. King probably sent the president's speech of Nov. 23, 1797, to the opening session of Congress as well as the answers to the envoys. For the speech and answers see, Nov. 23, 27, and 28, 1797, *Annals of Congress*, VII, 630–634, 642–648, 472–475.

7. This letter and its enclosure is printed in *Message of the President of the United States of 5th March, 1798: with a letter from our Envoys Extraordinary at Paris, With Other Documents* (Philadelphia, [1798]), and is also in *Amer. State Papers, Foreign Relations*, II, 150–151.

tory to the Council of Five Hundred, urging the necessity of a Law to declare as good prize all Neutral Ships met at sea, whose cargoes, in part or in whole shall consist, of Merchandizes or Commodities, the production of England, or of the English possessions, that the Flag, as they term it, may no longer cover the property. And declaring further that the ports of France, except in cases of distress, shall be shut against all Neutral Ships, which in the course of their voyage, shall have touched at an English port.

A Commission has been appointed to report on the message & it is expected that a Decree will be passed in conformity to it.

Nothing new has occurred since our last in date of the 24th. ultmo. We can only repeat that there exists no hope of our being officially received by this Government, or that the objects of our Mission will be in any way accomplished. We have the honor to be with great respect & esteem, Your most obt. Servts.

CHARLES COTESWORTH PINCKNEY
J MARSHALL
E GERRY

P:S: The Law above mentioned has been passed unanimously by the Council of Five Hundred & we enclose a Journal containing the account. There is no doubt but that it will be adopted without opposition by the Council of Ancients.

From James C. Mountflorence

Letterbook Copy, Franklin Collection, Yale University Library

Sir[8] Paris, January 16, 1798

I received yesterday a Letter from Mr Barnet[9] dated the 9th: inst. by which he informs me that he has received a Circular from from the Consul General covering the Copy of one from you,[1] authorizing the Consuls to make advances to our Seamen in certain cases, but without any provision for such as are detained as Prisoners of War, having been found on board English Vessels captured

8. This letter is address to Pinckney only, but all three envoys responded in the next document, Jan. 17, 1798. The duties of overseeing consular affairs were shared jointly by the three envoys.

9. Isaac Cox Barnet, of New Jersey, had been appointed U.S. consul at Brest, but before JM's arrival in Paris, the Directory had refused to accept Barnet's exequatur. He could not, therefore, undertake his consular duties.

1. See American Envoys to Fulwar Skipwith, Dec. 20, 1797.

by those of the french Republic. Several of our Seamen being in that predicament in the public jails of Brest, & Mr Barnet thinking he could procure them their Liberty at the rate of 24 li. per man, altho the Minister of Marine has lately issued orders to liberate neutrals but upon condition that they will embark on board french vessels, he would request your orders on that Subject.

The same Consul also informs me that Captain Samuel Burley of the Brig Sally of Boston, arrived at Brest the 1st December last, is about selling his Vessel, and has discharged his Crew, without paying the wages of all his men, and without supplying any one of them with the means of returning home; among them there is a Black that he has beaten in a cruel manner—this is a delicate and difficult matter for Mr. Barnet to manage, as he has not yet an *Exequatur* from this Government.

A Letter from Mr Fenwick[2] of the 8th: inst. informs me that the Brig Amiable Matilda of Philadelphia, Capt. Brown, carried sometime ago into Bayonne, and whose *Role d'Equipage* had been concealed by the people of the privateer, has been acquitted and given up. Arrived also at Bordeaux a Vessel from New-York, which place she left early in december last, but I have no letters by her. With great respect, I have the honour to be, Sir, Your most obedt. and most devoted humble Servant.

Js. C. Mountflorence

To Fulwar Skipwith

ALS, Miscellaneous Papers, New York Public Library

Sir Paris, January 17, 1798

Mr. Barnet the consul at Brest considers the general instructions which have been given respecting American seamen as not extending to those who have been capturd on board british vessels & are detaind in prison. He adds that there are many in this situation at Brest & that he beleives he coud liberate them at twenty four livres per man.

Our intention is that prisoners as well as others shall be liberated & returnd to their country. We are willing that the sum he mentions be advanced for this purpose. But especial care is to be taken

2. Joseph Fenwick had been appointed U.S. consul at Bordeaux by President Washington. Fenwick was a merchant and copartner of John Mason of the firm Mason & Fenwick in Georgetown, Md.

that the intervention of the United States be only usd for such sailors as will embark for their own country. We wish all proper measures to be taken to restore our fellow citizens to their friends their families & their liberty, but we can make no advances for those who would still continue in Europe. We are Sir very respectfully, Your obedt.

CHARLES COTESWORTH PINCKNEY
J MARSHALL
E GERRY

From Caron de Beaumarchais

LS, Pierpont Morgan Library

Messieurs [Paris], January 17, 1798

Jai lu avec la plus grande attention le discours Anglais du Président *John Adams*, traduit littéralement en francais que vous m'avès communiqué.[3] Je crois répondre a votre honorable confiance en vous disant avec véracité, que quoique les phrases du Président, dont quelques journaux français, se sont plaint, semblent n'avoir été placées par l'orateur dans son discours, que pour amener Et mieux faire sentir la nécessité dont il parle de prendre des mesures Energiques contre toute espèce d'agressions tant intérieures que Maritimes; et quoique, rigoureusement parlant, on puisse regarder ces phrâses, plutot comme un tableau fâcheux de L'Europe entière, que comme des reproches adressés directement au Gouvernement de la france; il est impossible Messieurs, de ne pas voir a *travers un voile léger*, que c'est le Directoire de france que le Président D'Amérique a eu en vue de désigner.

1. Parce que c'est dans l'article ou il parle de la négotiation entamée avec notre gouvernement, que ces phrases sont enchassées; Et que leur Véhémence est bien loin des ménagements qu'il employe plus loin, l'orsqu'il parle des plaintes qu'il croit devoir porter contre le Gouvernement Espagnol, relativement au séjour prolongé de ses troupes sur votre territoire, etc.

2. Parce qu'après les plaintes modérées du Président contre les Espagnols, il reprend toute son amertume pour dénoncer les tenta-

3. During their conference on Jan. 13, 1798, JM or Gerry probably gave Beaumarchais copies of Adams's speech to Congress of Nov. 23, 1797. See Journal, Dec. 17, 1797; Beaumarchais to Gerry, Jan. 13, 1798, Gerry Papers, Pierpont Morgan Library.

tives d'agens qu'il appelle *Etrangers* (mais qui désignent des français) pour entrainer, dit il, les Indiens enclavés chez vous, a des hostilités contre les Etats qu'il préside; surtout en appuyant sur l'urgente nécessité de porter un regard sévère, et de promulguer une loi rigoureusement répressible de ce qu'il nomme *un délit aussi grave!*[4]

3. Parce qu'ensuite, rappelant l'Etat respectif des deux peuples, d'après *le traité d'amitié* qui éxiste, dit il, entre le gouvernement Anglais, et celui des Etats unis; Le Président ne parle de l'angleterre, avec une douce abondance, que pour annoncer aux deux chambres qu'Elle a nommé des comissaires pour la fixation des limites, et des indemnités qui déja sont, dit il, en partie acquittées par elle.

D'ou il résulte, honorables amis, qu'on na pas pu se méprendre un instant sur l'intention de votre Président de faire peser ses graves plaintes sur le Gouvernement français, *sans que l'on puisse s'y méprende*. Et, sans vouloir entrer, de ma part, dans la question du plus ou moins de droit qu'il avait de porter ces plaintes; puisque l'avis que vous me demandés, est uniquement de vous dire si je crois que, *d'après votre traduction mesme*, le reproche du Président peut être regardé comme dirigé contre le Directoire de france; je vous réponds très nettement que *Oui*; Et que je crois qu'il est de votre Loyauté d'abandonner toute réclamation sur l'infidélité des traducteurs, qui ne serait, dans ma franche opinion, qu'un moyen de chicane au dessous de la dignité de négotiateurs tels que vous.

Peut être était il désirable, vu la mission très grave dont vous etes chargés près du gouvernement de France, qu'on Eut écarté avec soin de ce discours public prononcé par le Magistrat le plus important des Etats, tous ce qui pourrait fomenter, entretenir l'aigreur que votre honorable mission est de travailler a calmer! Mais puisqu'on ne peut empêcher que ce qui est fait ne soit fait; je crois, Messieurs, qu'il est de votre dignité de laisser là cette question; En vous occupant uniquement, Et franchement (comme vous m'avès assuré que que vous le faites) du fond des choses, sur

4. Adams said in his speech to Congress: "In connection with the unpleasant state of things on our western frontier, it is proper for me to mention the attempts of foreign agents to alienate the affections of the Indian nations, and to excite them to actual hostilities against the United States; great activity has been exerted by these persons, who have insinuated themselves among the Indian tribes, residing within the territory of the United States, to influence them, to transfer their affections and force to a foreign nation, to form them into a confederacy, and prepare them for war, against the United States." Nov. 23, 1797, *Annals of Congress*, VII, 632.

lesquelles vous ne devés laisser aucun doute a personne, que vous soyès volontairement en retard d'une réponse, *quelle quelle soit*, que l'on semble attendre de vous!

En[5] effet on en attend une, m'a-t-on dit, sur des objèts précis qui vous ont Eté remis, par Ecrit, au nom du Ministre, Et par la personne affidée avec qui vous m'avès permis d'en causer librement: tout retard de cette réponse, soit au ministre mesme, ou soit a la personne qui vous a remis cet écrit, ne peut que Nuire au Succès desirable de votre Négotiation.

Je vous en dirai davantage la 1ère. fois que J'aurai le plaisir En vous voir.

Je vous renvoye le discours anglais et français que vous m'avès remis. Salut honneur et respect bien Sincère.

CARON BEAUMARCHAIS

American Envoys to Talleyrand

EDITORIAL NOTE

The following document is a clear, comprehensive exposition of the American position during the mission to Paris. Marshall wrote it with the intention of "stating the objects of our mission and discussing the subjects of difference between the two nations in like manner as if we had been actually received and to close the letter with requesting the Government to open the negotiation with us or to grant us our passports."[6] As the scant Journal entries show, Marshall worked for the better part of a month preparing the statement. He divided it into two broad sections: one a "justification of the conduct of the American government"[7] and the other a statement of "the claims of the United States upon France."[8] As Marshall finished each portion he submitted it to the other envoys for suggestions and corrections. He apparently did not have difficulty securing Pinckney's consent to the final statement, but Gerry procrastinated, causing an outburst of temper from the usually mild Marshall. Gerry did not approve the document until January 22, 1798.[9] It then took nine days before the statement was copied in English and French for submission to Talleyrand.[1] The document shows that Marshall was, as John Adams observed, "learned in the Law of Nations."[2] In the document Marshall repeatedly tried to reconcile the provisions of the Jay Treaty with the French Treaty of Alliance of 1778. Rather than recognize that the definitions of contraband in the two treaties were inconsistent with each other,

5. The remainder of the letter is in Beaumarchais's hand.
6. See Journal, Dec. 18, 1797.
7. See *ibid.*, Jan. 2, 1798.
8. See *ibid.*, Jan. 10, 1798.
9. See *ibid.*, Jan. 20 and 22, 1798.
1. See *ibid.*, Jan. 31, 1798.
2. Adams to Gerry, July 17, 1797, Gerry Papers, Henry E. Huntington Library.

and that the Americans had in fact retreated from a policy of "free ships make free goods," as stipulated in the Treaty of Alliance, Marshall took refuge in international law in hopes of extricating the United States from a weak bargaining position.

In a paper designed to strengthen his country's position, Marshall resorted to arguments that he probably did not fully believe. Only the credulous would believe that "the United States did not apprehend that the treaty with Britain could be considered as affecting its relations to France" or that the Jay Treaty "had not changed, in the most minute circumstance, the preexisting situation of the United States, in relation either to France or Great Britain." To Marshall's credit, he included relatively few such assertions.

Despite Marshall's original intent, the American envoys did not end the document with an ultimatum for either formal negotiations or the return of their passports.[3] According to William Vans Murray, another strategy was adopted. The American envoys intended to wait for ten days after delivering their statement to Talleyrand and, if it went unanswered, then to submit a separate letter demanding their passports. Marshall drew up the second letter immediately after the submission of the letter to Talleyrand on January 31. But after what were to Marshall inexplicable and inexcusable delays, Gerry again refused to sign. Gerry's action prolonged the mission for another two months, since Pinckney and Marshall did not want to force an open break with him.[4]

Albert Beveridge possibly exaggerated when he wrote that "the statement by Marshall remains to this day one of the ablest state papers ever produced by American diplomacy."[5] But Marshall admirably delineated the American grievances, and if this paper, with its forceful statement of American rights, had been accepted as a basis of negotiations, the United States would have been in the stronger bargaining position, a point that did not go unnoticed by Talleyrand.[6] Although the initial strategy failed, Marshall could later take some consolation from the knowledge that the document was studied by the second American commsision to France in 1799 as the strongest statement of American rights and obligations toward France.

To Talleyrand

LS, Archives of the Ministry of Foreign Affairs, Paris

Citizen Minister, Paris, January 17, 1798

The undersigned Ministers Plenipotentiary & Envoys Extraordinary from the United States of America to the French Republic

3. See Pinckney to Rufus King, Dec. 27, 1797, and Mar. 14, 1798, King Papers, Library of Congress; JM to Charles Lee, Mar. 4, 1798.

4. See Murray to Timothy Pickering, Feb. 11, 1798, Diplomatic Dispatches, Netherlands, III, RG 59, National Archives; Murray to Pinckney, Feb. 9, 1798, Murray Papers, Pierpont Morgan Library; JM to Lee, Mar. 4, 1798; Pinckney to King, Mar. 14, 1798, King Papers, Lib. Cong.; Journal, Feb. 2, 6, 7, 10, 14, and 18, 1798; Pinckney and JM to Talleyrand, Feb. 26, 1798.

5. Beveridge, *Marshall*, II, 297.

6. See Talleyrand to American Envoys, Mar. 18, 1798.

have been hitherto restrained by the expectation of entering on the objects of their mission, in the forms usual among nations, from addressing to the Executive Directory through you, those explanations & reclamations with which they are charged by the Government they represent. If this expectation is to be relinquished, yet the unfeigned wish of the United States to restore that harmony between the two republics, which they have so unremittingly sought to preserve, renders it the duty of the undersigned to lay before the Government of France, however informal the communication may be deemed, some considerations in addition to those heretofore submitted, relative to the subsisting differences between the two nations.

Openly and repeatedly have France & America interchanged unequivocal testimonials of reciprocal regard. These testimonials were given by the United States with all the ardor and sincerity of Youth. It is still believed that on the part of France they were likewise the offspring of real esteem. They were considered on the other side of the Atlantic as evidencing a mutual friendship to be as durable as the Republics themselves. Unhappily the scene is changed, and America looks around in vain for the Ally or the Friend. The contrast both of language and of conduct, which the present so avowedly exhibits to a portion of the past, has been repeatedly attributed by France to a disposition, alledged to exist in the Government of the United States, unfriendly to this Republic and partial towards its enemies. That Government, astonished at a reproach so unfounded in fact, so contradicted by its declarations and its conduct, could scarcely consider the charge as serious, & has ever cherished the hope, that a candid review of its conduct founded on the documents, & aided by the arguments with which the Executive Directory has been furnished, would have rescued it from the injurious suspicion. This Hope seems not to have been realized. The undersigned, therefore, deem it proper to precede their application for that Justice which they claim from France by an effort to remove the cause, which is alledged to have produced the injuries of which they complain. With this view they pray the attention of the Executive Directory to a serious and candid reconsideration of the leading measures, adopted by the Government of the United States, & they persuade themselves that, however various and multiplied the channels may be through which misinformation concerning the dispositions of that Government may have been received, yet this reconsideration must remove unfounded prejudices & entirely exculpate the American Nation from an accusation, it knows to be unfounded, and believes to be supported by no single fact.

When that war, which has been waged with such unparalleled fury, which in its vast vicissitudes of fortune has alternately threatened the very existence of the conflicting parties, but which in its progress has surrounded France with splendor, and added still more to her glory than to her territory, when that war first involved those nations with whom the United States were in habits of friendly intercourse, it became incumbent on their Government to examine their situation, their connections, and their duties. America found herself at peace with all the belligerent powers. She was connected with some of them by treaties of Amity and commerce, and with France by a treaty of Alliance also. These several treaties were considered with the most serious attention, and with a sincere wish to determine, by fair construction, the obligations which they really imposed. The result of this Inquiry was a full conviction that her engagements by no means bound her to take part in the war, but left her so far the mistress of her own Conduct as to be at perfect liberty to observe a system of real neutrality. It is deemed unnecessary to analyze those treaties, in order to support the propriety of this decision, because it is not recollected ever to have been questioned, and is believed not to admit of Doubt.

Being bound by no duty to enter into the War the Government of the United States conceived itself bound by duties the most sacred to abstain from it. Contemplating man even in a different society as the natural friend of man, a state of peace, though unstipulated by treaty, was considered as imposing obligations not to be wantonly violated. These obligations, created by the Laws of nature, were in some instances strengthened by solemn existing engagements, of which good faith required a religious observance.

To a sense of moral right other considerations of the greatest magnitude were added, which forbid the Government of the United States to plunge them unnecessarily into the miseries of the bloody conflict then commencing. The great nations of Europe, either impelled by ambition, or by existing or supposed political interests peculiar to themselves, have consumed more than a third of the present century in war. Whatever causes may have produced so afflicting an evil, they cannot be supposed to have been entirely extinguished, and humanity can scarcely indulge the hope that the temper or condition of man is so altered as to exempt the next century from the ills of the past. Strong fortifications, powerful navies, immense Armies, the accumulated wealth of ages and a full population enable the nations of Europe to support those wars in which they are induced to engage by motives which they deem adequate and by interests exclusively their own. In all respects different is the situation of the United States. Possessed of an extensive unsettled territory, on which bountiful nature has bestowed with a lavish hand all the capacities for future legitimate greatness, they indulge no thirst for conquest, no ambition for the extension of their limits. Encircled by no dangerous powers, they neither fear or are jealous of their neighbours, and are not, on that account, obliged to arm for their own safety. Separated far from Europe by a vast & friendly ocean, they are but remotely, if at all, affected by those interests, which agitate & influence this portion of the world. Thus circumstanced, they have no motives for voluntary war. On the contrary, the most powerful considerations urge them to avoid it. An extensive undefended commerce, peculiarly necessary to a nation, which does not manufacture for itself, which is and for a long time to come will be almost exclusively agricultural, would have been its immediate & certain victim. The surplus produce of their labor must have perished on their hands, and that increase of population, so essential to a young Country, must with their prosperity have sustained a serious check. Their Exertions too could not have been considerable, unless the war had been transferred to their own bosoms. Great as are the means & resources of the United States for self defence, 'tis only in self defence that those resources can be completely displayed. Neither the genius of the nation, or the state of its finances admit of calling its citizens from the plough, but to defend their own liberty and their own firesides. How criminal must have been that Government, which could have plunged its Constituents into a war, to which they were neither impelled by duty or solicited by interest; in which they committed so much to hazard; in which they must suffer in order to act efficiently, and could only display their energies in repelling invasion? But motives, still more powerful than the Calamities of the moment, have influenced the Government of the United States. It was, perhaps, impossible to have engaged voluntarily in the existing conflict, without launching into the almost boundless ocean of European Politics, without contracting habits of national conduct, and forming close political connections, which must have compromited the future peace of the nation, &

have involved it in all the future quarrels of Europe. A long train of Armies, debts and taxes, checking the growth, diminishing the happiness, and perhaps endangering the liberty of the United States, must have followed the adoption of such a System. And for what purpose should it have been adopted? For what purpose should America thus burthen herself with the conflicts of Europe? Not to comply with any engagements she has formed; not to promote her own views, her own objects, her own happiness or her own safety; but to move as a satellite around some greater planet, whose laws she must of necessity obey. In addition to these weighty considerations, it was believed that France would derive more benefit from the neutrality of America, than from her becoming a party to the war.

The determination then of the Government of the United States to preserve that neutral station, in which the war found it, far from manifesting a partiality for the enemies of France, was only a measure of justice to itself and to others, and did not even derogate from that predeliction for this Republic, which it has so repeatedly expressed and displayed.

Having avowed this determination, increased motives of honor and of duty commanded its faithful observance. It is not a principle, which remains now to be settled, that a fraudulent neutrality is no neutrality at all, and that the nation, which would be admitted to its privileges, must perform also the duties it enjoins. Had the Government of the United States, declaring itself neutral, indulged its partialities by granting favors unstipulated by treaty, to one of the belligerent powers, which it refused to another, it could no longer have claimed the immunities of a situation, of which the obligations were forgotten; it would have become a party to the war as certainly as if war had been openly and formally declared; & it would have added to the madness of wantonly engaging in such a hazardous conflict, the dishonor of insincere and fraudulent conduct. It would have attained circuitously an object which it could not plainly avow, or directly pursue, & would have tricked the people of the United States into a war which it could not venture openly to declare.

It was matter of real delight to the Government and people of America to be informed, that France did not wish to interrupt the peace they enjoyed.

The undersigned have been induced to rest on this first necessary and decisive step taken by their Government, although its propriety may not be controverted, from a conviction that, if the right of the United States to observe a fair and honest neutrality be established, the general charges of an unfriendly disposition, made against them by France, must be relinquished, because the facts by which those charges are supported will be found to have grown inevitably out of that situation.

This measure was accompanied with another, which, in repelling so astonishing a charge as partiality for the enemies of France, deserves to be noticed. Soon after the Government of the United States had notified to its Citizens the duties, which its neutrality enjoined, Mr. Genet, the first minister from this Republic, arrived at Philadelphia. Although his conduct had been such as to give cause for serious alarm; although, before he was even acknowledged as a minister, or had reached the Authority which could inspect his credentials, he had assumed the functions of the Government, to which he was deputed, yet that Government, resolved to see in him only the representative of a Republic to which it was sincerely attached, gave him the same warm & cordial reception which he had experienced from its Citizens, without a single exception, from Charleston to Philadelphia. The then situation of France deserves to be remembered. While the recollection adds, Citizen Minister, to the Glory with which your nation is encircled, it establishes the sincerity of the United States. The most formidable combination, the world had ever seen, threatened the extermination of this Republic. Austria, Germany, Prussia, Britain, Spain, Holland & Sardinia were in Arms against France; and Russia was leagued in the Coalition. Nor was this all. The Republic, distracted by internal divisions, contained numerous enemies within its own bosom, & a considerable portion of its proper force was arrayed against itself. In such a state of things the most sanguine might fear & the most ardent hesitate. Confident in their strength & relying on success, the coalesced powers sought to arm in their cause the residue of the world, and deemed it criminal to acknowledge the Sovereignty of the Republic. The nations of Europe, even those who had not entered into the Contest, were either themselves unwilling to acknowledge this Sovereignty, or were deterred by fear from doing so. Had the partialities of America been against France this Example would have been followed. According to the rules of ordinary calculation the measure would have been safe, and consequently a Government, feeling the attachments now so unjustly attributed to that of the United States, would have indicated those attachments by its adoption. Far from pursuing such a System, the United States, unawed by the strength of the Coalition, received with open arms the minister of this Republic, acknowledged with enthusiasm the Government which had deputed him, overlooked his extraordinary attacks on their Sovereignty, and manifested a cordial friendship for his nation, and a sincere wish for its success.

Scarcely were the first ceremonies of his reception over, when mr. Genet displayed a disposition to usurp & exercise within the United States the choicest and most important duties and powers of Sovereignty. He claimed the privileges of arming and embodying the Citizens of America within their own Territory to carry on from thence expeditions against nations with whom they were at peace; of fitting out & equipping within their limits, privateers to cruize on a commerce destined for their ports; of erecting within their Jurisdiction an independent Judiciary; and of arraigning their Government at the bar of the people.[7] The undersigned will not ask in what manner France would have treated any foreign minister, who should have dared so to conduct himself towards this Republic. But in what manner would the American Government have treated such a minister, if the representative of a nation it viewed with coldness, or even indifference? In what manner would it have treated him had he been the representative of any other nation than France? No man acquainted with that Government can doubt how these enquires ought to be answered. From the minister of France alone could this extraordinary conduct have been borne with temper. To have continued to bear it without perceiving and feeling its extreme impropriety would have been to have merited the contempt as well of France as of the other Powers of the earth. The Government of the United States did feel it, but far from transferring to his nation that resentment which such conduct could not fail to excite, it distinguished strongly between the Government and its minister, and the representations it made were in the language of a friend afflicted, but not irritated by the injuries complained of.

7. JM was referring to Genet's authorization of expeditions against Spanish-held Florida and the Southwest, and his commissioning of privateers to attack British and Spanish shipping. The charge of setting up a private judiciary referred to the question of whether the French consuls could authenticate the validity of prizes. See Dumas Malone, *Jefferson and the Ordeal of Liberty* (Boston, 1962), 90–131; Melvin H. Jackson *Privateers in Charleston, 1793–1796: An Account of a French Palatinate in South Carolina*, Smithsonian Studies in History and Technology, I (Washington, D.C., 1969).

The recal of that minister was received with universal joy, as a confirmation that his whole system of conduct was attributable only to himself; and not even the publication of his private Instructions could persuade the American Government to ascribe any part of it to this Republic.

At the same time the exertions of the United States to pay up the arrearages of their debt to France, which had been unavoidably permitted to accumulate; their disinterested and liberal advances to the Sufferers of Saint Domingo, thrown suddenly upon them, without provisions or money, whose recommendation was that they were Frenchmen and were unfortunate, the perseverance with which they apologized for and ascribed any occasional injuries they sustained to the force of Circumstances, the interest which they continued openly to take in all the fortunes of this Republic, manifested partialities of a very different sort from those which have been so unjustly attributed to them.

At this period too a great principle was brought into discussion, the dispassionate consideration of which is essential to the fair estimate of the charges made by France against the Government of the United States. The property of French Citizens was taken by british cruisers & ships of war out of American bottoms, and the American Government submitted to the practice. The propriety of submitting to it depends entirely on the naked right of the Captors, under the existing circumstances of the Case to exercise such a power. The circumstances were these. In the Treaty of Commerce made between France and the United States in February 1778, it was stipulated in substance, that neither party should take out of the vessels of the other the goods of its enemy, but that the Character of the bottom should be imparted to its Cargo. With England the United States had made no stipulation on the subject. It follows then that the rights of England, being neither diminished or increased by compact, remained precisely in their natural state, & were to be ascertained by some preexisting acknowledged principle. This principle is to be searched for in the Law of nations. That Law forms, independent of compact, a rule of action by which the Sovereignties of the civilized world consent to be governed. It prescribes what one nation may do without giving just cause of war, and what of consequence another may and ought to permit without being considered as having sacrificed its honor, its dignity or its independence. What then is the doctrine of the law of nations, on this subject? Do neutral bottoms of right and independant of particular compact protect hostile goods? The question is to be considered on its meer right, uninfluenced by the wishes or the interests of a neutral or belligerent power.

It is a general rule, that war gives to a belligerent power a right to seize and confiscate the goods of his enemy. However humanity may deplore the application of this principle, there is perhaps no one to which man has more universally assented, or in which Jurists have more uniformly agreed. Its theory and its practice have unhappily been maintained in all ages. This right then may be exercised on the Goods of an enemy wherever found, unless opposed by some superior right. It yields by common consent to the superior right of a neutral nation to protect, in virtue of its sovereignty, the goods of either of the belligerent powers found within its jurisdiction. But can this right of protection, admitted to be possessed by every Government within its own limits, in virtue of its absolute sovereignty, be communicated to a vessel navigating the high seas? It is supposed that it cannot be so communicated, because the ocean being common to all nations, no absolute sovereignty can be acquired in it, the rights of all are equal, and must necessarily check, limit, & restrain each other. The superior right therefore of absolute sovereignty to protect all property within its own territory, ceases to be superior when the property is no longer within its territory & may be encountered by the opposing acknowledged right of a belligerent power to seize and confiscate the goods of his enemy. If the belligerent permits the neutral to attempt without hazard to himself thus to serve & aid his enemy, yet he does not relinquish the right of defeating that attempt, whenever it shall be in his power to defeat it. Thus it is admitted that an armed vessel may stop & search at sea a neutral bottom, & may take out goods, which are contraband of war, without giving cause of offence, or being supposed in any degree to infringe neutral rights. But this practice could not be permitted within the rivers, harbors or other places of a neutral, where its sovereignty was complete. It follows then that the full right of affording protection to all property whatever within its own territory which is inherent in every government, is not transferred to a vessel navigating the high seas. The right of a belligerent over the goods of his enemy within his reach is as complete as his right over contraband of war: & it seems a position not easily to be refuted, that a situation which will not protect the one would not protect the other. A neutral bottom then does not of right, in cases where no compact exists, protect from his enemy the goods of a belligerent power.

To this reasoning the practice of nations has conformed & the common understanding of mankind seems to have assented. Vattel B3. Sect: 115, says positively "that effects belonging to an enemy, found on board a neutral ship, are seizable by the rights of war." Vattel is believed to be supported by the most approved writers on the same subject. It is deemed unnecessary to multiply citations to this point, because France herself is supposed to have decided it. In her maritime ordinance of 1744 which is considered as having been in force in 1788, enemy goods in neutral bottoms generally are declared liable to seizure and confiscation. From the operation of this rule are excepted the vessels of Denmark and the United Provinces, to whom special treaties secured the exemption. In the ordinance too of the 26th. of July 1778, the first article of which is considered as forbidding the cruisers of France to stop and bring into port neutral vessels having on board the goods of an enemy, a power is reserved to revoke the privilege granted to neutrals by that article, if the enemy should not grant the same privilege within six months from the publication of that regulation. This clearly indicates a conviction, that the exemption from capture of the goods of an enemy, which should be found on board the vessel of a neutral power, not having stipulated such exemption by treaty, was a privilege granted by the Ordinance, and that the meer revocation of the Ordinance would abolish the privilege and restore the antient rule. It will not be contended that France has continued in a long course of practice and of legislation opposed to her own opinion of the law of nations. It must then be considered as the opinion of France, that under that law neutral bottoms give no protection to the goods of an enemy.

This principle, thus admitted to have been established, is supposed by some to have been changed by the armed neutrality. A new law of nations, it is contended, was introduced by that confederation. But who were the parties to that federation and what was its object? The nothern maritime powers of Europe united to protect by force in their own bottoms during the then existing war the goods of either and of all the belligerent powers. The compact in its own nature was confined with respect to its objects and its duration. It did not purport to change, nor could it change permanently & universally, the rights of nations not becoming parties to it. It did indeed hold forth the promise of future more permanent & more general engagements for the same object, but such engagements were never formed. How then can this temporary and partial convention be considered as altering radically & generally principles, which have been universally adopted, and in the modification of which all have an interest? Would France herself admit that a combination, such as that which constituted the armed neutrality, may rightfully change the law of nations & establish a new code of universal obligation? It is believed that no nation on earth would more perseveringly oppose such an invasion of its sovereignty.

There seems then to be no solid ground for maintaining, that the general law of nations has been at all varied by the armed neutrality.

It remains to enquire, whether the treaties between France & the United States pledge either nation to assert and establish the principle that free bottoms make free goods.

The treaty of amity and commerce, concluded the 6th. of February 1778, stipulates reciprocally for the right of trading with, and protecting the goods of the enemy of either party in the vessels of the other, and in turn surrenders its own goods, found in the vessels of an enemy; but contains no clause imposing on either party the duty of extending the principle, or of supporting its applications to other nations. The stipulations of that treaty are negative as well as affirmative. They specify as well the disabilities intended to be created & the duties to be imposed, as the privileges designed to be granted. Had it been intended that either nation should have been bound to maintain this principle in its intercourse with others, or should have been in any degree incapacitated from prosecuting freely that intercourse, without the previous admission of the principle, a stipulation to that effect would have been made. No such stipulation having been made, the parties cannot be presumed to have intended it. Indeed it would have been madness in the United States, under their actual circumstances, to have formed such an agreement. There being no express stipulation to this effect, it cannot be supposed to have been implied. Nations forming a solemn compact, which ought to regulate their conduct towards each other, which is to be resorted to as the standard for adjusting their differences, do not leave to implication such delicate and important points. Indeed, if a great principle not mentioned is permitted to be implied, the object of a written agreement, which is itself to evidence all the obligation it creates, is totally defeated. But who is to make the implication, and to what extent is implication to be allowed? It is very easy to perceive, that the doctrine of implying in contracts, stipulations never formed, would destroy all certainty of construction, and open a boundless field of controversy to the contracting parties.

It results from the very nature of a contract, which affects the rights of the parties, but not of others, and from the admission of a general rule of action binding independent of compact, which may be changed by consent, but is only changed so far as that consent is actually given, that a treaty between any two nations must leave to all others those rights, which the law of nations acknowledges, & must leave each of the contracting parties subject to the operation of such rights. For the truth of this position, believed to be so clear in itself, and which it is supposed the history of all Europe would illustrate, the Ordinance of 1744, already quoted, is considered as furnishing an unequivocal authority. By that ordinance the law of nations is applied to all those neutrals, with whom France had not stipulated, that the quality of their bottoms should be imparted to their cargoes, while those, with whom such stipulations had been made, are exempted from the application of that law.

The desire of establishing universally the principle that neutral bottoms shall make neutral goods is perhaps felt by no nation on earth more strongly than by the United States. Perhaps no nation is more deeply interested in its establishment. It is an object they keep in view and which, if not forced by violence to abandon it, they will pursue in such manner as their own judgement may dictate, as being best calculated to attain it. But the wish to establish a principle is essentially different from a determination that it is already established. The interests of the United States could not fail to produce the wish; their duty forbid them to indulge it, when deciding on a meer right. However solicitous America might be to pursue all proper means, tending to obtain for this principle the assent of all or any of the maritime powers of Europe, she never conceived the idea of obtaining that consent by force. The United States will only arm to defend their own rights; neither their policy nor their interests permit them to arm in order to compel a surrender of the rights of others.

These and other considerations, which have been submitted to the Government of France, produced on the part of the United

States, a decision that their bottoms could not of right protect the goods of a belligerent power from an enemy not bound to respect the principle. This decision was founded on the most perfect conviction that it was injoined by the law of nations, and that good faith, respect for truth, and for the duties of an upright and honest judge rendered it indispensable. This conviction remains unshaken. If those arguments, which still appear conclusive to the American Government, have not the same operation on the Judgement of France, they must at least be sufficient to evince the Sincerity with which that Government has acted, and to prove that its conduct in this respect was produced by a sense of duty, and not by any partiality for a Nation, against which it was at that time considerably irritated by other causes.

The undersigned, Citizen Minister, rely too implicitly on your candour and discernment to apprehend that you will estimate improperly the motives, which, on this essential point, have influenced and guided the United States.

The early decision of the American Government on this Subject was immediately avowed openly, & was amply supported by mr. Jefferson, the then Secretary of State, in his letter to mr. Genet, dated the 24th: day of July, 1793 and in his letter to Mr. Morris,[8] dated the 16th. day of August, in the same year. The arguments, which those letters contain, were supposed to have satisfied the Government of France, since its ministers in the United States no longer controverted the principle they supported. Indeed those arguments appeared too conclusive to permit a doubt, concerning the Success which would attend them.

In August 1794, when mr. Monroe, the then minister of the United States to this Republic, was received in the bosom of the Convention, France obviously did not consider the acknowledgement of this established principle of the law of nations, as indicating a partiality towards her enemy. The language used on that occasion could only have been used to the minister of a nation, whose friendship was valued, and whose conduct had evinced the sincerity of its professions. It was then declared, the "the sweetest, the frankest fraternity united in effect the two republics," and that "their Union would be forever indissoluble." These declarations, made long after America had avowed its neutrality & had avowed its acquiescence under the principle that a belligerent

8. Gouverneur Morris, a Federalist from New York and Pennsylvania, was then U.S. minister to France.

power, unrestrained by particular treaty, may of right take out of the bottoms of a neutral the Goods of its enemy, demonstrate that neither that neutrality nor that acquiesence evidenced the want of a proper regard for France. The Government of the United States still cherishes the hope that this true and fair estimate, then made of its conduct may be soon resumed by a nation, whose friendship it has assiduously and unremittingly cultivated by all those means which good faith and justice could permit it to use.

After the discussion of this interesting question was supposed to have been closed, and France was believed to have been intirely content with that System, in which the United States felt themselves bound to persevere, some complaints were made, not against the principles adopted by the Government, but against the application of those principles to particular cases, supposed not to come within them. The neutrality of the United States could not permit prize to be made of Vessels belonging to nations, with whom they were at peace, within their jurisdiction, or by privateers fitted out in their ports. Regulations to this effect were necessarily made, and to enforce the observance of those regulations was a duty not to be dispensed with. The right of one of the belligerent powers to obtain the release of a vessel, captured under such circumstances, was as sacred as the right of the Captor to a vessel taken on the high Seas, and which, according to the usages of war, was lawful prize. The United States were bound to respect the rights of both. To do so it was necessary to examine the facts, for which purpose a tribunal, in which both parties might be fairly heard, was unavoidable. Some complaints were made of particular vexations and each complaint has heretofore been particularly attended to. It is believed to be unnecessary to review these several cases, because the undersigned are entirely persuaded that explanations already given must have been completely satisfactory. Should any one of them be still considered as furnishing subject for complaint, the undersigned will proceed to its investigation with the most sincere desire to attain truth, and to redress the wrong, if any has been committed.

During this period the causes of complaint against France on the part of the United States were by no means inconsiderable. Their commerce was not exempt from depredations, believed to be entirely unwarrantable, made upon it by the Cruizers of this Republic.

On the ninth of May 1793 the national convention passed a Decree relative to the commerce of neutrals, the first article of which is in these words "The French ships of war and privateers may stop and bring into the ports of the Republic such neutral vessels, as are loaded in whole or in part, either with provisions belonging to neutrals, & destined for enemy ports, or with merchandize belonging to enemies." In consequence of the remonstrances of the American minister, the Convention on the twenty third of May declared "That the vessels of the United States are not comprized in the regulations of the decree of the ninth of May." On the twenty eighth of the same month, the Convention repealed the decree of the twenty third. On the first of July, they reestablished it. On the twenty seventh of July, it was again repealed. Under the decree of the ninth of May, the vessels of the United States were captured, brought into the ports of France & their cargoes disposed of. Could this decree, Citizen minister, be considered otherwise than as infringing the laws of nations, the rights of neutrals, & the particular engagements, subsisting between France & the United States? When on the eighth of June in the same year, the British Government issued a similar order, its injustice produced a ferment throughout America, indicating strong dispositions immediately to oppose its execution by force. The letter of mr. Jefferson, the then Secretary of State, to the minister plenipotentiary of the United States at London,[9] dated the seventh of September 1793, and remonstrating against the order of the eighth of June, contains so much justness of sentiment & strength of Argument, as to have been quoted by your predecessor in his letter to mr. Monroe of the ninth of March 1796. It cannot escape you, citizen minister, that the arguments of mr. Jefferson concerning the order of the eighth of June, apply conclusively to the decree of the ninth of May; and that to them are to be added those arguments which are drawn from the hardship of being absolutely compelled, without any alternative, to part with the cargo in France; and those too which are drawn from the duties imposed by an express and solemn treaty.

Nothing can demonstrate more conclusively the real temper of the United States than the difference between the reception given

9. Thomas Pinckney, of Charleston, S.C., a brother of Charles Cotesworth Pinckney, was U.S. minister to Great Britain. See Jack L. Cross, *London Mission: The First Critical Years* (East Lansing, Mich., 1968).

to the decree of the Convention, of the ninth of May, and that which was given to the order of the British Cabinet, of the eighth of June.

A large number of American vessels too were for a long time detained at Bordeaux very much to the injury of the owners, without assigning a motive for such detention, or putting it in the power of the government to conjecture the cause of a measure, which so deeply affected the interest of their fellow citizens.

These and other embarrassments were experienced; but they could not diminish the attachment of the United States to France. In the midst of them, prayers were offered up, through the whole extent of the American continent, for the success of this republic. The government feeling the same sentiment displayed it, at least as far as was compatible with the decent deportment, required from a nation not a party in the war, & professing neutrality. Such would not have been the conduct of a government and people in secret unfriendly to France.

Very strong and just resentments were at that time inspired by the hostile conduct of Britain. The instructions of June 1793, whereby American vessels, laden with provisions for France, were ordered to be brought into the ports of Britain, there to sell such cargoes, or to give security to sell them in other ports, in Amity with England; and the still more offensive order of November the sixth in the same year, whereby vessels laden with the produce of a French colony, or carrying provisions to such colony were ordered to be brought in for adjudication, added to the preexisting causes of mutual irritation, had produced such a state of things as to render it obvious, that the injuries complained of by America must be entirely done away, or that war was inevitable. This State of things was not so altered by the order of the eighth of January 1794, revoking that of the sixth of November 1793, as to promise a different result. But as a nation, prefering peace to war, will ever make a peaceful demand of reparation for injuries sustained, before that reparation is sought by the sword, and as the policy of America has ever been "to pursue peace with unremitting zeal, before the last resource which has so often been the scourge of nations, & could not fail to check the advanced prosperity of the United States, was contemplated," an envoy extraordinary was deputed to his Britannic Majesty. "Carrying with him a full knowledge of the existing temper & sensibility of his country," it was expected that "he would vindicate its rights with firmness & cultivate peace with sincerity."

Truly desirous as the American Government was of preserving peace with Britain, its determination was unalterable not to preserve it, nor to receive compensation for injuries sustained, nor security against their future commission, at the expence of the smallest of its engagements to France. Explicit and positive instructions to this effect were given to mr. Jay; & these instructions were freely communicated to the minister of this republic, then at Philadelphia. The negotiation of the American Envoy terminated in a treaty, in many respects desirable to the United States. But however desirable its objects might be, the Government of the United States would not have hesitated to reject them, had they been accompanied with any stipulation violating or weakening its engagements to France. But it has been able to discern no such stipulation. The twenty fifth article of that treaty guards the rights of this republic by the following clause, "Nothing in this treaty contained shall, however, be construed or operate contrary to former and existing public treaties with other Sovereigns or States." The treaty with France being a "former and existing public treaty," and it being thus provided that nothing contained in the treaty with Britain "should be construed or operate contrary to it," the government of the United States did not apprehend that the treaty with Britain could be considered as affecting its relations to France.[1] But such was its attention to its ally, that the instrument was, previous to its ratification, submitted to the consideration of the minister of this republic, who was invited to communicate freely to the government of the United States such observations upon it as he might judge proper. Mr. Adet in a Letter addressed to mr. Randolph, dated the 12th. Messidor, 3d. year of the French republic, one and indivisible, (30th. June 1795, old style) expressed his sense of this procedure in the following words, "This frank measure is to me a sure guaranty of the friendship of the American government towards France, and of the fidelity with which it always marks its conduct towards a faithful ally." He then stated those reflections to which the reading of the treaty had given birth. The articles which relate to enemy goods in neutral bottoms are

1. JM's reasoning at this point might be logical, but it was also unrealistic. The major issue between France and the United States was how the Jay Treaty had changed relations between the United States and France.

mentioned without a comment. He contended that the list of contraband was swelled and that the 23d. 24th. & 25th. articles of the treaty with Britain ceded to that power advantages inconsistent with previous cessions to France. This letter was answered by mr. Randolph on the 6th. of July following, who proves that no article was enumerated in the list of contraband in the treaty between the United States & Britain which was not of that description previous to its formation, and independent of it; notices briefly the subject of enemy goods in neutral bottoms; and demonstrates that the objections of mr. Adet to the 23d. 24th. & 25th. articles were entirely founded on a misconstruction of them.[2] This misconstruction was so apparent, that Britain has never claimed it, nor would the American government ever have admitted it. The letter of mr. Randolph closes the subject of contraband and of enemy property taken out of neutral bottoms with a paragraph to which, Citizen minister, your attention is solicited, "Hitherto, however (says he) I have spoken upon principles of right. Upon any other principles, & more especially upon those of hardship and injury to a friend, it shall be a topic of the negotiation now opening between us. With the temper which will pervade the whole of it, I cannot doubt, that some modification may be devised; and it may be separated from the general treaty, so as not to be delayed by it."

It was then apparent that the government of the United States, actuated by that friendship which transcends the line of strict obligation, was willing gratuitously to release her ally from those stipulations of a former treaty, which in the course of events were deemed to operate unfavorably to her. This readiness to concede marked that friendship the more strongly as the situation, in which the two nations found themselves, could not have been unforseen, but was the very situation for which the article provides. The answer of mr. Randolph concludes with requesting an opportunity to remove any remaining doubts, should there be such, by further explanations; no remaining doubts were stated, & therefore, as well as for its contents, the letter was believed to be entirely satisfactory to mr. Adet; and it was hoped that this government as well as that of America would consider the treaty with Britain as an accomodation desirable by the United States, & not disadvantageous to France.

It is not easy to express the chagrin felt by the American govern-

2. For a discussion of the contraband issue, see Timothy Pickering to American Envoys, July 15, 1797.

ment on learning, that in this treaty the United States were supposed to have "knowingly and evidently sacrificed their connections with this republic, and the most essential and least contested prerogatives of neutrality." With the firmness of conscious integrity, the United States aver that they have never knowingly sacrificed or impaired their connections with this republic, nor the prerogatives of neutrality, but that they have, according to their best judgement, invariably sought to preserve both.

The undersigned will endeavor faithfully to state the impressions of the government they represent on this interesting subject.

The objections made to this treaty by your predecessor in office, in his note to mr. Monroe dated 19th. of Ventose, 4th year of the French Republic, one and indivisible, (9th. March 1796) are

1st. That the United States, besides having departed from the principles established by the armed neutrality, have given to England, to the detriment of their first Allies, the most striking mark of an unbounded condescension, by abandoning the limit given to contraband by the law of nations, by their treaties with all other nations, and even by those of England with the greater part of the maritime powers.

2dly. That they have consented to extend the denomination of contraband even to provisions. Instead of pointing out particularly, as all treaties do, the cases of the effective blockade of a place, as alone forming an exception to the freedom of this article, they have tacitly acknowledged the pretensions raised by England to create blockades in the colonies, and even in France, by the force of a bare proclamation.

Mr. Adet in his letter to mr. Pickering, dated 25th. Brumaire, 5th. year of the French Republic, one and indivisible, (15th. November 1796, old style) has repeated the same objections, and has been pleased also to superadd some observations, relative to the formation of such a treaty generally, and the circumstances attending its negociation, in terms not to have been expected by the first & almost only voluntary friend of this republic.

These having been the only specific objections, officially made to the treaty with Britain by the Government of France, either in Paris or in Philadelphia, are necessarily supposed to be the only objections which have occurred.

They have often been discussed on the part of the United States, but that discussion will be renewed, because, although the undersigned may be unable to suggest any argument not heretofore urged, they cannot resist the hope that an attentive reconsideration of those arguments may give them a success, which has not yet attended them.

The first objection may be supposed to consist of two parts.

1st. The abandonment of the principle that neutral bottoms make neutral goods, an objection rather insinuated than expressed; and

2dly. The addition to the catalogue of contraband.

1st. On the first part of the objection it is observable, that the statements of the late minister of exterior relations & of mr. Adet seem to admit, but certainly do not controvert the position that previous to the formation of the armed neutrality, a belligerent power could rightfully take out of the bottoms of a neutral the goods of its enemy. This position is believed to be uncontrovertible. Some of the arguments in support of it have been already detailed, and it is deemed unnecessary to repeat or to add to them. To this principle of the armed neutrality, with a departure from which the United States seem to be impliedly charged, the note of Mr. de la Croix does not assign any obligation whatever; nor does he appear to consider it as having been engrafted by that confederation on the law of nations. On this point mr. Adet has not been more explicit. He seems to have been content with vague insinuations, and not to have been willing to commit himself by a direct averment that, in consequence of the armed neutrality, the law of nations on this subject is changed. The undersigned are unwilling to combat at length a proposition not positively advanced, which they deem so clearly indefensible, and will therefore refer to the brief observations already made respecting it.

It may not, however, be improper here to notice that in February 1778, when the treaty between France and the United States was entered into, the Armed neutrality had not been formed. Of consequence the state of things on which that treaty operated was regulated by the law of nations, as it clearly existed previous to the formation of the Armed neutrality. It is supposed to be admitted that, according to that state of things, neutral bottoms could afford no protection to the goods of an enemy. The stipulation then of the article of that treaty was understood at the time, by the contracting parties, to form an exception to a general rule, which would retain its obligation in all cases where it was not changed. If then the contracting parties had designed to impose on each other the necessity of extending this exception to other nations, so as to convert it into a general rule, they would have expressed this intention in their contract. Not having expressed it, they must be considered as intending that this exception should form a rule as between themselves, while the general rule should govern as with other nations who had not consented to change it.

It is also worthy of observation that when this treaty was made the United States were at war, and France at peace with Britain. In this state of things, which might have continued had not war been declared, or hostilities commenced by England, the bottoms of France would have protected from American cruizers English property, while they would not have protected from British cruizers American property. This was the necessary result of that state of things, under which the treaty was formed. America had consented to it, and neither could or would have complained.

It is also to be noticed that, before the negotiation with England had commenced, the government of the United States had openly avowed that opinion on this subject, which its best judgement dictated. This opinion, perfectly unconnected with that negotiation, was known by all to regulate and form the basis of its conduct. The letters of mr. Jefferson, already quoted, had stated to the world the perfect conviction of the United States that, by the law of nations, a belligerent power, not restrained by particular treaty, might rightfully take out of the bottoms of a neutral the goods of its enemy, as well as their determination that, they could not and ought not to oppose the exercise of this right. The right having been clearly & unavoidably admitted, and the determination to acquiesce under its exercise having been avowed openly, mr. Jay could only solicit its surrender. Had no treaty been formed, or had the treaty omitted to mention the principle, the right would still have existed, would still have been acknowledged, and would still have been exercised. The treaty does not in fact or in expression cede a new privilege—it regulates the exercise of one before existing and before acknowledged to exist. The harsh means of exercising this right, which are given by the law of nations, are modified and softened by the treaty, and this is the only effect, which the article on this subject has produced. It was the only motive, and it was a sufficient motive for introducing it.

The second branch of this objection seems more to be relied on, & comes forward in a more decisive shape. It is

That the United States have abandoned the limit given to contraband by the law of nations, by their treaties with all other nations, and even by those of England with a greater part of the maritime powers.

The limit of contraband is supposed to have been extended by inserting in the catalogue, naval stores & timber for ship building.

To estimate rightly a charge so warmly made, it becomes indispensable to ascertain whether these articles are, independent of treaty, by the law of nations, contraband of war. On this single point seems to rest the verity of the accusation.

It is to be regreted, that those who have averred the negative have not been pleased to furnish some authorities, in support of the opinion they advance. Such authorities would have been considered with candor, and any conviction they might have produced would have been freely acknowledged. But no such authorities are furnished, and it is believed that none exist.

America solicitous to confine as much as possible by common consent the list of contraband, but determined, however she might oppose its enlargement, not to attempt its diminution by force, was under the necessity of examining the subject, & of ascertaining the line of partition between the rights of neutrals & of belligerent powers. As guides in such a research, she could only take the most approved writers on the law of nations. These are believed to class timber for ship building, and naval stores for the equipment of vessels, among articles admitted to be contraband of war. Vattel (B.7. sect: 112) defines contraband goods to be "Commodities particularly used in war—such are arms, military and *naval* Stores, *timber*, horses, and even provisions in certain junctures, where there are hopes of reducing the enemy by famine." The treaty between France and Denmark concluded in 1742, places tar, rosin, sails, hemp, cordage, masts, and timber for shipbuilding on the catalogue of contraband; & Valin, in his commentary on the marine ordinances of France, (Vol. 2. page 264) says that "of right these articles are now contraband, and have been so from the commencement of the present century." In conformity with these opinions has been that of America; and, if the law of nations was understood by the most approved jurists, she has not erred.

But the modern public law of nations and modern treaties are said to have established a different rule. If the modern public law of nations has changed the principle, such change is yet unknown to the United States. It is much to be wished that more full and satisfactory information had been given in support of an opinion, a difference on which is alledged to have produced consequences so extremely calamitous.

It is not averred that the armed neutrality has constituted this modern public law. It is supposed that this cannot be averred, because France will never admit the right of a confederacy, whatever may be its power, to impose the law on those who are not parties to it. It is supposed also that this cannot be averred, for another reason. The members of the armed neutrality had not themselves agreed upon the articles, which should be deemed contraband. Russia, the power originating that celebrated, though short lived compact, published in 1780 the principles on which she would maintain the commerce of her subjects. One of these was, that the articles of contraband should be regulated by the 10th. & 11th. articles of her treaty of commerce with Great Britain.

Afterwards Denmark entered into a convention with Russia, for maintaining generally the principles agreed upon; but on the subject of contraband in particular, Denmark adopted, as the rule by which to be governed, her treaty of commerce with Great Britain, concluded the 10th: of July 1670, in the 3d. Article of which, contraband goods are described to be "*any provisions of war*, as soldiers arms, machines, cannon, ships, *or other things of necessary use in war*." But by a convention concluded at London, on the 4th. of July 1780 between Great Britain and Denmark, "To explain the treaty of commerce of 1670, between the two powers" "*Timber for shipbuilding, tar, rosin, copper in sheets, sails, hemp, and cordage, and generally whatever serves directly for the equipment of a vessel*, unwrought iron & fir planks excepted" are declared to be contraband.

Denmark having in her convention with Russia adopted her treaty with England, made in 1670, as declaratory of those articles which she should consider as contraband, & having by her explanatory agreement with England, substituted a particular enumeration of articles for a general description of them, not as an amendment, but as an explanation of the treaty of 1670, has taken a different rule, in the very compact referred to as establishing a modern public law of nations, from that taken by Russia. The rule of Denmark classes among contraband precisely the same articles which are enumerated as such in the treaty between the United States & Britain, and which are only found in that enumeration, because it is believed, that the law of nations has unquestionably so placed them. Sweden and Holland too, in acceding to the armed neutrality, adopt their own treaties, as the rule by which they will respectively be guided. There was then, even among the parties to this agreement, no fixed Law of contraband. Had the potentates of Europe designed to establish permanently and generally the principles of the armed neutrality, the war which originated that convention would not have terminated without some general agreement concerning it. The efforts of Sweden, to obtain a Congress for examining and terminating the different concerns, both of the powers at war and of the neutral States could not have proved entirely abortive.

No argument then can be drawn from the armed neutrality in support of the position that the modern public law of nations relating to contraband has been abandoned by the United States. No modern public law having been formed the rule remains unchanged, and at the present moment, as well as when the treaty with France was formed, is believed to ordain as contraband the articles enumerated as such in the treaty with Britain.

But it is alledged, that in this treaty the United States have abandoned the limits given to contraband by their treaties with all other nations, and even by those of England with a greater part of the maritime powers.

It is true that the United States, desirous of liberating commerce, have invariably seized every opportunity, which presented itself, to diminish or remove the Shackles imposed on that of neutrals. In pursuance of this policy, they have on no occasion hesitated to reduce the list of contraband, as between themselves and any nation consenting to such reduction. Their preexisting treaties have been with nations as willing as themselves to change the old rule, and consequently a stipulation to that effect, being desired by both parties, has been made without difficulty. Each contracting party is deemed to have an equivalent for the cession made in the similar cession, it receives from the party, with whom it contracts. Neither requires of the other as an additional consideration, that it shall propagate by the sword the principles which form the basis of their private agreement, and force unwilling nations to adopt them; nor that it should decline to regulate by treaty its interests with any other nation, which should refuse to accede to them. As little could either suppose that its particular contract contained anything obligatory on others, or was capable of enlarging or diminishing their rights. The treaties of the United States then with other nations can only establish the limits of contraband, as between the contracting parties, and must leave that subject, with nations not parties to the contract, to the law which would have governed had such particular stipulation never been made. According to the existing state of things, when the negotiations between the United States and Great Britain were opened, naval stores and timber for ship building were, as between America & Britain, contraband of war. They would have retained this character had the treaty never been made. They would have retained it had the treaty contained no provision on the subject. The United States were truly desirous of excluding them from the list—but Britain was unwilling to do so. Had the United States possessed the means of coercion, their established policy, founded on the basis of justice and their own peculiar situation forbids a resort to those means, for any other purpose, than the defence of their own rights, or a compliance with their own engagements. It was not a case in which force would have been deemed justifiable, and the object being unattainable by mutual consent was unavoidably relinquished for the moment. Yet it was proper to enumerate the articles, which were before contraband, and which continued to be so, because that enumeration notified to the merchants of the United States the hazard which those commodities would encounter on the seas, & because also it prevents those vexatious altercations, which might otherwise have been produced by the efforts of one party to swell and of the other to reduce the list.

If, on the refusal of Britain to substitute any other rule, concerning contraband, in the place of that established by the law of nations, France finds herself in a situation to be injured by an observance of her engagements with the United States, it is not the treaty with Britain, but that with France, which has produced this situation. This was foreseen when that treaty was entered into & did not prevent it. The stipulation concerning contraband was formed when France was at Peace & America at war. Although, that state of things did not long continue yet its continuance was by no means deemed impossible. Notwithstanding this the government of the United States has manifested a willingness to change this stipulation, as well as that which respects enemy's property in neutral bottoms, so soon as France complained of them. Of this the letter from mr. Randolph to mr. Adet, already quoted, affords conclusive testimony.

It appears then, on examining this objection to the treaty between the United States & Britain, that it has not added to the catalogue of contraband a single article; that it has ceded no privilege; has granted no right; and that it has not changed, in the most minute circumstance, the preexisting situation of the United States in relation either to France or to Britain. Notwithstanding these truths the Government of the United States has hastened to assure its former friend that, if the stipulations between them be found oppressive in practice, it is ready to offer up those stipulations a willing sacrifice at the shrine of friendship.

In vain will you search in this procedure for "a known and evident sacrifice, on the part of the United States, of their connections with this republic, and of the most essential and least contested prerogatives of neutrality." In vain will you search for evidence of their "having given to England, to the detriment of their first Allies, the most striking mark of an unbounded condescension, by abandoning the limits given to contraband by the law of nations, by their treaties with all other nations, and even by those of England with the greater part of the maritime powers." The United States feel these reproaches as conscious innocence feels the imputation of guilt.

2ndly. It is also alledged that "the United States have consented to extend the denomination of contraband even to provisions. Instead of pointing out particularly, as all treaties do, the cases of the effective blockade of a place as alone forming an exception to the freedom of this article, they have tacitly acknowledged the pretensions raised by England to create blockades in our Colonies, and even in France, by the force of a bare proclamation."

The objection to this article shall be considered according to its letter and according to its operation.

The objectionable words are "And whereas the difficulty of agreeing on the precise cases in which alone provisions and other other articles not generally contraband may be regarded as such, renders it expedient to provide against the inconveniencies and misunderstandings which might thence arise: It is further agreed, that whenever any such articles so becoming contraband, according to the existing laws of nations, shall for that reason be seized, the same shall not be confiscated, but the owners thereof shall be speedily and completely indemnified; and the captors, or in their default, the Government under whose authority they act, shall pay to the masters or owners of such vessels, the full value of all such articles, with a reasonable mercantile profit thereon, together with the freight and also the demurrage incident to such detention."

The admissions contained in this clause are

1st. That provisions are not generally contraband, and

2dly. That they are sometimes contraband.

An effort was made to establish the precise cases in which alone they should be subjected to seizure; but America would only consent to consider them as contraband in the case of an effective blockade, siege or investment of a place, while on the part of England this strict interpretation of the rule was not admitted; but it was contended that provisions became contraband when there were reasonable hopes of reducing the enemy by famine. In this opposition of sentiment to what have the United States consented? "To extend the denomination of contraband even to provisions?" "To acknowledge tacitly the pretensions raised by England to create blockades in your colonies & even in France, by the force of a bare proclamation?" "To secure to the English alone the carriage of meals?" In a word to have commerce only with England?" Reconsider the words themselves and it will require no comment to prove how inapplicable to them are these assertions. The Clause complained of, having stated the admissions and the difficulty already mentioned, proceeds to say: "It is further agreed that whenever any such articles so becoming contraband according to the laws of nations shall for that reason be seized the same shall not be confiscated but the owners thereof shall be speedily and completely indemnified."

It is too clear to admit of contestation that this clause does not declare provisions to be contraband, or admit of their seizure in any other case than where, "according to the existing law of nations, they should become contraband." In such case the right to seize them is not given by this article, but is admitted by France & by all the world to exist independent of treaty. In such case they would have been seized had this stipulation never been entered into, & would have been confiscated also. The only alteration, which is by the letter of the clause produced in the law of nations, is to exempt from confiscation goods which under that law would have been subject to it.

But it has been suspected to have an object & an operation in practice different from its letter. It has been suspected to cover a design to admit substantially certain principles with respect to blockades, which in theory are denied.

Incapable of duplicity, America with the pride of conscious integrity repels this insinuation, & courts an investigation of the facts on which it is founded.

The government of the United States and that of Britain, having construed the law of nations differently in this respect, each would have acted upon its own opinion of that law. The privateers of England would have seized as contraband any goods deemed such in their Courts of Admiralty; & the government of the United States would have reclaimed such goods, & would have supported the demand in such manner, as its own judgement dictated. This procedure is not changed. The right to make such reclamation has not been relinquished, nor has the legality of the seizure in any other case, than that of an attempt to enter a place actually invested, been in any degree admitted.

It is true that the british government renewed the order concerning provisions about the time of the ratification of this treaty; but it is not less true that the Government of the United States manifested a firm resolution to submit to no such construction, & remonstrated so seriously against it as to produce a revocation of the order. Nor is this all. Claims for provisions seized in cases of a meer proclamation blockade have been actually made and have been actually decided in favor of the claimants. The british government has acquiesced under such decisions by paying the sums awarded. These sums were not limited to a reasonable profit on the price of the commodity seized, but were regulated by its price at the port of destination, & consequently the actual as well as avowed principle of such decisions was, that the goods seized had not become contraband "according to the existing Law of nations."

The intention of the Government then and the practice under the article are in direct opposition to these injurious suspicions, the indulgence of which has produced such pernicious effects. It is even believed that the decision on this subject will be one step towards the establishment of that principle, for which America has never ceased to contend. It is also believed, and has ever been believed, that the article objected to would have a necessary tendency to increase, and did in fact increase the quantity of provisions imported from America into France, and her colonies. The american commerce, being intirely in the hands of individuals, is consequently conducted by them according to their own views of particular advantage. They will unquestionably endeavor to supply the highest market, unless restrained from doing so by other considerations, which render it unadvisable to attempt such a supply.

In their calculations the risk of reaching the market is too important an item to be passed over or forgotten. Every diminution of this risk adds to the number of those who will attempt the supply, and consequently a knowledge that the voyage should it even fail by the seizure of the vessel, would yet be profitable, must increase the number of those who would make it.

It is plain then that this article admits the seizure of provisions in no situation where they were not before seizable, & encourages their transportation to France & her colonies, by diminishing the risk of such transportation.

It is also complained of, that this treaty has not "as all treaties do, pointed out particularly, the cases of the effective blockade of a place" as alone forming an exception to the freedom of provisions.

Articles in a treaty can only be inserted by consent. The United States therefore can never be responsible for not having inserted an article to which the other contracting party would not assent. They may refuse to make any change in the existing state of things prejudicial to themselves, or to other powers, & they have refused to make any such change. But it is not in their power to insert as by common consent an article, though meerly declaratory of a principle, which they consider as certainly existing, & which they mean to support, if such common consent be unattainable. All that can be done in such a case is, to leave the principle unimpaired, reserving entirely the right to assert it. This has been done. The principle was left unimpaired & has been since successfully asserted.

The United States are at all times truly solicitous to diminish as much as possible the list of contraband. It is their interest, in common with all others nations, whose policy is peace, to enlarge so far as they can be enlarged, the rights of neutrals. This interest is a sure guaranty for their using those means, which they think calculated to effect the object, and which a just regard to their situation will permit. But they must be allowed to pursue the object in such manner as may comport with that situation. While they surrender no actual right in preserving which there is a common interest; while they violate no preexisting engagement, & these they have not surrendered nor violated, they must judge exclusively for themselves how far they will or ought to go in their efforts to acquire new rights, or establish new principles. When they surrender this privilege, they cease to be independent, & they will no longer deserve to be free. They will have surrendered into other hands the most sacred of deposits—the right of self government, and instead of the approbation, they will merit the contempt of the world.

Those parts of the treaty between the United States & Britain, which have been selected by France as injurious to her, have now been examined. The undersigned are too well convinced that they in no degree justify the enmity they are alledged to have produced, not to rely on a candid reconsideration of them as a sure mean of removing the impressions they are supposed to have made.

Before this subject is entirely closed, one other objection will be noticed. The very formation of a commercial treaty with England seems to be reprobated, as furnishing just cause of offence to France, & mr. Adet has permitted himself to say "It was a little matter only to allow the English to avail themselves of the advantages of our treaty; it was necessary to assure these to them by the aid of a contract which might serve at once as a reply to the claims of France, and as peremptory motives for refusals, the true cause of which it was requisite incessantly to disguise to her under specious pretexts. Such was the object of mr. Jays mission to London; such was the object of a negociation, enveloped from its origin in the Shadow of Mystery & covered with the veil of dissimulation."

Passing over this extraordinary language, the undersigned, being only desirous of producing accommodation by the exhibition of truth, will consider the opinion, which is obliquely hinted and the fact which is directly averred.

The practice of forming commercial treaties is so universal, among nations having any commercial intercourse with each other, that it seems unnecessary to discuss their utility. The right to form these treaties has been so universally asserted & admitted, that it seems to be the inseparable attribute of sovereignty, to be questioned only by those, who question the right of a nation to govern itself, and to be ceded only by those, who are prepared to cede their independence.

But the prosperity of the United States is in a peculiar degree promoted by external commerce. A people almost exclusively agricultural have not within themselves a market for the surplus produce of their labor, or a sufficient number & variety of articles of exchange, to supply the wants of the cultivator. They cannot have an internal, which will compensate for the loss of an external commerce. They must search abroad for manufactures, & for many other articles, which contribute to the comfort and convenience of life, and they must search abroad also for a market for that large portion of the productions of their soil, which cannot be consumed at home. The policy of a nation, thus circumstanced, must ever be to encourage external commerce, & to open to itself every possible market for the disposition of its superfluities, & the supply of its wants. The commercial and manufacturing character and capacities of England must turn into that channel a considerable portion of the commerce of any nation, under the circumstances of the United States. It is a market too important & too valuable to be voluntarily closed. In consequence a considerable portion of their commerce has taken that direction, & a continual solicitude has been manifested to regulate and secure it by contract. To abolish this commerce, or to refuse to give it permanence and security by fair and equal stipulations would be a sacrifice, which no nation ought to require, and which no nation ought to make. In forming her treaty of amity and commerce with the United States, France claimed no such prerogative. That treaty declares the intention of the parties to be "to fix, in an equitable & permanent manner, the rules which ought to be followed relative to the correspondence & commerce which the two parties desire to establish between their respective countries, states & subjects:" and that "they have judged that the said end could not be better obtained than by taking, for the basis of their agreement, the most perfect equality and reciprocity, and by carefully avoiding all those burthensome preferences which are usually sources of debate, embarrassment and discontent; by leaving also each party at liberty to make, respecting commerce and navigation, those interior regulations which it shall find most convenient to itself; and by founding the advantage of commerce solely upon reciprocal utility, and the just rules of free intercourse; reserving withal to each party the liberty of admitting at its pleasure, other nations to a participation of the same advantages." The treaty itself contains no stipulation in any degree contradictory to these declarations of the preamble, or which could suggest a suspicion that under those declarations was concealed a wish to abridge the sovereignty of the United States with respect to treaties, or to control their interests in regard to commerce. In forming a commerical treaty with Britain, therefore, in which no peculiar privilege is granted, the Government of the United States believed itself to be transacting a business exclusively its own, which could give umbrage to none, and with which no other nation on earth would consider itself as having a right to interfere. There existed consequently no motive for concealing from, or declaring to France, or any other power, that the negotiations of mr. Jay might or might not terminate in a commerical treaty. The declaration, therefore, was not made. Nor is it usual for nations about to enter into negotiations, to proclaim to others the various objects to which those negotiations may possibly be directed. Such is not, nor has it ever been the practice of France. To suppose a necessity, or a duty on the part of one government thus to proclaim all its views, or to consult another, with respect to its arrangements of its own affairs, is to imply a dependence to which no government ought willingly to submit. So far as the interests of France might be involved in the negotiation, the instructions given to the negotiator were promptly communicated. The minister of this republic was informed officially, that mr. Jay was instructed not to weaken the engagements of the United States to France. Further information was neither to have been required or expected. Indeed that which was given furnished reason to suppose that one of the objects of the negotiation with Great Britain was a commercial treaty. Why then such unnecessary & unmerited sarcasms against a cautious & unoffending Ally? Those objects which she pursued were such as an independent nation might legitimately pursue, & such as America never had dissembled, & never deemed it necessary to dissemble, her wish to obtain. Why should an effort be made to impress France with an opinion, that mr. Jay was not authorized to negotiate a commercial treaty with Britain, when the fixed opinion of America had ever been that France could not be, and ought not to be dissatisfied with the formation of such a treaty? Why should the minister of France have been informed officially, that mr. Jay was specially instructed not to weaken the engagements of the United States to France, if it was intended to convince that minister that his power did not extend to subjects in any degree connected with those engagements? To what purpose should the government of the United States have practised a deception deemed by itself totally unnecessary, & which its utmost efforts could not long continue? It requires an equal degree of folly and of vice to practise a useless fraud, which must inevitably & immediately be detected, and the detection of which must expose its author to general infamy, as well as to the enmity of those on whom the fraud had been practised. These considerations ought to have produced some hesitation concerning the fact. The testimony in support of it ought to have been very positive and very unexceptionable before it received implicit faith. It should have been very clear that there was no mistake, no misunderstanding, concerning the information communicated, before the charge was made in such terms as the minister of France has been pleased to employ. But the testimony is believed to be satisfactory, that the Government of the United States has not endeavored to impress on France any opinion on this subject which the fact of the case did not warrant. The declaration of mr. Randolph made July 8th. 1795, is full to this point. It is in these words, "I never could with truth have informed the French minister, that the mission, as set forth in the President's message to the Senate, contemplated only an adjustment of our complaints, if by this phrase it be intended to exclude commercial arrangements: I could have no reason for saying so, since the French republic could have had nothing to do with our commercial arrangements, if they did not derogate from her rights—it could have answered no purpose, when so short a time would develope the contrary—I never did inform the French minister as is above stated.

"The only official conversation which I recollect with mr. Fauchet[3] upon this subject, was when I communicated to him, with the President's permission, that mr. Jay was instructed not to weaken our engagements to France. Neither then nor at any other time in official or unofficial conversation did I ever say to him, that nothing of a commercial nature was contemplated; or that nothing but the controversies under the old treaty, and the spoliations were contemplated.

Mr. Fauchet some time ago said to me, that he understood from what I said that mr. Jay was not authorized to treat of commercial matters—I told him, that he misunderstood me—No letter has ever passed upon this subject."

If then mr. Randolph did give mr. Fauchet the information contended for, it is plain that he was never authorized to do so; but the considerations already detailed render it infinitely more probable that mr. Fauchet has misunderstood mr. Randolph than that mr. Randolph has misinformed mr. Fauchet.

The undersigned have taken, they trust, a correct view of the leading and influential measures, adopted by the government of the United States. They have endeavored to state, with plainness and with candor, the motives which have occasioned the adoption

3. Joseph Fauchet (1761–1834).

of those measures, & the operation they are believed to have. They have shown that if America is to be reproached with partialities irreconcileable with her neutral situation, it is not by France that those reproaches ought to be made. They have been induced to take this review by a hope, which they cannot relinquish without regret, that it may contribute to efface impressions, which misrepresentation may have made, and to take from the intentions and conduct of the government they represent, that false coloring which unfriendly pencils have so profusely bestowed upon them. They are anxious still to cherish the hope that, by exposing frankly & sincerely the sentiments which have hitherto guided their nation, they may restore dispositions on the part of France compatible with the continuance of those sentiments.

Complaints have been made, that in the application to particular cases of those general principles, which the neutral station of the United States rendered indispensable, inconveniencies and vexations which were unavoidable, have been sometimes sustained. These complaints have been separately and fully discussed. The undersigned persuade themselves that the explanations, which have been given respecting them if not entirely satisfactory, have yet been such as to prove the good faith and upright intention which have never ceased to direct the conduct of the United States. If notwithstanding this good faith and the purity of these intentions, the difficulty of their situation has in any case produced even an involuntary departure from those principles by which they profess to be guided, they are ready to consider that case and to repair any fault which may inadvertently have been committed. With these dispositions on their part, with this consciousness of having never ceased to merit the friendship and esteem of the French nation, with a conviction that a temperate & thorough review of the past cannot fail to remove prejudices, not warranted by facts, the United States have relied confidently on the Justice of France, for a discontinuance and reparation of those serious and heavy injuries, which have been accumulated on them.[4]

Desirous of establishing, not the dependence of a weak on a powerful nation, but that real & cordial friendship, the willing and spontaneous offering of generous minds, which can only be lasting

4. This is probably the end of the first part of the paper that JM referred to as "a justification of the conduct of the American government." The next part contains "the claims of the United States upon France." See Journal, Jan. 2 and 10, 1798.

when evidenced to be mutual, & can only be preserved when bottomed on reciprocal justice, the undersigned will now represent with candor and frankness the well founded complaints with which they are charged.

These complaints consist

Of claims uncontroverted by the Government of France, but which remain unsatisfied, and

Of claims founded on captures and confiscations, the illegality of which has not yet been admitted.

In the first class of cases are arranged

1st. Those whose property has been seized under the decree of the national convention of the 9th. May 1793.

2ndly. Those who are intitled to compensation in consequence of the long detention of their vessels at Bourdeaux in the years 1793, & 1794.

3dly. The holders of bills and other evidences of debts due, drawn by the colonial administrations in the West Indies.

4thly. Those whose cargoes have been appropriated to public use without receiving therefor adequate payment, &

5thly. Those who have supplied the Government under contracts with its agents, which have not yet been complied with on the part of France.

These well founded claims of American citizens, thus originating in voluntary and important supplies, in the forcible seizure of valuable property, accompanied with promises of payment, & in injurious detentions, constitute a mass of debt which the justice and good faith of the french government cannot refuse to provide for, and which is too considerable to be unnoticed by that of the United States. The undersigned are instructed to solicit your attention to this subject, and they would persuade themselves that they do not solicit in vain. So many circumstances concur to give force to the application, that they leave it to your government in the confidence that no additional representations can be necessary.

They pass to complaints still more important for their amount, more interesting in their nature & more serious in their consequences.

On the 14th. Messidor, 4th. year of the french republic, one and indivisible (July 2d. 1796) the Executive Directory decreed "That all neutral or allied powers shall without delay be notified, that the flag of the French republic will treat neutral vessels, either as to confiscation, as to searches or capture, in the same manner as they shall suffer the English to treat them." This Decree, in any point of view in which it can be considered, could not fail to excite in the United States the most serious attention. It dispenses at once as they conceive with the most solemn obligations which compact can create, and consequently asserts a right on the part of France to recede at her discretion from any stipulations she may have entered into. It has been demonstrated that governments may by contract change, as between themselves, the rules established by the law of nations, & that such contract becomes completely obligatory on the parties, though it can in no manner affect the rights of others; yet by this decree allies with whom such stipulations exist are to be treated, without regard to such stipulations, in the same manner as they are treated by others, who are bound by a different rule. This as it respects the United States is the more unfriendly, because a readiness has been manifested on their part so to modify by consent their treaty with France as to reinstate the rules established by the law of nations.

The general terms too in which this decree is conceived threatened but too certainly the mischiefs it has generated, and the abuses which have been practised under it. Neutrals are to be treated as they shall permit the English to treat them. No rule extracted from the practice of England is laid down, which might govern the cruisers of France, or instruct the vessels of neutrals. No principles are stated, manifesting the opinion entertained of the treatment received from England, which might enable a neutral to controvert that opinion, and to show that the English were not permitted to treat its flag as was supposed by the government of France. To judge from the decree itself, from any information given concerning it, or from the practice under it, those who were to be benefited by its abuse were to decide in what manner it should be executed, and the cruiser who should fall in with a valuable vessel had only to consult his own rapacity, in order to determine whether an English privateer, meeting a vessel under similar circumstances would capture and bring her into port. Multiplied excesses and accumulated vexations could not but have been apprehended from such a decree, and the fact has realized every fear that was entertained concerning it. It has been construed even in Europe to authorize the capture and condemnation of American vessels for the single circumstance of their being destined for a british port. At no period of the war has Britain undertaken to exercise such a power. At no period of the war has she asserted such a right. It is a power, which prostrates every principle of national sovereignty & to which no nation can submit without relinquishing at the same time its best interests & sacrificing its dearest rights. This power has been exercised by France on the rich and unprotected commerce of an Ally, on the presumption that that ally was sustaining the same injuries from Britain, at a time when it is believed that the depredations of that nation had ceased, & the principle of compensating for them had been recognized.

In the West Indies similar depredations have been experienced. On the first of August 1796, the special agents of the Executive Directory to the Windward Islands decreed that all vessels loaded with contraband should be seized & confiscated for the benefit of the Captors.

On the seventh Frimaire, 5th. year of the French republic, one and indivisible, (27th. November 1796) the commission, delegated by the French republic to the leeward islands, resolved that the Captains of french national vessels and privateers are authorized to stop and bring into the ports of the colony american vessels bound to English ports or coming from the said ports.

On the nineteenth Pluviose, 5th. year of the French republic, one and indivisible, (February 1st: 1797) Victor Hugues and Lebas, the special agents of the Executive Directory to the Windward islands, passed a decree subjecting to capture and confiscation neutral vessels destined for the windward & leeward islands of America, delivered up to the English & occupied and defended by the emigrants. These ports are said to be Martinico, St. Lucia, Tobago, Demerara, Berbice, Essequibo, Port au Prince, St. Marks, L Archaye, and Jeremia. The decree also subjects to capture all vessels which have cleared out for the West Indies generally.

The undersigned will not detain you, Citizen minister, for the purpose of proving how directly & openly these decrees violate both the law of nations and the treaty between France & the United States.

They have been executed on the officers & crews of the captured vessels, in a manner by no means calculated to mitigate their rigor.

The decree of the 14th. of Messidor was soon followed by another which has spared but little of the American commerce, except what has fortunately escaped the pursuit of the cruisers of France. On the 12th. Ventose, 5th. year, (12th. March 1797) the Executive Directory, considering the treaty of amity, commerce, and navigation, concluded at London the 19th. November 1794, between the said United States & England, as containing concessions of privileges to Britain which, under the treaty of February 1778, might be enjoyed by this republic also, proceeds to modify the treaty between France & the United States, by declaring enemy's goods in American bottoms liable to capture & confiscation, by enlarging the list of contraband, and by subjecting to punishment as a pirate any American citizen holding a commission given by the enemies of France, as well as every seaman of that nation making a part of the crew of enemies ships. The decree next proceeds to exact from Americans papers which had been made necessary to establish the neutrality of foreign vessels generally, by the ordinance of the 26th. of July 1778, but which had never been considered as applying to the United States; which required papers their vessels could not be supposed to possess, and which the treaty between the two nations was supposed to have rendered unnecessary.

The basis taken by the Executive Directory on which to rest their modification of the treaty of the 6th. of February 1778, is that by the treaty of the 19th. of November 1794, *particular favors in respect of commerce and navigation have been granted to England.*

It has been demonstrated that no particular favors in respect of commerce or navigation, have been granted to England. That treaty has been shown only to recognize, regulate & moderate the exercise of rights before possessed, and before openly acknowledged to be possessed—rights which France & America had reciprocally ceded to each other, without requiring as a condition of the cession that either should compel England to form a similar stipulation.

But to admit for a moment that the treaty with England might be considered as stipulating favors not before possessed yet the American government did not so understand that treaty, & had manifested a disposition to modify, by common consent, its relations with this Republic in such manner as to reinstate a rule which has been voluntarily changed. It cannot but be sincerely regreted, because it seemed to indicate an unfriendly temper, that France has deemed it more eligible to establish by force, in opposition to her treaty a principle which she deemed convenient, than to fix that principle on the fair basis of mutual and amicable agreement.

But the clause under which these modifications are justified is in these words. "The most Christian King and the United States engage mutually not to grant any particular favor to other nations, in respect of commerce & navigation, which shall not immediately become common to the other party, who shall enjoy the same favor, freely, if the concession was freely made or on allowing the same compensation, if the concession was conditional." If these stipulations unequivocally amounted to the grant of favors, still the grant is not gratuitous. The concessions on the part of the United States are made on condition of similar concessions on the part of Britain. If therefore France chuses to consider them as modifications of the treaty of 1778, she can only do it by granting the reciprocal condition; on this supposition she has either of the rules at her election, but she cannot vary from the first without a compact on her part to grant the reciprocal stipulation. Such a compact is in the nature of a national treaty.

But the rules laid down in the decree of the 12th. of Ventose 5th. year, (March 2d. 1797) as founded on the 17th. 18th. & 21st. articles of the treaty of the 19th. of November 1794 are materially variant from those articles. To demonstrate this it is only necessary to contrast the rules of the decree with the articles of the treaty on which those rules are said to be founded.

Articles of the treaty of the 19th. November 1794 as quoted by the Directory.

Article 17th.

It is agreed that in all cases where Vessels shall be captured or detained *on just suspicion* of having on board enemy's property, or of carrying to the enemy any of the articles which are contraband of war, the said Vessels shall be brought to the nearest or most convenient port; & *if any property of an enemy should be found on board such Vessel, that part only which belongs to the enemy shall be made prize* & the vessel shall be at liberty to proceed

Rules established by the arreté of the Directory.

Rule 1st.

According to the 17th. article of the treaty of London of the 19th. of November 1794 all merchandize of the enemy or *merchandize not sufficiently proved to be neutral*, laden under the American flag, shall be confiscated, but the vessel on board of which it shall be found shall be released and restored to the owner. It is enjoined on the Commissaries of the Executive Directory to accelerate by all the means in their power, the decision of contests which shall

with the remainder without any impediment. And it is agreed that all proper measures shall be taken to prevent delay in deciding the cases of ships or cargoes, so brought for adjudication; & in the payment or recovery of any indemnification adjudged, or agreed to be paid to the owners or masters of such ships.

arise either on the validity of the prize cargo, or on the freight and demurrage.

According to the article, when *on just suspicion* of having on board enemy's property, or of carrying to the enemy contraband of war, a vessel shall be brought into port, *that part only which belongs to the enemy* shall be made prize. According to the article then, the fact whether the property does or does not belong to an enemy is to be fairly tried. The party who would establish the fact must prove it. The captor must show *the justice of the suspicion* on which the capture or detention was founded. The burthen of the proof rests on him. If in truth & in fact the property does not belong to an enemy, or is not proved to belong to an enemy, it must be discharged. But the rule pursues a different course. The rule declares that merchandize of the enemy, or *not sufficiently proved to be neutral*, laden under the American flag, shall be confiscated. The burthen of the proof is shifted from the captor to the captured. The question to be tried is not solely whether the merchandize be in fact the property of an enemy, but also whether it *be sufficiently proved to be neutral.* The sufficiency of this proof is to be ascertained, not by general and satisfactory testimony, not by the great principles of truth & the common understanding of mankind, but by the exhibition of certain papers, demandable at the will of one of the parties, and not in the possession of the other.

This may be a regulation which France chuses to establish, but certainly it is a regulation, essentially variant from the article it professes to resemble.

Article 18.

In order to regulate what is in future to be esteemed contraband of war, it is agreed that

Rule 2d.

According to the 18th. article of the treaty of London of the 19th. of November 1794, to the

under the said denomination shall be comprised all arms & implements serving for the purposes of war, by land or by sea, as cannon, muskets, mortars, petards, bombs, grenades, carcasses, saucisses, carriages for cannon, musket rests, bandoliers, gunpowder, match, saltpetre, ball, pikes, swords, head pieces, cuirasses, halberds, lances, javelins, horse furniture, holsters, belts, and generally all other implements of war; as also timber for ship building, tar or rosin, copper in Sheets, sails, hemp & cordage, & generally whatever may serve *directly, to the equipment of vessels*, unwrought iron & fir plank only excepted.

articles declared contraband by the 24th. article of the treaty of the 6th. of February 1778, are added the following articles;

Timber for Ship building; pitch, tar & rosin; copper in Sheets; sails, hemp and cordage, and everything which serves directly *or indirectly* for the armament & equipment of vessels, unwrought iron & fir planks excepted. These several articles shall be confiscated whenever they shall be destined or attempted to be carried to the enemy.

The immense number of articles, which may serve indirectly for the armament and equipment of vessels, are made contraband by the rule of the Directory, though they are not so by the article it professes to cite.

Article 21st.

It is likewise agreed that the subjects and citizens of the two nations shall not do any acts of hostility or violence against each other, nor accept commissions or instructions so to act from any foreign prince or state, enemies to the other party, nor shall the enemies of one of the parties be permitted to invite, or endeavor to inlist in their military service any of the subjects or citizens of the other

Rule 3d.

According to the 21st. article of the treaty of London, of the 19th. of November 1794, every individual known to be an american, who shall hold a commission given by the enemies of France, as well as every seaman of that nation making a part of the crew of enemy ships, shall by that act be declared a pirate and treated as such, without being allowed in any case to alledge that he was forced to do it

party; & the laws against all such offences & aggressions shall be punctually executed. And if any subject or citizen of the said parties respectively shall accept any foreign commission or letters of marque, for arming any vessel to act as a privateer against the other party, it is hereby declared to be lawful for the said party, to treat and punish the said subject or citizen, having such commission or letters of marque, as a pirate.

by violence menaces or otherwise.

The government of the United States has never formed a treaty comprehending an article in any degree similar to this rule. It has never assented to such stipulations as they relate to its own citizens, or required them as they relate to those of other powers. The difference between the article and the rule requires no comment. Nor will the rule be commented on. The undersigned will only observe, that the article is by no means uncommon, but is to be found in most treaties of amity & commerce. The 21st. article of the treaty with France the 19th. of the treaty with the United Provinces, the 23d. of the treaty with Sweden, and the 20th. article of the treaty with Prussia contain similar stipulations. It is not easy to conceive a reason why it should not also be inserted in a treaty with England, or why its insertion should give offence to France.[5]

But the fourth rule of the decree is, in its operation, the most extensive & the most seriously destructive. That rule declares that "Conformably to the law of the 14th. of February 1793, the regulations of the 21st. of October 1744, and of the 26th. of July 1778, concerning the manner of proving the property of neutral ships & merchandize, shall be executed according to their form & tenor."

"Every American ship shall, therefore, be a good prize, which shall not have on board a list of the crew in proper form; such as is prescribed by the model annexed to the treaty of the 6th. of

5. For the treaties with France, the United Provinces, Sweden, Prussia, and Great Britain, see Miller, ed., *Treaties*, II, 19, 76, 142, 175–176, 260–261.

February 1778, the observance of which is required by the 25th. & 27th. articles of the same treaty."

This rule requires that American ships and merchandize, in order to prove the property to be american, shall exhibit certain papers, & especially a role d'equipage, which are required of neutrals generally, by the particular marine ordinances of France, recited in the Decree of the Directory. But France & America have entered into a solemn treaty, one object of which was to secure the vessels of either party, which might be at peace, from the cruisers of the other, which might be engaged in war. To effect this object, the contracting parties have not referred each other to the particular statutes or ordinances of either government, but have enumerated the papers, which should be deemed sufficient. They have done more: They have prescribed the very form of the passport, which should establish the neutrality of the vessel, & prevent her being diverted from her course. The 25th. & 27th. articles of the treaty between the two nations, which are quoted by the Directory, and are considered by the undersigned as conclusive on this subject, are in these words;

Article 25th.

"To the end that all manner of dissentions and quarrels may be avoided and prevented, on the one side and on the other, it is agreed, that in case either of the parties hereto should be engaged in war, the ships and vessels, belonging to the subjects or people of the other ally, must be furnished with sea-letters or passports expressing the name, property and bulk of the ship, as also the name and place of habitation of the master or commander of the said ship, that it may appear thereby that the said ship, really and truly belongs to the subjects of one of the parties, which passport shall be made out and granted according to the form annexed to this treaty; and they shall likewise be recalled every year, that is, if the ship happens to return home in the space of a year. It is likewise agreed, that such ships, being laden, are to be provided not only with passports as above-mentioned, but also with certificates, containing the several particulars of the cargo, the place whence the ship sailed and whither she is bound, that so it may be known whether any forbidden or contraband goods be on board the same; which certificates shall be made out by the officers of the place whence the ship set sail, in the accustomed form; and if anyone shall think it fit or advisable to express in the said certificates, the person to whom the goods on board belong, he may freely do so."

Article 27th.

"If the ships of the said subjects, people or inhabitants of either of the parties, shall be met with, either sailing along the coasts or on the high seas, by any ship of war of the other, or by any privateers, the said ships of war or privateers, for the avoiding of any disorder, shall remain out of cannon shot, & may send their boats aboard the merchant ship which they shall so meet with, and may enter her to the number of two or three men only, to whom the master or commander of such ship or vessel shall exhibit his passport concerning the property of the ship, made out according to the form inserted in this present treaty, and the ship, when she shall have shewed such passport, shall be free & at liberty to pursue her voyage, so as it shall not be lawful to molest or search her in any manner, or to give her chace or force her to quit her intended course."

It will be admitted that the two nations possess the power of agreeing, that any paper in any form shall be the sole document, demandable by either from the other, to prove the property of a vessel and cargo. It will also be admitted, that an agreement so made becomes the law of the parties, which must retain its obligation.

Examine then the words of the compact & determine by fair construction what will satisfy them.

The 25th. article states substantially the contents of a paper, which is termed a sea letter or passport, & which "it is agreed that in case either of the parties should be engaged in war the ships and vessels belonging to the subjects or people of the other ally must be furnished with." To what purpose are they to be furnished with this sea letter or passport? The article answers "To the end that all manner of dissentions & quarrels may be avoided and prevented, on one side and the other" "That it may appear thereby that the ship really and truly belongs to the subjects of one of the parties."

But how will the passport "prevent and avoid all manner of dissentions and quarrels, on one side or the other," if ordinances, both prior and subsequent to the treaty, are to be understood as controlling it, and as requiring other papers, not contemplated in the public agreement of the two nations? How is it to appear from the passport "that the ship really and truly belongs to the subjects of one of the parties," if it is denied, that the passport is evidence of that fact, and contended that other papers, not alluded to in the treaty, shall be adduced to prove it?

But the 27th. article is still more explicit. It declares that when a merchant ship of one of the parties shall be visited by the ships of war or privateers of the other, "the commander of such ship or vessel shall exhibit his passport, concerning the property of the ship, made out according to the form inserted in the present treaty, and the ship, when she shall have showed such passport, shall be free and at liberty to pursue her voyage, so as it shall not be lawful to molest or search her in any manner or to give her chace, or force her to quit her intended course." What is it that shall prove the property of the vessel? The treaty answers, the passport. But the decree of the Directory requires in addition certain other papers, perfectly distinct from the passport. The treaty declares that "the ship, when she shall have shewed" (not the role d'equipage or any other paper, required by the particular ordinances of either nation, but) "such passport, shall be free and at liberty to pursue her voyage, so as it shall not be lawful to molest or search her in any manner, or to give her chace or force her to quit her intended course." Yet the vessels of America, after exhibiting "such passport," are not "free and at liberty to pursue their voyage;" they are "molested;" they are "chaced;" they are "forced to quit their intended course;" they are captured and confiscated as hostile property.

It is alledged that the form of the passport, which is annexed to the treaty, manifests that certain acts were to be performed by the person to whom the passport is delivered, and that such person ought to prove the performance of those acts.

But the treaty, far from requiring such proof, absolutely dispenses with it. The treaty declares that the passport shall itself evidence the property of the vessel, and secure it from molestation of any sort. By consent of the parties then, the passport is evidence of all that either party can require from the other. Neither the right to give such consent, or the obligation of a compact formed upon it can as is conceived ever be denied. Nor can the form of the passport, whatever it may be, change the compact.

But let the words of the model be examined.

They are "A tous ceux qui ces présentes verront: soit notoire que faculté et permission a été accordée à . . . . . . maître ou commandant du navire appellé . . . . . . de la ville de . . . . . . de la capacité de . . . . tonneaux ou environ, se trouvant présentement dans le port de . . . . . . qu'après que son navire a été visité et avant son départ, il prêtera serment entre les mains des officiers de la marine, que le dit navire, appartient à un ou plusiers sujets de . . . . . . dont l'acte sera mis à la fin des présentes; de même qu'il gardera les ordonnances et règlemens maritimes, et remettra une liste signée et confirmée par témoins, contenant les noms et surnoms, les lieux de naissance, et la demeure des personnes composant l'equipage de son navire, et de tous ceux qui embarqueront, lesquels il ne recevra pas à bord sans connaissance et permission des officiers de marine; et dans chaque port ou hâvre, il montrera la présente permission aux officiers et juges de marine."

It is material to observe that the model requires the oath concerning the property of the vessel to be annexed to the passport, but does not require any other certificate or the annexation of any paper whatever. Why this difference? It is a solemn proof of that for which the article stipulates & therefore the model expresses that the evidence of this fact shall be annexed, but it does not require the production of the evidence of any other fact.

It seems then to be demonstrated that the sea letter or passport, a model of which is annexed to the treaty, is by solemn agreement to be received by each party as conclusive testimony, that the vessel producing such passport is the property of a citizen of the other, & is consequently to continue her voyage without molestation or hindrance.

But let it be supposed, that the treaty on this subject was less conclusive, & that its stipulations had been ambiguously expressed: Yet it is certain that it has been uniformly understood by both parties, as the undersigned have expounded it, and that neither France or the United States, previous to the decree complained of, considered the vessels of either nation, producing the passport agreed on, as liable to capture for want of a role d'equipage.

For more than four years after her treaty with the United States, France was engaged in a war with Britain; and in the course of that time, it was never suggested that a role d'equipage was necessary for the protection of an american vessel. It does not weaken the argument, that the United States were also parties to the war. The principle assumed is, that without the production of the papers required by the decree, the vessel does not appear to be, and cannot be considered as American property. If this principle be correct, it would not cease to apply because the United States were engaged in the war. Was America even engaged in the war on the part of France a British vessel carrying American colors would not be secured by the flag she bore. It would be necessary to prove by her papers, or other admissible testimony, that the vessel was American property. If this fact cannot appear without a role d'equipage, while the United States are at peace, neither could it appear without the same evidence, if the United States were parties to the war.

About four years of the present war had also elapsed, before this construction of the treaty, at the same time so wonderful and so ruinous, had disclosed itself. In the course of that time, the ports of France were filled with the vessels of the United States. Very many of them sailed under contracts made for the government itself by its minister, in Philadelphia. No one of them possessed a role d'equipage; no one of them was considered on that account as being liable to condemnation. Indeed in some instances, vessels have been captured and discharged, although this paper was not among those belonging to the ship.

Such a long course of practice appears to have evidenced unequivocally the sense of France on this subject.

It is too apparent to be questioned for a moment, that on the part of the United States, no suspicion had ever been entertained that such a paper could have been required. A role d'equipage could have been obtained with as much facility as that passport, for which the treaty stipulates. Could it have been imagined, that American Vessels incurred the possible hazard of being retarded only one day in a voyage for want of such paper, it would in every instance have been supplied. No vessel would have sailed without it.

Your own mind, Citizen Minister, will suggest to you, with irresistable force, the extreme hardship of thus putting a new construction on a long existing contract, or of giving a new & unexpected extension to antient municipal regulations, and of condemning thereby vessels taken on the high seas, for want of a paper not known to be required, when they sailed out of port. If a role d'equipage was really considered by France as a necessary evidence of any fact, the establishment of which was deemed essential, common usage & those plain principles of justice, which all nations should respect, indispensably require that the regulation should first be made known to a neutral & friendly nation, by other means than by the capture and confiscation of its property. If this measure had been announced to the Government of the United States, before it had been put in practice, & American vessels had sailed without a role d'equipage, they would have taken upon themselves the hazard of such a procedure. But in a moment, when the Ocean is covered with peaceful merchantmen, pursuing a just and lawful commerce, to bring into sudden operation a measure, which had never before been applied to them, which had for so many years slept unheard of, and by the force of this regulation, to confiscate unguarded property, which had been trusted to the seas, under the faith of solemn existing treaties, & without a conjecture that this, more than any other formula, would have been required, is to impose on unoffending individuals a ruin, from which no wise precautions, no human foresight could possibly have protected them. On this subject then, the undersigned appeal with confidence to the justice & equity of the French Government.

But could it be conceded for a moment, that the Executive Directory might rightfully modify the treaty of France with the United States by that of the United States with Britain, & might rightfully require a role d'equipage, in order to establish the neutrality of a vessel, for want of which the vessel might be confiscated, yet the cargo, being proved to be neutral, ought to be safe.

According to the law of nations, the goods of an enemy, found on board the ship of a friend, are liable to capture; & the goods of a friend, found on board the ship of an enemy, are safe. The United States and France have consented to change this rule as between themselves. They have agreed, that the goods of an enemy, found on board the vessels of either party, shall be safe; and that the goods of either, found on board the vessel of an enemy, shall be liable to capture. The one part of this rule is in consequence of, & dependent on the other. The one part cannot on any principle of justice be abandoned, while the other is maintained.

In their treaty with England, the United States retain unchanged the principle of the law of nations. If France modifies her treaty in this respect by that of England, she ought to take the principle intire. If in conformity to the treaty between the United States & England, France claims the right of taking enemy's property, found on board an American ship, then in conformity with that treaty also, France ought to spare American property found on board an enemy's ship. If therefore this extraordinary position could be maintained, that an American ship without a role d'equipage becomes the ship of an enemy, still the cargo, being proved to be the property of a friend, ought, on the principle of modifying the treaty between the two nations by that with England, to have been restored to the owners.

The result of these regulations has been, the most extensive and universal devastation of the American commerce. Not only vessels bound to and from the enemies of France, but vessels bound to and from her allies, & to & from her own ports, have been seized and confiscated.

The inevitable consequence has been, that direct commerce between the two nations is almost annihilated, & that the property of American citizens has been taken to a much larger amount than would have been possible in a state of actual war.

Yet[6] the Government of the United States wishing, if it be possible, to avoid even defensive measures, has sought assiduously and unremittingly, though hitherto without success, for such peaceful and amicable explanations, as might do away existing animosities, and restore between the two republics, that harmony which it so truly desires.

America has accustomed herself to perceive in France only the Ally & the friend. Consulting the feelings of her own bosom, she has believed that between Republics an elevated and refined friendship could exist, & that free nations were capable of maintaining for each other a real & permanent affection. If this pleasing theory, erected with so much care and viewed with so much delight, has been impaired[7] by experience, yet the hope continues to be cherished, that this circumstance does not necessarily involve the opposite extreme. It is believed that there exists no sufficient cause for solid & permanent enmity between France and the United States, but that on the contrary, the interests of both would be promoted by that friendly intercourse, which a reciprocal observance of the great & immutable principles of justice would certainly establish, & can alone preserve. Under this impression, America resists[8] the opinion, that the present state of things has grown out of a digested system to which France designs to adhere. She wishes and she endeavors to persuade herself, that temporary causes, which too often produce effects a sound and just policy must reprobate, connected with a misconstruction of the conduct of

6. There is a draft of the remainder of the dispatch in the Pinckney Family Papers, Library of Congress. The draft appears to be the last one prepared; the final changes in wording in it were inserted before it was recopied for the dispatch. The changes might possibly have been those suggested by Gerry, since they generally suggest a milder tone. See Journal, Jan. 20 and 22, 1798.

7. In the draft "destroyed" has been crossed out and "impaired" inserted above the line. Pinckney Family Papers.

8. In the draft "would yield reluctantly" has been crossed out and "resists" inserted. *Ibid.*

her government, as well as of the motives on which it has acted, may have occasioned those very serious aggressions of which she complains. She recedes therefore, even under the pressure of these aggressions, slowly & with difficulty from the attachments she has formed. So intertwined with every ligament of her heart have been the chords of affection which bound her to France, that only repeated and continued acts of hostility can[9] tear them asunder.

The Government of the United States, therefore, still searches the means of terminating peacefully, & in a manner which ought to be mutually satisfactory, the calamities of the moment, & of averting the still greater calamities which may be reserved for the future. Not even the discouraging and unusual events, which had preceded the present effort to negociate, could deter that government from repeating its endeavors for the preservation of amity & peace. Three citizens of the United States have been deputed as envoys extraordinary & ministers plenipotentiary to the French republic. Their instructions authorize & direct them to review the existing treaties between the two nations, & to remove by all proper means, the inequalities which have grown out of the stipulations of those treaties, in consequence of the refusal of England to adopt the principles they contain. They are also directed to give fair & complete explanations of the conduct of the government they represent; to state fully & truly the heavy[1] injuries which their fellow citizens have sustained; & to ask from the equity of a great & magnanimous republic, that compensation for those injuries which, we flatter ourselves, their justice will not refuse, & their liberal policy will not hesitate to give.

Bringing[2] with them the temper of their Government and conutry, searching only for the means of effecting the objects of their mission, they have permitted no personal considerations to influence their conduct; but have waited, under circumstances, beyond measure embarrassing and unpleasant, with that respect which the American government has so uniformly paid to that of France, for permission to lay before you, Citizen Minister, those important communications with which they have been charged.

9. In the draft "could" has been crossed out and "can" inserted. *Ibid.*

1. In the draft "unparalleled" has been crossed out and "heavy" inserted. *Ibid.*

2. Pinckney sent a copy of the ending of the dispatch to William Vans Murray in Amsterdam to forward to Pickering. The extract sent to Murray appears to be a draft that was made before the final changes in wording were inserted in the draft. *Ibid.* Murray to Pinckney, Feb. 9, 1798, Murray Papers, Pierpont Morgan Library. A copy of the extract is enclosed in Murray to Pickering, Feb. 4, 1798, Diplomatic Dispatches, Netherlands, III, RG 59, National Archives.

Perceiving no probability of being allowed to enter, in the usual forms, on those discussions which might tend to restore harmony between the two republics, they have deemed it most advisable, even under the circumstances of informality which attend the measure, to address to your government, through you, this candid review of the conduct, and this true representation of the sentiments and wishes of the government of the United States. They pray that it may be received in the temper with which it is written, & considered as an additional effort, growing out of a disposition common to the government and people of America, to cultivate and restore, if it be possible, harmony between the two republics. If, Citizen Minister, there remains a hope that these desirable objects can be effected by any means which the United States have authorized, the undersigned will still solicit, and will still respectfully attend the developement of those means.

If on the contrary no such hope remains, they have only to pray that their return to their own country may be facilitated; and they will leave France with the most deep felt regret, that neither the real and sincere friendship, which the Government of the United States has so uniformly and unequivocally displayed for this great republic, nor its continued efforts to demonstrate the purity of its conduct and intentions, can protect its citizens, or preserve them from the calamities which they have sought[3] by a just and upright conduct, to avert.

The undersigned pray you, Citizen Minister, to accept the assurances of their perfect respect and consideration.

CHARLES COTESWORTH PINCKNEY
J MARSHALL
E GERRY

To Timothy Pickering

LS, RG 59, National Archives

No. 6

Dear Sir, Paris, February 7, 1798

We transmit to you in this enclosure our last letter to the Minister of Foreign Relations; though dated the 17th. ultimo, it was

3. The extract Murray sent to Pickering has "seek in vain" for "have sought." Murray to Pickering, Feb. 4, 1798, Diplomatic Dispatches, Netherlands, III, RG 59. The draft in the Pinckney Family Papers has "have sought" inserted, but the crossed-out words are illegible.

not on account of the time taken to translate so long a letter, delivered untill the 31st.[4]

In all of our communications here, although we have agreably to your instructions written in our own language, we have at the same time taken the precaution, lest our meaning should be misrepresented or misunderstood, to accompany them with an accurate translation.

We have not yet received any answer to this communication, & should no notice be taken of it in a few days, we shall apply in a more explicit manner for our Passports.

The Councils have passed the Decree mentioned in our Number 5,[5] as having been recommended by the Directory, to capture, & condemn all Neutral vessels laden in part or in whole, with the Manufactures or Productions of England or it's possessions.

We enclose you the official copy of the Report on that subject, & shall represent to this Government, the injustice & injury which it must inevitably occasion us. We have the honor to be with great respect, Yours most Obt. Humble Servts.

CHARLES COTESWORTH PINCKNEY
J MARSHALL
E GERRY

Deeds

Deed Book Copies, Office of the Clerk of Hardy County, Moorefield, W. Va.

[*February 7, 1798* (*Hardy County, Va.*). By his attorney, Rawleigh Colston, JM conveys by release and quitclaim parcels of land in the South Branch Manor to: Anthony Baker, 224 acres for £78 19s. 9d.; Michael Carr, 89 acres for £41 5s. 4d.; Robert Darling, 241 acres for £58 9s.; Isaac Pancake, 90 acres for £47 17s.; John Rennicks, 215 acres for £85 11s. 4d.; Christopher Strader, 45 acres for £64 10s. 1d.; Isaac Vanmeter, 1,205 acres for £366 14s. 1d.; David Welton, 126 acres, 224 acres, 103 acres, and 129 acres for £40 each; Job Welton, 50 acres for £100 and 516 acres for £200. JM also conveys by grant and release with covenant 44.5 acres to David Welton for £12. All the deeds were recorded in the District Court at Hardy County in May 1798.]

4. See American Envoys to Talleyrand, Jan. 17, 1798. A printed copy of the neutrality regulations proposed by the Directory on Jan. 5, 1798, and passed by the Council of Five Hundred, Jan. 12, 1798, was also enclosed.

5. American Envoys to Pickering, Jan. 8, 1798.

From Nathaniel Cutting

ALS, Gerry Papers, Library of Congress

Gentlemen, Paris, February 17, 1798

In the present critical state of American affairs, I[6] hope you will not think ill of my taking the liberty, by this method, to communicate to you some ideas which the interesting nature of those affairs excite in my mind.

However you and myself may differ on unessential points of politics, where the whole problem ultimately resolves itself into an affair of individual opinion, yet I am persuaded that we all have the good of our Country at heart; and that it is only the *means of attaining* that desirable object, *which* we behold through different mediums.

You may perhaps think me impertinent in presuming, unasked, to offer you my opinion relative to measures calculated for the meridian of your present public character and Station; I beg you to be assured that I would not willingly offend you; but in addressing you on the present occasion, I think that I am discharging *a duty* which every good citizen ought to hold paramount to all personal considerations; I mean *Duty to one's* Country! I am also emboldened to take this step by the firm belief that the period will soon arrive when the free & independent Citizens of the United States will loudly proclaim that every American who has in any way exerted himself to maintain Peace and good-will with France, "*has deserved well of his Country*!"

Without further preamble, permit me to observe that your residence in that City has, doubtless, brought you acquainted with many *interesting circumstances* of which you previously were, and our Government now is, totally ignorant. This, in my humble opinion, ought to be an argument of sufficient weight to engage you to adopt measure which were never contemplated in America.

The irrecoverable lapse of Time, the infinite importance of the object of your mission, and the delicate Ballance on which the Peace and Prosperity of the United States are suspended, and of which I venture to flatter myself you still hold the counterpoise, all urge you to act with decision and firmness, and to take upon your-

6. Nathaniel Cutting (1756–1824), the brother of Dr. John Brown Cutting, was a Massachusetts merchant with business interests in the French West Indies. Nathaniel Cutting had served as U.S. consul at Le Havre.

selves a responsibility for which every true-hearted American would cordially indemnify you; for I trust they would all have reason to rejoice in its salutary consequences.

Taking into consideration all apparent circumstances relative to your present mission, it is natural for me to conceive that your *Discretionary Powers* must be very ample: for I cannot pay so bad a compliment to the Wisdom and Sagacity of the American Government as to suppose that it would send three Gentlemen of your respectability on so important a mission, across the Atlantic, and tie you up to future orders which must be the result of a slow and precarious correspondence! I therefore take it for granted that you are really and *bona fide* "Plenipotentiaries," in the most unlimitted sense of the term.

Many of the most important *existing circumstances*, which must influence your negociations, are *without example* in the annals of mankind; I conclude, therefore, that you will not seek a *precedent* for the exercise of your Powers.

Permit me, Gentlemen, to trace the outlines of that Conduct which *I* would pursue had I the "painful pre-eminence" to stand in your place.

I should despise the antiquated Farce of *Diplomatic etiquette*, and would leave *those* unsubstantial forms to moulder in the learned dust of *Royal Archives*, *where only* they, and the memory of the most zealous advocates for their observance, will, shortly, have an existence. I would come forward with that persuasive candour which would dignify Republican good-faith, and make a frank declaration to the French Nation, through the medium of its Directors, stating to them that it has never been the intention of the *United States* to measure Swords with France; on the contrary *their* most ardent wish is for Peace and goodunderstanding with her. I would say that from my own actual observations of the *Government* of *France*, and *its public concerns*, for months past, *both* appear in a different light from that in which they were seen in *America*. I would acknowledge candidly that want of early and accurate intelligence *there*, directly from this Country, has probably occasioned many well-meaning Citizens of the United States to imbibe erroneous opinions respecting the Government of France, its opperations and intentions. I would admit that malevolence, ever vigilant, had taken advantage of that ignorance of current events, had either distorted or given a false colouring to them, and had endeavoured, by the thick vapour of misrepresentation and the clamour of calumny, to obscure the light of Truth, and drown the voice of Reason. I would profess that I am convinced of the deceptions which designing men have attempted to practice upon our Government; that I am disposed amicably to discuss all those points which have given rise to mutual recriminations, and will concur in any rational measures for restoring reciprocal confidence, and preventing future misunderstanding. I would call to their recollection those first, great principles which form the Basis of both the American and the French Revolution. I would exhort the Directors, therefore, to join me in proving to all mankind the excellence of the Republican System by exhibiting that true magnanimity which can overlook unintentional offences, can without a blush acknowledge an error, and can chearfully make reparations proportionate to injuries. I would say to them in a manly tone, but without betraying any indication of ill-humour, that I have heavy claims against the nation for captures and detention of American property: but that being convinced of the necessity the Government is under to apply all the resources of France to the prosecution of the existing contest with England, I would only demand at present the full admission of the principle of compensation and the liquidation of the accompts: that so far from insisting on the immediate payment of the amount that may be found due to our Citizens, I would consent that it be funded as a Debt due to the United States. To prove further the amicable disposition of our Country, I would propose that in addition to the Debt abovementioned, *a Loan* of effective money should be made to France, under Guarrantee of our Government.

You know, Gentlemen, that for many years past I have resided principally in France; and of course have had opportunity to become pretty well acquainted with the natural *temper* and *disposition* of Frenchmen: I flatter myself that I have not been a very inattentive, or inaccurate, observer of their *public conduct*: and from comparing *both* with what I feel and know of human nature in other Countries, I am convinced that an address in the Spirit of that I have sketched above, would almost instantaneously calm the resentment which now effervesces in the bosom of the French Directory, and which the heat of contrary language may cause to burst into the most violent excesses.

With all due deference to your superiour Judgment, I am of opinion that the propositions I have hinted above, present *the only possible* mode of procuring to the Citizens of the United States the reimbursement of *one livre* of that immense amount of property now locked up from them in France. And, what is still a more melancholy consideration, I know of no other mode that will prevent a great deal more American property from being irrecoverably sunk in the same fathomless abyss!

In a Letter which I have recently written to a Gentleman[7] of the first consideration in the United States, I was led to make some observations on this unfortunate subject, which I beg leave here to transcribe.

"Many of the intrepid Citizens of the United States, who consult only their own liberal ideas of moral Rectitude, and who listen only to the dictates of that quick resentment which may be excited by any apparent offence to what they call '*National Honor and Dignity*,' are doubtless disposed rather to 'hurl back defiance in the teeth of France,' rather than to adopt that conciliatory language, both at home and abroad, which, at present, is much more consonant to the relative situation of the United States and this omnipotent Republic!

"If we calmly set down and count the cost of a war against France at this moment, and take into view all its frightful consequences, I believe we shall find that the true interest of our Country would dictate our rather making *very great* sacrifices to restore and maintain a good understanding between the two Republics.

"It may be said that it will degrade our national character to submit to purchase that justice which ought to be gratuitously rendered us. Before we decide, let us deliberately weigh the question.

"We may assure ourselves that if once we '*let slip the Dogs of War*,' *One hundred millions* of *Dollars* would not enable us to enchain them again. It should be remembered also, that the French Government and Cruizers acting under its authority already hold from our Citizens a property which may amount, perhaps, to *twenty millions of dollars*. It is probable that in case of a war, *that amount* would be irretrievably lost, in addition to the inevitable expence which hostile opperations would occasion, and which, like a rolling Snow-ball, would increase in magnitude in proportion to its progress; while the principal sources of our Public Revenue would diminish in an inverse ratio, if not be entirely exhausted. To these considerations a thousand other ill-consequences of the war might

7. Cutting to Thomas Jefferson, Feb. 19, 1798, Nathaniel Cutting Papers, Massachusetts Historical Society.

be added, which would demonstrate that this mode of supporting our '*national Honor and Dignity*' would prove a very dear bargain to us, and is totally incompatible with our present ability.

"Would it not be better policy to smother that useless Choler which almost suffocates us, and, instead of demanding what is justly due to us, come generously forward with *the offer of a Loan*? At first view, such a proposition may appear very extraordinary; but a slight examination of the subject will prove that the adoption of it might be productive of infinite advantage to the United States. At this critical period, when the Finances of France are so extremely extenuated by the prodigious Struggles she has been obliged so long to maintain against 'a World in arms,' such an aid would be peculiarly *apropos*, and the proposal dexterously managed, I am of opinion would retrieve the confidence and esteem of the Nation, would Sanctify the claims of our Citizens against the French Government, and would eventually be the most economical mode of effecting an accommodation.

"Let us suppose that, as a preliminary article, the French Government should agree to fund the *twenty millions* of *dollars* they may owe to our Commerce, as a Debt due to the United States; and of course that our own Government should undertake to satisfy each individual claimant; Suppose that in addition to this our Government should Loan to that of France, *Ten millions of Dollars more*, to be furnished in the course of a year; the whole *thirty millions of Dollars* to remain without interest during the continuance of the present war; but that both principal and interest should be reimbursed us within ten years after the establishment of a general Peace, at ten equal payments.

"The advantages the United States might derive from such an arrangement are almost as incalculable as the mischiefs that would inevitably result from their dashing into a War against France at the present moment.

"An important consideration is, that by adopting this measure immediately, we might do that with a tollerably good grace, which we may even be glad to do *essentially*, though perhaps under *another name*, at a later period, when we shall not be entitled to claim the smallest degree of merit from it.

"A strong suspicion is entertained by several Gentlemen of my acquaintance that whenever the *Directory* of *France* think proper to commence a negociation with our Commissioners, *It* will peremptorily make certain demands which will be *tantamount to a Loan*;

but probably the pecuniary aid *It* may *require* will never be placed on so favorable a footing for the United States as that which I have indicated above."

I must beg your pardon, Gentlemen, for the prolixity of this address. I hope you will do me the justice to attribute it to its true motives, an earnest solicitude for the success of your negociations, and the sincere wish that all your fellow-citizens may soon rejoice in the actual enjoyment of those advantages they have a right to expect from your acknowledged abilities and patriotism. Salut & Respect.

NAT. CUTTING.

From Caron de Beaumarchais

Draft, Private Collection

[*February 23, 1798, Paris.* Beaumarchais argues at length that the United States grant a loan to France because it would be less expensive than war. A refusal to grant the loan would reduce the United States to the status of Holland and Switzerland. He also suggests that one of the envoys be sent back to the United States to receive new instructions and the loan.[8]]

To Talleyrand

LS, RG 59, National Archives

Citizen Minister,[9] [Paris, February 26, 1798]

8. Beaumarchais indicated on this draft that he had sent a copy of this letter to Talleyrand.

9. This letter, which includes a request for the return of the envoys' passports, was never delivered to Talleyrand because Gerry refused to sign it. Pinckney sent the letter to Rufus King, asking him to send it on to Timothy Pickering, who had it filed with the regular dispatches in Diplomatic Dispatches, France, VI, RG 59, National Archives. See Pinckney to King, Mar. 14, 1798, King Papers, Library of Congress; King to Pickering, Apr. 7, 1798, Pickering Papers, Massachusetts Historical Society; Journal, Feb. 2, 5, 6, 14, 18, and 26, 1798.

JM and Pinckney had been waiting for Gerry to sign the letter, but Gerry refused after receiving what he considered a new proposition from Talleyrand. In a letter to his brother, Pinckney explained the circumstances of Gerry's refusal to sign. "After the letter to the Minister of foreign affairs, mentioned in our number Seven to the Secretary of State [see American Envoys to Pickering, Mar. 9, 1798], had been altered by Mr. Gerry in the manner he had thought proper, and it had been copied fair, translated and signed by General Marshall and myself, Mr. Gerry declined adding his signature, but told General Marshall he would do so when he arrived from the country, where he and General Marshall were going with a party for a few days. They returned

Since their letter of the 17th. of January[1] was prepared, the undersigned are informed by the journals that the legislative Councils of the French republic have decreed that

1st.[2] The condition of ships in every thing which concerns their character as neutrals or enemies shall be determined by their cargo; consequently every vessel, found at sea laden in the whole or in part with merchandize coming out of England or its possessions, shall be declared good prize, whoever may be the proprietor of such commodities or merchandize.

2ndly. No foreign vessel which in the course of its voyage shall have entered into an english port shall be admitted into any port of the french republic, but in the case of necessity; in which case such vessel shall be obliged to depart from such port so soon as the cause of entry shall have ceased.

---

on the twenty fourth of February, and on the twenty fifth I received a summons to meet my colleagues in the evening, when Mr. Gerry informed us, that a secretary [d'Autremont] of Mr. Talleyrand had called on him that morning, and had Suggested (though he said he was not authorised to do so by the minister, nor did he know whether he would approve it) a means of conciliation, which Mr. Gerry said he considered in a very different light from any that had been made us before: it was, to Stipulate a loan to the French government now, but not payable until after the war, in Supplies of our own, produce for St. Domingo and their Islands. . . . He would act with us, I believe, if General Marshall and myself would consent to take all the consequences which might possibly arise from our asking for our passports upon ourselves. This I should not hesitate to do, as I am convinced the French mean to amuse us until they see the event of their projected invasion on England; and if any thing could induce them to make a treaty with us at present, it would be an idea that we were earnest in departing, if we would not negociate on just and honorable terms, and that we were unanimous. We are restrained from demanding our passports without Mr. Gerry will really join us in it, on the apprehension of the division it might occasion in America, were it known we were divided on so important a measure." Pinckney to Thomas Pinckney, Mar. 13, 1798, Free Library of Philadelphia. Another copy is in the Pickering Papers.

Gerry wrote to Adams explaining his refusal to sign. "And here, it may be necessary to remark, that on the evening preceding the 22d of Feby when General Marshall & myself had agreed to visit Madam Villette, at her country seat, he informed me, that the letter to Mr. Talleyrand, demanding our passports, was ready, & proposed that we should sign it, & leave it with General Pinckney. I answered, that this was an unexpected proposition, that he knew we had engaged to go the next day to *Villette*, 30 or 40 miles distant, that on delivery of that letter to Mr Talleyrand, our passports would probably be sent to us, with an order to depart immediately, that my baggage was unpacked, & my bills were unpaid, that a day or two, at least would be requisite for these matters, but that I would send an apology to Madam Villette, would prepare immediately to leave the City, & would then sign the letter. This he declined, & preferred a postponement of the signature till our return. Soon after this, the proposition of a loan was made, to take place at the peace." Gerry to John Adams, July 8, 1799, Gerry Papers, Lib. Cong. For JM's comments on Gerry's refusal to sign, see JM to Charles Lee, Mar. 4, 1798.

1. See American Envoys to Talleyrand, Jan. 17, 1798.

2. This portion of the letter was included in American Envoys to Talleyrand, Apr. 3, 1798. Several words obscured by the binding have been supplied from that letter.

This decree too deeply affects the interests of the United States to remain unattended to by their ministers. They pray you, therefore, Citizen Minister, to receive their respectful representations concerning it.

The object of the decree is to cut off all direct intercourse between neutrals & Great Britain, or its possessions, & to prevent the acquisition, even by circuitous commerce, of those articles which come from England or its dominions.

The right of one nation to exchange with another the surplus produce of its labor, for those articles which may supply its wants or administer to its comfort, is too essential to have been ever classed among those admitted to be in any degree doubtful. It is a right in ceding which a nation would cede the privilege of regulating its own interests & providing for its own welfare. When any two nations shall chuse to make war on each other they have never been considered, nor can they be considered as thereby authorizing themselves to impair the essential rights of those who shall chuse to remain at peace. Consequently those rights, the free exercise of which is essential to its interests & welfare, must be retained by a neutral power, whatever nations may be involved in war.

The right of a belligerent to restrain a neutral from assisting his enemy by supplying him with those articles, which are defined as contraband has been universally submitted to; but to cut off all intercourse between neutrals & an enemy, to declare that any single article which may have come from the possessions of the enemy, whoever may be its owner, shall of itself be sufficient to condemn both vessel & cargo, is to exercise a control over the conduct of neutrals, which war can never give, & which is alike incompatible with their dignity and their welfare.

The rights of belligerents are the same. If this might be exercised by one, so might it be exercised by every other. If it might be exercised in the present, so might it be exercised in every future war. This decree is therefore on the part of France, the practical assertion of a principle which would destroy all direct or circuitous commerce between belligerent & neutral powers, which would often interupt the business of a large part of the world, and withdraw or change the employment of a very considerable portion of the human race.

This is not all. It is the exercise of a power which war is not admitted to give, and which may therefore be assumed in peace as well as war. It essentially affects the internal oeconomy of nations, and deranges that course of industry which they have a right to pursue, & on which their prosperity depends.

To acquiesce therefore in the existing state of things, under a principle so extensive & so pernicious, is to establish a precedent for national degradation, which can never cease to apply, & which will authorize any measures which power may be disposed to practise.

France therefore will perceive that neutral governments, whatever may be their dispositions towards this republic, are impelled by duties of the highest obligation to remonstrate against a decree, which at the same time invades their interests & their independence, which takes from them the profits of an honest and lawful industry, as well as the inestimable privilege of conducting their own affairs as their own judgment may direct.

It is hoped that the remonstrances of the United States on this subject will derive additional force from their subsisting engagements with France, and from a situation peculiar to themselves.

The twenty third article of the treaty of amity & commerce of the 6th. of Feby: 1778, is in these words, "It shall be lawful for all and singular the subjects of the most christian King, and the citizens, people and inhabitants of the said United States, to sail with their ships with all manner of liberty & security, no distinction being made who are the proprietors of the merchandizes laden thereon, from any port to the places of those who now are or hereafter shall be at enmity with the most christian King, or the United States. It shall likewise be lawful for the subjects and inhabitants aforesaid, to sail with the ships & merchandizes aforementioned, and to trade with the same liberty & security from the places, ports and havens of those who are enemies of both or either party, without any opposition or disturbance whatsoever, not only directly from the places of the enemy aforementioned to neutral places, but also from one place belonging to an enemy, to another place belonging to an enemy, whether they be under the jurisdiction of the same prince, or under several. And it is hereby stipulated, that free ships shall also give a freedom to goods, and that every thing shall be deemed to be free & exempt which shall be found on board the ships belonging to the subjects of either of the confederates, although the whole lading, or any part thereof should appertain to the enemies of either, contraband goods being always excepted. It is also agreed in like manner, that the same liberty be extended to persons who are on board a free ship, with this effect, that although they be enemies to both or either party, they are not to be taken out of that free ship, unless they are soldiers & in actual service of the enemy."

The two nations contemplating and providing for the case when one may be at war and the other at peace, solemnly stipulate and pledge themselves to each other, that in such an event the subjects or citizens of the party at peace may freely trade with the enemy of the other, may freely sail with their ships in all manner of security to and from any port or place belonging to such enemy. Nor is this all. Not only goods coming from the hostile territory, but the very goods of the enemy himself may be carried with safety in the vessels of either of the contracting parties.

You will perceive, citizen Minister, without requiring the undersigned to execute the painful task of drawing the contrast, how openly and entirely the decree of the Councils opposes itself to the treaty between France & the United States.

In addition to the hitherto unceded rights of a sovereign and independent nation, in addition to the rights stipulated by compact, the undersigned will respectfully submit other considerations growing out of the peculiar situation of the United States manifesting the particular hardships the decree complained of must impose on them.

In possession of a rich extensive & unsettled country, the labor of the United States is not yet sufficient for the full cultivation of its soil, and consequently but a very small portion of it can have been applied to manufactures. Articles of the first necessity & comfort are imported in exchange for provisions & for those raw materials, which are the growth of the country, & which its inhabitants are accustomed to raise. It is at any time extremely difficult, nor is it practicable without great loss, to change suddenly the habits of a whole people & that course of industry in which the state of their population & their real interests have engaged them. An agricultural cannot suddenly & at will become a manufacturing people; the United States cannot instantaneously, on the meer passage of a decree, transfer to the manufacture of articles heretofore imported, such a portion of their labor as will at the same time furnish a market for the surplus commodities, and a supply for the wants of the cultivator of the soil. It is therefore scarcely possible for them to surrender their foreign commerce.

Independent of the right they possess in common with others to search for & chuse the best markets, it is believed that the supplies they need could with difficulty, in the actual state of the world, be completely furnished without the aid of England and its possessions. It is not pretended that France manufactures at present for foreign consumption; nor do the undersigned suppose that there exists a market, where the citizens of the United States can obtain in exchange the articles they need & are accustomed to consume, if those coming out of England and its possessions be entirely excluded.

A variety of other considerations, & especially the difficulty individuals must encounter in suddenly breaking old & forming new connections, in forcing all their commerce into channels not yet well explored, in trading without a sufficient capital to countries where they have no credit, combine to render almost impossible an immediate dissolution of commercial intercourse between the United States & Great Britain.

If then the decree complained of shall be executed on American vessels, it can only increase grievances already but too considerable & transfer the carriage of english manufactures for american consumption from their own to british bottoms, sailing under the protection of a convoy. Instead of wounding England, it will probably aggrandize its marine by sacrificing the remnant of that of the United States, & by destroying that system of policy by which they have heretofore sought to give their own vessels that portion of their own carrying trade, which would otherwise be enjoyed by british merchants.

A[3] very essential object of the mission with which the undersigned are charged is to obtain a cessation of hostility against the commerce of their country. While under circumstances of painful humiliation, they are solliciting this cessation, a decree is passed, the necessary tendency of which is nearly to destroy that which they are deputed to save.

They can no longer resist the conviction, that under existing circumstances the demands of France render it entirely impracticable to effect the objects of their mission.

Not being permanent ministers, but Envoys extraordinary with full powers for particular purposes, they deem it improper to continue in Paris after the impossibility of effecting those purposes has been demonstrated. A due respect for the government of the United States commands them to retire from France, til the gov-

3. The remainder of the letter was not included in the letter to Talleyrand, Apr. 3, 1798.

ernment of the French republic shall be willing to consider and receive them as the representatives of their country, & shall be willing to enter upon an amicable discussion of the subjects of difference, which unhappily subsist between the two nations. America has uniformly displayed, in a manner not to be misunderstood, too much solicitude for this discussion, and for the accomodation which might result from it, to render it necessary for the undersigned to give any assurances of the promptness with which they would themselves return from any part of Europe for the purpose, or with which any fit occasion for entering on it will be embraced by the United States.

They now request that passports for leaving France may be furnished them; and beg leave to add that they are induced to this measure only by the conviction, that their longer continuance in this republic, while its government refuses to hear or to accredit them as ministers, would be improper, unavailing & inconsistent with the dignity of the United States. They trust therefore that their departure, which has become indispensably necessary, will not be considered as in any degree detracting from that earnest wish for reconciliation with France of which the government of the United States has given so many proofs, and which it will still continue to feel.

Accept, citizen Minister, the assurances of their respectful consideration.

CHARLES COTESWORTH PINCKNEY
J MARSHALL

To Talleyrand

LS, Archives of the Ministry of Foreign Affairs, Paris

Citizen Minister, Paris, February 27, 1798

The Envoys from the United States of America to the french Republic are solicitous of obtaining from you an interview on the objects of their mission. If this request meets your approbation, be pleased to name the time when they may have the honor to attend you.

Accept, citizen Minister, the assurances of their respectful consideration.

CHARLES COTESWORTH PINCKNEY
J MARSHALL
E GERRY

To Nathaniel Cutting

Letterbook Copy, Gerry Papers, Henry E. Huntington Library

Paris, February 27, 1798

We received your Letter of the 17th. at the time when Genl Marshall & Mr Gerry had formed the design of an Excursion for a day or two into the Country, which has delayed our answer.[4]

We are much obliged to you for your sentiment on the important objects of our mission, & assure you that we have viewed the subject with the utmost attention & solicitude in Every point of light which you have presented to us, & in many others, which the advantage of our situation has necessarily suggested. We have the honor to be, Your most obedt & very humbe Servts

Signed. C. C. PINCKNEY
J. MARSHALL
E. GERRY

To Charles Lee

AL, Free Library of Philadelphia

Dear Sir[5] Paris, March 4, 1798

4. JM and Gerry had gone to visit Madame de Villette at her country home. See Gerry to John Adams, July 8, 1799, Gerry Papers, Library of Congress; Mary Pinckney to Margaret Manigault, Mar. 9, 1798, Manigault Family Papers, University of South Carolina.

5. It has been assumed that John Adams was the recipient of this letter, but it is more likely that JM sent it to Charles Lee. There is no record of JM writing to Adams during the entire mission, but while in Europe he did write at least three letters to Lee. See JM to Lee, Sept. 22, Oct. 12, and Nov. 3, 1797. Neither Adams nor Timothy Pickering mentioned receiving any personal letters from the envoys with the set of dispatches carried by William Lee. Moreover, JM, with his usual style of deference and etiquette, would probably not have written to the president or secretary of state, "I have cursed a thousand times the moment when a sense of duty inducd me to undertake this painful embassy, but I must now make the best of it." Also, JM's explicit criticism of Gerry would not have been appropriate in a letter to President Adams.

The possibility that the letter might have been written to George Washington can be safely eliminated by JM's instructions for the recipient to read the enclosed letter of JM to Washington, Mar. 8, 1798. Moreover the code used in this letter is the same used in previous letters to Charles Lee, who, in addition to Pickering, was JM's only other correspondent in Philadelphia who had access to the official government code for the mission to France.

Pickering, in a marginal note on his deciphering of Pinckney to Thomas Pinckney, Mar. 13, 1798, Pickering Papers, Massachusetts Historical Society, identified d'Autremont as Talleyrand's secretary. Pickering stated that this information had come from

If[6] *you have received my former letters you will be surprised at the date of this. You will have expected that by this time we have either left Paris or are so near leaving it as not to think it worth*while *to write. Such has been my own opinion but I think it now perfectly uncertain what will be our course.*

We had prepared a letter remonstrateing against the late decree of the legislature concerning neutral vessells having on board any article coming out of England or its possessions which *letter Mr. Gerry corrected according to his own mind* and *it was translated. General Pinckney and myself signed it but Mr. Gerry refused to sign it. We had a serious conversation on the subject* and *he said he would sign it when we returned from a visit* in the *country we had agreed to make together and which was of three days continuanace. On our return Mr. Gerry said that he had received an accommodating proposition which changed the face of affairs* totally.[7] *Mr. Dutrimond the secretary of Mr. Taleyrand had called on him and spoken of a loan to be stipulated immediately and to be paid at the close* of the *present war. Dutrimond said he did not know that this government* would *agree to it but recommended it to Mr. Gerry to propose it as an accommodating proposition on our part. Mr. Gerry is decidedly in favor of it, General Pinckney and myself are decidedly* against *it. We think it a direct violation of our instructions and we think it impossible to stipulate a loan in such terms not to make the contract a security* on which *money may be raised for present purposes. Mr. Gerry is of opinion* that *our instructions rather imply power to make such a loan and that our refusal to make it will* inevitably *involve us in a war with France. Of consequence he refuses to join us in a determination against the loan. We have had a conversation with the minister, the result of* which will *be communicated in our public letter. We expect to see him in two or three days.*[8] *Finding it impossible to act in concert and dreading the consequence which an absolute division among ourselves may have in* the *United States and being uncertain what may be the will of our government I have proposed that Mr. Gerry and myself should return to the United States to lay the state of things before the government and obtain precise* instructions *how to act General Pinckney to remain here for orders. I am* induced *to make this proposition from a conviction that everything depends on the descent on England and that by going to the United*

a private letter, most likely this one. Lee probably gave the letter to Pickering, as he did other letters from JM.

6. Italics indicate words originally in code.

7. See JM and Pinckney to Talleyrand, Feb. 26, 1798, and Journal, Feb. 26, 27, and Mar. 3, 1798.

8. The meeting with Talleyrand took place on Mar. 6, 1798. See Journal, Mar. 6, 1798, and American Envoys to Pickering, Mar. 9, 1798.

States with our information *we shall put our country in a situation to defend itself as early and to take the same measures as if our negotiation was* absolutely *broken off and shall leave it perhaps the option to submit to the terms now offerred if such shall be its will. My proposition is agreed to by Mr. Gerry but we have no* absolute *confidence in* its *execution. We are so* convinced of the *importance of unanimity that we have made vast efforts to maintain it and would not have divided on* unessential *ground. But the question of a loan is one on which it is* impossible to *relinquish an opinion. When I see you I shall be able to demonstrate to you the value I set on our acting in union.*

I beg you not to mention the communication I now make as I am entirely unwilling *that our difference of opinion should be publicly known.*

March 10th.

We have had the Second conversation with the minister.[9] *It is now understood* completely *that the loan required is for immediate use, yet we shall not send our letter nor shall we demand our passports nor shall we go home (unless I go alone) to lay the actual state of things* fully *before our government nor shall we as I conjecture even press the French government in such a manner as to bring it to treat with us, if indeed it would treat* rather than *absolutely break off the* present *misarable negotiation unless we come to an open rupture among ourselves. Mr. Gerry* however *has agreed that a majority may decide* and *that he will not make known to this government our* differences *but he must be relieved in America respecting the war which our measure will produce. The point to which this leads is too apparent not to be seen by any person who knows the divisions of our country. Thus are we agreed. I have cursed a thousand times the moment when a sense of duty inducd me to undertake this painful embassy, but I must now make the best of it. I repeat my request that you will keep to yourself the conttents of this letter* except *so far as to let it be known that we wait the orders of this or our government.*

Read the inclosd & direct it to *General Washington.*[1]
The bearer Mr. Lee wishes a consulate in France. He is a gentleman of good connections & good character.[2]

9. JM was referring to the meeting of Mar. 6, 1798.

1. See JM to Washington, Mar. 8, 1798. These last three sentences are in JM's hand.

2. William Lee, of Boston, was later U.S. consul at Bordeaux. Lee also carried the official dispatch of American Envoys to Pickering, Mar. 9, 1798, back to Philadelphia. On Lee, see Mary Lee Mann, ed., *A Yankee Jeffersonian: Selections from the Diary and Letters of William Lee of Massachusetts, Written from 1796–1840* (Cambridge, Mass., 1958).

Memorandum

AD, Pinckney Family Papers, Library of Congress

[Paris, March 5, 1798]

Mem. of what was agreed by the Envoys to be said at a meeting with Mr: T.[3]

In answer to Mr: Talleyrand's proposition relative to a loan we consider it in effect the same as has been made at different periods by Mr: Hortinguer & Mr: Bellamy, & also directly to Mr: Gerry to be communicated to his Colleagues viz. a proposition of aid to be furnished by the United States to France during the present War; and we think it best candidly to declare to Mr: Talleyrand that this in addition to its being a measure amounting to a declaration of War against Great Britain is expressly forbidden by our Instructions. At the same time that we make this communication we shall consider it improper on all other occasions to be so explicit in what regards our Instructions.

If Mr: Taleyrand proposes a loan payable after the close of the War (& not negotiable directly or indirectly during the continuance of it),[4] the answer will be that ⟨we have maturely considered the subject, & that we cannot stipulate a loan in any form, we therefore hope that the Negotiation may proceed on its justice, but⟩ if a loan is an ultimatum with this Government such is our personal solicitude to accomodate subsisting differences between the two Republics that Genl: Marshall & Mr: Gerry will if that be agreeable to France immediately return to the United States to receive the instructions of our Government.

3. This is the written memorandum prepared by the envoys on Mar. 5 while discussing how to respond to Talleyrand's request for a loan. An abbreviated version appears in the Journal, Mar. 6, 1798, and in American Envoys to Timothy Pickering, Mar. 9, 1798. Gerry, in a marginal note in his letterbook copy, stated that the memorandum had been "committed to writing by Mr. Gerry in the morning before we met Mr. Talleyrand & repeated carefully by G Pinckney, who after the meeting said 'he thot he had got his lesson very well by heart.'" American Envoys to Pickering, Mar. 9, 1798, Letterbook, Gerry Papers, Henry E. Huntington Library. According to JM's Journal, Mar. 5, 1798, the envoys had written the memorandum the day before. The memorandum appears to be written in Pinckney's hand.

4. The section in parentheses was written as a footnote to the memorandum.

To George Washington

AL, Washington Papers, Library of Congress

Dear Sir[5] Paris, March 8, 1798

Before this reaches you it will be known universally in America that scarcely a hope remains of accomodating on principles consistent with justice, or even with the indepence of our country, the differences subsisting between France & the United States. Our ministers are not yet, & it is known to all that they will not be, recognizd, without a previous stipulation on their part, that they will accede to the demands of France. It is as well known that those demands are for money—to be usd in the prosecution of the present war. It was some little time past expected that, convinced of the unpracticability of effecting the objects of their mission, our ministers were about to demand their passports & to return to the United States. But this determination if ever made is, I am persuaded, suspended if not entirely relinquishd. The report has been that so soon as it shall be known that they will not add a loan to the mass of american property already in the hands of the government, they will be ordered out of France & a nominal as well as actual war will be commenced against the United States. My opinion has always been that this depends on the state of the war with England. To that object the public attention is very much turnd, & it is perhaps justly beleivd that on its issue is stakd the independence of Europe & America. The preparations for an invasion are immense. A numerous & veteran army lines the coast & it is said confidently that if the landing of 50,000 men can be effected, no force in England will be able to resist them. The often repeated tale that the

5. Washington read this letter to a small group of visitors at Mt. Vernon on June 13. According to one of the visitors, the ensuing conversation "aroused the passionate wrath" of Washington. "I have never heard him speak with so much candor nor with such heat. 'Whether,' he said, 'we consider the injuries and plunder which our commerce is suffering' (up to 50 million dollars) 'or the affront to our national independence and dignity in the rejection of our envoys, or whether we think on the oppression, ruin and final destruction of all free people through this military government, everywhere we recognize the need to arm ourselves with a strength and zeal equal to the dangers with which we are threatened. Continued patience and submission will not deliver us, any more than submission delivered Venice or others. Submission is vile. Yea, rather than allowing herself to be insulted to this degree, rather than having her freedom and independence trodden under foot, America, every American, I, though old, will pour out the last drop of blood which is yet in my veins.'" Julian Ursyn Niemcewicz, *Under Their Vine and Fig Tree: Travels through America in 1797-1799, 1805 with Some Further Account of Life in New Jersey*, trans. and ed., Metchie J. E. Budka (Elizabeth, N.J., 1965).

war is made not against the people but the government, maintains, in spite of experience some portion of its credit, & it is beleivd here that a formidable & organizd party exists in Britain ready, so soon as a landing shall be effected, to rise & demand a reform. It is supposed that England revolutionizd under the protection of a french army, will be precisely in the situation of the batavian & cisalpine republics & that its wealth, its commerce, & its fleets will be at the disposition of this government. In the meantime this expedition is not without its hazards. An army which arriving safe woud sink England may itself be encounterd & sunk in the channel. The effect of such a disaster on a nation already tired of the war & groaning under the pressure of an enormous taxation, which might discern in it the seeds of another coalition, & which perhaps may not be universally attachd to existing arrangements, might be extremely serious to those who hold the reins of government.

It is therefore beleivd by many who do not want inteligence that these formidable military preparations cover & favor secret negotiations for peace. It is rumord (but this is meer rumor) that propositions have been made to England to cede to her the possessions of Portugal in America, in consideration of her restoring the conquests she has made in France Spain & Holland & of her consent that Portugal in Europe shall be annexd to the spanish monarchy. This report is derivd from no source in any degree to be relied on, & is supported by no circumstance rendering it in any degree probable other than the existing disposition for partitioning & disposing of empires. I am however persuaded that some secret negotiation with England is now on the tapis. I know almost certainly that a person high in the confidence of this government, who is frequently employd in unofficial negotiation, has passed over into that island.[6] We can only conjecture his objects.

You probably know that the affairs of Rastadt are substantially decided. The Emperor & the King of Prussia have declard themselves in favor of ceding to France the whole territory on the left of the rhine on the principle of compensation in the interior of Germany. This woud seem to me to take from England the hope of once more arming Austria & Prussia in her favor, for certainly had those powers contemplated such an event they woud not have

6. JM was probably referring to Pierre Bellamy, who had gone to London. See Journal, Feb. 20, 1798; William Wickham to George Hammond, Feb. 16, 1798, F.O. 27/53, Public Record Office.

effected the pacification of the empire. This circumstance will probably influence the secret negotiations with England. It will probably too very much influence the affairs of Swisserland. The determination of France to revolutionize the helvetic body has been long known. In the pais de vaud belonging to the Canton of Berne the revolution has commenced & is completely affected under the protection & guidance of a french army for which that little country has already paid about 800,000 livres Swiss. France has insisted on extending the revolution throughout Swisserland. The existing governments in some of the cantons & especially in Bern declare their willingness to reorganize their constitution on the base of an equality of rights & a free representation, but they protest against foreign interposition & against a revolutionary intermediate government. In support of this resolution they have collected all their force & most of the cantons which have already changed their form of government have furnishd their contingents. The mass of the people in Bern are firmly united & seem to join the government in saying that they will to the last man bury themselves under the ruins of their country rather than submit to the intermeddling of foreigners in the formation of their constitutions. Such is the present truely interesting state of Swisserland. A powerful military force is advancing upon them & at the same time it is said that the negotiations are to be opend. The terms offerd however are supposd to be such as if accepted will place that country in the same situation as if conquerd. A revolutionary government is insisted on.

The Swiss have observd an exact neutrality throughout the late war on the continent & have even since the peace sought to preserve the forbearance of France by concessions not perfectly compatible with the rights of an independent nation.

On the side of Italy it is beleivd that materials are preparing to revolutionize Sardinia & Naples. Some jealousies exist with respect to Spain. Augereau has been orderd sometime since to Perpignan a position from which he may with advantage overawe that monarchy, invade Portugal or preserve order in the south during the insuing elections.[7] It is the common opinion that shoud the elections in any respect disappoint the wishes of the Directory it will be on the side of Jacobinism. The existing government appears to me to need only money to enable it to effect all its objects. A

7. JM was referring to Pierre François Charles Augereau (1757–1815), one of Napoleon's most trusted aides. Perpignan is in southern France.

numerous brave & well disciplind army seems to be devoted to it. The most military & the most powerful nation on earth is entirely at its disposal. Spain Italy & Holland with the Hanseatic towns obey its mandates. Yet there is a difficulty in procuring funds to work this vast machine. Credit being annihilated, the actual empositions of the year must equal the disbursements. The consequence is that notwithstanding the enormous contributions made by foreign nations France is overwhelmed with taxes. The proprietor complains that his estate yields him nothing. Real property pays in taxes nearly a third of its produce & is greatly reduced in its price. The patriotic gifts for the invasion of England to which men have been stimulated by all possible means have not exceeded by the highest calculation 100 000 livres. This is the amount stated by a person who charges the officers of the treasury with peculation. The treasury admits 65,000 livres. It is supposd that recourse will be had to a forced loan & that the neighbors of the republic will be requird to contribute still further to its wants. A very heavy beginning has been made with Rome.

March 10th.

The papers announce that the troops of France & Swisserland have had some severe encounters in which those of the latter have been worsted & the french have enterd Fribourg & Soleure.[8] Report (which as yet wants confirmation & indeed is disbeleivd) also says that Berne has submitted.

To Timothy Pickering

LS, RG 59, National Archives[9]

No. 7.

Dear Sir, Paris, March 9, 1798

Agreeably to what we represented to you in our No. 6,[1] we pre-

8. Fribourg is in western Switzerland; Soleure, or Solothurn, is in northwestern Switzerland on the Aar River.

9. A clerk wrote on the verso, "to Coll. Pickering, No. 7, Paris March 9, 1798, recd. June 1st., (forwarded by Mr. King from London Apl. 6.)."

Gerry believed that a copy of American Envoys to Talleyrand, Feb. 26, 1798, had been enclosed with this dispatch, but there is no evidence to confirm this. See American Envoys to Pickering, Mar. 9, 1798, Letterbook, Gerry Papers, Henry E. Huntington Library.

1. See American Envoys to Pickering, Feb. 7, 1798.

pared a letter to the minister of Foreign affairs on the subject of the late law authorizing the capture of neutral vessels on board of which any productions of Great Britain or its possessions should be laden, shewing how incompatible such law was with the rights of neutral nations and the treaty between France & America, its direct tendency to destroy the remaining commerce of our Country, and the particular hardships to which it would subject the agricultural as well as commercial interests of our Countrymen from the peculiar situation of the United States. We added that under existing circumstances we could no longer resist the conviction that the demands of France rendered it entirely impracticable to effect the objects of our mission, & that not being permanent ministers, but Envoys extraordinary with full power for particular purposes, we deemed it improper to remain longer in France after the impossibility of effecting those purposes had been demonstrated. Before however we took this measure and explicitly demanded our passports, we deemed it expedient to desire Major Rutledge to call on mr. Talleyrand on the 19th. ultimo to know if he had any communication to make to us in consequence of our letter dated the 17th. and delivered the 31st. of January. To this mr. Talleyrand replied, that he had no answer to make, as the Directory had not taken any order on the subject, and when they did, he would inform us of it. Still being anxious to hear explicitly from mr. Talleyrand himself before we sent our final letter whether there were no means within our powers of accomodating our differences with France on just and reasonable grounds, we wrote to him on the 27th: February soliciting a personal interview on the subject of our mission; he appointed the 2d. of March following. You will find in the exhibit A, herewith enclosed, what passed on that occasion. On the 4th: instant we requested another interview. We have detailed in the latter part of the same exhibit, for your information, the substance of that conversation. From these accounts you may observe that the views of France with regard to us, are not essentially changed, since our communications with its unofficial agents in October last. We have the honor to be with great respect, Your most obedt. hble. Servts.

CHARLES COTESWORTH PINCKNEY
J MARSHALL
E GERRY

Exhibit A[2]

⟦*March the second.* At *three o'clock we waited on Mr. Talleyrand*, and were *almost immediately introduced to him. General Pinckney commenced the conversation, by saying that our government* and *ourselves were extremely anxious to remove the subsisting difference between the two republics; that we had received many propositions, through Mr. Bellamy, to which we had* found it impracticable *to accede;* and *that we had now waited on him for the purpose of enquiring whether other means might not be devised, which would effect so* desirable an object. *The minister replied, that without doubt, the Directory wished very sincerely, on our arrival, to see* a *solid friendship established between France* and *the United States*, and *had manifested this disposition by the readiness with which orders for our passport were given.* That *the Directory had been extremely wounded by the last speech of General Washington, made to Congress when about to quit the office of President of the United States*, and by the *first and last speech of Mr. Adams.* That *explanations of these speeches were expected* and *required of us. General Pinckney expressed his surprize that the speech of General Washington was complained of;* and *said that this was a new complaint. Mr. Talleyrand merely observed, that the Directory was wounded at it;* and *proceeded. He said that the original favorable* disposition *of the Directory had been a good deal altered by the coldness* and *distance which we had observed.* That *instead of seeing him often*, and endeavoring to *remove the obstacles to a mutual approach, we had not once waited on him. General Pinckney observed, that when we* delivered *him our letters of credence, he informed us that the Directory in a few days would decide concerning us;* and that when the *decision was made, he would communicate it to us.*

That *this had for some time suspended any procedures on our part. He answered that this related only to our public character*, and not to *private visits. General Pinckney said, that on an application made by his secretary for a passport for an American under his care, he was told that he must apply to the office of police, for that America had no minister in France, since the recall of Mr. Monroe.* The *minister said that was very true:* and *then proceeded to say*, that *the Directory felt itself wounded by the different speeches of Mr. Washington and Mr. Adams, which he had stated*, and *would require some proof on the part of the United States of a friendly disposition, previous to a treaty with us. He then said that we ought to* search for and propose *some means which might furnish this proof:* that *if we*

2. Most of this exhibit was taken from the Journal, Mar. 2, 1798, and is printed here in open brackets (⟦ ⟧). Italics indicate words originally in code.

were disposed to furnish it, there could be no difficulty in finding it; and *he alluded very* intelligibly *to a loan. He said he had several conferences with Mr. Gerry on this subject, who had always answered, that we had no power. Mr Gerry said that he had stated other objections: that he had particularly urged that it would involve us in a war with Great Britain. He made no reply and General Pinckney observed that a loan had* repeatedly *been suggested to us that we had uniformly answered that it exceeded our powers. Mr. Talleyrand replied that persons at such a distance as we were from our government*, and *possessed as we were of the public confidence* must often *use their discretion* and *exceed their powers, for the public good.* That there was a material *difference between acting when instructions were silent, and doing what was particularly forbidden. That if indeed a loan was positively forbidden, we might consider ourselves as incapable of making one; but if as he supposed was the case, (he looked the question) our instructions were only silent at it* must *be* referred *to us to act in a case not* provided *for according to the best of our* Judgment, *for the public good: that in almost all the treaties made during the revolution, the negotiators had exceeded their powers* altho *the government* appointing *them was at no considerable distance. He particularized the treaty with* Prussia, *and several others. General Pinckney told him, that our powers did not extend to a loan,* and *perhaps* might *forbid it. The minister still urged the difference between an express* prohibition, *and meer silence. He then proceeded to state that the principal objection on the part of our government to* a *loan* must *be, that it would draw us out of the neutral* situation *in which we* wished *to continue: that there were* various *means of* avoiding *this; first, the secrecy of France which might be relied on;* and *secondly, means of* disguising *the loan might be devised which would* effectually *prevent its being considered as an aid during the present war: that if we were truly and sincerely* desirous *of effecting the thing we should* Experience *no difficulty in finding the means. He again stated a* proposition *of this sort on our part, as being* absolutely *necessary to prove that the Government was not about entering into a treaty with persons of a temper hostile to it.* Mr *Gerry, not well hearing* Mr *Talleyrand who* spoke *low asked him to explain himself with respect to the* proposition *which he had* alluded *to, supposing it to be* a *new one; and he* answered *that one of them was secrecy; but that there were besides* various *ways which might* easily *be suggested to cover the loan as an* immediate *one, by* limiting *the time of advancing it to distant instalments.* Mr *Gerry observed that Dutrimond had suggested that a loan was proposed to be made payable after the war* and in *supplies to* St. *Domingo.* Mr *Talleyrand* signified *that that might be one of the means used;* and *said that if we were only sincere in our wish it would be easy to bring about the end. General Marshall told* Mr *Talleyrand that if the ministers of the United States had manifested any* unwillingness *to take all proper measures to reconcile the two* republicks *or any indifference on the subject, they had very badly represented the* feelings *and wishes of their government; that the government of the United States was most sincerely* desirous *of preserving the* friendship *of France; and had, in his opinion* unequivocally *manifested that desire, by having deputed us, under the* extraordinary *circumstances attending our mission,* and *by having so long* patiently *borne the immense loss of property which had been sustained; that we had* endeavoured, *according to the best of our* Judgment *to represent truly this* disposition *of our government; but that we understood that France would consider nothing as an* Evidence *of friendship but an act which would transcend* and violate *our powers,* and *at the same time operate the most serious* Injury *to our country; that neutrality in the present war was of the last* importance *to the United States;* and *they had resolved* faithfully *to maintain it; that they had committed no act* voluntarily, *which was a breach of it; and could do nothing in secret, which, if known, would* Justly arrange *them among the* belligerent *powers; that in the present state of things, if America was* actually *leagued with France in the war, she would only be* required *to furnish money; that we had neither ships of war or men to be* employed *in it* and *could* consequently *as a* belligerent *power only be asked for money; that therefore, to furnish money was, in fact, to make war, which we could by no means consent to do, and which would absolutely transcend our powers; being an act* altogether *without the view and contemplation of our government, when our mission was decided on. That with respect to supplies to Saint Domingo, no doubt could be entertained that our merchants would furnish them very* abundantly, *if France would permit the commerce, & a loan really payable after the close of the war, might then be negociated. Mr. Talleyrand again marked the distinction between silence of instructions and an express prohibition; and again insisted on the necessity of our proving, by some means which we* must *offer, our friendship for the republic. He said he must exact from us, on the part of his government, some proposition of this sort; that to prove our friendship, there must be some immediate aid, or something which might avail them; that the principles of reciprocity would require it. General Pinckney* and *General Marshall understood him, by this expression, to allude to the loan formerly made by France to the United States. Mr. Gerry at the time thought he alluded to the treaty to be made; and said all treaties should be founded in reciprocity: and then asked him whether a loan was the ultimatum of this government? Mr. Talleyrand did not give a direct answer to the question. He said, as he was understood, that the government insisted on some act which would demonstrate our friendly disposition towards, and our good wishes for the republic. This once done, he said the adjustment of complaints would be easy: that would be matter of* enquiry *and if France had done us wrong, it would be repaired: but that if this was refused it would increase the distance and coldness between the two republics. The conversation* continued *in this stile until four o'clock: when we took our leave, and* agreed to *meet in the evening. In the course of it, and in reply to some observations of Mr. Talleyrand, respecting the proofs of friendship required by France, General Pinckney observed that our being here was a mark of the friendly disposition of our government, and that while we were here the government had passed a decree for seizing neutral vessels having on board any article coming out of England: which in its operation would subject to capture all our property on the ocean. Mr. Talleyrand replied, that this was not particular to us, but was common to all the neutral powers. At another time, in answer to his demand of some mark of our friendship, General Marshall observed that we considered the mutual interests of the two nations as* requiring *peace and friendship: and we relied on finding sufficient motives in the interest of France to preserve that friendship, without forcing us to an act* which *transcended our powers, & would be so injurious to our country. As we were taking our leave Mr. Talleyrand again noticed our not visiting him, and said, that he conceived our not having had an audience from the Directory ought not to have prevented it. General Marshall told him, that our seeing the Directory or not, was an object of no sort of concern to us; that we were perfectly indifferent with regard to it, but that we conceived that until our public character was in some degree recognized and we were treated as the ministers and representatives of our government, we could not take upon ourselves to act as ministers because by doing so we might subject ourselves to some* injurious *circumstance to which we could not submit. He said that was very true, but that we might see him as private individuals and discuss the objects of difference between us.*]

We requested of Mr. Talleyrand another interview at such hour *as might be convenient to him on the sixth instant. He answered, that he would receive us at half past eleven at which hour we attended him.*[3]

[*Immediately*[4] *after our* arrival *at his office we were introduced to the minister, and General Pinckney stated that we had considered with the most serious attention the conversation we had had the honor of holding with*

3. A marginal note in the Legation Book, Franklin Papers, Yale University, indicates that no copy was made of the note to Talleyrand in which the envoys requested another interview. No copy of the note has been found in the Archives of the Ministry of Foreign Affairs, Paris.

4. This is part of the Journal entry for Mar. 6, 1798.

him, a few days past, that the propositions he had suggested appeared to us to be substantially the same with those which had been made by Mr. Hottinguer, and by Mr. Bellamy, and also to Mr. Gerry, with an intention that they should be communicated to his colleagues: that we considered it as a proposition that the United States should furnish aid to France to be used during the present war: that though it was unusual to *disclose instructions yet we would declare to him, that in addition to its being a measure amounting to a declaration of war against Great Britain, we were expressly forbidden by our instructions to take such a step.*[5]

The minister said in the tone of a question, he supposed our instructions were to do nothing which would amount to a departure from our neutrality. General Pinckney said, that we were so instructed, and that they were still more particular. Mr. Talleyrand then proceeded to argue that it would be no departure from neutrality, to stipulate a loan payable after the war; and spoke of it clearly as admitting of application to immediate use. He said a good deal of the secrecy with which the transaction might be cloathed; *and observed further, that a loan payable after the war would be a proof of our faithful observance of the duties of neutrality, since it would be considered as proving that we had rejected propositions for an immediate loan. General Marshall replied, that we thought differently; that in our opinion any act, on the part of the American Government, on which one of the belligerent powers could raise money, for immediate use would be furnishing aid to that power, & would be taking part in the war. It would be, in fact, to take the only part which, in the existing state of things, America could take. This was our deliberate opinion; and in addition to it we considered our instructions as conclusive on this point.*

He observed, that we had claims on the French Government for property taken from American citizens. Some of these claims were probably just. *He asked, if they were acknowledged by France, whether we could not give a credit as to the payment,* say *for two years? We answered that we could. He then insisted that it was precisely the same thing; that by such an act we should consent to leave in the hands of France funds to which our citizens were intitled, and which might be used in the prosecution of the war. General Pinckney said there was a difference between the cases; that such prizes were now* actually *in the power of the French, without our consent; we could not prevent it, or get them out, but the granting or not granting a loan was in our own power. He repeated his observation: and General Marshall said, that the property for which money was due to American citizens from the French government, was taken into the possession of that Government*

5. See Memorandum, Mar. 5, 1798, and Journal, Mar. 6, 1798.

without any co-operation on the part of the United States. No act of any sort was performed by our Government, which in any degree contributed to place those funds in the hands of France; nor was there any consent towards it; but in the case proposed, the act would be the act of the Government; the Government would itself *place funds in the hands of France, and thereby furnish means which might be employed in the prosecution of the war. This was the distinction between the* cases; *and in a question of neutrality, it appeared to us to be all important. The minister then proceeded to state the case of our* assuming *the debt of our citizens; and of paying the money in that manner: but General* P[inckney] & Mr *Gerry told him we were positively forbidden to* assume *the debt to our own citizens, even if we were to pay the money directly to them. He seemed surprised at this. Genl.* P[inckney] *observed, that contrary to usage, we had deemed it proper, in the* existing *state of things, to state* candidly *our powers to him, that he might know* certainly *that we could not secretly, or under any* disguise *whatever, make* a *loan which might be used during the war.* Mr. *Talleyrand said he* must *resume his* position, *that there was a difference which he* must *insist upon between a loan payable* immediately, *and a loan payable in future,* and *he still* insisted *there was no difference between a loan payable in* future, *and a credit for the money which might be due to our citizens.* Mr. *Gerry observed, that his* colleagues *had* Justly *stated the distinction between the debt which will be due to the citizens of the United States from France, in* case *of her* recognizing *the claims which we shall make in their behalf, and a debt which might arise from a loan by the government of the United States to that of France, during the war. The one is the result of an arrest of the property without their consent, the other would be a* voluntary *act of the government of the United States, and a* breach *of their neutrality. There is an* additional *objection to the latter. If the United States should make such* a *loan, it would give too much reason to* suppose *that their government had consented, in a* collusive *manner, to the capture of the* vessels *of their citizens, and had thus been* furnishing *France with supplies to carry on the war. Our* instructions *are express not to stipulate any aids to France, either directly or indirectly, during the war. With respect to a secret* stipulation, *a loan cannot be made without an act of the* Legislature: *but if the Executive were* adequate *to it, we have had an* instance *of an* injunction *of secrecy on members of the Senate, on an important subject which one of the members thought himself warranted in publishing in the newspapers; and of frequent* instances *of secrets which have otherwise escaped. Secrecy in this* instance *might therefore be considered, if the measure was in itself* admissible, *as being impracticable. General Marshall observed, that we had considered the subject with great* solicitude, *and were decidedly of opinion, that we could not, under any form make a loan which could be used during the war; that we could not tell what our government would do if on the spot; but were* perfectly *clear, that without* additional *orders, we could not do what France requested.*

Mr. Gerry observed, that the government and nation of the United States as well as ourselves, were earnestly solicitous to restore friendship between the two republics; that, as General Marshall had stated, we could not say what our government would do, if on the spot, but if this proposition met the wishes of the government of France, General Marshall and himself had agreed immediately *to embark for the United States,* and *lay before our government the existing state of things here, as it respected our nation, to enable them to determine whether any, and what other measures on their part, were necessary. Mr. Talleyrand made no observation on this proposition: but enquired whether we expected soon to receive orders. Mr. Gerry mentioned an answer he had received to a letter sent by him in November; and General Marshall stated that our first dispatches were sent on board two vessels at Amsterdam on the twentieth of November; from which Mr. Talleyrand could form as just an idea as we could, when an answer might be expected: but he did not think it probable one would arrive before a month to come. General Marshall told him we knew that our government had not received our dispatches the eighth of January;* and *we could not tell when they might be received. He asked whether our* intelligence *came through England. General Marshall answered that it did not and General Pinckney said, that American papers as late as the eighth of January mention the fact.*

There was some *conversation about the time when these instructions might be expected; and General Marshall suggested a doubt whether our government might give any instructions. He asked with some surprise, whether we had not written for instructions?* and *we answered that we had not: and Mr. Gerry said that we had stated facts to our Government; and conceived that nothing more was necessary. General Pinckney observed, that the Government knowing the facts, would do what was proper;* and that *our applying or not applying for instructions would not alter their conduct. Mr. Talleyrand then enquired whether we had not sent any one to the United States. General Pinckney said no:* and *Mr. Gerry added, that soon after our arrival we made propositions to send one of our number which were not accepted, and General Marshall further added,* that those who had *communicated with us, had told us we should be ordered out of France* immediately and *we had supposed that we should be ordered out, before our letters could reach the Government. Mr. Gerry then observed, that the Government of France* must judge for itself; *but that it appeared to him, that a treaty on liberal principles, such as those on which the treaty of commerce between the two nations was first established, would be* infinitely more advantageous *to France than the trifling advantages she could derive from a loan. Such a treaty would produce a friendship* and *attachment, on the part of the United States, to France, which would be solid* and *permanent, and produce benefits far superior to those of a loan, if we had powers to make it.* To this *observation Mr. Talleyrand made no reply. We parted without any sentiment delivered by the minister on the subject of our going home to consult our government.*

As we were taking our leave of Mr. Talleyrand, we told him that two of us would return immediately *to receive the instructions of our Government; if that would be agreeable to the Directory: If it was not, we would wait some time, in the expectation of receiving instructions.*]

From Caron de Beaumarchais

Draft, Private Collection

[Paris, March 12, 1798]

Si Messieurs les Ministres de l'amerique ne se sont pas arrètés, en revenant de Passy, chez le Cn Beaumarchais.[6]

Il les prie pendant qu'ils sont dans le quartier, de [*ventôse*] bien lui faire l'honneur de repassée chez lui. Il a quelque chose qui les touche a [*leurs*] communiqués.

To Fulwar Skipwith

ALS, Collection of Justin G. Turner, Los Angeles

Sir Paris, March 13, 1798

We have receivd your letter of the 7th. inst.[7] accompanying a letter from Mr. Fenwick[8] to you & his accounts as Consul at Bordeaux.

We regret very much that any advances made for the citizens of the United States shoud not be immediately reimbursed but we have not the power, nor are we disposed to assume it, of settling

6. Beaumarchais wrote in the margin that the envoys were on their way to see Madame Dumas. For JM's description of the visit, see JM to George Washington, June 22, 1798.

7. Not found.

8. Joseph Fenwick.

or paying the accounts of the consuls. The Congress of the United States is about to act on the subject & we can not anticipate its resolutions. The liberation & restoration to their country of our distressed seamen is an object of so much magnitude that to attain it we have agreed to transcend our powers & have stated to you how far we can go. We cannot pass the limits markd in our letter to you of the 20th. of Decr. last.[9]

We trust that measures will soon be taken by the proper authority for liquidating all accounts against the United States. We are Sir very respectfully, Your obedt.

CHARLES COTESWORTH PINCKNEY
J MARSHALL
E GERRY

From Caron de Beauamrchais

Record Copy, Private Collection

Général Paris, March 16, 1798

Nous avons épuisé vous et moi tout ce qui concerne l'affaire de la réunion désirable de la france et de l'Amérique, Après que je vous ai montré mon profond désir du Succès de votre mission difficile, ⟨*et trop Courte*⟩

Ce n'est plus au Guerrier, ni au Ministre que je parle; C'est a mon deffenseur, sur l'amitié sur les talents duquel fonde mon nouvel espoir en Virginie. Je vous prie d'agréér de moi, Editeur de Voltaire, les oeuvres bien complettes du plus beau génie de la france.[1] Si je me hâte de vous les adresser; c'est pour que vous ayés le tems de les faire emballer avec Soin. Et qu'elles puissent, arrivant dans votre cabinet, bien conservéés, vous rappeler souvent quand nous nous Seront séparés l'ami de votre pays et le Vôtre.

To Caron de Beaumarchais

ALS, Private Collection

[Paris, *ca.* March 16, 1798]

Je reçoive votre Voltaire avec des sentimens que vous ne pouvez que faire elèver. Si j'ai senti des difficultés a cet egard, je vous prie

9. See American Envoys to Skipwith, Dec. 20, 1797.

1. Beaumarchais was referring to P. A. Caron de Beaumarchais *et al.*, eds., *Oeuvres complètes de Voltaire*, 70 vols. (Kiel, 1785–1789).

de croire que j'ai aussi senti trés fortement les motifs de ce don flatteur. Rien ne peutêtre plus èlégant que votre present ou plus delicat que votre maniere. Il n'y a que l'amité qui a mis Voltaire dans mes mains que je pourrois estimire encore plus que Voltaire. Ne jugez pas des mes sentimens de reconnaissance par mon François, mais croyez que je suis avec le plus haut estime & attachment. Votre

J MARSHALL

From Talleyrand

LS, Gerry Papers, Pierpont Morgan Library

Paris, March 18, 1798[2]

Le Soussigné Ministre des Relations extérieures de la République française a mis sous les yeux du Directoire exécutif le Mémoire que les Commissaires et Envoyés extraordinaires des Etats-unis de l'Amérique lui ont fait parvenir sous la date du 28 Nivôse der.,[3] et c'est en éxécution des intentions du Directoire, qui desire convaincre les Etats-unis des véritables dispositions qui l'animent à leur égard, que le Soussigné communique aux Commissaires et Envoyés extraordinaires les observations suivantes.

La premiere chose qui a dû frapper dans le Mémoire des Commissaires et Envoyés extraordinaires, c'est la méthode qu'ils ont jugé à propos de suivre dans l'exposition et dans la discussion des points qui sont en contestation entre les deux Etats.

Le Directoire éxécutif animé des dispositions les plus conciliantes et pénétré des intérêts qui doivent rapprocher les deux Nations autant qu'empressé de concourir au voeu bien connue des deux Peuples pour le maintien d'une intimité parfaite, avait lieu d'attendre que les Envoyés apporteraient au nom de leur Gouvernement des dispositions entierement analogues et un esprit préparé d'avance par les mêmes vues et par les mêmes desirs. Quel a dû être, d'après cela, l'étonnement du Directoire éxécutif quand le

2. A translated copy of this dispatch appears under June 18, 1798, *Annals of Congress*, IX, 3426–3433. The State Department copy was translated by Jacob Wagner and is in Diplomatic Dispatches, France, V, RG 59, National Archives. On Talleyrand's orders a copy of this dispatch was sent to Philadelphia with directions to have it published as soon as possible; it was published in the *Aurora* (Philadelphia), June 16, 1798. See Joseph Létombe to Talleyrand, June 29, 1798, Correspondance Politique, Etats-Unis, XLIX, Archives of the Ministry of Foreign Affairs, Paris.

3. See American Envoys to Talleyrand, Jan. 17, 1798.

Soussigné lui a rendu compte d'un mémoire dans lequel les Commissaries et Envoyés extraordinaires, en renversant l'ordre connu des faits, se sont attachés à passer en quelque sorte sous silence, les justes motifs de plainte du Gouvernement français, et a déguiser la véritable cause de la mésintelligence qui se prolonge entre les deux Républiques! Ensorte qu'il paraitrait, d'après cet exposé aussi partial qu'infidèle, que la République française n'a aucun grief réel a faire valoir, aucune réparation légitime à éxiger, tandis que les Etats-unis seraient les seuls admissibles à se plaindre, les seuls autorisés à réclamer des satisfactions.

Les intentions qui ont fait préferer cette marche à toute autre n'ont point échappé au Directoire éxécutif: et, c'est autant par un juste sentiment de la dignité de la République dont les intérêts lui sont confiés, que pour se prémunir éventuellement contre les vues qu'on pourrait se proposer par une semblable conduite, qu'il a chargé le Soussigné de faire disparaître ces vaines apparences, qui ne peuvent en effet subsister à l'instant que les faits auront été rétablis et que les véritables intentions du Directoire auront été solemnellement constatées, en opposition avec celles qu'on ne pourrait lui attribuer que gratuitement et en se prévalant de son silence.

Une vérité incontestable, et qui se trouve entierement écartée dans le Mémoire des Commissaires et Envoyés extraordinaires, c'est que l'antériorité des griefs et des plaintes appartient à la République française; que ces plaintes et ces griefs étaient aussi réels que nombreux, bien avant que les Etats-unis eussent la moindre réclamation fondée à élever, et par conséquent, avant que tous les faits sur lesquels les Envoyés appuient avec tant de détails, eussent existé.

Une autre vérité non moins incontestable, c'est que tous les griefs que présentent les Commissaires et Envoyés extraordinaires, sauf des exceptions que le Soussigné était prêt à discuter, sont une conséquence nécessaire des mesures que la conduite antérieure des Etats-unis avait justifiées de la part de la République française, et que ses traités avec les dits Etats unis autorisaient dans certains cas qu'il dépendait du Gouvernement général de l'Union de faire ou de ne pas faire éxister.

Il serait hors de propos d'entrer dans l'énumération des plaintes que le Gouvernement français avait lieu d'élever contre le Gouvernement fédéral depuis le commencement de la guerre suscitée à la République française, par une Puissance jalouse de sa prospérité et de sa régénération. Ces détails sont consignés dans les offices nombreux passés à Philadelphie par les Ministres de la République, et ils ont été récapitulés par le Prédecesseur du Soussigné, dans une note adressée sous la date du 19 Ventôse an 4e au Ministre plénipotentiaire des Etats-unis à Paris, et exposés très en détail dans l'office passé à Philadelphie par le Citoyen Adet le 25 Brumaire de l'an 5.[4] On se plaignait dans la note ci-dessus de l'inéxécution des traités conclus en 1778, dans les seules clauses où la france eut stipulé quelques avantages en retour des efforts qu'elle s'était engagée à faire pour l'utilité commune; et l'on y réclamait contre des insultes faites à la dignité de la République française.

Dès le commencement de la guerre, en effet les Tribunaux Américains ont prétendu au droit de prendre connaissance de la validité des prises menées dans les Ports des Etats-unis par des Croiseurs français. Il est résulté de cette prétention contraire à la lettre du Traité de Commerce de 1778 que les proprietés des Citoyens de la République ont été injustement détenues, et que l'on a totalement découragé la Course française dans les Mers de l'Amérique contre un Ennemi qui en fesait revivre les lois les plus barbares pour détruire et insulter le Commerce américain sous les yeux même du Gouvernement fédéral.

On ne se connait pas à favoriser les Ennemis de la République française dans un point aussi essentiel; point sur lequel il pouvait à la vérité survenir quelques abus, mais que le Gouvernement français se montrait disposé à prévenir; on allait encore jusqu'à permettre aux Vaisseaux ennemis, contre le sens textuel du Traité ci-dessus, de relâcher dans les Ports des Etats-unis après avoir capturé *des propriétés ou des Bâtimens appartenans à des Citoyens français*. Bientôt après, on arrêta, par ordre du Gouvernement, une Corvette nationale mouillée dans le Port de Philadelphie (Arrestation du Cassius Août 1795), et cette arrestation s'étendit ensuite jusqu'au Capitaine Commandant. Les Tribunaux américains se saisirent de même de la personne de l'Ex-Gouverneur de la Guadeloupe pour faits de son administration, et il a fallu que le Directoire éxécutif menaçat d'user de représailler pour faire prendre à cette affaire le cours que le droit des Gens lui assignait.[5]

4. The list of French grievances was included in Charles Delacroix to James Monroe, Mar. 9, 1796, Correspondance Politique, Etats-Unis, XLV. The Adet pamphlet, printed in French and English, is listed under Pierre-Auguste Adet to Timothy Pickering, Nov. 15, 1796, *ibid.*, XLVI.

5. Talleyrand was referring to Gen. George Victor Collot, the former governor of Guadeloupe who, while waiting to be exchanged as a prisoner of war of Great Britain, was sued for damages by a Philadelphia merchant for duties undertaken as governor.

Pendant tout l'espace de tems qu'on vient de parcourir le Gouvernement français fit de vains efforts pour déterminer le Gouvernement des Etats-unis à procurer aux Agens de la République les moyens légaux de faire éxécuter les clauses de la convention consulaire de 1788 qui accordaient à notre navigation et à notre Commerce des privilèges dont le principe était consacré par les Traités de 1778; et jamais on ne put obtenir, à cet égard, que des renvois infructueux aux Tribunaux. En général, toutes les matieres qui, avec des intentions sincèrement conciliantes, auraient pu se terminer par voie de négociation, étaient habituellement déférées aux autorités judiciaires: et celles-ci, Soit qu'elles fussent, ou non, soumises à une influence secrette, privaient, en derniere analyse, la République des droits fondés sur les Traités, ou bien en modifiaient l'éxercice selon qu'il convenait au systême du Gouvernement.

Tel était l'état véritable des choses au mois d'août 1795, époque où la ratification d'un Traité d'amitié, de Navigation et de Commerce signé à Londres dans le mois de Novembre précédent, entre les Etats-unis et la Grande-Bretagne vint mettre le comble aux griefs de la République.[6]

Quelle avait été jusques-là la conduite du Gouvernement français envers les Etats-unis? Le Soussigné, pour en faire voir le contraste avec celle des dits Etats, se contentera de rappeller des faits qui ne peuvent toutes fois avoir été oubliés.

Occupée des soins les plus pressans en Europe, la République n'avait porté ses regards sur les Etats-unis que pour leur donner constamment des preuves nouvelles de l'amitié et de l'intérêt les plus sincères, et elle laissait à ses agens à discuter à l'amiable avec le Gouvernement fédéral les contestations dont on vient de tracer une esquisse et qui, si elles eussent été traitées de part et d'autre avec un véritable esprit de conciliation, n'auraient pu altérer la bonne intelligence au point où elle l'est en ce moment. La République était à peine constituée qu'on envoya un Ministre à Philadelphie dont la premiere démarche fut de déclarer aux Etats unis qu'on ne les presserait point d'éxécuter les clauses défensives du Traité

On the suit, see Létombe to Delacroix, July 25, 1797, and Létombe to Talleyrand, Nov. 12, 1797, Frederick J. Turner, ed., *Correspondence of the French Ministers to the United States, 1791-1797*, American Historical Association, *Annual Report, 1903*, II (Washington, D.C., 1904), 1054–1055, 1078–1079; George W. Kyte, "The Detention of General Collot: A Sidelight on Anglo-American Relations, 1798–1800," *WMQ*, 3d Ser., VI (1949), 628–630.

6. Talleyrand was referring to the Jay Treaty.

d'alliance, quoique les circonstances représentassent de la maniere la moins équivoque, le *casus foederis*.[7] Loin d'apprécier cette conduite, le Gouvernement Américain la reçut comme la reconnaissance d'un droit, et c'est dans cet esprit encore que les Commissaires et Envoyés extraordinaires ont abordé cette question au commencement de leur mémoire. Le Ministre de la République à Philadelphie ayant donné de l'inquiétude au Gouvernement Américain fut rappellé avec empressement et même avec des circonstances extrêmement rigoureuses. Son Successeur porte aux Etats-unis toutes les réparations désirables ainsi que les déclarations les plus amicales et les plus sincères. Rien n'égale l'esprit de conciliation ou plûtôt de condescendance dans lequel ses instructions étaient rédigées relativement a tous les points qui avaient causé quelques inquiétudes au Gouvernement fédéral. Le Cit. Adet renforça encore, au nom de la Convention nationale, ces expressions de bienveillance; et cette Assemblée elle-même accueillit avec l'effusion d'une confiance et d'une sécurité sans bornes le nouveau Ministre que le Président des Etats-unis envoya auprès d'elle avec l'intention apparente de correspondre sincèrement aux dispositions que la République n'avait cessé de professer.

Ce qui doit paraître incroyable, c'est que la République et son alliance étaient sacrifiées au moment où elle redoublait ainsi d'égards pour son Alliée et que les démonstrations correspondantes du Gouvernement féderal n'avaient pour but que de la maintenir ainsi que son Gouvernement dans une fausse sécurité. Et cependant il est connu aujourd'hui que c'est à cette même époque que Mr. Jay qui avait été envoyé à Londres, seulement, disait-on alors, pour négocier des arrangemens relatifs aux déprédations éxercées sur le Commerce Américain par les Croiseurs de la Grande Bretagne, signait un Traité d'Amitié, de Navigation et de Commerce dont à Paris et à Philadelphie on a tenu la négociation et la signature dans le plus grand secret. Ce Traité ne fut avoué à notre Ministre plénipotentiaire qu'à la derniere extrêmité, et il ne lui fut communiqué que pour la forme et après, qu'il eut reçu la ratification du Sénat. Lorsque les Agens de la République se sont plaints de cette conduite mystérieuse, on a répondu en invoquant l'indépendance des Etats-unis solemnellement consacrée dans les Traités de 1778: maniere étrange de combattre un grief dont la dissimulation à laquelle on a eu recours démontre la réalité; subterfuge insidieux

7. On Genet's declaration, see Dumas Malone, *Jefferson and the Ordeal of Liberty* (Boston, 1962), 96–98.

qui substitue au vrai point de la question un principe général que la République ne pouvait pas être soupçonnée de contester, et qui détruit à l'aide d'un sophisme cette confiance intime qui doit éxister entre deux alliés, et qui surtout devait éxister entre la République française et les Etats-unis.

S'il est difficile de trouver dans cette conduite celle qu'on doit attendre d'un Ami, que doit-on penser du Traité même et de ses clauses? Ce Traité est aujourd'hui connu de toute l'Europe, et la faible majorité à laquelle il a passé dans les deux Chambres, ainsi que la multitude de voeux imposans qui se sont prononcés dans la Nation contre un tel acte, déposent honorablement en faveur de l'opinion qu'en a portée le Gouvernement français. Le Soussigné ne répétera point à l'égard de ce Traité ce que son Prédécesseur en a dit dans sa note du 19 Ventôse précitée et dans celle du 19 Messidor suivant et ce que le Ministre Plénipotentiaire de la République à Philadelphie a exposé très au long dans son Office du 25 Brumaire. Il se contentera d'observer sommairement que dans ce Traité, tout ayant été prévu pour faire tourner la neutralité des Etats-unis au désavantage de la République française et à l'avantage de l'Angleterre; que le Gouvernement fédéral ayant fait dans cet acte à la Grande Bretagne les concessions les plus inouies, les plus incompatibles avec les intérêts des Etats-unis, les plus dérogatoires à l'alliance qui éxistait entre les dits Etats et la République française; celle-ci a été parfaitement libre de se prévaloir pour parer aux inconvéniens du Traité de Londres, des moyens conservatoires que lui fournissaient le droit naturel, le droit des Gens et les Traités antérieurs.

Telles sont les raisons qui ont déterminé les arrêtés du Directoire dont se plaignent les Etats-unis, ainsi que la conduite de ses Agens aux Antilles. Toutes ces mesures ont pour principe l'article 2 du Traité de 1778 qui veut qu'en matiere de navigation et de commerce la France soit toujours à l'égard des Etats-unis Sur le pied de la Nation la plus favorisée. On ne peut s'en prendre au Directoire éxécutif si de l'éxécution de cette clause éventuelle il est résulté quelques inconvéniens pour le Pavillon Américain. Quant aux actes abusifs qui pouvaient sortir de ce principe, le Soussigné répète encore qu'il était prêt à les discuter de la maniere la plus amicale.

De cet exposé fidèle des faits qui ont progressivement amené entre les deux Etats la mésintelligence actuelle, il résulte, comme l'a dit le Soussigné en commençant cette réponse, que l'antériorité des griefs appartient à la République française et que celles de ses mesures qui ont pu motiver les plaintes des Etats unis sont, à quelques exceptions près, la conséquence naturelle d'un état de choses qu'il a dépendu d'eux de faire ou de ne pas faire éxister.

Le Soussigné, en terminant au Traité de Londres l'exposition des griefs de la République, ne remplirait qu'imparfaitement sa tâche, et il est de son devoir de porter plus loin ses regards.

Dès qu'une fois le Traité dont il s'agit eut été mis à éxécution, le Gouvernement de Etats-unis sembla se croire dispensé de garder aucune mesure envers la République, malgré l'assurance réitérée qu'on avait donnée à ses Ministres que ce Traité ne changerait rien à l'état préexistant de la neutralité des Etats-unis, on notifia dans le cours de l'année 1796 aux Croiseurs français qu'ils ne pouvaient plus, comme jusqu'alors cela s'était pratiqué, être admis à vendre leurs prises dans les Ports des Etats-unis. Cette décision fut rendue par la Cour fédérale de justice et motivée sur le Traité conclu entre les Etats-unis et la Grande Bretagne.

Les Journaux connus pour être sous le Contrôle indirect du Cabinet, ont depuis le Traité, redoublé d'invectives et de Calomnies contre la République et contre ses principes, ses Magistrats et ses Envoyés; des pamphlets ouvertement soudoyés par le Ministre de la Grande-Bretagne, ont reproduit sous toutes les formes, ces insultes et ces calomnies, sans que jamais un état de choses aussi scandaleux ait attiré l'attention du Gouvernement qui pouvait le réprimer. Au contraire, le Gouvernement lui-même s'est attaché dans ses actes publics à encourager ce scandale. Le Directoire éxécutif s'est vu dénoncer dans un discours prononcé par le Président dans le cours du mois de Mai der. (v:s:)[8] comme cherchant à propager l'anarchie et la division dans les Etats unis.[9] Les nouveaux Alliés que la République s'est faits et qui sont les mêmes qui contribuèrent à l'indepéndance des Américains ont été également insultés dans des correspondances officielles qui ont été rendues publiques, ou dans les Journaux. Enfin on ne peut s'empêcher de reconnaître dans le ton des discours et dans celui des publications qu'on vient d'indiquer, une inimitié sourde qui n'attend que le moment pour éclater.

Les faits ainsi rétablis, il est fâcheux d'avoir à penser que les instructions d'après lesquelles ils ont agi n'ont point été rédigées dans l'intention sincère d'arriver à des résultats pacifiques; puisque

8. Vieux style.

9. Talleyrand was referring to Adams's speech at the opening of Congress, May 16, 1797, *Annals of Congress*, VII, 54–59.

loin de partir dans leur mémoire de quelques principes avoués et de quelques faits reconnus, les Commissaires ont interverti et confondu les uns et les autres, de maniere à pouvoir imputer à la République tous les malheurs d'une rupture qu'on semble vouloir amener par une marche semblable. Il est évident que le desir bien prononcé de soutenir à tout prix le Traité de Londres qui est le principal grief de la République; d'adhérer à l'esprit dans lequel ce Traité a été conçu et éxécuté, et de n'accorder à la République aucun des moyens de réparation qu'elle a proposés par l'organe du Soussigné, ont dicté ces instructions. Il est également évident que l'on n'hésite pas à sacrifier à ces sentimens étranges ceux que devraient inspirer les Traités de 1778 et le souvenir des circonstances au milieu desquelles ils ont été conclus.

Les conséquences éloignées d'une pareille conduite n'ont point échappé à l'attention du Directoire. On desire, en n'omettant rien pour prolonger la mésintelligence et l'augmenter encore, en rejetter sur la République tout l'odieux aux yeux de l'Amérique et de l'Europe: on cherche à justifier par des apparences trompeuses les préventions dont on entoure à plaisir le nom de la République, et le systême d'éxasperation et d'éloignement qu'on suit à son égard avec la plus étrange obstination: on veut enfin saisir la premiere occasion favorable pour consommer une union intime avec une Puissance envers laquelle on professe un dévouement et une partialité qui sont depuis longtems le principe de la conduite du Gouvernement féderal.

Les intentions que le Soussigné attribue ici au Gouvernement des Etats-unis sont si peu déguisées qu'on semble n'avoir rien négligé à Philadelphie pour les manifester à tous les yeux. C'est vraisemblablement dans cette vue que l'on a jugé à propos d'envoyer vers la République française des Personnes dont les opinions et les relations sont trop connues pour en espérer des dispositions sincèrement conciliantes. Il est pénible pour le Soussigné d'être obligé de relever le contraste de cette conduite avec celle qu'on a tenue envers le Cabinet de St. James dans des circonstances analogues. On s'est empressé alors d'envoyer à Londres des Ministres bien connus par des sentimens conformes à l'objet de leur mission. La République aurait dû compter, ce semble, sur une déférence pareille, et si l'on n'a point observé à son égard les mêmes convenances, il est beaucoup trop vraisemblable qu'il faut l'attribuer aux vues indiquées plus haut par le Soussigné.

Il est impossible de prévoir où peuvent conduire de telles dispositions. Le Soussigné n'hésite point à croire que la Nation Américaine comme la Nation Française voit avec regret cet état de choses et n'en envisage les conséquences qu'avec douleur. Il estime que le Peuple Américain ne se méprendra ni sur les préventions qu'on a voulu lui inspirer contre un Peuple Allié, ni sur les engagemens qu'on semble vouloir lui faire contracter au détriment d'une Alliance qui a si puissamment contribué à le mettre au rang des Nations et à l'y maintenir, et qu'il verra dans ces combinaisons nouvelles les seules dangers qui peuvent courir sa prospérité et sa considération.

Pénétré de la justesse de ces réflexions et de leurs conséquences, le Directoire éxécutif a autorisé le Soussigné à s'exprimer avec toute la franchise qui convient à la Nation Française. Il était indispensable qu'au nom du Directoire éxécutif il dissipât ces prestiges dont on n'a depuis cinq ans cessé d'entourer à Philadelphie les plaintes des Ministres de la République pour les atténuer, les calomnier ou les travestir: il était instant enfin qu'en fesant connaître ses sentimens d'une manière non équivoque il éclaircît tous les doutes et toutes les fausses interprêtations dont ils auraient pu être l'objet.

C'est donc uniquement dans la vue d'applanir la voie des discussions que le Soussigné est entré dans les développmens qui précèdent. C'est dans la même vue qu'il déclare aux Commissaires et Envoyés extraordinaires que malgré la sorte de prévention qu'on a pu concevoir sur eux, le Directoire éxécutif est disposé à traiter avec celui d'eux trois dont les opinions présumées plus impartiales promettent dans le cours des explications plus de cette confiance réciproque qui est indispensable.[1]

Le Soussigné se flatte que cette ouverture ne souffrira de la part des Commissaires et Envoyés extraordinaires aucune difficulté sérieuse; il est d'autant plus naturel de l'espérer que par la teneur de leurs Pouvoirs les dits Commissaires et Envoyés extraordinaires sont autorisés à négocier conjointement ou *séparément*; ensorte que le desir seul de prévenir tout accommodement pourrait élever quelque objection contre cette mesure qu'on ne fait au reste qu'indiquer aux Commissaires eux-mêmes pour que rien ne porte ici un caractére de défaveur et qui évidement n'a d'autre objet que d'assurer à la négociation une heureuse issue en écartant d'abord tout ce qui

1. This was Talleyrand's primary purpose in answering the American envoys. He had submitted a memoir to the Directory, *ca.* Feb. 3–18, 1798, proposing that two of the envoys be sent home and that Gerry, the most favorably inclined, be retained. Stinchcombe, "WXYZ Affair," *WMQ*, 3d Ser., XXXIV (1977), 610–611.

pourrait de part et d'autre réveiller dans le cours de cette Négociation des sentimens capables de la compromettre.

Le Soussigné espère que les Commissaires et Envoyés extraordinaires le mettront bientôt en état de rendre compte au Directoire éxécutif de leur détermination. Quelle que puisse être cette détermination, le soussigné se flatte que les explications dans lesquelles il est entré auront mis la question dans son vrai jour; pourront éventuellement servir à dissiper aux yeux de tous les hommes impartiaux l'impression défavorable dont on chercherait à atteindre les intentions de la République Française et de son Gouvernement. Il termine par renouveller aux Commissaires et Envoyés extraordinaires l'assurance de sa Considération.

CH. MAU. TALLEYRAND.

To Caron de Beaumarchais

ALS, Private collection

Monsieur [Paris, *ca.* March 22, 1798]

Je vous prie de croire que la politesse & la bonté qui ont dicté le don trés élégant que vous m'avez offert, ont fait sur moi une impression que le tems ne peut pas effacer. Je ne vous ai pas dit jusqu'ici qu'il n'etoit pas possible de l'accepter parceque j'avais l'esperance la plus forte que l'etat relatif de nos deux pays me laisseroit le pouvoir d'y repondre. Cette esperance devient si foible que je n'ose pas m'y fier. Il faut donc que je vous prie de pardonner le renvoi de votre present & de croire que cette marque estimable de votre amitié a fait sur moi une impression aussi profonde que si ma situation m'avoit permis de la retenir.[2]

Acceptez les assurances trés vrais quoique fuites en tres mauvais françois de mon estime.

J MARSHALL

From Timothy Pickering

ALS, Gerry Papers, Pierpont Morgan Library[3]

Gentlemen, Philadelphia, March 23, 1798

On the 4th instant came to hand your first dispatches since your

2. The gift JM returned was probably the edition of Voltaire's works mentioned in Beaumarchais to JM, Mar. 16, 1798.

3. This letter has been transcribed from the quintriplicate copy that Gerry received on May 29, 1798; it is the only copy with a postscript. Gerry decoded an earlier copy.

arrival at Paris; these were your numbers 1. 4. & 5; and on the 6th instant your numbers 2 and 3 were received.[4] On the 5th. your No. 5, dated the 8th of January, and a translation of the message of January 4th from the Directory to the Council of Five Hundred, were laid before Congress. In this letter you "repeat, that there existed no hope of your being officially received by that government, or that the objects of your mission would be in any way accomplished."

This[5] opinion is sanctioned by the whole tenor of your communication and we trust that soon after the date of your number five you closed your mission by demanding passports to leave the territtories of the French Republic.

An official copy of your letters of credence having been delivered to the Minister for Foreign Affairs, and by him laid before the Directory, they were sufficiently informed of the great objects of your mission; & considering that you were an extraordinary delegation from an independent nation, you had a right to expect a prompt and respectful reception. The fair and honourable views of the American Government which dictated your appointment and your powers, entitled you to expect the early appointment of a commission by the French Government, with equal powers, to negociate on all the matters in controversy between them. *Had the french Government been influenced by similar views the object of your mission would long since have been accomplished to the advantage and peace of both nations but instead of coming forward on such equal and proper ground they have treated you and thro you your country with extreme neglect.*

Under these circumstances the president presumes that you have long since quited Paris and the French dominions. Yet actuated as you were with an ardent desire to preserve peace which you knew would be so grateful to your country and having for this object manifested unexampled patience and submitted to a series of mortifications as you also propose to make one more direct attempt subsequent to the date of your last letter to draw the French government to an open negotiation, there is a bare possibility that this last effort may have succeeded. The president therefore thinks it proper to direct:

First, that if you are in treaty with persons duly authorised by the Directory on the subject of your mission then you are to remain and expedite the completion of the treaty. If it should not have been concluded before this letter gets to hand you will have ascertaind whether the negotiation is or is not conducted with candour on the part of the French Government. And if

4. See American Envoys to Pickering, Oct. 22, Nov. 8, 27, Dec. 24, 1797, and Jan. 8, 1798.

5. Italics indicate words originally in code.

you shall have discoverd a clear design to procrastinate you are to break off the negotiation, demand your passports and return; for you will consider that suspence[6] *is ruinous to the essential interest of your country.*

Second, that if on the receipt of this letter you shall not have been received, or whether received or not, if you shall not be in treaty with persons duly authorised by the Directory with full and equal powers you are to demand your passports and return.

Third, in no event is a treaty to be purchased with money by loan or otherwise. There can be no safety in a treaty so obtained. A loan to any republic would violate our neutrality and a douceur to the men now in power might by their successors be urged as a reason for annulling the treaty as a precedent for further and repeated demands.

It is proper to apprize you that a motion has been made in the Senate and will doubtless be repeated in the House of Representatives to desire the president to lay before them your communications and he will probably be under the necessity of doing it only withholding the two[7] *names which you promised should in no event be made public.* I have the honor to be, with great respect, Gentlemen, your obedient Servant,

TIMOTHY PICKERING

April 9.[8] Pursuant to a call of the House of Representatives, the President laid before Congress your dispatches No. 1. to 5. in confidence; *submitting it to their wisdom when to make them public. In a few days the Senate ordered them to be printed; and the House of Representatives afterwards did the same. This morning they have been published.* I have received no letter from you later than your No. 5.

T. PICKERING.

From Rufus King

LS, Gerry Papers, Pierpont Morgan Library

Gentlemen, London, April 2, 1798

It[9] *should be known to you that South America is on the eve of revolution. England has prepared; she waits only for the events that the march of the French army into Spain will effect to send an expedition to commence the*

6. This word is underlined in the manuscript.
7. Pickering made a coding error here; five names were withheld.
8. This postscript has been decoded by the editors from the quintriplicate copy.
9. Italics indicate words originally in code. King made several minor encoding errors that the editors have silently corrected.

revolution which shall make South America independant. If it is not assisted to become independant by England, the work will be done by France who will introduce there her detestable principles, divide it into small republics, put bad men at their head, and by these means facilitate her meditated enterprizes against us. We have an immense interest in the event as well as in the manner in which it shall be accomplished. England will at Philadelphia ask the cooperation of the United States. France has formed and will not be diverted from her plan respecting the United States. Your mission must therefore fail and if so the sooner the better. Tho I understand that Humphries[1] *has received assurances that our treaty with Spain shall be carryed into execution I do not believe it.*

France expects to find un point d'appui *in Louisiana and to begin from thence her operations against the United States. The treaty must then remain inexecuted it will serve the same purpose as* the obsolete Treaty respecting the Pays de Vaud or the ancient Disputes between Rome and Naples.

The French system once established in South America and the West Indies we shall be in perpetual risque. On the other hand the independance of South America only will put an end to the old colony and commercial system and with obvious combinations presents wealth and security to the United States and a new balance among nations. This communication *is most strictly confidential.* With sincere attachment, I am, Gentlemen, Your ob: & faithful Servant,

RUFUS KING

P.S. Your No. 6 went with the Convoy which sailed on the 18. ultimo. Your No. 7. is still in my hands and will be sent in a day or two.[2]

From Charles Cotesworth Pinckney

Copy, Pinckney Family Papers, Library of Congress

Gentlemen, Paris, April 2, 1798

I think it of importance, that no longer delay should take place, in transmitting our reply to the Minister of Foreign Affairs.[3]

Duty to our Country & justice to ourselves require, that this

1. David Humphreys.

2. See American Envoys to Timothy Pickering, Feb. 7 and Mar. 9, 1798.

3. See Talleyrand to American Envoys, Mar. 18, 1798, and American Envoys to Talleyrand, Apr. 3, 1978.

letter should not remain unanswered, & I am very apprehensive, if we do not make it soon, we shall be prevented from making it at all. The latter part of the letter which Mr Gerry took with him, to consider, he said should be attended to immediately. If he cannot join his Colleagues in what is there expressed, & cannot suggest such alterations as they can accede to, we ought then to determine what prudence & duty may dictate, but I am for avoiding an apparent admission by our silence, of the unjust & injurious charges, made against our Country our Government & ourselves. I see so much danger resulting from delay, that I am unwilling it should be imputable to me, I therefore think it incumbent on me, to give you my sentiments freely on this subject, & hope by tomorrow morning we shall come to some decision.[4]

Mr. Burling[5] requests to have any Dispatches we may wish to transmit by him, to America, the day after tomorrow. I have the honor to be very respectfully, Your most Obt. Servt.

(Signed) CHARLES COTESWORTH PINCKNEY

Response to Talleyrand

EDITORIAL NOTE

In the following document the American envoys summarized the failure of their negotiations. The French had persistently refused to open formal or reciprocal discussions of any of the outstanding issues, and this refusal called for an answer. Marshall and Pinckney thought it imperative that they set the record

4. Gerry answered Pinckney that afternoon. "Mr. Gerry presents his compliments to General Pinckney & informs him that he is ready at any moment to finish the letter proposed as an answer to the minister of foreign affairs. He has made one attempt to obtain this object, but his propositions not having been altogether acceptable to General Marshal, he thot it best to present in one point of view the draft, as he proposes it, & it is now ready. He has suggested no alterations but such as appear to him indispensibly necessary to prevent further irritation on the part of this government: the charge on our part of wantonly plunging the U States onto a war: & future embarrassments to our government & ourselves. He shall certainly accord in this final measure with his collegues, if possible: as he deprecates a difference of opinion with them, in the important & embarrassing affairs of the embassy. Mr. G's health is not good at present, but he has not from that or any consideration, neglected a moment, the business alluded to." See Gerry to Pinckney, Apr. 2, 1798, Pinckney Family Papers, Library of Congress. In a note to Gerry, Pinckney specified that the envoys meet at seven that evening. See Pinckney to Gerry, Apr. 2, 1798, *ibid.*

5. Walter Burling, of Boston, was in France attempting to recover claims for a condemned cargo ship. Burling was a partner in Perkins, Burling & Co., of Boston. See Thomas Perkins to Joseph Perkins, Sept. 21, 1797, Extracts from Letterbooks of Joseph and Thomas Perkins, Perkins Papers, Massachusetts Historical Society.

straight before being ordered to leave Paris.[6] By this time the two envoys knew that Gerry intended to remain in Paris and to negotiate separately.[7]

According to the Journal, Marshall started to write the paper on March 22, finishing it on March 30.[8] Working rapidly and without his usual care, he incorporated major sections of previously printed documents on French-American disputes over maritime rights.[9] He also repeated the bulk of the undelivered note to Talleyrand that Gerry had refused to sign.[1] Given these circumstances, it becomes understandable how Marshall could have included such awkward and questionable sentences in his discussion of freedom of the press as, "It is a calamity incident to the nature of liberty and which can produce no serious evil to France; it is a calamity occasioned neither by the direct nor indirect influence of the American Government. In fact that government is believed to exercise no influence over any press."

To secure Gerry's assent, which Pinckney and Marshall still considered important, the two envoys accepted, with revisions, Gerry's conclusion rather than Marshall's.[2] Gerry insisted upon and achieved a change of emphasis concerning the means of breaking off negotiations. Whereas Marshall and Pinckney wanted a direct statement demanding their passports, Gerry rephrased the section in an attempt to shift the burden to the Directory. Gerry's version stipulated that if the Directory was unwilling to negotiate, the passports should be returned to the envoys. Gerry and his colleagues differed over tactics rather than substance. While sharing Marshall's and Pinckney's assessment of French unfairness to the United States, Gerry believed that only the envoys' continuing effort to negotiate prevented France from going to war with the United States. Marshall and Pinckney did not fear or expect war. They believed that since the negotiations were hopelessly deadlocked, the only honorable alternative was to leave Paris and allow the government in Philadelphia to decide on the next step.

Despite his constant refrain of seeking open, formal negotiations on all points of difference, Marshall was in this document more argumentative, more tendentious, than in previous papers—a sign of his mounting frustration over the mission. He had naively hoped to be home by Christmas; yet he was spending spring in Paris, as Talleyrand continued to procrastinate and evade even the simplest questions. Marshall later summarized the attitudes of the envoys at the end of the mission: "It was their duty, unmindful of personal considerations, to pursue peace with unabating zeal, through all the difficulties with which the pursuit was embarrassed by a haughty and victorious government, holding in perfect contempt the rights of others, but to repel with unhesitating decision, any propositions, an acceptance of which would subvert the independence of the United States. This they have endeavored to do."[3]

6. See Pinckney to JM and Gerry, Apr. 2, 1798; Journal, Mar. 22 and 23, 1798.
7. See Journal, Mar. 23, 1798.
8. *Ibid.* Mar. 22, 23, and 30, 1798.
9. See Timothy Pickering to American Envoys, July 15, 1797.
1. See JM and Pinckney to Talleyrand, Feb. 26, 1798.
2. *Ibid.*, See "Gerry Draft of Conclusion of American Envoys to Talleyrand," Apr. 2, 1798, Gerry Papers, Library of Congress.
3. See Citizens of Richmond to JM, and JM to Citizens of Richmond, Aug. 11, 1798.

To Talleyrand

LS, Archives of the Ministry of Foreign Affairs, Paris

Citizen Minister, Paris, April 3, 1798

Your letter of the 28th Ventose (18th of March) in answer to a memorial of the undersigned dated the 17th. of January, was received the day after its date, & has been considered with the most respectful attention.

In that memorial the undersigned, without furnishing cause of reproach, might have limited themselves to a statement of the numerous and well founded complaints of the nation they represent. They have been induced to extend their observations to other subjects, by that sincere desire to reestablish harmony & mutual confidence between the two Republics, which the government of the United States has never ceased to feel and to express. Supposing that those misrepresentations to which human action & human sentiment must ever continue to be exposed, might have impressed on the mind of the french government, occupied with the great and interesting events of Europe, the unfounded suspicion of partiality on the part of America for the enemies of France; the undersigned cherished the hope, that a complete review of the conduct of their government, accompanied with a candid and thorough investigation of the real principles on which that conduct was founded, by removing prejudices, might restore sentiments which the United States have ever sought, & still seek to preserve.

In taking this review it was obvious, that a minute discussion of every particular fact might incumber the examination with details, which previous explanations had rendered unnecessary, and therefore it was confined to those leading measures, of which the particular cases were the necessary results. The undersigned however declared & they still declare that if the government of the United States has given just cause of complaint to that of France in any case, they are ready to consider and to compensate the injury. That negotiation, the opening of which they have for nearly six months unremittingly solicited & patiently attended, would, if entered upon, demonstrate the sincerity of this declaration.

Still animated by the same spirit which has dictated all their efforts to approach this Republic; still searching to remove unfavorable impressions by a candid display of truths and a frank manifestation of the principles which have always governed the United States, and still endeavoring thereby to facilitate the restoration of harmony between two nations which ought to be the friends of each other, the undersigned will lay before you the result of their reflections on your letter of the 28th. of Ventose.[4] Whatever force you may be pleased to allow to their observations, the relative situation of the two Republics it is hoped, will not fail to convince you, that they proceed from the most perfect conviction of their justice.

You contend, citizen Minister, that the priority of complaint is on the part of France, and that those measures which have so injured & oppressed the people of the United States, have been produced by the previous conduct of their Government.

To this the undersigned will now only observe, that if France can justly complain of any act of the government of the United States, whether that act be prior or subsequent to the wrongs received by that Government, a disposition and a wish to do in the case what justice and friendship may require, is openly avowed and will continue to be manifested.

Your complaints against the United States may be classed under three heads.

1st. The inexecution of their treaties with France

2dly. The treaty of amity, commerce & navigation formed with Great Britain.

3dly. The conduct of their Government since that treaty.

If the undersigned shall be disappointed in their hope to convince you that on no one of these points can their government be justly inculpated, they yet persuade themselves that the demonstration of the good faith & upright intention, with which it has ever acted, will be complete and satisfactory. This being proved, and a tender of compensation for any unintentional wrong being made, a base for accommodation is offered which we must yet hope will be acceptable to France.

1st. The inexecution of the treaties between the United States & France.

Under this head you complain

1st. That from the commencement of the war the American tribunals have in effect pretended to the right of taking cognizance of the validity of prizes brought into the ports of the United States by French cruisers.

4. See Talleyrand to American Envoys, Mar. 18, 1798.

2dly. That against the textual sense of the treaty the government has permitted the ships of the enemy to come to in their ports after having captured property or vessels belonging to french citizens.

3dly. That it has ordered the arrest of a national corvette anchored in the port of Philadelphia and that the arrestation has extended to the captain commandant.

4thly. The refusal to provide the means to execute the consular convention.

These complaints shall be considered in the order in which they are made.

1st. From the commencement of the war the American tribunals have in effect pretended to the right of taking cognizance of the validity of prizes brought into the ports of the United States by French cruisers.

You have not been pleased to state a case in which this right has been asserted, and the undersigned are persuaded that no such case exists. Far from asserting it the Government of America has expressly disclaimed it. Mr Jefferson, the then Secretary of State, in his letter to Mr. Morris of the 16th of August 1793, which letter was laid before the french Government, declares that "The United States do not pretend to any right to try the validity of captures made on the *high seas* by France or any other nation, over its enemies. These questions belong, of common usage, to the sovereign of the captor, and whenever it is necessary to determine them, resort must be had to his courts. This is the case provided for in the 17th. article of the treaty, which says, that such prizes shall not be arrested, nor cognizance taken of the validity thereof; a stipulation much insisted on by mr. Genet & the consuls, & which we never thought of infringing or questioning."

Mr. Randolph, the successor of mr. Jefferson, in his letter to mr. Fauchet of the 29th. of May 1795, says "As to prizes made by legal cruisers on the high seas, it never was the intention of the President to interpose, he having abstained (as the 17th. article of our treaty of commerce imports) from examining into their lawfulness."

Mr. Monroe in his letter to your predecessor of the 15th. of March 1796 says "You will observe that I admit the principle if a prize was taken upon the high sea and by a privateer fitted out within the republic or its dominions, that in such case our Courts have no right to take cognizance of its validity. But is any case of this kind alledged? I presume none is or can be shewn."

But the United States have deemed it an indispensable duty to prevent, so far as they could prevent, the practice of hostility against nations with whom they were at peace, within their own limits, or by privateers fitted out in their own ports.

For the reasoning of their government in support of this decision, the undersigned will again refer to the letter of mr. Jefferson already quoted.

"Another doctrine advanced by mr. Genet is, that our Courts can take no cognizance of questions, whether vessels held by theirs as prizes, are lawful prizes or not: that this jurisdiction belongs exclusively to their consulates here, which have been lately erected by the National Assembly, into complete Courts of Admiralty.

"Let us consider, first, what is the extent of the jurisdiction which the consulates of France may rightfully exercise here. Every nation has of natural right, entirely and exclusively all the jurisdiction which may be rightfully exercised in the territory it occupies. If it cedes any portion of that jurisdiction to judges appointed by another nation, the limits of their power must depend on the instrument of cession. The United States & France have, by their consular convention, given mutually to their consuls, jurisdiction in certain cases specially enumerated. But that convention gives to neither the power of establishing complete courts of Admiralty within the territory of the other, nor even of deciding the particular question of prize or not prize. The consulates of France then cannot take judicial cognizance of those questions here. Of this opinion mr. Genet was when he wrote his letter of May 27th., wherein he promises to correct the error of the consul at Charleston, of whom in my letter of the 15th., I had complained, as arrogating to himself that jurisdiction, though in his subsequent letters, he has thought proper to embark in the errors of his consuls.

"The real question is, whether the United States have not a right to protect vessels within their waters and on their coasts? The Grange was taken within the Delaware between the Shores of Jersey and of the Delaware State, and several miles above its mouth. The seizing her was a flagrant violation of the jurisdiction of the United States. Mr Genet, however, instead of apologizing, takes great merit, in his letters, for giving her up. The William is said to have been taken within two miles of the shores of the United States. When the admiralty declined cognizance of the case, she was delivered to the French consul, according to my letter of June 25th., to be kept till the executive of the United States should examine into the case; and mr. Genet was desired, by my letter of June 29th. to have them furnished with the evidence on behalf of the captors, as to the place of capture. Yet, to this day, it has never been done. The brig Fanny was alledged to be taken within five miles from our shore. The Catharine within two miles and a half. It is an essential attribute of the jurisdiction of every country to preserve peace, to punish acts in breach of it, and to restore property taken by force within its limits. Were the armed vessel of any nation, to cut away one of our own from the wharves of Philadelphia, and to choose to call it a prize, would this exclude us from the right of redressing the wrong? Were it the vessel of another nation, are we not equally bound to protect it, while within our limits? Were it seized in any other waters, or on the shores of the United States, the right of redressing is still the same: And humble indeed would be our condition, were we obliged to depend, for that, on the will of a foreign consul, or on any negociation with diplomatic agents. Accordingly this right of protection within its waters and to a reasonable distance on its coasts, has been acknowledged by every nation, and denied to none; and if the property seized be yet within their power, it is their right and duty to redress the wrong themselves. France herself has asserted the right in herself & recognized it in us in the 6th. article of our treaty; where we mutually stipulate that we will, *by all the means in our power*, (not by negociation) protect & defend each other's vessels and effects, in our ports or roads, or on the seas near our countries, and recover and restore the same to the right owners. The United Netherlands, Prussia & Sweden have recognized it also, in treaties with us; and indeed it is a standing formula, inserted in almost all the treaties of all nations and proving the principle to be acknowledged by all nations."

In the letter of mr. Randolph to mr. Fauchet already cited, that gentleman resumes this subject & mr. Fauchet in answer to him says "The admiralty courts have already ceded to the intreaties of our enemies for their intervention in prize causes, in truth, frequently and almost constantly by using the double plea, of which you spoke to me, that is to say, by arguing either of seizure within the jurisdictional line of the United States, or of armament or of augmentation of armament of the capturing vessels, in their ports. On this subject, Sir, you request me to specify to you a circumstance in which a prize was arrested which did not come under that denomination, and you take the trouble to establish that they have a right to intervene in every case that can be brought under those heads. In the first place, sir, *I never have, at least to my recollection, contested the right of your courts or of the government to interfere in matters of the nature of those you mention.*"

It would seem then to be incontestible that the principle asserted by the United States, which indeed is an unquestionable principle, has been admitted in its utmost latitude by France.

It is believed that in the execution of this principle, the government and tribunals have only been guided by a sense of duty & the obligations of justice. If in any case which can be selected wrong has unintentionally been committed, that wrong has grown inevitably out of the situation of the United States, out of the conduct of persons they have been unable to control, & will with readiness be corrected.

2dly. That against the textual sense of the treaty the Government has permitted the ships of the enemy to come to in their ports after having captured property or vessels belonging to french citizens.

It is to be regretted that you have not been pleased to state some particular case; if the complaint be founded on a fact, which has manifested this permission; or if it be founded on principle, the precise difference between the construction given by the President of the United States to the article of the treaty of the 6th. of February 1778, relative to this subject & that for which you may contend. For want of such a guide, the undersigned may discuss unnecessary points without giving you complete satisfaction on that which in your mind may constitute the real difficulty.

The 17th: article of the treaty is in these words "It shall be lawful for the ships of war of either party, and privateers, freely to carry whithersoever they please, the ships and goods taken from their enemies, without being obliged to pay any duty to the officers of the admiralty or any other judges; nor shall such prizes be arrested or seized when they come to and enter the ports of either party; nor shall the searchers or other officers of those places search the same, or make examination concerning the lawfulness of such prizes; but they may hoist sail at any time & depart & carry their prizes to the places expressed in their commissions, which the commanders of such ships of war shall be obliged to shew: on the contrary, no shelter or refuge shall be given in their ports to such as shall have made prize of the subjects, people or property of either of the parties; but if such shall come in, being forced by stress of weather; or the danger of the sea, all proper means shall be vigorously used that they go out and retire from thence as soon as possible."

Do you contend, citizen minister, that this article ought to be rigidly construed according to its letter? If you do it becomes necessary to ascertain what are the disabilities to which its letter really subjects the vessels belonging to the enemies of France. They are

1st. That no shelter or refuge shall be given in the ports of the United States to the ships of war or privateers belonging to the enemy *which shall have made prize* of the subjects people or property of France:

2ndly. That if such ships of war or privateers shall come in, being forced by stress of weather or the danger of the sea, all proper means shall be vigorously used that they go out and retire from thence as soon as possible.

The letter of the article does not exclude generally the ships of war belonging to the enemy, but those only *which shall have made prize* of the subjects people or property of France. That the vessel shall have made a prize is a part & an essential part of the description.

Whether the vessel be or be not within this description, is a fact the ascertainment of which must precede the measures to be taken in consequence of that fact.

When the fact shall have been ascertained, the letter of the article denies refuge or shelter to the ship of war or privateer, but not to the prize which may have been made.

You well know, citizen minister, that if the letter of the article is to be set up against its spirit when the former is most favorable to the views of France, the letter must still be adhered to, though it should counteract those views.

The situation of the United States bound them to observe between the belligerent powers an exact neutrality in all cases, where their previous treaties had not stipulated advantages or imposed disabilities. They could not refuse to one belligerent power those rights of ordinary hospitality which were enjoyed by others, which the common usages of nations permit, and which were forbidden by no particular treaty. Such refusal would have been manifestly partial, & a plain departure from that neutral position in which the United States found themselves, and which good faith, integrity & their best interests impelled them religiously to maintain. Thus circumstanced, it was the duty of the government to give its true construction to a treaty, granting advantages to one of the belligerent powers, and imposing certain disabilities on another. In searching for this true construction, its best judgement ought to be exercised, and the dictates of that judgement ought to be obeyed. The United States have done so. They have refused shelter in their ports to the prizes made on the french republic, or to the ships of war belonging to the enemy & accompanying such prizes. They have permited ships of war not bringing prizes with them, to remain in their ports, without instituting tribunals to enquire, whether such ships have at any time captured french citizens or french property. The reasoning on which this decision was founded, and which appears to the undersigned to have been conclusive, will not now be repeated. It has been detailed in several letters from the Secretary of State of the United States to the minister of France in Philadelphia. The undersigned will only observe, that the construction supposed to be just, and for that reason actually put upon the article, is believed to be more favorable than the literal construction, to the interests of France. Ships of war which may have made prizes on this Republic, if they enter the ports of the United States without such prizes, ought indeed under the letter of the article, to be ordered to depart, so soon as the fact can have been ascertained, but the prizes themselves are permitted to remain in safety. By the actual construction a ship of war entering without a prize is permitted to remain, but all shelter is refused to a ship of war, which shall be accompanied by a prize, & also to the prize itself. It would seldom happen that a ship of war, not driven in by stress of weather or the dangers of the sea, would wish to continue in port longer than the time which would be unavoidably consumed, in ascertaining the fact of her having made a prize, but it must often happen that a prize, now excluded from the ports of the United States, would find shelter in them if the literal construction of the treaty should be adopted.

This exposition given by the United States to this article was made known in 1793. France has never signified a wish that the literal construction throughout should be pursued. This strengthens the opinion entertained by the undersigned, that the rule on this subject, so early established by the American Government, is considered by this republic as more favorable to its interests, than a rule conforming entirely to the letter of the article.

3dly. The government of the United States has ordered the arrest of a national corvette anchored in the port of Philadelphia, and the arrestation has been extended to the Captain commandant.

The undersigned beg leave to state the case which is the foundation of this complaint. In the statement itself, they trust, will be found a complete justification of the conduct of the United States.

The Cassius, under the name of les Jumeaux, was fitted and armed for a vessel of war in the port of Philadelphia, in violation of a law of the United States. In December 1794, having escaped from the port to descend the river, orders were given to the militia of the State of Delaware to intercept her. The attempt was made and failed—the crew of les Jumeaux, which was unexpectedly found to be very numerous, resisted the officers who went on board, manned their cannon, and brought them to bear on the cutter in which the militia (about forty in number) were embarked. Their force being inadequate to the enterprize they retired, with an intention to return the next day with a reinforcement. They did so: but les Jumeaux had sailed and gone to sea. The agent Mr. Guerret, by whom les Jumeaux had been fitted out, was tried in the Circuit Court at Philadelphia, convicted of the offence, & received sentence of fine and imprisonment.

Les Jumeaux proceeded to St. Domingo. Samuel B. Davis, a citizen of the United States, there took the command of her, with a commission from the french government. Davis probably sailed from Philadelphia in les Jumeaux, for the purpose of finally taking the command of her. Her name was now changed to le Cassius; and on a cruise she took a schooner called the William Lindsay, belonging to Messrs. Yard and Ketland of Philadelphia: Mr. Ketland having purchased an interest in her after her sailing. The schooner & her cargo were condemned as prize at St. Domingo. In August 1795, Capt. Davis, commanding le Cassius, came with her to Philadelphia. She was immediately known. Mr. Yard, with a view of obtaining an indemnification for the loss of the schooner and her cargo libelled le Cassius in the District Court, and caused the Captain to be arrested. Soon after, the Supreme court being in Session, captain Davis's council applied for and obtained a prohibition to the district Court, to stop its proceedings; by which the suits both against him and le Cassius were defeated. The Prohibition was granted on this principle; that the trial of prizes, taken without the jurisdiction of the United States, and carried into places within the jurisdiction of France, for adjudication, by french vessels, and all questions incidental to it, belong exclusively to the french tribunals: and consequently that its vessels of war and their officers, are not liable to process of our courts, predicated upon such capture & subsequent proceeding within the jurisdiction of the french government.

Messrs. Yard and Ketland having failed to obtain indemnification in this mode, procured new process on the information of mr. Ketland, to be issued from the circuit court, by which le Cassius was attached as a vessel armed & equipped as a ship of war in the port of Philadelphia, with intent to cruise and commit hostilities against nations with whom the United States were at peace; in violation of the act of Congress prohibiting such armaments. Mr. Adet complained that the process was taken out of the circuit court: because as he alledged, it had no jurisdiction, and that it would be attended with delay, that court sitting but twice a year: whereas the district court, in which it was said the prosecution (if at all permitted) should have been commenced, was always open. Gentlemen of legal knowledge were consulted on the point of jurisdiction in this case, and they were decided in their opinion, that the circuit court had jurisdiction, and exclusively of the district court. The Government of the United States had no part in originating this prosecution; and the district attorney, in behalf of the United States, took measures at each term of the circuit court, to prepare the cause for trial, and on a plea calculated to defeat the prosecution. At length, in October term 1796, the cause was brought to a hearing. In the course of the argument, the question of jurisdiction presented itself. The court adjourned 'till next day to consider of it, and on the following morning dismissed the suit.

The undersigned may be permitted to ask whether in a change of situations, placing France precisely in the circumstances of the United States, either the Corvette or her Captain would have escaped?

4th. The refusal to provide the means to execute the consular convention of the 14th. of November 1788.

As you have not selected the particular parts of this convention, supposed to remain unexecuted, the undersigned must necessarily consider the more definite charges heretofore made on the same subject, as being adopted by you.

Your predecessor in office in his letter to mr. Monroe of the 19th. Ventose, 4th. year (9th. March 1796) complains

1st. That the clause granting to French consuls the right of judging exclusively in disputes between Frenchmen is become illusory for the want of laws giving them the means of having their decisions executed.

2dly. The right of causing mariners who desert to be arrested is rendered ineffectual, because the Judges charged by the laws with issuing the mandates of arrest have lately required the presentation of the *original* roll of the crew in contempt of the 5th. article admitting in the tribunals of both powers, copies certified by the consul.

It is then understood to be required

1st. That the Officers of the United States should execute the judgements of the consuls; &

2dly. That the Judges of the United States should issue mandates of arrest against persons charged with being deserters, without a view of the original roll of the crew.

It is very justly observed by mr. Jefferson in his letter to mr. Morris, which has been already cited, that "Every nation has of natural right entirely and exclusively, all the jurisdiction which may be rightfully exercised in the territory it occupies. If it cedes any portion of that jurisdiction to Judges appointed by another nation, the limits of their power must depend on the instrument of cession." The parties to the convention profess its object to be "to define and establish in a reciprocal and permanent manner the functions & privileges of Consuls and Vice-consuls."

It is to be expected then, as well from the intention of the Convention establishing the tribunal, as from the nature of the tribunal itself, which is a foreign court, constituted by a foreign authority, governed by foreign laws, and amenable for its conduct to a foreign government, that no power is to be implied, and that it possesses no capacity which is not expressly given to it.

To ascertain then the precise extent of the stipulation, let the Convention itself be considered.

The first point rests exclusively on the 12th. article, which is in these words. "All differences and Suits between the subjects of the most christian King, in the United States, or between the citizens of the United States, within the dominions of the most christian King, & particularly all disputes relative to the wages and terms of engagement of the crews of the respective vessels, & all differences of what ever nature they be, which may arise between the privates of the said crews, or between any of them and their captains, or between the captains of different vessels of their nation, shall be determined by the respective consuls and vice-consuls, either by a reference to arbitrators, or by a summary judgement, and without costs. No officer of the country, civil or military, shall interfere therein, or take any part whatever in the matter: and the appeals from the said consular sentences shall be carried before the tribunals of France or of the United States, to whom it may appertain to take cognizance thereof."

In this article no engagement is made to furnish the means of executing consular judgements. If therefore the preceding positions be just there is an end of the question. But other arguments present themselves in support of the construction contended for by the United States. The consular authority in a foreign country is usually either voluntary or enforced by the laws of the nation to which the consuls belong, and which may bind its own citizens or subjects under penalties to be inflicted on their return, or otherwise. Upon this idea, it was sufficient to stipulate a permission of the jurisdiction in exclusion of the courts of the country; on any other idea it would have been necessary to have stipulated explicitly and perhaps in detail, the manner in which its sentences should be executed. To accede to the demands of France would be to erect in a foreign country complete courts of justice, with effectual process to compel the appearance of parties and witnesses, and to execute their decisions. And as the transactions in commerce & navigation could not in the nature of things be confined to the foreigners alone, the citizens of the country must often be necessary witnesses to those transactions and of course rendered amenable to this foreign jurisdiction in their own country; whereas the jurisdiction granted by the article is only of french consuls over french citizens in the United States; & reciprocally of american consuls over the citizens of the United States in France. This would be to extend by implication the authority of a foreigner over persons not contemplated by the treaty as subject to it. The article declares too "That no officer of the country civil or military shall interfere therein or take any part in the matter." But Sheriffs, Marshalls & their deputies or any other persons appointed by and acting under the laws of the country are "officers of the country," and consequently cannot aid in the execution of consular decisions, because they are expressly forbidden "to interfere therein or take any part whatever in the matter." But was it meant that the laws should give consuls the power to appoint such executive officers of their own nation? Should it be conceded that a person so appointed could not be considered as an officer of that nation by virtue of and according to whose law he held his office, still we find no such thing in the convention. On the contrary, in the case of deserters from vessels mentioned in the 9th. article, whom the consuls are authorized to cause to be arrested, they are expressly directed to apply in writing to the "courts Judges and officers competent" to make the arrests; meaning the courts Judges and officers of the country where the consuls reside. In addition to this, if power could be given to Consuls to appoint officers to execute their decisions, these officers must of course have their fees of compensation to be paid by one or other of the parties. But the article giving the jurisdiction declares that the consular judgment shall be "without costs."

The second complaint is that the Judges of the United States have required the exhibition of the *original* roll of the crew as the testimony which would authorize the issuing a mandate to apprehend a french mariner charged as a deserter.

The right to require these mandates is founded entirely on the 9th. article of the consular convention. That declares that "the consuls and vice-consuls shall address themselves to the Courts Judges & officers competent and shall demand the said deserters in writing, proving by an exhibition of the *registers of the vessel or ships roll* that those men were part of the said crews, and on this demand, *so proved* (saving however where the contrary is proved) the delivery shall not be refused." It would be an idle waste of time to attempt to prove to you, citizen minister, that "the register of the vessel or ships roll" is not a copy of that paper, or that the exhibition of a copy does not satisfy a law, which peremptorily requires the exhibition of the original. Your predecessor has thought proper to refer to the 5th. article of that instrument; but a slight perusal of that article will convince you, citizen minister, that it does not apply to the case.

When then the Judges of the United States determined that the mandate of arrest could not be issued on the exhibition of a copy of the "register of the vessel or ships roll" they did not so decide for the purpose of giving effect to the system of the Government, but because the treaty was clearly understood by them positively to require the presentation of the original.

The undersigned regret, citizen minister, that your researches concerning the United States have not extended to their Courts. You would have perceived & admired their purity. You would have perceived that America may repose herself securely on the integrity of her Judges; & your justice would have spared the insinuations concerning them, which have closed this part of your letter.

The undersigned will next consider what you have stated with respect to the treaty of Amity Commerce & Navigation formed with Great Britain.

You complain, citizen minister, in very strong terms of the deception alledged to have been practised with respect to the objects of mr. Jay's mission to London, and also of the contents of the treaty which that mission produced.

You are pleased to observe that it was then said, that mr. Jay had been sent to London *only* to negotiate arrangements relative to the depredations committed on the American commerce by the cruisers of Great Britain.

By whom, citizen minister, was this said? Not by the President in his message to the Senate, announcing the nomination of mr. Jay, nor by the then Secretary of State, in communicating to mr. Fauchet the subjects of that mission. The documents with respect to this assertion have been stated & have been fully commented on. It has been demonstrated that the American government did not seize this occasion to practise a deception so unnecessary, so foreign from its well known character, and which could produce only mischief to itself. As you have in no degree weakened the testimony which is relied on as disproving this allegation, or produced any sort of evidence in support of it, the undersigned cannot but mingle some degree of surprize with the regrets they feel at seeing it repeated, accompanied with the charge of that "dissimulation" of which all, who examine well the conduct of the government of the United States, will so readily pronounce it to be incapable.

You also criminate the secrecy which attended this negotiation. To this complaint, when formerly insisted on, it was answered that so much of it as was material to this republic was immediately communicated to her minister, and that she had no right to enquire further, or to be dissatisfied that other objects were not disclosed. That it is not the practice of France, nor of any other nation, to communicate to others the particular subjects of negotiation which may be contemplated; and that no nation could be independent which admitted itself to be accountable to another for the manner in which it might judge proper to regulate its own concerns, on points in which that other was not interested, or which was bound to give previous intimation of every article which might be inserted in a treaty formed on the avowed principle of leaving in full force all preexisting engagements. This reasoning is only answered by terming it "a sophism" "an insiduous subterfuge." May not any reasoning on any subject be answered in the same manner? But can such an answer impair its force? Without doubt, citizen minister, the Government of the United States, when it informed France that the negotiations of mr. Jay would not in any respect weaken its engagements to this republic, would have added that they might eventually extend to a commercial treaty, if it had been supposed that the omission to give such information could really be considered as a breach of legitimate obligation, or as an evidence of diminished friendship. The information was most probably not given because it was unusual, & because it could neither be considered as proper, as necessary or as material. The undersigned trust that the painful and unavailing discussions on this subject, rendered so unpleasant by the manner in which it has been treated, will never again be renewed.

Passing to the treaty itself, you say that the small majority by which it was sanctioned in the two houses of Congress, and the number of respectable voices raised against it in the nation, depose honorably in favor of the opinion which the French government has entertained of it. But you must be sensible, citizen minister, that the criterion, by which you ascertain the merits of the instrument in question, is by no means infallible, nor can it warrant the inference you draw from it. In a republic like that of the United States, where no individual fears to utter what his judgement or his passions may dictate, where an unrestrained press conveys alike to the public eye the labors of virtue & the efforts of particular interests, no subject which agitates and interests the public mind can unite the public voice, or entirely escape public censure. In pursuit of the same objects, a difference of opinion will arise in the purest minds from the different manner in which those objects are viewed, & there are situations, in which a variety of passions combine to silence the voice of reason, and to betray the soundest judgements. In such situations, if the merits of an instrument are to be decided, not by itself, but by the approbation or disapprobation it may experience, it would surely be a safer rule to take as a guide the decision of a majority, however small that majority may be, than to follow the minority. A treaty too may be opposed as injurious to the United States, though it should not contain a single clause which could prejudice the interests of France. It ought not to be supposed that a treaty would for that reason be offensive to this republic.

Had you been pleased to state any objections to this instrument drawn from the compact itself, the undersigned would have given to those objections the most serious and respectful consideration. But it is supposed that you adopt without adding to the complaints made by your predecessor & by mr. Adet, when you observe that you will not repeat what they have said. These complaints have been amply discussed in the memorial the undersigned had the honor to transmit you, bearing date the 17th. January. It is believed to have been demonstrated that the stipulations complained of, do not in the most remote degree, wound the interests of France, affect the preexisting engagements of the United States, or change their situation in relation to the belligerent powers. Such incontestably was and is the opinion of the American Government, and in this opinion only would the treaty have been agreed to. As no one of the arguments, which have at various times been urged on this subject, on the part of the United States, has ever yet been noticed, the undersigned deem unnecessary, any attempt to reurge or to strengthen them.

You say that you will content yourself "with observing summarily that in this treaty everything having been provided to turn the neutrality of the United States to the disadvantage of the French republic and to the advantage of England; that the federal government having in this act made to Great Britain concessions the most unheard of, the most incompatible with the interests of the United States, and the most derogatory from the alliance which existed between the said United States and the French republic, the latter was perfectly free to avail itself of the preservatory means with which it was furnished by the laws of nature and of nations, and by its anterior treaty, for the purpose of parrying the inconveniencies of the treaty of London. Such are the reasons which have determined the Arretés of the Directory of which the United States complain, as well as the conduct of its agents in the Antilles." But you have not shown a single provision "which turns the neutrality of the United States to the disadvantage of the french republic and to the advantage of England"; you have not shown a single concession "incompatible with the interests of the United States" or "derogatory from their alliance with France."

It is considered as having been demonstrated that this treaty leaves the neutrality of the United States, with respect both to

France and England precisely in its former situation, and that it contains no concessions which are either unusual or derogatory from their alliance with this Republic.

But if in forming this judgement the American Government has deceived itself, still it ought to be remembered that it has ever manifested a readiness to place France on the footing of England, with respect to the articles complained of.

You suppose that the second article of the treaty between the United States & France justifies the Arretés of which the former power complains. But that article only entitles either of the contracting parties to a participation of any particular favor in respect of commerce or navigation, which might thereafter be granted by the other to other nations, on allowing the same compensation, if the concession was conditional. It has never been pretended to extend to preexisting rights held and exercised under the law of nations, and barely recognized by any subsequent treaty. If this could be insisted on, still it was shown incontestibly by the undersigned, that the arreté particularly complained of, so far as it professes to found itself on the treaty with England, greatly transcends that treaty, and in its most noxious article, that requiring a role d'equipage, has no relation to it. This all-essential circumstance you have not been pleased to notice, and it is with infinite regret the undersigned observe that the discussions at which you hint, are to be limitted to the abuses of the principle established by the Arreté, and not extended to the compatibility of the principle itself either with justice, the laws of nations, or existing treaties. It is well known that such a discussion, if indeed the undersigned could be permitted to enter upon it, would avail but little, since the vast mass of American property, captured by the cruisers and condemned by the courts of France, has been found in vessels not furnished with a role d'equipage.

The undersigned have been minute in their attention to every syllable you have uttered on this interesting subject, because it has been often considered as having given cause of just irritation to France & they are sincerely desirous of probing to the bottom every subject which may have assumed that complection. Their wish is unaffected, to give to every complaint its real value, in order thus to prepare the way for accommodation by the relinquishment of such as are not well founded, and the admission of those which may have a real existence.

The third head of your complaints relates to the conduct of the government of the United States since their treaty with England.

You observe that "so soon as the treaty in question had been put in execution, the government of the United States seemed to think itself dispensed from the observance of any measures towards this Republic, & you adduce in support of this general observation

1st. The refusal to permit in the ports of the United States the sale of prizes made by french cruisers.

2dly. The invectives and calumnies against the french government, its principles, & its officers, contained in certain journals and pamphlets published in the United States; and

3dly. The speech of the President of the United States to Congress in may last.

1st. The Government of the United States does not permit the sale in their ports of prizes made upon England by the cruisers of France.

The fact is admitted. To erect it into an offence, it becomes necessary to prove that this measure violates either the engagements, or the neutrality of the United States. Neither is attempted. To show that it violates neither, had this been rendered necessary, would by no means have been deemed an arduous task. It will now only briefly be observed that the 17th. article of the treaty of commerce of the 6th. of February 1778, which alone relates to this subject, so far from stipulating for the sale of prizes in the ports of either nation, limits itself to a declaration that the captors shall have liberty to bring them into port free from duties, arrests, or searches, and to depart with them to the places expressed in their commissions; thereby evidently contemplating the then existing regulations of this nation. France has manifested her own opinion on this subject in her treaty with Great Britain of the 26th. of September 1786. The 16th. article of that treaty declares that "it shall not be lawful for foreign cruisers who shall not be the subjects of one or the other crown, and who shall have a commission from any other Prince or State, enemies of the one or the other, to arm their vessels in the ports of one or the other of the said two kingdoms, *to sell there what they shall have taken, or to change the same in any manner whatever*." In a war with England then, France being neutral, the cruisers of the United States are forbidden to sell their prizes in the ports of this Republic.[5] The 17th. article of the treaty

5. For the text of the article JM was quoting, see Clive Parry, ed., *The Consolidated Treaty Series*, L (New York, 1969), 81.

of February 1778, being reciprocal France has pronounced her decision that it does not give her cruisers a right to sell their prizes in the ports of America. If this right had been given by the treaty of February 1778, that between the United States and England could not be construed to impair it.

Nor is the prohibition a departure from the neutrality of the United States. A nation to violate its neutrality must manifest a partiality for one of the belligerent powers, must accord favors not stipulated by preexisting treaties to one, which it refuses to the other. This is not even alledged in the present instance. Far from permitting British cruisers to sell, in the United States, prizes they have made on the French, they are not even allowed to bring them into port.

A candid consideration of this subject will prove, that the withdrawal of a favor, the grant of which manifested so strongly the attachments of the United States, far from justifying the resentments which have been expressed in consequence of it, can only be attributed to the solicitude of the American government, to render perfectly unexceptionable, its observance of that neutrality which it professes to maintain. It has been shown unequivocally to have been the opinion of the contracting parties that the treaty of commerce of the 6th. of February 1778, did not give to either, being at war, a right to sell its prizes in the ports of the other, being at peace. It is not pretended that this is one of the rights accruing, without special stipulation, under the laws & usages of nations. It is not then a right at all. If granted it is a voluntary favor. But a voluntary favor essential in the prosecution of the war, if granted by a neutral to one belligerent power and of necessity refused to the other, affords to that other, at least, a more plausible pretext for complaint, than has been given by any other act of the Government of the United States. What in such a situation woud be the language of France? Would this republic permit a neutral nation, not bound thereto by any obligation whatever, to allow in its ports as a voluntary favor, the sale of prizes made on french citizens, while the same favor was of necessity denied to the cruisers of France? It is believed that such a use of neutrality would not be permitted, & the undersigned felicitate themselves & their country, that the government they represent has never intentionally given to this republic, any cause of dissatisfaction as serious as this would have been. You will not fail to observe, citizen minister, that this heavy accusation when analyzed, is nothing more than the refusal of a meer favor on the part of the American government, the grant of which might have been dangerous to itself, might have drawn it from that neutral station, which it is its duty to observe, and which favor France had previously, in the most explicit terms, declared its determination not to grant, under similar circumstances, to the United States.

2ndly. Your second allegation is "that the journals known to be indirectly under the control of the cabinet have redoubled their invectives & calumnies against the Republic, its magistrates and its Envoys, and that pamphlets openly paid for by the minister of Great Britain have reproduced under every form those insults and calumnies without having ever drawn the attention of the government to a state of things so scandalous, & which it might have repressed."

The Genius of the Constitution & the opinions of the people of the United States cannot be overruled by those who administer the government. Among those principles deemed sacred in America, among those precious rights considered as forming the bulwark of their liberties, which the Government contemplates with awful reverence; and would approach only with the most cautious circumspection, there is no one, of which the importance is more deeply impressed on the public mind, than the liberty of the press. That this liberty is often carried to excess, that it has sometimes degenerated into licentiousness, is seen and lamented; but the remedy has not yet been discovered. Perhaps it is an evil inseparable from the good to which it is allied, perhaps it is a shoot which cannot be stripped from the stalk, without wounding vitally the plant from which it is torn. However desirable those measures may be, which might correct without enslaving the press, they have never yet been devised in America. No regulations exist which enable the government to suppress whatever calumnies or invectives any individual may chuse to offer to the public eye, or to punish such calumnies and invectives otherwise, than by a legal prosecution in courts, which are alike open to all who consider themselves as injured.

Without doubt this abuse of a valuable privilege is matter of peculiar regret when it is extended to the Government of a foreign nation. The undersigned are persuaded it has never been so extended with the approbation of the Government of the United States. Discussions respecting the conduct of foreign powers, especially on points affecting the rights and interests of America, are unavoidably made in a nation, where public measures are the results of public opinion, & certainly do not furnish cause of reproach; but it is believed that calumny & invective have never been substituted for the manly reasoning of an elightened & injured people, without giving pain to those who administer the affairs of the Union. Certainly this offence, if it be deemed by France of sufficient magnitude to be worthy of notice, has not been confined to this Republic. It has been still more profusely lavished on its enemies, and has even been bestowed with an unsparing hand on the federal government itself. Nothing can be more notorious than the calumnies & invectives with which the wisest measures & the most virtuous characters of the United States have been pursued and traduced. It is a calamity incident to the nature of liberty and which can produce no serious evil to France; it is a calamity occasioned neither by the direct nor indirect influence of the American Government. In fact that government is believed to exercise no influence over any press.

You must be sensible, citizen minister, with how much truth the same complaint might be urged on the part of the United States. You must know well what degrading & unworthy calumnies against their government, its principles, & its officers, have been published to the world by french journalists and in french pamphlets. That government has even been charged with betraying the best interests of the nation, with having put itself under the guidance of—nay more—with having sold itself to—a foreign court. But these calumnies atrocious as they are, have never constituted a subject of complaint against France. Had not other causes infinitely more serious and weighty interrupted the harmony of the two republics, it would still have remained unimpaired, & the mission of the undersigned would never have been rendered necessary.

3dly. You complain of the speech of the President of the United States made to Congress in may last. It denounces, you say, the executive Directory as searching to propagate anarchy & division in the United States.

The constitution of the United States imposes on its President this important duty—"He shall from time to time give to the Congress information of the state of the Union."

It having been deemed proper to recall the minister from the United States to this republic, and to replace him by a citizen, the objects of whose mission, as expressed in his letters of credence, were "to maintain that good understanding which from the commencement of the alliance had subsisted between the two nations; & to efface unfavorable impressions, banish suspicions & restore that cordiality which was at once the evidence & pledge of a friendly union,"[6] the President of the Directory addressed the recalled minister in the following terms.

"In presenting today to the executive Directory your letters of recall you give to Europe a strange spectacle.

"France rich in her liberty, surrounded with the train of her victories, strong in the esteem of her allies, will not abase herself by calculating the consequences of the condescensions of the American government to the suggestions of her antient tyrants. The french republic hopes, moreover, that the successors of Columbus, Rawleigh & Penn, always proud of their liberty, will never forget that they owe it to France. They will weigh in their wisdom the magnanimous good will of the French people with the crafty caresses of certain perfidious persons, who meditate to bring them back to their antient slavery. Assure, mr. Minister, the good people of America that like them we adore liberty, that they will always have our esteem and that they will find in the french people that republican generosity which knows as well how to grant peace as to cause its sovereignty to be respected."[7]

The change of a minister is an ordinary act for which no government is accountable to another and which has not heretofore been deemed "a strange spectacle" in France or in any other part of Europe. It appears to be a measure not of itself calculated to draw on the government making such change, the strictures or the resentments of the nation to which the minister is deputed. Such an effect produced by so inadequate a cause could not fail to command attention while it excited surprize.

This official speech addressed by the government of France to that of the United States through its minister, charges that government with condescensions to the suggestions of their antient tyrants, speaks of the crafty caresses of certain perfidious persons, who meditate to bring back the successors of Columbus of Raw-

6. JM was quoting from the initial instructions given to Pinckney when Washington first appointed him to succeed James Monroe as minister to France. See Timothy Pickering to Pinckney, Sept. 14, 1796, Pickering Papers, Massachusetts Historical Society.

7. Barras's speech of Dec. 30, 1796, is printed in *Amer. State Papers, Foreign Relations*, I, 746.

leigh & of Penn to their antient slavery, and desires the minister to assure (not his government but) the good people of America' that they will always have the esteem of France, and that they will find in the french people that republican generosity which knows as well how to grant peace as to cause its sovereignty to be respected.

That a minister should carry any assurances from a foreign government to the people of his nation, is as remarkable, as the difference between the manner in which his government and his people are addressed.

His government is charged with condescension to the suggestions of the antient tyrants of his country but the people are considered as loving liberty, and they are to be assured of the perpetual esteem of France. This esteem they are to weigh against the crafty caresses of those perfidious persons, who meditate to bring them back to their former slavery.

When this speech, thus addressed directly to the Government and people of the United States, in the face of Europe and the world, came to be considered in connection with other measures—when it came to be considered in connection with the wide spreading devastation to which their commerce was subjected, with the severities practised on their seamen, with the recall of the minister of France from the United States, and the very extraordinary manner in which that recall was signified by him both to the Government and people, with the refusal even to hear the messenger of peace, deputed from the United States for the sole purpose of conciliation, it could not fail to make on the american mind a deep & serious impression. It was considered as a fact too important to be withheld from the Congress by that department of the Government, which is charged with the duties of maintaining its intercourse with foreign nations, and of making communications to the legislature of the Union.

The President therefore did communicate it in the following words, "With this conduct of the french government, it will be proper to take into view, the public audience given to the late minister of the United States, on his taking leave of the executive Directory. The speech of the President discloses sentiments more alarming than the refusal of a minister, because more dangerous to our Independence and union; and at the same time studiously marked with indignities towards the government of the United States. It evinces a disposition to separate the people of the United

States from the Government: to persuade them that they have different affections, principles & interests from those of their fellow citizens, whom they themselves have chosen to manage their common concerns; and thus to produce divisions fatal to our peace. Such attempts ought to be repelled, with a decision which shall convince France and the world, that we are not a degraded people, humiliated under a colonial spirit of fear and sense of superiority, fitted to be the miserable instruments of foreign influence, and regardless of national honour, character and interest.

"I should have been happy to have thrown a veil over these transactions, if it had been possible to conceal them: but they have passed on the great theatre of the world in the face of all Europe & America; & with such circumstances of publicity & solemnity that they cannot be disguised and will not soon be forgotten; they have inflicted a wound in the American breast. It is my sincere desire however that it may be healed."[8]

It is hoped that this communication will be viewed in its true light: that it will no longer be considered as a denunciation of the executive Directory, but as the statement of an all important fact by one department of the American government to another, the making of which was injoined by duties of the highest obligation.

The undersigned have now, citizen Minister, passed through the complaints you urge against the government of the United States. They have endeavored to consider those complaints impartially, & to weigh them in the scales of justice and of truth. If any of them be well founded France herself could not demand more readily than America would make reparation for the injury sustained. The President of the United States has said "If we have committed errors, & these can be demonstrated, we shall be willing to correct them: if we have done injuries, we shall be willing on conviction to redress them." These dispositions on the part of their government have been felt in all their force by the undersigned, & have constantly regulated their conduct.

The undersigned will not resume, citizen Minister, the painful task of reurging the multiplied injuries, which have been accumulated on their country, and which were in some degree detailed in their memorial of the 17th. of January last. They cannot, however, decline to remonstrate against a measure which has been announced since that date.

8. JM was quoting from John Adams's speech of May 16, 1797, *Annals of Congress*, VII, 54–59.

The legislative Councils of the French republic have decreed that[9]

1st. The condition of ships, in everything which concerns their character as neutrals or enemies, shall be determined by their cargo; consequently every vessel, found at sea laden in the whole or in part with merchandize coming out of England or its possessions, shall be declared good prize, whoever may be the proprietor of such commodities or merchandize.

2dly. No foreign vessel which in the course of its voyage shall have entered into an english port shall be admitted into any port of the french republic, but in the case of necessity, in which case such vessel shall be obliged to depart from such port so soon as the cause of entry shall have ceased.

This decree too deeply affects the interests of the United States to remain unattended to by their ministers. They pray you, therefore, citizen Minister, to receive their respectful representations concerning it.

The object of the decree is to cut off all direct intercourse between neutrals and Great Britain, or its possessions, and to prevent the acquisition, even by circuitous commerce, of those articles which come from England or its dominions.

The right of one nation to exchange with another the surplus produce of its labor, for those articles which may supply its wants or administer to its comfort is too essential to have been ever classed among those admitted to be in any degree doubtful. It is a right in ceding which a nation would cede the privilege of regulating its own interests & providing for its own welfare. When any two nations shall chuse to make war on each other they have never been considered nor can they be considered as thereby authorizing themselves to impair the essential rights of those who shall chuse to remain at peace. Consequently those rights, the free exercise of which is essential to its interests and welfare, must be retained by a neutral power, whatever nations may be involved in war.

The right of a belligerent to restrain a neutral from assisting his enemy by supplying him with those articles, which are defined as contraband, has been universally submitted to; but to cut off all intercourse between neutrals & an enemy, to declare that any single article, which may have come from the possessions of the

9. JM took this section from the undelivered note of JM and Pinckney to Talleyrand, Feb. 26, 1798.

enemy, whoever may be its owner, shall of itself be sufficient to condemn both vessel and cargo, is to exercise a control over the conduct of neutrals, which war can never give & which is alike incompatible with their dignity & their welfare.

The rights of belligerents are the same. If this might be exercised by one, so might it be exercised by every other. If it might be exercised in the present, so might it be exercised in every future war. This decree is therefore on the part of France, the practical assertion of a principle, which would destroy all direct or circuitous commerce between belligerent and neutral powers, which would often interrupt the business of a large part of the world, & withdraw or change the employment of a very considerable portion of the human race.

This is not all. It is the exercise of a power which war is not admitted to give, and which may therefore be assumed in peace as well as war. It essentially affects the internal economy of nations and deranges that course of industry which they have a right to pursue and on which their prosperity depends.

To acquiesce therefore, in the existing state of things, under a principle, so extensive & so pernicious is to establish a precedent for national degradation, which can never cease to apply, and which will authorize any measures, which power may be disposed to practise.

France, therefore, will perceive that neutral governments, whatever may be their dispositions towards this Republic, are impelled by duties of the highest obligation to remonstrate against a decree, which at the same time invades their interests and their independence—which takes from them the profits of an honest & lawful industry, as well as the inestimable privilege of conducting their own affairs as their own judgement may direct.

It is hoped that the remonstrances of the United States on this subject will derive additional force from their subsisting engagements with France, and from a situation peculiar to themselves.

The twenty third article of the treaty of amity and commerce of the 6th. of February 1778, is in these words, "It shall be lawful for all & singular the subjects of the most christian King, and the citizens, people and inhabitants of the said United States, to sail with their ships with all manner of liberty & security, no distinction being made who are the proprietors of the merchandizes laden thereon, from any port to the places of those who now are or hereafter shall be at enmity with the most christian King or the United States. It shall likewise be lawful for the subjects and inhabitants aforesaid, to sail with the ships & merchandizes aforementioned, and to trade with the same liberty & security from the places, ports and havens of those who are enemies of both or either party, without any opposition or disturbance whatsoever, not only directly from the places of the enemy aforementioned to neutral places, but also from one place belonging to an enemy to another place belonging to an enemy, whether they be under the jurisdiction of the same prince, or under several. And it is hereby stipulated, that free ships shall also give a freedom to goods, & that everything shall be deemed to be free and exempt which shall be found on board the ships belonging to the subjects of either of the confederates, although the whole lading, or any part thereof should appertain to the enemies of either, contraband goods being always excepted. It is also agreed in like manner, that the same liberty be extended to persons who are on board a free ship, with this effect, that altho they be enemies to both or either party, they are not to be taken out of that free ship, unless they are soldiers and in actual service of the enemy."

The two nations contemplating & providing for the case when one may be at war and the other at peace, solemnly stipulate and pledge themselves to each other, that in such an event the subjects or citizens of the party at peace may freely trade with the enemy of the other, may freely sail with their ships in all manner of security to & from any port or place belonging to such enemy. Nor is this all. Not only goods coming from the hostile territory, but the very goods of the enemy himself may be carried with safety in the vessels of either of the contracting parties.

You will perceive, citizen minister, without requiring the undersigned to execute the painful task of drawing the contrast, how openly & entirely the decree of the Councils opposes itself to the treaty between France and the United States.

In addition to the hitherto unceded rights of a sovereign & independent nation, in addition to the rights stipulated by compact, the undersigned will respectfully submit other considerations growing out of the peculiar situation of the United States, manifesting the particular hardships the decree complained of must impose on them.

In possession of a rich, extensive & unsettled country, the labor of the United States is not yet sufficient for the full cultivation of its soil and consequently but a very small portion of it can have been applied to manufactures. Articles of the first necessity & comfort are imported in exchange for provisions & for those raw materials, which are the growth of the country, and which its Inhabitants are accustomed to raise. It is at any time extremely difficult, nor is it practicable without great loss, to change suddenly the habits of a whole people and that course of industry in which the state of their population & their real interests have engaged them. An agricultural cannot suddenly and at will become a manufacturing people; the United States cannot instantaneously, on the meer passing of a decree, transfer to the manufacture of articles heretofore imported, such a portion of their labor as will at the same time furnish a market for the surplus commodities, and a supply for the wants of the cultivator of the soil. It is therefore scarcely possible for them to surrender their foreign commerce.

Independent of the right they possess in common with others to search for & chuse the best markets, it is believed that the supplies they need could with difficulty, in the actual state of the world be completely furnished without the aid of England and its possessions. It is not pretended that France manufactures at present for foreign consumption; nor do the undersigned suppose that there exists a market, where the citizens of the United States can obtain in exchange the articles they need & are accustomed to consume, if those coming out of England & its possessions be entirely excluded.

A variety of other considerations, & especially the difficulty individuals must encounter in suddenly breaking old and forming new connections, in forcing all their commerce into channels not yet well explored, in trading without a sufficient capital to countries where they have no credit, combine to render almost impossible an immediate dissolution of commercial intercourse between the United States and Great Britain.

If then the decree complained of shall be executed on American vessels, it can only increase grievances already but too considerable and transfer the carriage of english manufactures for american consumption from their own to british bottoms, sailing under the protection of a convoy. Instead of wounding England, it will probably aggrandize its marine by sacrificing the remnant of the United States and by destroying that system of policy by which they have heretofore sought to give their own vessels that portion of their own carrying trade, which would otherwise be enjoyed by british merchants.[1]

You have made some general animadversions on the government of the United States, which the undersigned feel themselves bound briefly to notice.

You[2] have charged that government with giving instructions not in the sincere intention of arriving at the pacific results; and yet the undersigned have offered to change those clauses in the treaty of 1778, which have become inconvenient to France[3] and to repair any injuries which may have been commited.

You have charged that government with omitting nothing to prolong and augment the misunderstandings between the two republics; but does not the fact that the undersigned are now in Paris furnish persuasive evidence to the contrary?

You have charged it with searching to justify by deceitful appearances the prejudices with which it surrounds at pleasure the name of the republic & the system of exasperation and separation pursued in this respect with the strangest obstinacy; but has not this republic in terms the most cordial been again & again intreated to enter into a candid investigation of the mutual complaints of the two nations? Have not these intreaties been unnoticed while the ministers deputed to make them remain unaccredited?

You have charged it with wishing to seize the first favorable occasion for consummating an intimate union with a power towards which a devotion & a partiality are professed which have long constituted the principle of the conduct of the federal government; but whilst no devotion or partiality has been expressed for any nation except France, have not the United States made & are they not still making the most extraordinary efforts to restore the broken relations between the two republics?

In[4] a letter discussing the important interests of two great nations the undersigned are unwilling to introduce what relates personally

1. This is the end of the passage JM copied. *Ibid.*

2. The remainder of the dispatch is a modified version of the closing section of Gerry's draft. See "Gerry Draft of Conclusion of American Envoys to Talleyrand," Apr. 2, 1798, Gerry Papers, Library of Congress.

3. The ending of this sentence was changed by the envoys from what Gerry had written originally. Gerry's draft read: "& have only refused to stipulate for their country contributions which must at the same time oppress & plunge it into a war with which it has no concern & which to it must be pecularly distressing." *Ibid.*

4. In the Gerry draft this was the opening paragraph, but it was shifted, without change, and inserted at this point. *Ibid.*

to themselves. This unwished for task has been rendered a duty by ascribing to them opinions & relations which exist in imagination only, and adducing those supposed opinions & relations as proofs of an indisposition on the part of the government which has deputed them, towards that accommodation which has been sought so unremittingly, through all those difficulties and impediments with which the pursuit has been embarassed.

After the strictures on the designs & intentions you have attributed to the government of the United States which have been already noticed, you are pleased to add that these intentions are so little disguised, that nothing seems to have been neglected at Philadelphia to manifest them to every eye. It is probable with this view that it has been judged proper to send to the french republic persons whose opinions & relations are too well known to hope from them dispositions sincerely conciliatory.

The opinions and relations of the undersigned are purely american unmixed with any particle of foreign tint. If they possess a quality on which they pride themselves it is an attachment to the happiness and the welfare of their country; if they could at will select the means of manifesting that attachment, it would be by effecting a sincere & real accommodation between France and the United States, on principles promoting the interest of both, & consistent with the independence of the latter.

It requires no assurance to convince that every real American must wish sincerely to extricate his country from the ills it suffers & the greater ills with which it is threatened; but all who love liberty must admit[5] that it does not exist in a nation which can not exercise the right of maintaining its neutrality. If "opinions & relations" such as these are incompatible with "dispositions sincerely conciliatory" then indeed has the federal government chosen unfit instruments for the expression of its pacific disposition.

You contrast the conduct observed by the United States under analogous circumstances towards the cabinet of St. James, with that which is observed towards this republic. You say that on that occasion there was a solicitude to send to London Ministers well known to possess sentiments conformable to the object of their mission. That the republic had a right to count upon a similar deference, and that if a like attention has not been observed with re-

5. In the Gerry draft the ending of the sentence read: "that quiet may be purchased at too high a price." *Ibid.*

spect to it, it is too probable that it must be attributed to the views already indicated.

If unfortunately the cases shall exhibit a contrast, it is not to be found in the characters, the United States have thought proper to employ,[6] or in the conduct of their government, otherwise than by the superior attention manifested towards this republic, & never shown to any other nation, in deputing to it with ample powers three envoys extraordinary and ministers plenipotentiary, from the three great divisions of the United States. The ministers sent to the cabinet of St. James greatly deserved the confidence of their country, but they did not possess sentiments more conformable to the objects of their mission than those deputed to this republic. They did not wish more ardently to effect reconciliation nor is it believed that any persons who could have been deputed to that cabinet would have submitted to greater sacrifices in order to obtain it. Had their application for compensation for past injuries, & security against their future commission, been only met by requisitions a compliance with which would involve their nation in ills, of which even war might not perhaps be the most considerable; had all attempts to remove unfavorable impressions failed & all offers to make explanations been rejected, can it be believed that other ministers, (the first having been ordered out of the nation) would have waited six months unaccredited, soliciting permission to display the upright principles on which their government had acted and the amicable sentiments by which it was animated.

The undersigned are induced, citizen minister, to pray your attention to these plain truths, from a conviction that they manifest unequivocally the friendly temper of the federal government, and the extreme reluctance with which the hope of an accommodation with France would be relinquished.

The undersigned observe with infinite regret that the disposition manifested to treat with the minister who might be selected by this government, is not accompanied with any assurances of receding from those demands of money, heretofore made the consideration on which alone a cessation of hostility on American commerce could be obtained; to which the undersigned have not the power to accede; with which the United States would find it extremely difficult to comply; & a compliance with which would violate their

6. The remainder of the paragraph was not included. *Ibid.*

faith pledged for the observance of neutrality, & would involve them in a disastrous war with which they have no concern.

Nor do you answer to the applications which have been made for compensation to the citizens of the United States for property which shall be proved to have been taken contrary to the law of nations & existing treaties otherwise than that you are willing to discuss cases where there has been a departure from certain principles, which principles in fact involve almost every case.

You have signified, citizen Minister, that the executive Directory is disposed to treat with one of the envoys & you hope that this overture will not be attended on the part of the undersigned with any serious difficulty. Every proposition of the executive Directory is considered with the most minute & respectful attention. The result of a deliberation on this point is that no one of the undersigned is authorized to take upon himself a negotiation evidently entrusted by the tenor of their powers & instructions to the whole: Nor are there any two of them who can propose to withdraw themselves from the task committed to them by their government while there remains a possibility of performing it. It is hoped that the prejudices said to have been conceived against the ministers of the United States will be dissipated by the truths they have stated.

If[7] in this hope they shall be disappointed, and it should be the will of the Directory to order passports for the whole or any number of them, you will please to accompany such passports with letters of safe conduct which will entirely protect from the cruisers of France the vessels in which they respectively sail, & give to their persons, suite & property that perfect security to which the laws & usages of nations entitle them.

They pray you, citizen Minister, to receive the renewal of their assurances of profound respect and consideration.

CHARLES COTESWORTH PINCKNEY
J MARSHALL
E. GERRY

7. In the Gerry draft this paragraph read: "If in this hope they shall be disappointed the will of the Executive directory concerning their departure will be chearfully obeyed so soon as it shall be signified. If it shall be determind to direct passports for the whole or any number of them you will please to accompany those passports with letters of safe conduct, which will entirely protect from the cruisers of France, the Vessels in which they may respectively sail & give to their persons & suite that perfect security which the laws & usages of nations afford." *Ibid.*

To Timothy Pickering

LS, RG 59, National Archives

No. 8.

Dear Sir, Paris, April 3, 1798

We herewith transmit you the copy of a Letter written to us by the Minister of foreign affairs, dated the 28th. Ventose, (18th. March) and purporting to be an answer to our memorial of the 17th. of January.[8]

We also send you in this enclosure a copy of our reply, which has been presented this morning. As soon as we certainly know what steps the French Government mean to pursue in consequence of this reply, you shall be informed of them. We remain with great respect & esteem, Your most obedt. Servts.

Charles Cotesworth Pinckney
J. Marshall
E Gerry

To James H. Hooe

ALS, Marshall Papers, Library of Congress

Dear Sir[9] Paris, April 9, 1798

I declind answering your letter[1] by the last post in the expectation that it woud be in my power to inform you by this that I shoud be happy to take my passage in Mr. Dobrées vessel.[2] I have however still the mortification to remain perfectly uncertain when I shall quit France & from what port I shall sail. These are events which do not depend on my will—if they did I coud speak positively concerning them.

If I sail from a port in France I shall carry with me a letter of safe conduct for the vessel as well as myself. Consequently it will be an object to any vessel in which I may take my passage—for

8. See Talleyrand to American Envoys, Mar. 18, 1798, and American Envoys to Talleyrand, Apr. 3, 1798.

9. James H. Hooe (1772–1825), a merchant, is identified as being from Alexandria, Va., in John Mitchell to Rufus King, July 30, 1798, King Papers, XXXVIII, New-York Historical Society.

1. Not found.

2. Pierre Frédéric Dobrée. JM addressed this letter "Au citoyen James H. Hooe, Aux soins du citoyen Dobrée, Consul, Nantes."

the affair of papers being en regle will perhaps be but a weak protection. Will you my dear Sir favor me with a statement of any other vessels about to sail from Nantz or its neighborhood? Perhaps tho that of Mr. Dobrée shoud be gone there may be others in which I can sail.

Adieu my dear Sir. I wish you a great deal of happiness & am, your obedt

J MARSHALL

From Rufus King

Letterbook Copy, King Papers, New-York Historical Society

My Dear Sir, London, April 13, 1798

I have considered my Letters to Genl. Pinckney as written jointly to you and him, and therefore have not particularly acknowledged the Letter that you Sometime past wrote me.[3]

By General Pinckney's last Letter I have reason to apprehend that I may not see him before his return:[4] the object of this Letter is to entreat you to take England in your way, and to give me the opportunity and advantage of confering with you not only upon what has passed but what is likely to occur respecting our Connection and affairs with Europe.

Ships will be leaving England almost every week for several months to come, and your stay here may therefore be as short as you chuse. Accept the assurance of the sincere attachment and respect of

R K.

From Talleyrand

Copy, Archives of the Ministry of Foreign Affairs, Paris

Paris, April 13, 1798

Le Ministre des relations extérieures envoye à Monsieur Pinckney[5] son Passeport. Il Croit que Cette Piece est une precaution

3. See JM to King, Dec. 24, 1797.

4. Pinckney informed King that he planned to go to the south of France because of his daughter's health and then to depart from Bordeaux for the United States. See Pinckney to King, Mar. 27, 1798, King Papers, LXIII, New-York Historical Society.

5. A note on the copy indicates that identical notes were delivered to JM and Pinckney.

Suffisante pour que Monsieur Pinckney n'ait pas la Crainte d'être arrêté par des Corsaires francais. Mais Comme il a appris qu'il désiroit pour plus grande Sureté un Sauf Conduit du Ministre de la Marine, le Ministre des relations exterieures a l'honneur de lui adresser l'une et l'autre piece.[6]

To Talleyrand

AD, Archives of the Ministry of Foreign Affairs, Paris

[Paris], April 13, 1798

Genl. Marshall has the honor to acknowledge the receipt of the letter of the minister of exterior relations inclosing his passport & a letter of safe conduct.

Though he had expected that the letter woud have been more special yet he trusts that it will protect him, & will prevent the vessel in which he may sail from being turnd out of her course. In this confidence he embarks from one of the ports of France.

To Caron de Beaumarchais

ALS, Private Collection

Paris, April 15, 1798

J'ai reçu mon cher ami, avec beacoup de sensibilité votre lettre trés obligiante d'aujourd'hui. Je vous remercie infiniment pour son accompagniment. C'est un morceau d'esprit bien precieux.[7]

J'ai perdu mon passage de Nantes & par consequence je chercherai un autre a Bourdeaux. Je part demain matin. Plut a Dieu que mes desirs pour un rapprochement entre les deux republics pourroient reussir. On verroit aussitot le fin des ourages qui menacent notre tranquilité.

Adieu Monsieur je vous souhaite beaucoup de bonheur quand

6. The letter of safe conduct has not been found.

7. Beaumarchais wrote in the margin that the parting gift was a letter of Voltaire to the king of France. The letter was probably one written on Apr. 15, 1760, that had been published in Geneva in 1775. Beaumarchais was the editor of the major edition of Voltaire's letters and had many transcripts in his possession. See Theodore Besterman *et al.*, eds., *Les Oeuvres complètes de Voltaire*, XLI (Geneva, 1968), 204-206; Besterman, "The Beaumarchais Transcripts of Voltaire's Correspondence," *Times Literary Supplement*, Apr. 23, 1949, 272.

je vous souhaite la justice & dans Fotre pais & dans le mien. Je suis votre

J MARSHALL

To James H. Hooe

[*April 18, 1798.* JM writes about his travels in France and his plans to return to the United States. Listed in Parke-Bernet Galleries, Inc., Auction Catalog (New York, Dec. 3, 1963), item 159. Not found.]

To Charles Cotesworth Pinckney

ALS, Pinckney Family Papers, Library of Congress

My dear Sir[8] Bordeaux, April 21, 1798

I arrivd at this place to day which is the sixth after my departure from Paris. The journey was in nothing remarkable since as usual two wheels broke down on the road. I do not however think this must of necessity be communicated to the Secretary of State & consequently my broken wheels will be saved the circuit of the United States. It is fortunate for me that I pressed on so expeditiously. The Alexander Hamilton, (a very excellent vessel but for the sin of the name which makes my return in her almost as criminal as if I had taken England in my way) has fallen down the river & woud have saild tomorrow had not I arrived to day. My baggage has not yet made its appearance but I hope to see it tomorrow or the next day & in that case I go on board so soon as a boat can take me to the vessel & shall bid I beleive an eternal adieu to Europe, (I wish to add) & to its crimes. Mark I only mean its political crimes, for those of a private nature are really some of them so lovely that it requires men of as much virtue & less good temper than you & myself to hate them.

If you have given me a line before your departure from Paris I hope I shall receive it here. If you have deferd writing till your journey has commenced you will probably have the pleasure of bringing your letter with you to the United States as you will have a chance to find it here.

8. JM addressed this letter to Pinckney, "Care of Messrs. Vanderyrer Villemint & Schwartz, bankers, Paris," the Paris agency of Willink, Van Staphorst & Hubbard, of Amsterdam.

I will hope that the health of your daughter improves. Present me very respectfully to Mrs. Pinckney & beleive me to be with sincere & affectionate esteem, Your obedt

J MARSHALL

My baggage is here & I sail today the 23d. No letter from you.

To Fulwar Skipwith

ALS, Dreer Collection, Historical Society of Pennsylvania

Dear Sir Bordeaux, April 21, 1798

The inclosed papers I have designd for more than three months to deliver to you but have never thought of doing so & seen you at the same time.[9] The day before I left Paris I put them in my pocket for that purpose but was too much occupied with my departure to take them out again. I am happy in beleiving that the omission has produced no inconvenience.

I reachd this place to day at 3 o Clock. The Alexander Hamilton has fallen down the river & her captain woud have gone on board tomorrow had not my arrival to day induced him to wait til Monday for my baggage. If it arrives I shall take my passage in her for New York.

Present me to my friends in Paris & have the goodness to say to Madam Vilette in my name & in the handsomest manner, everything which respectful friendship can dictate. When you have done that You will have renderd not quite half justice to my sentiments. Farewell. I wish you a great deal of happiness & am, yours etc.

J MARSHALL

My baggage is arrived.

Deeds

Deed Book Copies, Office of the Clerk of Hardy County, Moorefield, W. Va.

[*April 25, 1798* (*Hardy County, Va.*). By his attorney, Rawleigh Colston, JM conveys parcels of land in the South Branch Manor to: Anthony

9. See Timothy Pickering to American Envoys, July 15, 1797, for the papers that JM might have been carrying for months from Philip Felichy to Pickering. See Felichy to Pickering, July 7 and Sept. 14, 1796, Miscellaneous-Miscellaneous, F 44, Envelope 1, RG 76, National Archives.

Baker, 28 acres for £7 and 29 acres for £7 5s.; Moses Hutton, 32 acres for £8; David Welton, 14.5 acres for £4; Jesse Welton, 35 acres for £8 15s.; Job Welton, 56 acres for £35 5d. All the deeds were recorded in the District Court at Hardy County in either May or Sept. 1798.]

Deeds

Deed Book Copies, Office of the Clerk of Hardy County, Moorefield, W. Va.

[*May 4, 1798* (*Hardy County, Va.*). By his attorney, Rawleigh Colston, JM conveys parcels of land in the South Branch Manor to Jonathan Hutton, 20 acres for £5 and 53 acres for £13 5s. Both deeds were recorded in the District Court at Hardy County on May 9, 1798.]

From Thomas W. Griffith

ALS, Pickering Papers, Massachusetts Historical Society[1]

Sir, Paris, May 20, 1798

I hope this will find you safe & well in a land of real Liberty, However things have taken such a turn in Europe since this few weeks that I am about to address you on a subject, which I thought by no means apropos at the moment of your departure from here.[2]

The manner in wh. republicanism is used of late will I think accomplish a suspension of that moral force which has decided the fate of so many Countries, for the natural Consequences must be indifference & difficulties on the one side, Union & Vigour on the other, indeed too much success tends evidently to create causes wh. finally combat it and a Ballance must ensue sooner or later. We have only I think to look well into what passes around us just now to be convinced that this epoque has arrived or is near at hand, for many details and for reasons known to you, I must beg leave to refer you to the papers inclosed, wh. are perhaps worth the postage.[3]

It is then I think highly probable that some Terms will be offerd from here much more consistant with the Honour of the United States, Govrt. & poeple, than any wh. have appeared in public

1. JM sent this letter to Timothy Pickering in September. See JM to Pickering, Sept. 15, 1798.

2. Griffith was a Baltimore merchant. For an account of his experience in France, see Elizabeth Wormeley Latimer, ed., *My Scrap-Book of the French Revolution* (Chicago, 1899), 9-69; and F 7, 4733, dossier 1, Archives Nationales, Paris.

3. Enclosures not found.

yet, or even than those wh. we suppose were made to you whilst here, and it is under this Conviction Sir, that I am induced to offer myself to Gouvernment a Candidate for the important place of Consul genl. here, place wh. has now lately become vacant as it appears,[4] taking the liberty to solicit your good offices in my favour.

Soon after my arrival in this Country, that is to say in 1794 most of the respectable Merchants in Baltimore, place of my nativity, petitioned the then president to give me the Consulship for Havre de Grace, But, whatever might be the dispositions of Gouvernment toward me Mr. N. Cutting who you have seen in this City was previously named to that place & holds it still. A long residence in this Country, and some application to the Study of its Deeds, the revolution & the french Gouvernment will I trust enable me if favord with the Confidance of my Countrymen to give due satisfaction as well to the executive as to individuals, such at least would be my views and I hope you know enough of me to think so.

I offer you anew every assurance of my esteem & respect, as well as any services here I can possibly render you or yr. friends, having the Honour to be, Sir, Yr. mo. Obedt. Hble Servt.

THO WATERS GRIFFITH

You will have heard that Threilhard one of the fr. Ministers at Rastadt. goes into the directory in the place of Francois de neufchateau.[5]

I trust that Doctor McHenry Minister at War & Genl. Saml. Smith, both of Baltimore & to whom I have written by this opportunity, would join you in any recommendation in my favor.[6]

4. Fulwar Skipwith had long since resigned his post as consul general, but with the break in French-American relations no action was taken on his resignation and he continued to serve until 1799.

5. Jean-Baptiste, comte de Treilhard (1742–1810), formerly a negotiator for France at Lille, was elected to replace Nicholas-François de Neufchâteau on May 15, 1798, and took office on May 22, 1798.

6. James McHenry. Samuel Smith (1752-1839) was a prominent merchant and politician from Baltimore. On Smith, see Frank A. Cassell, *Merchant Congressman in the Young Republic: Samuel Smith of Maryland, 1752–1839* (Madison, Wis., 1971).

To Timothy Pickering

ALS, Vail Collection, New-York Historical Society

Dear Sir New York, June 18, 1798

I arrivd at this place yesterday & shall set out to day for Philadelphia.

With the last letters addressd to you by the envoys from the United States to the French republic was transmited a copy of their answer to the letter receivd by them from the minister of exterior relations.[7] On the 14th. of april a passport & letter of safe conduct were deliverd to me & on the 16th. I set out for Bordeaux at which place I embarked for the United States. Genl. Pinckney receivd his passport on the 13th & proposd setting out from Paris for the south of France about the 17th. or 18th. of the same month. The ill health of his daughter to whom a residence of a month or two in the south is prescribed by her Physicians as indispensible will postpone his embarkation for some little time.[8]

Mr. Gerry remains in Paris. I am the bearer of a [*letter*] from that Gentleman to the President[9] which I pres[*ume*] communicates far fully than is in my power his sit[*uation*]. I am Sir with much respect & esteem, Your obedt. Servt.

J MARSHALL

To George Washington

ALS, Washington Papers, Library of Congress

Dear Sir Philadelphia, June 22, 1798

Your letter to Genl. Dumas was deliverd by me to his lady from whom in consequence of it I receivd during my stay in Paris the

7. See American Envoys to Talleyrand, Apr. 3, 1798. The letters had arrived in Philadelphia on June 14 and were transmitted to Congress the day after JM's arrival in New York City. The dispatch included Talleyrand's letter of Mar. 18, 1798. June 18, 1798, *Annals of Congress*, IX, 3125-3159

8. The Pinckneys left Paris in mid-April and spent two months in the congenial southern climate near Lyons until their daughter Eliza was well enough to attempt the voyage to America. Mary Pinckney to Margaret Manigault, Apr. 15 and May 28, 1798, Manigault Family Papers, University of South Carolina; Marvin R. Zahniser, *Charles Cotesworth Pinckney: Founding Father* (Chapel Hill, N.C., 1967), 190, 198.

9. See Gerry to John Adams, Apr. 16, 1798, Adams Papers, Massachusetts Historical Society. The letter was communicated to Congress by President Adams on June 21, 1798. *Annals of Congress*, IX, 3459–3460.

most polite & flattering attentions.[1] She deliverd me the inclosd answer which was written in Copenhagen & forwarded to her.[2] Having heard that Mrs. Marshall is in Winchester I shall immediately set out for that place.[3]

Permit me Sir to acknowledge the receipt of your very polite & obliging letter in answer to that which I did myself the honor to address to you from the Hague.[4] I had not sir expected to draw you into a correspondence which might intrude on your leisure but merely to do myself the pleasure of communicating to you occasionally such facts as it might be agreeable to you to receive. With the most sincere respect & attachment, I remain Sir your obedt. Servt.

J MARSHALL

From the Grand Jury

Printed, *Philadelphia Gazette and Universal Daily Advertiser*, June 25, 1798, 2

SIR,[5] Philadelphia, June 22, 1798[6]

THE members of the grand inquest for the County of Gloucester, in the State of New-Jersey whilst in sessions received the pleasing information of your return to the land in which you were born, which you have so ably and faithfully served, and which receives to its bosom the citizen who deserves well of his country.

Accept, sir, on this occasion the congratulations of us, a portion of the people, whose dignity you have so nobly maintained and whose rights, unawed by power and uncorrupted by seduction,

1. See JM to Washington, July 7, 1797.
2. Letter not found.
3. During JM's absence, Mary W. Marshall had given birth to their fourth child, John Marshall, on Jan. 13, 1798. She had gone to Winchester in early summer to recuperate from a recurring nervous condition, no doubt staying with JM's brother, James Markham Marshall. JM departed for Winchester on June 25; he arrived there on June 28. *Philadelphia Gazette and Universal Daily Advertiser*, June 25 and July 11, 1798.
4. See JM to Washington, Sept. 15, 1797, and Washington to JM, Dec. 4, 1797.
5. This document is printed here as an example of many similar addresses and replies that resulted from JM's visits to cities as he traveled to Virginia. Most of these were reprinted in local newspapers. On Friday, Samuel Kennard, David Harker, and Michael C. Fisher, a committee from the grand jury of Gloucester County, N.J., waited on JM at Oeller's Hotel in Philadelphia and delivered the address.
6. JM arrived in Philadelphia amidst much celebration on Tuesday evening, June 19. See Thomas Jefferson to James Madison, June 21, 1798, Madison Papers, Library of Congress; *Philadelphia Gazette and Universal Daily Advertiser*, June 19 and 20, 1798.

you would not surrender to vindictive and profligate men. At a wide distance from your government, surrounded with the glare of power, and assailed by the acts of misrepresentation, or bolder falsehood, it is possible you experienced many painful solicitudes for the fate of that country, rendered dear to you by all the ties of nature, friendship and allegiance—those fears must now be removed. It must afford you infinite pleasure, to behold on your arrival, the unconquerable spirit of Americans rising into action prepared for every event: a spirit which will never submit, and which will only expire when liberty herself shall die.

In proffering to you, sir, this tribute of our respect and affection, we embrace the occasion to express the high confidence we repose with all true Americans, in the talents and integrity of the President of the United States; whose vigilance and wisdom, conspicuous through every period of a splendid and useful life, did not forsake him in the selection for your important mission. Long may you live, sir, in the enjoyment of all the felicities of this life (in the memory and gratitude of your countrymen and their posterity you will ever live); and when called to the skies, may you receive a crown of glory which fadeth not away. By order of the Grand Jury

JAMES HOPKINS, Foreman.

To the Grand Jury

Printed, *Philadelphia Gazette and Universal Daily Advertiser*, June 25, 1798, 2

GENTLEMEN, Philadelphia, June 22, 1798

I RECEIVE with sentiments, I feel myself unable to display, the very flattering address with which I am honored by the grand inquest for the county of Gloucester, in the state of New-Jersey.

That my return to the bosom of my native country, an event so grateful to myself, should afford pleasure to so respectable a portion of my fellow-citizens, excites sensations in a mind alive to esteem honourably and virtuously to be acquired, which more than compensate the painful and embarrassing circumstances to which, during my absence from the land which gave me birth, I have been unavoidably exposed.

That the efforts of the Envoys of the United States in the service of a beloved country receives your matured approbation, an approbation founded on a perfect knowledge of their conduct, is a sweet reward for exertions, the failure of which, they can never cease to lament.

In making those exertions they have been uniformly governed by the most sincere and ardent desire for peace, regulated and tempered by the firm determination, that not even peace was to be purchased at the price of national independence. Although uninformed of the particular sentiments which prevailed in America, or of the judgments which might be entertained of their measures, they ever estimated too highly the virtue, the patriotism and the justice of their fellow-citizens, not to believe that a system of conduct, founded entirely on the principles which have been stated, would, however unsuccessful, be viewed with indulgence. It is pleasing to believe, that in this the American character has not been mistaken.

Participating entirely your sentiments concerning the President of the United States, allow me to add to my felicitations on the happiness of possessing at a period critical as the present, a chief magistrate believed to be so worthy of the public confidence, my grateful acknowledgments for the instance you have selected of his continuing vigilance and wisdom.[7]

Permit me, gentlemen, to mingle with my thanks for your obliging expressions concerning my personal happiness, the most sincere wishes of my heart that the good solicited for me may be long, very long possessed by the grand inquest for the county of Gloucester in the state of New-Jersey.

JOHN MARSHALL.

From Militia Officers

Printed, *Philadelphia Gazette and Universal Daily Advertiser*, June 25, 1798, 2

[*June 22, 1798, Philadelphia.* A committee of officers from the Gloucester County, N.J., militia meets JM at Oeller's Hotel and congratulates him on his safe return from France. "We are sensible, that what truth, reason, and eloquence could do, has been done already. As it seems to remain

7. This is the only known instance in which JM publicly acknowledged his confidence in President Adams by direct reference to him in an address. George Cabot (1751–1823) reported at a later date that JM expected war with France but thought that the United States should wait for a declaration of war by France. Cabot to Rufus King, Oct. 6, 1798, King Papers, XLI, New-York Historical Society.

only for our country to try the last resort, we hope it will be grateful to your heart to be informed, that, armed in honesty, and impelled by that courage which American freemen possess, we are resolved, when called upon by our country, to contribute our part, to enforce by the sword, those injured rights which the milder means of negociation have failed to secure."]

To Militia Officers

Printed, *Philadelphia Gazette and Universal Daily Advertiser*, June 25, 1798, 2

[*June 22, 1798, Philadelphia.* JM responds with gratitude to the address of the Gloucester County, N.J., militia officers for their praise of his conduct. Referring to their mention of the sword, JM cautions that "the permanent and real interests of our country require at all times that all honorable means of avoiding war should be essayed before the sword be appealed to. The well-known moderation of our government and of our national character assures us that these means will ever be essayed. When they fail, it is flattering and consoling to believe that the people of the United States consider every calamity as light when only to be avoided by the loss of national independence—an object which must be dear to the militia of New-Jersey who have contributed so much to its acquisition."]

From Thomas Jefferson

ALS, Collection of the Association for the Preservation of Virginia Antiquities, on deposit at the Virginia Historical Society

[Philadelphia], June 23, 1798

TH: JEFFERSON presents his compliments to General Marshall.[8] He had the honor of calling at his lodgings twice this morning, but was so un-lucky[9] as to find that he was out on both occasions. He

8. Jefferson had planned to leave for Virginia on Wednesday, June 20, 1798. On Tuesday morning the news of JM's arrival in New York City reached Philadelphia, and Jefferson remained at the capital to await the news from France. Jefferson to James Madison, June 21, 1798, Madison Papers, Library of Congress; Jefferson to Thomas M. Randolph, June 21, 1798, Jefferson Papers, Massachusetts Historical Society.

9. Jefferson first wrote "so lucky" but inserted "un-" before sending this note to JM. Many years later, JM was reported to have said that Jefferson's initial omission of the prefix "un" to the word "lucky" was one occasion where Jefferson had come close to telling the truth. Sallie E. Marshall Hardy, "John Marshall, third Chief Justice of the United States, as son, brother, husband and friend," *The Green Bag*, VIII (1896), 482–483; Beveridge, *Marshall*, II, 347.

wished to have expressed in person his regret that a preengagement for to-day which could not be dispensed with would prevent him the satisfaction of dining in company with Genl. Marshall,[1] and therefore begs leave to place here the expressions of that respect which in common with his fellow citizens he bears him.

To Thomas Jefferson

AL, Jefferson Papers, Library of Congress

[Philadelphia, June 24, 1798]

J MARSHALL begs leave to accompany his respectful compliments to Mr. Jefferson with assurances of the regret he feels at being absent when Mr. Jefferson did him the honor to call on him.

J MARSHALL is extremely sensible to the obliging expressions containd in Mr. Jeffersons polite billet of yesterday.

He sets out tomorrow[2] for Winchester & woud with pleasure charge himself with any commands from Mr. Jefferson to that part of Virginia.

From Caron de Beaumarchais

Record Copy, Private Collection

Mon honorable Ami Paris, July 7, 1798

Quand M. Gerry arrivera en Amérique avec ce mot d'un homme qui vous aime, Et l'un de ceux qui vous ont le mieux apprécié en France. Il y aura déja longtems que vous aurès revu vos pénates obéris.

Aprés votre 1er repos, Et le 1er coup d'oeuil que vous aurés donné a vos propres affaires; après tous vos comptes rendus a vos commettans; n'oubliés pas que vous avés laissé a Paris l'un des Francais qui a le plus contribué a rendre l'Amérique libre, il y a 20 ans; qui desire le plus la franche réunion de nos deux grandes Républiques; qui y travaille constament malgré l'etrange ingratitude

1. The members of Congress gave a dinner for JM at Oeller's Hotel on June 23. See Invitation, June 21, 1798, John Rutledge, Jr., Papers, Duke University Library; Beveridge, *Marshall*, II, 348–349.

2. Albert Beveridge mistakenly noted that JM left Philadelphia on June 22. Beveridge, *Marshall*, II, 351 n. 1.

dont votre pays a payé ses Services. N'oubliés pas, ami, que S'il est écouté dans ses demandes au Directoire; ce Sera votre ami, lui mesme qui ira travailler avec vous a ce rapprochement utile. N'oubliés pas qu'il est dans la détresse en France, parce que rien ne Si termine pour lui en amérique, Et que vous etes Son deffenseur en appel de la Virginie, comme vous l'avés été au 1er tribunal ou il a gagné ce procès.

Je vous salue, vous honore vous aime, Et compte pouvoir vous embrasser, Sous quelques mois.

Signé CARON BEAUMARCHAIS

Post Script; A l'instant ou je fuies ces 4 mots pour vous; on m'apporte le journal de ce jour. Je vous l'envoye, pas gaiété, comme si vous étiés encore dans la Rue de Vaugirard, chez Madme. de Villette et vous l'aimera l'idée du véritable esprit de votre gouvernement aujourd'hui.

Dieu! ne Souffrons pas *Vous de votre coté*; moi du mien; que les deux republiques se brouillent. Depuis votre départ bien des intrigues ignorées, obscures, se sont eclairciés au sujet de votre reunion. Bref, le gouvernement francais ne veut pas que l'on croye qu'il est dans des dispositions hostile, a l'égard des américains; puisqu'il autorise de pareils détails dans tous les journaux—qu'il fait aimer la France et notre état republicain.

Rappellés vous que vous m'avés promis de faire de vrai éfforts pour le rapprochement puis, ai je y concourir avec vous!

L'étonnante créature qu'on nomme *Bonaparte*, a pris en 24 heures, *l'isle et le fort de Malthe*, le second Gibraltar de notre Méditerranée, que le grand Soliman Second, avec toutes ses forces d'Europe, d'Asie et d'Affrique, abbandonner apres 3 mois de siege. Il a donné la liberté a 46500 turcs esclaves pour la Vie; lesquels, dans leur enthousiasme, ont juré de le suivre partout, comme leur puissant bienfaiture. Le 1er article du journal que je vous envoye, vous donnera la juste idée des projets de Bonaparte.[3]

Et l'on commence a dire que le *Gouvernement anglais* veut faire Sincerement la paix. Il est bien tard pour cette grande idée. Je crois qu'ils ne garderont pas plus l'Irlande qu'ils n'ont de garder l'Amérique. L'insurrection est générale dans cette isle, comme elle

3. The official report of the capitulation of Malta to Napoleon was reported in *Moniteur Universel* (Paris), July 6, 1798. Suleiman the Magnificent (1494-1566), of the Ottoman Empire, had failed to capture the island in 1565.

l'était dans votre continent en 1776, quand *Silas Deane* vint un Sollicitter pour Son pays. J'echauffai, mon ami, toutes les cervelles francaises pour la cause des américains; et grace a mes travaux de touts guerir, les ministres glacés d'un Roi trop jeune alors, consentirent qu'un commercant, qui était moi S Nouât a votre service, et multipliât des moyens de secours, lesquels me Sont encore liés après vingt ans.

Adieu mon cher Marshall, jusqu'au moment ou j'irai me rejoindre a tous pour achever la réunion, si l'on ni autre.

Signé BEAUMARCHAIS

From George Washington

ALS, Williams College Library

Dear Sir, Mount Vernon, July 15, 1798

Your favour of the 22d. Ulto. from Philadelphia,[4] came duly to hand, and I regretted exceedingly that it would not be in my power to see you in your way to Richmond. I hope your return will give perfect restoration of health to Mrs. Marshall, and that you found all the rest of your family & connections well.

I was glad to find that the *only* letter I wrote to you, while you were in France, had got to your hands.[5] I should at least have acknowledged the receipt of the several letters[6] you were so good as to favour me with, after your arrival at Paris, but judging from the situation in wch. you were placed, by the Directory of that Country, that they would not find you there, I declined it on that account; and now offer you my sincere congratulations on your safe return to your own Country, family & friends, among whom I pray you to class him who is with very sincere esteem and regard, Dear Sir, Your Most Obedt. Servant

G: WASHINGTON

From Timothy Pickering

Presscopy, Pickering Papers, Massachusetts Historical Society

Dear Sir, Philadelphia, July 24, 1798

It will be acceptable to you to receive, in a compact form, a

4. See JM to Washington, June 22, 1798.
5. See Washington to JM, Dec. 4, 1797.
6. See JM to Washington, Sept. 15, Oct. 24, 1797, and Mar. 8, 1798.

complete copy of all the papers relating to your late mission to the French Republic; and to distribute a few among your friends. Herewith I send you half a dozen copies for those purposes.[7] I intend to send 1800 to be distributed in Virginia, pursuant to a late resolve of Congress; and shall forward them as soon as I receive some information, which by this mail I request, of Colo. Carrington.[8] I am very respectfully, dear sir, your obt. servt.

TIMOTHY PICKERING

Deed

Deed Book Copy, Office of the Clerk of Hardy County, Moorefield, W. Va.

[*August 6, 1798* (*Hardy County, Va.*). By his attorney, Rawleigh Colston, JM conveys 24 acres in the South Branch Manor to Jonathan Hutton for £6. The deed was recorded in the District Court at Hardy County on Sept. 6, 1798.]

From Hanover Soldiers

Printed, *Virginia Gazette, and General Advertiser, Supplement Extraordinary* (Richmond), August 14, 1798, 2

[*August 7, 1798, Hanover, Va.* Upon JM's arrival from Fredericksburg,[9]

7. President Adams transmitted dispatch No. 8 to Congress on June 18, 1798. See American Envoys to Pickering, Apr. 3, 1798. The House of Representatives moved to print for the use of its members 1,200 copies of all the dispatches received from France to counteract what the Federalists termed "seditious publications" by Francophile printers in America who were the alleged agents of the French Directory. Robert Goodloe Harper suggested that "5000 at least" of the dispatches should be printed for public distribution. Harper observed that "it had long been manifest to him that France had her secret agents in this country." June 18, 1798, *Annals of Congress*, VIII, 1972. The implication of a French conspiracy in America came after Benjamin Franklin Bache published Talleyrand's message to the American envoys, dated Mar. 18, 1798, in the *Aurora* (Philadelphia), June 16, 1798, two days before President Adams submitted the document to Congress. See Talleyrand to American Envoys, Mar. 18, 1798; Gerry to John Adams, Apr. 16, 1798, Talleyrand to Gerry, Apr. 3, 1798, Gerry to Talleyrand, Apr. 4, 1798, under June 21, 1798, *Annals of Congress*, IX, 3459–3461.

8. Pickering wrote to Edward Carrington: "I shall be under the necessity of troubling one or two gentlemen in each state to make the distribution. You will permit me to send a large portion of those destined for Virginia to your care. Those for the northern and northwestern parts of the State, it will doubtless be best to send to Alexandria and Winchester. That as you can better judge what portions of the State should form the districts for distribution, you will greatly oblige me by pointing them out to me." Pickering to Carrington, July 24, 1798, Pickering Papers, Massachusetts Historical Society.

9. JM had left Winchester on Aug. 3. He passed through Fredericksburg on Aug.

the officers and soldiers of the Hanover Troop of Horse deliver a note of thanks to JM for his "public services" during his mission to France. Having read the dispatches published in Philadelphia, they believe that the failure of the mission "may be ascribed to the rapacious and inadmissible demands of the French Republic; and that your acquiescence therewith would have branded the United States with indelible dishonor."]

To Hanover Soldiers

Printed, *Virginia Gazette, and General Advertiser, Supplement Extraordinary* (Richmond), August 14, 1798, 2

[*August 7, 1798, Hanover, Va.* JM expresses appreciation for the reception given him by the Hanover Troop of Horse. In reference to the dispatches that had been published, he concludes: "The impression which the publication of the papers relative to the late mission to France has made on your minds, is such as might be expected to have been made on genuine Americans loving exclusively their own country, and devoted to its liberty and independence. It is unhappily but too true that the demands of the French republic were rapacious and inadmissible, and that a submission to them would have reduced the United States to the humble, dishonorable condition of a tributary and dependent nation."]

From Richmond Cavalry

Printed, *Virginia Gazette, and General Advertiser* (Richmond), August 14, 1798, 2

[*August 8, 1798, Caroline County, Va.*[1] Addressing JM as "fellow citizen and commander," this unit of the Richmond militia congratulates JM

---

4 where, while attending the theater, he witnessed a fight that broke out when the musicians played the "President's March," a popular tune identified with the Federalists. The *Aurora* (Philadelphia), Aug. 20, 1798, commented that JM's friends got "drubbed" in the foray. See also *Virginia Gazette, and General Advertiser, Supplement Extraordinary* (Richmond), Aug. 14, 1798.

1. JM arrived in Richmond on Wednesday, Aug. 8, 1798. The Richmond Troop of Horse under the command of Capt. William Austin met JM about 40 miles from the city and presented him with this address read by Dr. John Adams (1773-1825). When the entourage reached Richmond, Capt. Richardson's company of Light Infantry Blues, Gov. James Wood, several members of the Council of State, former officers who had served in the Revolution, and a number of the city's inhabitants greeted JM. As the column entered the city, Capt. Dunscomb's artillery company fired a salute in JM's honor. *Virginia Gazette, and General Advertiser* (Richmond), Aug. 14, 1798.

It is unclear how the Hanover address could have been delivered the day before the Richmond troop met JM in Caroline County. JM should have passed through Caroline County before reaching Hanover.

upon his return to Virginia. The cavalry emphasizes the significance of its close relationship to JM and concludes that "we owe you a debt of gratitude for your manly support of our rights;—and that when the voice of our country shall call us to the field under your command, we will alike manifess our attachment to your person and to our independence—our *pass word* shall be, to live *free or die gloriorsly*."]

To Richmond Cavalry

Printed, *Virginia Gazette, and General Advertiser* (Richmond), August 14, 1798, 2

[*August 8, 1798, Caroline County, Va.* JM replies to the address of the Richmond cavalry, expressing appreciation for their kindness and approbation of his conduct while in France. Because they know him personally, their "sentiments are believed to be permanent, and I love to think that no vicissitude in human affairs will induce you to regret having displayed them. . . . I delight to perceive that I was not mistaken in believing that when your duty as the citizens of a free republic—'when the voice of your country should call you to the field—you would manifest your attachment to its independence, and your pass word would be, *to live free* or *die gloriously*.' . . . I cannot view you without exulting in the recollection, that you are attached to the brigade I have the honor to command."]

Deed

Deed Book Copy, Office of the Clerk of Hardy County, Moorefield, W. Va.

[*August 8, 1798* (*Hardy County, Va.*). By his attorney, Rawleigh Colston, JM conveys 13 acres in the South Branch Manor to Teakman Our for £10. The deed was recorded in the District Court at Hardy County on Sept. 7, 1798.]

From Richmond Common Hall

Printed, *Virginia Gazette, and General Advertiser* (Richmond), August 14, 1798, 2

[*August 9, 1798, Richmond.* The mayor, recorder, aldermen, and Common Council of Richmond congratulate JM upon his safe return from France. They praise him for teaching them "to beware of a government whose influence at a distance can enfeeble and almost paralize; but whose touch is death. Perhaps we may owe to you the preservation of our excellent constitution . . . and of our well-earned liberties. . . ."]

To Richmond Common Hall

Printed, *Virginia Gazette, and General Advertiser* (Richmond), August 14, 1798, 2

[*August 9, 1798, Richmond.* JM thanks the Richmond Common Hall for its expressions of appreciation and congratulations. He writes: "I do not think that either policy or patriotism require me to conceal from you the firm and deep conviction of my mind, that accommodation with the French Republic on terms consistent with the independence of the United States has been long impracticable, and that you judge rightly when you say that 'peace was unattainable by any just and honorable means.'"]

To James McHenry

Copy, Lightfoot Papers, Swem Library, College of William and Mary

Dear Sir Richmond, August 10, 1798

Mr. Philip Lightfoot of the County of Culpeper is desirous of obtaining the commission of Captain among the 10000 to be raised for national defence.[2]

He is a young Gentleman of excellent character, considerable influence, sound american principles & turn & temper which is firm & as is believed well fitted for a military character. I am Sir very respectfully, Your obed Servt.

J MARSHALL

From Citizens of Richmond

Printed, *Virginia Gazette, and General Advertiser* (Richmond), August 14, 1798, 2

Richmond, August 11, 1798

RECEIVE, Sir, the affectionate congratulations of your fellow-

2. Philip Lightfoot (1774–*ca.* 1865) had been a lieutenant in the Virginia militia and a court clerk in Virginia in 1798. Lightfoot received the commission on Jan. 10, 1796, and served in the Eighth U.S. Regiment. James McHenry to Lightfoot, Jan. 10, 1799, Lightfoot Papers, Swem Library, College of William and Mary.

On June 22, 1798, Congress had authorized President Adams to appoint officers for the Provisional Army of 10,000 men that had been sanctioned by Congress on May 28, 1798. May 28 and June 22, 1798, *Annals of Congress*, IX, 3729-3733.

citizents of Richmond, and its vicinity,[3] on your safe return to this city, after having honorably and faithfully discharged your duty in the important mission to which you were called by the wisdom of the executive councils of America—Having been accustomed to esteem your known integrity and many amiable qualities in private life, we are proud to acknowledge that we feel our attachment and respect considerably heightened and increased by your virtuous exertions abroad, in maintaining the dignity, the honor, and independence of your country. We retrace your conduct with pleasure, and rejoice to think that one of our most distinguished patriots went forth at the public call from this city to advocate the cause of his injured country, and that he maintained it with ability, fortitude, and manly freedom, against the insiduous designs of her enemies, at the very seat of their empire, notwithstanding the numerous difficulties to which he was exposed.

For we are sensible, Sir, of the critical situation in which you found yourself placed upon that occasion. Removed at an immense distance from the councils of your country, and cut off from the benefits of a free correspondence with them by the vigilance of your adversaries, you had displayed before your eyes one of the most anxious scenes that ever agitated the human mind.—On one side you beheld France respecting no laws, human or divine, but glorying in her might, elated with successes, and frantic with ambition, meditating universal conquest, and grasping at the empire of the earth.—On the other, you beheld your infant country but just emerged from late and serious difficulties, desirous of maintaining neutrality, of cultivating peace, and pursuing a system of faith and justice towards all nations, menaced with hostilities and internal dissentions by an imperious government, which is callous to the dictates of morality and justice, and knows no laws but those of force and violence; a government which repaid all your efforts for justice and reconciliation with contumely and disdain, and threatend, unless committing the dignity of your country, you would purchase for her a frail and temporary peace by exhausting her resurces, to deluge her plains with blood, and

3. Two hundred citizens of Richmond, Manchester, and the surrounding vicinity held a banquet at Rev. John Buchanan's spring outside the city limits. The governor, members of the Council of State, and officers of the old Continental army attended. Mayor John Barret of Richmond, presided at the dinner. *Philadelphia Gazette and Universal Daily Advertiser*, Aug. 25, 1798; *Virginia Gazette, and General Advertiser* (Richmond), Aug. 14, 1798.

confound her amidst the misery and ruin in which they had involved some of the deluded nations of Europe. This was a scene calculated to excite all the most powerful passions of the heart, and to embarrass the judgment with their conflicts, but a generous mind did not hesitate to decide, and we have the satisfaction to say that, relying on the candor, virtue, and long tried perseverance of your countrymen, you nobly disdained the profligate proposal, and with honest firmness rejected every proposition which tended to commit the safety, honor, and independence of the nation you represented, declaring to despotism itself, that America, equal to every difficulty, would brave every dandger, and submit to every calamity, rather than yield up her liberty, or surrender her independence—But, Sir, we have the satisfaction to believe your anxiety is relieved, upon returning to a grateful country which receives you back again into its bosom with delight, to find you were not deceived in the opinion which you had formed of the candor, virtue, and firmness of your fellow citizens; that your predictions have been literally verified, and that every preparation is already making by a wise and virtuous government to repel the danger;—that France, though terrible to her neighbours, by her arms and intrigues, will find in this distant region virtue superior to both, and a hardy race of men united in sentiment, impregnable to seduction, and prepared to endure all the labor, fatigue, and danger of the longest and bloodiest war to maintain their Independence, and to transmit unshackeled to posterity, that hallowed liberty which they adore.

We believe too, sir, that to a mind like yours, it must afford the highest consolation to remark the immense difference there is between the dignified conduct and manly virtues of those who administer your own government, and the detestable vices of those who have usurped the government of France:—Between the order and Liberty which exist here, and the violence and despotism that prevail there; between that Justice, moderation, and anxious attention to the public good, which form the characteristic of those who administer our own government, and the injustice, violence and scandalous pursuit of their own private aggrandizement, which distinguish those who in France have put all liberty, authority, and safety under their feet.

Return therefore, sir, to this Land of Freedom, and into a country, which glories in your virtues and repays your generous exertions with thanks and approbation, the highest rewards to a virtuous mind; and may the manly and dignified conduct which you have displayed upon that occasion, and which justly excites the gratitude of your country, serve to convince future generations, that he who would acquire the approbation and affections of a brave and free people, should never hesitate to expose them to war and difficulty, rather than commit their independence or surrender the smallest portion of their liberty. For possessed of these, the temporary difficulties of a war, which is resisted in order to support them, are easily sustained, but deprived of them, men who aspire to the exalted character of Freemen, would view all other joys as poisoned and embittered, and would turn with loathing and disgust from every other comfort in life. But, Sir, permit us to observe, that whilst we applaud your conduct, we approve likewise of the wisdom of that government which selected you; whilst we receive you with affection and gratitude at the place of your residence, and rejoice to see you restored to the arms of a virtuous family, we praise, we admire and ardently love that government which you have so ably defended; and so far from agreeing to prostrate its independence at the feet of another nation, we will with united hands and hearts rally round its standard, and court danger and death under all their forms, sooner than permit its measures to be controlled by forreign influence.

In fine, we will never consent to survive the government and Independence of America which we have covenanted to maintain, but we will transmit them safe and unimpaired to posterity, or perish in the struggle to preserve them.—Permit us also to express, Sir, the high satisfaction which we have in an opportunity of proving by this public testimonial of our confidence in your integrity, judgment and veracity, how greatly the despots of France have deceived themselves when they ventured to believe that a candid country would not sooner confide in the representations of their own ministers and fellow citizens, than in the insiduous relations of the despicable emissaries of falsehood, faction and intrigue, endeavored to be disseminated amongst them by the contrivances of a gloomy despotism, which hates and plots the destruction of that happiness abroad, which it has annihilated at home.

Be pleased, Sir, to accept our sincere wishes for your future health and welfare; and as we trust that you will continue to merit the esteem of mankind, so we hope that you will always receive the benedictions and most unqualified approbation of your country.

To Citizens of Richmond

Printed, *Virginia Gazette, and General Advertiser* (Richmond), August 14, 1798, 2

Richmond, August 11, 1798

I WILL not, Gentlemen, attempt to describe the emotions of joy which my return to my native country, and particularly to this city, has excited in my mind; nor can I paint the sentiments of affection and gratitude towards you, which my heart has ever felt, and which the kind and partial reception now given me by my fellow citizens, cannot fail to increase. He only who has been long absent from a much loved country and from friends greatly and deservedly esteemed—whose return is welcomed with expressions which, dictated by friendship, surpass his merits or his hopes, will judge of feelings to which I cannot do justice.

The situation in which the late envoys from the United States to the French republic found themselves in Paris, was indeed attended with the unpleasant circumstances which you have traced. Removed far from the councils of their country, and receiving no intelligence concerning it, the scene before them could not fail to produce the most anxious and disquieting sensations. Neither the ambition, the power, nor the hostile temper of France, was concealed from them:—nor could they be unacquainted with the earnest and unceasing solicitude felt by the government and people of the United States for peace. But amidst these difficulties, they possessed as guides, clear and explicit instructions, a conviction of the firmness and magnanimity, as well as of the justice and pacific temper of their government, and a strong reliance on that patriotism and love of liberty, which can never cease to glow in the American bosom. With these guides, however thorny the path of duty might be, they could not mistake it. It was their duty, unmindful of personal considerations, to pursue peace with unabating zeal, through all the difficulties with which the pursuit was embarrassed by a haughty and victorious government, holding in perfect contempt the rights of others, but to repel with unhesitating decision, any propositions, an acceptance of which would subvert the independence of the United States. This they have endeavored to do. I delight to believe that their endeavors have not dissatisfied their government or country, and it is most grateful to my mind to be assured that they receive the approbation of my fellow citizens in Richmond, and its vicinity.

I rejoice that I was not mistaken in the opinion I had formed of my countrymen. I rejoice to find, though they know how to estimate, and therefore seek to avoid the horrors and the dangers of war, yet they know also how to value the blessings of liberty and national independence: They know that peace would be purchased at too high a price by bending beneath a foreign yoke, and that peace so purchased could be but of short duration. The nation thus submitting, would be soon involved in the quarrels of its master, and would be compelled to exhaust its blood and its treasure, not for its own liberty, its own independence, or its own rights, but for the aggrandizement of its oppressor. The modern world unhappily exhibits but too plain a demonstration of this proposition. I pray Heaven that America may never contribute to its still further elucidation.

Terrible to her neighbors on the continent of Europe, as all must admit France to be, I believe that the United States, if indeed united, if awake to the impending danger, if capable of employing their whole, their undivided force—are so situated as to be able to preserve their independence. An immense ocean placed by a gracious providence, which seems to watch over this rising empire, between us and the European world, opposes of itself such an obstacle to invading ambition, must so diminish the force which can be brought to bear upon us, that our resources, if duly exerted, must be adequate to our protection, and we shall remain free, if we do not deserve to be slaves.

You do me justice, gentlemen, when you suppose that consolation must be derived from a comparison of the administration of the American government, with that which I have lately witnessed. To a citizen of the United States, so familiarly habituated to the actual possession of liberty, that he almost considers it as the inseparable companion of man, a view of the despotism, which, borrowing the garb and usurping the name of freedom, tyrannizes over so large and so fair a portion of the earth, must teach the value which he ought to place on the solid safety and real security he enjoys at home. In support of these, all temporary difficulties, however great, ought to be encountered and I agree with you, that the loss of them would poison and embitter every other joy; and that deprived of them, men who aspire to the exalted character of free men, would turn with loathing and disgust from every other comfort in life.

To me, gentlemen, the attachment you manifest to the government of your choice, affords the most sincere satisfaction. Having no interests separate from, or opposed to, those of the people, being themselves subject in common with others, to the laws they make, being soon to return to that mass from which they are selected for a time in order to conduct the affairs of the nation, it is by no means probable that those who administer the government of the United States can be actuated by other motives than the sincere desire of promoting the real prosperity of those whose destiny involves their own, and in whose ruin they must participate. Desirable as is at all times a due confidence in our government, it is peculiarly so in a moment of peril like the present, in a moment when the want of that confidence must impair the means of self defence, must increase a danger already but too great, and furnish, or at least give the appearance of furnishing, to a foreign real enemy, those weapons which have so often been so successfully used.

Accept, gentlemen, my grateful acknowledgements for your kind expressions concerning myself, and do me the justice to believe, that your prosperity, and that of the city of Richmond and its vicinity, will ever be among the first wishes of my heart.

J. MARSHALL.

To Timothy Pickering

ALS, Pickering Papers, Massachusetts Historical Society

Dear Sir Richmond, August 11, 1798

On my return to Richmond a very few days past I had the pleasure of receiving your letter of the 15th. of July inclosing the copy of one addressed to Mr. Gerry[4] & also that of the 24th.[5] of the same month transmiting several copies of the dispatches from the late envoys to the french republic, for both of which I thank you.

I shoud scarcely suppose it possible that the letter to Mr. Gerry

4. Pickering's letter of July 15 has not been found. In the letter to Gerry, Pickering wrote: "It is presumed that you will consider the instructions of the 23d. of March . . . as an effectual recall: lest, however, by any possibility, those instructions should not have reached you, and you should still be in France, I am directed by the President to transmit to you this letter, & to inform you that you are to consider it as a positive letter of recall." Pickering to Gerry, June 25, 1798, Pickering Papers, Massachusetts Historical Society. See Pickering to American Envoys, Mar. 23, 1798.

5. See Pickering to JM, July 24, 1798.

coud find him in France, but as I know he is so extremely cautious as often to be dilatory I am apprehensive that complete information of the present temper of the United States will be acquird by the french government before he sails & that possessd of such information insiduous propositions will be hinted, not with real pacific views, but for the purpose of dividing the people of this country & separating them from their government. I shall therefore continue to feel considerable anxieties on this subject until I hear of his arrival & that he has brought with him either real peace which I am sure is impossible, or no seductive intimations. The people of this country generally, so far as I can judge in the very short time I have been here, are pretty right as it respects France. Few are desperate enough to defend her conduct or to censure that of our government with respect to her. Some leading characters have reprobated slightly the conduct of the envoys for not having in a more explicit manner offerd to abandon the claim for spoliations on our commerce on condition of an abandonment on the part of France of the demand of a loan, & others have endeavord to spread the opinion that the fairest prospect existed of an accomodation through the means of Mr. Gerry with whom there was every reason to beleive that a negotiation was opend so soon as Genl. Pinckney & myself left Paris. These representations however make so little impression that I beleive France will be given up & the attack upon the government will be supported by the alien & sedition laws.[6] I am extremely sorry to observe that here they are more successful & that these two laws, especially the sedition bill, are viewd by a great many well meaning men, as unwarranted by the constitution. I am entirely persuaded that with many the hate of the Government of our country is implacable & that if these bills did not exist the same clamor woud be made by them on some other account, but there are also many who are guided by very different motives & who tho less noisy in their complaints are seriously uneasy on this subject.

I am extremely anxious to hear from Genl. Pinckney & cannot restrain a fear that his distance from Paris may prevent his sailing til his embarkation may be opposed by serious difficulties.

The derangements produced by my absence & the dispersion of

6. The Alien and Sedition Laws were four measures passed between June 18 and July 14, 1798. June 22, 25, July 6, and 14, 1798, *Annals of Congress*, IX, 3739–3746, 3753–3754, 3776–3777. See also James Morton Smith, *Freedom's Fetters: The Alien and Sedition Laws and American Civil Liberties* (Ithaca, N.Y., 1956).

my family oblige me to make either sales which I do not wish, or to delay payments of money[7] which, I ought not to delay, unless I can receive from the treasury. This state of things obliges me to apply to you & to ask whether you can furnish me either with an order from the Secretary of the treasury on Colo. Carrington or with your request to him to advance money to me. The one or the other will be sufficient. With very much respect & esteem, I am dear Sir your obedt. Servt.

J MARSHALL

When you can with convenience do so you will much oblige by forwarding to me the hastyly sketchd journal which I kept in France.[8]

To Mary W. Marshall

ALS, Marshall Papers, Swem Library, College of William and Mary

My dearest Polly Richmond, August 18, 1798

I reached this place about a week past & have scarcely had time to look into any business yet there are so many persons calling every hour to see me. I have been a little indisposd by the hot & disagreeable ride but am now perfectly well & if I coud only learn that you were entirely restord I shoud be happy. Your mama & friends are in good health & your mama is as chearful as usual except when some particular conversation discomposes her.[9] Your sweet little Mary[1] is one of the most fascinating little creatures I ever beheld. She has improved very much since I saw her & I cannot help agreeing that she is a substitute for her lovely sister. She talks in a way not easily to be understood tho she comprehends very well every thing that is said to her & is the most coquetish little prude & the most prudish little coquet I ever saw. I wish she was with you as I think she woud entertain you more than all the rest of your children put together. Poor little John[2] is cuting teeth & of course is sick. He appeard to know me as soon as he saw me.

7. See Fairfax Lands: Editorial Note, Vol. II, 140–149.

8. See Paris Journal: Editorial Note, *ca.* Oct. 4, 1797.

9. Polly's father, Jaquelin Ambler, had died on Jan. 10, 1798. This may account for JM's comment about Polly's mother, Rebecca Burwell Ambler. *Virginia Argus* (Richmond), Jan. 12, 1798.

1. Mary Marshall was JM's only surviving daughter.

2. John was seven months old.

He woud not come to me but he kept his eyes fixed on me as on a person he had some imperfect recollection of. I expect he has been taught to look at the picture & had some confusd idea of a likeness. He is small & weakly but by no means an ugly child. If as I hope we have the happiness to raise him I trust he will do as well as the rest. Poor little fellow, the present hot weather is hard on him cutting teeth, but great care is taken of him & I hope he will do well.

I hear nothing from you my dearest Polly but I will cherish the hope that you are getting better & will indulge myself with expecting the happiness of seeing you in october quite yourself.[3] Remember my love to give me this pleasure you have only to take the cold bath, to use a great deal of exercise to sleep tranquilly & to stay in chearful company. I am sure you will do every thing which can contribute to give you back to yourself & me. This hot weather must be very distressing to you—it is so to every body—but it will soon be cooler. Let me know in time every thing relative to your coming down. Farewell my dearest Polly, I am your ever affectionate

J MARSHALL

From Caron de Beaumarchais

Record Copy, Private Collection

Mon honorable ami Paris, August 24, 1798

Le Cn DesMourgues[4] qui vous rend cette lettre, en vous portant cette nouvelle assurance de mon estime et de mon affection, vous dira avec quel plaisir j'ai appris la belle réception que vos compatriotes vous ont faite, a votre arrivée, au Continent.

J'ai toujours Eté loin de partager. L'injuste opinion que l'on s'etait plu a répandre chez nous, de votre partialité en faveur des anglais, contre la République francaise. Je vous ai toujours regardé comme un penseur profond, ami de la paix entre nos deux nations; Et non comme un homme de parti.

3. The long absence of JM, the recent death of her father, and the chronic melancholia from which she suffered had prevented Polly from returning to Richmond. Eliza Carrington to Frances Caines, *ca.* 1802, Eliza Jaquelin Ambler Papers, Colonial Williamsburg Foundation, Williamsburg, Va.

4. Des Mourgues was the son of Jacques Augustin Morque (1743-1818). See Talleyrand to Moreau de Saint Méry, Sept. 8, 1798 [Médéric Louis Elie] Moreau de Saint Méry, *Voyage aux Etats-Unis de l'Amérique*, ed. Stewart L. Mims (New Haven, Conn., 1913), 395.

De votre côté vous m'avés rendu la justice de croire que mes mécontentemens particuliers sur la conduite de votre Gouvernement envers moi, n'altéraient point le vif desir de concourir a la réunion si desirable des deux plus grandes Républiques du monde.

Quoiqu'il puisse arriver, mon honorable ami, des semences de division qu'on a fait éclare entre nos deux nations; je ne varierai pas plus sur la majeure utilité d'un sincère raprochement que sur les sentimens personels que vous m'avés inspirér. N'oubliés pas que vous etes mon défenseur en Amérique, comme je me suis rendu courageusement le Vôtre en France. Obtenés moi, de votre cour d'appel, la mesme justice que votre Eloquence a fait rendre en première instance a celui qui vous a voué estime et gratitude. Je vous salue, vous honore et vous aime.

From Wilson Cary Nicholas

Draft, Nicholas Papers, University of Virginia Library

My Dear Sir [Charlottesville, *ca.* August] 1798

The letter you wrote me after your arrival in Holland came to hand some time in December.[5] I should immediately have answered it but for the uncertainty of my letter reaching you. Your letter was a source of infinite pleasure to me, I considered it as a sure pledge of your friendship, at such a distance, with so many objects to occupy your attention, and so many persons in this country who would expect to hear from you; that you should write me so long a letter was a gratification that I little expected, but one that gave me infinite satisfaction, for be assured there (1)[6] is not a man whose esteem I value more, whose friendship I reciprocate with more sincerity, I sincerely lament the difference of opinion that has existed between us as to some great political events, but flatter myself that you will give me full credit when I assure you, that my confidence in you, my affectionate regard for you, has not been for one moment in the smallest degree impaired. I have myself conscientiously pursued that course which seemed to me best calculated to promote the happiness, and secure the liberty of my country men, I am confident that your motives are equally pure;

5. Not found.

6. The numbers and word in parentheses appear above the line in the manuscript. It is unclear what these numbers mean.

and your only object the public good, actuated by the same motives, having the same object in view there is there can be no motive to distrust each other. I will faithfully give you my opinion of the present state of (2) our affairs that if we can reconcile it to our interest, we have no cause to fear, the [*reproaches*] of other nations, that they have carried their aggressions beyond what we ought. I have been long convinced that we have sufficient cause for War with France according to the usage of nations but I believe the best interests of this country would be sacrificed by going to War, the only pretence for it is the protection of commerce, and I have no doubt that our commerce would be more impaired by war, than it will be without it, and that we shall have in addition to greater commercial injury, an immense accumulation debt a dangerous increase of executive power and influence and at length be obliged to submit to at terms highly disadvantageous, for I do not see a possible injury that we can do the nations that we are to go to war with so as to force them to make peace upon equal terms, ⟨commerce is more necessary to us than to them ⟨⟨nations that we are to war with,⟩⟩ and they have it in their power to do us infinitely more mischief than we can do them we indeed could do them no injury but in conjunction with the British to a connection with whom I think there are insuperable objections who I have no doubt would gladly accept of peace at any moment that France will grant it,⟩ and almost upon terms, I am confident that the abandonment of us would be no obstacle, I would not have you to suppose from what I have said that I would pay money to France to induce (3) her to treat with us, or even to accommodate existing differences, this I would not do, as I believe that would be a sure means of exhausting ourselves without securing the object, I would be prepared for defence at home by means of an efficient Militia, I would let our own citizens or others who were willing to encounter the risk, export and import, in doing only this I should by no means consider that we sacrificed the commercial part of the community, for as I have said I believe a state of war would be worse for them than any other situation the fact is that the great shock produced by the present state of things is over the magnitude spoliation of our loss as was owing to our merchants not being apprized of their danger so as guard against it by the usual means of insurance and deduction from the price of the articles exported it is not true that the inconvenience would in future fall upon that class of citizens, it would be divided among (borne 4) all who either buy what is imported or sell what is exported, the price of imports would be enhanced in proportion to the premium of in insurrance, as the price of exports would (5) be reduced in the same proportion.

Greatly as I deprecate war, I dread its effects more from a strong conviction that it will be made a pretence for an increase of executive power that I fear will destroy the liberty of my country, than from any apprehension from a foreign foe, for all the purposes of defence of our territory, of our right of self government, I think our means fully competent, beyond these objects I believe we can not go, and that every effort will tend only to exhaust our resources that ought to be reserved, and exclusively appropriated to those great, those all important objects.

If I know myself the first the most ardent wish of my heart is the happiness of my country, uninfluenced by any other consideration I will steadily pursue that course that best promises to secure the object that is dearest to me. A man who loves his country must feel at this moment the deepest anguish we are inveloped in difficulties and dangers that threaten our best interests. I have written thus fully and freely, from a belief that however we may differ about the means, our objects are the same, and form an anxiety that a man whose good opinion I value at so high a rate should not hear from others (who might perhaps misrepresent me) but from myself, what my opinions are, upon the present awful state of our affairs. Accept my sincerest congratulations upon your safe return to your country, your family, and friends and be assured that there is no man who feels a warmer interest in every thing that relates personally to you than your affectionate friend

W. C. N

From Timothy Pickering

Presscopy, Pickering Papers, Massachusetts Historical Society

D Sir, Trenton, September 4, 1798

Your letter of the 11th ulto. was mislaid. I have just found it.[7] If Colo. Carrington will be so obliging as to make to you the ad-

7. See JM to Timothy Pickering, Aug. 11, 1798. JM's letter had been mislaid when the government moved to Trenton, N.J., in mid-August to escape the yellow fever epidemic in Philadelphia. Pickering to John Adams, Aug. 18, 1798, Pickering Papers, Massachusetts Historical Society.

vances you request I will reimburse him. In the mean time I shall be obliged to you for your account stated for settlement at my office.[8] On the receipt of it, I will lose no time to place the balance in your hands. I am fearful the delay of this answer may have exposed you to some inconvenience.

By the first good private conveyance I will return your journal.[9]

You will have seen Mr. Gerry's correspondence with Talleyrand about W. X. Y. & Z: This is the finishing stroke to his conduct in France by which he has dishonoured & injured his country and sealed his own indelible disgrace.[1] I am very respectfully, sir, your obt servt.

TIMOTHY PICKERING.

To Timothy Pickering

ALS, Pickering Papers, Massachusetts Historical Society

Dear Sir Mount Vernon,[2] September 5, 1798

Soon after my arrival in Richmond I wrote to you acknowledging the receipt of two letters with which you had favored me & requesting your attention to a subject which I take the liberty again to mention. You informd me when I had the pleasure of seeing you in Philadelphia that you coud probably transmit me a

8. See Envoy Account, Sept. 30, 1798.

9. See Paris Journal: Editorial Note, *ca.* Oct. 4, 1797.

1. The correspondence between Talleyrand and Gerry appeared in the French newspaper *Bien Informé* (Paris), June 9, 1798. In the exchange of letters between May 30 and June 4, 1798, Talleyrand asked Gerry to divulge the names of the foreign intriguers who had solicited a bribe from the American envoys. For his own political purposes, the French foreign minister attempted to place himself above suspicion by pretending that he had no knowledge of the bribery attempt. After several insistent letters, Gerry complied with Talleyrand's request and furnished the names of the XYZ agents. Pickering expressed disgust with Gerry for having submitted to Talleyrand's demand, since Gerry knew that the foreign minister was behind the bribery attempt in the first place. The correspondence was sent to Congress on Jan. 18, 1799. *Annals o Congress*, IX, 3465–3484. It was reprinted in the *Aurora* (Philadelphia), Aug. 30 and Sept. 1, 1798.

2. While on a business trip, JM visited at Mt. Vernon and discussed the congressional elections in Virginia with the former president. George Washington to Bushrod Washington, Aug. 27, 1798, Washington Papers, Ser. 4, Library of Congress (microfilm ed., reel 112). The two visitors had arrived the morning of Sept. 3. John C. Fitzpatrick, ed., *The Diaries of George Washington, 1748-1799*, IV (Boston, 1925), 283-284; JM to James Kirk Paulding, Apr. 4, 1835, Charles J. Tannenbaum Collection, N.Y.; John Stokes Adams, ed., *An Autobiographical Sketch by John Marshall . . .* (Ann Arbor, Mich., 1937), 25–26. See also Congressional Election Campaign: Editorial Note, at Sept. 19, 1798.

draft on Colo. Carrington & it was relative to that draft I had written to you. Colo. Carrington says that a letter from the secretary of the treasury or yourself will be a sufficient document for him & I requested such a letter. As I am apprehensive that in consequence of your removal the request may not have reachd you I beg leave to repeat it.

The General has been really ill but seems now to be perfectly restored.[3] With very much respect & esteem, I am dear Sir your obedt.

J Marshall

To Timothy Pickering

ALS, Pickering Papers, Massachusetts Historical Society

Dear Sir Richmond, September 15, 1798

I had the pleasure of receiving by the last post your two favors of the 4th. & 6th. inst. Altho the letter you inclosd relates to a subject on which I have no conception that the government will act I suppose I ought to lay it before you. Mr. Griffith supported the character of an American—in other respects he is better known to the Gentlemen he refers to than to me. His letter shows the impression at Paris relative to our future inter course with France.[4]

I have seldom seen more extraordinary letters than those of Mr. Talleyrand to Mr. Gerry. He must have known in what manner they woud have been answerd before he coud have venturd to have written them. That he shoud have founded a demand to Mr. Gerry for the names of certain persons on a document proving that Mr. Gerry had asserted Mr. Talleyrand to have recognizd those very persons as his agents was as pointed an insult as coud have been given. There is a fact relative to this business not mentiond in the dispatches which deserves to be known. The company at the private dinner to which Mr. Gerry was invited by Mr. Talleyrand consisted of X. Y. & Z. After rising from the table X & Y renewd to Mr. Gerry in the room & in the presence (tho perhaps

3. Washington contracted malarial fever on Aug. 19, 1798. G. Washington to B. Washington, Aug. 27, 1798, Washington Papers, Ser. 4, Lib. Cong. (microfilm ed., reel 112); Fitzpatrick, ed., *Washington Diaries*, IV, 283.

4. Pickering's letter of Sept. 6 and its enclosures have not been found. For the Griffith letter, see Thomas Griffith to JM, May 20, 1798.

not in the hearing) of Talleyrand, the money propositions which we had before rejected.[5]

I inclose you the copy of the account you gave me at Philadelphia.[6] It will be convenient to Colo. Carrington to settle it here. I am Sir with much respect & esteem, your obedt. Servt

J MARSHALL

Shoud Genl. Pinckney arrive present him with my congratulations & tell him we expect him here with anxiety.

Address and Reply

Printed, *Virginia Gazette, and General Advertiser* (Richmond), September 25, 1798, 3

[*September 17, 1798, Albemarle County, Va.* Nine prominent young Federalists in behalf of "two hundred and eighty two subscribers" in Albe-

5. For an account of the dinner, see Journal, Dec. 2, 1797. Timothy Pickering used JM's disclosure in his "Reply to the Freeholders of Prince Edward County," *Aurora* (Philadelphia), Nov. 6, 1798. The controversy over the dinner set off a personal dispute among the envoys with JM silently siding with Pickering against Gerry. See Pickering to JM, Sept. 21, 1798; Pickering's copy of his address, dated Sept. 29, 1798, is in the Pickering Papers, Massachusetts Historical Society; see also Gerry to John Adams, Oct. 20, 1798, Adams Papers, Mass. Hist. Soc.; Pickering to JM, Nov. 5, 1798, JM to Gerry, Nov. 12, 1798, JM to Pickering, Nov. 12, 1798; "Pinckney Certificate on Dinner," *ca.* Nov. 25, 1798, Pickering Papers; Gerry to Adams, June 24 and July 8, 1799, Adams Papers.

Gerry's recollection of the dinner was confused and sometimes contradictory. In a letter to his wife he stated he was scheduled to have dinner with Talleyrand on Nov. 26, 1797. In his first defense of his mission to France, Gerry claimed that he had dined twice with Talleyrand, once at Talleyrand's and once at his own residence on Dec. 30, 1797. Later Gerry stated that he had dined only once with Talleyrand, at Gerry's residence on Dec. 30, 1797. In one of a series of defenses made to Adams when Gerry was attempting to refute JM's and Pickering's statements about the dinner, Gerry recalled: "The company consisted, not only of Mr. Talleyrand, X, Y, Z, myself, & the secretaries, but also of Mr. [Richard] Codman who came to the lodging of General Martial & myself to accompany me to the dinner; a circumstance which he [JM] has undoubtedly forgot: & Mr. [Fulwar] Skipwith & many others." Gerry to Adams, June 24, 1799, Adams Papers. See Gerry to Ann Gerry, Nov. 25, 1797, Gerry Papers, Library of Congress; Gerry to Adams, Oct. 20, 1798, Pickering Papers; Gerry to Adams, July 8, 1799, Adams Papers.

The only other contemporary evidence on the dinner in addition to the Journal entries for *ca.* Dec. 2 and 17, 1797, is Pinckney's comment that the French were showing civilities to one of the envoys while ignoring the other two. See Pinckney to Rufus King, Dec. 14, 1797, King Papers, Lib. Cong. Gerry did attend a major fete given by Talleyrand for Napoleon on Jan. 3, 1798, but it is clear that the dispute over the dinner party did not involve Gerry's attendance at this event. See Mary Pinckney to Margaret Manigault, Jan. 23, 1798, Manigault Family Papers, University of South Carolina.

6. See Envoy Account, Sept. 30, 1798.

marle County express appreciation to JM for his service to the country during the mission to France. They also "declare our full and unequivocal approbation" of measures taken by President Adams to repair relations with France and to strengthen the nation's defenses. The address is delivered to JM by Bushrod Washington. JM replies, acknowledging the role of his colleagues in Paris, and asserting that their "temperate and repeated supplications for peace having been rejected with a haughtiness unexampled in the history of nations," they could only submit or defend the nation. JM supports the latter course and praises steps taken by President Adams to improve national defense.]

Congressional Election Campaign

EDITORIAL NOTE

Marshall's election to the Sixth Congress is a classic example of a private citizen being thrust into elective office as a result of becoming a national hero. As the first of the envoys to return to the United States, Marshall became the focus of public attention and a symbol of republican virtue in the New World.[7] When the residents of Richmond feted him upon his return to that city, one of them said, "When future generations persue the history of America, they will find the name of Marshall on its sacred page as one of the brightest ornaments of the age in which he lived."[8] It is not surprising, therefore, that George Washington recognized the political wisdom in having Marshall challenge the Republican incumbent in the spring 1799 congressional elections.

Upon returning from France, Marshall did not wish to continue in public service.[9] He was aware that further absence from Richmond would make it very difficult for him to maintain his neglected law practice, and his investment in the Fairfax lands made him especially conscious of his need to earn more money than he could realize from a political career. When Marshall notified George Washington that he wanted to call on him in early September while on a trip to Frederick County, Washington replied that he was most anxious to discuss politics with him. Washington urged his nephew Bushrod to accompany Marshall and encouraged the pair to come even though the former president was himself ill.[1] When they arrived at Mount Vernon, Washington pressed both men to run for Congress. Bushrod Washington agreed to become a candidate for the Westmoreland County district, but Marshall was reluctant to make a similar declaration

7. See Grand Jury to JM and JM to Grand Jury, June 22, 1798. The best study of the election campaign is Nancy M. Merz, "The XYZ Affair and the Congressional Election of 1799 in Richmond, Virginia" (M.A. thesis, College of William and Mary, 1973). The editors wish to acknowledge the assistance of her work.

8. *Virginia Gazette, and General Advertiser* (Richmond), Aug. 14, 1798.

9. JM to James Kirk Paulding, Apr. 4, 1835, Charles J. Tannenbaum Collection, N.Y.; John Stokes Adams, ed., *An Autobiographical Sketch by John Marshall* . . . (Ann Arbor, Mich., 1937), 25.

1. George Washington to Bushrod Washington, Aug. 27, 1798, Washington Papers, Ser. 4, Library of Congress (microfilm ed., reel 112).

for the Richmond district. After several days of extensive conversation among the three men and a heady experience at an Alexandria banquet in Marshall's honor, Marshall agreed to become a candidate. He later commented that it was primarily Washington's example of public service that pursuaded him to enter the political arena.[2]

Virginia had become the stronghold of Republican sentiment. Such leaders as Thomas Jefferson, James Madison, and James Monroe were prominent at the national level, and state politics was directed by Republicans preeminent in the state legislature. By 1798 Federalists held only four of the nineteen congressional seats in Virginia. While the four congressmen generally supported the administration's defense program, only one, Thomas Evans, of the Eastern Shore, voted for the Alien and Sedition Laws.[3]

The Republican domination of Virginia was shaken, however, after the publication of the XYZ dispatches by Congress in April 1798. As copies of the account of the diplomatic mission circulated throughout the nation, public sentiment rallied in support of President Adams. Memorials and addresses condemning Talleyrand and his agents flooded the executive office.[4] In Congress the Federalists rode the wave of popular support and launched their legislative program to prepare the nation's defenses in the event of war with France. During the summer of 1798 the Federalists reached the zenith of their popularity. The black cockade of Federalism replaced the tricolor of revolutionary France in the hat brims of Americans outraged by the conduct of France toward the United States.

Republicans and Federalists in Virginia prepared for the congressional elections at least seven months before election day, and although structured political parties did not exist in Virginia, each group had developed its campaign strategy by the late summer of 1798. The Federalists hoped to reduce Republican dominance in the state by selecting prominent candidates in each district who could win the support of the electorate. They also attempted to discredit the Republicans by showing that the French sympathizers who criticized the defense measures introduced in Congress had been blinded by the perverted Republicanism of seditious organizers in the United States.[5] After December 1798 the Federalists also used the Kentucky and Virginia Resolutions to suggest that the Republicans were encouraging disunion. The Republicans planned to combat these Federalist attacks by showing that the Federalist warhawks were attempting to establish an American "monocracy" with close ties to Great Britain and that the Federal-

2. John C. Fitzpatrick, ed., *The Diaries of George Washington, 1748–1799*, IV (Boston, 1925), 283–284; Adams, ed., *Autobiographical Sketch*, 25–26; *Columbian Mirror and the Alexandria Gazette*, Sept. 6, 1798.

3. See Harry Ammon, "The Jeffersonian Republicans in Virginia: An Interpretation," *Virginia Magazine of History and Biography*, LXXI (1963), 153–167; Manning J. Dauer, *The Adams Federalists*, rev. ed. (Baltimore, 1968), 236, 311–314; Merz, "XYZ Affair," 3.

4. Hundreds of memorials addressed to the president, as well as his replies, are in the Adams Papers, Massachusetts Historical Society. These documents have been studied in John William Kuehl, "The Quest for Identity in an Age of Insecurity: The XYZ Affair and American Nationalism" (Ph.D. diss., University of Wisconsin, 1968), 89–133.

5. Alexander DeConde, *The Quasi-War: The Politics and Diplomacy of the Undeclared War with France, 1797–1801* (New York, 1966), 74–108; James Morton Smith, *Freedom's Fetters: The Alien and Sedition Laws and American Civil Liberties* (Ithaca, N.Y., 1956), 3–21.

ists had used the XYZ dispatches to create a war scare and thus gain approval for the creation of a standing army to suppress domestic insurrection. They also pointed to the Federalists' abrogation of the principles of free speech and freedom of the press in the Alien and Sedition Laws, and argued that the constitutional safeguards outlined in the Kentucky and Virginia Resolutions were necessary to prevent government by executive decree.[6]

Marshall's Republican opponent in the Richmond district was John Clopton, of New Kent County. A former officer in the American Revolution and a one-term member of the House of Delegates, Clopton had been a successful lawyer prior to his election to the Fourth Congress in 1795. As the incumbent in a Republican state and district, Clopton possessed the advantage of majority party status in a political system where incumbents were returned to office with predictable frequency. The electorate voted for a familiar name or relied upon a general knowledge of a candidate's character, and Clopton was as well known within the district as Marshall. Moreover the Republicans were able to use their dominance in the state legislature to spread Republican views throughout the state. But the advantages of incumbency notwithstanding, Clopton had returned to Virginia disheartened by the war fever that had swept the nation in the summer of 1798.[7]

Marshall benefited politically from his newly acquired fame as one of the envoys in the mission to France and from the support of George Washington and later, Patrick Henry, two of Virginia's honored statesmen. The Richmond congressional district tended to vote Republican, but it included a large Federalist minority. If he could attract moderate voters in the district, Marshall could win the election. Moreover, Marshall, unlike Clopton, did not have to explain or qualify the implications of the Virginia Resolutions of 1798. Marshall held the moderate middle ground between the High Federalists who advocated war with France and the disunion implied in the Republican challenge to the constitutionality of the Alien and Sedition Laws.

Marshall and Clopton agreed on certain issues. Both men criticized the Alien and Sedition Laws—Clopton considered the laws unconstitutional and Marshall thought them useless, since each state had statutes to punish seditious libel and to regulate the activity of aliens. Both men shunned permanent alliances and favored the neutrality policy recommended by Washington. Clopton ignored the issue of the French alliance but supported George Logan's peace mission. Unpersuaded by the revelations of the XYZ mission, Clopton did not believe war was imminent.[8] Marshall had publicly expressed his opposition to permanent alliances, but advocated a temporary connection if necessary to protect the nation from foreign invasion. Marshall urged the nation to prepare for war in the event

6. Myron F. Wehtje, "The Congressional Elections of 1799 in Virginia," *West Virginia History*, XXIX (1968), 252, 257.

7. Samuel J. Cabell, John Clopton, William B. Giles, and John Nicholas, members of the Virginia congressional delegation, left Congress in low spirits before the end of the session in 1798 because the Federalists controlled the Congress.

8. In a printed circular letter dated Jan. 24, 1797, Clopton declared his regret for the deterioration in the relations between the U.S. and France, but he was careful not to state his unqualified support for France. Noble E. Cunningham, Jr., ed., *Circular Letters of Congressmen to Their Constituents, 1789–1829*, I (Chapel Hill, N.C., 1978), 72–78.

of a French invasion, but, unlike New England Federalists, he did not wish the United States to declare war because of the experiences of the XYZ mission.[9]

Less than a month after he decided to run for office, Marshall's campaign began with the publication of a letter from "A Freeholder" asking about his views on foreign and domestic policies. It is possible that Marshall wrote the letter himself; it was written only two weeks after he decided to run for office, and the questions were phrased in a sympathetic manner that enabled him to respond favorably. In his reply Marshall voiced his moderate position on the Alien and Sedition Laws, thus disturbing the High Federalists in New England but apparently causing him no political harm in Richmond. This was Marshall's only public statement during the campaign; he ignored the Republican attempt to sustain public debate through publication of an additional "Freeholder" letter.[1]

Federalists and Republicans continued to level charges and countercharges at each other in the newspapers. A Federalist using the pseudonym Buckskin attacked letters Clopton had written to his constituents. Clopton's public letters incited fear and discontent among the people, and his private letters were "too violent to be made Circular," Buckskin contended. More serious was Buckskin's charge that Clopton had libeled the president and had called Adams a traitor who grasped at absolute power by bribing the majority of the House of Representatives. The letter containing the evidence was in the hands of William Pollard, of Hanover County, Buckskin alleged. Clopton denied the charge and appealed to Pollard, who corroborated Clopton's denial that such a letter existed.[2]

The Virginia Federalists avoided one stratagem that would have spelled disaster for Marshall. Secretary of State Timothy Pickering learned of the Buckskin-Clopton exchange and wanted to initiate legal action against Clopton on the grounds of seditious libel. He wrote Edward Carrington for full details of the matter and asked Carrington to obtain the letter in Pollard's possession. Carrington replied that there was not a shred of evidence to support Buckskin. With a cooler head and an eye to the election, Carrington, who was Marshall's brother-in-law, advised Pickering to drop the matter. Had Pickering proceeded with his plan and the federal government prosecuted Clopton, the legal action would have given voters a vivid example of the dangers of the Sedition Act and placed Marshall at a disadvantage in the election.[3]

In December 1798 and January 1799, John Thompson, a young Republican lawyer from Petersburg, devoted five essays to a criticism of Marshall's reply to "Freeholder." The *Letters of Curtius* called Marshall a member of the British party in America and considered him vain and two-faced in his "feeble" criticism of the Alien and Sedition Laws.[4] Following each letter there appeared a reply written

9. See JM to Citizens of Richmond, Aug. 11, 1798.

1. Freeholder to JM, Sept. 19, 1798, and Freeholder to JM, calendared at Oct. 11, 1798; JM to Freeholder, Sept. 20, 1798. See also Merz, "XYZ Affair," 25; Beveridge, *Marshall*, II, 286.

2. *Va. Gaz., & Genl. Adv.*, Oct. 9 and 16, 1798; Cunningham, ed., *Circular Letters*, xxv, xxxvii–xxxviii.

3. Pickering to Carrington, Oct. 23, 1798, Carrington to Pickering, Oct. 30, 1798, Pickering Papers, Mass. Hist. Soc.

4. *The Letters of Curtius* appeared in the *Aurora* (Philadelphia) between Dec. 15 and 26, 1798. A postscript to Curtius appeared in the same newspaper on Jan. 22, 1799.

by an unknown Federalist using the pseudonym Procopius. Procopius, in a rather defensive style, refuted each charge Curtius leveled at Marshall and concluded that Curtius had misrepresented Marshall's opinions by "cleverly turned phrases" intended to confuse the public.[5]

The *Letters of Curtius* prompted other writers to defend Marshall by attacking John Thompson's character. A writer, identified only as Hodge, wrote an essay in a colloquial, backwoods dialect that cleverly reminded readers of Marshall's close association with George Washington and their attachment to the principles of 1776. "You is rite again in the argument of the thing," Hodge told Curtius, "when you says this Marshall's principals is proved by none but tories and refugees, for Washington luvs the same principals, and you nose what a tory he was bout 20 yeres ago."[6] In more direct terms Thersites observed that Curtius had overreached his talent when he presumed to criticize a man of Marshall's abilities. Philo-Curtius considered Curtius a deranged man who imagined himself persecuted by the Federalists.[7] Another writer urged Thompson to cultivate the virtues of sincerity and truth, features the writer found noticeably absent in Thompson's letters to Marshall. The tone of the letter was that of a father writing to an impetuous son warning him that "dissimulation in youth, is the forerunner of perfidy in old age."[8]

In December 1798 the focus of the Republican attack shifted from the newspapers to the floor of the Virginia legislature. The Kentucky legislature had passed a series of resolutions written by Thomas Jefferson that labeled the Alien and Sedition Laws unconstitutional. The resolutions called for the legislatures of other states to use their sovereignty to prevent the enforcement of the laws. On December 25, 1798, the Virginia legislature passed similar resolves drafted by James Madison. The immediate political purpose for this elaboration of the theory of states' rights was to promote the Republicans as the champions of individual liberty and of freedom of speech and press. Several state legislatures rejected the constitutional interpretations expressed in the Kentucky and Virginia Resolutions on the grounds that the resolutions weakened the government by the threat of secession and defied the Constitution at a time when many believed the threat of foreign invasion existed.[9]

The Federalists in the Virginia legislature could not prevent the passage of the Virginia Resolutions, but led by John Marshall's brother-in-law, George Keith Taylor, Henry Lee, and perhaps Marshall himself, the Federalists drafted a

---

Thompson had delivered a rousing speech against the Jay Treaty in Aug. 1795. He actively supported the Republican cause until his death, caused by pleurisy, at age 21. *The Letters of Curtius* were reprinted as a pamphlet in 1798 and again in 1804. See John Thomson, *The Letters of Curtius Written by the Late John Thomson of Petersburg* (Richmond, 1804).

5. *Va. Gaz., & Genl. Adv.*, Dec. 25, 1798, Jan. 1, 18, and 25, 1799.

6. *Ibid.*, Dec. 11, 1798.

7. *Ibid.*, Jan. 1, 1799.

8. *Ibid.*, Jan. 15, 1799. See also the following essays supporting JM that appeared in March and April: Fabius, Trump, and Humble Farmer, *ibid.*, Apr. 16 and 19, 1799; Simples echoed Henry Lee's theme, *ibid.*, Mar. 22, 29, Apr. 5, and 12, 1799.

9. On the Kentucky and Virginia Resolutions, see Harry Ammon and Adrienne Koch, "The Virginia and Kentucky Resolutions," *WMQ*, 3d Ser., V (1948), 145–176; James Morton Smith, "The Grass Roots Origins of the Kentucky Resolutions," *WMQ*, 3d Ser., XXII (1970), 221–245.

minority address in defense of the Alien and Sedition Laws.[1] They claimed that the Alien Law was an elaboration of extant legal statutes in Virginia and did not impinge upon state power; the Sedition Act was merely an authorization for the federal government to exercise its power to safeguard citizens against seditious persons. The minority address was a statement of principles that fell midway between the alternatives of disunion implied in the Virginia Resolutions and the bellicose views advanced by the hawkish High Federalists north of the Potomac. The address urged Virginians to redress their grievances through constitutional means.

Apprehensive over the implications of the Virginia Resolutions and their effect on his constituents,[2] Clopton outlined his position in a letter addressed to John Allen, of Richmond:

> I have never knowingly deviated from the Constitution; but my votes were always such as I have conscientiously believed were in support of the Constitution. I have not ceased to entertain ardent wishes to preserve those CHECKS and BALANCES in the Constitution, in which consists much of its excellence. . . . I have considered it my sacred duty, to which I was bound, and with which my inclination has ever coincided, to dissent from measures which, I did believe, were not compatible with the constitutional distribution of powers. . . . For thus acting . . . I have been represented by some persons as an enemy to the government.[3]

Clopton's defense of his conduct received a strong rebuttal from Henry Lee, of Westmoreland County, a candidate for Congress and a hero of the American Revolution. Lee, in his *Plain Truth* essays, written in February and March 1799,

1. Scholars have attributed authorship of the address to JM on the basis of its style and language and two remarks by Theodore Sedgwick who suggested that JM wrote the document. The content of the address suggests that Henry Lee was the author. The reasoning is akin to the views Lee expressed in *Plain Truth* (Richmond, 1799). If JM authorized the minority address, his views on the Alien and Sedition Laws had changed. JM considered the laws useless, because remedy against seditious libel was available in common law. The minority address strongly supports the Alien and Sedition Laws and considers them useful, constitutional, and necessary. JM had never made a public statement in favor of the laws. Moreover, it was Henry Lee who submitted the address to the Committee of the Whole in the House of Delegates. Perhaps JM played both sides of the political fence to gain votes, but if he was so firmly attached to a belief in the common law, it is unlikely he would have abandoned this belief for purposes of political expedience. See *JVHD*, Dec. 1798, 90-95; *Address of the Minority in the Virginia Legislature to the People of that State; containing a Vindication of the Constitutionality of the Alien and Sedition Laws* (Richmond, 1799); *Va. Gaz., & Genl. Adv.*, Feb. 1 and 5, 1799; Sedgwick to Rufus King, Mar. 20, 1799, King Papers, LXI, New-York Historical Society; Sedgwick to Alexander Hamilton, Feb. 7, 1799, Harold C. Syrett, ed., *The Papers of Alexander Hamilton*, XXII (New York, 1975), 469–472. See also Stephen G. Kurtz, ed., *The Federalists: Creators and Critics of the Union, 1780–1801* (New York, 1972), 176–177. Kurtz attributes authorship to both Lee and JM.

2. Clopton's views were given in several letters that identify the men chiefly responsible for Clopton's reelection in the district. See Clopton to John C. Littlepage (Hanover), Clopton to Capt. Nicholas Syme (Hanover), Clopton to James Apperson (New Kent), Dec. 23, 1798, Clopton to Richard Apperson (New Kent), Clopton to William Foushee (Richmond), Dec. 30, 1798, Clopton to William Chamberlayne (New Kent), Dec. 29, 1798, Clopton to Col. C. Travis (Williamsburg), Jan. 1, 1799, Clopton to Philip N. Nicholas (Richmond), Jan. 7, 1799, John Clopton Papers, Duke University.

3. Clopton to John Allen (Richmond), Feb. 22, 1799, *ibid.*

questioned the core of Republican constitutional theory. He denied that the state legislature possessed the authority to speak for the people of Virginia concerning the constitutionality of the Alien and Sedition Laws. The people had created the government in a separate convention and ratified it in conventions called for that purpose. The state legislature did not possess sovereignty because the union was created by the people, not the legislatures, of the states. While the legislature was at liberty to express its opinion on the matter, Lee added, it would be guilty of infringing upon the sovereignty of the people if it attempted to prevent the enforcement of the Alien and Sedition Laws within the borders of Virginia.[4] Lee had turned the tables on his opponents. *Plain Truth* was a strongly reasoned, nationalist interpretation of the Constitution that forced the citizens of Virginia to consider if the state legislature had usurped their sovereignty. The argument forced Clopton and other Republicans to define the limits of their attachment to the principles of state sovereignty as expressed in the Virginia Resolutions.

Another blow to Republican fortunes came from an unanticipated source. Archibald Blair, clerk of the Executive Council of Virginia and a friend of Marshall's, informed the ailing Patrick Henry that members of the Republican party had spread the rumor that Henry opposed Marshall's election because Marshall belonged to the aristocratic party in the state.[5] Henry responded with characteristic energy. In answer to Blair's letter Henry lamented the growth of faction and party in the nation. He feared that the architects of the Virginia Resolutions contemplated the breakup of the union. Henry endorsed Marshall's candidacy in glowing terms:

> Independently of the high gratification I felt from his public ministry, he ever stood high in my esteem as a private citizen. His temper and disposition were always pleasant, his talents and integrity unquestioned. These things are sufficient to place that gentleman far above any competitor in the district for Congress. But, when you add the particular information and insight which he had gained, and is able to communicate to our public councils, it is really astonishing that even blindness itself should hesitate in the choice. . . . Tell Marshall I love him, because he felt and acted as a Republican, as an American. . . .[6]

After Henry's declaration George Washington wrote to Henry and urged him to return to politics as a candidate either for Congress or the state legislature.[7] Henry announced his decision to seek a seat in the Virginia legislature as a delegate from Charlotte County. With the renowned Patrick Henry in the Federalist camp supporting Marshall, Republican alarm over the outcome of the election increased.[8]

4. *Plain Truth* appeared in *Va. Gaz., & Genl. Adv.*, Feb. 5, 8, 12, 15, 19, 22, 26, Mar. 1, and 5, 1799.

5. Blair had written Henry on Dec. 28, 1798. See Archibald Blair to Patrick Henry, Jan. 13, 1799, William Wirt Henry, *Patrick Henry: Life, Correspondence and Speeches*, III (New York, 1891), 427–428.

6. Henry to Blair, Jan. 8, 1799, Moses Coit Tyler, *Patrick Henry* (Boston, 1887), 409–411.

7. Washington to Henry, Jan. 15, 1799, Washington Papers, Ser. 4, Lib. Cong. (microfilm ed., reel 113); John Taylor to [James Madison], Mar. 4, 1799, Madison Papers, Lib. Cong.

8. Madison observed that the "opinion still prevails that Marshall will be disappointed, but it is agreed that the maximum of effort will be used in his favor, and we know that in that case, the issue must be attended with some uncertainty." Madison

As election day approached the political tension gave rise to rumors that the Republican legislature had collected and stored arms in the Richmond armory to resist the enforcement of the Alien and Sedition Laws. The rumor was not true, but it created suspicion and distrust among partisans in both camps.[9] On polling day, in accordance with the usual practice, candidates treated the voters to refreshments. One report noted that whiskey in abundance was to be had at the courthouse green for the friends of either party. As the liquor warmed the spirits of the crowd, fights erupted among the citizens assembled to witness the result of the election. Seated at the justices' bench, Marshall or Clopton thanked each citizen personally for his vote while partisan observers in the crowd shouted applause or yelled insults as each voter expressed his preference.[1]

Marshall defeated John Clopton by 108 votes. While no official returns have survived, newspapers reported aggregate returns for three of the counties in the district. Clopton defeated Marshall in Hanover County by a margin of 7 votes, 317 to 310. In Henrico County, Marshall defeated Clopton by 49 votes, 299 to 250. The vote in Clopton's home county of New Kent registered a plurality for Marshall of 162 to 137. In James City County, Marshall's margin was 12 votes.[2]

In Philadelphia, Timothy Pickering expressed satisfaction with the results in Virginia. Expectations exceeded results, Pickering noted, but the successes "give joy to all the real friends of the U. States."[3] The Federalists had made significant gains statewide. They captured eight of Virginia's nineteen congressional seats for a net increase of four over the previous session. The Virginia legislature, however, remained solidly Republican.[4] Federalists had hoped that Patrick Henry's return to politics would provide the rallying point to offset the ruling triumvirate of Republicans—Madison, William B. Giles, and John Taylor. Unfortunately for Federalist aspirations, Henry died on June 6, 1799.

---

to Thomas Jefferson, Jan. 25, 1799, Madison Papers. Jefferson remained cautiously optimistic throughout the campaign. He distributed campaign literature, urged Republicans at Philadelphia to write anti-administration pamphlets, drew up the Kentucky Resolutions, tried to found a Republican newspaper in Virginia by soliciting subscriptions, and in several letters reminded his fellow Republicans of the moral purpose of the Republican cause. Jefferson to Edmund Pendleton, Feb. 14, 1799, Jefferson Papers, Lib. Cong.; Ralph Ketcham, *James Madison: A Biography* (New York, 1971), 393–397; Noble E. Cunningham, Jr., *The Jeffersonian Republicans: The Formation of Party Organization, 1789–1801* (Chapel Hill, N.C., 1957), 128–135.

9. Philip G. Davidson, "Virginia and the Alien and Sedition Laws," *American Historical Review*, XXXVI (1931), 336–342.

1. Charles S. Sydnor, *Gentlemen Freeholders: Political Practices in Washington's Virginia* (Chapel Hill, N.C., 1952), 18–26. An imaginative account of election day in Richmond in 1799 is found in George Wythe Munford, *The Two Parsons; Cupid's Sports; The Dream; and the Jewels of Virginia* (Richmond, 1884), 202–211.

2. There are no vote totals for the district, and Merz's research is the most reliable on the subject. Merz, "XYZ Affair," 52; *Va. Gaz., & Genl. Adv.*, Apr. 26 and 30, 1799. The *Gazette of the United States and Philadelphia Daily Advertiser*, May 2, 1799, reported a margin of 114 votes. *Porcupine's Gazette* (Philadelphia), May 6, 1799, also gave JM a margin of 114 votes. In Hanover County, Clopton had a majority of 7 votes, while JM carried Henrico County by 48, New Kent County by 25, Charles City County by 35, and James City County by 12 votes.

3. Pickering to JM, May 16, 1799. See also Pickering to King, May 4, 1799, King Papers, Lib. Cong.

4. Merz, "XYZ Affair," 52–54.

Marshall's victory was part of the temporary resurgence of Federalism that had swept the southern and New England states.[5] Federalist manipulation of the XYZ dispatches for partisan political purposes unleashed a temporary wave of nationalist sentiment that carried many Federalists, including Marshall, into office. The gains made in Virginia represented a deviation in the voting habits of the citizens of the Old Dominion but not a permanent shift in their political allegiance. They had cast their ballots in 1799 for political moderation and not for Federalism.

Marshall's victory over Clopton was also a personal triumph in that Marshall's reputation for integrity and wisdom counted as much in the outcome as his stand on the issues in the campaign. Other factors, however, contributed to Marshall's victory and Clopton's defeat. Federalist newspapers were superior to the Republican press in the quality of their arguments. Republicans did not produce a writer who matched the cogency of the *Plain Truth* essays. Also, nascent American nationalism played a part in the formation of public attitudes during the campaign, a theme that Marshall exploited. Clopton's incumbency does not in itself appear to have been a significant obstacle to Marshall's election.

Finally, Marshall's conduct as an envoy to France influenced voters in his favor. A resident of Hanover County who did not know Marshall wrote a letter to a newspaper in which he criticized Clopton and announced his decision to vote for Marshall because he was a man of integrity. The writer reminded voters of France's attempt to ferment "division Amongst us in her favor against our own government." He further commented that "having threatened to discredit this very gentleman in the estimation of his countrymen his rejection must have a tendency to revive and encourage her [France's] hope of dividing and ruling us and may cause that prospect of reconciliation with which you [Clopton] flattered us to disappear again."[6] Another writer said, "Should he miss his Election, what must those against whom his abilitys are to shield the Union, think?"[7] Marshall's defeat would have been interpreted as a public rejection of his conduct overseas, and would have encouraged the French in their belligerence to the Federalist administration. Marshall thus owed his election largely to the national prominence and popularity he gained for his performance in the mission to France.

From a Freeholder

Printed, *Virginia Herald* (Fredericksburg), October 2, 1798, 2

Dear Sir, Richmond, September 19, 1798[8]

Under a conviction that it will be of utility, should the answers to the following questions be such as I anticipate; I state them

5. Cunningham, *Jeffersonian Republicans*, 134; but see also Merz, "XYZ Affair," 61–63.

6. *Va. Gaz., & Genl. Adv.*, Apr. 12, 1799, quoted in Merz, "XYZ Affair," 57.

7. George Gairdner to Francis Jerdone, Mar. 24, 1799, Jerdone Papers, Swem Library, College of William and Mary, quoted in Merz, "XYZ Affair," 59.

8. This letter is incorrectly dated Sept. 12 in Beveridge, *Marshall*, II, 574.

with a confidence of your readiness to give replies: They will, at all events, greatly satisfy my mind.

1st. Do you not, in heart and sentiment, profess yourself an American—attached to the genuine principles of the constitution, as sanctioned by the will of the people, for their general liberty, prosperity and happiness?

2nd Do you conceive that the true interest and prosperity of America is materially, or at all, dependant upon an alliance with any foreign nation? If you do, please state the causes, and a preference, if any exists, with the reasons for that preference.

3d. Are you in favor of an alliance, offensive and defensive with Great-Britain? In fine, are you disposed to advocate any other, or a closer connection with that nation, than existed at the ratification of the treaty of '94? If so, please state your reasons.

4th. By what general principles, in your view, have the measures of our administration and government, in respect to France, been consistent with true policy or necessity? And could not the consequences have been avoided by a different line of conduct on our part?

5th. Are you an advocate for the alien and sedition bills? or, in the event of your election, will you use your influence to obtain a repeal of those laws?

A FREEHOLDER.

To a Freeholder

Printed, *Virginia Herald* (Fredericksburg), October 2, 1798, 2

DEAR SIR, Richmond, September 20, 1798

I have received your letter of yesterday, and shall, with equal candor, and satisfaction, answer all your queries.[9] Every citizen has a right to know the political sentiments of the man who is proposed as his representative; and mine have never been of a nature to shun examination. To those who think another gentleman more capable of serving the district than myself, it would be useless to explain my opinions, because whatever my opinions may be, they will, and ought, to vote for that other; but I cannot

9. This is the only public political statement JM made during the election campaign. The Freeholder replied to this letter but JM declined to continue the debate in the newspapers. See Freeholder to JM, calendared at Oct. 11, 1798.

help wishing, that those who think differently, would know my real principles, and not attribute to me those I never possessed, and with which active calumny has been pleased to asperse me.

Answ. 1. In heart and sentiment, as well as by birth and interest, I am an American, attached to the genuine principles of the constitution, as sanctioned by the will of the people, for their general liberty, prosperity and happiness. I consider that constitution as the rock of our political salvation, which has preserved us from misery, division and civil wars;—and which will yet preserve us if we value it rightly and support it firmly.

2d. I do not think the interest and prosperity of America, at all dependent on an alliance with any foreign nation; nor does the man exist who would regret more than myself the formation of such an alliance. In truth, America has, in my opinion, no motive for forming such connections, and very powerful motives for avoiding them.—Europe is eternally engaged in wars in which we have no interest; and with which the soundest policy forbids us to intermeddle. We ought to avoid any compact which may endanger our being involved in them. My sentiments on this subject, are detailed at large, in the beginning of the memorial addressed by the late envoys from the U. States to the minister of foreign affairs of the French republic, where the neutrality of the United States is justified, and the reasons for that neutrality stated.

3d. I am not in favor of an alliance offensive and defensive with G. Britain, nor for any closer connection with that nation, than already exists. No man in existence is more decidedly opposed to such an alliance, or more fully convinced of the evils that would result from it. I never have, in thought, word or deed, given the smallest reason to suspect I wished it; nor do I believe any man acquainted with me does suspect it. Those who originate and countenance such an idea, may (if they know me) design to impose on others, but they do not impose on themselves. The whole of my politics respecting foreign nations are reducible to this single position. We ought to have commercial intercourse with all, but political ties with none. Let us buy as cheap and sell as dear as possible. Let commerce go wherever individual, and consequently national interest, will carry it: but let us never connect ourselves politically, with any people whatever. I have not a right to say, nor can I say positively, what are the opinions of those who administer the government of the U. States; but I believe firmly, that neither the President, nor any one of those with whom he advises, would consent to form a close and permanent political connection with any nation upon earth. Should France continue to wage an unprovoked war against us, while she is also at war with Britain, it would be madness and folly not to endeavour to make such temporary arrangements as would give us the aid of the British fleets to prevent our being invaded; but I would not, even to obtain so obvious a good, make such a sacrifice as I think we should make, by forming a permanent political connection with that, or any other nation on earth.

4th. The measures of the administration and government of the U. States with respect to France, have in my opinion, been uniformly directed by a sincere and unequivocal desire to observe, faithfully, the treaties existing between the two nations, and to preserve the neutrality and independence of our country. Had it been possible to maintain peace with France without sacrificing those great objects, I am convinced that our government would have maintained it. Unfortunately it has been impossible. I do not believe that any different line of conduct, on our part, unless we would have relinquished the rights of self-government, and have become the colonies of France, could have preserved peace with that nation. Be assured that the primary object of France is, and for a long time past has been, dominion over others. This is a truth only to be disbelieved by those who shut their eyes on the history and conduct of that nation. The grand instruments by which they effect this end, to which all their measures tend, are immense armies on their part, and divisions, which a variety of circumstances have enabled them to create, among those whom they wish to subdue. Whenever France has exhibited a disposition to be just towards the United States, an accurate attention to facts now in possession of the public, will prove, that this disposition was manifested in the hope of involving us in her wars as a dependent and subordinate nation.

5th. I am not an advocate for the alien and sedition bills: had I been in congress when they passed, I should, unless my judgment could have been changed, certainly have opposed them. Yet, I do not think them fraught with all those mischiefs which many gentlemen ascribe to them. I should have opposed them, because I think them useless; and because they are calculated to create, unnecessarily, discontents and jealousies at a time when our very existence, as a nation, may depend on our union—I believe that these laws, had they been opposed on these principles by a man, not suspected of intending to destroy the government, or of being hostile to it, would never have been enacted. With respect to their repeal, the effort will be made before I can become a member of congress. If it succeeds, there will be an end of the business—if it fails, I shall, on the question of renewing the effort, should I be chosen to represent the district, obey the voice of my constituents. My own private opinion is, that it will be unwise to renew it for this reason: The laws will expire of themselves, if I recollect rightly the time for which they are enacted, during the term of the ensuing congress. I shall, indisputably, oppose their revival; and I believe that opposition will be more successful, if men's minds are not too much irritated by the struggle about a repeal of laws which will, at the time, be expiring of themselves.

J. MARSHALL.

From Timothy Pickering

Letterbook Copy, RG 59, National Archives

Dear Sir, Trenton, September 20, 1798

I have just received a letter from the President directing me to make out a Commission for you to fill the Seat vacant on the Bench of the Supreme Court by the death of Judge Wilson.[1] The Commission I shall send this day to Quincy for the President's Signature. I wish in the meantime to be informed whether it will be agreeable to you to accept the appointment. Your acceptance will gratify the President, all the public men whose opinions I am acquainted with, and your fellow citizens, at large throughout the United States. If there were any more persuasive motive, I would present it to your view. I request an early answer.

I received your letter from Mount Vernon, and wrote you that any arrangement you should make with Colo. Carrington for the payment of the balance due you from the U. States should be complied with on my part.[2] I have the honor etc.

TIMOTHY PICKERING

1. Adams to Pickering, Sept. 13, 1798, Adams Papers, Massachusetts Historical Society. On Sept. 6, 1798, Pickering learned of the death of Justice James Wilson (1742-1798) from Judge James Iredell and promptly informed Adams who had removed to Quincy, Mass.

2. See JM to Pickering, Sept. 5, 1798.

From Timothy Pickering

ALS, Gray-Glines Collection, Connecticut State Library

(private)
Dr. Sir, Trenton, September 20, 1798

Your last conversation with me the evening before your departure from Philadelphia[3] makes me apprehensive that you will decline the vacant seat in the supreme court: For this reason I request your opinion (information, if you can give it) whether Mr. Bushrod Washington will accept it?[4] I have understood that he has thought of quitting the bar; and that this place on the Bench would probably be acceptable to him. Respectfully yours

T. PICKERING.

From Timothy Pickering

Letterbook Copy, RG 59, National Archives

Dear Sir, Trenton, September 21, 1798

Last night I received your favour of the 15th. and a copy of the paragraph respecting Talleyrand and Mr. Gerry I have sent to the President: it contains an important fact which ought to be on record, and made as public as the Envoy's dispatches.

I now inclose a statement of your account,[5] in which an article of credit is introduced on the supposition that Colo. Carrington will pay you the balance and receive your draught on me for his reimbursement. You will be pleased to give your receipt on the account upon the balance being paid you, and return the account to me, as it will exhibit the only document in my office of the monies paid you in Europe—until the Banker's accounts arrive; and independent of them it will be proper.

Private letters received at Boston intimate that Hauteval[6] is coming over with Mr. Gerry. I am very respectfully, Dear Sir, etc.

TIMOTHY PICKERING

3. June 24, 1798.
4. See JM to Pickering, Sept. 28, 1798.
5. See Envoy Account, Sept. 30, 1798.
6. Lucien Hauteval.

To William S. Crawford

ALS, Cabell Papers, Swem Library, College of William and Mary

Dear Sir[7] Richmond, September 26, 1798

I have receivd yours by Mr. Camden. I shall certainly resume my practice in the superior courts & will very readily engage in the business you mention. I am Sir very respectfully, your obedt. Servt.

J MARSHALL

To Timothy Pickering

ALS, Adams Papers, Massachusetts Historical Society

Dear Sir Richmond, September 28, 1798

By the mail of last night I had the pleasure of receiving your two letters of the 20th. & 21st. inst. I pray you to make my respectful & grateful acknowlegements to the President for the very favorable sentiments concerning me which are indicated by his willingness to call me to so honorable & important a station as that of a Judge of the United States. The considerations which are insurmountable oblige me to decline the office. I can assure you that I shall ever estimate properly both the dispositions of the President & the polite & friendly manner in which you have communicated them. I am confident that Mr. Washington woud with pleasure accept the appointment & I am equally confident that a more proper person coud not be named for it.[8]

My account will be adjusted with Colo. Carrington & transmited to you.[9]

I am astonishd at the delay of Mr. Gerry's arrival. He must have been detained in Paris longer than was expected. The motives for this detention may easily be conjecturd. If Logan[1] arrives before

7. The letter is addressed to Crawford, "Atty. at law, Amhurst." Crawford was clerk of the Amherst County Court in 1792.

8. JM's letter in which he declined appointment to the U.S. Supreme Court was forwarded to John Adams on Oct. 5, 1798. Adams to Pickering, Sept. 29, 1798, Domestic Letterbooks, XI, RG 59, National Archives; Pickering to Adams, Oct. 5, 1798, Adams Papers, Massachusetts Historical Society.

JM refused the appointment because he wished to return to his law practice. John Stokes Adams, ed., *An Autobiographical Sketch by John Marshall . . .* (Ann Arbor, Mich., 1937), 26.

9. See JM to Pickering, Oct. 1, 1798.

1. George Logan (1753–1821). See Frederick B. Tolles, *George Logan of Philadelphia* (New York, 1953), 153–204.

his departure that event will probably have its influence. Do you hear any thing of Genl. Pinckney? I am extremely anxious to know of his arrival. I am dear Sir with much respect & esteem, your obedt.

J MARSHALL

Mr. Hauteval[2] is a conciliatory character. There are few french men who are as well disposd to our country—but yet he is devoted to Mr. Talleyrand.

Envoy Account

Copy, RG 53, National Archives

Richmond, September 30, 1798

Drs.

		Dollars.	*Cents*
1797. July.	To my outfit as Envoy aforesaid	9 000	"
1798. June 23.	" my salary from the 20th: of June 1797, to the 14th of July 1798 comprehending three months after I received my Passport in Paris to return to the United States, being 1 year & 24 days at 9.000 dollars per annum	9 591	78
	" the Salary of my Secretary (John Brown) from the 8th: of July 1797 to the 14th: of July 1798, comprehending three months subsequent to the delivery of the passport above mentioned, 1 year and 6 days at 1350 dollars per annum	1 372	19
	Dollars	19 963	97

2. This comment on Hauteval's character is noteworthy in view of JM's public vilification of the French government. For Hauteval's defense of his conduct in the affair, see Hauteval to Talleyrand, June 1798, communicated to Congress, Jan. 18, 1799. *Annals of Congress*, IX, 3526–3527.

Crs.

1797.			
July 15.	By Cash received from Timothy Pickering Secretary of State in part of my Outfit	3 500	"
	" my Drafts on Messrs: W & J Willink N & J Van Staphorst & Hubbard, Bankers for the Department of State at Amsterdam from the of 1797 to the of [3]1798		
1798.	amounting to 20,000 Guilders at 40 Cents per Guilder are equal to	8 000[4]	"
	" My Ditto on Ditto for 50 Louis d'or equal to	222	"
June 23	" Cash from Timothy Pickering Secretary of State	2 000	"
Octr.	My Draft on Ditto dated this day, in favor of Edward Carrington Esqr. for six thousand two hundred and forty one dollars & ninety seven cents which when paid will be in full of this account	6 241	97
	Dollars.	19.963	97.[5]
	Errors Excepted		

J MARSHALL

3. The inclusive dates, Oct. 13, 1797, to Apr. 15, 1798, are supplied in the accounts of the Amsterdam bankers upon whom JM drew money for the mission. See Willink, Van Staphorst & Hubbard to Timothy Pickering, June 30, 1798, "Letters Received from Amsterdam Bankers," RG 59, National Archives.

4. In a footnote to this figure and the one following, a clerk wrote, "These two sums are passed to the credit of the Willinks, per their acct. no. 114."

5. Prior to his departure from Philadelphia in July 1797, JM received $500.00 in cash and $3,000.00 in drafts on banks in Amsterdam. Between Oct. 13, 1797, and Apr. 15, 1798, JM drew the remainder of his outfit, or expense money, $5,500.00. During the same period he received an additional $1,372.19 for the salary of his secretary, John Brown, and $1,349.81, a portion of his own salary. When JM returned to Philadelphia he received $2,000.00 in salary from State Department funds on June 23, 1798, and the balance of his salary, $6,241.97, was given to him after he reached Richmond in the form of a draft on Col. Edward Carrington on Oct. 1, 1798.

Gerry had great difficulty settling his account with the State Department; his problem was largely attributable to Pickering's obstinate dislike of Gerry's role in the XYZ imbroglio. Based on the accounts of the three envoys, the cost of the mission was $58,552.80. Pinckney's account shows expenses and salary totaling $20,342.61. Gerry's account amounts to $18,246.22. The salary of each envoy was $9,000.00, prorated for

Law Papers, September 1798

U.S. Circuit Court, Va.

Rawle v. Byrd, declaration, ADS, U.S. Circuit Court, Va., Ended Cases (Unrestored), Virginia State Library.[6]

To Timothy Pickering

ALS, Pickering Papers, Massachusetts Historical Society

Dear Sir Richmond, October 1, 1798

I now inclose you the account[7] you were so good as to prepare for me. I have drawn on you in favor of Colo. Carrington for the sum expressed to be receivd from him.

The conflict of parties in this state is extremely ardent. Considerable efforts are making to change essentially our delegation & I am not without hopes that in some instances those efforts will be successful.

I am beyond measure sollicitous to know the state of our affairs with France. The delays of Mr. Gerry strenghten my opinion that some half handed negotiation will be commenced which will not give us peace but will serve to divide us. With much respect & esteem, I am dear Sir your obedt.

J MARSHALL

---

any service beyond the 12-month period. See "Statement by Register of the Treasury on Expenses of the XYZ Mission and Ellsworth Mission," Sept. 2, 1796–Aug. 1801, RG 53, Natl. Arch.; "U.S. in Account with Charles C. Pinckney," Oct. 1798, Pinckney Family Papers, Library of Congress; "U.S. in Account with Elbridge Gerry, 1797–1799," Records of Bureau of Accounts, RG 53, Natl. Arch.; John Adams to Pickering, Aug. 3, 1799, and Willink, Van Staphorst & Hubbard to Pickering, June 30, 1798, "Letters Received from Amsterdam Bankers," RG 59.

6. JM represented William Rawle, a Pennsylvania resident, who had sued Mrs. Mary Byrd on a writing obligatory in the amount of £4,000. On Dec. 1, 1798, the jury found for Rawle. See U.S. Circuit Court, Va., Record Book, VII, 129–138, Virginia State Library; Receipt, Oct. 10, 1798, and Receipt, Nov. 6, 1798.

7. Original enclosure not found. See Envoy Account, Sept. 30, 1798.

From Timothy Pickering

Presscopy, Pickering Papers, Massachusetts Historical Society

Dear Sir, Trenton, October 4, 1798

Yesterday I recd. from Mr. H. M. Rutledge, who is arrived at N. York in the Ship Factor, a letter dated there the 2d. of which the inclosed is an extract. This morning appears Mr. Gerry's letter of July 20th to Talleyrand appears, & I now inclose it.[8] It is, I suppose, the *wonderful spirit of resentment*, and *severity* of *animadversion* on the conduct of Talleyrand, that alarmed Mr. Gerry, when pursued by the English row-boat, and induced him to tell Mr. Rutledge that he had "every thing to dread from the enmity of the French Government"! We may daily look for his arrival.[9]

I wish you could find time to make some *proper animadversion* on the infamous conduct of the French Government in relation to the mission of the three envoys extraordinary: and I beg you to consider whether the importance of correct information to the American citizens does not require it. Not that the part acted by you & General Pinckney will need vindication with men of sense, even among the French partisans; but these have baseness and malice enough to use the *bare assertions* of Talleyrand as evidences of your indisposition to effect a reconciliation. I am very respectfully your

T. PICKERING.

P. S. A letter from Mr. King by the Factor states a piece of very important news, the authenticity of which he says is not to be doubted. Austria and Naples have concluded a treaty of defensive alliance, for their mutual protection against France; and have

8. Enclosures not found, but see *Philadelphia Gazette and Universal Daily Advertiser*, Oct. 4, 1798; a copy of the letter to Talleyrand is enclosed in Gerry to Pickering, Oct. 1, 1798, Gerry Papers, Henry E. Huntington Library. Henry M. Rutledge was Pinckney's secretary in Paris during the XYZ mission. Rutledge told Pickering that Gerry had sailed from Le Havre but had put in at Portsmouth, England, after having been pursued by an open boat Gerry thought had been sent by the Directory to take him prisoner. The incident delighted Gerry's Federalist foes, confirming their low esteem of his courage and general character. Rutledge to Pickering, Oct. 2, 1798, Pickering Papers, Massachusetts Historical Society; Pickering to Rutledge, Oct. 4, 1798, Dreer Collection, Historical Society of Pennsylvania; Pickering to John Adams, Oct. 3, 1798, Domestic Letterbooks, XI, RG 59, National Archives; George Washington to Pickering, Oct. 15, 1798, Washington Papers, Ser. 4, Library of Congress (microfilm ed., reel 113). See also Rufus King to Secretary of State, Aug. 14, 1798, King Papers, LII, New-York Historical Society; Pickering to King, Oct. 3, 1798, Pickering Papers; Gerry to Ann Gerry, Oct. 1, 1798, Gerry Papers, Mass. Hist. Soc.

9. Gerry departed on Aug. 8, 1798, and arrived in Boston on Oct. 1, 1798.

agreed that if the latter should attack the Neapolitan dominions for supplying provisions etc. to the British ships of war (which the Neapolitan Government have engaged to do) it shall be deemed a casus foederis. This he remarkes, is expected to produce a war, and that Austria is preparing for it. He suggests also that a better prospect had just appeared of a new coalition against France. His latest letter is to Augt. 5.[1]

Genl. Pinckney was at Bordeaux, embarrassed by the embargo on all American vessels: but he had written to the Minister of Marine, to obtain a passport for the Ship in which Dupont the Consul & Volney,[2] with a cargo of other French people, went from America; for she being a flag of truce might be presumed to form an exception to the order for an embargo; and if successful, he will take his passage in her: She was the ship Benjamin Franklin.

T. P.

Bellamy's vindication must not be forgotten: it appears replete with misrepresentations, & some falsehood: I have his original French as printed at Hamburg.[3]

Receipt

ADS, Virginia Historical Society[4]

[Richmond], October 10, 1798

Recd. this 10th. of October 1798 from Mr. William P. Byrd one thousand & seventy dollars in part discharge of a bond given by Mrs. Mary Byrd to William Shirtliff for £2000 dated the 31st. day of Jany. 1778, recd. also an order on Thomas Willing esquire in favor of William Rawle esquire for thirteen hundred & thirty

1. See King to Secretary of State, Aug. 5, 1798, King Papers, LXIV, N.-Y. Hist. Soc.

2. Victor Marie Dupont and Constantin-François Chasseboeuf Boisgivais, comte de Volney (1757-1820). Volney, a French scientist and author, arrived in Philadelphia on Oct. 12, 1795. Because of his interest in science, he corresponded with Jefferson and other notable American scientists. See Durand Echeverria, trans., "General Collot's Plan for Reconnaissance of the Ohio and Mississippi Valleys, 1796," *WMQ*, 3d Ser., IX (1952), 513.

3. A copy of Pierre Bellamy's vindication, dated Hamburg, June 25, 1798, is in Correspondance Politique, Etats-Unis, Supplement, II, Archives of the Ministry of Foreign Affairs, Paris.

4. This is item no. Mss2M3567b4 in the society's collections.

three & a third dollars which if paid is to be credited as of this date on the said bond.[5]

J MARSHALL

From a Freeholder

Printed, *Virginia Argus* (Richmond), October 12, 1798, 3

[*October 11, 1798, Richmond.* In response to JM's letter of Sept. 20, this writer asks him to justify article 9 of the Jay Treaty and to state whether he believes the Alien and Sedition Laws are constitutional. He asks other rhetorical and polemical questions. Apparently JM did not respond.]

From Timothy Pickering

Presscopy, Pickering Papers, Massachusetts Historical Society

Dear Sir Trenton, October 13, 1798

Last evening I received a letter from Monsr. Hory dated Bordeaux Augt. 27th of which a copy is inclosed:[6] you will be happy to find that General Pinckney sailed from Bordeaux about the middle of that month: and in order to give joy to others, especially his nearest friend, I have put the copy under cover to Major Pinckney,[7] to be sealed and forwarded by you from Richmond, without losing a post.

On the 10th instant Mr. C. Humphreys[8] arrived here with Mr. Gerry's budget, forwarded by the President. There is a manifestation of some spirit in his correspondence with Talleyrand: but he also manifests his folly, or something worse, in his repeated professions of his belief that the French government was sincere in its desires of preserving peace & settling all differences with the U. States on terms that we could accept. Perhaps I express myself too strongly in saying he "professes his belief," but he uses this phrase.

5. See Rawle v. Byrd, Declaration, listed at Law Papers, Sept. 1798, and Receipt, Nov. 6, 1798.

6. Enclosure not found, but see Louis Hory to Pickering, Aug. 27, 1798, Adams Papers, Massachusetts Historical Society.

7. Maj. Thomas Pinckney, of Charleston, S.C., was the younger brother of Charles Cotesworth Pinckney.

8. Clement Humphreys (1777–1803) had been sent to France in Mar. 1798 as a special courier to the envoys at Paris. While in France, Humphreys worked to secure the relief of American seamen stranded in French ports. Pickering to Humphreys, Mar. 28, 1798, Domestic Letters, X, RG 59, National Archives.

Mr. Talleyrand appeared sincerely desirous of effecting a reconciliation, *before the arrival of the Envoys' dispatches.*

There is a new fact respecting X. Y. & Z. which should be added to that which you communicated to me & which you will see I have published in my letter to P. Johnston & the Freeholders of Prince Edward County:[9] The bearer of Talleyrands letter to Mr. Gerry demanding the names of the intriguers designated by the letters X. Y. & Z. was told by Gerry, that there were other means by which Mr. Talleyrand might know their names. Yes answered the man, by the efforts of the Bureau and of the officers of Police, their names were discovered—*and then he named them all*—but this is a serious affair, & the government want your letter of *con*firmation. This fact is given by Mr. Gerry in his letter to me which contains a narrative of his proceedings.[1]

On the 21st of August Skipwith at Paris wrote Fenwick at Bordeaux that on that day he recd. an official copy of the arrete of the Directory taking off the embargo on American vessels: but the arrete was not then published. Fenwick in his letter of Augt. 28. to me, incloses a copy of Skipwith's letter: but adds, "Some apprehensions are entertained that if the late accounts from Philaa. by the flag vessel the Liberty (Volney embarked in her) that sailed about the 18th of July and arrived at Bordeaux a few days past should reach Paris before the execution of the arrette raising the embargo, it may be delayed." *

By a Paris Paper of the 23d or 24th of Augt. I see they had recieved information of the most important acts of Congress in relation to France. I am very respectfully, dear sir, your obt. servant

TIMOTHY PICKERING

*I have a private letter from a merchant of reputation at Bordeaux,[2] who says "The news brought by the liberty has made no great sensation." This letter is dated Augt. 27th.

9. Peter Johnston (1763–1841), of Farmville, Va., sent the secretary of state an address from Prince Edward County on Aug. 21, 1798. The document criticized the president's management of foreign and domestic affairs. Pickering considered the address an insult to the president and he refused to forward it to Adams in Quincy, Mass. On Sept. 29, 1798, Pickering published a reply to Johnston's letter in which he lectured the Virginian on his inappropriate language and lack of respect for the president. Pickering's reply was widely reprinted. See Johnston to Pickering, Aug. 21 and Oct. 26, 1798, Pickering to Johnston, Sept. 29, 1798, Pickering Papers, Mass. Hist. Soc.

1. Gerry to Pickering, Oct. 1, 1798, Gerry Papers, Henry E. Huntington Library.

2. Theodore Peters was a Dutch merchant. See Pickering to Adams, Oct. 13, 1798, Adams Papers.

To Timothy Pickering

ALS, Pickering Papers, Massachusetts Historical Society

Dear Sir   Richmond, October 15, 1798

I thank you for your letter of the 4th. inclosing an extract from a letter addressd to you by Major Rutledge.[3] We are now informd of the arrival of Mr. Gerry & are extremely anxious to know what opinions he will deliver relative to the situation of our affairs with France. Whatever those opinions may be they will very speedily be communicated throughout the continent to all the members of the opposition who appear to me to be perfectly prepard to seize & avail themselves of every sentiment he may utter which can be applied to their purposes. They seem to hold themselves in readiness to receive him into their bosoms or to drop him entirely as he may be French or American.

I had proposd to myself to make some comments on the letters of Talleyrand & Bellamy & to publish them but I have been restraind from doing so by my having, as a punishment for some unknown sins, consented to be named a candidate for the ensuing election to Congress. In consequence of this the whole malignancy of Antifederalism, not only in the district where it unfortunately is but too abundant, but throughout the state, has become uncommonly active & considers itself as peculiarly interested in the reelection of the old member.[4] The jacobin presses which abound with us & only circulate within the state teem with publications of which the object is to poison still further the public opinion & which are leveld particularly at me. Any thing written by me on the subject of French affairs woud be ascribed to me whether it appeard with or with out my signature & woud whet & sharpen up the sting of every abusive scribler who had vanity enough to think himself a writer because he coud bestow personal abuse & coud say things as malignant as they are ill founded. To protect myself from the vexation of these news paper altercations so far as it may be in my power, I wish if it be possible to avoid appearing in print myself. Another very powerful consideration restrains me. The superior courts which I attend have been for some time & will continue till the middle of December to be in session. My absence has

3. Henry M. Rutledge.

4. John Clopton (1756–1816). See Congressional Election Campaign: Editorial Note, at Sept. 19, 1798.

placed my business in such a situation as scarcely to leave a moment which I can command for other purposes.

If Mr. Gerry is really of opinion that an accommodation coud not be formd with France on terms compatible with the honor & independence of the United States it will be important to draw him fully out upon the subject. At present the disposition to relapse into dangerous foreign attachments shows itself in too many & may very easily be encouraged to strong efforts. With much respect & esteem, I am dear Sir your obedt

J MARSHALL

Bond

ADS, Executive Papers, Virginia State Library

[*October 17, 1798, Richmond.* JM cosigns a bond with James Markham Marshall executed in compliance with an act of Dec. 27, 1794, regarding the disposition of parcels of land in Romney, Va. In order to clear title to the land in the Hampshire County town, the act vested in the town's trustees all land not previously deeded by Thomas Lord Fairfax. The trustees evaluated the parcels and sold them to persons claiming prior right of possession. The law provided for the return of the purchase money when the purchaser posted bond to refund the money to anyone proving better title. James M. Marshall claimed title to land in Romney worth £1,000. See 1 Shepherd 317.]

From Timothy Pickering

Presscopy, Pickering Papers, Massachusetts Historical Society

(Private)

Dear Sir, Trenton, October 19, 1798

Meeting with no private conveyance, and having taken a copy of your journal, I now transmit it to you by the mail, in which I did not care to trust it, without having a copy.[5] But I deemed it important in another point of view: the President ought to be acquainted with Mr. Gerry's whole conduct. Your journal shows it to have been characterised, not only with timidity, indecision and meanness, but with *treachery*: yes, I have no doubt that he com-

5. See Paris Journal: Editorial Note, *ca.* Oct. 4, 1797.

municated to Talleyrand the train of your and General Pinckney's thoughts and determinations, and thus betrayed the Commission. His refusal to sign the letter demanding your passports is one evidence of it—assigning (unwittingly) as a reason, that Talleyrand said, *if the letter was sent*, a war would immediately take place.[6] He attempts, it is true, a correction of his words: but his first expression is correct—he had most certainly told Talleyrand the tenor of the letter. His frequent private & exclusively confidential conferences with Talleyrand, under injunctions of secrecy in regard to his colleagues, is another proof, and is besides, of itself, such a violation of his duty as ought to subject him to an impeachment: I hope he will be impeached.

In a former letter I suggested to your consideration the expediency of your writing a short history of the mission of the Envoys Extraordinary:[7] I think it cannot be questioned: or if there be any doubt, it can arise only from the display it must make of your own efficiency, that might to the envious appear marked with egotism. The President I know has formed (for he has expressed it to me by letter)[8] a correct opinion of *your* conduct, & thinks it unexceptionable. Yet in his answer to an address from Machias (in the District of Maine) there is a censure of all the envoys.[9] He subjoins an apology for them: but the world (the American World I mean) ought to know that every thing really wanting in spirit & dignity, is to be ascribed to his own *protegé*, Gerry. When he shall have read your journal, he is too just to retain his good opinion of him, or to withhold the distinction which truth and fact require to be made between him on one part and General Pinckney & you on the other.

6. See Journal, Feb. 26 and 27, 1798; Pinckney and JM to Talleyrand, Feb. 26, 1798.

7. Pickering to JM, Oct. 4, 1798.

8. See John Adams to Pickering, Sept. 17, 1798, Domestic Letterbooks, X, RG 59, National Archives; Adams to Pickering, Sept. 26, 1798, Adams Papers, Massachusetts Historical Society.

9. Pickering was referring to the following passage in President Adams's reply to the inhabitants of Machias, Me.: "Your country I presume will not meanly Sue for Peace, or engage in War from motives of Ambition Vanity or Revenge. I presume further that she will never again suffer her ambassadors to remain in France many Days or hours unacknowledged without an Audience of the Sovereign, unprotected and unpriviledged, nor to enter into Conferences or Conversations with any Agents or Emissaries, who have not a regular Commission, of equal Rank with their own and who shall not have shewn their Original Commission and exchanged official copies with them. While extraordinary circumstances are our Apology for the past deviation from established Rules, founded in unquestionable reason and propriety, the odious consequences of it will be an everlasting admonition to avoid the like for the future." Adams to the Inhabitants of Machias, District of Maine, Oct. 5, 1798, Adams Papers.

The General is at Newark, where he proposes to stay about ten days.[1] I am, dear Sir, with great respect & esteem, your most obt. Servt,

TIMOTHY PICKERING.

Oct. 20. This morning I received from Mr. King a letter in which is the following passage.[2]

"Notwithstanding his pretended delicacy, Hauteval by no means denies the agency ascribed to him in soliciting the bribe required by Talleyrand. Colonel Trumbull, who was at Paris soon after the arrival there of the Commissioners, has more than once informed me that Hauteval told him that both the Douceur and the Loan were indispensable, and urged him to employ his influence with the American Commissioners to offer the bribe as well as the loan." But I suppose Mr. Trumbull must have told you this at Paris.

General Pinckney accepts his commission of Major General.[3]

T. P.

To Timothy Pickering

ALS, Pickering Papers, Massachusetts Historical Society

Dear Sir Richmond, October 22, 1798

I had the pleasure of receiving in due course your letter of the 18th. inclosing one to Major Pinckney[4] which I forwarded immediately, since then I learn with real joy that Genl. Pinckney has arrivd with his family. For his own sake & for the sake of his country I rejoice at this event.

I have feard that Mr. Gerry woud be disposd to impress an

1. Pinckney had sailed from Bordeaux on Aug. 7, 1798. He and his family landed at New York on Oct. 13 and traveled to Newark on Oct. 19, 1798. Louis Hory to Pickering, Aug. 17, 1798, *ibid.*; Mary Pinckney to Margaret Manigault, Apr. 15, 1798, Manigault Family Papers, University of South Carolina; Pickering to George Washington, Oct. 13, 1798, Pickering Papers; Mass. Hist. Soc.; Pickering to Adams, Oct. 15, 1798, Adams Papers; Marvin R. Zahniser, *Charles Cotesworth Pinckney: Founding Father* (Chapel Hill, N.C., 1967), 190.

2. See Rufus King to Pickering, June 15, 1798, Diplomatic Dispatches, Great Britain, VII, RG 59, Natl. Arch.

3. Pinckney accepted the commission as major general in the Provisional Army on July 18, 1798. *Annals of Congress*, VII, 621–623. See also Pickering to Washington, Oct. 20, 1798, Pickering Papers.

4. JM meant the 13th. Thomas Pinckney.

opinion that the success of his negotiation was prevented by the publication of the dispatches. But how can this be the fact? Mr. Gerry's own letter to Talleyrand shows that he did not consider the claim for money as having been relinquished. If then Mr. Talleyrand was desirous of effecting a reconciliation on what terms was it to have been effected? Certainly on the condition of our submiting to the payment of money & a consequent engagement in the war under the coercion of & in subordination to the french republic. No person ever questiond the sincerity of Mr. Talleyrands wish to effect a reconciliation on those terms. The envoys woud have found no difficulty in making a treaty on such a basis. We never doubted that if our country was prepard to surrender its independence France was prepared to receive it.

I am anxious to know the course of conversation which Mr. Gerry pursues. The real french party of this country again begins to show itself. Publications calculated to soften the public resentiments against France, to excite an apprehension of Britain as our natural enemy, & to diminish the repugnance to pay money to the French republic are appearing every day. There are very many indeed in this part of Virginia who speak of our own government as an enemy infinitely more formidable & infinitely more to be guarded against than the french Directory. Immense efforts are made to induce the legislature of the state which will meet in Decr. to take some violent measure which may be attended with serious consequences. I am not sure that these efforts will entirely fail. It requires to be in this part of Virginia to know the degree of irritation which has been excited & the probable extent of the views of those who excite it. In this state of things the language of Mr. Gerry is material.[5]

I take the liberty to inclose a note to Genl. Pinckney & to Major Rutledge in the expectation that they may yet be in Trenton. If they have come on the inclosd may be destroyed.[6]

Your letter to the people of Prince Edward the contents of which are so highly approvd of by the friends of the government will probably for a short time releive me from abuse by substituting yourself as the object at which malevolence will for a time direct its shafts.[7] This however will be but a temporary releif. The charge

5. Rather than take his case to the public, where it would have played an important role in the political campaigns then being waged, Gerry remained silent and explained his conduct privately to John Adams.

6. Enclosure not found.

7. See Pickering to JM, Oct. 13, 1798.

against me will soon recommence. I am dear Sir with much respect & esteem, Your obedt

J MARSHALL

To John Hopkins

Printed extract, Walter R. Benjamin Autographs, Inc., *The Collector*, LXXIV (New York, 1971), item 10

[*October 22, 1798.* JM writes a receipt for "thirty dollars on account of a suit in the Court of Chancery concerning the division of Mr. Curtis's estate."]

Law Papers, October 1798

U.S. Circuit Court, Va.

Gist v. Hill, declaration, ADS, U.S. Circuit Court, Va., Ended Cases (Unrestored), Virginia State Library.

Kennedy v. Anderson, declaration, ADS, U.S. Circuit Court, Va., Ended Cases (Unrestored), Va. State Lib.

From Timothy Pickering

Presscopy, Pickering Papers, Massachusetts Historical Society

Dear Sir, Trenton, November 5, 1798

The inclosed letter to you is mentioned as committed to the care of Mr. Gerry: but I suppose it had a different conveyance: I received it within a day or two.[8]

Mr. Gerry is displeased with that part of my letter to P. Johnston of Prince Edward County, in which he is introduced. He recites the anecdote of the private dinner with Talleyrand, and X & Y renewing the money propositions. You will have seen that I gave it to the public in your own words. I call it an "important fact," and say that I have "incontrovertible evidence" of it: but Mr. Gerry, in a letter dated the 20th. of Oct. to the President, says this important fact "never existed."[9] And how do you imagine he main-

8. Enclosure not found.

9. Gerry to John Adams, Oct. 20, 1798, Pickering Papers, Massachusetts Historical

tains his denial? He says it was not a *private* dinner; that besides X. Y. & Z., 15 or 16 other persons were present; therefore the company could not consist of X Y & Z; and therefore—what? *that the money propositions were not renewed, and in Talleyrands own room & presence? and that X.Y.&Z. were not known to Talleyrand?* No; but that X. Y. & Z. did not compose the *whole* of the company, and "the proposition then made by X & Y was (*he thinks*) relative to the loan only"! But Genl. Pinckney (to whom I have shown Gerry's letter) says the proposition clearly and decidedly embraced the douceur as well as the loan.

Gerry desires his letter may be promptly published: the President has sent it to me: But I shall answer the President to-day, that I cannot publish it without exposing its quibbles and absurdities, but that if Gerry thinks proper to publish it himself, he may do it; and then I shall follow him; and display, not his meanness only, but his *duplicity* and *treachery*. He *betrayed* the counsels of his country's mission to Talleyrand; and for this as well as his engaging in *private* communications with him, and under an injunction of *secrecy towards his colleagues*, he ought to be impeached.

Seeing your correctness and veracity are called in question, I will have a copy of Gerry's letter made out, and inclose it. Your remarks upon it will be gratefully received by me. I very much suspect that Gerry, like Randolph & Monroe, wants to figure in print.[1] I am very truly & respectfully yours.

TIMOTHY PICKERING.

Society. A note on the envelope in Pickering's hand states that he "returned the original to the President the 11th Decr. 1798, at his request, that he might send it to Mr. Gerry, to publish it if he pleased. It was on this occasion that I said to the President, that I had no time to engage in a newspaper dispute with Mr. Gerry & did not desire it, but if he would publish, that I would follow him. The President then remarked—If you do engage in the newspaper with Mr. Gerry, you will find that you had never had such an antagonist in your life!!! Oh Sir, I replied, I have no apprehensions of difficulty in a controversy with Mr. Gerry." The note does not appear on the letter under the same date in the Adams Papers, Mass. Hist. Soc. See also Pickering to George Cabot, Nov. 6, 1798, Pickering Papers, and JM to Pickering, Sept. 15, 1798.

1. See [Edmund Randolph], *A Vindication of Mr. Randolph's Resignation* (Philadelphia, 1795); W. Allan Wilbur, "Oliver Wolcott, Jr., and Edmund Randolph's Resignation: An Explanatory Note on an Historic Misconception," Connecticut Historical Society, *Bulletin*, XXXVIII (1973), 12–16; John J. Reardon, *Edmund Randolph: A Biography* (New York, 1974), 321–334; James Monroe, *A View of the Conduct of the Executive, in the Foreign Affairs of the United States, Connected with the Mission to the French Republic, during the Years, 1794, 5 and 6* (Philadelphia, 1797); Harry Ammon, *James Monroe: The Quest for a National Identity* (New York, 1971), 157-173.

Receipt

ADS, Virginia Historical Society[2]

[Richmond], November 6, 1798

Recd. from Mrs. Byrd on account of a bond given by her to William Shirtliff on the first day of January 1778 the sum of one hundred & fifty dollars. Recd. by Mr. Parker.

J MARSHALL

Deed

Deed Book Copy, Office of the Clerk of Hardy County, Moorefield, W. Va.

[*November 8, 1798* (*Hardy County, Va.*). By his attorney, Rawleigh Colston, JM conveys 100 acres in the South Branch Manor to John Hay for £25. The deed was recorded in the District Court at Hardy County on May 6, 1799.]

To Timothy Pickering

ALS, Pickering Papers, Massachusetts Historical Society

Dear Sir Richmond, November 12, 1798

I have receivd your two letters of the 19th. of October & 5th. of November. My journal transmitted with the first came safe to hand.[3]

I have had so much reason to be more than satisfied with the conduct of the President towards me, that I shoud not have been wounded at the implied censure, in his answer to the people of Machias, on the long stay of the envoys in Paris. I am however & shall ever be happy to know that my public conduct while employed by him meets his approbation.

I have ever been & still am unwilling that my hasty journal which I had never ever read over until I receivd it from you, shoud be shown to him. This unwillingness proceeds from a repugnance to give him the vexation which I am persuaded it woud give him.

2. This is item no. Mss2M3567b3 in the society's collections. See Rawle v. Byrd, Declaration, listed at Law Papers, Sept. 1798, and Receipt, Oct. 10, 1798.

3. See Paris Journal: Editorial Note, *ca.* Oct. 4, 1797, for a discussion of the probable fate of the original journal.

The letter of Mr. Gerry astonishes me. It is written in a temper which the paper complaind of need not have excited, & threatens a state of things which from considerations of a public nature I wish very much to avoid. It is proper for me to notice this letter if I am to be supposed to have seen it, & I therefore transmit the inclosd to you open, which, (after reading it,) you will please to seal & forward to Mr. Gerry or retain as you shall judge right.[4] I wish Genl. Pinckney also to read it. I inclose you likewise a certificate of which as well as of the letter giving you the information which has been published you will make what use you please. I think it most adviseable & I desire that Genl. Pinckney may add his certificate to mine on the same paper if he is willing to do so.[5] I am confident he recollects the circumstance because we have each of us more than once mentiond it to the other.

While in Paris I did not beleive that any system of conduct which the envoys coud have adopted woud have given to their negotiation a successful issue. The conduct of France since the United States have displayed a determination to defend themselves & to assert their rights as an independent nation, produce in me doubt respecting this opinion. It now appears to me not absolutely

4. See Pickering to JM, Nov. 5, 1798. Gerry's dinner with Talleyrand was the source of considerable disagreement between JM and Gerry. See Journal, Dec. 2, 1797, JM to Pickering, Sept. 15, 1798, and Pickering to JM, Oct. 19, 1798. See also Deposition, Nov. 12, 1798. Pickering retained JM's deposition and did not send it to Gerry.

5. Pinckney's deposition was obtained about Nov. 25, 1798. This letter from JM, in which he enclosed his deposition, arrived at Philadelphia on Nov. 21, 1798. Pinckney was in Philadelphia to meet with the major generals of the Provisional Army, and he undoubtedly wrote the following deposition at Pickering's request: "I remember perfectly well Mr. Gerry's informing me when in Paris of what passed when he dined with Mr. Taleyrand. I did not understand from him that it was a public dinner but on the contrary the impression made on my mind was that it was a private unofficial dinner. Mr. Gerry was the only foreign Minister present. Mr. Danchet [Anton Dorsch] & Mr. Pichon two of Mr. Taleyrand's Secretaries who spoke English Mr. Z & W & Mr: Y & I think some other persons were present. X was not in the company when they sat down to dinner, he came in during dinnertime & took a seat at the Table. After dinner when the company rose from the Table X took Mr. Gerry aside to one of the windows & said to him 'Well have you got the Money ready?' To which Mr. Gerry answered 'Sr. I came from America with an honest Character & mean to return there with one.' X to this made no reply but immediately spoke to Y. Mr. Taleyrand was in the room during this conversation but I understood that he was not within hearing. This is the account I had from Mr. Gerry himself. I am confident the impression made on Mr. Gerry's mind at that time was that the money alluded to was the 50,000 and he frequently expressed himself in mentioning the transaction as if he was hurt at the indelicacy of renewing the proposition at that time." Pinckney to [Pickering, *ca.* Nov. 25, 1798], Pickering Papers, Massachusetts Historical Society. Pinckney is the only minister to place Mr. "W," or Hubbard, at the dinner, and he is incorrect in this assertion.

impossible that a negotiation in the usual forms might have been enterd into had no hope been entertaind of dividing the envoys or of obtaining the inadmissible terms which were demanded & so long deliberated on. With much respect & esteem, I am Sir your obedt.

J MARSHALL

Deposition

ADS, Pickering Papers, Massachusetts Historical Society[6]

[Richmond, November 12, 1798]

While the envoys of the United States were in Paris Mr. Gerry was invited to a private inofficial dinner by Mr. Talleyrand. On his return he stated to Genl. Pinckney & myself that the persons designated in the dispatches as publishd by government by the letters X. Y. & Z. had dind with him, & that after rising from table the money propositions which had before been made were repeated in the room & in the presence of the minister. Mr. Gerry stated this fact very explicitly & more than once manifested some degree of resentment that such a time shoud have been chosen for repeating on him the corrupt & vicious attempts which had before been made on us all.

On seeing Mr. Talleyrands letter demanding from Mr. Gerry the names of the persons designated by the letters W, X, Y, & Z, I was so struck with the shameless effrontery of affecting to Mr. Gerry ignorance of the persons so designated & of demanding their names from him that I stated to Colo. Pickering the fact which I now certify & which was afterwards published by him in a letter to Mr. Peter Johnston of Prince Edward.[7]

J MARSHALL

To Elbridge Gerry

ALS, Marshall Papers, Swem Library, College of William and Mary

Sir, Richmond, November 12, 1798

A copy of your letter to the President of the United States com-

6. JM enclosed this deposition in his letter to Timothy Pickering, Nov. 12, 1798. Pickering retained the original and used the information in his attack upon Gerry's handling of the informal negotiations with Talleyrand.

7. Pickering to Peter Johnston, Sept. 29, 1798, Pickering Papers, Massachusetts Historical Society. See notes at Pickering to JM, Oct. 13, 1798.

plaining of some clauses in the answer given "*by the Secretary of State*" to Mr. Johnston of Prince Edward was transmitted to me by the last post.[8]

The regret I coud not but feel on perceiving your dissatisfaction at the manner in which the circumstance that occurred at Mr. Talleyrands table was mentioned, is not a little increasd by my conviction that you must have supposed the information *on which Colo. Pickering* so *entirely relied* proceeded from me. This imposes on me the necessity of noticing particularly this part of your letter to the President. Before I do so I will, to prevent any continuance of misconception on your part, observe on the general impression you have permitted yourself to receive from the statement complaind of.

I know not sir why you shoud suppose the publication of the conversation alluded to a stigma on yourself. It was not stated to have been in your power to have avoided the application nor was it insinuated that you approvd or receivd it favorably. You were not censured for not having made the communication to the government, nor coud I have intended such censure since I must myself have participated in it. You did not withhold this conversation from your collegues & consequently, as our letters were joint, it was nearly as incumbent on me as on you to have suggested the propriety of mentioning it to the Secretary of State. The truth is that our dispatches contained so much testimony concerning the unprincipled attempts of France on the Envoys of the United States, that it was then deemd unnecessary to add this fact to the collection, "nor woud it have been brought into view but in consequence of the astonishing impudence manifested by Mr. Talleyrand in demanding of you the names of W. X. Y. & Z———of you sir who had stated yourself to have accompanied Y to Mr. Talleyrand & to have been assurd by him that "the information given by Mr. Y was just & might always be relied on."[9]—of you who had dined with X. Y. & Z. at the table of Mr. Talleyrand & had immediately after rising from that table been again attackd by them on the subject of money. "It was" I repeat to give additional evi-

8. Gerry to John Adams, Oct. 20, 1798, Pickering Papers, Massachusetts Historical Society. Timothy Pickering forwarded a copy of Gerry's letter to JM in his letter of Nov. 5, 1798.

9. This was Gerry's second visit to Talleyrand. The first was on Oct. 28, 1797, in the company of Mr. "Z," Lucien Hauteval. The visit referred to by JM took place on Dec. 17, 1797, with Mr. "Y," Pierre Bellamy. See Apr. 3, 1798, *Annals of Congress*, IX, 3350–3351, 3366–3367.

dence of that impudence & "not in the expectation of wounding you, that, on the publication of Mr. Talleyrands letter I mentiond this conversation" to Colo. Pickering. I am yet of opinion that the publication of it contains nothing indelicate or with which you have a right to be displeasd.

Permit me now sir to advert particularly to your letter.

Colo. Pickering had on my information stated as a fact that at a private dinner to which you was invited & at which the company was X. Y & Z., X & Y, after rising from table, renewd to you in the presence, tho not perhaps in the hearing of Mr. Talleyrand, the money propositions which had before been rejected.[1]

This fact you say never existed.

In support of a denial to me still more wonderful than the fact itself you say that

1st. The dinner was not a private dinner.

2dly. There were other persons that X Y & Z who formd part of the company.

3dly. You think the proposition was confind to the loan.

In answer to these assertions I beg leave to observe that

1st. The dinner was a private dinner.

You know well sir that the minister, occasionally, gives what may be termd official dinners to which he invites officers of government, foreign ministers etc. These are considerd & spoken of as public dinners. On other occasions he entertains his friends inofficially in like manner as any private gentleman woud entertain them—& these are properly termd private dinners. It was to one of the latter sort that you, according to your information to Genl. Pinckney & myself, was invited.

2dly. I cannot pretend to say how many persons may have dined with you but do not recollect to have heard you mention any other than X Y & Z & secretaries who are the family of Mr. Talleyrand.

3dly. If the application was confind to the loan you misinformed Genl. Pinckney & myself. You stated it to us as a repetition "of the money propositions" which had been rejected, & you expressed a good deal of indignation that such a time shoud have been chosen for the purpose, & you spoke in strong terms of the unblushing front with which the application was made.

But sir of what importance is it whether the dinner was public or private & whether the company consisted of seven or seventeen?

1. See Journal, *ca.* Dec. 2 and 17, 1797.

The fact was communicated by me to show that X, Y, & Z were perfectly known to Mr. Talleyrand. Do these circumstances in any degree change its substance? They change it no more than the number of courses served up for the dinner.

I must hope sir that you will think justly on this subject & will thereby save us both the pain of an altercation I so much wish to avoid. I am respectfully your obedt.

J MARSHALL

To Caron de Beaumarchais

ALS, Private Collection

Dear Sir Richmond, November 20, 1798

I have received with real pleasure your letter of the 18 messidor an 6.[2] I rejoice & shall always rejoice to hear of you & of your happiness. I can never forget your goodness & friendly attentions to me while in Paris, nor can your gay metropolis ever present itself to my imagination without bringing with it yourself & your amiable family.

It will give me infinite delight to see you in America provided you can be here in a situation which will be agreeable to yourself. No man will rejoice more than I shall to learn that France, listening at length to the too long neglected dictates of justice & of a sound policy, will consent to permit the United States to remain at peace with her on terms compatible with our independence; nor coud any thing add more to the pleasure such an event woud give me, than to see employed as the instrument of such an accomodation, a man I so much esteem personally & who, tho an enthusiastic frenchman is yet a moderate friend of—or at least not an absolute enemy to—the liberties of my own country.

Your cause my dear Sir is not yet decided. It is continued until april next when I expect the judgement of the court will be renderd.[3] I wish very sincerely it may be favorable to you. No effort

2. See Beaumarchais to JM, Aug. 24, 1798. Beaumarchais wrote on the verso, "Dernière lettre du gal. Marshall, Pour etre vue par le directoire."

3. Beaumarchais had won a decree in the High Court of Chancery on Sept. 29, 1796, and it had been appealed by the Commonwealth in James Innes, attorney general, and John Pendleton, auditor of public accounts, v. Caron de Beaumarchais. Apparently the Court of Appeals took no action in Apr. 1799; the case was revived in Oct. 1801 and because all parties to the suit had died the names of successors of the parties were supplied. On May 10, 1803, the court set aside the 1796 decree and entered

I am capable of making will be wanting to promote what I really think the justice of the case.

As I formed very few friendships in Paris those I did form were proportionably strong. I think of my few friends with much gratitude & affection, am anxious to hear of their happiness, & to give them marks of my recollection & esteem. I pray you sir to say this & much more for me in your own amiable & accomplished family & in the rue [des fonès] du temple & rue vaugirard.[4] With real esteem & affection, I remain your obedt. Servt.

J MARSHALL

To Robert Morris

ALS, Marshall Papers, New Hampshire Historical Society

Dear Sir Richmond, December 1, 1798

The vast pressure of my business during the sessions of our supreme courts & my sollicitude to form a more favorable opinion of your case have prevented my giving an earlier answer to your enquiries concerning it.[5] I wish it was now in my power to be more explicit than I am but it is one of those subjects on which rules do not seem to have been absolutely fixed & on which much will depend on the particular mode of thinking of the Judges who will decide the question. The fraud practiced on you to obtain both tracts ought not to prevail. If that can be establishd it makes the case a clear one. It certainly ought not to be lost sight of for a moment as it forms a most essential part of your case.

I condole with you very sincerely on the heavy calamity you have sustaind in the loss of your Son.[6]

---

a substitute that favored the Commonwealth. Court of Appeals Order Book, IV, 100–101, 102, 115, 267, 274–275, Virginia State Library.

4. These were the current residences of Beaumarchais and Madame de Villette. The words in brackets have been supplied from Beaumarchais's copy of this letter that was translated into French for the Directory.

5. Upon returning to Philadelphia, JM agreed to help Robert Morris in a dispute over Genesee lands in New York. Morris claimed he had given the Holland Land Company nothing more than a mortgage on the property, while the company insisted they had purchased the land outright. Alexander Hamilton was the lawyer for the Holland Land Company in this dispute. See Théophile Cazenove to Pieter and Christian Van Eeghen, June 6, July 14, Aug. 27, and Oct. 17, 1798; Morris to Cazenove, Feb. 9, 1799, Holland Land Company Papers, 302, 81, 83, Gemeentearcheif, Amsterdam.

6. William White Morris, Robert Morris's third son, died in 1798 during a yellow

Present me respectfully to Mrs. Morris & beleive me to be dear Sir with very much esteem, your obedt. Servt.

J MARSHALL

To Henry Banks

ALS, Virginia Historical Society

Dear Sir[7] Richmond, December 10, 1798

I have receivd yours of the 20th. Novr. & really regret that the situation of my affairs is such as absolutely to render it impossible for me to undertake the execution of the trust you woud confide to me.[8] I wish very sincerely to see your affairs arranged to your own satisfaction & woud contribute towards such an arrangement any efforts I coud make which were consistent with my other avocations —but those avocations are so various that I am certain it woud be impossible for me to attend to the duties of the trust. Shoud I undertake them I shoud be compeled to neglect them the consequences of which might be serious. I am dear Sir with much regard, Your obdt

J MARSHALL

From George Washington

ALS, Collection of the Association for the Preservation of Virginia Antiquities, on deposit at the Virginia Historical Society

My dear Sir, Mount Vernon, December 30, 1798

If General Pinckney should have left Richmond, let me request the favor of you to forward the packet here with sent, in the manner he may have directed; or, as your own judgment shall dictate, to ensure its delivery to him in Hallifax, or on the Road through North Carolina.[9]

---

fever epidemic in Philadelphia. He had studied law with Edward Tilghman and had helped his father as he struggled with his financial accounts.

7. This is item no. Mss2M3567b2 in the society's collections. The letter is addressed to Banks in Philadelphia.

8. Letter not found.

9. Pinckney had traveled from Newark to Philadelphia to meet with the major generals of the Provisional Army and with George Washington to discuss appointments and enlistments. Pinckney left for South Carolina on Dec. 17, 1798. The Pinck-

The Alien & Sedition Laws, having employed many Pens—and we hear a number of tongues, in the Assembly of this State,—the latter, I understand, to a very pernicious purpose.[1] I send you the production of Judge Addison on these subjects.[2] Whether any new lights are cast upon them by his charge, you will be better able to decide when you have read it. My opinion is, that if this, or other writings flashed conviction as clear as the Sun in its Meredian brightness, it would produce no effect in the conduct of the leaders of opposition, who, have points to carry, from which nothing will divert them in the prosecution.

When you have read the charge give it to Bushrod Washington, or place it to any other uses you may think proper. I wish success to your Election, most sincerely; and if it should fail (of which I hope there is not the least danger) I shall not easily forgive myself for being urgent with you to take a Poll. I offer you the compliments of the Season, and with much truth remain, Dear Sir, Your Most Obedt. and Affecte. Hble Servant

Go: WASHINGTON

---

neys spent Christmas with the Washingtons at Mt. Vernon and New Year's Day with JM in Richmond. *Virginia Gazette, and General Advertiser* (Richmond), Jan. 1 and 3, 1799; John C. Fitzpatrick, ed., *The Diaries of George Washington, 1748–1799*, IV (Boston, 1925), 291.

1. On Dec. 25, 1798, the Virginia Assembly adopted the resolutions declaring the Alien and Sedition Laws unconstitutional. See *JVHD*, Dec. 1798, 38–39; Harry Ammon and Adrienne Koch, "The Virginia and Kentucky Resolutions," *WMQ*, 3d Ser., V (1948), 145–176.

2. Alexander Addison (1759–1807), of Washington County, Pa., was a U.S. District Court judge. His pamphlet, *Liberty of Speech and of the Press. A charge to the grand juries of the county courts of the Fifth circuit of the state of Pennsylvania* (Washington, Pa., 1798), was a spirited defense of the Alien and Sedition Laws. Addison's pamphlet became the target of Republican writers during the election of 1800. *Aurora* (Philadelphia), Dec. 6, 1800; Beveridge, *Marshall*, II, 385; Elizabeth K. Henderson, "The Attack on the Judiciary in Pennsylvania, 1800–1810," *Pennsylvania Magazine of History and Biography*, LXI (1937), 118–119; see Richard E. Ellis, *The Jeffersonian Crisis: Courts and Politics in the Young Republic* (New York, 1971), 164-165.

INDEXES

LEGAL INDEX

GENERAL INDEX

The indexes for this volume were prepared with the assistance of CINDEX, an indexing program developed for the computer by the University of South Carolina. The editors wish to thank David R. Chesnutt, editor of the Papers of Henry Laurens, for making this program available and for helping modify it for this project. They would also like to thank Michael K. Donegan and David Reed of the College of William and Mary for their special aid to the editors.

LEGAL INDEX

The Legal Index contains both legal digest entries and case titles that appear in John Marshall's correspondence and papers. For names of individuals, including authors of books, and general subject entries, see the General Index, which begins on p. 539.

GENERAL INDEX

The General Index contains names of individuals that appear in this volume, as well as general subject entries. Dates of individuals, if known, may be found at their first page reference; if in an earlier volume, the volume number and page reference will follow the name in parentheses. For legal digest entries and case titles, see the Legal Index which appears on p. 535.

D

N

O